Talking Cures

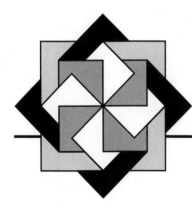

Talking Cures

A History of Western and
Eastern Psychotherapies

C. Peter Bankart

Wabash College

Brooks/Cole Publishing Company
I**T**P® An International Thomson Publishing Company

Pacific Grove ▪ Albany ▪ Belmont ▪ Bonn ▪ Boston ▪ Cincinnati ▪ Detroit ▪ Johannesburg ▪ London ▪ Madrid
Melbourne ▪ Mexico City ▪ New York ▪ Paris ▪ Singapore ▪ Tokyo ▪ Toronto ▪ Washington

 A CLAIREMONT BOOK

Sponsoring Editor: *Eileen Murphy*
Marketing Team: *Jean Thompson and Romy Taormina*
Editorial Assistant: *Lisa Blanton*
Production Coordinator: *Fiorella Ljunggren*
Production: *Scratchgravel Publishing Services*
Manuscript Editor: *Rebecca Smith*

Permissions Editor: *Fiorella Ljunggren*
Interior Design: *Anne and Greg Draus, Scratchgravel Publishing Services*
Cover Design: *Roger Knox*
Indexer: *James Minkin*
Typesetting: *Scratchgravel Publishing Services*
Printing and Binding: *Quebecor Printing, Fairfield*

For more information, contact:

BROOKS/COLE PUBLISHING COMPANY
511 Forest Lodge Road
Pacific Grove, CA 93950
USA

International Thomson Publishing Europe
Berkshire House 168-173
High Holborn
London WC1V 7AA
England

Thomas Nelson Australia
102 Dodds Street
South Melbourne, 3205
Victoria, Australia

Nelson Canada
1120 Birchmount Road
Scarborough, Ontario
Canada M1K 5G4

International Thomson Editores
Seneca 53
Col. Polanco
11560 México D. F. México

International Thomson Publishing GmbH
Königswinterer Strasse 418
53227 Bonn
Germany

International Thomson Publishing Asia
221 Henderson Road
#05-10 Henderson Building
Singapore 0315

International Thomson Publishing Japan
Hirakawacho Kyowa Building, 3F
2-2-1 Hirakawacho
Chiyoda-ku, Tokyo 102
Japan

Printed in the United States of America

10   9   8   7   6   5   4   3   2   1

Library of Congress Cataloging-in-Publication Data
Bankart, C. Peter
    Talking cures : a history of Western and Eastern psychotherapies / C. Peter Bankart.
        p.   cm.
    Includes bibliographical references and index.
    ISBN 0-534-34383-X (alk. paper)
    1. Psychotherapy—History.   2. Psychotherapy—Cross-cultural studies—History.   I. Title.
RC438.B36   1997
616.89'14'09—dc20   96-2816
                                                                    CIP

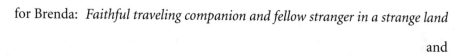

for Brenda: *Faithful traveling companion and fellow stranger in a strange land*

and

for Charlie: *May your life be full of interesting choices.*

These pages are also dedicated to the memory of Professor George Lovell,
a master of the Zen prod.

A professor has two functions: (1) to be learned and distribute
bibliographic information; (2) to communicate the truth.
The first function is the essential one, officially considered.
The second is the only one I care for.

WILLIAM JAMES

More true knowledge comes by meditation than by reading;
for much reading is an oppression of the mind,
and extinguishes the natural candle, which is the reason
of so many senseless scholars in the world.

WILLIAM PENN

For the student of Zen, a weed is a treasure.

SHUNRYU SUZUKI

Contents

PART I

The Discovery of the Unconscious: Mind Revealed   23

CHAPTER 2

The Search for the Meanings of Madness: From Demonology to Moral Therapy   24

Let There Be Light

CHAPTER 3

The Triumph of Reason, the Rise of Mental Science, and the "Mystery of Mysteries"   41

Toward a Science of the Mind

CHAPTER 4
The Rise and Fall of the Hypnotic Cure:
The Talking Cure in the French Tradition

CHAPTER 5
The Beginnings of Psychoanalysis: The Strange Case of Anna O.

CHAPTER 9
Carl Jung's "Analytical Psychology"   147

The Marriage of the Sun and the Moon

CHAPTER 10
Ego Psychology: Anna Freud, Erik Erikson, Karen Horney, and Erich Fromm   175

Let a Hundred Flowers Bloom, Let a Thousand Thoughts Contend

PART II

Psychotherapy in America: From Walden Pond to Walden Two

CHAPTER 11
William James and American Psychology

A Psychology of Use

CHAPTER 12
The Radical Behaviorisms of John Watson and B. F. Skinner   221

Pragmatism Triumphant

CHAPTER 13
The Behavioral Revolution in Psychotherapy   239

The Construction of Heaven on Earth

CHAPTER 14

Cognitive (Behavioral) Psychotherapy   259

Second Thoughts

PART III

Psychology on Trial   **281**

CHAPTER 17

Existential Psychotherapy: R. D. Laing, Viktor Frankl, and Rollo May   324

A Psychology of Humans Being

CHAPTER 18

Toward a Feminist Psychotherapy   346

Talking Back

CHAPTER 19
The Metaphysics of the Talking Cure   373

Soliloquy

PART IV

Non-Western Approaches to Psychotherapy: The Tao Is Silence

393

CHAPTER 22
Contemporary Japanese Psychotherapies: Morita and Naikan   440

Right Thought

CHAPTER 23
Therapies Based on Behavioral Self-Regulation:
Yoga and Other Techniques   463

Right Practice

CHAPTER 24
Final Thoughts

If You Meet the Buddha on the Road, Kill Him!

Bibliography

Author Index

Subject Index

Preface

The purpose of this book is, essentially, to explore the cultural, historical, and intellectual foundations of the theory and practice of psychotherapy—the enterprise I refer to in my title and in these pages as the "talking cure."

I have written this book primarily out of my experience teaching psychology for a quarter century to intellectually curious, bright, and wonderfully perceptive undergraduate students in the liberal arts. My "audience" is my former and future students, especially those who most enjoy learning when they come into direct contact with the world of ideas encountered in primary sources. My pedagogical goal is to show you how the very idea of a psychotherapeutic talking cure came about, how it became institutionalized in our society, and how it continues to evolve as millions of people every year look to psychology for answers to life's most perplexing dilemmas and challenges.

Talking Cures thus integrates, practically and philosophically, the histories of European and North American psychology, the history of madness, a variety of personality theories, the philosophy of science, current data from clinical psychology, examination of the effects of culture and gender, and my own experiences as a practicing therapist. As you read this book, I hope you will judge that I have preserved the intellectual integrity of the widely diverse ideas at the heart of the psychotherapeutic enterprise. I hope as well that I have succeeded in communicating at least a modicum of the wonder and mystery of the therapeutic process, which is the common experience of both the seasoned practitioner and the beginning student of the talking cure.

Like many books in the college bookstore, *Talking Cures* was conceived in frustration. Students who took my Theories of Personality course had only the vaguest sense of the intellectual and philosophical antecedents of the theories they studied and of their implications for the practice of psychotherapy. Students in History and Systems of Psychology courses rarely heard clinical psychology discussed and were too often persuaded that "real" psychology was rarely a "psychology of use." Most frustrating for me as a teacher was what happened in the Abnormal Psychology course: Students rarely perceived any connection between "disorders" and the ideas they encountered in other psychology courses. The failure of psychologists to integrate their field into a dynamic, meaningful, functioning whole led my students in

Abnormal Psychology to advocate a one-sided biological reductionism, usually in the form of Prozac or "genetics."

In truth, the psychology taught in these courses often doesn't seem any more integrated for me than for my students. I teach Principles of Psychotherapy, but I know that the subject matter is about as close to the real thing as a sex education course is to falling in love for the first time. Zillions of principles and labels must be mastered, but precious little context is provided for understanding them. And too often the fundamental human context is notably missing. My students remind me more and more often of a senior biology major I once counseled. He could recite the fundamentals of evolutionary theory backward and forward, but he graduated from college as committed to creationism as the day he first matriculated. It never occurred to him, just as it never occurs to many of my students, that some profound and even troubling ideas are hiding in those textbooks and hundreds of hours of lecture they endure in the name of becoming well educated. What I found most troubling about this young man was less that he was a well-educated young scientist who still believed in a literal interpretation of the Bible than that he had so compartmentalized the contents of his own consciousness. He appeared to me unlikely ever to engage his own creative, intellectual powers to comprehend, let alone resolve, the contradictions between his faith and his intellect.

In writing this book, I have therefore often found it necessary to challenge the ways we have thought about and taught students about psychotherapy in North America since the end of World War II. In the chapters that follow, I have attempted to identify and integrate a great many of the metaphysical themes within modern clinical psychology—to produce, in essence, an intellectual autobiography of this field of human endeavor. If I have succeeded, you will encounter in *Talking Cures* a social history at the intersection of the ideas and ideals that have shaped the professional identities of most contemporary practicing psychotherapists.

Talking Cures also attempts to address the gap between academic psychology and real-life psychotherapy. I believe that I have made more extensive use of case materials than most other authors in this field. More importantly, however, this book tries to communicate about psychology and psychotherapy by the extensive use of narrative. It is chock-full of stories, anecdotes, and what Freud would have called reminiscences (but which might more accurately be called true confessions). Those who enjoy teaching and learning in this style of discourse might actually enjoy this book. Others, however, may agree with the anonymous reviewer of some early drafts, who wrote that he had "devoted his whole career to keeping people like [me!] from influencing the field of psychology."

Who This Book Is For

Talking Cures is written for anyone who wants to learn something about the historical, cultural, and intellectual origins of a wide variety of contemporary approaches to psychotherapy. It is appropriate for any graduate or undergraduate psychology course where the object is to explore the relationships among culture, history, psychopathology, and up-to-date "treatments." I use the book in a senior capstone course for undergraduate majors interested in clinical and applied psychology, in a course on cross-cultural perspectives on psychotherapy, and in a research seminar on human change processes. I also believe that *Talking Cures* is accessible and of interest to the general reader with an interest in psychology and psychotherapy—a textbook that might be read for pleasure!

My hope is that more advanced students and general readers will couple their reading of this book with generous selections from the primary literature. Much of that literature is well written and culturally significant. Moreover, as Paul Ricoeur (1977/1992) noted, ultimately any aspect of the literature of psychotherapy can be verified only in the larger context of a particular theorist's "articulation of the entire network: [case histories], theory, hermeneutics, therapeutics, and narration" (p. 361).

My goal in *Talking Cures* is not to teach the mechanics of psychotherapeutic approaches; I assume that a substantial literature is already devoted to the application of therapeutic ideas and that nobody ever really learned how to do psychotherapy from a book anyway. Individual theories are not discussed in as much detail as many instructors will have come to expect from a textbook in this area of psychology, especially in the chapters that look at the work of Freud, Jung, Rogers, and the behaviorists. My assumption throughout is that theoretical details can be introduced, to the degree desired, by individual instructors. In my experience, it is more valuable for students to see the connections and the contradictions between competing ideas than to have a detailed working knowledge of the mechanics of the individual theories. Then, too, my students seem to be grateful for a textbook that consistently challenges them to make up their own minds and that does not invite massive amounts of memorization.

Instructors with an eclectic worldview especially ought to appreciate *Talking Cures*. When I teach this material, I become convinced of the great value and astute insights of each approach, without any worry about the massive contradictions implicit in my enthusiasm. Indeed, the most common question I am asked both out of class and in the last class discussion of the semester is: "What do you *really* believe?" Well, I guess I believe whatever I just said. I can appreciate all the approaches. But I hope that whatever I just said makes sense because of the context I am saying it in. Besides, foolish consistencies are the hobgoblins of too many narrow minds.

In Chapter 7 you will find a case history of my treatment of "Luke," a painfully confused and suicidal undergraduate who profoundly influenced the way I think about, teach, and apply the basic principles of psychoanalysis. But in Chapter 20, from the perspective of Zen Buddhism, I interpret the tragic life and stubborn survival of a former client, "Vivian," who has endured years of incestuous sexual abuse. To me, both interpretations are equally true and valid, and I "believe" them both equally. You, on the other hand, may well be inclined to apply a psychodynamic interpretation to Vivian's life and fate in Chapter 20, or a Zen interpretation to young Luke's dilemma in Chapter 7. To appreciate this book, in fact to tolerate its resistance to the question "What do you *really* believe?" it is probably necessary to agree with, or at least to be open to the possibilities in, George Lakoff's (1987) assertion that for we mere mortals there is no ultimate "God's eye view of the world—a single correct way of understanding what is and what is not true" (p. 9).

Unique Features of This Book

First off, yes, the ideas of a lot of "dead white guys" are represented in this book. But maybe fewer "dead white gods" are represented. If there is a way for an honest history of the practice of psychotherapy to be written with less emphasis on the patriarchs, I hope someone will tell me how. At least in this book you get some different dead white guys, a few dead white women, and a collection of dead Indian, Chinese, and Japanese guys—in addition to an interesting collection of living men and women—which is more than you usually get in many standard psychology textbooks.

In Part I, *Talking Cures* focuses extensively on the struggle during the Enlightenment to promote humanistic ideas, over religious beliefs and practices, for understanding and treating people with emotional and psychological disorders. Father Johann Gassner and Franz Anton Mesmer may be dead white guys, but they were genuine pioneers in developing psychological cures for the psychologically afflicted (even though neither of them knew it and in fact would both have despised me for saying so). The extraordinarily important role of the French scientists Jean-Martin Charcot and Jean-Pierre Janet is also recognized in these pages, as it is in few other books on psychotherapy, where Sigmund Freud is too often presented as the solitary founding father of dynamic psychology. I hope you will come away from the first few chapters of this book fascinated and intrigued by the "discovery of the unconscious," which changed the face of 19th-century psychiatry and set the stage for the development of psychoanalysis. This book's coverage of the discoveries of Joseph Breuer, Anna Freud, and Karen Horney is perhaps not as unusual, but I hope you will appreciate the distinct roles these pioneers played in the development of a scientifically based talking cure.

In Part II, it is a pleasure to pay tribute to the ideas of William James and to give them the fuller credit they deserve. They set the context for the century of North American psychology that was to follow. However else could one begin to understand John B. Watson and Mary Cover Jones?

In a similar vein, Part III introduces Mary Calkins's nearly forgotten work on the self and Gordon Allport's seminal writings on propriative growth and development, without which there may never have been a humanistic "third force" in American clinical psychology. I am especially happy with the range of ideas and perspectives introduced in the later chapters in Part III and hope you will have as much fun reading about Wilhelm Reich and Fritz Perls as I had in writing about them. Chapter 18 was the most difficult chapter to write, not because there is any question of the importance of feminist psychotherapy but because it is extraordinarily difficult to describe any particular approach as clearly and convincingly "feminist." As Mary Daly pointed out, many feminist critics question whether "mind gynecology" (Freud's term, not Daly's, although it serves her purpose brilliantly) is appropriate for victims of oppression. Chapter 19 represents my own psychotherapeutic worldview at the moment. It is 10% inspiration and 90% homage to the writings of those who have done the most to illuminate my own journey through life. Frankly, it is a chapter on metaphysics. If the spirit of William James approves of even a little bit of Chapter 19, I will be certain that I have not entirely wasted my time.

Part IV focuses on non-Western approaches to psychotherapy and personal growth, and it is rooted in the teachings and practices of Zen. I hope that we will see more and more attention paid in the West to the "quiet therapies" described in these chapters. I would rather have spent a month writing about Morita and Naikan therapies and the tea ceremony than an hour contemplating "managed care" and the politics of prescription privileges.

Acknowledgments

A number of people read and provided helpful suggestions for various drafts of *Talking Cures*. Christian Bates (Wabash '96), in his capacity as the Psychology Department's Parks Intern in the summer of 1995, read all the chapters and contributed significantly to both the chapter introductions and the chapter summaries. Brenda Bankart read most of the manuscript and provided valuable counsel throughout the process of preparing the manuscript for publication. Steve Morillo, Hall Peebles, and Emmy Peebles also provided help in times of need and welcome breaks from the solitary tasks of writing and revision. Debbie Polley, our interlibrary loan librarian, Jeff Beck, our reference librarian, and Diane Enenbach, the tsar of library circulation, all provided crucial help, usually in times of crisis. Speaking of crisis, special thanks to Scott Hemmerlein, who kept several computers up and running while I was working on this project—and on more than one occasion bailed me out of some electronic catastrophe. Judy Oswalt, Marcia Caldwell, and Debbie Bourff all helped produce the drafts of this book that my students read. Thanks to one and all. And thanks also to the several cohorts of students whose feedback has contributed so much to make this project a success.

The members of the production team that worked on *Talking Cures* have been wonderful collaborators. Becky Smith is an awesome force as a copy editor, and I am truly pleased to have had the opportunity to work so closely with the book's designers, Anne and Greg Draus of Scratchgravel Publishing Services, who also carried out the production of the book, and Kelly Shoemaker at Brooks/Cole. Finally I want to acknowledge the support and hard work of the three people at Brooks/Cole whose faith in this project made such an enormous difference. Eileen Murphy was my editor and guardian angel; Fiorella Ljunggren served as production supervisor and director of the pep band; and Claire Verduin was my publisher, therapist, and risk management counselor. I didn't find it at all peculiar that Claire fled into retirement after she accepted *Talking Cures* for publication, but it is a miracle that we finally all agreed on a single title for this book.

I am grateful to the reviewers of the manuscript for their constructive criticism and useful suggestions. They are Arthur Borhart, California State University–Dominguez Hills; Timothy Dickel, Creighton University; Sam Gladding, Wake Forest University; Wayne Lanning, University of Nevada–Las Vegas; John C. Lewton, University of Toledo; Beverly B. Palmer, California State University–Dominguez Hills; and Bill Thornton, University of Southern Maine.

Throughout this manuscript there are references to materials from my case files. In every case—with the exception of Rob in Chapter 12, who asked to have his name included—the names of the clients have been changed and their identifying characteristics substantially altered. Wherever possible, I have obtained permission from each of these persons to tell their stories. Several former clients have assisted me in recalling details of their cases. No person described in this book is currently a student or employee of Wabash College.

C. Peter Bankart

To the Student and the General Reader

The single most important realization I hope you will get from this book is that this metaphysical business called psychotherapy, this "talking cure," has to be comprehended ultimately as a powerful, distinctly personal relationship between two essentially similar human beings (or "humans being," as I say on my more existential days). My knowledge of students tells me that 99% of most students' energies are tied up, one way or another, in relationships. So I expect you to be profoundly good at reading between the lines in these pages. I hope you will never lose sight of the fundamental observation that all psychotherapy comes down to two human beings having a relationship that is so intensely real and important to both of them that at times nothing else will seem to matter.

So far, about half the student readers of various drafts of this book have concluded that Joseph Breuer must have been involved more than just clinically with poor sweet Anna O. (Chapter 5). And who knows what was going on between wifeless Franz Mesmer and 18-year-old Maria Theresa Paradis, who was his patient and houseguest for six long and lonely months in Vienna during the winter and spring of 1877 (Chapter 3), or between Sigmund Freud and Wilhelm Fleiss (Chapter 6). Not a shred of evidence that I am aware of would let me argue convincingly that there was more to these stories than Victorian propriety would have permitted. But I suspect that students are generally more perceptive of these things than any scholar, and you may well be right, especially after you read the data presented in Chapter 18 on sexual intimacy between therapists and their patients.

But I hope you will focus on the idea of relationships a bit more broadly. I hope that you will develop a real sensitivity for the central role played in all forms of psychotherapy by the core values that must be shared and communicated between a therapist and a client before any psychotherapy will succeed. In Chapter 19 I refer to these values as essential for the ultimate purpose of psychotherapy—namely, the mutual and courageous search for truth. But I want you to understand that the "truth" I thus speak of is not just some finite, load-bearing, mathematically probable statement about reality as we know it. From where I stand, this notion of truth must be extended to some active process whereby we make sense of the world we actively construct. This "making sense," or, as I prefer, "having the world truthfully," requires achieving a clear understanding of both one's self and one's world. As Paul Watchel (1984/1992) observed:

The situations one finds oneself in can often be understood not as thoroughly external events but as products of one's subjective particularities. That is, the events do not simply "happen" to us but are a predictable consequence of our internal state and the behavior it leads to. The stark impassiveness of a dominating husband, for example, both contributes to the wife's fear of assertiveness and stems from it. One woman I worked with was stunned to discover how much of a "pushover" her husband was once she started asserting herself. As she spontaneously put it, "I thought he was the situation I faced, but he was the situation I *made.*" (p. 430)

The result of a successful therapeutic partnership that helps people to see, think, and behave more truthfully is a reduction in pain and an increase in well-being. But beyond that, a successful therapeutic partnership involves a fuller realization of our potential happiness, a rediscovered capacity to love, to relate openly, and to live more creatively—a way of living that Sigmund Freud characterized as reflecting the "terminal stage" of human development, the ideal "genital character."

Thus the therapeutic relationship is no ordinary marriage of convenience, nor (although money usually changes hands) is it simply the "purchase of friendship." It is a relationship founded on profoundly moral terms. As Joseph Margolis (1966/ 1992) pointed out, in fact it is a relationship "doubly subject to moral review" (p. 89). First, it is a professional alliance, subject to ethical scrutiny (confidentiality, informed consent, professional licensure, and so forth). And second,

it is directly and professionally concerned with influencing changes in human action and motivation, a matter that ordinarily falls within the domain of morality. . . . The enterprise of psychotherapy, whatever the variety or doctrinal conviction, clearly presupposes a set of values in the name of which the alteration of the lives of patients is undertaken. (Margolis, 1966/1992, p. 89)

The therapeutic relationship is thus based on a set of values that are profoundly *eudaimonistic,* a 50-cent word that refers to a metaphysical theory of happiness. Following the lead of Aristotle, most of Western psychotherapy's eudaimonia is based on the value of actively living one's life fully and rationally. Probably no psychologist has expressed this function of psychotherapy more eloquently than Carl Rogers (Chapter 15), who wrote:

Both the subjective experience of psychotherapy and the scientific findings regarding it indicate that individuals are motivated to change, and may be helped to change, in the direction of greater openness to experience, and hence in the direction of behavior which is enhancing of self and society, rather than destructive. (1955, p. 277)

Will *Talking Cures* lead you to fashion your own eudaimonia? Perhaps not, but it may offer a rough guide to where you may want to look further. The ideas in this book have the potential to change your life in important and enriching ways. Happy hunting!

PRELUDE

Until philosophers are kings in their cities, or the kings
and princes of this world have the spirit and power of
philosophy . . . cities will never have the rest from
their evils—no, nor the human race, as I believe,
and then only will this our ideal State have a
possibility of life and behold the light of day.

PLATO

CHAPTER 1

Basic Considerations for Undertaking a History of the Talking Cure

Eat a Bowl of Rice

Talking Cures *is a book about people and places, ideas and images. More than that, this book is about the process of understanding the human condition across continents and centuries. This ongoing human pursuit is traced through the long history of the search for an all-encompassing, reasoned therapeutic ideal that will speak to the psychological and emotional needs of human beings. In this book, psychotherapy is viewed as an art practiced by individual "artists"—although at the same time its practice is limited both by ethics and values and by the sometimes rigid restraints of science. Psychotherapy is itself about change. Enjoy yourself as you learn about the historical and cultural roots of psychotherapy and explore your own path into the world of people and ideas that is psychotherapy.*

The Triumph of the Therapeutic

Modern scientific psychology and its extraordinary product—systematic emotional and behavioral treatment of disordered individuals by means of a formalized therapy constructed around two human beings talking with each other—is scarcely one hundred years old. We might, in fact, date the formal origins of the talking cure to Sigmund Freud's seminal psychological exploration of the mysteries of the unconscious mind, *The Interpretation of Dreams,* which was published in 1900. Yet within that relatively short period, modern psychotherapies and the men and women who have defined and developed them have had a profound impact on our culture and all the human lives contained within it.

It is not an exaggeration to say that Western civilization's acceptance of the "talking cure" has permanently and profoundly influenced the way we think about ourselves, understand others, raise our children, and anticipate the future. We impose "therapeutic" interpretations on practically every aspect and important event in our lives. One could even seriously argue that the language and concepts of psychotherapy have largely supplanted both the doctrines and rituals of religion and the dictates of civil authority as the common cultural context for our separate lives.

In the past, religious doctrines provided a common, inclusive bond among all members of relatively homogeneous communities. These days, however, social analyses based on religion tend to divide us into exclusive enclaves of fellow believers that barely coexist within the larger culture. For example, when students get together to form Bible study groups, I have witnessed heated debates over whether Catholics can rightfully be considered Christians.

It is similarly difficult for us to understand our society and ourselves from a class-based economic and political perspective, probably because of the moral and ethical disrepute Marxism fell into after World War I. If nothing else, the infusion of issues of race and ethnicity into any discussion of social class muddies the waters of understanding. In addition, as the raging public debates over "political correctness" demonstrate, a great many people today are determined to resist social analyses that explore race, gender, and ethnicity as coherent explanations about the course of our lives.

Metaphors for Our Time

Today, it is perhaps only within the secular, supposedly objective, scientific context of terms like *diagnosis, treatment,* and *recovery* that we find it possible to see, understand, and truly comprehend one another. Psychology and, more particularly, psychotherapy have become our common language of discourse. Psychotherapy provides the central metaphors for conversation among "Christians," "feminists," "African Americans," "neoconservative Democrats," "gay men and lesbians," "environmentalists," and "secular humanists."

Even for the confirmed and enthusiastic psychologist, this development is not altogether wonderful. Too much that is important cannot be comprehended in the language, the methods, and the metaphors of the discipline. We can't, for example, come to terms with spiritual forces that are strong enough to compel people to give up their freedom and their lives in the service of extremist "cults"; but we can understand that a Jimmy Jones or a David Koresh was a "psychopath" who controlled the "minds" of his "sick" followers. We don't recognize the economic and political causes of the epidemic of crack cocaine use throughout the United States; but we can say that we know that "addictions" are a "disease," a form of "mental illness." We no longer have a common moral authority to show us where our lives have lost their meaning, their purpose, or their certainty. But we can "understand" that 52 million adult Americans (28%) will suffer from a "diagnosable mental disorder" within the next twelve months (Regier et al., 1993). Thus we depend almost exclusively on the language of psychology and psychotherapy to convert the personally and morally unimaginable and unfathomable into the culturally and even scientifically understandable and manageable.

A Language for Insults

We often attempt to apply the psychological tools we use for understanding others to ourselves, in the hope that these tools will permit us to "know" ourselves. Most of us, I think, are unaware of how distorting and narrowing such psychologized self-knowledge truly is. Just about every reader of this book, for example, could compose a long list of psychological attributes that describe his or her own personality. The task is even easier if I ask you to describe only your negative attributes.

Probably because of their fascination with the pathological in human nature, psychologists have not been very successful at teaching people a vocabulary and category system to describe positive and healthy human qualities. However, we all are more or less articulate psychological experts at the fine art of describing the negative side of our experience as being human beings. Perhaps one of psychology's greatest triumphs has been in teaching so many of us the psychobabble vocabulary that we use to call ourselves and others bad names!

The Idea Behind This Book

The goal of this book is to uncover the historical roots of our love affair with the psychological and the therapeutic. My plan over the next 24 chapters is to trace the historical and cultural roots of the "science of the mind." Out of them has grown our current awareness of what it means to become, as well as what it means to fail at becoming, a fully functioning human being.

The struggle of humankind to understand itself is a fascinating journey. It has a great many dead ends, quite an extraordinary cast of characters, and a moral lesson or two to teach as well. It reveals no more absolute "truth" than any other field of human endeavor, but with the self as its focus, its hints at truth and suggestions of wisdom make it perhaps the most compelling story of our age.

Philosophical Roots of the Talking Cure

At their intellectual roots, all formal Western approaches to psychotherapy are products of the Enlightenment. Each presents a reasoned response to the emotional and psychological costs of the Darwinian struggle to survive the social competition brought on by the industrial age. Each school of psychotherapy offers a distinctive solution to the challenges posed by 19th-century "modernization," with its intense focus on individualism and the individual's struggle to live humanely in a difficult world.

The central focus of *Talking Cures* is the intellectual, scientific, philosophical, and practical foundations of modern psychotherapies. Our study will lead us from their beginnings in the prayers and incantations of ancient priest-healers in Mesopotamia, Persia, and Egypt to the emergence of the 18th-century philosophers' faith in the power of reason and science, the modern-day formulation of the cognitive therapies, and our postmodern understanding of the elusiveness of the Truth.

Talking Cures will also address how the assumptions, goals, and methods of every new psychotherapy reflect the hopes and the beliefs of the times and cultures from which it is derived. My hope is that *Talking Cures* will leave every interested reader with a clearer appreciation for the simple idea that everything we understand of the human condition and every assumption we make about human nature is ultimately a reflection of the historical, political, and cultural forces that have shaped our ways of seeing, and even being, in the world.

A Focus on People

This is also a book about the ways psychotherapists like myself make a living. It is about the lessons we can learn from others about the sources of human joy, suffering, and understanding—both in our own lives and in the lives of those closest to us. *Talking Cures*, in a real way, is an homage to the lives of several hundred people who, over the past 25 years, have shared their humanity—their despair, their hopes, their fears, and their victories—with me, a perfectly ordinary human being who calls himself a therapist. This book is an effort to share the insights I have gleaned from learning about these lives, these common, everyday lives full of question and remorse, often sad and sometimes tragic secrets, uncommon joy, and common everyday unhappiness. *Talking Cures* is a meditation on 25 years of shared triumphs and defeats, a quarter century of wisdom glimpsed and lost and then, sometimes, regained.

I make my living largely by listening to people tell me the stories of their lives and by telling and retelling my own stories in return. Each story is distinct and unique;

yet at the same time each story is universal and part of our shared experience as human beings. Often my job as a therapist is to try to help the story teller sort out which is which. Sometimes I can help that person find the universal within his or her particular life experience. Sometimes our shared task is to reveal the unique and the exceptional that lie embedded within the universal. Our quest is to uncover the emotional truth, the spiritual truth, and the intellectual-historical truth within each person's story.

The Fine Art of Learning to Listen

Therapists learn to listen to silences as well as words, to the nonverbal as well as the verbal. The meaning in a person's eyes may reveal a truth unfathomable by language alone. Therapists also learn to listen for the errors and distortions that invade the stories that are told. We try to understand why someone has chosen to tell this particular fellow human being this particular story at this particular time. A fully attuned psychotherapist is in large measure a professional riddle solver—a hopeful traveler, like the mighty Oedipus, trying to outsmart the wily sphinx that may be encountered at almost any turn along the road. It's a preposterous way to make a living. Some days I wonder why all therapists aren't turned into pillars of salt, as a cosmic protest against the arrogance and presumption inherent in the practice of the profession.

A Cautionary Note Concerning Your Source

Perhaps I have already started to lead you down a path that I must constantly remind myself and my fellow therapists not to travel. I said that this book is about the lives of the people who have trusted their stories to me. But in reality, this book is not so much about those lives, as about what I remember (or think I remember) and value and keep of the stories I am told.

The truth is largely that psychotherapy is about the reconstructions individual therapists make of people's lives based on the fragments we think we understand in the deeply flawed process of trying to hear and comprehend another human being. Every psychotherapeutic encounter is defined by the categories and the schemata of understanding that a therapist brings to that relationship by virtue of his or her own training and life experience. Thus the process and the substance of psychotherapy is fundamentally shaped by the values that therapists employ to give their own lives meaning. This book merely gives you an idea of the sort of "engineering diagrams" we use in that creative and constructive process. The task of attempting genuine understanding of every person who enters the consulting room is perhaps better left to the gods.

This point is neither particularly profound nor especially controversial. It is, however, absolutely crucial to your ability to learn anything significant from these pages. For it is critically important that you obey this book's primary directive: "*If you meet the Buddha on the road, kill him!"* When you travel the road of life actively in pursuit of wisdom, you will encounter many charlatans and many smiling people offering facile solutions to even the most complex dilemmas. The only way to encounter the true Buddha on the road, however, is to obliterate all the false Buddhas from your heart and mind. What needs to be "killed" is not the false prophet or the slick New Age huckster, of course, but the part inside you that wants to find THE answer, the part that demands an external authority provide quickly satisfying, easy answers. If you meet the illusion of a true Buddha in these pages—or anywhere else, for that matter—you need to strike down your own pretense and resume your journey. In psychotherapy as in most of life, it is far better to travel hopefully than to arrive at your destination prematurely and full of conceit and self-satisfaction.

There are no absolute truths in this book, and it will not reveal to you the secrets of the human heart. Any part of this book that seems to make a claim of infallibility should be instantly dismissed as at best an intriguing clue. If it persists in asserting dominance over your thinking, destroy it utterly by considering the source: a middle-aged professor sitting at his desk in the middle of Indiana writing a book that he hopes you'll read but not take too seriously. Then ask yourself, "Would I really invite anyone, let alone a *professor,* to change the way I really think?" And then go out and "kill" the false prophet before he silences your own thoughts.

The View From the Consulting Room

"Psychotherapy Is About Change" is written in foot-tall invisible letters on the walls of my consulting room. Most of my clients recognize the necessity of change, of course, but all begin the psychotherapeutic journey with the firm conviction that therapy will empower them to effect that change in other people. The classic case is the distraught person who makes an appointment with a therapist and demands that the therapist "Fix my rotten kid/spouse/boss/lover!" Once this other person has been transformed through the magic of psychotherapy, the client is convinced, life will be vastly richer and more fulfilling for everyone.

As a therapist, I enter into each new relationship knowing that what the client really wants is impossible. There is no technology for miraculously turning a rotten kid into a perfect child, a no-good spouse into a model of domestic partnership, a selfish, shortsighted boss into a paragon of enlightened stewardship, or a disinterested lover into a paragon of devotion.

People in an unhappy relationship who come to therapy motivated by the wish to have things change so that they can remain in that relationship ultimately must accept the necessity and the inevitability of change in themselves. Even more difficult to accept, perhaps, is the reality that none of them will completely control the process or direction of change. Most aspects of the therapeutic process are thoroughly reciprocal, and most change is conservative and incremental. In the end, if therapist and client are successful in achieving their goals, it will be impossible to say who is responsible for changing what in whom. As a therapist, I know in my mind and in my heart that there is no way to overcome unhappiness or despair without addressing the need for fundamental change within oneself.

Certainly, if the client changes in some remarkable way, a great number of other people and situations will change. But neither the client nor I have any way of predicting either the direction or the extent of subsequent changes. Will she fall in or out of love? Will she bring back into conscious memory painful events long buried in a self-protective amnesia? Will she recognize that she has been socialized to think bizarrely and irrationally about herself and her most important and intimate relationships? Will she come to recognize how selfishly she has turned her back on the obligation she owes her parents? Will she come to realize that she has never been able to love herself without feeling guilty and ashamed?

Historical and Cultural Contexts in Psychotherapy

The most important question for the present discussion is whether each of these distinct outcomes is equally likely. If not (and in my experience they aren't), then what accounts for the patterns that emerge when we conduct research on the experience of hundreds or even thousands of people engaged in the therapeutic process?

A major portion of the variance has to be assigned to social, cultural, and historical processes. It is within these contexts that we live our lives. Even the most basic facts of existence—one's gender, social class, race, developmental level, physical health, sexual orientation, temperament, and central psychological traits—make sense and have genuine significance only as they are played out within the unique frame of a specific society, culture, and historical context. Throughout this book I will thus attempt to identify and explore the role of societal, cultural, and historical variables in the development and practice of each of the psychotherapies under study. An additional reason for doing so will be to try to show how fully psychotherapies mirror the cultures they originate within.

A genuine understanding of Freud's psychoanalysis, for example, requires (and at the same time provides) a reasonably deep understanding of middle-class life in turn-of-the-century Europe. In practical terms, to understand Freud's theory of the sexual basis of neuroses, one must first understand Freud's biological explanation for the preeminence of the sex drive. This explanation must be understood in turn within the context of the importance attached to instincts, especially sexual instincts, in the late-19th-century European science of biology.

I want to push this point one step further: To fathom Freud's near-obsession with the sexual foundations of emotional distress is also to come to a fuller awareness of the sexual repression and hypocrisy in the lives of the Austrian middle class at the turn of the last century and the effect of this repression on the mental health of adolescents and young adults during the time when Freud derived his theories.

In a similar fashion, as you will see in Chapter 22, unmet reciprocal personal obligation is perceived in contemporary Japan to be at the root of many common emotional disorders. Knowledge of this bit of cultural anthropology helps us to understand why Japanese psychotherapies are constructed the way they are and how they operate therapeutically within Japanese culture. Understanding these psychotherapies also provides us with a window through which we can view both the organization of traditional values within Japanese culture and the way the stresses and strains of contemporary urban life affect the people living within that value system.

Asked why he studied emotionally disturbed individuals when his goal was to achieve an objective science of the normal mind, Freud replied that he studied neurotics for the same reason that geologists study shattered crystals: because the broken-apart examples reveal the structure of the intact members of the group. We might say that we study the psychotherapies and the psychopathologies of a society within a culture at a specific moment in time in order to see where the lines of fracture exist in that society. Our goal as psychologists and students of psychology is both to study the individuals living within that cultural-historical moment and to try to understand that moment itself.

An Answer to Paradox

What insights into our own social organization do we gain from the following apparently contradictory findings from contemporary research into depression?

The data from hundreds of studies of psychotherapy outcomes suggest that "cognitive therapy" is the most effective psychotherapy for unipolar depression in contemporary North America. Cognitive therapy (see Chapter 14) consists largely of helping clients learn to identify and correct systematic "errors" in the way they think when they are depressed. At the same time that therapists are crediting the success of the therapy to its focus on "cognitive behavior modification," however, most psychotherapy clients attribute the benefits they feel they have gained from therapy to the warm, authentic, caring acceptance of a supportive therapist. In fact, clients tend to feel this way regardless of the therapeutic techniques applied by and subscribed to by the therapist.

My answer to this conundrum, and you are welcome to your own, is that from an objective, "scientific" perspective, contemporary middle-class Americans—whether they have any awareness of this fact or not, and contrary to the most closely held beliefs of humanistic psychologists (see Chapter 15)—find their lives most manageable and harmonious when they live in accord with the ideals of the stoic philosophers of antiquity. That stoic ideal states that a rational, scientific explanation of life can make psychological pain bearable and emotional loss sustainable. The therapist who is most successful in helping clients understand this ideal and who is most clever at helping depressed people mend their cognitive ways will, therefore, be the most successful therapist.

On the other hand, ordinary people within our culture more or less implicitly embrace a "truth" that is completely contrary to the fundamental assertions of contemporary cognitive therapies (see Chapter 14). Contrary to the hair-shirt philosophy of the stoics, this "naive" view, which is powerfully reinforced by both popular culture and popular psychology, is that how you feel at any given point is determined by the state of your relationships with those people who are closest to you and are the most intimately involved with your well-being. Accordingly, if your relationship with the therapist results in your feeling less depressed and helpless, your explanation for the improvement is not focused on the therapist's technique but on his or her relationship with you.

This interpretation of the data might lead to this resolution of the paradox: Optimal recovery from unipolar depression requires thinking in new ways (an observable "fact" from the data); such new thinking appears to become more likely when a depressed person experiences acceptance and support within the context of a strong therapeutic relationship (a second observable "fact" in the data). Thus we can conclude objectively that, within our culture, both the stoic philosophical ideal and our personal relationships are important factors in our psychological well-being.

These two assumptions—although apparently mundane and obvious—are, in fact, defining aspects of our culture and are not universal to the human condition. For a great many cultures, stoicism and "interpersonalism" are not central ideals. My own theory is that interpersonalism is most critically important in times and cultures that value romantic love. I would argue likewise that "reason" is a relative value. In all probability, reason becomes more important with the development of an industrial economy based on the principles of an objective, scientific worldview.

A "Postmodern" View of Causation

The foregoing discussion illustrates a few other points that need to be made before we get down to cases. Perhaps the most compelling idea is that within the psychotherapeutic process even highly reliable and seemingly objective "facts" are open to interpretation, conjecture, belief, and even taste. Reality is thus phenomenologically constructed—by each person involved in the therapeutic process. This view of reality, which honors diverse and even contradictory interpretations of human experience, is the essence of a "postmodern" worldview.

For example, in the case of a therapist treating a client diagnosed with depression, the therapist may attribute the reduction in Tom's depression scores on the Beck Depression Inventory and the improvement in Tom's relationships at work and at home to her success in teaching Tom to perceive his world more rationally. Tom, by contrast, may attribute his improvement to the caring quality of his relationship with the therapist and to the growth he has achieved through the insights he has gained about himself and his relationships with others. Meanwhile, Tom's therapist's supervisor sees Tom's improvement as evidence that basic laboratory research into the dynamics of depression are starting to have a major payoff in the culture. She may also have a private moment to acknowledge that all those years of the therapist's doctoral training and postdoctoral supervision are really starting to pay off. The chain of possible explanations and attributions is potentially endless and radiates in all directions from every element of the initial situation.

The postmodern view of this dynamic exchange of narratives is that all three versions of events are potentially equally "true" and valid, and they don't fatally contradict one another. Rationality, relationship, and professional training are *all* implicated in Tom's struggle with depression. All are vital in coming to terms with the needs of the 20 million Americans who become clinically depressed each year (Regier et al., 1993); it follows that both reason and intimacy must be in painfully short supply in this culture. For psychology to serve people in some consistent and meaningful fashion, it must address as best it can questions associated with both cognitive and interpersonal processes.

Meanwhile, we can have great fun debating as cognitivists, humanists, logicians, poets, theologians, disbelieving students, and doctrinaire professors. Within professional psychology, this ambiguity becomes the stuff of a thousand doctoral dissertations. And of course it can be transformed into a giant turf war between competing scholarly enclaves, each of which hopes to entice the really big dollars from the federal granting agencies and the legal right to prescribe psychotropic medications.

The Buddha on the Road, Revisited

I hope you will begin, and end, your reading of *Talking Cures* resigned to the complex fact that no single Big Truth exists to explain the mystery and the reality of psychotherapy. In therapy, as in every other field of human endeavor, it is not even logical to think everyone will agree on one Truth for all people for all time. Anyone who tries to persuade you otherwise, or any part of yourself that wants to believe otherwise, is a false Buddha.

Psychotherapy as Art Based on Science

Corsini (1989) wrote "Psychotherapy is an art based upon science." I am particularly fond of this description, because it gives me the only opportunity I will ever have to call myself an artist. I suspect that every practicing psychotherapist also thinks of herself or himself as engaged in a creative, self-expressive art. Our vocation isn't mechanical; we don't fear being replaced by computers or any other bit of technology.

But what is this "art"? Do I create the client sitting in front of me? Does a client become mine in the sense that a statue is a Rodin or a Michelangelo or a novel is a Charlotte Brontë or an Alice Walker? How will the therapeutic process engage and reflect my creative talents? How will I leave my signature on the finished piece? For that matter, will it ever be finished? Perhaps the client becomes a canvas that passes from studio to studio during its life—never completed, only "finished" when time runs out.

As you can see right away, I hope, the metaphor of psychotherapy as art is problematic. But I think we can consider the therapist an artist primarily because what goes on in the consulting room is a spontaneous, creative process of discovery and self-expression that operates according to a set of rules and principles previously laid down by those who established the basic parameters of its presentation.

Great Masters and Their Therapeutic Schools

The great masters of the talking cure were those who established these basic parameters—and in many cases inspired whole schools of devoted followers. Often the great masters challenged their culture's fundamental assumptions about what it means to possess genuine self-knowledge and how that knowledge is obtained. In the process they invented new methods of self-exploration and self-expression, which over time became the trademarks of various schools of psychotherapy.

With careful reading, you will come to recognize the characteristic signatures in their work. You will also come to discover a special affinity for the style and power of one or two specific approaches. Certainly, finding the medium that best speaks to your own penchants and tastes can be of intellectual and practical significance to you in the years ahead. However, I also hope that you will come away from your study with new appreciation for some schools that you may have known little or nothing about before reading these chapters. Perhaps you will also gain a better appreciation for the skill required of those who work within a framework that you had previously dismissed as uninteresting or simple-minded.

But the point we need to address here is more practical than aesthetic. The artistry associated with every school of psychotherapy is specific and highly refined. Each produces a likeness of the person that is to be read and evaluated according to the accepted standards of its tradition. How your portrait looks when the artist is done has less to do with how skinny or short or bald or old you are than with whether the painter was Picasso in his Blue period, van Gogh at the height of his powers, or a Zen monk painting you with his eyes closed.

Psychotherapeutic Narratives

The metaphor of the narrative portrait has become an increasingly important idea in contemporary writing about this creative constructive process in psychotherapy (Bruner, 1990). As when you have your portrait painted on a canvas, the "you" that emerges in a psychotherapeutic narrative bears some essential relation to you as a living creature, but to some extent it is also a product of the therapist's creative process of perceiving you—a process called *apperception*. In more formal psychological terms, we could say that you are the stimulus but that the creative power of the therapist turns the sensation of that stimulus into a coherent perception. You might prefer a fairly superficial but highly accurate factual narrative, or perhaps a more insightfully written one that reveals some deep essence of your character, or a narrative that portrays much of your life as an essential mystery. In the end, however, the text of the narrative that will be constructed depends in large measure on the interpretation of the events of your life by the creative person to whom you reveal yourself. In psychotherapy, as in art, you may reject that interpretation if you find it disagreeable (you probably cannot avoid having to pay for it, unfortunately). If it is a narrative that you find genuinely informed, you can use it as a starting point for deep self-discovery.

Why is this point important? It is because the therapist is ultimately going to "read" the constructed narrative back to you as your own story. The therapist will proceed with no small enthusiasm to help you comprehend and accept the psychological complexity, emotional power, and human truth that is embedded within the narrative.

Refer back to the example of a man selecting therapy for depression. A cognitive psychotherapist is going to develop a narrative of Tom as a person who needs to recognize how pervasively influenced he has been by profoundly distorted, maladaptive, and even irrational cognitions about life and its outcomes. A therapist in the Japanese tradition of Zen would want Tom to hear the narrative of a selfish neurotic who is intimidated by the challenge of engaging the web of obligation that motivates all human life. An Adlerian psychotherapist would write the story of a profoundly discouraged man who is failing in the essential task of making a constructive contribution to the future of society.

Are all three narratives equally valid? If we assume the integrity of the therapeutic relationship in each instance, then we would have to concede that each account of Tom's life is as valid and as potentially therapeutic as any other. We might want to question the applicability of a Zen interpretation in west-central Indiana or the usefulness of a purely rational interpretation in Victorian Vienna, but we would not necessarily question the significance or the sincerity of the narrator's perception.

We must be actively aware, however, that the therapist-as-narrator is imposing his or her perceptions on our reality. Further, we must recognize that the therapist's narratives are a product of a specific culture, time, and worldview, and that they may or may not fit especially well with the original phenomenologically constructed narrative the patient initially brought to therapy. We must always hope that the construction of the narrative has been a thoroughly collaborative effort between the client and the therapist, but we will almost never know that for certain.

The idea of the psychotherapeutic narrative is important in another sense too. If we are reading these narratives a decade or a century later, it may be especially hard for us, in perhaps a completely different cultural setting, to understand that we can look at the story of a neurotic person's suffering as revealing something of that time and culture to us. As you read the various narrative accounts of psychotherapy in this book, I hope you will develop the ability to see the work of the various therapists as windows on culture and history, at least as much as they are clinical portraits.

Dawes (1994), using the metaphor of a "personal story" in the place of Bruner's use of the term *narrative,* cautions us, however, to remain skeptical about wholly accepting the therapist's constructed narrative. He issues a strong warning to the readers of these therapeutic reconstructions, stating that such narratives may present a feel-good trap that may in fact distort the realities of people's lives:

> Unfortunately, no research has been conducted on the extent to which the "good story" is a liberator or a trap—at least none of which I am aware—so the question is unresolved. Even if such a "good story" is liberating, however, we may still question whether it is really the role of the therapist to encourage a belief in a story that is predictably incorrect. Do clients come to therapy to become deluded in the interests of their liberation? Would we really choose to believe an incorrect "explanation" of our own behavior simply because it made us happy—especially if this explanation negated the role of our own deliberate choice in what we did? (p. 217)

A Note on Therapeutic Objectivity

Like all other human beings, psychotherapists live in a world largely of their own creation. In the creative exploration of a human life, they may take vows of scientific objectivity, radical humanism, or antivitalism (see Chapter 2), but they surrender all genuine prospect for objectivity at the gates of their perception. I suspect that we begin psychotherapy, whether as therapist or client, with the hope of finding a person who sees and constructs the world pretty much as we do.

Sometimes the expectations that clients bring to therapy offer an embarrassing view of how psychotherapists are viewed in popular culture. I still have occasional conversations with a young man I'll call Todd who originally called about a problem he was having with insomnia. The first time Todd came into my consulting room, he looked around briefly and then lay on the office sofa with his head toward my chair. There was an awkward silence as I struggled for something appropriate to say, which was broken when Todd asked me to tell him what age he should begin trying to remember.

Alas for Todd, I had to tell him that I didn't believe we could have a productive conversation unless he was sitting up and we were looking at each other face-to-face. Todd was completely taken aback by the "normality" I imposed on our meeting. He had rehearsed the scene a thousand times in his mind before coming to the appointment, and it never occurred to him that he would not almost immediately be led to discover the repressed memories that he assumed had to be at the root of all psychological difficulties. I have had other clients who never could quite accept that therapy can be conducted face-to-face, and I can only hope that they eventually found a therapist whose "picture" of the therapeutic hour more closely matched their own. Todd's initial anticipation of what therapy would be was common enough, by the way, that I ended up selling the couch and replacing it with chairs.

Clients' initial assumptions often reveal odd beliefs about psychotherapy. They sometimes also reveal peculiar, if not bizarre, aspects of their previous experiences with psychotherapists. Not too long ago, for example, I had an initial session with a new client who began with a detailed dissertation on her most lurid and graphic sexual fantasies. "Stop!" I cried, after about 15 seconds. "Why are you telling me these things, Pat? We hardly know each other!"

Pat explained that in her only other therapeutic experience, revealing and discussing sexual fantasies was the sole content of all the conversations she had engaged in. When Pat had initially resisted her therapist's pressure to engage in this rather unconventional behavior, she had been told that she was "regressing into denial, repression, and hysterical avoidance."

Some Practical Advice

The number-one item of business between Pat and me became a rather careful and thorough exploration of what else had happened in this previous "therapy." It didn't appear that Pat had been sexually exploited by her previous therapist, but she had lost a lot of valuable time in getting to the real issues that brought her to therapy. In the interim, her therapist had, of course, benefited financially from indulging in pseudotherapeutic voyeurism.

Pat's experience with an incompetent therapist shows both how trusting many people are of the mysterious power of their therapist and how much bizarre behavior passes as therapy in our do-your-own-thing age of all sorts of psychomagic. Some of the more imaginative New Age scams being offered as therapy these days are described in the last chapter of *Talking Cures.*

Dawes (1994) addressed the issue of the scientific legitimacy of a wide range of "diagnostic" and "therapeutic" practices still in common use by therapists of all stripes, but especially by psychologists. As one example, after reviewing the scientific literature concerning the validity of projective tests, most specifically the Rorschach ink blot test, Dawes concluded:

> I would like to offer the reader some advice here. If a professional psychologist is "evaluating" you in a situation in which you are at risk and asks you for responses to ink blots or to incomplete sentences, or for a drawing of anything, walk out of that psychologist's office. Going through with such an examination creates the danger of having a serious decision made about you on totally invalid grounds. If your contact with the psychologist involves a legal matter, your civil liberties themselves may be at stake. If you have been mandated to see the psychologist by court order, quietly object to the test if possible, and ask to make an appointment later. Immediately consult a lawyer. (pp. 152–153)

As a rule of thumb, I strongly recommend that, if you meet a person claiming to offer psychotherapy who seems more "out of it" than you are and who expects you to do things that seem eccentric and strange, you immediately follow the immortal words of Monty Python: "Run away! Run away! Run away!"

Psychotherapy as Persuasion

The point of this lengthy digression is simple. As the former president of the American Psychological Association, Albert Bandura, wrote, psychotherapy is basically a process of persuasion (Bandura, 1969). The goal of the therapist is to get you to see that if you adopt the therapist's view of life, psychology, and being—then you will for all practical purposes be relieved of your psychic troubles.

These prescriptions come in dozens of different forms: Think logically! Discover your past! Embrace your obligations! Be here now! Reinforce discriminatively different responses to the stimulus! The personal is political! Listen to your anima speak!

I too seek to persuade my clients to a way of thinking, and perhaps of being, that will release them from their pain and unhappiness. At least initially, they try to persuade me that they aren't responsible for the state they are in. I try to persuade them that they are. Once I win the argument, they are "cured"—or at least much recovered. When they refuse to be persuaded, it is not because I am wrong but because (obviously!) they are stubborn, resistant, unenlightened, and unreachable. If I cannot persuade, cajole, or otherwise convert my clients to my way of thinking, my duty is to refer them to another therapist. I do so with the hope that the next therapist will be more successful than I have been in moving these particular clients toward more productive ways of thinking and behaving.

Cosmetic Psychopharmacology

A lot of my clients come in already persuaded that they have a "chemical imbalance." What they want is a magic pill, and indeed a lot of these clients discover the magical powers invested in and offered up by chemical science. They respond to the drug-induced biological changes in themselves by feeling better, becoming more hopeful and less helpless.

Is the use of chemicals cheating? Perhaps not. But a reactivated neuron isn't much of a metaphor for living one's life more productively and more humanely.

What's more, the mighty placebo, the all-powerful sugar pill, or the hopeful weekly phone call from the front-office receptionist, could potentially put a lot of hardworking, honest psychotherapists out of work. Let's face it, hysterical misery is something that every red-blooded psychotherapist can develop an enthusiasm for—but hysterical relief? Not that I would for one second disavow any of the placebo effects that occur every day in my own work with clients. Indeed, the placebo effect has a long and well-documented history, even in the treatment of physical ailments like angina pectoris (Bleich, Moore, Benson, & McCallie, 1979). But must I as a psychotherapist compete with every mountebank appearing in cable television infomercials who will lift depression and cure warts for anyone who will send $25 to the Tower of Hope?

The Science of Psychotherapy

Several readers of early drafts of this book commented that although I might make a persuasive case for the art of psychotherapy, I had not given enough credit to its scientific foundations. I hope that in subsequent drafts I responded adequately to most of these criticisms. Ultimately, you will have to judge the merits of this criticism on your own. But I do have a defense of being less scientific in *Talking Cures* than some would expect, which I hope will help set the tone for the rest of the chapters.

In my view, this entire book is about the "scientific" foundations of psychotherapy. Franz Anton Mesmer and his fellow magnetists in 18th-century Europe were among the leading scientific thinkers of their age. Freud was one of the most brilliant neurologists of his generation, and he followed the rules of the science of his day with precision and determination. Carl Rogers, probably the greatest humanistic psychologist in history, insisted that psychotherapy could develop only in accord with a rigorous new "science of the person." Meanwhile, B. F. Skinner propounded a revolutionary behaviorism that declared virtually everything Rogers was concerned with to be outside the legitimate realm of science. And in 1988 Roger Sperry, the father of experimental neuroscience, wrote an article in *American Psychologist* declaring that the "new" science of cognitive psychology need not exclude matters of religion, "freedom of will, conscious purpose, subjective value, morality, and other subjective phenomena which are vital to religion" (p. 607).

The problem with evaluating the contribution of science to the development of the talking cure (and its sibling problem, the "scientific merit" of psychotherapy) is that very few of us are going to agree on what the nature of science is, what its logical boundaries are, and whether and how often the definition of science changes.

I agree wholeheartedly that psychotherapy absolutely must be grounded in science. At the very least, the process psychotherapists go through in deriving answers to their questions must be public, be open to criticism, and result in "truths" subject to correction, modification, and even rejection.

By those standards, even the long-lost specialty of phrenology and its lifelong champion, Franz Joseph Gall (1758–1828), deserve respect. Phrenology was the science of reading character traits and temperament and predicting behavior on the basis of the morphology of the skull and facial features. Phrenology was such a perfect science that it put itself right out of business. Phrenologists offered precise quantification of data, exact scientific predictions, public access to noninvasive dependent variables, and complete falsifiability. The only problem was that phrenology was to-tally, absolutely, and unambiguously wrong.

Still, no theory or therapy in this book is as "scientific" as phrenology. So what can we say about science and the healing arts of psychotherapy? Must psychotherapy be quantifiable? Should it claim to be objective? Must it obey the laws of Newtonian physics? Should it be beautiful or elegant or optimistic? Should it appeal to "com-mon sense"? Should it attempt comprehensive understanding of the mysteries of nature, or should it, like Skinner's behaviorism, boldly exclude from analysis those parts of life that are private and inaccessible to our common observation? Should it assume a static, "created" world or a dynamic, "constructed" world? Should it explore the questions of humankind from the point of view of men, or women, or the ruling classes, or the government health care planner? Should it celebrate human diver-sity, delve into the mysteries of complex statistical interactions, or champion only bottom-line, main effects? These questions yield no fixed answers in human science. We simply must be able to live with the ambiguities they create.

But aren't some therapies "better" than others, more efficacious, less expensive, quicker, more permanent, more widely applicable? At least tell us, some plead, what is true. If Uncle Paul is depressed, little Jimmy is afraid of spiders, my sister has re-fused to eat anything but tofu for the past six months, and my life doesn't seem all that inspired either, surely there are scientific answers to be found. If not, what do those thousands of psychology graduate students do with all those years they spend chained to computer terminals and locked inside research laboratories?

What the Data Reveal

We may never truly get very far beyond the goals of the original 18th- and 19th-century French physician-alienists, whose primary goal was to "console and clas-sify." But modern psychotherapy has produced some "scientific," or at least quanti-fiable, answers.

First, the overwhelming statistical evidence is that theoretical orientation, thera-peutic method, choice of technique, and professional allegiance are variables of al-most no real weight in determining the degree of success a client will encounter in a course of psychotherapy. What a client does in therapy and, to some degree, which practical benefits the client will derive from therapy, depend on the theoretical per-suasion of the therapist. Nevertheless, "most reviews of psychotherapy outcome re-search show little or no differential effectiveness of different psychotherapies" (Stiles, Shapiro, & Elliott, 1986, p. 165).

Are all psychotherapy experiences essentially, therefore, equivalent? Does any-thing predict when psychotherapy will be meaningful, and effective and leave the cli-ent with productive long-term changes in his or her ability to live life fully?

The answer may surprise you. Virtually all psychotherapy outcome research agrees that one variable predicts the relative success of the therapeutic process: personality, personal style, and "psychological presence" of the therapist (for an extended discussion of this point see Gurman & Razin, 1977; Lambert, 1989). The scientific literature is extensive and relatively unambiguous on this point; a nicely detailed review of this literature can be found in Mahoney's book *Human Change Processes* (1991).

The shape and texture of the therapeutic experience is determined, far more than by technique or theory, by what Mahoney called "the three Rs of helping": a role-defined *relationship*, a *rationale* or metaphor for the personal change process, and the *rituals* enacted by the therapist and the client during the course of the relationship (Mahoney, 1991, p. 288).

The second "truth" about psychotherapy revealed by research is that a client who is working with a caring, competent, and skilled practitioner (with whom the client can establish a cooperative and trusting relationship) almost can't go wrong. A comprehensive study analyzed the statistical patterns found within the results of over 300 published research reports. Here is what the authors concluded:

> Conventional reviews of research on the efficacy of psychological, educational, and behavioral treatments often find considerable variation in outcome among studies and, as a consequence, fail to reach firm conclusions about the overall effectiveness of the interventions in question. In contrast meta-analytic reviews show a strong, dramatic, pattern of positive overall effects that cannot readily be explained as artifacts of meta-analytic technique or generalized placebo effects. Moreover, the effects are not so small that they can be dismissed as lacking practical or clinical significance. Although meta-analysis has limitations, there are good reasons to . . . conclude that well-developed psychological, educational, and behavioral treatment is generally efficacious. (Lipsey & Wilson, 1993, p. 1181)

A review in the journal *Psychological Science*, the flagship journal of the American Psychological Society (an organization representing the scientific side of psychology, many of whose members broke away from the American Psychological Association's identification with clinical psychology), raised the issue of "the status and challenge of non-professional therapies" (Christensen & Jacobson, 1995). These authors reviewed the literature that reveals the lack of substantiated difference in psychotherapeutic outcome attributable to therapist experience in terms of years or training. Furthermore, whatever differences exist between professional and paraprofessional therapists "surprisingly, favor paraprofessionals" (p. 9).

How the Data Affect Us

As disappointing as these results may be to colleagues who treasure the idea of possessing special healing gifts, the results ought to be reasonably reassuring to the consumers of both professional and paraprofessional psychological services. For as Christensen and Jacobson (1995) documented, existing demand for psychological services cannot be met by the limited number of professional therapists; indeed, they estimated that roughly one in five persons in need of services actually receive treatment.

Part of the reason for this discrepancy is financial. Large numbers of the population are without adequate health insurance, and for even more, access to mental health services is radically curtailed by "managed care." In addition, however, millions of people are turning to self-help groups, self-administered dietary and exercise therapies, and support groups instead of professional therapists. To substantiate this movement within our society, all one has to do is to look at the amount of space devoted to psychological self-help books in any bookstore. The important point to remember is that, rather than looking at the positive results achieved by "nonscientific" therapies as threatening, a scientific psychology ought to be open both to the potential cost savings of nonprofessional interventions and to the lessons these methods can teach us about refining and extending scientific understanding.

Please keep these ideas in mind as you think about the science behind the talking cures described in the following pages. I will endeavor to be as scientifically helpful and up to date as I can be. However, like many members of my generation, I was profoundly influenced by George Miller's 1969 presidential address to the American Psychological Association. He called on psychologists to "discover how best to give psychology away" in order to improve the lives of the people who truly need it (p. 1074). My fondest hope is that this book will at least indirectly serve that cause.

Rollo May's Nightmare

All the great people described in this book are my heroes, but one is a special hero. He is Rollo May (1909–1995), one of North America's preeminent existential psychotherapists. Here is a story he told in 1979 (pp. 4–5):

> A psychologist—any psychologist, or all of us—arrives at the heavenly gates at the end of his long and productive life. He is brought up before St. Peter for his customary accounting. Formidable, St. Peter sits calmly behind his table looking like the Moses of Michelangelo. An angel assistant in a white jacket drops a manila folder on the table which St. Peter opens and looks at, frowning.
>
> The silence is discomfiting. Finally the psychologist opens his briefcase and cries, "Here! The reprints of my hundred and thirty-two papers. And let me submit the medals I received for my scientific achievement."
>
> But St. Peter's frown is unabated as he silently continues to stare into the psychologist's face. At last he speaks. "I'm aware, my good man, of how industrious you were. It's not sloth you're accused of. Nor is it of unscientific behavior. It's not unethical behavior that's down on this document. You're as ethical as the next man. Nor am I accusing you of being a behaviorist or a mystic, or a functionalist or an existentialist or a Rogerian. Those are only minor sins.

"You are charged with nimis simplicando! You have spent your life making molehills out of mountains—that's what you are guilty of. When man was tragic, you made him trivial. When he was picaresque, you called him picayune. When he suffered passively, you described him as simpering; and when he drummed up enough courage to act, you called it stimulus and response. Man had passion; and you called it 'the satisfaction of basic needs.' You made man over into the image of your childhood Erector Set or Sunday School maxims—both equally horrendous.

"In short we sent you to earth for seventy-two years to a Dantean circus, and you spent your days and nights at sideshows! *Nimis simplicando!* What do you plead, guilty or not guilty?"

As the author of this book, I assume the role of the defense attorney for the accused. And I invite you to be the judge and the jury. You need to examine each defendant individually, on a case-by-case basis, each on his or her own merits. But then you also need to judge the defendants as a group.

My only special pleading is that, before reaching a verdict, you take the time to do some reading in the works of the master therapists I introduce to you. Any obvious oversimplification you find in these pages is most likely mine—not theirs.

A Caution and a Modest Invitation

Now let us begin our intellectual journey by going back half a millennium to the beginnings of Western psychiatry and psychology. We travel to Europe—the ancestral home of many readers of this book, the locus of centuries of oppression for others, and a curious, backward place full of bearded barbarians from the perspective of the ancestors of still other readers. We go first to Europe to establish a historical and cultural context, and because every journey needs a beginning, we begin with the discovery of the unconscious.

One final warning about meeting the Buddha on the road: My best friend has a bumper sticker on his truck that reads, "Indians Discovered Columbus." Let's heed the warning. Nineteenth-century European physicians no more discovered the unconscious than John Rogers Clark "discovered" Indiana. Indeed, a stronger argument could be made for the reverse, as the bumper sticker states so elegantly.

But the "discoverer's" power to name is a powerful prerogative indeed. It is because of this prerogative that we honor our trespassing, lost, and hapless European forebears. They defined and named our consciousness and fired our imagination about the secrets that lie within the vast, newly "discovered" human psyche.

And now it is time for me to reveal the meaning of the enigmatic invitation with which I began this chapter: Eat a bowl of rice. It is an invitation to enjoy this simple but basic product of my labor. Throughout much of the world, a good bowl of rice is simultaneously an unextraordinary and common thing, a sacred offering, a fundamental source of life, and an extremely revealing and personal statement. As

Ohnuki-Tierney (1993) wrote, "The symbolic importance of rice has been deeply embedded in the Japanese cosmology . . . as soul, as deity, and ultimately as self" (p. 8). Each grain of rice—an analogy to the ideas you will find in this book—is alive with potential significance; for the Japanese, each rice grain contains *nigitama*, the peaceful, positive power of deity. Pure white rice embodies the sacred power each of us possesses for the possibility of complete self-rejuvenation in an ever-changing process of self-discovery (Ohnuki-Tierney, 1993).

So I say to you: "Come. Sit at my table. Eat a bowl of rice. Welcome to the extraordinary world of a most ordinary man. Please enjoy."

PART I

The Discovery of the Unconscious: Mind Revealed

Neither at that time, nor indeed later in my life, did I feel any particular predilection for the career of a physician. I was moved, rather by a sort of curiosity, which was however, directed more towards human concerns than towards natural objects; nor had I grasped the importance of observation as one of the best means of gratifying it.

SIGMUND FREUD

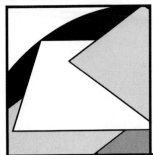

CHAPTER 2

The Search for the Meanings of Madness: From Demonology to Moral Therapy

Let There Be Light

From the time of the ancient Babylonians and Egyptians and perhaps even earlier, specialists have been charged with the task of "healing" the abnormal and socially malfunctioning members of society. Many of the techniques developed by these therapeutic pioneers—the laying on of hands, for example—continued in active use throughout the Enlightenment and even into the modern era. The American and French Revolutions initiated the intellectual, moral, and philosophical discourse that laid the foundations for the scientifically based psychotherapies, which emerged a century later. Through the stories and histories told in this chapter, you will learn about the origins of Western psychotherapy and observe the intricate connections between psychotherapy and the society that created it.

Madness in the Era of Witches, Devils, and Demons

Consider the plight of "a certain well-born citizen of Spires" (a city in the southwest of Germany on the Rhine River). It was well known throughout the province that Squire Spires, as we shall call him, had married unfortunately. Despite all hopes that the merciful Lord might call Frau Spires home prematurely, she was born with a cast-iron constitution—and a tongue of pure venom. Everyone in the village loved the squire, and everyone feared the wrath of his overbearing, contentious, evil-tempered mate.

It was said for miles around that Squire Spires had devoted most of his life to placating his black-hearted wife, that he had tried in every possible way to please her and to put an end to her constant abusive taunts.

A Demonological Account of Mental Illness

Life went on this way for years, and then one day the unthinkable happened. The parish priest told the story:

> Spires had gone into his house one day, and his wife railing against him as usual with opprobrious word, he wished to go out of the house to escape from quarreling. But she quickly ran before him and locked the door by which he wished to go out; and loudly swore that, unless he beat her, there was no honesty of faithfulness in him. At these heavy words he stretched out his hand, not intending to hurt her, and struck her lightly with his open palm on the buttock; whereupon he suddenly fell to the ground and lost all his senses, and lay in bed for many weeks afflicted with a most grievous illness. (Kramer & Sprenger, 1486/1971, p. 87)

Suspecting foul play, the priest called in the local physician, who had treated such cases before. The old man withdrew from his medicine bag an intensely hot iron pot containing molten lead. He held it over the stricken man and slowly poured its contents into a bowl of river water. Miraculously, as it hardened in the cold water, the molten lead took the form of a near-perfect swan. Witnesses were amazed. The doctor explained that when molten lead is poured over the body of a victim of witchcraft, it forms an image, an image cast by the powerful work of devils. The lead obeys the power of Saturn, the influence of that planet being entirely evil.

In short, the good and noble Squire Spires had succumbed to the power of the devil, applied through the agency of one of the devil's witches. Without question that witch was the dastardly Frau Spires herself.

History does not reveal what happened either to the squire or to his wife, but the results could not have been positive in either case. The most likely outcome for the unfortunate woman was a two-stage public trial. In the preliminary phase, everyone in the town would have been encouraged to do their Christian duty and speak of all their suspicions and animosities toward the suspected witch. They almost certainly would have told of other strange infirmities that had befallen people who tangled with Frau Spires.

This evidence being sufficient, in the second part of her trial the bishops and priests almost certainly would have first excommunicated Frau Spires for consorting with Satan. Then they would have delivered the doomed woman to the civil authorities for punishment as a heretic, her crimes being Satanism, sorcery, apostasy, and sodomy (having had sex with a devil) (Summers, 1928/1971, p. xvii). Frau Spires's punishment would probably have been the usual for convicted Satanists: to be separated from her family, the church, and her community "with extreme prejudice."

Exorcism. As for the squire, his fate was perhaps more kindly intended but scarcely less drastic. He most certainly would not have received psychological counseling. To start with, had there been a proto-psychotherapist in the neighborhood, he or she would certainly have been branded a necromancer, a term applied to any person who attempted to converse with a devil. Such a heretic would be denying the basic teaching of St. Thomas "that it must not be believed that devils are subject to any corporeal powers; and therefore they are not to be influenced by invocations or other acts of sorcery" (Kramer & Sprenger, 1486/1971, p. 178). In fact, even to attempt such a "talking cure" would be accepted as proof that one was in league with the Prince of Darkness.

With psychotherapy not very likely, what was left? The short answer is exorcism, a righteous casting out of the devils that had captured the good Squire Spires. Depending on the severity of the case, a priest might have tried some or all of the following exorcism techniques:

- One popular technique was the laying on of hands, a practice known 400 years later as "the concentration technique," when Sigmund Freud used it with some success while treating some of his first hysterical patients (Breuer & Freud, 1883/1955a, p. 110).
- The natural power of music, especially harp music, was thought to chase away demons, as it did for Saul in the Bible. The effects of music were thought to be enhanced by combining it with treatment by herbs and stones possessing "natural virtue."
- Treating the patient with the heart and liver of a fish, applied either as a paste or, in more resistant cases, as smoke, was believed to sometimes drive demons from the afflicted.
- If all else failed, treating the afflicted person with the smoke from holy incense was believed to sometimes work. But the afflicted must first have made a good confession (which could be a sticking point for the unconscious squire), received Holy Communion, and remained bound and naked to a holy candle of the length of Christ's body or of the cross while a mass of exorcism was said (Kramer & Sprenger, 1486/1971, p. 183).

Witch-Hunting with *The Malleus Maleficarum*. All this information, and a good deal more, was available to Squire Spires's priest in *The Malleus Maleficarum*, a sort of witch-hunter's handbook first published in 1486 by two German Dominican monks, Heinrick Kramer and James Sprenger, under the direction and supervision of Pope Innocent VIII. In a reign of eight years (1484–1492), Innocent managed to put the term *Inquisition* firmly into the history books. An estimated 100,000 heretics, witches, and "deviates" met their mortal end in just the first year of Innocent's papacy.

The *Malleus* was published in more than thirty editions over the next two centuries and was the central authoritative source at witchcraft trials in England, Italy, Germany, and France. Its last recorded appearance in a capital trial was in June 1782 at Glaris, Switzerland, when Anna Goeldi was convicted of witchcraft and executed by hanging.

Whatever compassion we may feel for their hundreds of thousands of victims, the Inquisition and the *Malleus* itself are only indirectly related to the history of psychotherapy. Most of the victims of the Inquisition were perfectly sane political criminals whose real crime was questioning and conspiring against the power of the Church—which is to say the ruling structure of society. Summers (1928/1971), a 20th-century theologian, wrote in the introduction to the 1928 edition of the *Malleus* of those persecuted by the Church for their political activities during the Inquisition:

> The wild fanatics who fostered the most subversive and abominable ideas aimed to put these into actual practice. To establish communities and to remodel whole territories according to the programme which they had so carefully considered in every detail with a view to obtaining and enforcing their own ends and their own interests. These heretics were just as resolute and just as practical, that is to say just as determined to bring about the domination of their absolutism as any revolutionary today. The aim and objects of their leaders . . . were exactly those of Lenin and Trotsky. (p. xvii)

Lenin and Trotsky! That's pretty strong stuff, especially in 1928.

What about the fact that vast numbers of the persecuted included common peasant women and adolescent girls? Should we understand them all to have been dangerous anarchists and radicals? Isn't it more likely that they, like poor Frau Spires, were desperately unhappy women who annoyed and intimidated their husbands, fathers, and neighbors? Summers had an answer, which doesn't altogether deny the speculation. He said (of the *Malleus*):

> Possibly what will seem even more amazing to modern readers is the misogynic trend of various passages, and these are not the briefest nor the least pointed. However exaggerated as these may be, I am not altogether certain that they will not prove wholesome and needful antidote in this feministic age, when the sexes seem confounded, and it appears to be the chief object of many females to ape the man, an indecorum by which they not only divest themselves of such charm as they might boast, but lay themselves

open to the sternest reprobation in the name of sanity and common sense. (1928/
1971, p. xxxix)

This theologian and I are not eating from the same rice pot!

As many contemporary writers have pointed out, the witch hunts were little more than organized institutional violence against women who were perceived as a threat to the established patriarchal order. Witches were "wicked women," whose insatiable carnal lust led them to "kill with a look, tear an unborn baby from the womb of its mother, ruin crops, destroy livestock, and alter men's minds to inordinate love or hate" (Ussher, 1991, p. 44).

Witchcraft in Colonial New England. In colonial America, in one twelve-month period (1691–1692), 250 persons were arrested for witchcraft in Salem, Massachusetts. Fifty of these unfortunates were condemned; 19 were executed; 2 died in prison; and 1 was tortured to death (Deutsch, 1949). One of those executed was Martha Carrier, whose 8-year-old daughter provided the necessary evidence to send her mother to the gallows:

> *How long hast thou been a witch?*
> Ever since I was six years old.
> *How old are you now?*
> Near eight years old.
> *Who made you a witch?*
> My mother. She made me set my hand to the book [presumably the *Devil's Book*].
> *You said you saw a cat once. What did the cat say to you?*
> It said it would tear me to pieces if I would not set my hand to the book.
> *How did you know it was your mother?*
> The cat told me so, that she was my mother. (Deutsch, 1949, p. 35)

The sad irony is that, as far as we can tell, the majority of these "witches" were depressed and lonely old women who lived in melancholic isolation away from the rest of their community. We can only imagine what fear these eccentric old crones struck in the hearts of the village children and how often they were suspected of being responsible for the deaths of women in childbirth, the diseases that killed valuable farm animals, and even their accusers' own lewd and wicked thoughts.

It is clear from the historical record that the evil represented by witches was very highly eroticized. Six women from Andover, Massachusetts, under torture in Salem, confessed to "riding broomsticks through the air, consorting with devils and having carnal relations with them, pinching and otherwise annoying their neighbors abed by means of their 'specters,' and visiting illness and death on others through their black magic" (Deutsch, 1949, p. 36). Not only were witches believed to possess an insatiable sexual lust for all sorts of animals, children, and spirits, they were also responsible for stealing men's sexual potency. As explained in the *Malleus*:

When the member is in no way stirred and can never perform the act of coition, this is a sign of frigidity of nature; but when it is stirred and becomes erect, yet cannot perform, it is a sign of witchcraft. (Kramer & Sprenger, 1486/1971, p. 115)

It is hard to imagine the level of institutionalized mystery and paranoia that surrounded men's understanding of women during this era. Menstruation, for example, was considered part of the "natural craft of women" which was symbolic of their unnatural powers and lusts. As the Reverend Reginal Scot, an English cleric, wrote in 1584:

Women are also monthly filled full of superfluous humours, and with them the melancholic blood boils; whereof spring vapours, and are carried up, and conveyed through the nostril and mouth, etc., to the bewitching of whatsoever it meet. For they belch up a certain breath, wherewith they bewitch whomever they list. And of all other women, lean, hollow-eyed, old beetle-browed women are the most infectious. (quoted in Ussher, 1991, p. 49)

In an era when celibacy was held to be pure Christian virtue, to the righteous Christian man, every woman must have seemed a potential temptress, a daughter of the Biblical seducer, Eve. In fact, any woman

who was openly or actively sexual was in danger of being considered a witch. Sexuality, womanhood, and witchcraft became synonymous. The combined fear, disgust, and suppressed sexual attraction felt for all women is clearly reflected in the fantasies and accusations surrounding the witches. The representation of a woman's sexuality was linked to her alleged weakness, her closeness to animals and to creatures of the lower order. . . . All women could be witches—their sexuality and fecundity made this so. (Ussher, 1991, p. 49)

It is probably also the case that a great many "old hags" were also medicine women, who practiced healing arts with herbs, potions, and incantations. It is also very probable that many of these early nurse-practitioners mixed potions for arousing the interest of neglectful husbands, preventing and enhancing conception, assisting in labor and childbirth, and inducing abortion. As Ussher pointed out, these women may also have kept alive a community of goddess worship, which perpetuated ancient mystic traditions of women as "the guardians of sacred fire and the givers of life" (1991, p. 58).

For all these reasons, "mad" women were feared and loathed, as many radical feminists are today. It was the responsibility of the Church to regulate the social order, and so for several hundred years throughout Europe and during the last stages of the Church's supremacy even in the New World, it hunted down, tried, and executed deviate "madwomen" to preserve the spiritual and sexual safety of the established order.

As early as 1563 a tiny number of physicians attempted to persuade the courts that many of the accused women were deranged and deluded but essentially harmless.

There is little evidence that their testimony was given much credence, however. The issue was one of public safety and public order. These women were disruptive. They lived outside the control of husbands, fathers, and even Church authority. Destroying a madwoman or two sent a powerful message to other dissidents. As at least one historian explained, the whole episode undoubtedly had a cathartic and thus "therapeutic" effect on the entire community (Midelfort, 1972, cited in Ussher, 1991, p. 59).

I began our search for the roots of modern psychotherapy with publication of the *Malleus* 500 years ago because the *Malleus* provides the first "modern," socially relevant means for approaching, understanding, and perhaps even treating (if smoked fish livers are your thing) the widest range of that involuntary nonconformity that is today called mental illness. Of course, as you will see later in this book, we have no better reason to think of the behavior of the emotionally and psychologically different as "sick" than we have to think of it as "sinful," or as a consequence of demons. But in the quest to distinguish between the medieval and the modern, the *Malleus* is a convenient and, as we have seen in the words of various religious sources, an appropriate place to draw the line.

Mental Illness in the Ancient World

If you read a comprehensive textbook in the field of abnormal psychology, you will learn that evidence has been found of trephination (surgical removal of a circular piece of skull bone) in the Neolithic period, at the end of the Stone Age. Some have interpreted this discovery as evidence of "treatment" thousands of years ago for some undetermined form of emotional or psychological distress.

More than 4000 years ago, the Babylonians (who resided in the area that is now Iraq), under the leadership of the great "law giver" Hammurabi, described in detail the ethical and moral obligations of their priestly healers. Those healers classified human disorders according to the demons responsible for each one.

These early psychotherapists were devoted followers of the healing god, Ninurta, and his goddess wife, Gula. The chief mission of the healer was precise diagnosis, which was based on a detailed case history. Only if the disorder was correctly identified could the healer give the incantation that would evoke the god who was efficacious in combating the specific demon responsible for that disorder.

> The gods had seven enemies, the evil demons, who headed an army of lesser demons devoted to Ishtar, the goddess of witchcraft and darkness. Each disease had its specific demon. Insanity was caused by the demon Idta. The demons were served by sorcerers, who used the evil eye, special concoctions, and certain ceremonies. (Alexander & Selesnick, 1966, p. 20)

The remarkable thing about the psychiatric practices of these ancient priests is the evidence that they recorded in significant detail, on clay cuneiform tablets, the first systematic application of the talking cure. As one medical historian noted,

[Their] system of medicine . . . was dominated by magic and religion . . . the purpose of which was to rehabilitate an individual and to reconcile him with the transcendental world. . . . The soul searching of the patient who was convinced that he had suffered because he has sinned had a liberating effect; and the rites performed and the words spoken by the incantation priest had a profound suggestive power. (Sigerist, quoted in Alexander & Selesnick, 1966, p. 19)

By the time the ancient Egyptians began to learn the principles of spiritualist medicine from the Babylonians, the Egyptians had already made one of their great healers, Imhotep (circa 2850 B.C.E.), their god of medicine. The Egyptians had long recognized the importance of caring for the body as well as the soul. So in addition to practicing psychotherapy through religious incantations and solemn rituals, their healing temples advocated cultural enrichment by way of concerts, dances, and artistic self-expression; an early form of what is today known as occupational therapy; and "incubation sleep." The term *incubation sleep* probably signifies a hypnotic state induced by ingestion of a mild narcotic, the purpose of which was to elicit visions and mild hallucinations that would then be divined by the priests of Imhotep's temple.

It was the Egyptians who introduced into Western medicine the belief that hysteria, an emotional condition, was a gynecological disorder, caused by a malpositioned or wandering uterus. Treatment required fumigation of the uterus by way of the vagina to lure the wandering uterus back to its proper position. In time, fumigation became a widely accepted medical practice throughout the Greek world, championed by no lesser lights than Hippocrates, Plato, and Galen (Alexander & Selesnick, 1966). This gender-specific view of the cause of hysteria was still in vogue in eastern Europe during the time of Freud's medical training, in the late 19th century.

Persians (people of the area that is now Iran) developed their first formal talking cures under the reign of Darius the Great, who reigned between 521 and 486 B.C.E. Led by the teaching of the religious prophet Zoroaster (also known as Zarathustra), Persian physicians recognized that health required actively combating demonic forces. Their primary weapons in the war against impurity were purity of mind and body, good deeds, and adherence to the holy word. Spiritual healers—who emphasized the importance of living one's life with virtue, courage, humility, and charity—were considered the most powerful physicians. Many of these teacher-healers were probably also priests of Mah (pronounced "Mag"); these "greatest ones" dedicated their lives to combating the evil effects of Satan in the world. Reference is made to them in the New Testament, where it tells of the Christ child being visited by three Magi.

Hebrew and Greek Views of Madness

As hard as it may be for us today to imagine the infant Jesus of Nazareth receiving gifts from three practicing holy men–psychotherapists, it may not have seemed that unusual to the Hebrews of the Holy Land 2000 years ago. For although the Hebrew

Bible declared that there was but one God, He was known to be the source of all health, as well as all affliction. All sickness, including madness, was visited on humankind by this God. Thus the Hebrews were familiar with the idea that priests were solemnly charged with evoking God's healing powers. In fact the most important Hebrew physicians were priests who had special ways of appealing to the Great Healer (Alexander & Selesnick, 1966).

Detailed psychiatric accounts appear throughout the Old Testament, including those describing the afflictions of Kings Asa and Saul of the Hebrews as well as King Nebuchadnezzar of Babylon, who was afflicted with the psychotic delusion that he was a wolf (*lycanthropy*). Hebrew priests were empowered to fight the "unclean" spirits that caused madness, melancholy, catatonia, and epilepsy. By 490 C.E. the Hebrews had established a mental hospital in Jerusalem. Throughout the rest of history, many of the most important developments in the talking cure would come from the work of men and women of Jewish descent.

Temples of Asclepius. The Greek epic poet Homer, eight centuries before Christ, had sung of the madness that the gods inflicted on those who offended them. The classical Greeks probably acquired most of what they practiced as psychiatry from various peoples of the Middle East. For instance, they borrowed the cult of Imhotep from the Egyptians; gave him a Greek name, Asklepios (also spelled Aesculapius), and birthplace; and converted several old temples to Apollo to hospitals for cure and convalescence. Many of these temples eventually evolved into prosperous health spas frequented by health-conscious, upper-class patrons.

As Greek influence spread throughout the Mediterranean, hundreds of Asclepian temples were established as spas and as centers for the treatment of the physically and mentally ill. The temples themselves were generally magnificent compounds that also served as centers of learning and culture. People admitted to a temple for treatment found everything necessary for the body (baths and springs with medicinal properties, gymnasiums), the mind (large libraries of great works, wonderful gardens), the emotions (magnificent theaters), and the soul (the sacred temple itself, with its priests and sacred images and objects.) The greatest of these temples was constructed at Epidauros on the Peloponnesian peninsula around 420 B.C.E.

> The temple took 4 years and 8½ months to build. . . . The doors were of ivory and the cult statue [was] in gold and ivory. . . . Asklepios was represented seated on a throne, grasping a staff in one hand, and holding the other over the head of a serpent; a dog crouched by his side. (Rossiter, 1981, p. 284)

In its prime, an Asclepian temple I visited outside Pergamum in southwestern Turkey was probably fairly typical of these total-health communities. A "sacred way," a long walkway into the precincts, was flanked by examining priests who rejected anyone too sick or too poor to be likely to benefit from the therapeutic regimen. The temple itself was linked with the rest of the compound by underground tunnels, including an underground labyrinth that brought the patient to the source of the "sacred fountain," which provided the community with its healing waters. (Local folklore claims today that the spring is slightly radioactive, which may explain its healing powers.) Emerging aboveground at the spring, the pilgrim would have found herself at the entrance to the theater and the library. But the sacred waters were at the geographical and spiritual center of the entire compound.

There are varying theories of how treatment proceeded for those admitted to the temple for relief of emotional and mental distress. The theory that seems to make the most sense, given the architecture of the grounds, is that treatment began with a thorough purging of the digestive tract, a cleansing bath in the sacred waters, and a massage. Then patients were probably given a powerful narcotic drink derived from the opium poppies that abound in this part of the world and taken underground for an incubation sleep. The purpose of this sleep was to elicit the sleeper's dreams for interpretation by the temple priests.

Evidently, Asclepian priests took quite an active role in overseeing all elements of the cure, including this incubation sleep. At various places throughout the underground labyrinth of chambers are false walls with circular holes, through which priests could observe and comment to their patients.

Asclepian priests appear to have been well versed in the uses of snakes in healing rituals. Snakes were considered sacred by the Asclepians, who frequently treated physical ailments with application of live snakes to afflicted limbs. Just as the snake could shed its skin and gain "new life," so the patients at the Asklepion were supposed to shed their illnesses. The Asclepian staff with a snake entwined around it continues to be the symbol of physicians in the Western world.

At the rear of one Asclepian temple we visited near Delphi in Greece there was, according to archeologists, a windowless chamber where mentally ill persons were detained. In pits under their feet, hundreds of snakes slithered and hissed. This was, evidently, an early and at least occasionally quite successful form of shock therapy.

Claudius Galen. The Greeks practiced a fascinating blend of therapeutic techniques within the compounds of their Asclepian temples. They combined hygiene, nutrition, exercise, cultural enrichment, and rest with a healthy dose of exorcism, dream interpretation, and self-examination, all probably mixed with at least a small dose of theatrical charlatanism. The healer-priest was at the center of all these activities, and his advice was the absolute word.

However, spiritualist interpretations of illness (including dream interpretation) gradually gave way to scientifically based, materialist explanations among the classical Greeks. By the age of Hippocrates (460–337 B.C.E.), the treatment of emotional illness and even madness had evolved into a practice based on naturalistic observation and a distinctly materialist philosophy of science. In time, the Asclepian temples became the world's first great modern medical schools.

Claudius Galen (circa 130–200 C.E.), the father of modern medicine, was born at and spent his life practicing and teaching medicine in the Asclepian temple in Pergamum. Galen's medicine continued to be practiced throughout the Western world well into the 16th century.

Demonology in the Current Era

A few years ago, my hometown newspaper carried this story:

> At 12:56 A.M., John Leslie Keller, Colorado Springs, hit a shrub in the 100 block of Vermont ave. His brother told police that Keller had been freed of the devil by exorcism but was now "possessed by seven demons" who caused the crash. Mr. Keller was taken to Methodist Hospital. ("Police Blotter," 1989, p. 2)

Demonology continues to be a favored explanation for bizarre behavior even in modern, postindustrial, postfeminist, politically correct North America. Among its adherents, demonology apparently still provides highly satisfying answers to life's most perplexing problems.

At this point I need to insert a cautionary note to those sophisticated readers who think they can safely ignore the subject of demonology. Medical psychiatry is less than 100 years old, and truly modern psychiatry is less than perhaps 50 years old. In the history of *Homo Sapiens,* flogging, starvation, prayer rites, noise, smoke, totems, charms, amulets, talismans, exorcisms, and faith healings have more often been considered answers to the puzzle of mental illness than anything I will introduce in this book. It is probably wishful thinking to believe that science always marches forward and that what has been gained can never be lost.

Consider what happened between about 400 B.C.E. and 300 C.E. In addition to defining a code of ethics for healers that is still in use today, Hippocrates had worked out a psychiatry based on natural science and reason by at least 400 B.C.E. He insisted that medical training be based in biology and anatomy, and using that system, he classified abnormal psychology into scientific categories. Hippocrates also oversaw establishment of the first comprehensive mental hospital, in the modern sense of that term, in a Temple of Saturn (the same Saturn who had condemned Frau Spires by causing molten lead to take the shape of a swan) in Alexandria, Egypt. His system of science lasted at least six centuries and led to the establishment of psychiatry as a medical specialty.

During the Roman Empire, Hippocrates' psychiatric work was advanced under the direction of the Greek physician Aslepiades, who also wrote the first comprehensive textbook of psychiatric medicine. Ever heard of *him*? No? That's precisely my point. By the 3rd century C.E. psychiatry was lost and abandoned. In the so-called Dark Ages, anyone who might have thought to revive it was warned away:

> They err who say there is no such thing as witchcraft . . . who do not believe that devils exist except in imagination of the ignorant and common, and are the natural accidents

which happen to a man [which he] attributes to some devil. But this is contrary to the true faith which teaches us that some angels fell from heaven and are now devils [and such] infidelity in a person who has been baptized is called heresy, therefore such persons are plainly heretics. (Kramer & Sprenger, 1486/1971, p. 8)

In 25 years of teaching I've never met a student who would voluntarily admit that he or she would renounce "science" if Kramer and Sprenger came to the door. But I've known dozens, probably hundreds, of students who keep a sort of preintellectual explanation in reserve to be called on when the debate turns to evolution, the biological basis of schizophrenia, the social damage done by restrictive gender roles, the "naturalness" of homoeroticism, or the "place" of women in modern society.

I suspect that many of us who superficially do not seem to believe in demonology are often surprisingly tentative in accepting the global legitimacy of psychology-psychiatry-psychotherapy as a scientific response to common, everyday mental illness. My hunch is that we hold to our secular human "science" a lot less firmly than we think we do. The talking cure as it has developed in the past century probably holds at best a tentative place in our understanding of the world.

Is that Kramer and Sprenger at the door? Or just a couple of sales reps from the folks who make Prozac?

Madness in England at the Time of Henry VIII

Our story would end here (as probably would the mortal life of your author) had Innocent VIII and his successors retained their worldly power. Alas, even as Catholic Europe celebrated its final victory over the Moslem Moors in Spain in 1492 (and sent Christopher Columbus off to be discovered by the Indians), the end of the Church's hegemony was already in sight. Martin Luther, father of the Protestant Reformation, was already 9 years old. Perhaps more significantly, Henry "Defender of the Faith" VIII was already a year old and destined to assume the throne of England in less than 20 years.

The declining power of the Catholic Church in Europe after the 17th century is important to our history, but probably equally important was the view of mental illness embedded in British common law dating back to the 13th century. Under the legal tradition of *parens patriae,* the English monarch was the "parental" guardian of all his subjects. Therefore, the Crown was also ultimately responsible for caring for "the property and person" of all mentally incompetent persons.

Thus when the 18-year-old Henry VIII inherited the throne in 1509, he became the legal custodian of all the mentally ill, brain-damaged, and severely retarded "fools, lunatics, and natural idiots" of his kingdom. Under the circumstances, it was reasonably unlikely that the mentally ill would be dispatched as witches and heretics. Also, as Neugebauer (1979) pointed out, the "problem" of the mentally ill became an administrative and financial responsibility of the government.

Having been largely a matter of faith in Catholic Europe, the plight of the mentally ill in Anglican England became a matter of policy and politics. Lawyers replaced priests in deliberations on the subject of mental illness. Had Squire Spires been an Englishman, he might well have had the political clout necessary to get the local sheriff to convene a jury to determine that his dear wife was so out of control that she was no longer mentally competent. If the squire had been able to persuade the jury, the right and responsibility for the person and property of Frau Spires might have been transferred to the Crown. The Crown, of course, would have fought back in order to save itself the expense and inconvenience of caring for her. But under the doctrine of *parens patriae,* many such emotionally distressed persons came to reside in Crown-supported asylums.

More realistically, however, the Squire himself would probably have ended up in the asylum. By the time of his unfortunate collapse, English common law had a fairly sophisticated system, even by today's standards, for adjudicating claims of mental incompetence. Neugebauer (1979) reported that most of the findings in these trials were apparently quite sound: John Norwick "lost his reason due to a long and incurable infirmity"; Bartholomew de Sadewill's insanity was cause for his coming under the king's care "after a blow received on the head"; John Barry's "fear of his father" had caused him to become incompetent; James Benok had been "afflicted by reason of a fright on 20 October 1556 and has so continued from that time to the present."

The Asylum Movement

Commitment to an asylum was surely a one-way ticket to a horrible life, but it must have seemed infinitely better to the afflicted person's friends and family than torture and burning at the stake. The asylums were, however, a financial burden on the Crown. The establishments themselves were relics from the times of the Crusades, when the men came back from their foreign adventures with all sorts of horrendous diseases—especially leprosy. So very little capital expenditure was required to establish these asylums, but the overall expense of keeping thousands of people at least minimally alive and under lock and key was considerable.

The case of the Hospital of St. Mary of Bethlehem in London, established in 1243, is illustrative. Bedlam, as it was known, was one of more than 200 asylums for returning leper-soldiers built in England and Scotland during the Crusades. In 1403 the population of Bedlam comprised mostly lepers and assorted beggars, but six insane men had also been sent there by the courts. By 1547, when Henry VIII transferred responsibility for maintenance of the hospital and its inmates to the London city government (note parallels with the mental health policy of the U.S. federal government in the 1980s), Bedlam had become an asylum exclusively for the insane and a place of extreme human misery. It remained open under continuous operation until 1948.

If you haven't seen the film *Amadeus,* now is the time for you to do so. Pay attention to the opening and closing shots, which are supposed to be in Vienna's "Lunatic's Tower" around 1800. The human misery of the lunatic asylum was literally a chamber of horrors that attacked all the sense organs simultaneously. The incredibly inhuman noises, the pervasive stench, and the horrible sight of the most helpless and hopeless of all humanity must have been beyond human reckoning.

To finance these "snake pits," creative "revenue enhancements" were required. The Hospital of St. Mary of Bethlehem sold tickets to the rich to come and watch the antics of the lunatics. Bedlam soon became one of the great tourist attractions in London, rivaling the Tower of London and Westminster Abbey in popularity among holiday makers. You might think about the issue of financing the next time you pass a mentally ill homeless person on the street begging for money. She may well be testimony to long-standing government policy with respect to the financial support of institutions caring for the chronically mentally ill.

Clearly, the warehousing of the mentally ill in asylums throughout Europe was a matter of financial and political necessity. Whatever humane impulse led to the establishment of these institutions, "treatment" was not part of the motive. It is equally clear, however, that the rediscovery of psychiatry as a medical specialty was in large measure a consequence of the need to deal with the social and medical problems that arose in high-density populations of deranged and demented persons. Medically legitimate theories began to be developed about the cause of insanity, and the large populations of afflicted souls in asylums facilitated research into the causes of and treatments for psychiatric disorders. By late in the 19th century, medical psychiatry was established in Europe, most notably in the persons of Franz Anton Mesmer in Austria, Phillipe Pinel in France, and William Tuke in England. It also had a solid beginning in North America in the person of Benjamin Rush, who enjoyed the solid support of his fellow Philadelphian and co-signer of the Declaration of Independence, Benjamin Franklin.

Moral Therapy: The Impact of the Enlightenment on Madness

In Chapter 1, I tried to persuade you of the intimate connection between psychotherapies and their historical context. The late 18th century provides a clear instance of this reciprocal determinism. The French Revolution of 1789—dedicated to liberty, fraternity, and equality, and inspired by the "new idea" that human beings could govern themselves through their inherent powers of reason—was to shape profoundly the foundational ideas of psychology and psychiatry.

> There was a kind of optimism in the eighteenth century, resting on a faith in the harmony of natural or unregulated events. In sharp contrast to the Calvinists, the major

writers of the Enlightenment believed that if everyone just followed his own natural tendencies and sought his own happiness things would work out well for everyone. A common will would emerge, and the result would be a more widespread enjoyment of the riches of life. (Coan, 1977, p. 38)

The changes in treatment of the mentally ill that were empowered by the French and American Revolutions and inspired by the writings of the Enlightenment philosophes and contemporary Quakers came collectively to be known as the *moral therapy movement.* This admirable effort to improve the lot of the mentally ill by releasing them from the sickness of industrial society and corrupt human institutions marks the beginning of the modern era of psychiatry.

Enlightenment psychiatrists like Phillippe Pinel, inspired by the writings of Jean Jacques Rousseau and Denis Diderot, believed in the natural goodness of human beings. They believed the "noble savage" and the "simple peasant" were archetypes of Natural Man—that is, humankind uncontaminated by society and its constraints, unbowed by the pressures of conformity or the yoke of repressive government.

So the French stormed the Bastille to free the victims of political, economic, and social repression. And in 1792, led by Pinel himself, the revolutionaries unchained the mental patients in the Paris asylums, where the patients were

shackled to the walls of their cells, by iron collars which held them flat against the wall and permitted little movement. . . . They could not lie down at night , as a rule. . . . Oftentimes there was a hoop of iron around the waist of the patient and in addition . . . chains on both the hands and the feet. . . . These chains [were] sufficiently long so that the patient could feed himself out of a bowl, the food usually being a mushy gruel-bread soaked in a weak soup. . . . They were presumed to be animals . . . and not to care whether the food was good or bad. (Selling, 1940, p. 54, quoted in Davison & Neale, 1982, p. 21)

We will explore the French roots of moral therapy in more detail in Chapter 3.

The Circulating Swing, the English Coffin, and the Water Cure

Even after Pinel unchained the insane in Paris, living conditions for the chronically mentally ill were scarcely better than they had been in the early days of the asylums. And although treatment was a concept with some medical authority to it, the "treatments" of this period were not necessarily better than the illnesses they were intended to eliminate.

Many of the new treatments were based on prevailing views about the sensitivity of the brain to disorders of the blood. Dr. Benjamin Rush, who had established the first humane hospital for the insane in the United States (in Philadelphia in 1783), favored a treatment that required withdrawing up to 6 quarts of blood from a patient over a few weeks. What was left of the afflicted person would then be "spun" in a variety of devices that looked like medieval instruments of torture. As Rush proclaimed: "No well-regulated institution should be unprovided with the circulating swing."

A treatment favored for a while in Europe featured the "English coffin." The patient stood inside a device like the case of a grandfather clock, and the door was locked until the patient came to her or his senses.

Following Rush's advice that many lunatics could be cured through fright, one New England doctor invented a cure that was sure at least to separate the malingerers from the genuinely afflicted:

> On his premises stood a tank of water, into which a patient, packed into a coffin-like box pierced with holes, was lowered by means of a well-sweep. He was kept under water until the bubbles of air ceased to rise, after which he was taken out, rubbed, and revived—if he had not already passed beyond reviving! One wonders if this "water-cure" was not a direct descendant of the old witch-hunting water tests, whereby suspected witches were bound and dragged through water in the belief that if they floated, they were guilty, and if they sank—let God have mercy on their souls! (Deutsch, 1949, p. 82)

This treatment may have been a surefire cure-all for witches, but it probably didn't relieve anyone's depression or do much of anything else.

Tea Party Therapy

Perhaps because I married a staunch tea-drinking English-Canadian, my favorite creative treatment of this period is "tea party therapy," introduced by the very British William Tuke. Tuke's treatment was not only humane, it anticipated what would be called today a "social role theory" interpretation of mental illness and reminds one a bit of modern "milieu therapy."

Tuke reasoned that taking one's tea properly was what separated the enlightened from the savage. If taking tea in a genteel way maintained standards of decent behavior and thought, then surely learning how to take one's tea would help the chronically mad. Tuke therefore grouped large numbers of hapless mental patients around tea tables and instructed them in the appropriate verbal and nonverbal behaviors to engage in when taking tea. (Before you pass off this treatment as a bit of pure whimsy, keep in mind that every Japanese person with any hope of maintaining social acceptability learns the same thing to this very day.) When the patient was capable of sitting through several tea parties without committing any obvious faux pas, he or she was clearly well enough to be released back into society.

I love this story, first because it would make perfect sense to virtually all my wife's Canadian and British relatives and second, because it is a wonderful reminder of how our notions of normality, abnormality, treatment, and psychotherapeutic outcome are tied up with the day-to-day world in which we live our lives. If you are a college student living away from home in a residence hall, you are surely aware of the somewhat bizarre norms and rituals every college student has to learn to survive institutional life. When, as a college counselor, I assure the dean and your parents that you are "sane" enough to live in your dormitory, sorority, fraternity, or co-op, what am I saying? I am saying that you are capable of behaving in ways and under conditions that your parents should never know about. The point is, you have to be "sane" enough to adjust to your world, which is, however, less than a picture of middle-class sanity and decorum.

Somehow I think Tuke intuitively understood the importance of adapting to the social milieu. A practical man was Tuke. At least he didn't try to drown people to cure them.

Before we leave Tuke's tea parties, I should reveal that a great many of his patients were hatmakers by trade. The solvents used in those days in making hats were quite toxic to the fellows who had to inhale them all day. Many hatters went mad from organic brain damage. As you have probably already figured out, Dr. Tuke's tea party therapy became Lewis Carroll's inspiration for the Mad Hatter's tea party in *Alice in Wonderland.*

Hospitals as Warehouses

What is most remarkable about the moral therapy movement is how well it worked. Pinel, for example, claimed a cure rate of 95%. People really did recover once they were removed from the asylums to the countryside where they could enjoy nutritious food, clean air, and the support of concerned practitioners. It was, alas, an expensive and therefore doomed effort. The mentally ill were too many, and the resources too few; and the mentally ill rarely enjoy either political or economic clout.

So in the middle of the 19th century the insane were increasingly repopulating old asylums, now called hospitals, without much hope of receiving effective treatment. There was a light in the land, however: psychiatry. It would grow and prosper and become a powerful social and cultural force over the next century. But it did little to help chronically mentally ill people until the development of powerful new tranquilizers in the 1950s (in France). Not until then did the fundamental position of the seriously mentally ill change again. Even today, it is a distinctly minority view that the talk therapies (which are about to be "discovered" in the following chapters) have any place at all in the treatment of the mad.

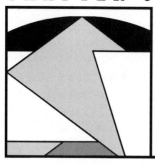

CHAPTER 3

The Triumph of Reason, the Rise of Mental Science, and the "Mystery of Mysteries"

Toward a Science of the Mind

The development of modern Western scientific thought is generally considered to have its origins in the Enlightenment, when reason began to overcome faith. Better systems of education allowed for the emergence of secular scientists, such as Charles Darwin, Jean-Jacques Rousseau, and Hermann von Helmholtz. For the masses, though, faith was still very important, and religion still played a major role in common people's views on psychopathology and psychotherapy. Controversial figures such as Father Johann Gassner gained wide notoriety as religious healers.

Meanwhile, Franz Anton Mesmer's theory and therapeutic practice of magnetism started to challenge Church doctrine and created a legitimate opportunity for the systematic study and treatment of non-physical, nondemonic illness. This work in turn paved the way for competing reason-based, scientific theories and therapeutic practices in the 19th century.

The Struggle for the Hearts and Minds

By late in the 18th century, the time of the French and American Revolutions, the old feudal European order was under relentless attack from many sides. Enlightenment notions about the supremacy of reason in the conduct of human affairs were rightly perceived as frontal attacks on the powers of the monarchy and its landed aristocracy and on the unquestioned authority of the established Church.

The universal application of human reason held out the promise of wiping away despotism, superstition, ignorance, irrational control by passion, and oppressive government. Society could be re-created to end the servitude of the people to the elite power of the few. Nowhere would the liberating effects of the application of the powers of human reason be more stunningly demonstrated than in the conduct of science. As the English poet Alfred Tennyson wrote, science would "follow knowledge like a sinking star, beyond the boundaries of human imagination." However, throughout Europe in the 17th and 18th centuries and to varying degrees, depending on the country, through the 19th century, genuine scientific research was basically a private pursuit by independently wealthy individuals. Some research went forward within church-based universities and monasteries, but much of this research was based on the contemplation of nature (Taylor, 1989). Moreover, the results of research in the life sciences during this period were very likely to be suppressed if they contradicted scriptural evidence or church dogma.

European modern science is generally accepted to have become established in the middle of the 17th century with the writing of Francis Bacon, an English philosopher. Bacon advocated scientific investigation by rigorous experimentation, not simply for edification regarding the wondrousness of God's creation but also for the furtherance of benefits to all persons. Bacon envisioned an active, dynamic, empirical, and largely inductive science, which would be dedicated to solving social problems and eliminating the sources of suffering. For Bacon and his followers, it was not sufficient to pursue science to glorify the "providential order." To be worthy of their inheritance, humankind had to become the stewards of the Creator and strive to perfect the divine plan on earth. This task, they thought, was the very reason humankind had originally been endowed by God with reason, will, and intelligence.

The struggle between independent-thinking natural philosophers like Bacon and conservative religious authority had been an ongoing story since the Reformation. Church fathers had never been comfortable with independent scientific inquiry, and independent empiricist researchers—such as Bacon, Copernicus, Galileo, Johannes Keppler, and Gregor Mendel—were constantly skirting the edges of excommunication and charges of heresy. This pattern continued into the 19th century. For example, the Austrian monk Mendel's pioneering work with genetic transmission and mutation was suppressed for more than 50 years. His data were discovered only by accident in 1900, 16 years after his death.

Jean-Jacques Rousseau and the Age of Enlightenment

With the coming of the Enlightenment, there was a nearly complete divorce between the endeavors of scientists and any religious authority. Philosophers who called themselves "radical utilitarians" rejected any connection between the work of science and any alleged "providential order" (Taylor, 1989). Reason was responsible only to itself, they felt; its full exercise demanded complete freedom from all authority. Scientists served only one ideal: the universal pursuit of a state of happiness that would be the common legacy of all human beings. Nature itself was regarded as an impartial, benevolent force; the only evil in the world was ignorance. The active pursuit of science would bring about an era of human perfection; the only limitation acting on human beings was the blindness of ignorance.

At the forefront of this movement was the Swiss-born French philosopher Jean-Jacques Rousseau (1712–1778). Himself a Deist (one who believes in the existence of a creator God although not in the subsequent supernatural regulation of that creation by that God), Rousseau advocated a doctrine of "enlightened naturalism," a rigorous pursuit of truth through the unflinching application of human reason (Taylor, 1989). Perfectibility, according to this view, depended on the transformation of humankind's wild, blind, and uncontrolled will into a force working single-mindedly for the common good. This dedication of the self, which almost required an absolute renunciation of the wild energy of human nature, would advance the human condition. Rousseau called such self-dedication "the social contract."

Under the social contract, scientists would no longer be isolated. All people of reason would be united within dynamic networks, "scientific societies" that would support, integrate, and extend scientific investigation. Human progress would proceed under the flag of free and deliberate inquiry. The collective organization of science and scientists would even be extended to medicine, where it would result in the creation of medical specialties like pediatrics and orthopedics (Ellenberger, 1970). Eventually medical science would become engaged in discovering the causes and cures of a wide range of dread diseases, such as smallpox, rabies, and typhoid.

As Rousseau had envisioned, learned societies emerged and provided a forum for the wide dissemination of scientific findings. Scientific journals began to be produced; subscription fees were collected to further research by professionals and amateur scientists. Promising young students from well-to-do families became tuition-paying research assistants on scientific expeditions.

This is precisely how the young Charles Darwin ended up on the *Beagle* in 1831 and the equally young William James found himself in the Amazon basin in 1865 in the company of the great biologist Louis Aggasiz. Both Darwin and James were taken aboard scientific expeditions to assist in the collection of biological and geological specimens in the southern hemisphere. The collecting expedition up the Amazon River was an episode in James's young life that would have profound effects on the future of psychology, as you will see in Chapter 11.

Enlightenment thinking eventually persuaded thousands of the best minds of the 19th century to turn to science as the most reliable way to create the knowledge required for thorough social, economic, political, educational, and religious reform. Progress was a practical affair, of course; but it was also a social and moral idea. Ellenberger (1970) noted:

> The historical and cultural importance of the enlightenment can not be overestimated; it constitutes the background of modern Western civilization. The principles of freedom of religion, thought, speech, and the principles of social justice, equality, the social state, the notion of public welfare as being a normal function of the state rather than an act of charity, the principle of compulsory and free education . . . all sprang from the Enlightenment. (pp. 197–198)*

And so did the modern notion of psychotherapy, the "art based on science" that would free humankind from the oppression of hysterical and melancholic misery.

Father Johann Gassner: Champion of the Faithful

By 1775 the European stage was set for the first truly dramatic confrontation between the old order and the heresy of the Enlightenment "new thinkers." Representing 1700 years of Church dogma was a 48-year-old Austrian Catholic priest who made his home in Switzerland. Father Johann Joseph Gassner (1727–1779) had earned an international reputation as probably the foremost exorcist of his day. In 1774 he had performed a successful exorcism of the wealthy and powerful Countess Maria Beradine von Wolfegg, which had brought him to the favorable attention of the Empress Maria Theresa of Austria. With the publication of his book on the detection and treatment of demonic illness in that same year, his good works had become known to virtually all the faithful, and he developed a following appropriate to his fame—much to the consternation of some of his fellow townspeople, who resented having their quiet little community turned into a major tourist attraction and exorcism center.

Gassner's Exorcisms. Gassner revealed that the "Evil One" worked three forms of affliction on people. At the lowest level were preternatural illnesses, which were caused by the devil and mimicked ordinary physical illnesses. More advanced demonology was evidenced in people who had been bewitched by sorcery and thereby developed psychological disturbances. The worst cases were those of outright possession by a devil—which I suppose meant actual psychotic episodes.

---

*Selected excerpts in this chapter from *The Discovery of the Unconscious: The History and Evolution of Dynamic Psychiatry,* by H. F. Ellenberger. Copyright © 1970 by Henry F. Ellenberger. Reprinted by permission of Basic Books, a division of HarperCollins Publishers, Inc.

The first problem Gassner faced was how to tell the difference between one of those "circumsessio" psychosomatic illnesses and actual physical illness (a problem that plagues therapists today at least as much as it did then). Gassner's ingenious answer was that when in doubt, one should go ahead with the exorcism anyway. No harm would be done, and if a demon was exorcised, well, that was a fine thing indeed. If no demon made his presence known, the victim could then go to a physician. More severe cases of possession, manifesting delusions and hallucinations, were of course obvious.

Gassner's exorcisms involved the laying on of hands, the invocation of the name of Jesus Christ, and the recitation of prayers—standard stuff, for the most part. But Gassner also demanded, in front of large and enthusiastic crowds, that his patients produce their symptoms in their fullest form.

> In his laying on of hands, Gassner was sometimes very vigorous and even cruel; for example on one occasion he repeatedly flexed the fingers of a sufferer from arthritis of the finger joints and caused much pain. His dialogues with the devils inhabiting his raving and suffering patients furnished a grim entertainment for his audience. . . . Those afflictions which did not respond to exorcism he declared to be of natural origin and problems for physicians only. (Pattie, 1994, p. 54)

The second problem Gassner had to confront was how to deal with the heretics who seemed to be challenging his work every time he arrived in a town to perform one of his highly publicized exorcisms. One particularly vexatious group of new-thinking troublemakers had once been members of the independent-minded order of Jesuits, which had been abolished by vigilant Church officials in 1773. But most of the heretics were far more dangerous than even the Jesuits. Many of them were not even communicants of the Church. They were a spiritual plague threatening to destroy the Christian world.

These were troubled times for good men like Father Gassner. He enjoyed great support from the masses, but the adulation and notoriety also made him increasingly suspect in the eyes of his religious superiors. The good news was that the aristocracy wasn't too much of a problem. The rich and powerful were smart enough to figure out that whatever happened to the Church was going to happen to them too. Besides, the Church was the least of the problems Louis XVI and his Austrian bride Marie Antoinette and their court were facing in Paris.

No, the real problem was the new and troubling bourgeoisie class of merchants, manufacturers, and traders. They read too much; they thought too much. And they talked too much. They were a threat to everything that Christianity had built. They had to be shown.

So show them he did. Father Gassner began traveling through the provinces performing public exorcisms in front of huge crowds. He cured Catholics, of course. But even more spectacularly, he cured Protestants too. He cured the rich and the poor.

He cured two nuns who had been possessed by devils; one of the nuns collapsed after the demon fled, and the other said that although she didn't have much memory of what had happened, she hadn't suffered from the cure. He then cured a high-born lady with melancholia and gave her advice as to how to keep the demons of her affliction away in the future. Pattie (1994) estimated that at the height of Gassner's popularity, in 1774 and 1775, Father Gassner was treating 2700 patients a month.

The Rebuke of Father Gassner. Over the ensuing months, Gassner's bishop grew increasingly alarmed by his priest's spreading fame and notoriety. Vatican officials became increasingly unhappy with Father Gassner's notoriety and finally persuaded his bishop to step in to avert what could become a major uncontrollable public situation. In the eyes of many, Father Gassner was becoming more important to the people than the Church itself; the possibility of heresy was even rumored in some Church circles.

An official Church inquiry took place in June 1775. The inquisitors' conclusion was that the exorcisms had all been conducted under the fullest exercise of Church law. They were satisfied that Gassner had never claimed he himself had anything to do with the cures, which would have been a major heresy. They took official note that Father Gassner had always been extremely careful to make sure people understood that the cures were entirely due to the spirit of the Lord working through him.

However, the tribunal concluded, the social disruption created by the public healings, especially those performed on nonbelievers, posed a serious threat to public order and Church discipline. Father Gassner was ordered to henceforth perform his miracles only on true believers who were sent to him directly by their own parish priests. Soon thereafter Pope Pius VI banned all of Gassner's writings.

As Ellenberger (1970) pointed out, Gassner's only real problem was timing. Had he been working his miracles in 1675 or even in 1725, he might have been canonized after his death. But this was 1775, and the Enlightenment was in its fullest glory. Ellenberger noted, "Curing the sick is not enough; one must cure them with methods accepted by the community" (p. 57). Gassner died in Church-ordered silence and complete obscurity in 1779 (Pattie, 1994).

In the midst of his problems with the Church, however, Father Gassner's reputation and authority were being convincingly challenged by forces far beyond the authority of the Pope in Rome. The person doing the deed was a 41-year-old German-born Viennese physician who personified everything the Enlightenment stood for and the established Church stood against.

Franz Anton Mesmer and the Scientific Theory of Madness

Franz Anton Mesmer (1733–1815) did the unthinkable. In 1775 he literally set out from Paris on Father Gassner's trail, following him around from town to town. Mesmer not only cured more people than the priest, he cured those whom Gassner had found untreatable. He treated the nobility, and he treated the common people. He overtly ridiculed the religious basis of Gassner's exorcisms and told anyone who would listen that it was science, not superstition, that saved people from their misery. Father Gassner, Mesmer reported to the Munich Academy of Sciences, was a man possessed not of the holy spirit but of an unusually high degree of "animal magnetism," which Mesmer believed to be "a subtle physical fluid [which] fills the universe and forms the connecting medium between man, the earth, and the heavenly bodies, and also between man and man" (Mesmer, 1779, quoted by Ellenberger, 1970, p. 62). Although the unenlightened old priest was sincerely unaware, he was in reality, according to Mesmer, "a tool of nature" (Pattie, 1994, p. 55).

In Munich Mesmer performed his cures in front of the crown prince of Germany. For his efforts he was nominated to be a member of the Bavarian Academy of Science. He amazed the other members with feats like the following:

> Mesmer performed some experiments before the Munich Academy, in which he produced various symptoms in several persons by applying a magnet and also by pointing his finger toward his subject. He showed also that magnetic effluvia were perceptible as a wind, sometimes warm and sometimes cold, when the tip of a finger was placed near Mesmer's index finger and that the magnetic influence penetrated closed doors and thick walls, was reflected by a mirror, could be felt as wind coming from a mirror, and could be transmitted for a distance of ten feet or more by means of a walking stick. He produced a recurrence of convulsive twitching in the Rev. Father Ildefonso Kennedy, Secretary of the Academy, whenever he pointed his finger toward him. (Pattie, 1994, p. 55)

The Case of Baron Horeczky de Horka. Perhaps you will forgive my enthusiasm for this largely forgotten man of science when you read the following commentary from the momentous year 1775. It tells what transpired when Mesmer paid a house call on the Hungarian nobleman Baron Horeczky de Horka. The finest physicians in Vienna had declared the baron's chronic nervous spasms of the throat incurable and the product of his imagination. Their treatment consisted of various herbal teas, which had no demonstrable effect on the affliction. Desperate for relief, and in defiance of his closest political advisers (who feared offending powerful members of the clergy), the baron invited Mesmer, with his magnets and a machine for producing static electricity, to the baron's castle for a long weekend:

> Shortly after Mesmer's arrival, several of the castle's inhabitants began to feel pains or peculiar sensations in their bodies as soon as they came near him. Even the skeptical Seyfert [the keeper of the journal recording this event] noticed that he was seized with an invincible sleepiness when Mesmer played music. [Mesmer played a glass harmonica, the effects of which, according to Ellenberger, could be "shattering."] It was not long before he became convinced of Mesmer's extraordinary powers. He saw how Mesmer could elicit morbid symptoms from people around him, particularly those whom he

had magnetized. A lady who was singing lost her voice as soon as Mesmer touched her hand and recovered it when he made a gesture with his finger. As they were sitting together Seyfert saw that Mesmer was able to influence people sitting in another room simply by pointing at their images reflected in a mirror, even though these people could see him neither directly nor indirectly in the mirror. At another time when two musicians were playing the horn, Mesmer touched one of the instruments; immediately a group of people—who could not see him—began to have symptoms that disappeared when Mesmer removed his hand. Meanwhile the rumor had spread that an extraordinary healer had arrived from Rohow, and patients came from neighboring areas to see him. Mesmer magnetized many of them, while sending others to see their own doctors.

On the sixth evening, Mesmer announced that the Baron would have a crisis on the following morning—which actually happened. The crisis was unusually violent, and it was reported that the fever had increased or decreased according to whether Mesmer came closer to the patient or drew away from him. A second, less violent crisis occurred a few days later, but the Baron found the treatment too drastic, and Mesmer left Rohow, though not without healing, at the last minute, a peasant who had suddenly lost his hearing six weeks before. (Seyfert, 1856, quoted in Ellenberger, 1970, pp. 59–60)

It is not clear if Mesmer could ultimately claim credit for curing the baron. At one point during the magnetic treatments, it was reported that the baron was "frisking about and playing merry tunes on his violin." However, the baron's personal physician, who held no fondness for Mesmer or his methods, attributed the baron's "frisking about" to a fever-induced delirium. This malady was probably caused by Mesmer's practice, even in the dead of winter, of having his patients' feet submerged in a basin of cold water, the better to conduct Mesmer's static electricity.

The physician and the baron's wife became solidly opposed to Mesmer's interventions. The patient was something of an unwilling participant as well:

On the third or fourth day [after the "merry tunes" episode] Mesmer wanted to magnetize the Baron again, but the patient would hear nothing of it. After long and repeated remonstrances, the Baron did, however, lie down. The magnetizing began just as before. The effects were soon visible, but they were now somewhat weaker than before. The Baron endured it for barely a quarter of an hour; just before he entirely lost his senses, he leaped out of bed, saying he would prefer to keep his throat trouble or even to die rather than suffer such torments again. No arguments could induce him to get into bed again. (Pattie, 1994, p. 51)

It is to be noted, however, that Seyfert reported that his master never again had either a fever or a throat spasm.

The Case of Maria Theresa Paradis. At the peak of his powers, Mesmer frequently entertained the rich and famous of Vienna—including Leopold Mozart and his family, which included the 20-year-old Wolfgang Amadeus (who immortalized both Mesmer and his magnets in the opera *Cosi Fan Tutte*). Mesmer treated a steady stream of the superpowerful and superrich, including the king and queen of France (Marie Antoinette was the Austrian empress's daughter) and the Marquis de Lafayette. True to his vision of the social contract, Mesmer also went from town to town magnetizing trees so the poor would have free access to effective treatment whenever they needed it.

In his most celebrated case, Mesmer restored the sight of a young favorite of the Empress Maria Theresa, the blind musician Maria Theresa Paradis. Maria, the only child of an Austrian court official, had been struck blind in her sleep at the age of 3 years and 7 months. Pronounced incurable by the royal physicians, she nevertheless endured bleedings by leeches, purgatives, diuretics, and electric shocks applied to the eyes. The results of the treatment, according to Pattie (1994):

> The electricity increased her irritability [as well it might!] and eye spasms to such an extent that it was possible to preserve her from harm only by repeated bleedings. The eyes protruded unpleasantly from their sockets and were continuously moving and turned upwards, producing a most disagreeable appearance. (p. 58)

Mesmer began his treatment of the girl, who was now also clinically depressed, when she was 18 years old. He treated her as a guest in his private villa for more than 5 months in 1777, with startling results. Her vision began to return, but she showed no signs of being able to comprehend what she saw. She was frightened by the faces of those she had previously known only from their voices and was frightened by any source of artificial light or bright sunlight. A wide variety of medical experts confirmed the partial restoration of the patient's sight under Mesmer's magnetic treatments, but her depression grew steadily worse.

Ultimately Mesmer took to wrapping his patient's eyes with up to 25 layers of gauze to protect her eyes from painfully bright lights and "disagreeable impressions." All this time the girl was in residence at Mesmer's villa, which had become a sort of public place, with young Maria Theresa its principal attraction. As Mesmer wrote, "People came in crowds to my house to make sure for themselves, and each one, after putting the patient to some kind of test, withdrew greatly astonished and saying the most flattering things to me" (1781, quoted in Pattie, 1994, p. 61).

Mesmer had created a miracle cure—sort of. The royal physicians later reported to the empress that the girl was just as blind when she left Mesmer's villa as she had been when she entered.

"Nonsense!" exclaimed Mesmer, and he had the girl brought back to him. In one short treatment, her sight was once again restored. Only to be lost again once she again left the villa. It seemed that the girl quite literally only had eyes for her "Uncle Franz."

Her family was incensed and accused Mesmer of trickery. Mr. Paradis entered Mesmer's rooms by force with sword unsheathed. In the ensuing struggle, Mesmer's servant disarmed the father and ejected him from the house. The father left screaming threats; the mother fainted; Maria Theresa was cast once again into blindness.

Mesmer once again treated his patient and restored her vision; but as soon as she returned home, her blindness returned. In fact, Pattie (1994) discovered, Marie Theresa Paradis spent the rest of her life as a completely blind person. She died in 1824 at the age of 65.

Was the girl truly blind? Blindness can be induced by hypnosis, and it is a common hysterical complaint. But would hypnosis or hysteria explain blindness in a 3-year-old? Mesmer's "proof" was sufficiently public to persuade us that for some period during her treatment she could indeed see. Furthermore, the way in which she recovered her vision is roughly consistent with modern evidence of how previously blind people recover their sight. Still, the girl experienced no lasting benefit from Mesmer's treatments. In fact, her temporary improvement appears to have brought her little joy and much emotional suffering. It was also recorded that her musical abilities declined drastically when she recovered any degree of vision, so the "cure" must be considered as highly debatable.

His reputation under severe attack, Mesmer eventually accused the girl and her family of what we would today call Ganser's disorder, involuntary faking of a psychological illness. It was an outrageous publicity stunt, he charged, because her parents supported themselves with the money they collected from the concerts of the famous "blind" musician. The truth will probably never be known. But the interested reader can pursue the case further by reading a wonderful short novel, *The Strange Case of Mademoiselle P.*, by Brian O'Doherty (1992), which re-creates the entire history of Mesmer's relationship with his most famous patient.

The Paris Board of Inquiry. Father Gassner's credibility had been demolished by Mesmer's famous 1775 tour. But by 1784 Mesmer's own credibility hung by a slender thread. The hysterically blind musician's fate had proved to be commonplace. Patients often experienced profound recoveries when in Mesmer's presence but then relapsed soon after treatment. Mesmer maintained, however, that even when his patients did relapse, they did so less and less severely after each treatment. But his practice and his reputation were clearly in trouble.

An international panel of almost 20 distinguished men of science was convened in Paris to conduct a full investigation into Mesmer's claims for the miraculous powers of animal magnetism and into the charges that had been mounting against him. At the inquiry Joseph Guillotine, inventor of the famed instrument designed to carry out more humane state executions, was one of the representatives of France. Apparently as a concession to Mesmer, Benjamin Franklin, then age 78, represented the United States on behalf of Dr. Benjamin Rush, the "father" of American psychiatry.

All methods of physical science available to the commission failed to document any evidence of the existence of animal magnetism. They decided, however, to conduct clinical field trials before coming to any final conclusions. In the first phase of

the experiments, the commissioners subjected themselves to magnetization, each for
2½ hours a day for a week. The results were ambiguous.

In the next phase, experienced magnetism patients were tested for observable effects during treatment, but the commission remained unconvinced of the regimen's
effectiveness. Below is the description of one such test conducted at Benjamin
Franklin's country estate. The subject was a boy of 12 who had previously shown
"great sensitivity to magnetism":

> While the boy remained in the house, d'Eslon magnetized an apricot tree in the orchard.
> The boy was then brought out, blindfolded, and asked to touch four trees in succession,
> one of which had been magnetized. . . . At the first tree, he said he was sweating and
> had some slight pain in his head. At the second, he felt dizzy, and the head pain contin-
> ued. At the third, these symptoms grew worse, and he said that he thought he was
> getting nearer to the magnetized tree. Finally, at the fourth non-magnetized tree, 24-feet
> from the magnetized one, he fell in a convulsion, losing consciousness. (Pattie, 1994,
> p. 149)

The results of all the experiments came out solidly against magnetism. Transcribed
below is a portion of the commission's final report:

> The commissioners, having found that the fluid animal magnetism cannot be perceived
> by any of the senses and that it has no effect either upon themselves nor upon the
> patients submitted to them; having assured themselves that [any] produced changes
> [are a product of] the imagination; . . . have unanimously concluded, on the question of
> the existence and utility of magnetism, that there is no proof of its existence, that this
> fluid without existence is consequently without utility, and that the violent effects ob-
> served in public clinics are to be attributed to the touching, to the aroused imagination,
> and to that mechanical imitation which leads us in spite of ourselves to repeat that
> which strikes our senses. (The Royal Commission, 1784, quoted in Pattie, 1994, p. 151)

Ultimately Mesmer was branded a charlatan and barred from further medical
practice. As if to add insult to injury, the French Faculty of Medicine then required
all practicing physicians to sign an oath: "No doctor shall declare himself to be a par-
tisan of animal magnetism in his writings or in his practice under penalty of removal
from the list of *docteurs-regents*" (Faculty of Medicine, 1799, quoted in Pattie, 1994,
p. 155).

By utter coincidence, the not-quite-so-young blind harpsichordist Maria Theresa
Paradis arrived to give a concert in Paris at precisely the moment the Paris Board of
Inquiry's official verdict was being read. Her presence revived all the old stories and
gossip about Mesmer's failed treatments.

The final straw was added to Mesmer's disgrace when, after being invited to Lyons,
France, to give a much-needed face-saving demonstration of his powers to the visiting Prince Henry of Prussia, "to his own consternation and to the dismay of his disciples, he failed utterly" (Ellenberger, 1970, p. 67). Mesmer retreated to Switzerland a

broken and devastated man. He lived for another 31 years, but he was never heard of again by the public. They had lost interest in him anyway, after he had what the artist Andy Warhol would have recognized as his "15 minutes of fame."

The First Psychotherapist. I am not going to provide a complete recapitulation of Mesmer's discredited scientific theories. You already know that they involved animal magnetism. Mesmer believed in the universality of magnetic fluids, the connective material among human beings, the earth, and the heavenly bodies. Mesmer also believed that magnetic fluids connected human beings to one another, that disease was caused by unequal distribution of these fluids in the human body, and that cure was effected when an equilibrium of magnetic fluids was established within the body. With the help of "Mesmerisms"—techniques for channeling, storing, and conveying this fluid to other persons—certain "crises" could be precipitated (recall the account of Baron Horeczky de Horka's unsuccessful treatment) that would have a curative effect on the system.

This principle would be reintroduced in the 1930s, and once again rejected by the scientific community, by the radical young psychoanalyst Wilhelm Reich (see Chapter 16). Reich's theory of a sexual "orgone energy" is similar in many respects to Mesmer's theory of a "magnetic fluid." I can easily imagine that this basic idea has sufficient archetypal power that it will come around again and again, in ever-new forms. Perhaps it is what gives so many people faith in the power of healing crystals today. Meanwhile, "May the Force be with you."

Nevertheless, Mesmer was the first person in modern times to establish a scientific theory of nonphysical illness and the first person to establish a thriving practice of interpersonal therapy based on that theory. And if that isn't good enough for you to erect a little shrine to Mesmer, consider that he established the first philosophical and professional societies dedicated to the pursuit of practical therapies for psychological disorders. His dream was to make magnetic cures so widely available to the masses that within his lifetime the practice of medicine (which in those days was an ugly business) would wither away from disuse. Magnetism, he believed, "brings medicine to its highest point of perfection." "There is only one illness, and one healing," Mesmer said (1779, quoted in Ellenberger, 1970, p. 63). He used no potions or incantations, no salve of fish innards, no superstitions; and no people of high social rank needed to be empowered to administer treatments.

Mesmer's group therapy equipment consisted of his trademark "baquet," a large oak wine cask containing double rows of slender tubes of magnetized water. Up to 20 persons could sit around this 18th-century hot tub, making physical contact with the steel rods protruding through its lid. When there were enough people to form a circle around the baquet, they were instructed to hold hands "to create a more favorable circumstance for the passage of the magnetic fluid" (Szasz, 1978, p. 49). When Mesmer treated patients individually, he would sit in front of his patients with his knees touching the patient's knees, pressing the patient's thumbs in his hands, looking into his eyes, then touching his hypochondria and making passes over his limbs [and] this is what was supposed to bring forth the cure. (Ellenberger, 1970, p. 63)

And of what was Mesmer found guilty? Of being the first psychotherapist, as far as I'm concerned. Mesmer probably wasn't the last person to go into hiding at the suggestion that he'd make a pretty good psychologist, but he almost surely was the first. The Paris Board of Inquiry accused him of curing people by stimulating their imaginations. They concluded that Mesmer was a charlatan precisely because he had discovered that psychological and interpersonal factors can be systematically manipulated to bring alleviation of overwhelming psychological, emotional, and physical distress.

A Threat to Women's Virtue. We also know now of a second, secret report submitted to the king but not published until 1799. This report, which was written after careful consultation with the chief of the Paris police, revealed that magnetizing treatments had a rather obvious sexual side as well and thus "were a threat to the virtue of women" (Pattie, 1994, p. 154). I would conjecture that Maria Theresa's mother was determined to remove her daughter from Mesmer's therapeutic influence for the most obvious reason of all—namely that her 18-year-old daughter had been a houseguest of a wifeless gentleman-physician for more than 5 months. The report disclosed that magnetized female patients, with their "more mobile nerves" and more excitable and vivid imaginations, often felt "attracted" to their magnetizer. Furthermore, the report speculated, the small "convulsions" often observed in women undergoing magnetization may in fact have been "crises of a different kind . . . caused by the power nature has given one sex over the other to attract and excite it" (Pattie, 1994, p. 154).

The commission confided to the king that most women who sought magnetizing treatments were not even sick. They seemed to suffer from a certain excess of "charm," creating a severe moral danger for both themselves and their physicians, by "the reciprocal attraction of the sexes act[ing] in full force." In severe cases, especially in the treatment of "lively and sensitive women," the report observed, there is

a total disorder of the senses; the eyelids become damp, respiration is short and interrupted, the chest rises and falls rapidly, convulsions begin, [and in the] last degree, the most pleasant termination of the emotions, is often a convulsion . . . followed by languor and a sort of sleep of the senses. (Pattie, 1994, p. 155)

No wonder magnetizing treatments had to be suppressed! No wonder all those aspiring medical students had to sign the oath! As the commissioners themselves concluded, the human imagination is wondrously powerful.

This shocking, highly eroticized "side effect" of psychologically based therapy would be rediscovered a century later as "transference" by Joseph Breuer and Sigmund Freud. It would become a central clue to unlocking the secrets of the unconscious mind.

Sociétés de l'Harmonie. What was even more dangerous about the work of Mesmer and his followers, I suppose, was how seriously they took their Enlightenment notions of the social contract and the worth of common people. French Mesmerists started something like magnetism franchises, *Sociétés de l'Harmonie,* which were also training schools and near-secret societies. These societies, which operated throughout France, were dedicated to liberating common people from the oppression of any form of physical or nervous disorder.

One group of Mesmerists in the province of Alsace opened the doors to their clinics to provide free outpatient magnetic treatments to anyone who needed them but did not have the means to pay for them. Talk about *heresy!* Old Mesmer is lucky the medical society didn't burn him on a mound of used tongue depressors at a stake made from the trunk of a magnetized tree.

With Mesmer in disgrace and his followers reduced to carrying out their pursuits as a band of social activists practicing healing without medical or scientific sanction, the future of the nascent field of psychiatry was in grave doubt throughout Europe. Rousseau's high rhetoric about the equality of all citizens stood in stark contrast to the realities confronting the mentally ill and their families.

The Rise of Moral Treatment

During this time, the prevailing treatments for institutionalized "lunatics" were supervised by *physician-alienists* and other "charlatans." (Anyone who practiced psychiatry without any medical training was called a charlatan, and thus the term did not have the same wholly negative connotations it has today.) "Medicine for the insane" amounted to little more than frequent purging and bleeding (up to 70 times a week) of the thousands of inmates of vast bureaucratically controlled state asylums. As late as the close of the 18th century, these unfortunates lived, often four or more to a single bed, under the same conditions as had their predecessors a century and a half earlier under the rule of King Louis IV.

This Louis, in the spirit of his historic get-really-tough-on-welfare reform campaign known as the Great Confinement, had established a network of "hospitals-general" between 1656 and 1676. They were designed to confine

a wide assortment of the idle and potentially unruly poor—not only lunatics but also vagrants, beggars, invalids, and prostitutes. Despite its name, the hospital-general was not a hospital; it had no medical aim whatsoever. It aimed only at maintaining political control over urban agglomerations (which had, as Paris had shown, an alarming capacity for growth) by segregating those elements identified as undesirable and forcibly setting them to work, so they would earn their own keep and might even return a profit to the state. (Goldstein, 1987, pp. 41–42)

Under this policy of "enlightened absolutism," virtually everyone who presented the state with a "social problem" was rounded up and deposited in one of these large "total institutions." By the mid-18th century, this population included women with venereal diseases, lunatics, melancholics, those mentally deficient persons whose families were unwilling or unable to care for them, and those afflicted with "frenzy" (probably manifestation of mania). As Goldstein (1987) pointed out, this wholesale warehousing of the misfits and most marginal members of society probably led to the first connection between insanity and the medical concept of disease.

During this period, men with political connections could acquire from the monarch a *lettre de cachet* that authorized the arrest and imprisonment of a son, daughter, or wife who misbehaved or brought discredit to a family's good name. These unfortunates would remain locked up with the lunatics "during the King's pleasure," without appeal and without any opportunity to defend themselves from the charges their patriarch had brought against them.

Phillippe Pinel's Moral Therapy

By the time of the French Revolution, medical science had joined forces with the state bureaucracy to work toward some system of treatment that would "cure" alleged mental diseases and the excesses of the state hospital system. Phillippe Pinel (1745–1826), introduced briefly in Chapter 2, became the man of the hour. His book, *Traite medico-philosophique sur l'alienation mentale, ou la manie [A Medical and Philosophical Treatise on Madness, or Mania]*, published in 1801, argued that a proper scientific view of madness required engaging and operating directly on the intellect and the emotions of the mentally ill. This radical new form of treatment was an important part of the larger moral therapy movement, which was also introduced in Chapter 2.

Pinel declared that moral therapy was to be applied equally "among all classes of society." Indeed, the new methods were used to treat the incarcerated insane in the Salpêtrière (the great Paris hospital-general for women) and the Bicêtre (for men), as well as King George III of England, whose mind had been destroyed by syphilis (Goldstein, 1987, p. 65, n. 4).

By 1802 Pinel had succeeded in having large numbers of the incarcerated inmates of the hospitals-general screened. Those found to have "treatable" mental disorders were transferred for further care and moral treatment to special wards at the Salpêtrière. There Pinel not only researched the case histories of his patients but also studied with intense interest the techniques employed by the more successful nonmedical charlatans working within the system.

An excellent example of the work of the charlatans is provided by Goldstein (1987), who described the success of the purging and bleeding treatments of an assistant surgeon by the name of Dufour:

> In one room, partitioned by boards, [a panel of scientific examiners] found three patients confined to a bed. The first, whose "delirium" was his belief that he was a monarch, was talkative and cheerful. The second, thin and of a melancholic complexion and bearing, replied aptly to all their questions, sighed a great deal, and recognized himself to be ill. The conversation of the third revolved wholly around the conviction he was Christ; he, like the first, was cheerful and of a gentle humor. . . . [T]he surgeon stated that these three manifestly peaceable patients had, before his treatment of them, been "in a habitual and extreme furor." (p. 8)

Pinel proudly declared that in pursuit of cures for the insane, he had learned valuable information from people of all walks of life. He cited the experience of his American colleague Benjamin Rush, who had gained profound insights into healing techniques for madness from "ordinary people, in every walk of life, . . . quacks, nurses, old women, . . . [e]ven negroes [*sic*] and Indians" (Rush, 1789, quoted in Goldstein, 1987, p. 76). Moral treatment was thus politically correct (for its time) populism.

Moral treatment also avoided any prohibitively narrow definition of science. Central to the application of moral therapy according to Pinel, were the case study method, because it revealed the gradual course of recovery under attentive care; a certain theatricality on the part of the physician, including "display, pomp, show, [and] appearance"; gentleness, encouragement, and philanthropy; authority of presence; "idea combat" and "forceful language" against the fixed ideas of the patient; moral instruction in managing and releasing the natural passions; doctor/patient rapport and camaraderie; and the fostering of courage in patients. "The lunatic was not to be considered 'absolutely deprived of reason,' inert and inaccessible to motives of fear and hope, to sentiments of honor" (Goldstein, 1987, p. 85). The essence of Pinel's treatments was in the person of the therapists, the "authority of their presence," and in the relationship between a therapist and a patient, in what Pinel referred to as the "physical and moral qualities" (Goldstein, 1987, p. 86). These factors enabled the physician to command the patient back to health and reason.

Moral treatments sought to "inspire and fortify the imagination" and to "school the passions" toward that which was natural, noble, and right. They were therefore in accord with Rousseau's teaching that the "artificial social passions" block people's natural moral progress and ultimately turn people against themselves and create human misery. For Pinel, the talking cure was about unlocking and freeing the inner humanity of each person, about restoring each person's true nature and overcoming the destructive effects of an alienating social order.

According to the careful statistics Pinel kept, compared with a base recovery rate of under 20% under the old methods, fully 95% of the insane recovered their ability to live as free and independent men and women following a course of moral treatment. Such is the power of the liberated human spirit.

The "New Men" of Science

Most historians agree that the Age of Reason, which had been the great creation of the Enlightenment philosophies, came to a crashing end with the excesses that followed in the wake of the French Revolution and the Reign of Terror. These were the events chronicled in Charles Dickens's novel *A Tale of Two Cities.* Even Pinel came to argue against continued revolution as a benefit to his patients when he saw that prolonged social instability simply inflamed passions and clouded the powers of reason.

However, the Enlightenment had foreshadowed the end of feudalism in Europe and the immense power enjoyed by the established Church and a highly privileged aristocracy. A group of writers and thinkers known as the Philosophes played an important role by attacking centuries-old Church dogma as the product of ancient superstition and myth and branding it devoid of reason and intellectual merit. In effect, they declared humankind's independence from God.

The Philosophes. The faith of these "new men" was in the power and glory of nature. And they understood nature as a scientifically knowable, rational and lawful system composed of real material—atoms—that could be studied and understood by human beings with the help of Newtonian physics.

> The Philosophes, rejecting Christianity, wanted to complete Newton's work, that is, to provide a rational account of humankind and its relation to the world. . . . [In this] *naturalism* [people were to be understood] in natural rather than supernatural terms. People were to be considered part of nature, not forever outside it in a world of God, angels, and souls. (Leahey, 1992, p. 127)

René Descartes (1596–1650) had argued that animals were really no more than biological machines and that their various forms and functions were simply variations on a materialist theme. So what could one rightfully conclude about human beings? This metaphysical problem had been around for a long time, but with the vast change in thinking during the Age of Reason, the problem had to be confronted anew. If humans were just another mechanical aspect of the materialist world, what was to become of ethics, of the "higher" emotions like romantic love, and of reason? Was everything arbitrary? Was the savagery of the Reign of Terror as "natural" as a mother's love for her child or a man's defense of his honor? Were the natural laws governing human affairs as capricious and indifferent to human suffering as the laws of physics? Was a person's violent disregard for the rights and property of another simply a material manifestation of a law as natural as the laws that cause a tornado or an earthquake?

Various writers answered in the affirmative. Thomas Malthus (1766–1834) wrote about the inevitable struggle for survival as population growth outstripped food supply. The Marquis de Sade (1740–1847) declared the moral nihilism implicit in the pursuit of pleasure. Arthur Schopenhauer (1788–1860) proclaimed, "In the heart of every man there lives a wild beast." These writers all perceived humankind to be at the mercy of a wild biological energy of an instinctive, amoral nature. Schopenhauer in particular perceived human life as a vast struggle to gain control over the "great reservoir of unbridled power which underlies mental life" (Taylor, 1989, p, 446). They all looked on reason as the only vehicle for control over this essential wildness.

Charles Darwin. Perhaps the most important scientific voice to be heard on this subject belonged to Charles Robert Darwin (1809–1882). Darwin's position was expressed in 1856 when he published the results of his analysis of the biological and fossil material he had collected during the voyage of HMS *Beagle,* which began in December 1831 and concluded 5 years later. The problem that Darwin addressed was an old one for biologists; it even had a nickname: the Mystery of Mysteries.

The mystery was how to account for the millions and millions of different species that inhabit the earth. The accepted view of the day, the so-called "argument from design," was summarized by P. H. Gosse as follows:

> I assume that each organism which the Creator educed was stamped with an indelible specific character, which made it what it was, and distinguished it from everything else, however near or like. I assume that such a character which distinguishes species from species *now,* were as definite at the first instant of their creation as now, and are as distinct now as they were then. (quoted in Fancher, 1990, p. 192)

My favorite elaboration on this theme came in response to the Creationist dilemma: how to explain the existence of fossil remains of creatures that no longer exist on earth. The politically, or perhaps piously, correct answer in Darwin's time was that these were the remains of all the creatures that had not made it on time to the sailing of Noah's arc.

Darwin first deepened the Mystery of Mysteries and then attempted a reasoned answer. He deepened the mystery by showing that in addition to species variety there is also geographic diversity to the distribution of species, with highly different members of common species living on either side of mountain chains and on different isolated islands miles and miles off the mainland of South America. The answer that he provided, of course, was the principle of natural selection. Through the process of Malthusian competition for scarce food resources, those members of the species whose biological variations made them most successful at securing food and avoiding predation reproduced most successfully and thus were "naturally" selected to continue the gene pool.

Darwin's grandfather, Erasmus (1731–1802), had embarrassed his family and scandalized the faithful by proclaiming the doctrine of evolution two generations before. His free-thinking speculations were inspired by perceptive strolls around England's seacoasts. Erasmus was said to have had the effrontery to paint the Latin phrase *E conchis omnia*—"Everything from shells"—on the side of his traveling carriage (Fancher, 1990, p. 193). His grandson's revolutionary claims about the origins of the species, which Charles himself said was "like confessing to a murder," contin-ued and renewed the family heresy.

The younger Darwin's claim, however, was supported by a small mountain of painstakingly collected and meticulously organized biological evidence. His revolu-tionary thesis was convincingly presented to an increasingly radical scientific com-munity, which was by and large already prepared to accept responsibility for the moral consequences of revolutionary, destabilizing ideas.

Official minutes of the scientific meetings where Darwin first presented his her-esy provide an interesting footnote: "The meeting had not produced any of those striking discoveries which at once revolutionize, so to speak, the definition of science on which they bear" (published in the proceedings of the Linnean Society, 1858, quoted in Fancher, 1990, p. 197). This assessment probably reflected the worldview of an older and more reserved scientific establishment. This generation had seen the horrible destabilizing effects of unbridled and unchecked "enlightened" thinking. Rather than throwing its lot with the freethinkers, anarchists, and revolutionaries of 1776 and 1783, this community of scholars made its peace with the sober forces of the moral order. They did so by sliding into intellectual subjectivism. Taylor (1989) characterized their reaction to the perceived social and moral dangers of objective science as a retreat into "Victorian piety, sentimentality, and self-congratulation" (p. 458). Thus many established scholars reverted to the pre-Baconian idea that all science was more or less about discovering the design of "the invisible hand of God." Members of the Linnean Society were not so insecure in either their religious or their scientific beliefs that they were in any danger of having their worlds overturned by a heretical gentleman-scholar whose entire theory was as disturbing and shamefully irresponsible as his grandfather's had been.

But the times were rapidly changing, and evolution was much in the air. As Hilgard (1987) pointed out, Darwin's theory of natural selection wasn't even the most scientifically sophisticated theory of evolution of its day. That honor probably belongs to Jean-Baptiste Lamarck (1744–1829). In fact, even in presenting his data, Darwin had to share the stage with the much younger Alfred Russel Wallace (1823–1913), who had also traveled extensively in South America and come to the same conclusions that Darwin had.

T. H. Huxley. If Darwin felt that he was almost confessing to a murder, the scientific community was willing to testify that the victim had been sick for a long, long time before the death blows were administered. Darwin's theory soon took on a life of its own. It was seized by "progressive" thinkers and promoted on campus and in town in pitched battles with religious authorities.

Thomas H. Huxley (1825–1895), also known as "Darwin's bulldog," became the foremost champion of evolution as revolutionary doctrine. In 1860 Huxley engaged the Bishop of Oxford, Samuel Wilberforce, to debate the theory at a public meeting of the British Association for the Advancement of Science. At the peak of the debate the bishop asked Huxley whether it was his grandfather or his grandmother whom Huxley believed to have descended from a monkey. Huxley replied,

> If the question is put to me, "would I rather have a miserable ape for a grandfather, or a man highly endowed by nature and possessed of great means of influence, and yet who employs these facilities and that influence for the mere purpose of introducing ridicule into a grave scientific discussion"—I unhesitatingly affirm my preference for the ape. (quoted in Fancher, 1990, p. 198)

And so the argument raged. But the preponderance of data was so overwhelming that soon any person who denied evolution as an established fact of nature was considered to be living in the prescientific, superstitious past. The significant point for the discipline of psychology, however, was that human beings were demystified; more importantly, they were a source of data.

The Mechanists Versus the Vitalists

The single most momentous question confronting the nascent field of psychology at midcentury was not whether the study of human behavior could be or would be scientific but what the assumptions and methods of that science would be. Those who remained truest to the Enlightenment's radical conception of humankind as part of nature, the ones who most zealously guarded the victories of the evolutionists in proclaiming humankind's common ancestral origin with all living matter, were called *mechanists*. They were by and large biologists, but their interests were closer to those of Newtonian physicists than to those of the biologists of the previous generation. The glory of mechanism was to discover the physical laws that explain human actions.

On the other side was a generally older, more conservative cohort of scientists, many of whom still remembered the horrors of the French Revolution and the somewhat more recent threats of social and political disorder in England. This was a generation of natural philosophers who had probably experienced more intellectual change in their lifetimes than any generation of scientific thinkers before them. Collectively they were the *vitalists*. Vitalists rejected the metaphor that a human being is a machine in favor of a more romantic view. They believed that intellect, emotions, and passions set human beings apart from the rest of creation. Vitalists were interested in mind more than brain, and they recognized that conscious mind had to be differentiated from unconscious mind. Vitalists also tended to be teleological: They believed that life evolved toward something and that all life was organic and growing. Vitalists could not accept a disciplined study of human life that did not include such fundamentally unique human attributes as freedom, choice, will, and spirit.

The battle between the mechanists and the vitalists grew in intensity as the credibility of their more traditional, theologically based rivals diminished. The mechanists resolved more and more of the old mysteries with data derived from new techniques in neurology and with more and more sophisticated understanding of the function and anatomy of the nervous system. The vitalists appealed to everyone who believed in transcendental truth of the sort professed by Thomas Jefferson—that some ideas are higher than ordinary ideas and that some aspects of the human condition are self-evident and not decipherable from dissecting a machine.

The battle raged throughout the learned quarters of society. The distinction became a matter of debate in the organization of government (see, for example, the writings of England's Edmund Burke) and in economics (see, for example, Adam Smith and John Maynard Keynes), in the worldwide debate over slavery and the treatment of Native Americans, and of course in medicine.

The question in medicine came down to a rather fundamental one: Is there a necessary, logical limit to the scientific understanding of biological processes in living organisms? Are some essential "mysteries" about vital creatures canceled by death and dissection? Or was it time to abandon the pathetic wish of the Creationists and accept the idea that all living matter goes through a life cycle at the end of which it returns to the earth from which it came? Do you have a soul or don't you? And would you want your best friend to marry someone who believed just the opposite?

The Antivitalist Oath

By midcentury the lines had been so clearly drawn that it was possible to use a person's position in this debate as grounds for scientific employment, acceptance to the university, and access to scientific publication. The great Hermann von Helmholtz, arguably the most brilliant physical scientist of his century, went so far as to ask his students and assistants to sign an antivitalism oath:

> I pledge a solemn oath to put into power this truth: No other forces than the common physical-chemical ones are active within the organism. In those cases which can not at the time be explained by these forces one has either to find the specific way or form of their action by means of the physical-mathematical model, or to assume new forces equal in dignity to the chemical-physical forces inherent in matter, reducible to the force of attraction and repulsion.

I have presented this oath to the students in my psychology classes every year for over 20 years. In all that time, no more than two or three students—advanced philosophy, natural science, and psychology majors—have been willing to sign the document. Many more students have actually expressed anger at my request to consider the oath and have refused even to discuss it with me.

Would you sign the oath? Would you accept therapy from someone who had signed it? Or from someone who had not? Would you accept medical treatment from someone who got angry and couldn't or wouldn't even talk about the oath? I'm 99% certain that Mesmer would have signed it in an instant. I'm equally certain that by the end of his life Darwin would have refused.

Crusaders for the Mechanistic Faith

The four originators of the antivitalism oath had an astonishing impact on the course of 19th-century science in Europe. Helmholtz became the pioneer of all sensory psychology and, according to Leahey (1992), "the greatest natural scientist of the nineteenth century . . . having formulated the law of conservation of energy when he was only twenty-six" (p. 51). Emil du Bois-Reymond, who according to Bolles (1993) drafted the text of the oath, became the preeminent physiologist of his day, arguing that there were no essential differences between humans and machines—save for the composition of their respective "parts." The third antivitalist was Carl Ludwig, whose most famous student was a young Russian physiologist named Ivan Pavlov, a name that should ring a bell with you if you remember any psychology at all.

The fourth member of this group was Ernst Brücke, whose students included both Joseph Breuer, whom you will meet in Chapter 5, and Sigmund Freud. The impact of Brücke's antivitalism was, therefore, especially profound. As a student, Freud could not imagine a scientific neurology that was anything other than absolutely mechanistic.

Brücke must have been a fascinating human being. He wrote about everything from anatomy to fine arts and developed a logical system for analyzing German poetry. He had a fierce reputation around the university and was considered a rigid, authoritarian Prussian by at least one unadmiring biographer. Here is what Ellenberger (1970) wrote about Freud's esteemed teacher:

> The scientific level of his teaching was far too high for his students, and he never deigned to teach at their level. Most dreaded of all examiners, he asked only one question, and if the candidate did not know the answer, he was never asked a second one. Brücke waited in impassive silence until the allotted fifteen minutes were through. (p. 431)

How many readers of this book would apply to the administration of their university for the privilege of working with such a professor on a daily basis—as Freud did? We see evidence here of a toughness of mind and character that many people have not fully recognized in Freud. I think we may safely assume that young Freud and his closest associates took their antivitalism quite seriously and quite passionately. Little wonder that Bolles (1993) called this generation of young scientists "vigorous crusaders for the mechanistic faith" (p. 45).

So we end this chapter at the dawn of modern psychiatry, with the people most intimately involved in its beginnings identifying themselves with the most radically humanistic, mechanistic, and antispiritualist elements in science and medicine. Modern dynamic psychiatry becomes heir to the Enlightenment and to all the contradictions, conflicts, and utopian dreams that era produced.

CHAPTER 4

The Rise and Fall of the Hypnotic Cure: The Talking Cure in the French Tradition

Preparing the Way

Subsequent to the French Revolution, the great asylum just outside Paris known as the Salpêtrière gained recognition because of the great scientific reforms being undertaken there in the diagnosis and treatment of mentally ill women. Its director, Jean-Martin Charcot, was among the leading men of scientific medicine of his age. Charcot was famous throughout the Western world for his remarkable work with hypnosis in the treatment of hysteria, in both men and women. This work profoundly impressed a young medical student named Sigmund Freud, visiting from Vienna. Another of the brilliant young men influenced by Charcot was Pierre Janet, who eventually took over Charcot's responsibilities at the Salpêtrière.

Janet and Freud were contemporaries, and many of their basic principles and observations of the mentally ill were comparable. They both agreed, for example, on the importance of the unconscious and the influence of sex on the human psyche (the latter an idea championed by Charcot). Ultimately, however, Janet was belittled for his ties to Charcot and for his continued therapeutic use of hypnotism. Much of his work has subsequently been overlooked or dismissed. Freud and his followers, on the other hand, were supremely successful in spreading the idea of a distinctly "Freudian" psychodynamic analysis.

Jean-Martin Charcot

Imagine a hospital as big as a town. Within its 45 buildings, spread out over 125 acres, live 5000 indigent, hapless, profoundly impaired people. The majority of the town's residents are women. The place has been asleep for decades. It's run with the discipline of a religious order; the rule of the nuns is the absolute law of the land. It is a terrible place, full of despair. The women are sick with every disease known to science and some other diseases that are just a mystery. Lunatics howl at the moon; hysterics sit mute, deaf, and blind. Screaming schizophrenics are restrained to prevent them from doing physical damage to anyone, including themselves. It is hell but a managed hell. At least these women have someplace to go, at least they are fed and kept warm in the winter.

The hospital, the Salpêtrière, was in the middle of Paris, but you might never have known from walking its grounds. It was established by Louis IV, who transformed it from a poorhouse into an asylum for beggars, prostitutes, and the insane. It grew and grew over the years. It even entered the history books briefly when Phillipe Pinel came at the start of the revolution and unshackled the chains of the insane within its walls.

Enter 36-year-old Jean-Martin Charcot (1835–1893), the neurologist son of a Parisian carriage maker. As a youth, Charcot may have been "cold, silent, shy, and aloof," with a speech impediment and a bad mustache (Ellenberger, 1965), but by the time he was 40 he was widely considered one of the most powerful and eminent men in all of European medicine (Fancher, 1990). Charcot had trained at the Salpêtrière as a medical student. Now, having been appointed chief physician of one of the largest sections of the Salpêtrière in 1862, Charcot demonstrated a genius for bureaucratic manipulation. In short order he transformed what had been for decades a vast warehouse of human misery into what Charcot could proudly call his "temple of science."

Under Charcot's leadership the Salpêtrière became one of the leading institutions in the world for treatment of and research on mental disorders. Always a dedicated neurologist, Charcot and his staff began collecting detailed case histories, performing autopsies, and developing world-class scientific laboratory facilities.

One of the very first things Charcot did was to cleanse his temple of science of the vestiges of the old order. In a move that would be the envy of many contemporary state mental hospital treatment directors, he fired all the old nurses—many of whom were nuns, medically unqualified—and replaced them with a team of lay nurses who shared his enthusiasm for the principles of enlightened medicine.

A new golden age of science was dawning all across Europe, but the Salpêtrière that Charcot had returned to was in most respects a relic of the past. It did not have a laboratory, a classroom, or even an acceptable facility for postmortem examinations. It didn't have a single modern medical examination room, and most of its medical equipment belonged in a museum. Yet this was the place where Charcot would show the world that the French were second to none in the medical arts.

Systematic Study of Hysterias

The women under Charcot's care were radically diverse. The hysterics as a group were rather young, and some were even quite pretty. They had to be separated from the strictly medical cases: the epileptics, the organically paralyzed, and the syphilitics.

Some of the epileptics, Charcot discovered, were misdiagnosed hysterics—a fact discovered when he observed them faking their seizures. His staff learned to tell epileptics and hysterics apart by observing their symptoms very carefully. Hysterics always had their seizures when they had an audience and somehow never managed to hurt themselves.

Hysteria, Charcot came to be convinced, is a lot like hypnotism. In fact, a clever physician could be trained to diagnose hysteria with hypnotism. It was Charcot's experience that virtually all hysterics could be easily hypnotized. The link between hypnosis and hysteria, Charcot came to perceive, was an organic weakness of the nervous system, a lack of "cohesive power."

Also central to hysteria was the patient's evident need to exaggerate and create a performance around her symptoms:

> The patient voluntarily exaggerates real symptoms or even creates in every detail an imaginary symptomatology. Indeed, everyone is aware that the human need to tell lies, whether for no reason at all other than the practice of a sort of cult . . . or in order to create an impression, to arouse pity, etc., is a common event, and this is particularly true in hysteria. (Charcot, quoted in Alexander & Selesnick, 1966, p. 172)

Charcot was able to demonstrate by means of systematically controlled observation that hysterical symptoms were always the carefully managed and narrowly produced creations of an active mind. By inducing paralyses in otherwise healthy subjects through hypnotic suggestion, Charcot was able to demonstrate that the resulting paralyses resembled in every detail those that resulted from traumatic emotional experiences. Perhaps more importantly, Charcot demonstrated that these hypnotically induced "conversion symptoms" could also be removed through the process of hypnotic suggestion.

These demonstrations, which had become almost routine at the Salpêtrière by the mid-1880s, provided the first irrefutable evidence that paralysis of the limbs could have a psychological basis. Prior to Charcot's discovery of the link between hypnosis and hysteria, all paralysis was assumed to result from traumatically induced nervous system lesions. By 1890 Charcot would be able to demonstrate a similar psychogenic basis for many cases of amnesia. Unlike cases of amnesia caused by neurological damage, persons with hysterical or "dynamic" amnesia could actually be induced to recover lost memories under hypnosis.

A note on the powerful cohort effects that influence the manifestation of psychopathology: By the early 1800s in France, cases of demonic possession had become extremely rare. In the place of possession, the physicians of the asylums were being increasingly confronted by a new form of madness with clear roots in the historical events of recent years. By 1820 most of the new patients in the Salpêtrière and the Bicêtre were beset with "monomania," a fixed delusion that induced them to act and think like the recently deposed (and decapitated) royalty. A Paris newspaper, "appalled" by the psychopathology generated by the violence of the revolution of 1789, proclaimed itself to be resolutely in favor of new efforts to incarcerate the insane. It laid the blame for this social disintegration on the "alternation of fears and hopes . . . , the condition of fever and over stimulation produced by an all-consuming politics," and demanded that the government repair at once the damage done to "civilization" by the revolution (Goldstein, 1987, p. 317). According to the science of the day, the events of the revolution and its aftermath had simply proved too overpowering for patients whose "sensibilities had been perverted" and whose weak minds, undeveloped intellects, and intrinsically mistrustful natures were simply not up to the demands placed on them by the events of history.

Gradually over the next 50 years, the symptomatology of French mental patients went through another transition. The diagnosis of monomania gave way to hysteria. By 1882 fully 20% of the women confined in the Salpêtrière were diagnosed hysterics, and the diagnosis of hysteria among male patients at the Bicêtre was beginning to climb as well (Goldstein, 1987, p. 322).

Hysteria, however, had a very poor reputation among midcentury continental physician-alienists. Although it is probably the oldest established psychiatric diagnosis in the Western world, dating back to the Egyptians in the time of Imhotep (who recommended vaginal fumigation, as you may recall), hysteria was considered by most science-practitioners of the mid-1800s to be a diagnosis based on a "wastepaper basket of unemployed symptoms." Symptoms of hysteria included convulsions, seizures, feelings of strangulation, fainting, swooning (called "the vapors"), limb paralysis, anesthesias, muscle spasms, mutism, stuttering, intractable hiccuping, inability to stand or walk erect, anorexia, frequent urination, tunnel vision, coughing, trancelike states, and a variety of other neurological and physical conditions unified solely by the fact that there was absolutely no evidence of any underlying biological pathology (Goldstein, 1987, pp. 323–324).

"One studies hysteria with repugnance and only as a matter of duty," declared Pierre Briquet, one of the leading lights of French psychiatry in 1859, after whom the hysteria-like somatization disorder was named (see the case of Martin in Chapter 13). However, like it or not, hysteria was sweeping the continent. In celebration of the widespread hysteria and in recognition of its bizarre symptomatology, in 1928 the Surrealists even gave hysteria an official birth date: 1878 (Goldstein, 1987, p. 322).

Flight Into Illness

Why did hysteria become such a pervasive form of female disability late in the 19th century? Keep in mind that, as Goldstein (1987) pointed out, virtually all French hysterics were working-class women and thus not at all like the upper-middle-class hysterical women that Sigmund Freud would encounter in his practice in Vienna. Still, hysteria apparently is and was a passive-aggressive response to the systematic exploitation of women by a patriarchal culture that had profoundly schizophrenic views of women and women's place in society. The Hungarian-American psychiatrist Thomas Szasz has called hysteria "the language of the powerless," a view supported by several feminist historians.

In this view, hysteria is essentially a "flight into illness" provoked by

> the contradiction between the relentless stress of . . . domestic life and the prevailing feminine ideal of frailty, docility, and subordination to men [in which] hysteria [is] an appealing form of indirect dissent, a way of entering covertly into a power struggle with the male world. The symptoms of hysteria—really parodies of femininity—enabled women to take to their beds, thus defeating both their husbands, whose households they left untended, and their male physicians, whose remedies they showed to be ineffi-cacious. . . . Fin-de-siècle hysteria, it appears, was a protest made in the flamboyant yet encoded language of the body of women who had so thoroughly accepted that value system that they could neither admit their discontent to themselves nor avow it publicly in the more readily comprehensible language of words. (Goldstein, 1987, p. 325)

Without benefit of these postmodern insights, Charcot held that hypnosis, amnesia, and hysteria were one and the same. It was essential, in Charcot's approach, to differentially diagnose organic from hysterical causation. This rule applied equally to amnesiacs, mutes, the paralyzed, and even the deaf. Hysterical patients, in Charcot's view, were still "fundamentally normal," which meant that with proper treatment they could be expected to recover all their lost faculties.

Charcot was not arguing that nothing was wrong with these patients or that they were purposely faking their symptoms. He believed that both hypnosis and the hysterical disorders, amnesias, and so forth that his patients displayed were caused by pathological weaknesses in the nervous system. He even conjectured that these weaknesses were probably the physiological basis for cases of so-called demonic possession and stigmata.

Perhaps, he argued, the two great debilitations of the day—hysteria among women and neurasthenia (psychopathological weakness and fatigue) among men—were some form of "universal neurosis," a reflection of the sedentary labor in the new mechanical age. Psychiatric treatment was no longer restricted to meeting the needs of the "privileged classes, softened by culture, exhausted by the abuse of pleasures, by preoccupation with business affairs and by excessive intellectual labors" (Charcot, 1891, quoted in Goldstein, 1987, p. 336) and of the overwhelmed poor. These disorders could be found "on a grand scale among urban proletarians and artisans" as well as among the ever-growing bourgeoisie. What was required was a new comprehensive system of outpatient psychotherapy, psychological counseling services for people from all walks of life and all social strata. And if neurosis was more or less universal, then the provision of physician-alienists to attend to the neurotic masses of men and women was nothing short of a public necessity.

An individual who could pass for an ordinary citizen, who certainly did not disturb the public peace, and who could live at home while making periodic visits to the psychiatric doctor [could visit a psychotherapist] in private office practice, within reach [of his or her home]. "You will be cured," says a doctor to his neurasthenic female client [in a popular play written by a French physician in 1905], "you will be cured as soon as you resolve to abdicate all personal control. . . . Do not get discouraged, put yourself in the hands of a doctor, obey him blindly." (Goldstein, 1987, p. 338)

The "Great Man"

By 1870 Charcot was being called "the greatest neurologist of his day" by the newspapers. His students and his contemporaries called him by a more memorable name, "the Napoleon of the neuroses." Short, brooding, obsessed, ambitious, a tyrant to anyone close to him—the name Napoleon was a good fit. But you couldn't find a more brilliant physician in all Europe. His cures were small-scale miracles. Those with a memory said there had been no one like him since the great Mesmer.

Many patients were brought to Charcot from all over the world, paralytic on stretchers or wearing complicated apparatuses. Charcot ordered the removal of those appliances and told the patients to walk. There was, for instance, a young lady who had been paralyzed for years. Charcot bade her stand up and walk, which she did under the astounded eyes of her parents and of the Mother Superior of the convent in which she had been staying. Another young lady was brought to Charcot with a paralysis of both legs. Charcot found no organic lesion; the consultation was not yet over when the patient stood up and walked to the door where the cabman, who was waiting for her, took off his hat in amazement and crossed himself. (A. Lyubimor, 1894, quoted in Ellenberger, 1970, p. 95)*

On Tuesdays the "Great Man" would make general rounds of the hospital. Followed by attending physicians, aspiring medical students, and more often than not a visiting member of a royal family or an international celebrity, Charcot would go from bed to bed astonishing everyone with his diagnostic skill. His knowledge of disease syndromes and complexes, his ability to cut right to the center of the disorder with no more than a question or two, and his penetrating style left onlookers in awe.

But the greatest attraction were his solemn lectures given on Friday mornings, each of which had been prepared with utmost care. Long before the beginning of the lectures, the auditorium was filled to capacity with physicians, students, writers, and a curious crowd. The podium was always decorated with pictures and anatomical schemata pertaining to the days' lecture. His bearing reminding one of Napoleon or Dante, Charcot

*Selected excerpts in this chapter from *The Discovery of the Unconscious: The History and Evolution of Dynamic Psychiatry,* by H. F. Ellenberger. Copyright © 1970 by Henry F. Ellenberger. Reprinted by permission of Basic Books, a division of HarperCollins Publishers, Inc.

entered at 10:00 A.M. often accompanied by an illustrious foreign visitor and a group of assistants who sat in the first rows. Amidst the absolute silence of the audience, he started speaking in a low pitch and gradually raised his voice, giving sober explanations that he illustrated with skillful colored chalk drawings on the blackboard. With an inborn acting talent he imitated the behavior, mimicry, gait, and voice of a patient afflicted with the disease he was talking about, after which the patient was brought in. The patient's entrance was sometimes also spectacular. When Charcot lectured on tremors, three or four women were introduced wearing hats with very long feathers. The trembling of the feathers allowed the audience to distinguish the specific characteristics of tremors in various diseases. (Ellenberger, 1970, p. 96)

Influence on Sigmund Freud

Two young men of great promise spent part of their formative years under Charcot's influence and tutelage. One of them, Pierre Janet, is discussed in some detail later in this chapter. Suffice it for now to say that the Great Man decided to choose the fresh-out-of-college Janet to be his right-hand man at the Salpêtrière.

The other young man of note was Sigmund Freud, but he seems never to have come to the busy and famous Charcot's attention. Freud spent four months in 1885 and 1886 at the Salpêtrière, just at the time when the Great Man was undertaking his most astonishing research. What Freud saw was that Charcot could induce hysterical paralyses in patients through posthypnotic suggestion. The very idea shattered everything Freud had just learned about hysteria in medical school in Vienna. He wrote to his fiancee back in Vienna,

> I think I am changing a great deal. Charcot, who is one of the greatest physicians and a man whose common sense borders on genius, is simply wrecking all my aims and opinions. . . . [N]o other human being has ever affected me in the same way. (Freud, 1960, quoted in Sulloway, 1979, pp. 30–31)

Freud went on to develop a theory based on Charcot's discovery that the form of a hysteric's symptoms—paralyzed speech or hearing or touch, for example—"behaves as though anatomy does not exist, or as though it has no knowledge of it" (Freud, 1892–1894, vol. 1, p. 169). Freud went on to appreciate, as Charcot did from his own research, that the hysteric's choice of symptoms revealed much about the nature of the psychological trauma that had given rise to the hysteria. Clearly, it was Charcot who discovered that posttraumatic paralysis could be distinguished from other causes of paralysis, but the true significance and importance of that observation remained to be discovered by Freud once he began his own career in Vienna.

The other thing that Freud took away from his brief time with Charcot was the realization that established medical science was incomplete and sometimes completely wrong. Charcot delighted in debunking established scientific "facts." The instance that impressed Freud the most had to have been Charcot's demonstration that a hysterical symptom could just as easily be induced by hypnosis of a male subject as a female subject. Freud had learned in medical school that hysteria was a "female disorder," caused by a displacement of the uterus, a theory essentially unchanged since the days of the Egyptian Imhotep 3000 years earlier (see Chapter 2). So when Freud saw a male patient who had developed a classical hysteria after an occupational injury, he was astounded. Frustratingly, when he tried to talk to his senior colleagues back in Vienna about what he had seen in Paris, the older men shrugged their shoulders and dismissed it as a typically wild and outrageous French story.

Charcot planted three seeds in Freud's mind about the origins of neurosis:

- Charcot taught that "sleep-life," or dreaming, was a potential key to understanding hysterical thinking. In short, Charcot believed that the world of dreams and daydreams held clues about the contents of the unconscious mind (Ellenberger, 1965).
- Charcot had preached and even proved that hysterical paralyses were "the result of ideas which had dominated the patient's brain at the moment of a special disposition" (Freud, 1893/1962, p. 22). As if this assertion wasn't radical enough, Charcot added that it was well established that behind all such dominating ideas were ideas about sex. More on this topic, much more in fact, will be presented in Chapter 5.
- Probably the most enduring lesson that Freud, and a great many of his contemporary neurologists, learned from Charcot was the importance of questioning long-standing medical doctrines. Charcot's dictum was "La théorie, c'est bon, mais ça n'empeche pas d'exister." Fancher's (1990) translation is "Theory is fine, but it doesn't prevent things from existing." A more colloquial translation might be "Believe what you see, not what someone tells you to see."

Triumph and Decline

In 1882 Charcot went before the French Academy of Science and presented his scientific theory of hypnosis. Ever since the findings of the "Franklin Commission" a century earlier, hypnotism had been a discredited relic of the age of Franz Anton Mesmer. Now Charcot appeared before the academy and presented his great unified theory of hypnosis, based on experimental evidence collected in public with the assistance of the hysterical inmate-subjects of the Salpêtrière.

To get a feel for the evidence presented to support the use of hypnotism, consider an experiment conducted by the young Alfred Binet (who later founded the psychological testing movement and whose name is associated with one of the most powerful intelligence tests in use today) and his associate Charles Fere:

> Harkening back to Mesmer, [Binet and Fere] introduced the magnet into hypnotic sessions. With [their subject, Blanche Wittmann,] in the somnambulistic stage [one of the three stages of hypnosis identified by Charcot], they induced paralyses or other effects

on one side of her body, and then reversed the polarity of a large magnet they held in front of her. Wit's effects immediately transferred to the other side. The hypnotists similarly reversed emotional states: After telling the hypnotized Wit that she felt very sad, for example, they transformed her piteous sobs into gay laughter with a simple flick of their magnet. . . . While admitting some of their results seemed implausible, they assured their readers that the effects had been "entirely unexpected" and had "issued from nature herself, . . . showing an inflexible logic." (Fancher, 1990, pp. 344–345)

Charcot won the day. The Academy of Sciences greeted Charcot's theory with enthusiastic approval, and the "pure" state of *grande hypnotisme* was accepted as a foundational construct in the blossoming field of neurology. Not only had Mesmer been vindicated, but France was brought to the center of the world stage of medicine.

Charcot's victory proved sadly short-lived, however. By the 1890s, though his mind was as sharp as ever, Charcot's health was failing badly. He died as one of the most powerful men of science in French history.

He also died a hated and despised man. The Catholic Church held Charcot in nearly complete contempt for his heretical views and for his complete disregard for theological accounts of human behavior. He was despised by the therapeutic heirs of the great Mesmer, many of whom had become professional magnetists—and had been ridiculed and ignored by the Great Man. Meanwhile, they claimed, Charcot had stolen their technology with his "hypnosis." On the other hand, the young antivitalists of the day considered Charcot a throwback to a superstitious past, rightly seeing all the vestiges of the old spiritualism in Mesmer's methods and assertions about hypnosis. By the time of Charcot's death in 1893, hypnosis had once again fallen out of favor, and demonstrations of hypnotic trances were largely relegated to parlor tricks and performances by professional spiritualists.

Hippolyte Bernheim and the Nancy School

The source of this striking turnaround was the group of dedicated skeptics, largely scientist-physicians, associated with what is known as the Nancy school (because it was located in the town of Nancy, France). Led by a scientist with the wonderful name of Hippolyte Bernheim (1840–1919), members of the Nancy school set out to test Charcot's claims about hypnosis with rigorous experimentation.

The results that came out of Nancy were unambiguous and were in complete opposition to Charcot. Hypnosis, Bernheim declared, was the product of a general human trait: suggestibility, which was defined as the "aptitude to transform an attitude into an act." Persons who were good hypnotic subjects, it was found, did not differ from others in the constitution of their nervous system but in the degree of their susceptibility to suggestion.

Hysterics, Bernheim observed, were excellent hypnotic subjects; it followed that they were also extremely suggestible. He argued that hysteria could therefore be successfully treated with straightforward nonhypnotic suggestion. The only real therapeutic challenge, Bernheim argued, was in finding ways to make people with hysterical disorders believe they could be cured (Fancher, 1990). Once this belief was established, the removal of symptoms was based on the authority the physician brought to his relationship with the patient. Bernheim also suggested that the reason hysteria was more prevalent among women and members of the middle classes is that these people had been brought up "more conditioned toward strict obedience" (Fancher, 1990, p. 337), a position that anticipated by a century the view that hysteria is symbolic of powerlessness.

Because of his profoundly authoritarian tendencies and despotic manner, which frequently resulted in episodes of ferocious meanness (Ellenberger, 1965), Charcot had accumulated not only a large following of devoted enemies but a large number of fellow scientists who despised him passionately and with what Ellenberger called "undying hatred." To the three great rules that Charcot had taught his students, his enemies added a fourth: "Deception always goes further than suspicion" (Ellenberger, 1965). When his critics successfully attacked the very heart of his theory by showing that there were no fixed stages to hypnotic induction and that most of the results Charcot had reported had been manufactured by his trembling assistants, his professional reputation was all but permanently destroyed.

Trances and Performances

What really killed Charcot's reputation was his theatricality. In the final years of his life, he had become more a performer than a healer. His patients were longtime inmates of the Salpêtrière who had been extensively and carefully rehearsed in how they were to respond under the spell of the Great Man. In case they should forget any of the ordained stages or miraculous features of the hypnotic trance, large, precise diagrams of patients in varying stages of hypnosis had been strategically hung all over Charcot's stage and even the walls of his auditorium. At the end, Charcot's patients were doing little more than joining him on a public stage to create entertainment. They had become part of a gigantic act that the old man was probably unable to distinguish from reality.

Who knows how long it had been since Charcot had actually hypnotized a naive subject, let alone cured anyone of a psychological disorder. It was apparent to Freud, who witnessed several of the public healing sessions, that the performances of the patients were completely staged. And of course Freud, as well as anyone else who cared to look, was appalled that these artificial displays were the only form of "treatment" available from the Great Man. Not only that, but Charcot appeared to have completely lost his critical intellectual abilities. He appeared no longer to care.

The example of Blanche Wittmann, whom we first met performing for Binet and Fere, reveals the extent of Charcot's self-deception. Wit, as she was known, had become a patient at the Salpêtrière when she was a young girl. Nobody knows exactly what was wrong with her, because Charcot ordered that all his patients' files be burned upon his death, and that order was carried out. Known among staff members as "la riene des hysteriques," or "the queen of the hysterics," Wit was described as "authoritarian, capricious, and unpleasant" toward other patients as well as hospital employees. But she was Charcot's favorite demonstration subject for his public exhibitions of hypnosis. She became so famous that oil paintings of her were commissioned to be painted in the various stages of trance, and these decorated the halls of the Salpêtrière hospital.

Essentially Wit remained a professional patient for the rest of her life. She spent her later adult years playing the part of a multiple-personality patient at the many public demonstrations staged at the Salpêtrière by Charcot's ranking staff members. She died of cancer as a tragic result of early experimentation with X-ray equipment, with which she had voluntarily assisted. Some said that when she died there was not a trace of insanity about her.

The fate that had befallen Mesmer also came to Charcot. Magnetism had evolved into hypnosis and offered stunning insights into the mind, but it had failed to establish a solid claim of scientific legitimacy. Many felt that both Mesmer's and Charcot's cures were primarily a by-product of the force of their personalities. Recognition of this fact by the men of the Nancy school destroyed Charcot's reputation.

But the times were changing. By 1890 the Salpêtrière offered the finest research facilities and the richest source of psychiatric subjects in the world. If he had done nothing else worth remembering, Charcot had set the stage for the formal discovery of the talking cure.

Pierre Janet

They called the man Achilles. The provincial authorities had brought him by stagecoach to the great Charcot as a last desperate act before abandoning all hope that he could be rescued from insanity. Apart from cursing and shrieking, Achilles was mute.

Achilles was 33; the year was 1890. The great Charcot shook his imperious head. Such an advanced case of neurological weakness was probably beyond any meaningful treatment. The officials should not hope for much.

The physical examination found nothing of importance—except for remarkable stigmata. When was the last time anyone had seen stigmata? Most of the Salpêtrière physicians in these days had seen stigmata only in textbooks. Stigmata were relics of a long-forgotten era of religious superstition and demonology. Achilles was a throwback; the Enlightenment had passed him by.

There was not, in truth, any real hope that even the Great Man could hypnotize him. Achilles was much too psychotic.

Charcot was tired. He was barely 65, but he felt more like 90, and his heart was so weak it might not last another winter. Achilles was work for a younger man, one with fewer responsibilities—and less obvious and numerous enemies.

Perhaps Pierre Janet was the man for the job. He was almost Achilles' age. As a man of enlightened views, Janet would be fascinated by the classical symptoms of demonic possession. The stigma alone might be enough for a short monograph. One had to tell Achilles' poor wife something, and Janet was a good man, as good as they come. Chest pains—the Great Man had to rest.

The Case of Achilles

The young physician was not particularly surprised when the Great Man asked him to have a look at the new case. Janet knew he was good. Had he not been chosen to present his doctoral research to the International Congress for Experimental and Therapeutic Hypnotism at the 1889 Universal Exposition in Paris? After the presentation, had not even the distinguished American philosopher-psychologist William James congratulated him on his work? Even that unhappy-looking Freud fellow from Vienna looked impressed. It was, perhaps, immodest to say so, but it was true: If modern, positivist science was going to be extended to psychiatric disorders, Janet, and rigorously trained young scientists like him, were going to be the ones to do it. And they were going to have to do it with tough, messy cases like the new lunatic in the east wing.

Achilles was babbling. Once in a while he would roar obscenities in an odd guttural voice—probably, Janet noted, in what was supposed to be the voice of the devil himself. No wonder the old man didn't think he could handle the case himself. Charcot didn't even suspect how deeply people hated him—they were jealous, of course. But timing was involved too. The key to success in science is to be in the right place at the right time—with the right set of ideas.

The Examination. Janet began by examining the patient. Soon every physician at the Salpêtrière would be required to use this method, but not until the old man was gone.

- *Step one: medical examination.* Conduct it in private, with no crowds, no spectators, no performance. Just conduct a routine but thorough medical examination.
- *Step two: "the fountain pen method."* Write down every single word the patient says, no matter how irrelevant or ridiculous it sounds. The key is always in the words. The trick is to recover it, like a precious gem lost in a coal pile.
- *Step three: interview.* Talk to the wife; talk to the physicians who have been treating the patient. Get the full story; find out the slightest details. The answer is always right in front of us, but we must learn to see it.

Here's what Janet and his colleagues learned from the examination process. Achilles' parents had been very much of the old school. They were full of religious superstitions, the father even more so than the mother. The father's favorite story was about his famous encounter with the devil—under a tree, no less. He was nothing short of obsessed, a raving lunatic on the subject of devils. The mother evidently agreed without exception to everything the old fool said.

Still, Achilles had been normal enough as a young man, and his wife reported that there really hadn't been anything remarkable about him until 6 months ago.

Achilles had returned home from a brief business trip and seemed troubled. His wife said he was "gloomy" and "preoccupied"; he stopped talking to her, as if something dreadful was weighing on his mind. She persuaded Achilles to visit the physician, but the physician could find nothing wrong. On their way home from the physician's residence, suddenly Achilles had a terrific fit of laughter, which lasted about 2 hours. During that episode, he exclaimed that he could see Hell, Satan, and demons.

Achilles then jumped out of the carriage, hastily tied his legs together with a piece of rope, and threw himself headfirst into a pond alongside the road.

Fortunately, people nearby were attracted by the commotion, and they rescued Achilles at once. By then he was raving about having passed "the test" and announced that the demons had fled him as soon as he entered the water. But a minute later he was shrieking that they had repossessed him at the very moment the strangers pulled him out.

Achilles remained in a state of extreme agitation for some months thereafter. Finally, after all the local doctors had failed to improve the deranged man's condition, his wife had been persuaded that Achilles' only hope, and hers too, was to deliver him to the Salpêtrière. There was an outside chance that the once Great Man, old Charcot, could cure him with his hypnotic sessions.

The Treatment. Janet pondered the evidence, formed a hypothesis, and decided to put it to a test. Because Achilles could not be hypnotized, Janet could not break into his self-imposed mutism. But perhaps there was another way. Janet put a pencil in Achilles' right hand and a writing tablet in his lap. As Janet had hoped, the man began automatically writing, although what he wrote was all "demonic" nonsense.

Janet then slowly rose from his chair and stood behind his patient. Janet whispered, "Who are you?" And the hand wrote, "I AM THE DEVIL." At which point Janet whispered, "Good, then we can talk together."

But first Janet would require proof of the devil's power. He first asked the devil to raise Achilles' arm against the patient's will. With apparent great struggle, the arm rose over Achilles' head. Apparently unpersuaded, Janet asked the devil to prove the fuller depths of his power. Janet challenged the devil to hypnotize Achilles against his will. The devil fell for the trick, and Achilles fell into a deep hypnotic trance.

Once the hypnosis was effected, the rest was routine. True to Charcot's dictum that "Sex is always at the bottom of neurosis," Achilles recounted under hypnosis that while he had been away on his business trip he had been sexually unfaithful to his young wife. He was so overcome by regret and disgust that he was unable to speak. He became obsessed with the memory of his infidelity and began to have vivid dreams about the devil. He was hardly surprised when he discovered that he had become possessed.

Just as the Great Man had expected, Janet published the case. Then in 1894 Janet reported that, as a result of further hypnotic treatments, Achilles had not only fully recovered but had remained completely symptom-free for over 3 years. The psychiatric principle manifest in this case, according to Janet, was that in treating hysterical illness,

> one has to search for the basic fact which is at the origin of delusion. . . . The illness of
> our patient does not lie in the thought of the demon. That thought is secondary and
> is rather the interpretation furnished by his superstitious ideas. The true illness is re-
> morse. . . . Man, all too proud, . . . has a propensity to comfort [himself] against dull
> reality by telling . . . fine stories. In some people these stories take the upper hand, to
> the point where they assume more importance than reality. (quoted in Ellenberger,
> 1970, p. 370)

Contributions to the Talking Cure

Janet's report, published a century after Mesmer's disgrace, is remarkable in at least a couple of respects. In the first place, we can marvel at the ingenuity of the physician and the effectiveness of the treatment. I wonder what the chances are today that Achilles would encounter a drug-free talking cure for his troubled mind. I wonder whether I, or many readers of this book, would have been as clever in working with the client's delusions, actually creating the cure out of the manifestation of the illness.

Janet's therapy was extraordinary, even by today's standards. But the real revelation is perhaps what it shows about how far psychotherapy had come in less than a century. This is the second aspect of the Achilles case that seems remarkable. By 1890 treatment of the mentally ill had become routinely medicalized. The Great Man, Charcot, had been the foremost neurologist of his day, and it was advances in this specialty field that supported and nurtured the great advances that were about to be made in the development of psychotherapy, both in France and in Austria.

Who had trained Janet, this pioneer in the talking cure? He had been trained by philosophers. In fact, his first scholarly presentation was a philosophical study titled "Foundations of Private Property," a thesis on the metaphysics of ownership. It concluded that scientific, rational thought should continue to refine the concept of property to achieve a "sublime reconciliation" of private interest and social justice.

Then one day Janet's dream and driving ambition came true, and he received the invitation to join the great Charcot in Paris. Janet would be able to turn his enlightened philosophical attention, his life's passion, to extend the metaphysical foundations of "truth and justice through reason" to treatment of the insane.

In Janet's hands hypnosis, and all of psychiatry, would become a medical specialty to be applied with the skill and precision of a true science. He was the New Man of his age.

Janet brought the painstaking rules of minutely reasoned scientific inquiry, which he had acquired as a philosopher, to the medical specialty of treating the mentally ill. Evidently, without being aware of the parallel, Janet was bringing to the new discipline of "abnormal psychology" the same scientific values and methods that his German counterparts—Wilhelm Wundt, Edward Titchener, and Gustav Fechner—were bringing to the study of human sensory processes. A new scientific psychology was being born.

The Nature of Madness. The essence of Janet's theory was consistent with the teachings of his mentor, Charcot. Janet believed that the lack of "psychic cohesiveness," which Charcot had seen as the common link between hypnosis and the neuroses, was in fact a neurological condition that Janet called "psychasthenia." Psychasthenia could be caused either by nervous exhaustion or by shock; its consequence was a failure of the nervous system to integrate fully all aspects of consciousness. Hysterical manifestations, Janet argued, were the result of aspects of consciousness splitting off from the rest of the mind, causing "the individual to behave as if he were completely motivated by . . . separate ideas" (Alexander & Selesnick, 1966, p. 173).

Even more interesting, perhaps, was Janet's claim that under hypnosis patients like Achilles could often remember the traumatic events that had precipitated the outbreak of their neurotic symptoms. He claimed that sometimes, when the recollection of these events was accompanied by a cathartic emotional release, the recovery of these memories led not to temporary but to permanent removal of neurotic symptoms. This idea was nothing short of revolutionary.

We can safely argue that the greatest contribution to come out of Janet's work with Achilles was new theories about the nature of madness. In describing his work with Achilles, Janet brought to maturity a number of concepts that would form the basis of dynamic modern psychiatry, which would in turn shape the thinking of the entire world in the 20th century. Foremost among these concepts were the following:

- The active role of the unconscious in shaping human affairs
- The importance of early experience in shaping both conscious and unconscious reality
- The scientific legitimacy of hypnosis as a method for accessing the unconscious
- And most importantly of all, the value of reconstructing the contents of the unconscious mind in order to cure psychopathology

For Janet, all these concepts were subject to the utmost scientific scrutiny—in terms of the laws of reason and logic and in terms of their applicability to human affairs.

Persecution by Ideas. Janet believed that the promise of progress—which had been the wellspring of the Enlightenment and had inspired the likes of Charles Darwin, Karl Marx, and Friedrich Engels—would be applied to the affairs of the common people to give them greater power over their own destinies. Janet was pioneering a science that, he believed, would liberate people from persecution by their own un-reasoned ideas. One contemporary observer wrote,

> When I went to Paris to study Janet's techniques . . . I found housed together many persecutionist patients who fired one another emotionally with fantastic tales. When I asked Janet what his therapeutic approach here was, I received the strange reply: "I believe those people until it is proven to me that what they say is untrue. You see, these people are persecuted by something, and you must investigate carefully to get to the root." What he wanted to make me see was that one ought not discard persecutional fantasies as ridiculous, or view them only symptomatically; one ought to take them seriously and analyze them, until the causal conditions are revealed. (Ernest Harms, 1959, quoted in Ellenberger, 1970, p. 351)

Janet's great and lasting contribution to the history of psychotherapy is simply this: He was the first modern scientific medical practitioner to recognize the extraordinary power of ideas as determinants of the overall physical, emotional, and psychological well-being of human beings.

Ideas could be seen as the central symptoms of a disorder, as its central cause, and ultimately as its solution. From having his patients "automatically write" these ideas, as he had with Achilles and most of his early patients, Janet developed the technique of having them talk about their "subconscious fixed ideas," as he called them, at random.

The Therapeutic Relationship. In marked contrast to most of his peers, Janet always insisted that his patients be treated with respect, patience, and kindness. After a short time spent working with patients, Janet came to understand that patients' feelings of trust and their perceptions of the physician's understanding and sympathy have a powerful influence on the outcome of any therapeutic technique.

Janet was therefore, without serious question, the first psychotherapist to take note of the sometimes dramatic but predictable changes that take place in the relationship between the client and the therapist as their association deepens over the course of their many conversations. Janet noticed that often, for example, patients would behave toward the therapist in ways they would not with anyone else. They would see the therapist as a uniquely kind and beneficent person, uniquely able to understand and communicate with them. Out of this special relationship would come the ability to share secrets and intense feelings that had never before been re-vealed to anyone.

As Janet modestly concluded, these advances in the relationship between patient and therapist made it possible for the therapist to offer much more substantial and effective help with the difficulties the patient had to face.

At first Janet was interested in the content of patients' talk as a way of discover-ing the ideas beneath the surface of conscious awareness. He believed that "free talk-ing" would give a therapist the mental clues needed to solve the puzzle of the person's hysterical suffering. But Janet soon came to see that there was cure in simply talking. He theorized that through the process of "substitution," old embedded ideas could gradually be changed, and hallucinations could slowly be transformed back to ordi-nary perception as the patient recovered the capacity for normal attention and in-formation processing.

An Obscure and Bitter Death

By 1900 the 41-year-old Janet seemed poised to become the central figure of Euro-pean psychiatry (Ellenberger, 1970). He had been recognized around the world for his contributions to science. In 1906 he visited Harvard University for the second time, for an unprecedented series of 15 distinguished lectures on the cause and treat-ment of hysterical disorders. He had developed a systematic, scientifically testable psychology of personality and psychopathology that took into account both the con-scious and the subconscious elements of mind. By the outbreak of World War I he had published more than 20 scientific books, some of which even went so far as to relate his psychiatric findings to the rapidly advancing science of evolution.

So why is Janet such an obscure figure today? Ellenberger (1970) suggested sev-eral reasons. The most important one is that he was the victim of at least three forces working against widespread acceptance of his work:

- The first was probably the most cruel: Janet's work was savagely attacked by his fellow French neurologists, who either wouldn't or couldn't accept a psycho-logical basis for nervous disorders. They attacked Janet for his association with Charcot and for his lifelong use of hypnosis, which was a perfectly acceptable psychological tool but a discredited medical one. They universally refused to accept a purely psychological interpretation of hypnotic phenomena, instead ridiculing it as a vestige of the old schools of magnetism. The fact that mag-netism had gradually devolved into spiritualism throughout Europe and the United States only made Janet's case more difficult.
- The medical establishment rejected Janet out of a combination of intellectual rigidity and professional jealousy, but his second foe attacked him on what seems like age-old grounds. The Catholic Church continued to have enormous

influence in France, and Janet's nominal Catholicism did not insulate him from the charge that his work was fundamentally antireligious, heretical, and especially anti-Catholic—which of course it was, being a direct product of Enlightenment thinking.

▪ The third force allied against Janet was the devoted followers of Freud, the founder of the new science of psychoanalysis. Janet had staked a solitary claim to territory that the Freudians also exclusively claimed as their own. Unfortunately, their attacks on Janet's integrity and scientific honesty went unanswered. Ellenberger (1970) suggested that the 86-year-old Janet may not even have been aware that he was accused of stealing Freud's ideas. At any rate, the charges went unanswered, and the history of modern psychiatry ended up being written by the loyal followers of psychoanalysis. Completely devoted to his work and his patients, Janet had never built a loyal following of enlightened disciples. It appears to have never occurred to him that he would have to fight a political battle within the field of psychology for the survival of his ideas. In this respect he was much like the great American psychologist William James. Evidently both thought their work would stand on its own merit, but both saw their work overtaken by political realities.

Janet died in relative obscurity in 1947 in Paris. His life's work was, and largely remains, abandoned and neglected. He outlived his rival, Freud, but the Freudians had emerged triumphant. Thus the stage is set for us to make our way to Vienna.

CHAPTER 5

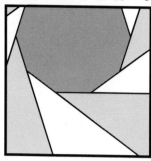

The Beginnings of Psychoanalysis: The Strange Case of Anna O.

La Reine des Hysteriques II

Controversial and incomplete, the case of 21-year-old Anna O. provided the foundations for the emerging discipline of psychoanalysis. Anna's physician, Dr. Josef Breuer of Vienna, recorded in minute detail several hundred distinct symptoms of her hysterical illness in 1880. Breuer also took note of Anna's fantastic memory under self-hypnosis of the traumatic details of her life, details of which she had no conscious awareness during her normal waking state. A decade later, intrigued by his older friend's account, a young neurologist by the name Sigmund Freud became fascinated by the case. Breuer and Freud published the case together in 1895; however, they disagreed completely about the underlying issues.

The story of Anna O. is fogged with ethical issues, many revolving around the nature of the relationship between the patient and her doctor. The historical record is also marred by incomplete evidence and insufficient proof of a meaningful cure. The case of Anna O. was, however, the first published example of a revolutionary idea: scientific analysis of the psyche.

Clinical Interlude

Anna O. was 21 years old when Dr. Josef Breuer first met her in 1880. The strong-willed, somewhat moody daughter of an upper-middle-class Jewish family, she was conceivably the brightest patient Breuer had ever treated, with an astonishingly quick grasp of things and penetrating intuition. She had wonderfully developed poetic and creative gifts, which Breuer described as "under the control of sharp and critical common sense." She was certainly also the most theatrical person the doctor had ever met; she spent much of her waking hours living through fairy tales in her imagination—though her puritanical family had little awareness of the depths of her private "indulgences." Her feelings, whether of joy or sadness, were always just a bit exaggerated. Somewhat unusual for a girl of her social class, she was extraordinarily kind to her family's household servants. Even more remarkably, she demonstrated an earnest, compassionate interest in the poor.

The family, on the other hand, was unremarkable in most respects. As was common among people of their social position in Vienna at that time, family life was monotonous. Anna's parents were exceedingly moralistic. She was allowed none of the cultural and social diversions so widely enjoyed by girls on the edge of womanhood. She had been largely deprived of even the opportunities afforded by close friendships with other girls for the sharing of intimacies and adolescent secrets. The only excitement and entertainment available to her was what Anna called the "private theater" of her imagination. She spent many long hours every day enveloped in her own private world of daydreams and fantasies.

The only thing extraordinary about Anna from a medical perspective, and this was actually quite astonishing, was how undeveloped the element of sexuality was in her. She had never known romantic love, and throughout her long illness, her enormous number of hallucinations, and the subsequent treatment that would eventually set her free, that element of mental life never emerged.

At the time of Anna's nervous breakdown, Dr. Breuer was both a colleague of Ernst Brücke at the University of Vienna and Sigmund Freud's most important benefactor in the early days of his career as a practicing physician. The following case study was one of several published in *Studies in Hysteria* (1955b), which was written jointly by Breuer and Freud in 1893, some 13 years after Anna's treatments were finished; all otherwise unattributed quotations and case details in this chapter are from this source. Breuer's detailed observations showed a progression of Anna's disease through four phases.

Phase One: Latent Incubation

The first phase of her illness, "the period of latent incubation," began in July 1880 and lasted until December 10. Anna had been engaged in the full-time occupation of nursing her sick father, who would die from his malady the following spring. The doctor had been consulted initially to treat Anna for a severe cough. It was obvious from the outset that the girl's health was severely compromised by an advanced case of nervous exhaustion.

When the doctor examined her, he discovered that she was suffering, apparently without anyone in the household noticing, from the beginning stages of anorexia nervosa (voluntary self-starvation). Given her already weakened condition, the eating disorder rapidly sapped her of all her remaining energies.

Phase Two: Manifest Psychosis

On December 11, 1880, Anna took to her bed. She remained there until April 1, 1881. This was the second phase of her illness, "the period of manifest psychosis." She suffered from paraphasia (loss of the ability to understand spoken or written language), a convergent squint, severe disturbances of vision, paralysis in the form of contracture of both the arms and the legs, paresis (partial paralysis) of the neck muscles, left-side occipital headaches, vertigo, anesthesia of the elbows, and complete rigidity of the shoulders.

The degree of psychical disturbance was equally alarming. Anna had developed a split personality, with two distinct phases alternating in rapid succession. The first phase was her usual personality—somewhat more melancholy and anxious than usual, yet relatively normal. The second appeared as a "naughty" (her word), unpleasant, and uncouth personality that was abusive toward other people and highly agitated. Her normal self experienced her naughty self as what she called "absences," periods of lost time when she would have no memory of what had transpired or who had been in the room with her.

Throughout the winter of 1880–81, Anna's condition worsened with a frightening intensity. The alternations occurred with greater and greater frequency, and her absent periods became more and more horrifying. During these absences she usually hallucinated horrible black snakes, which her normal self, whenever her mind momentarily cleared, would recognize as only the braids of her own hair. She complained of being blind and deaf. Next she felt she was two different persons, one of which was being controlled by the "Evil One," who forced her to behave badly.

Anna's inability to speak was gradually replaced by her own made-up language, composed of bits and pieces of five different languages. Eventually, even when she attempted to communicate by writing, the meaning of what she wrote was masked by this same unintelligible combination. Dr. Breuer developed the impression that her speech difficulty was an unconscious effort to avoid speaking of something that had strongly offended her and alienated her sensibilities.

To the doctor's complete surprise, in March 1881, when he asked Anna about his suspicion, she responded with a dramatic change in her condition and appeared to become decidedly less psychotic. In silent response to the physician's probing questions about the powerful aversion locked in her thoughts, Anna eventually experienced a complete return of the power of movement to the extremities of her body. Simultaneously her paraphasia receded and was transformed. In its place she now spoke only English, and only during her lucid state. She could, thankfully, still understand her native German, but she could no longer speak it. This development greatly vexed Anna's personal maid, who could not communicate in any language but German. Meanwhile, during her more and more frequent "absences," Anna spoke only in French and Italian. Total amnesia of the absent periods prevailed during her lucid episodes.

Further progress was noted on April 1, when Anna rose from her bed for the first time since December. Then, sadly, on April 5 her adored father died.

Phase Three: Continuous Somnambulism

Upon hearing the news, Anna exhibited a violent outburst of excitement immediately followed by a profound stupor. It lasted for two days, and then Anna emerged in an entirely new state. This was the beginning of the third period of her illness, "the period of continuous somnambulism alternating with more normal conditions."

Now she was much calmer, but Anna had developed a severe restriction of her field of vision; for instance, she could see only one flower at a time in a bouquet. Nor could she recognize anyone who came to visit her. She complained that everyone around her was nothing but a wax figure. This delusion deepened until she entirely denied the presence of any other person in the world, save one. That singular exception was her trusted and adored physician, Dr. Breuer.

At this time Anna continued to speak only in English. However, she now had lost her ability to comprehend German, although she could still read some French and Italian. She began to write only in English and only with her left hand.

The only encouraging news was that Anna's anorexia started to show signs of attenuation. She began to permit her doctor to hand-feed her, but she still always refused bread.

Dr. Breuer brought another physician (probably the famous sexologist Richard von Krafft-Ebbing) to examine Anna one day during this period. Anna, true to form, refused to acknowledge his presence in any way. This "negative hallucination," of a sort that can also be produced with hypnosis, receded only when the visitor broke into her consciousness by blowing a great cloud of cigar smoke in her face. There followed a great burst of spontaneous "feminine rage." She threw herself from her bed and raced for the door of her bedchamber, only to collapse unconscious on the carpet.

The next time Dr. Breuer visited her, she was much worse. She was hallucinating almost continuously and refusing all food in her doctor's absence. Anna was manifestly suicidal, and a decision was made to move her to the family's country house outside Vienna. Dr. Breuer visited her bedside at least twice a week and was pleased to note that his visits seemed to bring Anna significant peace of mind. Their conversations were increasingly focused on the sources of her many symptoms.

Meanwhile, her psychical condition continued to deteriorate quite severely, and it became necessary to medicate her with increasingly large doses of morphine, to which she subsequently became addicted. This state of affairs persisted through late

December 1881. Anna spent heavily medicated days sleeping and hallucinating. But every day at dusk, she returned to her lucid state in preparation for her evening "chimney-sweeping" sessions with her devoted physician.

During this period, except when Dr. Breuer was unavailable for consultation, the patient gradually improved, eventually to the point where she could return home to Vienna. At the end of December 1881, however, Anna experienced a significant relapse and had to be returned to the country house. There Dr. Breuer called on her in the early evening each day.

The essential feature of Anna's symptoms at this stage was an intensification of her "absences" into full-blown states of self-hypnosis. Anna even gave a pet name to these states: She called them "clouds." The doctor later wrote this account:

> The regular order of things was: the somnolent state in the afternoon, followed after sunset by the deep hypnosis for which she invented the technical name "clouds" [in English]. While in this trance-like state if she was able to narrate the hallucinations she had had in the course of the day, she would wake up clear in mind, calm and cheerful. She would sit down to work and write or draw into the night quite rationally. At about four she would go to bed. Next day the whole series of events would be repeated. It was a truly remarkable contrast: in the day-time the irresponsible patient pursued by hallucinations, and at night the girl with her mind completely clear. (Breuer & Freud, 1893/ 1955b, p. 66)

In the early evening, in the company of her trusted physician, and holding his hands "to satisfy herself of my identity," Anna seemed to develop an uncanny ability to understand and perceive what was happening to her, an ability quite separate from the torments she was going through during her long days of hallucinations. As Dr. Breuer noted, "She aptly described this procedure [the self-hypnosis], speaking seriously, as a 'talking cure,' while she referred to it jokingly as 'chimney sweeping.'"

After the doctor left, Anna would stay up until dawn occupied with her normal activities. She noted that her good nights were those that followed when she was particularly successful at getting some fixed delusion or hallucination "unstuck" in her therapeutic session. But there was little carryover from these successful sessions to her psychological state the next day.

Phase Four: Gradual Cessation of the Pathological States and Symptoms

In December 1881 the fourth and final stage of Anna's illness and therapy commenced when she presented her physician with a dramatic turn of events. Quite suddenly, her daytime behavior became dramatically more normal, but her nighttime behavior suffered drastic changes as well. Anna now lived her daytimes in the present and her nighttimes precisely 365 days earlier.

Night after night, Anna and her physician relived the "lost" days of 1881. It was as if she was driven to recover every minute detail of the period of her father's last illness and the subsequent months of mourning. Moreover, she felt compelled to recover those events in precisely the reverse chronological order from which they had occurred.

> Obviously, this was an extremely time-consuming procedure. Breuer gives as an example of one of the symptoms, the patient's transient state of deafness; he found seven subforms of this symptom and each one of them constituted one of the "series" that Breuer had to treat separately. The first subform, "not hearing when someone came in" had occurred 108 times, and the patient had to tell the detail of each one of these 108 occurrences in reverse chronological order, until Breuer reached the first manifestation: she once had not heard her father come in. But the six other subforms of the "not-hearing" symptom as well as each other symptom had to be treated for itself with a similar procedure. (Ellenberger, 1972, p. 270)

The hallucinations and delusions of the earlier phase were replaced with these memories of astonishing accuracy (Anna's mother had kept a detailed diary of Anna's illness).

Ultimately Anna's memories became even more complicated. She began weaving into her accounts of her father's final months memories of events that had taken place during the dreadful months, 2 years earlier, when she had first become afflicted with her psychological condition: "These [memories] were the psychical events involved in the incubation of the illness between July and December, 1880; it was they that had produced the whole of the hysterical phenomena, and when they were brought to verbal utterance the symptoms disappeared."

One particularly graphic example is illustrative. During one session on an exceptionally hot night in the late spring of 1882, the patient was suffering from acute thirst, which had become a somewhat regular complaint. Without being able to account for the problem in any way, Anna had found it impossible over the previous 6 weeks to drink any fluids. She would repeatedly take up the glass of water she longed for, but as soon as she touched it to her lips, she would push it away with disgust. Each time this happened, she fell into an absence of a few seconds' duration. But on this night, suddenly, a wrenching memory flooded back to her. All at once she remembered that her English governess, whom she loathed, had owned a tiny dog, which Anna also despised. One day Anna had seen the dog drinking from the governess's water glass, and the sight of it had made her nauseous. She had stifled her disgust and made no comment about it at the time, wanting to be polite. But now, "after giving energetic expression to the anger she had held back," she asked for and drank a large tumbler of water. As suddenly as it had come on, the disturbance entirely vanished, never to return.

The way was now clear for a series of major therapeutic breakthroughs:

> In this way her paralytic contractions and anaesthesia, disorders of vision and hearing of every sort, neuralgias, coughing, tremors, etc., and finally her disorders of speech were "talked away." Amongst the disorders of vision, the following, for instance, were disposed

of separately: the convergent squint with diplopia; deviation of both eyes to the right, so that when her hand reached out for something it always went to the left of the object; restriction of the visual field; central amblyopia; macropsia; seeing a death's hand instead of her father; inability to read. (Breuer & Freud, 1893/1955b, p. 72)

In exact reverse order, this remembering-and-talking cure removed the effects of (in addition to the 108 instances of not hearing when someone entered a room) 27 instances of not being able to follow a conversation when several people were talking, 50 instances of deafness when she was being directly addressed, 15 instances of being deaf while in a carriage, 37 instances of deafness brought on by sharp noises, 12 instances of sleep deafness, and 54 instances of deafness brought on by concentration.

Dr. Breuer also recounted how Anna was freed from some of her language problems and hysterical paralysis of her right arm when she recalled a horrible nightmare or hallucination she had experienced while sitting in her dying father's sickroom:

She fell into a waking dream and saw a black snake coming towards the sick man from the wall to bite him. . . . Her right arm over the back of the chair, had gone to sleep and had become anaesthetic and paretic; and when she looked at it the fingers turned into little snakes with death heads (the nails). (It seemed probable that she had tried to use her paralysed right arm to drive off the snake and its anesthesia and paralysis had consequently become associated with the hallucination of the snake.) When the snake vanished, in her terror she tried to pray. But language failed her: she could find no tongue in which to speak, till at last she thought of some children's verses in English, and then found herself able to think and pray in that language. (Breuer & Freud, 1893/1955b, p. 38)

In what would be their final formal therapeutic sessions, Anna took her beloved and trusted physician back through her memory of her father's sickroom on the day of his death. She relived all the trauma of his passing, as well as the terrible hallucinations that had overtaken her at the time. With that unburdening accomplished, we are told, she recovered her ability to speak and pray in German.

She was moreover free from the innumerable disturbances which she had previously exhibited. After this time she left Vienna and travelled for a while; but it was considerable time before she regained her mental balance entirely. Since then she has enjoyed complete health. (Breuer & Freud, 1893/1955b, p. 39)

Followup and Report

Anna O. was, in actuality, Bertha Pappenheim, who went on to a distinguished career as a campaigner for women's rights and a brave crusader against first the oppression of women and then the violent anti-Semitism of the Nazis. She established and managed a group home for illegitimate children, which also served as a safe house for young girls who had run away from forced prostitution. She was honored for her contributions to humanity by the West German government in 1954, and several biographies of her life have been published. At her funeral in 1936, the great theologian Martin Buber eulogized her:

> I not only admired her but loved her, and will love her until the day I die. There are people of spirit and people of passion. Rarer still are people of spirit and passion. But rarest of all is passionate spirit. Bertha Pappenheim was a woman with just such a spirit. (quoted in Dawes, 1994, p. 188)

A Psychological View of Hysteria

As Alexander and Selesnick (1966) documented, Freud had returned to Vienna from Paris in 1886 full of enthusiasm for Charcot's radical new ideas about the nature and treatment of hysteria. We can imagine the 30-year-old Freud earnestly talking to his colleagues in Vienna about Charcot's discoveries about the meaningfulness and even logic of hysterical symptoms. The most radical development in Freud's thinking turned on the nearly discredited phenomenon of hypnosis and the relationship of the purely "psychological" to the behavioral manifestations of nervous disease.

The reigning theory of the day attempted to demonstrate specific cause-and-effect connections between brain anatomy and hysterical symptoms. One of Freud's chief rivals, Theodore Meynert, for example, had proposed a direct link between hysterical aphasia and pathology in distinct areas of the cerebral cortex. How could Freud, one of the most brilliant neuroanatomists of his generation, reject a perfectly straightforward physicalist interpretation of hysteria in favor of one propounded by a French hypnotist?

Freud's dear friend and mentor, Josef Breuer, was more than receptive to these exciting new ideas. He was fascinated by Freud's accounts of what he had witnessed in Paris, and Breuer even accepted at face value the seemingly impossible idea that in France some significant minority of diagnosed hysterics were men.

What happened next caused history to happen. Breuer pulled out his old notebooks and asked Freud if he remembered the strange case of Bertha Pappenheim, which he and Freud had talked about back in 1882. Freud not only remembered the case, he said he had tried to give Charcot a full account of the case to get the old man's opinion about it. Charcot had taken not the least notice of the young Austrian's secondhand account; after all, Freud had never set eyes on the girl. "Typical grandstanding young medical student" may have been the weary Charcot's private thought.

Back in 1882, Breuer and Freud had both been completely at a loss to understand either what had caused Bertha's bizarre symptoms or what effects were responsible for the seeming miracle of her "cathartic" cure, as Breuer had called it at the time. At that time, Breuer and Freud were both as convinced of a physicalist, material explanation for hysteria as was Meynert. Their discussions 5 years earlier had been intriguing, and it was an intense joy for Freud to find an older physician who valued his opinions so highly, but in the end their conversations were entirely fruitless. But now, in light of what Freud had seen at the Salpêtrière, the strange case of the young Pappenheim girl seemed to embed every aspect necessary to establish the validity of a complete theory of the psychological etiology of hysterical disease.

At once Breuer and Freud set out to establish their claim. They would write up the case and establish the scientific legitimacy of the talking cure before the rest of the pack worked it out for themselves. But first Breuer and Freud had to develop a solid body of case study evidence based on their own work with the patients who visited their practice.

Then the bottom seemed to drop out of their plans: "From 1886 to 1889 Freud and Breuer continued their work on cathartic hypnosis but found that some patients could not be hypnotized and others were not permanently relieved of their symptoms" (Alexander and Selesnick, 1966, p. 192). They decided the problem was in their hypnotic technique. With what must have felt like sweet revenge, they decided that Freud would travel again to France, but not to the Salpêtrière, where he had felt so ignored. He would go instead to Nancy, the Salpêtrière's "enemy camp."

The decision proved to be crucial. As explained in Chapter 4, the physicians at Nancy, under the direction of Hippolyte Bernheim, were in the process of refuting Charcot's physicalist theory that hysteria was based on weakness of the nervous system. Their new theory propounded a completely psychological view of hypnosis and related phenomena; "suggestibility," a psychological trait, was at the center of their proposed system.

Freud never did become a clinically successful hypnotist, but he returned from Paris with a plan in his mind for the book with Breuer. And in 1895 the world received its first glimpse of the first comprehensive theory of the psychological foundations of hysterical disorder.

At the heart of Breuer and Freud's *Studies in Hysteria* was the assertion that hysterical symptoms result from the debilitating psychological effects of repressed memories of upsetting and often traumatic events. What empowers an event to have such a devastating effect on the unconscious mind? The answer appeared to be that the magnitude or importance of the trauma is not the determining consideration; what is responsible for the presence of hysteria, Breuer and Freud argued, was the strangulation of the expression of emotion at the time the trauma originally occurred. In some sense, the very niceness of girls like Bertha Pappenheim, the degree of highly controlled propriety that characterized their Victorian manners, set them up to become the victims of hysterical dysfunction.

There is a wonderful poetic justice in the fact that ultimately the "cure" for hysteria was not discovered by some high-powered masculine agent of Victorian culture. The victims of hysterical illness were by and large young middle-class women caught up in the repressive demands of a hypocritical, bourgeois society. How much better that the "cure" was conceived by one of their own, Bertha Pappenheim, who discovered that when she could give free, sometimes violent, expression to pent-up emotional memories, her tortured symptoms would at least temporarily subside.

Breuer's gifts as a physician and a human being had given his patient the opportunity and the support to find her way back from madness. And Freud's insatiable curiosity and driving scientific ambition had resurrected the case 13 years after the fact. But the unschooled intuitive wisdom of one 21-year-old woman lit the first candle in the darkness of 19th-century psychiatry and brought the reality of the talking cure to the world's attention.

A Second Look at the Case of Anna O.

That would be the end of this chapter, except for a famous controversy over the case report, which Freud's followers published in the 1920s. Permit me to quote from the footnote to the case written many years later by Freud's official translator and devoted disciple, James Strachey:

> At this point (so Freud told the present editor [James Strachey], with his finger on an open copy of the book) there is a hiatus in the text. What he had in mind, and went on to describe, was the occurrence which marked the end of Anna O's treatment. It is enough here to say that, when the treatment had apparently reached a successful end, the patient suddenly made manifest to Breuer the presence of a strongly unanalyzed positive transference of an unmistakable sexual nature. [Behind these technical terms lies a dramatic story: after Breuer had said good-bye to his patient, about to go off on a trip with his wife who had become jealous of her husband's interesting patient, he was suddenly called back to discover that she was in the throes of a hysterical pregnancy, claiming to be carrying Breuer's child] (E. Jones, 1953, quoted in Gay, 1989, p. 76n)

Freud further revealed that Breuer had in fact confessed to him that Anna O. had been, in truth, far from being fully recovered when he terminated her treatment. The young patient was essentially no better than she had been in the months before her talking cure. One aspect of her treatment that has escaped the attention of most writers is that they involved heavy sedation by powerfully addicting drugs: chloral hydrate (a hypnotic and sedative) and morphine.

In a bit of medical detective work, Ellenberger (1972) revealed that according to some Swiss medical records he was able to recover, the 22-year-old Bertha Pappenheim was placed in the Sanatorium Bellevue in Switzerland following her unsuccessful treatments with Dr. Breuer. After being hospitalized, Bertha received intensive treatment under the supervision of one of the continent's preeminent psychiatrists, Dr. Robert Binswanger.

According to Gay (1988), even after several months of treatment in Switzerland, Bertha was, in her own recollection, "totally deprived of the faculty to speak, understand or read German . . . with strong neuralgic pain . . . [and still suffering] shorter or longer absences . . . really nervous, anxious, and disposed to cry" (Gay, 1988, p. 66). The sanatorium discharge report noted:

She continued to be irritated with her family, exhibiting hysterical symptoms, and continued to disparage medicine and science as modalities of treatment. She remains in childish opposition to her physicians [and a confirmed addict to high doses of both morphine and chloral]. The general feeling of her physicians at the hospital was that she was an unpleasant person who exhibited hysterical behavior and who had neurological symptoms. (Rosenbaum, 1984, quoted in Dawes, 1994, p. 193)

As I noted earlier in this chapter, Bertha Pappenheim did eventually make a full recovery and go on to a full and rich life dedicated to the service of others. In fact, even during her terrible emotional ordeal Bertha continued to look after the needs of a number of poor, sick people—an activity Breuer attributed to her need to "satisfy a powerful instinct." You may interpret for yourself an interesting historical footnote reported by Sulloway (1979), who said that Bertha Pappenheim "never spoke to anyone of her experience with Breuer, and she later refused to allow the girls under her care to be psychoanalyzed" (p. 57).

The discrepancies between these various accounts of the case of Anna O. are of crucial historical importance, because there is widespread agreement among scholars that the case, in the words of Breuer himself, "contains the germ cell of the whole of psychoanalysis."

Alternatives to the Talking Cure for Treating Hysteria

As controversial as Breuer's treatments might seem today, they were a radically humanistic departure from the accepted treatments of his era:

At the peak of his [medical] career in 1874, Silas Weir Mitchell advocated as a treatment for hysteria: seclusion, enforced bed rest, and the absence of medical activities such as reading, as well as plenty of regular bland food and daily massage. . . . Mitchell's guiding philosophy was that the hysteric should be broken, almost like a wild horse, which will be cowed and tamed. In his own words: "There is often no success possible until we have broken up the whole daily drama of the sick room, with its selfishness and its craving for sympathy and indulgence. . . . A hysterical girl is . . . a vampire who sucks the blood of the healthy people about her." (Ussher, 1991, pp. 75–76)

These Victorian "rest cures" have earned a special place of dishonor in the feminist literature. Books such as Charlotte Perkins Gillman's *The Yellow Wallpaper* and Kate Chopin's *The Awakening* recount with chilling accuracy the deliberate blindness of the male Victorian medical establishment to the psychological and emotional needs of the women of their day. Showalter (1987) charged that the Victorian medical attitude toward "mad" women was

a microcosm of the sex war intended to establish the male doctor's total authority . . . [over] the hysterical woman, a feminist heroine, fighting back against confinement in the bourgeois home. Hysteria was the "daughter's disease"—a mode of protest for women deprived of other social and intellectual outlets or expressive options. (pp. 137, 147)

The "treatments" devised by these Victorian gentlemen included "incarceration in the asylum, treatments with leeches, solitary confinement, clitoridectomy, frequent [sexual] intercourse, or a good beating from a 'concerned' husband" (Ussher, 1991, p. 88). Ussher concluded after an extensive review of this literature that "each [treatment] can be deconstructed, and seen to act to pathologize the woman, treating her as the person who is sick, whilst ignoring the route she has travelled to arrive at the position of madness" (Ussher, 1991, p. 301).

It would be a mistake to conclude that codification of the talking cure quickly eliminated the use or seriously diminished the popularity of these older treatments. Nor were these treatments reserved exclusively for the complaints of women. Recent scholarship on the life of Adolf Hitler, for example, proposes that hypnotism's Germanic roots kept it alive and "fashionable" as a treatment for battle fatigue in the wake of Germany's defeat in World War I. The following story is based on fragmentary evidence from Hitler's autobiography, *Mein Kampf*, and other contemporary sources:

> Blinded by a poison gas attack on the Western front, Hitler was admitted to a military hospital in October of 1918. He appears to have recovered his sight for a while and then suffered a relapse—perhaps a form of "hysterical blindness"—when the news of Germany's humiliating defeat reached him. To others, Hitler described what happened next as a kind of miracle. In his blind, bedridden despair, he received a vision (or had a hallucination), heard a voice from above summoning him to a great destiny—to save Germany. It was then, the story goes, that he miraculously recovered his sight and vowed himself to avenging Germany's defeat. . . . However, the voice Hitler heard was not a voice from above. . . . [I]t was the voice of a hypnotist . . . Dr. Edmund Forster, and he was the ranking psychiatrist at Hitler's hospital . . . Dr. Forster cured Hitler's blindness by using then fashionable mesmeric techniques to put him in a trance and implant the belief that his beloved Germany needed him to recover his sight in order to serve the cause of national resurrection. (Rosenbaum, 1995, pp. 54–55)

Evidently believing that "in trying to cure Hitler, he transformed a previously obscure corporal into a monster" (Rosenbaum, p. 55), Forster committed suicide in 1933 while being pursued by the Gestapo.

Historical Significance of the Case of Anna O.

In many historians' eyes, the primary importance of the case study of Anna O. is that it was the first publication in the new medical specialty of psychoanalysis. We can only marvel at the undisputed fact that a document of such historic value is so marred by politics, intrigue, deception, personal vanity, and scientific ambition. We can only wonder what the history of science would look like if we knew the total, objective truth of every other historically important scientific report.

No doubt the basic idea of a hypnotically induced talking cure for hysterical patients would have made its way to Vienna from France in time. Even though the Franco-Prussian War of 1870–71 had slowed down scholarly exchange between Austria and France, reports of Pierre Janet's work would certainly have been circulating in Vienna by the turn of the century. But the early publication of Breuer's case gave Austrian neurology, and especially the new psychoanalytic profession, a much valued prior claim over reports published by Janet of his clinical work with Achilles. In fact, as you saw in Chapter 4, within a short time the work of Breuer and Freud totally eclipsed Janet's claim to prominence in the field. Timing is everything.

In my own view, what stands as more important historically is that the Anna O. case at last gave scientific and thus medical respectability to the connection between hypnosis and catharsis. For decades, neurologists had routinely used hypnosis in the treatment of their hysterical patients and had routinely observed patients' cathartic emotional experiences while under hypnosis. But were the positive effects due to the hypnosis or to the catharsis the hypnosis had provoked?

The case of Anna O. seems to turn that question on its head. Breuer clearly perceived that it was the cathartic re-remembering and reliving of painful emotional trauma that freed Anna O. from her symptoms. Because Breuer had never hypnotized the girl himself, it seemed clear to him that the primary instrument was emotional catharsis and that hypnotism was window dressing. In fact, hypnosis was imposed on the situation by the willful and highly suggestible young patient, who probably considered it a necessary, face-saving part of treatment.

Thus Anna O. became the first thoroughly documented case study that clearly revealed the mechanism of the cures effected by the magnetists and other hypnotizing faith healers of an earlier day. So when Breuer says that this case was the "wellspring for all of the psychoanalysis which followed," I think his focus is the catharsis his patient experienced in her self-initiated talking cure.

But when Freudians talk about this case, they see something quite different. What they see is the terrible relapse the girl suffered when Breuer left the case. They focus on the hysterical pregnancy and on her declaration "Now comes Dr. B's child." It was at that moment, I think most Freudians would say, that psychoanalysis was born. At that precise moment, in Freud's words, "Breuer held the key in his hand. And he dropped it." (1932, quoted in Gay, 1988, p. 67). That key would come to be called *transference,* and Freud and his followers would come to understand it as a powerful interpersonal force driven by the enormous demands of human sexual desire.

Which story is more honest: that of Breuer or of Freud's followers? We may never know. Ellenberger, who researched both the Pappenheim family papers and all the surviving medical records, concluded that the false-pregnancy story is highly improbable. On the other hand, Ellenberger also acknowledged that Breuer withheld vital information about the case and seriously distorted the historical record. Here is what Ellenberger (1972) concluded:

The newly discovered documents confirm what Freud, according to Jung, had told him: the patient had not been cured. Indeed the famed "prototype of the cathartic cure" was neither a cure nor a catharsis. Anna O had become a severe morphinist and had kept a part of her most conspicuous symptoms [especially her English/German aphasia]. . . . [T]he illness was a creation of the mythopoetic unconscious of the patient with the unaware encouragement and collaboration of the therapist. . . . Anna O's illness was the desperate struggle of an unsatisfied young woman who found no outlets for her physical and mental energies, nor for her idealistic strivings. (pp. 277–278)

The story of Anna O. became the sacred legend of the talking cure and the first proof of its powerful healing remedy, emotional catharsis. But more than that, the case was the basis for two of the deepest foundations of the entire psychoanalytic movement: the sexual basis of mental disorders and the primacy of the therapeutic relationship in effecting a cure.

But we are getting ahead of ourselves by a decade or so. It is time to meet the master.

CHAPTER 6

An Introduction to the Principles of Psychoanalysis

Prometheus: The Gift of Fire

The early story of Sigmund Freud is a tale of unrealized dreams, delayed gratification, and self-struggle. His early career was marked by strong influences and lasting friendships, despite his sometimes autocratic and very strong personality. Coping with his internal struggles and with a brief interlude with cocaine, Freud combated the conflicts between his own deeply held mechanistic, antivitalist views as a neurologist and the more humanistic ideas spawned by his observations of patients.

Freud's scientific companion, Wilhelm Fleiss, corresponded with him frequently as they tried to uncover together the dynamic properties of the human mind. However, Freud soon broke with Fleiss much as he had broken with Josef Breuer and began to work alone.

In personal crisis, Freud embarked on self-analysis, which ended with the revelation of the grand unifying theory of human existence that we know today as psychoanalysis. He described his 1900 masterwork, The Interpretation of Dreams, *as "an insight such as falls to one's lot but once in a lifetime—the most valuable of all the discoveries it has been my good fortune to make."*

Psychoanalysis: The Early Years

The year is 1924. Sigmund Freud is 68 years old, and his clinical work, for all intents and purposes, is complete. In the 15 years remaining to him, he will write sweeping works about the neurotic quality of religious beliefs (*The Future of an Illusion*, 1924) and about the challenge to civilization posed by humankind's base instincts (*Civilization and Its Discontents*, 1930/1961). But the great medical-therapeutic work is behind him. It is time for reflection.

Sigmund Freud's Memories

Freud decides to take a rather perfunctory request from a medical journal for a short personal profile as an invitation to think autobiographically. His memory travels back to his medical school days.

Remembering Paris. He remembers his first professional trip to Paris and the hope that he could pick up enough practical information at the Salpêtrière to make a success of a private practice in neurology back home in Vienna. What he remembers of that long-ago time is that

> in the distance shone the great name of Charcot; so I formed a plan to . . . go to Paris to continue my studies. . . . I became a student at the Salpêtrière, but, as one of the crowd of foreign visitors, I had little attention paid me to begin with.
> 	[Subsequently] I wrote to him and offered [to translate his lectures into German]. Charcot accepted the offer, I was admitted to the circle of his personal acquaintances, and from that time forward I took a full part in all that went on at the clinic. (1925/1964a, p. 6)

According to contemporary French accounts, this is perhaps a self-glorifying exaggeration. But Freud was invited to several of the lavish salon parties Jean-Martin Charcot held regularly for the high society of Paris, to which his friends, students, and colleagues at the hospital were invited.

At this point in his autobiographical essay, Freud paused to take level aim at those critics who were at that time openly writing in the French newspapers that Freud had stolen the discoveries of the great psychiatric pioneer Jean-Pierre Janet while both were at the Salpêtrière. Freud interrupted his story to defend himself against charges that he had misappropriated Janet's discovery of the talking cure. Freud unequivocally proclaimed the discovery as truly his own and asserted, somewhat unconvincingly in the eyes of later historians, "I should . . . like to say explicitly that during the whole of my visit to the Salpêtrière Janet's name was never so much as mentioned" (1925/1964a, p. 7). This statement is the equivalent of saying that you studied at the University of Vienna Medical School and never heard the name Freud mentioned.

This nasty piece of business having been dealt with, at least to Freud's satisfaction, he continued:

What impressed me most of all while I was with Charcot were his latest investigations upon hysteria, some of which were carried out under my own eyes. He had proved, for instance, the genuineness of hysterical phenomena and their conformity to laws . . . , the frequent occurrence of hysteria in men, the production of hysterical paralyses and contracture by hypnotic suggestion and the fact that such artificial products showed, down to their smallest details, the same features as spontaneous attacks, which were often brought on traumatically.

Many of Charcot's demonstrations began by provoking in me and in other visitors a sense of astonishment and an inclination to skepticism, which we tried to justify by appeal to one of the theories of the day. He was always friendly and patient in dealing with such doubts, but he was also most decided; it was in one of these discussions that (speaking of theory) he remarked, "Ça n'empêche pas d'exister" [one can not deny reality], a *mot* which left an indelible mark upon my mind.

No doubt the whole of what Charcot taught us at that time does not hold good today; some of it has become doubtful, some has definitely failed to withstand the test of time. But enough is left over and has found a permanent place in the storehouse of science. Before leaving Paris I discussed with the great man a plan for a comparative study of hysterical and organic paralyses. . . . He agreed with [my] view, but it was easy to see that in reality he took no special interest in penetrating more deeply into the psychology of the neuroses. When all is said and done, it was from pathological anatomy [organic lesions, traumatic injuries, and the like] that his work had started. (Freud, 1925/ 1964a, p. 7)

Returning to Vienna. Upon returning to Vienna, Freud began a private practice in neurology, with the aim of making sufficient money to marry his long-time fiancee. During this period he also experimented with cocaine, which for a brief time he, like most of the medical community, considered a "miracle substance." Throughout the 1880s cocaine was used as a tonic (mixed with red Bordeaux wine and sold by prescription), as a treatment for opium and morphine addiction, and as a stimulant to counter the effects of physical and nervous exhaustion. Freud published three well-received papers on the beneficial uses of cocaine, including one on its experimental use as a local anesthetic in ocular surgery by the title *"On Coca."*

According to Andrew Weil (1995), probably today's foremost authority on psychoactive natural substances, Freud became an enthusiastic habitual user of cocaine. Under its influence, Freud told his fiancee Martha, he experienced new confidence in social situations and relief from his chronic neurasthenia (nervous weakness). But his enthusiasm for the drug disappeared when he saw how its abuse brought ruin to some of his peers, including one of his close friends, who eventually died of cocaine poisoning. Freud ended up repudiating his previous enthusiasm for cocaine, branding it "the third scourge" following alcohol and morphine. He ultimately ordered his "cocaine papers" excluded from his published collected works.

By 1885 Freud had almost completely turned his attention away from scientific research in recognition of the growing need to support his family through the development of his medical practice. As he wrote in his autobiography,

> Anyone who wanted to make a living from the treatment of nervous patients must clearly be able to do something to help them. My therapeutic arsenal contained only two weapons, electrotherapy and hypnotism, for prescribing a visit to a hydropathic establishment [a trip to a therapeutic mineral spring] after a single consultation was an inadequate source of income. (Freud, 1925/1964a, p. 9)

Electromassage was widely recognized to be virtually useless with nonorganic, hysterical patients, and by his own admission, Freud, who had learned hypnotism from watching a public demonstration by an itinerant magnetist, was at best a marginally successful hypnotist. Freud was compelled by honesty to acknowledge that he could not hypnotize many patients and that even those he could hypnotize rarely developed a very deep or convincing hypnosis. Personally, I've always wondered if the problem was the cigar; I'd find it pretty hard to "completely relax" while gagging on secondhand cigar smoke.

Abandoning Hypnosis. Fortunately there was an alternative to hypnotism, a practical technique championed by Janet's archrivals at the Nancy school in France. You may recall from Chapter 4 that practitioners of the Nancy school had supplanted hypnotism with "verbal suggestion" in their therapy with hysterical patients. In fact, the physicians at the Nancy school had begun to develop a large number of purely psychological interventions for the treatment of hysteria; in a sense they were perhaps not even practicing medicine any longer. Thus Freud could write 35 years later of his trip to Nancy: "This implied of course, that I [was] abandoning the treatment of organic diseases; [which] was of little importance" (1925, p. 9). It seems extraordinarily unlikely that the ambitious Dr. Freud consciously intended to abandon physical treatment when he left for France, but there can be little doubt that Freud's thinking was fundamentally transformed by what he observed at Nancy:

> I witnessed the moving spectacle of old Liebault working among the poor women and children of the labouring classes; I was a spectator of [Professor] Bernheim's astonishing experiments upon his hospital patients, and I received the profoundest impression of the possibility that there could be powerful mental processes which nevertheless remained hidden from the consciousness of men. (Freud, 1925/1964a, p. 10)

Freud had traveled to Nancy with one of his patients, a young woman he described as "a highly gifted hysteric, a woman of good birth, who had been handed over to me because no one knew what to do with her" (Freud, 1925/1964a, p. 10). He persuaded Hippolyte Bernheim to examine her and to attempt treatment. But "Bernheim too failed. He frankly admitted to me that his great therapeutic successes by means of suggestion were only achieved in his hospital practice, and not with private patients" (Freud, 1925/1964a, p. 10).

Marrying and Making a Living. I think we need to read between the lines a bit to understand more fully what was happening to Freud at this juncture. Freud had married in September 1886 at the age of 30. His dreams of a life of academic research in neurophysiology under the esteemed Ernst Brücke, who had been a student of Hermann von Helmholtz (see Chapter 3) at the Helmholtz School of Medicine at the University of Vienna, had been crushed in 1881.

There is great controversy among historians as to why Freud was not kept on in the laboratory. Anti-Semitism was clearly a part of university politics and thus played a role in the decision, but funding problems probably played the greater part. At any rate, Freud's work up to that time showed great promise and was highly valued by Brücke. Nevertheless, he was released from his research position with the advice to secure a medical degree so he could support himself as a private practitioner. The experience was a terrific blow to Freud's self-esteem and to his dream of a career in medical research.

Meanwhile, Freud had strung out his engagement to Martha Bernays for 4 years. To accept the financial responsibility of marriage and family would mean completely foreclosing on his vision of becoming a man of science. Eventually, however, he was rescued from his own resistances by Josef Breuer, a fellow graduate of the Helmholtz School. Breuer's private practice in neurology was so successful that he could afford to refer some wealthy clients to his younger friend. From this early contact Freud learned of the case of Anna O., the subject of Chapter 5, whom Breuer had treated some years earlier.

We can imagine how deeply frustrated Freud must have been in private practice, toiling away at the mundane labor of applying standard neurological treatments of the day for pinched nerves, stressed backs, migraine headaches, menstrual complaints, and other neurological maladies. He was only in his thirties, discouraged, and fundamentally miserable in his work. But with the financial pressure that comes from producing six children in 5 years, what were his choices?

As a less than convincing hypnotist, Freud's choice to try to specialize in the treatment of hysterics must have struck most of his fellow neurologists as exceedingly eccentric, if not downright foolish. If his wife, Bertha, had known anything of the secrets of his heart, she must have feared for their financial survival. But she endured the years of secret engagement, the years of waiting, the great professional disappointments he suffered at the university, and his long absences away from home. And most of all, I imagine, she endured his friendship with the eccentric Wilhelm Fleiss.

Passionate Scientists: Freud and Fleiss

Fleiss, I believe it is fair to say, was the person at the center of Freud's life after Freud returned from his second trip to France. A mediocre ear, eye, nose, and throat specialist from Berlin, Fleiss was almost exactly Freud's age and, more importantly, shared his intense interest in neurology. Fleiss too was a frustrated scientist-turned-practitioner and, most significantly, a fellow antivitalist.

Breuer, always the father figure to aspiring young physicians, had met Fleiss while Fleiss was taking some postgraduate medical training in Vienna. Breuer encouraged his two young friends to meet, and toward the end of 1886 they instantly struck up a powerful rapport. Fleiss filled the intellectual and collegial vacuum in Freud's life that had been created by Freud's dismissal from the university. The two men met frequently, talking for hours and hours and sometimes entire weekends, sharing their revolutionary scientific ideas.

Freud's practice was picking up, but he was frustrated by the boredom of daily medical routines. His connection to Fleiss was his main outlet for his intellectual and scientific interests. He wrote his friend in 1888:

> My practice, which, as you know, is not very considerable, has recently increased somewhat by virtue of Charcot's name. The carriage is expensive, and visiting and talking people into or out of things—which is what my occupation consists in—robs me of the best time for work. The brain anatomy is where it was, but the hysteria is progressing and the first draft is finished. (quoted in Freud, 1985, pp. 18–19)

Their meetings were so fervent and full of mutual admiration that Freud took to referring to them with some seriousness as "our scientific congresses."

But the relationship was clearly more than just a meeting of two disembodied intellects. In 1894 Freud acknowledged "Your praise is nectar and ambrosia to me," and on June 30, 1896, he wrote to Fleiss that he was "looking forward to our Congress as to the slaking of hunger and thirst" (quoted in Freud, 1985). And in April 1898:

> After each of our Congresses I was strengthened anew for weeks, ideas kept crowding in thereafter, pleasure and hard work was reestablished, and the flickering hope that the way through the underbrush will be found burned quietly and radiantly for a while. Instructive it is not for me, this privation; I always knew what our meetings meant to me. (quoted in Freud, 1985, p. 306)

The passionate feelings expressed in this correspondence seem quite extraordinary. I've often wondered if there wasn't an unconscious, or perhaps even a conscious, homosexual bond between the two men. During this period, both men and women of the European middle classes were granted a certain latitude, which we don't seem to have today, to invest themselves in what has been called "passionate friendships." There is no evidence of a sexual bond between the two men, but would not a Freudian analysis permit the interpretation that the erotic bonds between the two men were sublimated into an almost feverish shared intellectual bond?

Certainly, too, much of their shared interest was in what one of Freud's biographers (Sulloway, 1979) called their common interest in sex. Fleiss was a strong advocate for the then radical view that bisexuality is an inherent property of all animals, including human beings. He argued that bisexuality was the primary motive behind unconscious mental repression:

The dominant sex of the person, that which is more strongly developed, has repressed the mental representation of the subordinated sex into the unconscious. Therefore the nucleus of the unconscious (that is to say the repressed) is in each human being that side of him which belongs to the opposite sex. (Fleiss, 1905, quoted in Sulloway, 1979, p. 183)

Freud evidently found this view intriguing and consistent with his own observations. He wrote to Fleiss in 1905 that the bisexuality theory "is the decisive factor" in understanding the psychoneuroses. "Without taking bisexuality into account I think it would scarce be possible to arrive at an understanding of the sexual manifestations that are actually to be observed in men and women" (quoted in Sulloway, 1979, p. 184).

Because so much of the correspondence between Fleiss and Freud has been lost, destroyed, and censored by their families, we will probably never know the true extent of their personal relationship or, more interestingly, all the reasons it fell irreparably apart in 1901. We do know that in his private life Freud espoused thoroughly conventional, if not prudish, views about sex, and he brought up his own children with very negative attitudes about masturbation and "other perversions." So I think we can fairly safely assume that whatever the sexual feelings between Fleiss and Freud, they were probably never openly expressed or acknowledged.

What is completely clear is that Freud had discovered a true scientific colleague in Fleiss at a time when Freud's professional and personal life were in turmoil. His father died in 1896, and Freud reacted to that loss very badly. He was perhaps influenced by Fleiss's interest in numerology, which had led Freud to believe he himself would die before he was 60.

What sustained Freud through all these difficulties was his conviction, powerfully supported by Fleiss's encouragement and enthusiasm, that modern science was on the edge of unlocking the mysteries of neurotic syndromes. The secret, Freud was certain, was hidden in the enigma of hysteria. If he could solve the puzzle of hysteria, Freud knew he would be recognized as the foremost neurological mind of the day—and perhaps of all time.

The "Project"

This driving ambition explains why, at this point in his life, Freud undertook his most ambitious intellectual venture: *"A Project for a Scientific Psychology."* In this work Freud and Fleiss proposed to attempt a completely mechanistic explanation for hysterical paralyses, which would demonstrate that all psychological processes within the organism are "rigidly and lawfully determined by the principle of cause and effect" (Sulloway, 1979, p. 94).

With the spirited support of Fleiss, whose contribution was a comprehensive master plan of the nervous system using a numerology based on the periodicity of the human menstrual cycle, Freud had the dream of surpassing even the great Charcot in the history of psychiatric medicine. Freud would be remembered, if he was successful, as the person who drove the final stake through the heart of vitalism.

Drafts of the "Project" were constantly in the mail between Vienna and Berlin. Freud believed that neurotics were being "neurologically poisoned" by the abnormal secretions of sexual toxins emanating from their reproductive organs. These toxins were often produced by unnatural external stimulation—for example, masturbation or coitus interruptus. Breuer added the observation, based on his clinical experience, that many married women suffered from hysterias as a direct consequence of their husbands' "perverse demands and unnatural sexual practices."

Freud also speculated that sexual toxins were unavoidably released as a consequence of the damage done to the nervous system when the immature sexual nerves of a child were stimulated. This damage could occur if a child witnessed the sex act. Freud documented this phenomenon in the case of Katharina, the first case he published in *Studies in Hysteria,* his book with Breuer. Neurological damage to a child's delicate system would, of course, be even worse when a child was the victim of sexual molestation.

What was most challenging to Freud's theorizing was that by 1900 hysteria had reached "almost epidemic proportions" (Ussher, 1991, p. 61) throughout Europe. Hysteria had become, along with anorexia nervosa and pervasive neurasthenic weakness, the main manifestations of what some authors have called "the cult of female invalidism."

Neither masturbation nor molestation could explain so many severe cases of hysteria among so many unmarried women and girls. Indeed, Freud reasoned, there were so very many hysterics that it must also be possible to produce sexual toxins "neurotically," by internal stimulation—perhaps even by thinking illicit, sexually stimulating thoughts.

In advancing this idea, Freud had proposed an ingenious solution to a great intellectual puzzle. But he had also come right to the edge of his commitment to antivitalism. He had come face to face with the unsolvable problem of the connection between the psychological mind and the physical body. Looking back in 1924, Freud could retrospectively side with the pioneering "psychologizing" of the Nancy school, but in the late 1800s, when the Project was being written, he was still thinking in the widely accepted physicalist tradition championed by Charcot.

Freud the Psychologist

Freud's intellectual adventure in trying to complete the Project is fully described in fascinating detail in Sulloway's (1979) *Freud: Biologist of the Mind.* For our purposes, it is enough to note that Freud's assertion that physical organic nervous disorders were caused by the toxicological consequences of improperly used libido (sexual energy) was hardly a novel idea in 1895. That hysteria was caused by a displaced uterus and that masturbation caused a variety of neurological disorders were well-established medical beliefs of the day.

What was truly extraordinary was that Freud had begun, through his new method of psychoanalysis, a scientific explanation of how this process operated psychobiologically. The Project proposed to explain in purely mechanistic terms how ideas could adversely affect the body. Thus Freud seemed to be on the verge of using psychology to resolve the mind/body dilemma, which had frustrated science since the days of René Descartes.

The Infantile Seduction Hypothesis

In 1895 Freud quite suddenly rejected the entire idea behind the Project. He wrote to Fleiss that he had begun to doubt the adequacy of the model, that perhaps it was taking him too far from the strict demands of their commitment to antivitalist science. In its place he developed the *infantile seduction hypothesis,* which argued that it wasn't the idea of sexual molestation, but actual illicit sexual experience, that produced the sexual toxins evident in neurosis. When imposed on an child's immature nervous system, this sexual excitation was the source of the neurological damage manifested in the madness of so many middle-class women.

Although this explanation restored the Project to the antivitalist, mechanist masterpiece it was originally supposed to be, the infantile seduction hypothesis was at variance with at least three major "facts":

- It wasn't even remotely possible that all hysterical neurotics had been sexually molested. That idea would implicate hundreds and probably thousands of solid, upper-middle-class families as sexual monsters.
- Even if all those girls had actually been molested, why didn't any of his patients remember the trauma they had experienced? How could such global amnesia be understood in purely physical terms?
- How could the talking cure be accounted for in this system? How could talk, even cathartic talk, remove sexual toxins from the nervous system?

The idea that human beings can restore themselves to psychological and emotional well-being by talking out their problems is, for most intellectual Westerners, an article of faith. We encourage our loved ones and friends to talk about their problems, and if they refuse to do so, we often consider their refusal as one indicator of a serious personal problem. On the other hand, such a public display of feelings to a relative stranger and such a total violation of the rules of personal privacy would probably strike most contemporary Japanese as symptomatic, in and of itself. If such self-indulgent confessional talking is not a clear sign of the loss of personal control, it is at least "very American"—that is, a strange, abnormal, self-indulgent practice. From what I have read of bourgeois life in the Europe of Freud's day, I have gathered the impression that Victorian Europeans would have more in common with the Japanese in this respect than they would with their great-great-grandchildren in Europe or North America.

The reality, of course, is that Freud's own writing largely brought this "therapeutic age" to fruition in Western Europe and North America. The question is how it happened and what Freud's role was. By 1900 the idea of a talking cure had been around for quite some time. Practitioners since Franz Anton Mesmer had healed the sick with words—as had the priests, I suppose one could argue, throughout centuries of exorcisms and prayer rituals. Mesmer, of course, hadn't recognized the verbal nature of his "magnetism," and I'm not sure Charcot understood his hypnotic treatments as the verbal cures they really were either. Surely, however, the physicians in Nancy understood the verbal nature of their "suggestion" cures, and Janet was obviously using the talking cure in a major way as early in his career as his work with Achilles (see Chapter 4), at the time Freud was visiting the Salpêtrière.

Freud's problem with the idea of a talking cure, I suspect, was that it was profoundly "politically incorrect." The very idea of it defied medical and scientific analysis. It evoked poetic images of a richly textured inner life and a creatively empowered source of self-expression. It was not, perhaps, theism or even an aspect of deism. But it reflected an offshoot of vitalism known as "romantic expressionism" (Goldstein, 1987; Taylor, 1989) and would have been regarded as reactionary in the extreme by the progressive New Men of medical science at the dawn of the 20th century.

The idea of a talking cure must therefore have sounded like a lot of sentimental, antiscientific, vitalist rot to radical scientists like Freud and Fleiss. It raised the specter of ancient superstition wrapped in poetic fantasy. All such conjecture, they thought, was yet another way to deny that the human organism can be exclusively understood as operating according to the laws of chemistry, mathematics, and physics.

I hope you can see that once Freud had promulgated his mechanistic theory of the sexual causation of madness, the infantile seduction hypothesis, all conjecture about a talking cure was really part of a much larger political struggle about the nature of human life. For Freud and his fellow antivitalists, all forms of romanticism were a denial of the absolute control over behavior exerted by biology. Most of those who opposed Freud's theory were, the antivitalists thought, propping up an ideology largely dedicated to denying socially inconvenient and politically dangerous biological facts.

Freud's Dilemma

In the closing years of the 19th century, Freud had a monumental problem: Despite his antivitalist loyalties, he knew that the talking cure worked. He knew because he had seen it firsthand in the work of his fellow psychiatrists (even if, as he later claimed, he had not actually seen it displayed by Janet) and because he had seen evidence of its effectiveness in his own patients.

At the very least, Freud had to fully accept the idea that the cathartic, explosive discharge of bottled-up ideas and memories through hypnosis was a powerful way to learn a patient's psychiatric history. Freud was an inept hypnotist—but he said so himself only because he could not get his patients to demonstrate the various levels of hypnosis that Charcot's hypnotic "science" had described. Still, Freud used hypnosis routinely as an interviewing technique, as a way to elicit the truth of patients' sexual experiences. These hypnotically recovered memories were the basic data on which the infantile seduction hypothesis had been built. Freud had become convinced on the basis of his own observations that the great Charcot had been right: Sexuality is always the irreducible source of the neurotic patient's symptoms. Hypnosis was merely the strongest available technique for recovering those memories.

As frustrating and inefficient as it must have been for him, by 1890 Freud had come to appreciate that hypnotic induction was worth its considerable trouble. Hypnosis was "immense help in the cathartic treatment," Freud (1925/1964a, p. 17) testified; in fact, he had no alternative in the treatment of hysterical patients. Thus hypnosis remained for several years at the center of the treatment methodology practiced by pioneering psychoanalysts.

Yet hypnosis strikes most of us as mumbo jumbo. It's a second cousin of magnetism, and magnetism's other second cousins are spiritualism and parlor games. Hypnotism had no foundation at the time in anatomy or physiology. We can imagine, therefore, that Freud was inordinately enthusiastic when he discovered the "concentration technique" to replace it.

This technique, which may have been inspired by what Freud saw on his trip to Nancy, required him to place his hand on the patient's head and then command the patient to remember the forgotten past. As you can imagine, this was physically a difficult thing to do all day (and Freud was addicted to his cigars). And it wasn't much better scientifically than hypnotism. No doubt Fleiss could make something of the concentration technique within the terms of his bisexuality theory, but its only real advantage was that it freed Freud once and for all from hypnosis.

After this development, it was evidently more or less by accident that Freud discovered his famous "couch technique." By "requiring the patient to lie upon a sofa while I sat behind him, seeing him, but not seen myself" (Freud, 1925/1964a , p. 17), he was able to get his patients to reveal the contents of their unconscious minds with only minimal probing and prodding. Freud wrote that, while undergoing this treatment, patients revealed

> everything that had been forgotten [that] had in some way or other been painful; it had been either alarming or disagreeable or shameful by the standards of the subject's personality. [Note the shift from *patient* to *subject* in the retelling.] The thought arose spontaneously: that was precisely why it had been forgotten, i.e., why it had not remained conscious. In order to make it conscious again in spite of this, it was necessary to overcome something that fought against one in the patient; it was necessary to make an expenditure of effort on one's own part in order to compel and subdue it. (1925/1964a, p. 17)

A moment of personal triumph! Freud had finally rid himself of the albatross of hypnotism, and he no longer needed to retain actual physical contact with each patient in order to get past the effects of the patient's amnesia.

Had Freud made any substantive progress? Well, he had the beginnings of a scientific explanation of the talking cure as catharsis; and catharsis in turn could be given the scientific-sounding function of physiologically "abreacting" neurological energy left over by traumatic events. Evidence of the force of this stored-up energy could be seen in the explosive power with which "forgotten" events could be recalled and even relived during the analytical sessions.

But what caused and accounted for the strength of the "resistance" to such memories? And why did people so often so desperately cling to dreadful, painful memories that made them crazy? How could any of this behavior be explained in terms of the neuroanatomy or the neurophysiological organization of the mind?

And then there were the patients, the biggest problem of all. In addition to being rather uninteresting, if not actually depressing, the vast majority of them lacked the intellectual sophistication, courage, and determination required to overcome their problems. The human perversity they demonstrated disturbed Freud; it flew in the face of what he knew as a scientist about the orderliness of the physical, mechanical world.

The Great Discovery

I don't think anyone really knows what happened next. Some writers have simply but mysteriously referred to it as the period of Freud's "creative illness." In September 1887 Freud wrote to Fleiss to tell him that Freud was completely abandoning the infantile seduction theory and with it his commitment to a completely physicalist interpretation of madness. One month later he wrote another enigmatic letter to Fleiss telling him that he now finally understood "the gripping power" of Sophocles' *Oedipus Rex.*

Six weeks later, another letter disclosed that Freud was beginning to realize how "deeply neurotic" his own life and fears were.

And then there was silence.

Freud tells us that he spent the better part of the next 2 years engaged in searing self-analysis. He turned the lens of psychoanalysis on himself and discovered a long series of powerful repressed memories from his own childhood. Most of these memories centered around infantile yearning for his mother and equally powerful infantile feelings of resentment and jealousy toward his father. While he was recovering these lost memories, Freud also became aware of the intense resistance his unconscious mind mounted against a full revelation of these long-repressed and deeply painful childhood memories.

The story of Freud's self-discovery through the process of self-psychoanalysis is told in fascinating detail by Christopher Monte (1991) in his book *Beneath the Mask.* Time invested in reading Monte's research would be well invested.

For our purposes, we need only note the self-analysis as a time of radical transformation for Freud—both in his person and in his theory. For what emerged from this self-analysis was the complete theory of psychoanalysis, which Freud would spend the next quarter century refining and elaborating.

The Interpretation of Dreams. The results of Freud's Promethean struggle are presented in the book *The Interpretation of Dreams* (1990), which for the rest of his life Freud considered his outstanding achievement, his singular gift to the world. (Prometheus was the Greek god who confined all human troubles within Pandora's box and suffered torture at the hands of Zeus for the sin of giving fire to humankind.)

The Interpretation of Dreams resolved virtually every intellectual problem that had haunted Freud for the first 15 years of his career as a practicing neurologist. Its most immediate and liberating consequence was that it permitted Freud to abandon the strict physicalist, mechanistic, antivitalist straitjacket that had so controlled and dominated his scientific thinking.

What replaced it was a system of thought—psychoanalysis—that in some significant measure accepted the deep mystery of human beings. Their actions could be understood and interpreted but not really predicted and controlled. Newtonian physics was abandoned as the theoretical tool for explaining human behavior and replaced by Darwinian biology, which allowed the search for processes and laws that could account for the variability and diversity of behavior.

The Project was essentially abandoned. The Fleiss friendship was broken—ostensibly because Freud came to believe that Fleiss was stealing his ideas but in reality because Freud emerged with a theory that made Fleiss's mathematically based antivitalism irrelevant. A new society of Freud's closest and most trusted associates was formed to disseminate and perpetuate the ideas of psychoanalysis around the world. Unfortunately, however, part of this mission was met by systematically denouncing and destroying the credibility of anyone whose ideas rivaled or challenged Freud's.

Intellectually, because of the power of Freud's personality and his almost pathological need for loyalty from his followers—his "small group of gallant supporters," as he called them—his theory of psychoanalysis was in many important ways stillborn. You have to take it or leave it as you find it, because it is not open to modification and correction.

But what an impact on the Western world psychoanalysis was to have. Anna O.'s mysterious madness was the seed of an idea that fundamentally changed the way people in the Western world understand what it means to be a human being and affected virtually every aspect of the social sciences and the humanities for at least the next century.

The Unconscious Mind. Where had Freud found the truth that would influence all of us so profoundly? He had found it within his own unconscious mind. But to get there he had first to discover the tools that would give him access to the human psyche. Hypnotism and concentration had not proved powerful enough. Freud claimed that he found the tool when he discovered the answer to the Greek playwright Sophocles' Oedipal conundrum: How can a human being come to know the truth about the self without in the process being self-destructive?

The answer came to Freud while he was engaged in his own self-analysis. He described an intellectual breakthrough, "an insight . . . such as falls to one's lot but once in a lifetime." He judged it "the most valuable of all of the discoveries it has been my good fortune to make." And he published it in 1900 in *The Interpretation of Dreams*, the book that was to mark the formal beginning of the psychoanalytic movement.

Freud's insight was as old as it was revolutionary. "The interpretation of dreams," he wrote, "is the royal road to a knowledge of the unconscious mind" (1900/1953, p. 68). The thesis of the book was that, in unlocking the meaning of dreams,

> psychoanalysis succeeded in achieving one thing which appeared to be of no practical importance but which in fact necessarily led to a fresh attitude and a fresh scale of values in scientific thought. It became possible to prove that *dreams* have a meaning, and to discover it. . . . [B]y disregarding the excommunication pronounced [by modern science] upon dreams, by treating them as unexplained neurotic symptoms, as delusional or obsessive ideas, by neglecting their apparent content and by making their separate component images into subjects for free association, psycho-analysis arrived at a different conclusion. The numerous associations produced by the dreamer led to the discovery of a mental structure which could no longer be described as absurd or confused, which was on an equality with any other product of the mind, and of which the *manifest* dream was no more than a distorted, abbreviated and misunderstood translation and usually a translation into visual images. (Freud, 1925/1964a , p. 28)

What psychoanalysis revealed about the inner reality of dream life was that the unconscious stores up and saves every important emotional aspect of childhood. Dreams preserve every childhood wish and fantasy. Contrary to popular opinion, they are not lost but are transformed into the universal human metalanguage of "primary-process thinking." These universal dream symbols are then called into the conscious memory of a dream when some aspect of our current life puts us in a situation that is metaphorically or symbolically similar to one we experienced as children. Dreams may thus be understood as providing us with an unconscious solution to our contemporary frustrations and disappointments, a psychical outlet for discharge of the tension in a troubling situation.

The discovery that within every human being the past lives in the unconscious gave Freud the power to uncover and recover the hidden secrets of the mind. Dream analysis is the excavating tool for psychoanalytic archeology. But dream analysis really is just a tool.

Freud's truly Promethean gift was the use to w¹
scious life. Freud believed that the psychoanalytic
the primal secrets of human psychology and mo
within our highly evolved nervous systems.

The Primacy of the Sexual Motive

In the years following World War I, Freud revise
a death instinct, "thanatos": All living things ye
striving through death. The conflict between thanatos and eros, the
fundamental source of human conflict. Freud regarded thanatos as responsible for
all destructive and sadistic urges and inclinations.

But in the beginning, through psychoanalytic interpretation of Freud's own and
his patients' free associations to their dreams, one overwhelming and overpowering
truth emerged. That truth proved to be capable of unlocking all the secrets of psychic
life. What Freud discovered, as everyone in the literate universe now knows, was sex.

Sex—the mother of all motives, the father of all instincts, the force that defines
every aspect of our mental lives.

The truth had been right in front of Freud all along. As he later recognized in
looking back over Breuer's work with Anna O., "Breuer had found the key, but he had
foolishly dropped it" (quoted in Jones, 1953, p. 224). Breuer had said:

> The case which I described in the *Studies on Hysteria* as "No. 1; Anna O.," passed
> through my hands, and my merit lay essentially in my having recognized what an un-
> commonly instructive and scientifically important case chance had brought me for inves-
> tigation. . . . Thus at that time I learned a very great deal; much that was of scientific
> value, but something of practical importance as well—namely, that it was impossible for a
> "general practitioner" to treat a case of that kind without bringing his activities and mode
> of life completely to an end. I vowed at that time that I would not go through such an
> ordeal again. . . . *I confess that the plunging into sexuality in theory and practice is not
> to my taste.* But what have my taste and feeling about what is seemly and what is un-
> seemly to do with the question of what is true? (Breuer, 1907, quoted in Monte, 1991,
> p. 36; emphasis added)

Twenty-five years later, in 1907, Breuer was still insisting that "the case of Anna O. . . .
proves that a fairly severe case of hysteria can develop, flourish, and be resolved without having a sexual basis" (Breuer, 1907, quoted in Monte, 1991, p. 36). But how
could Breuer claim that sex was not involved, knowing that his relationship with the
girl had ended with her accusations of a sexual liaison with the doctor?

One reason was that Breuer was still smarting from Freud's repudiation of him.
Breuer had refused to accept Freud's "Promethean insight" that sex was the single
universal motive behind all neurotic behavior. And Breuer was not prepared to
retract what was his own almost-Promethean insight, which he and Freud had

ir *Preliminary Communication* ("preliminary" to the later full pre-
Studies in Hysteria): "The hysteric suffers mostly from reminiscences"
5a, p. 7).

rong second reason for Breuer's "resistance" was that from his perspective
e was no sexual motive in the case of Anna O. You may recall that almost the very
st "fact" Breuer told us about her (see Chapter 5) was that "the element of sexuality was astonishingly undeveloped in her." Anna O. was virtually asexual and reclu-
sive in her life and interests. There is no trace of evidence that she was ever sexually
abused or molested, and it is quite certain that given her parents' puritanical, Victorian view of such matters, she had not been exposed either to parental nudity or to
the primal scene as a child. Breuer also continued to overlook the unfortunate matter of the phantom pregnancy and the obvious fact that the girl was totally infatu-
ated with him.

For Freud it was precisely Anna O.'s "astonishingly undeveloped sexuality" that
had precipitated her long and tortured illness. Anna O. was a perfect living model of
Victorian sexual repression and the psychic difficulties such oppression precipitates.
Suppression of the girl's sexual element had terrible biopsychological consequences
in her life, which were manifest initially in her hysterical illness and eventually in her
classic (actually, *the* classic) case of transference neurosis with her physician, Josef
Breuer.

In a significant extension of his theory, Freud eventually recognized that by trans-
ferring her enormously frustrated needs for sexual and affectionate love to the relationship with her therapist, Anna effectively released herself from all her other neurotic symptoms. The problem was that Breuer had no knowledge this transference
was happening. He had decided that the whole business was "not to his taste" and
thus "abandoned" his patient without recognizing the absolute necessity of "working through" those transferred sexual feelings. The result was that Anna O. plunged
into madness.

Looking Ahead, Looking Back

In the next chapter I will lay out the psychoanalytic theory of the neuroses, their
treatment, and their cure. I'll do so without much further intellectual elaboration.
But I hope you will be able to trace the various elements introduced thus far as
Sigmund Freud selects, integrates, and weaves them into a coherent theory.

Please do two things when you read the next chapter. First, don't read it to see
whether you "agree" or "disagree" with it, like it or dislike it. I can almost guarantee
that you will find Freud's theory less attractive in a great many respects than alternative theories presented in the remaining chapters. Rather than doing battle with
Freud, you might better focus on what he is trying to accomplish—which is nothing
less than the liberation of the human psyche. You too may not think his methods

appeal to your tastes, but he presents the principal problems of living creatively and well in a difficult world as brilliantly as anyone who has ever walked the earth.

Second, try to see the elegance of Freud's approach from the perspective of 19th-century science. He was able to fuse the Enlightenment's most cherished views about the supremacy of human reason with the hard-headed scientific realities of Darwin's theory of natural selection. Freud presents us with a difficult, combative world within which we must struggle to control our passions (instincts) in order to survive. He presents us with a psychology of courage. Though we may at root be savages, we truly have the capacity to become noble savages, through the fullest exercise of that which makes us distinctly human: the exercise of reason.

CHAPTER 7

Psychoanalysis: Prototype of the Talking Cure

Mind Revealed

Through his work with neurotics, Freud hoped to reveal the true organization of the unconscious mind. Freud also aimed to restore his patients to full emotional and occupational functioning through the process of psychoanalysis. When this task was accomplished, the result was what Freud called a "sadder but wiser" human being. The powerful force called repression, which Freud believed blocked awareness of unacceptable ideas and impulses, was the cornerstone of his theory of the unconscious. He thought abreaction, or cathartic release of pent-up emotions, and the exploration of dreams, symptoms, resistances, and repetition compulsions would reveal the fracture lines of the psyche and thus lead to healing.

In Freud's view, however, psychoanalysis is not equally applicable to everyone. It is revealing and restorative to only those members of the cultural and intellectual elite who can understand the true nature of their feelings and who have the natural capabilities to explore them.

The case study of Luke is an abbreviated example of the process of psychoanalysis. Luke was a fairly typical, unhappy U.S. college student. The complex process of coming to terms with the repressed contents of his unconscious, which ultimately required reliving some of childhood's most painful experiences, released Luke from a life of hysterical misery. Luke worked out the problems of the past within the context of his "transference" relationship with me, his therapist. These powerful emotional experiences, which are at the heart of the psychotherapeutic application of psychoanalysis, have the power to transform the lives of both the patient and the therapist.

The Dynamic Organization of Mind

The Will's opposition to let what is repellent to it come to the knowledge of the intellect is the spot through which insanity can break through into the spirit. (Schopenhauer, 1819, p. 460)

We probably ought to begin exploring the psychotherapeutic application of psychoanalysis with a brief overview of what Sigmund Freud would expect us to learn about neurotic misery from his theory of the structure and function of the psyche.

As the great Jean-Martin Charcot had recognized, hysterics suffer mainly from reminiscences. Their symptoms are not the bizarre and meaningless products of a diseased mind but a coherent display of meaningful behaviors structured by a recondite, or deeply hidden, emotional logic. In essence, the outward manifestations of hysteria are the meaningful products of powerful emotions that have been strangulated within the unconscious.

Psychoanalysis of dream life reveals to the trained observer a hidden but inescapable conflict of human needs played out on the stage created by human psychosexual development. The self-defeating helplessness, self-deception, and despair we see in people in their crises reveal deep structural fault lines within the human psyche—and within civilization itself.

Repression: Cornerstone of Psychoanalytic Theory

The one central concept you must accept in psychoanalysis, which appears in virtually all Freud's writings on the talking cure, is the idea of *repression,* "the corner-stone on which the whole structure of psycho-analysis rests" (Freud, 1914c/1957a, p. 14). The existence of repression, a kind of motivated amnesia or willful forgetting, was revealed to Freud in the powerful *resistances* his patients displayed during word-association tests. Freud wrote,

Repression is a preliminary stage of [self] condemnation, something between flight and condemnation . . . a necessary condition [for which] must clearly be that the instinct's attainment of its aim should produce unpleasure instead of pleasure. . . . *[T]he essence of repression lies simply in turning something away, and keeping it at a distance from the consciousness.* (1915/1957b, pp. 146–147)

Repression is essential to our everyday emotional equilibrium. As Dawes (1994) pointed out, Freud believed, like Schopenhauer (see the quote that begins this chapter), that madness and neurosis break through to consciousness when repression fails to hold in check our most painful ideas and unacceptable impulses. Repression is both automatic and unconscious. It is also cumulative. As Monte (1991) put it:

Freud's most profound discovery about the nature of defensive repression was that it is not any *one* unacceptable thought that causes its removal from awareness; it is the

combination of thoughts or feelings and their interrelationships that intensify psychological pain to the point where it cannot be consciously borne. Moreover, *each* element of
the conflict clashes powerfully with the individual's ethical self-image. (p. 56)

The only other point I need to make about the concept of repression before we
proceed is that it is relatively expensive in terms of the energy dynamics of the
psyche. It takes great psychic energy to "not know," to "not see," and to "not remember." The defense mechanisms employed by the ego to protect us from conscious
awareness of the painful can in fact become overwhelmed by the dimensions of the
task. At such points we experience what Freud referred to as a breakdown of the defense system:

The problem now facing the personality is how to "show" the mental conflict in a way
that is not consciously understandable even though it is, in a sense, out in the open at
last. To accomplish this feat, said Freud, we are able to substitute one form of overt
expression (physical) for another (psychological), thereby deflecting the course of an
intention by way of a compromise that satisfies all sides. . . . The [competing] wishes
strike a bargain and find some mutually expressive way to make themselves known in a
[neurotic] symptom of some sort. (Rychlak, 1981, pp. 84–86)

The Wisdom of Neurotics. If the goal of psychoanalysis is to uncover universal, deep,
structural, characterological, and historical sources for human motivation, behavior,
and even civilization, why does it choose to study the disordered behavior of those
who have cracked under the pressures of civilization? What can the study of the neurotic psychotherapy patient tell us of the human condition? The answer:

If we throw a crystal to the floor, it breaks; but not into haphazard pieces. It comes apart
along its lines of cleavage into fragments whose boundaries, though they were invisible,
were predetermined by the crystal's structure. Mental patients are split and broken structures of this same kind. Even we can not withhold from them something of the reverential awe which peoples of the past felt for the insane. They have turned away from external reality, but for that very reason they know more about the internal, psychical reality
and can reveal a number of things to us that would be otherwise inaccessible to us.
(Freud, 1933/1964b, p. 59)

The neurotic misperceives, misinterprets, and responds inappropriately to current experience because unconscious fantasy overwhelms the thin veneer of civilized,
conscious control. Neurotic symptoms must be understood as "negative perversions"
blocking expression of the most fundamental human instincts.

Hypnosis may bring a patient some temporary relief, but true relief of suffering
comes only through *abreaction*, cathartic discharge of pent-up emotions. Abreaction
takes place when the patient goes through the process of emotionally reexperienc-
ing and even reliving the psychic trauma of childhood. The beneficial consequence
of this painful process is that the demands of the adult's fully developed sex drive will
be no longer thwarted and the patient may ultimately find satisfaction in daily life.

How is the individual, once freed from the oppression of psychic blockage, to satisfy the fundamental but primitive, instinctual needs of the organism? They are to be discharged through love and work, the common debts to civilization owed by every man and woman. Our evolutionary endowment includes the capacity to reason and to delay gratification. The agent of this process is the ego.

What becomes of psychic trauma after it is discharged through abreaction of the repressed emotional residue of childhood experience? The answer, according to Freud, is that hysterical misery is transformed into common, everyday unhappiness. Once neurotic obstacles have been removed from the unconscious, the patient will be "sadder but wiser," at long last free from infantile illusion as well as adult delusion and obsession.

The Struggle to Overcome Resistances. Psychoanalysis requires that today's problems be resolved within the context of the patient's unique psychosexual history. By becoming the "archeologist of her own experience," guided gently but firmly by the analyst, the patient discovers the darkest, least reflected parts of her childhood memories. In this process, the patient encounters various crystallized *resistances*— areas of memory visited only in sleep and even then only in the dream language of *primary-process thinking.* The exploration of resistances is, in fact, the mapping of crystallized libido, life's sexual, generative energy.

Resistances to memory or to free association are dynamic and active. Just as a kidney stone lets the patient know of its existence by sending strong messages of pain and discomfort, so too the energy of a repressed impulse sends its telltale signals. In normal, everyday life, these signals are dreams, jokes, quirks of personality, and slips of the tongue. The symptoms of repression become more obvious in the neurotic, especially at times of emotional stress.

What characterizes neurotic resistance is *repetition compulsion,* a repeating of certain patterns over and over again. Repetition compulsion is the endless reliving of experiences and attitudes that do not bring us pleasure and may even bring us pain. It is the obsessive and compulsive quality of these experiences that reveals them for what they are. The compulsion to repeat isolates from conscious awareness repressed memories of traumatic experiences. To achieve a psychoanalytic cure, the patient must have the courage to take hold of the repressed memories. Ultimately the therapist will transform this compulsion to repeat, this resistance to acknowledging reality, into a motive for remembering.

In psychoanalysis the psyche is, in Freud's words, a text to be deciphered. And the psychoanalytic cure is "a work of mourning, which far from striking down the fantasy, recovers it as a fantasy in order to situate it clearly with the real" (Ricoeur, 1977/ 1992, p. 359).

Psychoanalytic treatment is essentially, in Freud's famous words, a struggle against resistances. It requires hundreds of hours of remembering, repeating, and working through—of remembering our past in order to gradually overcome the emotional resistances that prevent us from truly knowing ourselves. Freud worked out the underlying dynamics of the psychoanalytic talking cure in a seminal essay with the title "Remembering, Repeating, and Working Through" (Freud, 1914/ 1958d). Here is the essence of Freud's insights in this essay:

> [The cure] begins with the precise moment . . . when the memory of traumatic events is replaced by the compulsion to repeat which blocks remembering. Focusing on the compulsion to repeat, resistance, and transference, [Freud] writes, "The greater the resistance, the more extensively will acting out (repetition) replace remembering. . . . [T]he patient repeats instead of remembering and repeats under the conditions of resistance" (p. 151). Then he introduces transference, which he describes as "the main instrument . . . for curbing the patient's compulsion to repeat and to turn it into a motive for remembering" (p. 154). Why does transference have this effect? . . . If the resistance can be cleared away and remembering made free to occur, it is because the transference constitutes something like "a playground in which [the patient's compulsion to repeat] is allowed to expand in almost complete freedom" (p. 154). Extending this analogy of the playground Freud more specifically says: "The transference thus creates an intermediate region between illness and real life through which the transition from one to the other is made" (p. 154). . . . What is thereby singled out or sifted out from human experience is the immediately intersubjective dimension of desire. (Ricoeur, 1977/1992, pp. 348–349)

The "Psychopathology" of Everyday Life

An obvious example of repetition compulsion comes to mind. A young man of my acquaintance was terribly disturbed by the idea of homosexuality. He even wrote me letters about how repulsive and disgusting he found the images in his own mind about the intimate behavior of homosexual couples. He lived in a fraternity and spent literally hundreds of hours each year trying to find out who in his fraternity had engaged in homosexual behavior. He was instrumental in convincing his peers to convene several secret tribunals of the fraternity chapter to ferret out suspected homosexuals from among the brotherhood. He also had strong suspicions about many other students on the campus and was fairly certain that some members of the faculty and administration were homosexually inclined.

One interesting aspect of this student's paranoia was that people who were "out of the closet" as openly gay or lesbian didn't bother him at all. In fact, he claimed several good relationships with gay men both at work and in his home community, and he refused to participate in the harassment of the gay students' organization on his campus.

I was not this young man's therapist, and I know little about his personal or sexual history. But I was honest enough with him to tell him that his fascination with discovering who was "secretly" (I would say "privately") experiencing homosexual fantasies and behaviors was far more interesting as a window on his psyche than it was as a window on any of the targets of his suspicions. Yet, even after confronting him several times with my feelings that his curiosity about secret homosexuality was both unpleasant and in a way embarrassing to both of us, he continued to want to share his latest "discoveries" with me once or twice a semester.

I would not like to make any presumption about the roots of this peculiar pattern of behavior. In fact, I could reasonably explain his behavior in terms of the approval he received from many of his peers and some of his family members. Prejudice against homosexuals is after all just another prejudice in a society full of religious, ethnic, and social prejudices. But I can say that this person was an extraordinarily fine example of what Freud meant by repetition compulsion—of the seemingly mindless repetition of neurotic sequences without conscious awareness of motive or recognition of any personal experience that might make sense of it.

Should my acquaintance ever choose to get to the root of his problem—perhaps if someday his morbid fascination with "secret" homosexuality is perceived as a threat to his continued employment—a careful psychoanalysis of his resistances would help him think about and remember those childhood experiences that contributed to his fascination. If that source were recollected in an immediate, dynamic, and emotional way—if it were abreacted—then the energy bound up in that early experience would be discharged, and his obsession would be broken.

Please recognize that we all have resistances. We all have amnesic "absences"; we are all at least a little neurotic. We all experience a taxing day-to-day struggle with our unconscious resistances and our neurotic defenses. When we are stressed by the burdens and responsibilities of daily life, those resistances come more clearly to the surface of our behavior for all to witness. Our enemies see these aspects of our personalities as our enduring weaknesses and character flaws. Our friends see them as the qualities that make us uniquely who we are.

The Promise and the Limits of Psychoanalysis

Psychoanalysis is most fundamentally an invitation to deep, characterological change. Persons who seek psychoanalysis must make a profound commitment to engage in an unrelenting process of self-examination, self-discovery, and reappraisal of some of the most important and enduring parts of themselves. They pledge to uncover every forgotten secret of their childhood and to come to adult terms with images and impressions stored as the recollections of a small and innocent child.

Freud recognized that this method would never appeal to everyone. People who are too psychotic or too uneducated, who are "low-minded" or "repellent," who are "worthless," have nothing to gain from psychoanalysis of their mental lives. Freud kindly referred to these people as "beyond" the scope of his new science. But I think the truth is that psychoanalysis was designed for the culturally and intellectually elite.

Thus I also think it is a serious mistake to try to think of psychoanalysis as a panacea for the oppressed people of the world. This notion became quite the rage in the United States in the 1920s and for a while even influenced legal thinking in the criminal justice system. Ultimately, however, the legal machinery of society cannot function without being able to assess guilt and assign blame. It should be evident by now that finding fault would be an impossible task for psychoanalysis, however intuitively appealing the prospect is of understanding both the crime and the criminal in their full psychological context. I have become persuaded that psychoanalysis, rather than offering any social panacea, offers what is in essence individual salvation.

A Secular Doctrine of Salvation. I mentioned in Chapter 1 that I am married to an English-Canadian. I should now also reveal that she is a fellow psychologist. We were both trained in the most radical, fundamentalist, Skinnerian behaviorism you could imagine. (I recommend such training very highly and think it prepared us brilliantly for the future, but it was so extreme that most of the intellectual questions we were assigned to struggle with as graduate students are not even considered intellectually interesting today.)

We were warmly received when we arrived at our first teaching assignment and were invited to a great round of welcoming dinner parties. One of the first was a large dinner for all new faculty, and my wife was given the seat of honor next to the host, an older and very distinguished senior member of the faculty.

"Tell me, Brenda," the distinguished scholar asked my wife during the soup course, "have you much interest in the writings of Sigmund Freud?" "Not really," responded my bride quite honestly. "That surprises me," he answered, "especially since you are interested in children's development and behavior." "Well," she answered a little too quickly, "as De Beauvoir recognized, Freudianism is just another religion; and religion is just a waste of time as far as I'm concerned."

There was a pall of silence around the table. But life went on, as it does, and my wife and the host both found other conversational topics and partners. "Who was that guy?" Brenda asked as we drove home. "Him?" I replied. "Well first off, he is one of the members of the tenure and promotion review committee. And oh, yes; he is also the chairman of the religion department."

So let me make it clear that I do not use the term *salvationist* loosely. And it is a serious error, I now believe, to think of psychoanalysis as a religion—no matter how dogmatically and with how much mystery Freud "revealed" the doctrine to his followers. Psychoanalysis does, however, explicitly offer its adherents a life "saved" from superstition, illusion, ignorance of the self, neurosis, and ultimately madness. In this sense I think I might agree with Firestone's assertion that psychoanalysis has become, in some sense, "our modern church" (1970, quoted in Donovan, 1985, p. 104).

Reason, Humanism, and Psychoanalysis. I may get myself into trouble for saying this, but I'm not persuaded any more than Freud was that psychoanalysis offers much of a widely applicable "therapy" for emotional and mental illness. I have not been persuaded by any of the data I have seen that psychoanalysis can liberate a person from, for example, depression, alcoholism, or agoraphobia. If it is therapeutically effective at all, its effectiveness is relative to no therapy at all and probably restricted largely to hysterical disorders of the sort described in various case studies in this book.

Yet if you ask practicing psychotherapists, and even behavior therapists, where they would turn if their lives became disrupted to the point where they would seek psychotherapy, the largest percentage of them answer "psychoanalysis" or "psycho-analytically oriented therapy" (Lazarus, 1971; Norcross & Prochaska, 1984). Psycho-analysis offers enormous assistance to well-educated, affluent, middle-class Western people who lead thoughtful lives. In their quest to live humanely and deliberately, to succeed in some measure in the taxing day-to-day struggle of "love" (maintaining the primary relationships of one's life) and "work" (being productive but competing with the rest of the community), they find sustenance and support in the genuine self-knowledge that psychoanalysis makes possible.

This belief in the importance of self-knowledge was implicit in the transforma-tion of society brought about by the Enlightenment. It is an essential component of post-Enlightenment belief in the forceful drive of "progress" generated by free, self-determined, self-governing people. Through self-knowledge and reason, humankind can uncover, overcome, and resolve base savage instinct.

The soulmates of psychoanalysis are 19th-century communism and free-enterprise capitalism and 20th-century behaviorism and existentialism. Like them, psychoanalysis offers a new solution to ancient dilemmas and mysteries. That an-swer is humanism.

Humanism in psychology (a much broader construct than humanistic psychol-ogy, which is discussed in Chapter 15) is faith that reason, applied in a scientific con-text, will yield genuine self-knowledge. My thesis is that psychoanalysis remains one of the greatest driving forces of Western thought, and the "treatment" of choice for thousands, because the humanism it advances speaks directly to the "lives of quiet desperation" that so many of us lead.

I will return to this theme in Chapter 11, which introduces Part II of this book. There I will argue that the history of the New World required a different interpreta-tion of the human struggle and thus a different approach to psychotherapy. Never-theless, psychoanalysis was THE humanistic doctrine of individual salvation for edu-cated Western persons in the early years of the 20th century. This point is summed up in one elegant seven-word sentence: Where id was, there let ego be. Thus Freud expressed the central mission of the practice of psychoanalysis. Let reason replace instinct. Let civilization replace chaos. Let the mind control and restrain the passions. Let us all discover the redemptive power of love. And work.

Case Study of the Psychoanalytic Method: Luke

In my career I have treated only one person with a relatively orthodox psychoana-lytic method. And like Josef Breuer in his work with Anna O., I neither intended the treatment to proceed in this fashion, nor did I particularly welcome the opportunity once it had presented itself. But perhaps if I tell you the story, you will understand both the therapeutic secrets of the psychoanalytic method and its metaphysics, which will allegedly rescue Western civilization from misery, despair, rage, illusion, and superstition.

When I met "Luke," I was reasonably fresh out of graduate school and still a card-carrying Skinnerian behaviorist. I believed in reinforcement and in classical conditioning and worked out everything by constructing models using only these two mechanist, antivitalist principles. I was roughly in my career where Freud was in his when he began the "Project" with Wilhelm Fleiss. My doctoral dissertation had explored conditioned cardiac responses "in anticipation of painful electric shock" in marginally willing volunteer subjects recruited from undergraduate psychology courses. I was also in clinical training under the supervision of a wise and kind much-older psychologist who observed far more than he let on.

My client was a desperately depressed and increasingly self-destructive college sophomore. Luke had the usual midwestern American family: a mom and a dad who were pretty seriously religious and still married to each other, a younger brother who was 15 years old, and a sister who was 11. Luke also had a girlfriend who maybe was, or maybe wasn't, his fiancee. All I really knew about "Sharon" was that she was in college studying to become a social worker, that she was very religious, and that she had promised God she would remain a virgin until she married.

Luke had "accidentally" lost his virginity at a fraternity party during his freshman year. He had been drunk at the time, and the woman had taken all the initiative in both the decision and the manner in which they had sex. Luke had never even learned her name; all he knew about her was that she attended a nearby college. He never made contact with her again after their one-night stand. He had, however, made it well known among his newly acquired fraternity brothers that he had "scored" at the party.

Stage One: Where Is It Going?

When he came to see me, more than 12 months after the party, Luke told me he had made the appointment because, though he tried and tried, he was simply unable to get this sexual episode out of his mind. He had remained faithful to Sharon ever since that fateful night, but he could never tell Sharon what had happened. Because he had taken a vow of chastity with her, she could never forgive his "breaking his word to God." Nor could he forgive his betrayal of his promise to God and to Sharon.

Luke was increasingly unable to sleep. He had completely lost his appetite and was losing weight so fast that his clothes hung on him in an almost clownlike way. He confessed that he was no longer drinking alcohol—he was bingeing on it. He was terrified that Sharon would become so alarmed at the changes that had overtaken him that she would dump him in favor of another guy.

We worked together for weeks and weeks. Eventually he stopped attending his classes. Then he stopped seeing or writing to Sharon (he told her he was too busy with school). He became more and more heavily involved with alcohol.

Luke now slept almost all day and stayed up all night writing morbid poetry and long, long self-hating confessional letters. We used those letters as starting points for our three-times-a-week sessions.

My supervisor seemed to take a real interest in the case. We talked about it every week. The older man kept asking me where the case was going. I kept telling him I didn't know. This pattern kept on so long that I began to wonder if the old guy was getting senile.

The sessions were getting to be an ordeal for both Luke and me. For 3 hours each week, he would come in and tear into himself verbally and emotionally, always rehearsing what a horrid and unworthy person he was. At my supervisor's suggestion, I tried being very Rogerian (see Chapter 15) with him. I earnestly tried to practice the difficult skill of mirroring back the feelings behind the words I heard Luke say.

My supervisor listened to the tapes and said he found what I was doing to be something he had never heard before. He called my approach with Luke "quite interesting," but he couldn't tell what it was I was doing or trying to accomplish.

For sure, whatever I was doing, it was more "interesting" than it was Rogerian. Looking back, I think I was doing a sort of primitive, early form of cognitive behavior therapy (see Chapter 14). I didn't know that at the time, however, because cognitive therapy hadn't been invented yet.

Stage Two: A Cure?

The second stage of therapy came on quite suddenly. One day Luke appeared in my office with a brand-new set of clothes, which actually fit him. He had shaved and had a new haircut. He had lost so much weight that he had been forced to buy his new clothes in the boys' department, and his haircut matched the look. He looked like he was about 12 years old. I kept staring at his Prince Valiant haircut, not able to figure out what I found so fascinating about his physical appearance.

He informed me that he was starting a new life. The depression was behind him, and he now knew what was wrong. This was a radical change in his personality to go along with his new look.

My very first cure! Or, at least, a sort of cure. I didn't have a clue what had happened, but as a behaviorist I assumed that Luke's contingencies of reinforcement had changed in some fundamental, earth-shattering way.

My supervisor asked me if Luke had changed his sleeping pattern. "Yes." And had he started going to his classes again? Was he arranging to make up for lost work? "Ouch." I forgot to ask—and because of professional confidentiality, I really had no way to check with his professors. Luke had asked not to schedule another appointment for several weeks. "I guess I screwed up a bit, eh?"

I didn't have to wait too long to find out. I received a call from the emergency room at the local hospital around 3:00 A.M. the next Saturday night. Luke had gotten totally wasted on alcohol and had then nearly succeeded in throwing himself in front of a passing freight train. Fortunately, another student had been in the vicinity, figured out why Luke was lurking behind a tree near the tracks, and tackled Luke just as he was about to throw himself in front of the train.

When I went to the hospital, I discovered that Luke was a complete mess, physically and emotionally. I stayed with him all day on Sunday and spent most of Monday listening to his story.

After our last session, he had removed himself to a neighborhood tavern where, within an hour or so, he had been picked up by a female patron who was older than he was. They had gone back to her place and had sex for a couple of days. When that was over, he had gone to another bar and repeated the pattern with a new partner. Luke had continued in this fashion for about 10 consecutive days. He couldn't remember exactly how many women he had slept with or how much he had drunk, but it was a considerable quantity in both cases.

Luke had embarked on this adventure to see if the devil possessed him. Convinced that he was possessed, Luke had gotten royally wasted on Saturday night in preparation for exorcising the demon by taking his own life. The rest of the story I have told you.

Stage Three: Abreaction

Thus began the third phase of our association. Today I would probably have called Luke's parents from the emergency room and recommended or even demanded an in-patient stay at a stress center near his home. But then I was young and foolishly confident that we could work out Luke's problems. Besides, we didn't have any stress centers in those days, just vast old state mental hospitals.

My supervisor shook his head with sorrow as I told him the story. He looked at me for a long time and then asked again, "Where is it going?" This time I didn't think he was senile.

This time, I acted on my instincts. When Luke was released from the hospital, he came to see me. The first question I asked him was about his appearance. What kind of game was it to dress up like a precious little boy to go to bars to get picked up by older women?

Luke hotly denied my accusation. I hit him broadside. I asked him if he denied the pretty obvious fact that because of the way he had chosen to dress and groom himself he had half the homosexual and bisexual men on campus following him around hoping to get his phone number. Luke just stared at me. Was it his new goal in life to try to seduce the entire world? Would he or could he deny it?

This approach wasn't exactly what Freud would have done, but it worked. Luke broke down and wept for almost an hour. Then, for the first time in all the hours we had spent together, we began serious therapy.

We did some dream analysis. He revealed to me a recurrent dream, in which he was at a large track meet. He was in a race, and he was winning his event. But then he would come to a dead stop just before the finish—just stop, as everyone else ran past him to the finish line.

"And are there any spectators at this track meet?"

"Yes."

"Who?"

"Sharon."

"Good. Who else?"

"Nobody."

"I don't believe you."

Tears.

Me again: "Who else?"

Mumbling.

"Who?"

Shouting: "My f——ing father!"

"Let's talk about it."

The theme that subsequently emerged was Luke's refusal to give in to his father or to accede to any of his father's wishes. In all his dreams, Luke would defiantly not let his father take pride in him. He would always stop at the finish line, drop the ball, receive the exam and have his mind go blank, marry Sharon and then discover at the wedding that Sharon was a man. And in every instance—there was Dad. Watching, boasting, taking the credit. And in every instance Luke sabotaged the plan.

One day while we were talking about some dream imagery, a crushing memory suddenly flashed into Luke's head, and he began to cry with great feeling. In the image that flashed through his mind, Luke was 3 or 4 and playing with his dog, Lucky. They lived out in the country, and Lucky was the best and only friend Luke had. It was after supper. Dad was playing poker in the kitchen with some of his pals. Dad had lost a lot of money and seemed drunk. Dad was out of money, so on the next hand he bet Lucky. And he lost. The winner took Lucky away, and Luke never saw the dog again.

When little Luke cried about losing Lucky, his father gave Luke the only beating he ever received in his life.

Talk about abreaction! It was as if the entire episode were replayed right there, 15 years later. The experience was as emotionally fresh as the day it had happened. By the end of the story we were both in tears.

But so Luke's dad was a bastard. So what? He had had a drinking problem then, but he was reformed now, Luke said. Luke and his dad were "good buddies" now. The painful images of childhood didn't connect in any way with the present. Luke hadn't thought of Lucky or even the beating for years and years. His emotional reaction to remembering didn't make any sense.

We weren't finished. Now it was time for the therapist to get an education. "Where is it going?" the almost-smiling wise old man asked me.

"Only one place left," I replied.

He looked me straight in the eye and said gravely: "Take it slow."

Slow? I never would have gotten this far by "slow," I thought. The elderly lose their touch. I "knew" the answer; I had solved the puzzle. The entire case was about the rage, the utterly consuming rage Luke felt toward . . .

Can you figure out the puzzle? The answer is as obvious as the nose on your face. The answer is so obvious it's almost trite. But it was Luke's terrible, awful secret.

It wasn't Lucky. And it wasn't Sharon. It had something to do with . . . What did Charcot say was at the bottom of all neurosis? Sex?

I knew now where we were going. But I also knew I had to let Luke take me there. And so we began the fourth and final stage of our work together.

Stage Four: Transference and Countertransference

Luke and I became awesomely close. He shared every ounce of himself with me. Each of us discovered that we "loved" the other. For me he became the son I hoped my infant child would grow up to become. In turn I was the parent who understood and accepted him. I didn't know about Freud's absolute commandment that the "analyst must never permit himself to love the patient," and I probably would have rejected the advice anyway.

Positive Transference. Let's listen to what Freud had to say about the patient/therapist relationship:

> The outcome is that [the patient and the therapist] enter into a love-relationship which is illicit [I certainly didn't tell my supervisor about it] and which is not intended to last forever [who can argue with that?]. But such a course is made impossible by conventional morality and professional standards. . . . It is clear that a psycho-analyst must look at things from a different point of view. . . . This phenomenon, which occurs without fail and which is, as we know, one of the foundations [Anna O. again!] of the psycho-analytic theory, may be evaluated from two points of view, that of the doctor who is carrying out the analysis and that of the patient who is in need of it.
>
> For the doctor the phenomenon signifies a valuable piece of enlightenment and a useful warning against any tendency to a counter-transference which may be present in his own mind. (1912/1915/1958a, p. 160)

My "falling in love" with Luke was my *countertransference*. My emotional need to be a competent and skillful psychotherapist—my need to offer something vital from within myself to help other people—created the love I felt for Luke. I was becoming his parent in the fullest emotional sense, and Freud acknowledged that one outcome of this state of affairs is "a permanent legal union among them." But I don't think my wife was ready to adopt a 20-year-old college student to be a brother to our 2-year-old.

Further, Freud pointed out,

[the therapist] must recognize that the patient's falling in love is induced by the analytic situation, and is not to be attributed to the charms of his own person; so that he has no grounds whatever of being proud of such a "conquest," as it would be called outside analysis. And it is always well to be reminded of this. (1912/1915/1958a, pp. 160–161)

A contemporary psychoanalyst has suggested that transference phenomena may have profound effects on the relationships between therapists and patients, as well as on society's treatment of the mentally ill:

A troublesome aspect of narcissistic transference, as many analysts will attest, is that [the patients] don't experience themselves as being in that state when they are. Time and time again, while working with preoedipal patients [patients who have not yet resolved their "oedipal complexes" by renouncing their claims to the opposite-sex parent in favor of identification with their same-sex parent] I have felt like getting rid of one as incurable, or felt maybe I ought to marry that wonderful female patient or have a homosexual affair with an attractive male, before recognizing that I was being swayed by the *induced* feelings. Unless you are alert to the possibility that feelings that you experience as your own and that seem to have nothing to do with the patient may actually be the *patient's feelings,* that danger exists.

Over the centuries, the phenomenon of emotional induction appears to have contributed to society's dismal handling of those suffering from acute mental illness. One explanation of why these individuals have been mutilated, shackled, sexually abused, burned at the stake, even killed, is that they felt that they deserved such treatment and induced those feelings around them. (Spotnitz, 1984, p. 137; italics added)

Luke's love for me was *transference* love. My love for him was what Freud called countertransference. While transference lasted in this "positive" state, we had a grand time, although Luke seemed to be progressing in this new stage of therapy rather slower than I had hoped.

Negative Transference. Luke was progressing slower than he had hoped, too, evidently. One day he came to our session once again dressed in his little-boy clothes and wearing his hair in the seductive Prince Valiant style.

I was astonished, flabbergasted, speechless. Finally, I blurted, "What gives with the Lolita costume?"

The reply was a stream of invective and nastiness that nearly blew me out of my chair. I was, he now revealed to me, incompetent, uncaring, only using him so I could get my license to practice, cold, more screwed up than he was, and probably a closet homosexual.

Welcome to *negative transference.* Suddenly all those warm, loving, intimate feelings that Luke had transferred from his unconscious to our relationship were all the vile, nasty, and disgusting things stored in the dark recesses of his emotional memory.

Luke's outburst was like a blinding flash of light. It was an example of not only what I had been taught but also what I was at that very moment, ironically enough, teaching my students in class.

I felt as if the scales of blindness were literally falling away. Were Luke and I so close to the final showdown?

Still, I wasn't really a Freudian. I didn't know about the elaborate process Freud had described for "working through the transference" in the same way that one "works through" resistances earlier in therapy.

Resolution. "Luke," I asked "are you really sure it's me you are talking to?"

"D—— right I am. I sure as hell know."

"OK, give me a 'for instance.'"

"Alright, d—— you, let's take all the pressure you are putting on me to become a f——ing doctor."

"OK, let's."

"You son of a b——."

"How?"

Crying furiously and almost convulsively for a few seconds: "I don't know; I don't know; I don't know."

"Luke, did you wear that outfit for me?"

"Yes! . . . NO! . . . I don't know . . . I don't think so."

"Well, what were you thinking when you put it on?"

"I was thinking about how you treat me like a child, so I was going to dress like a child. I wanted to make you realize how unfair you have been to me. I wanted to tell you that if you wanted to keep me as a child, this is how I am going to live."

"And is that what you really think? Is that how I really make you feel?"

"No!"

"Who are you really talking to, Luke? Do you trust me enough to tell me?"

One-way tickets to graduate school are sewn in the binding of this book for anyone who has already figured out who Luke was talking to.

It was his mother—she whom we had never even mentioned in nearly a year of therapy. Luke was unconsciously harboring an enormous reservoir of anger and resentment toward his mother for "abandoning" him to the rough-and-tumble, hard-drinking, and hard-driving world of his father. She hadn't intervened to "save" Lucky. She had never stood up to protect him from his father's insensitivities, or from the drunken beating. She had seemed to him to become cold and puritanical once Luke ceased being a weak and dependent child.

Reflection

Luke now saw how his relationship with Sharon had carried forward some of those puritanical themes into his current life. The vow of chastity he had taken with Sharon had basically been coerced from him by another strong, puritanical woman in his life. He had been given a simple choice: Either forswear his adult sexual identity or lose a woman's love—again.

Luke quickly understood that he had a lot to resolve with his mother and with Sharon. He had a lot to come to terms with, too, in terms of his own sexuality, which he now realized was pretty ravenous.

Recognition of the necessity to sort out who was who in the transference relationship came without any great emotional disturbance. The hard work was now done. Luke's only hard-core and explosive abreactive experience was when he remembered the incident about Lucky. That memory worked on him and worked on him until his unconscious mind was able to sort out where he really felt the responsibility for that episode lay.

When Luke's therapy was over, we parted warmly and promised to keep in touch. We even managed to exchange Christmas cards for a year or two. He graduated from college in time, resolved his relationship with Sharon in a mutually agreeable manner, and went on to become a very successful professional man. Our mutual transference "love" evaporated. It just vanished.

Except, of course, it didn't. You never forget your first love—or your first case.

I am now certain that my supervisor knew all along both what was happening and what was going to happen. This book is dedicated in part to his memory.

The bottom line? Know thyself. But try not to self-destruct in the process. Luke lifted his veil of repression and completed therapy, "sadder but wiser." As I confessed in the first pages, this is a book about how I make my living. There are probably easier ways. But until the philosophers all become kings in their cities, somebody has to do this job.

CHAPTER 8

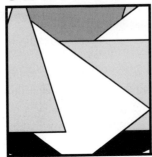

Alfred Adler's "Individual Psychology"

The Search for Significance

Did Alfred Adler feel inferior to his contemporary, the great Sigmund Freud? Is that why he radically challenged Freud in front of the entire Psychoanalytic Society in Vienna, calling into question some of Freud's most dearly held ideas? This chapter may help you answer these questions for yourself.

For Adler, the essential quest of human beings has four elements: the search for significance, the struggle to overcome feelings of inferiority, the formation of personality "complexes," and lifestyle choices. A key aspect of Adler's theory is encouragement. The encouragement Adler gained from his father helped him to overcome his physical inferiorities as a child. Central to Adlerian psychotherapy is the idea that every human being must be given encouragement if he or she is to find the courage to live life most fully—in an occupation, in love and marriage, and on a broader social level.

The First Dissenter

January 4, 1911: President Alfred Adler opened the meeting of Vienna's Psychoanalytic Society by reporting that the move to the society's new offices was almost complete and that members would enjoy perusing Professor Sigmund Freud's writings at their leisure in the expanded space. Vice President Wilhelm Stekel announced that the February 1 meeting would be devoted entirely to a presidential address titled "The Masculine Protest," which would present ideas challenging and stimulating to all. Stekel then called on the president to read his paper "On Some Problems for Psychoanalysis."

After a brief discussion of the paper, Freud rose to thank Adler for his remarks. Freud was pleased that in the press of assuming his new duties as president, Adler had found sufficient time to begin drafting such an interesting paper. Freud expressed hope that the president would soon be freed from competing responsibilities so that he might resolve the difficulties in his paper regarding the theory of neuroses, the universality of the sexual motive, and the universal significance of penis envy in the neurotic strivings of women. The difficulties with Adler's presentation, Freud concluded, came from a faulty understanding of the role of unconscious sexual motives in the development of neuroses and of the defensive role of the ego. Freud concluded by thanking the president again for his service and expressing hope that his administrative duties would not be discharged with the same "trivial and methodologically deplorable" result as the present "sterile" paper.

The meeting was adjourned at 10:28 P.M. Thus began the end of the 4-month administrative reign of the first president of the Psychoanalytic Society.

One of Freud's first and most devoted followers, Adler had been meeting weekly with the rest of Freud's small group since its beginnings in 1902. Freud had nominated him for the presidency of the society and had appointed him editor of the association's official journal, *Centralblatt,* as a token of his appreciation for a decade of loyal service to the developing field of psychoanalysis.

But even as he did this, Freud knew that Adler's unresolved neurotic ambitions were a danger to the intellectual integrity of the movement. Freud kept his concerns to himself, of course, but if Adler was a traitor, it was better to find out sooner rather than later. And it would be wise to find out as early as possible who would join Adler in plunging the dagger into his master's back.

It didn't take long to find out. At the February 1911 meeting Adler read his paper "The Masculine Protest," arguing that the striking frequency of secondary sexual characteristics of the opposite sex among neurotic patients—"a pronounced psychological hermaphroditism"—is attributable to the structural inequalities of power accorded the sexes by society. Women in particular, Adler had observed, demonstrate rejection of their subordinate status in society by rejecting the suffocating and demeaning place assigned them as helpless, passive creatures. The resulting "masculine protest" of some women could be seen in their dressing and acting like men and rejecting their most sacred and important role: that of mother.

Apparently unaware of the consternation he was arousing in his listeners, Adler read on. He had also observed that boys and men are equally damaged by outmoded views of gender inequality. Boys reveal their masculine protest either by glorifying and exaggerating the masculine traits of aggression and antisocial behavior or by completely rejecting the impossible restrictions assigned to them on account of their gender and thus becoming passive. In some extreme cases, their masculine protest is manifested in a stated desire to dress and behave like girls.

The masculine protest, in Adler's view, constitutes the nucleus of homosexuality in both boys and girls. It is also the factor most responsible for failed marriages, poisoned human relationships, and a wide variety of interpersonal dysfunctions.

Adler exhorted his fellow psychoanalysts, as the only authentic champions of the common people, to demonstrate the intellectual, political, and ethical leadership needed to overthrow the corruption of entrenched male privilege. "All our institutions, our traditional attitudes, our laws, our morals, our customs, give evidence of the fact that they are determined and maintained by privileged males for the glory of male domination" (Adler, 1927, p. 123).

Adler's paper was the unambiguous outrage that Freud had feared yet secretly expected it would be. By advocating "social reform," Adler had betrayed the very core of psychoanalysis, the very essence of Freud's life work. He had taken the single biological fact of mental life—the oedipal conflict—and made it a bit of arbitrary social engineering.

After Adler's address, the members of the society were in an uproar. There were pointed heckling and shouted abuse. Some were even threatening to come to blows. And then, almost majestically, Freud rose from his seat. He surveyed the room with his penetrating eyes. He told them there was no reason to brawl in the streets like uncivilized hooligans. The choice was simple. Either he or Dr. Adler would remain to guide the future of psychoanalysis. The choice was the members' to make. He trusted them to do the right thing. And, by his lights, they did.

Psychoanalysis, "that other religion," had spawned its first official heretics. After the vote, Adler and Stekel resigned their posts, calling on those who believed in "freedom of inquiry" to join them. They left the building silently and retired to a nearby cafe. Those who left were seven in number. They resolved immediately to form a new society—The Society for Free Psychoanalytic Research—and pledged to each other never to shirk the courage it would take to follow Truth, wherever it led them.

The Society for Free Psychoanalytic Research (or "Free Psychoanalysis," according to Ellenberger, 1970) soon thereafter changed its name to the Society for Individual Psychology, but it remained remarkably true over the years to the ideals of its founding. Adler and his followers devoted the rest of their lives to developing a psychology that would reveal the social and cultural foundations of neuroses. Their response to human problems was characteristically ethical and practical—an orientation that stood in dramatic contrast to the biological and theoretical focus of psychoanalysis.

Adler's Childhood

Alfred Adler was born a second son in 1870. His brilliant, successful, extroverted, handsome, and altogether successful older brother was named Sigmund. Sigmund Adler was the very model of the self-made man. Although the Adler family background was only marginally even lower middle class, Sigmund counted among his friends a rich assortment of doctors, lawyers, bankers, and successful merchants. He maintained a large private library, enjoyed the best food and music, played a sharp game of chess, and was adored and respected by everyone in his family. As a young man he used the fortune he had made to rescue his parents and siblings from the bankruptcy courts and then went on to make a second fortune. It was said that he was extremely fond of his little brother, Alfred, and as a youth went out of his way to protect the younger, weaker boy from numerous neighborhood bullies.

Alfred was only a year and a half younger than Sigmund, but the differences between them were profound. Alfred was a sickly child whose early memories of his big brother verged on the pathetic:

> One of my earliest recollections is of sitting on a bench bandaged up on account of rickets, with my healthy elder brother sitting opposite me. He could run, jump, and move about quite effortlessly, while for me movement of any sort was a strain and an effort. Everyone went to great pains to help me, and my mother and father did all that was in their power to do. At the time of this recollection I must have been about two years old. (quoted in Bottome, 1939, p. 30)

Several times during his childhood, Alfred became so ill and weak that the family physician gave him up for lost. A younger brother was even more sickly than Alfred and died in early childhood. Alfred spent a lot of his childhood with doctors, and it seemed doctors were always around the house. They became his heroes; from them he said he learned the greatest lesson of his life: "One must always challenge death."

Alfred was the great favorite of his father Leopold, who was an unremarkable man in most respects. Leopold managed his wife's family's grain business for a while, until he almost ran it into the ground. At that point Leopold began his own grain-trading business and indeed did run it into the ground. The family survived primarily through the unceasing efforts of Alfred's mother, who raised almost all the food they ate, took care of all the children, managed the family business when it overwhelmed her husband, and kept the family house, which was soon lost to creditors. The house had been her parents' ancestral home.

It is thus understandable that Mrs. Adler was not a particularly happy or joyful person. She was described as nervous and gloomy and exhausted from the work of taking care of their large household. She died at age 61 "worn-out by illness and overwork" (Bottome, 1939). Alfred never found in her the intimate nurturance that Freud had found with his mother. This is probably the singular reason why the centerpiece of Freud's theory, his insistence on the primacy of the oedipal relationship, never made much sense to Adler as a scholar or as a practicing therapist.

Freud's and Adler's fathers were likewise mirror opposites. Freud's father was a patriarch, a devout Jew, a man of mystery and power. Although as merchant Jews in Vienna Freud's and Adler's fathers were of essentially the same social class, Freud's father would not have recognized any commonality with Leopold Adler. Adler's father, only a nominal Jew with Hungarian ethnic roots, was anything but patriarchal and aloof. He is described as carefree and happy with a wide sense of humor and a special devotion to his hapless son Alfred. Leopold was a failure in the life of the marketplace, but unlike Freud's father, whom no one could ever please, Leopold sheltered his boy with the philosophy "Never believe what anyone tells you about yourself." Leopold even supported his son unconditionally when the boy was required to repeat a grade at the gymnasium, the same middle school Freud had attended as a boy. Probably most importantly of all, from Alfred's later perspective, Leopold showered his boy with encouragement.

In later years Alfred Adler said that neurotics suffer mainly from discouragement. Surely he had in mind his happy, self-confident father, who would not be bowed down by even the heaviest trials of everyday life.

Perhaps because Adler interpreted his mother's solitary pessimism as the result of her special burden of motherhood and still unconsciously resented his mother's critical detachment, he later came to hold somewhat contradictory views about women. On the one hand, he was a solid champion of progressive reform, which advocated equal rights for women. But on the other hand, he also believed that a mother's foremost obligation is to raise her children with generosity of spirit, optimism, and encouragement.

Adler also believed that a child's character and disposition are a product of that child's place in the family constellation. This belief is a direct consequence of Adler's own birth position. He was sandwiched between an older all-star brother and a string of five younger siblings, at least one of whom was weaker and more sickly than he and one other who was as ambitious and successful as their older brother, Sigmund.

The Struggle to Survive

Probably much to everyone's surprise, little Alfred survived both childhood illnesses and the rigors of an Austrian education. He grew up to become a physician and to engage his childhood prototype: he who would fight death professionally.

As a young trainee at the medical college, Adler extensively volunteered his services at the general hospital, Beckh-Widmanstetter (which would not have him on its paid staff because he was technically a Hungarian citizen), and in a free clinic for the poor. By making these connections Adler not only received advanced medical training, which would otherwise not have been within his financial reach, but also met the "best and the brightest" specialists among the Viennese medical establishment of the last decade of the 19th century. Through his contacts with this circle, Adler became interested in Josef Breuer's and Freud's revolutionary work with hysterics. Freud and Adler eventually met, in 1901 or 1902. But more significantly for his later convictions, Adler made the acquaintance of other progressive, social-minded physicians by volunteering his time at the free clinic. These contacts rekindled an intense interest in socialism in him and in turn brought him into contact with the circle of young, well-educated idealists who read and debated the theories of Karl Marx, Friedrich Engels, and the other socialist revolutionaries of the day.

One of these young socialists was a beautiful young woman named Raissa Epstein. As a woman interested in obtaining a university education, she had had no choice but to leave her native Russia. She and Adler met, fell madly in love, and married almost immediately. The young couple moved in with his parents and produced a daughter 9 months later.

Adler opened a medical practice, specializing in nervous disorders, in one of the working-class sections of Vienna. His patients were the working poor.

Circus People. Adler was particularly impressed by the circus people he treated, who had their permanent winter quarters in his part of the city. He marveled at their wonderful skills, their enthusiasm for life, and their unbridled optimism. He also marveled at the way so many of them had successfully compensated for the accidents of nature and hazards of the world that had left their bodies maimed and distorted.

Adler was also deeply impressed with the tightly knit community in which circus people lived. Every person was valued for what he or she could contribute to the good of all. Even if all a grotesquely deformed person could do was to stand on a stage as a "freak," he or she was still able to make an active contribution and to enjoy a significant life.

Tailors. Another group of people Adler worked with was tailors. Adler studied the case histories of his tailor patients with great care. He came to realize that most of their illnesses were due to the occupational hazards of their trade.

In 1898, the same year as the birth of his daughter, Adler published his first book, *Health Book for the Tailoring Trade.* This was probably the first book ever published in the field of occupational medicine. Adler attempted to show in its 31 pages "the relationship of economic situation and disease in a given trade, and the resulting prejudice to public health" (Ellenberger, 1970, p. 599).*

The thesis of the book was that the forces of the marketplace forced tailors to work for less and less money under more and more dangerous conditions. Adler chronicled the 18-hour days worked by tailors, their wives, and their children under

---

*Selected excerpts in this chapter from *The Discovery of the Unconscious: The History and Evolution of Dynamic Psychiatry,* by H. F. Ellenberger. Copyright © 1970 by Henry F. Ellenberger. Reprinted by permission of Basic Books, a division of HarperCollins Publishers, Inc.

conditions that he described as "damp, dark, airless, overcrowded, and which favor contagion of infectious diseases" (1898, quoted in Ellenberger, 1970, p. 600).

Under these appalling conditions, the tailors of Vienna were afflicted with a wide range of chronic diseases:

> Pulmonary tuberculosis is twice as frequent among them as in the average of other trades. Another result [of their working conditions is] circulatory disturbances such as varicose veins and hemorrhoids, as well as frequent stomach and intestinal diseases [and] scoliosis, cyphosis, rheumatism, arthritis of the right arm, callousites of the ankles and so on. . . . Their type of close work determines shortsightedness and cramps of the eye muscles. They are the victims of slow poisoning through toxic dyes and infectious diseases transmitted to them through the old clothes they are brought for repair. . . . According to statistics, disease frequency among tailors is higher than in any other trade and the average life expectancy is the lowest of all trades. (Adler, 1898, quoted in Ellenberger, 1970, p. 600)

Adler concluded his book with a call for government regulation of working conditions, accident insurance, old-age and unemployment insurance, the prohibition of piecework, and adequate lodging and eating houses for the workers.

Other Crusades. Adler was soon publishing a variety of tracts in popular and medical journals, both under his own name and under pseudonyms. In these publications he advocated drastic reform within the medical profession. He called on physicians to educate their patients about the dangers of the workplace and demanded that physicians demonstrate social responsibility by leading the movement for public health education and reform. He demanded that the state collect funds to pay for medical treatment of the poor, asserting that society could no longer trust individual physicians to take their fair share of responsibility for the destitute sick. He would not tolerate the claim "We have no money" from government officials. He further demanded the establishment of a permanent bureaucracy that would ensure adequate health care for everyone—"current to the latest standards of science"—as a matter of basic human rights.

Another cause that captured the young physician's attention and energy was the plight of young soldiers impressed into military service for political causes they didn't understand and that were not in their true economic or political interests. Adler knew firsthand about the military. He had been conscripted into the military medical reserve corps, which still regularly called on him to treat soldiers wounded in training and in battle. He was particularly disturbed by the apparent ignorance of the soldiers,

> the paradox of the common people going to war with such a show of enthusiasm to endure so many sufferings for a cause which was not their own. The answer is that they acted in that way in order to escape the distressing feeling of helplessness. (Adler, 1918, quoted in Ellenberger, 1970, p. 587)

In a pamphlet with the title "The Other Side," Adler wrote:

> But what about the mass enthusiasm at the beginning of war and the numerous volunteers? Many . . . went to war because they were dissatisfied with their position or their family life. These were often the ones who were the most rapidly disenchanted. But the people should not be held responsible for their attitude at the beginning, because they had no means of assessing the situation, having been thoroughly deceived by their leaders. [Their] only salvation was to fight under the banner of the oppressor [which is what] psychoanalysts . . . call the "identification with the enemy." (1919, quoted in Ellenberger, 1970, p. 588)

A Champion of Women's Rights

As an impassioned champion of equal rights for women, Adler was drawn into the fierce battle being waged at the turn of the century over sexuality and reproductive freedom. As you might surmise, Adler was all for it. "Nobody can bear a position of inferiority without anger and disgust," Adler said (1931, p. 267). That woman must be submissive was utter "superstition," in Adler's view. "All that we ask of conduct, of ideals, of goals, of actions and traits of character, is that they should serve towards our human cooperation" (p. 69).

Adler believed passionately that physicians had a special obligation to advise women of the latest scientific information about human sexuality and reproduction. He was a champion of contraceptive birth control when it was a socially and medically revolutionary cause all over Western Europe and in North America.

Leading medical authorities of the day told women who actively practiced birth control—most notably coitus interruptus (withdrawal)—that the practice was dangerous to the female nervous system. These physicians gravely advised women that, in terms of damage to their nervous and reproductive systems, contraception was hardly better than masturbation. Both practices were "proven," at least in the thinking of these masculine experts on women's reproductive health, to be gravely dangerous. All efforts at contraception, women were routinely told, inevitably resulted in nervous exhaustion, hysteria, and in severe cases insanity. This was a widely shared point of view among the medical community at the time.

At about this period in U.S. history, these views became incorporated into the wider doctrines of the "Cult of Pure Womanhood," which preached marital chastity and temperance. As disagreeable as this viewpoint sounds, the efforts of crusaders to preserve "pure womanhood" dramatically lowered the death rate of women, whose reproductive rate began to decline precipitously.

In fiery response, Adler attacked one of the leading antisex medical authorities. Max Gruber, in his book *Hygiene of Sexual Life*, had cautioned women about the dangers of their sexuality. Gruber was one of the leading proponents of the view that a woman endowed with too strong a sexual appetite would weaken her husband's fragile nervous system until he became chronically neurasthenic. In fact, any woman who did not exercise strict control over her sexual appetites, Gruber warned, would find herself responsible for her husband's early and untimely death from nervous exhaustion.

Adler wrote the following in a review of Gruber's book:

> Adler opposes the views of Max Gruber in regard to a topic much discussed. Adler contends that sexual abstinence can cause inconveniences for emotional health, with some rare exceptions. In regard to sexual excesses, Adler thinks Gruber has exaggerated their noxious effects, and there is no evidence that they can cause neurasthenia. Adler also states that the alleged dangers of birth control have been much overstated. As for homosexuality, Adler agrees with the author that it is not a congenital abnormality, and argues that it should be punished only if it brings prejudice to another party and to protect minors. Adler sees the dangers of masturbation in another perspective than the author. They do not exist so much in regard to physical health as they do in regard to harmonious emotional development. [For him, "the masturbator" was a solitary, unhappy child.] (1904, quoted in Ellenberger, 1970, p. 603)

The Mild-Mannered Revolutionary

Adler expected Freud to actively support and encourage such nonconventional views towards workers, medicine, government, military conscription, sexual expression, masturbation, birth control, and the rights of women. His mistake was forgivable. Many of Freud's contemporary readers (and not a few of his modern ones, in my experience) expected him to possess a radical, revolutionary spirit. But in truth Freud was a deeply conventional man in almost every respect.

What few people understood about Freud was that he had discovered the sexual etiology of nervous disorders as an act of science, not of politics. He had a lifelong, abiding distaste for "the masses" and was not even particularly keen on the idea of democracy. He believed in stability and balance. He believed in harnessing the forces of nature, including the sexual instincts—not in celebrating them.

Perhaps because my childhood had many of the same elements as Adler's, I have always felt an affinity for him and his work. In my mind's eye I see him as he was described by a former neighbor in Vienna:

> There was nothing conspicuous about him. He was modest and made no particular impression. You would have taken him for a tailor. Though he had a country house, he did not look as if he had a large income. His wife was a normal decent housewife. There was only one maid in the house. Although he traveled much and received many visitors, I never even realized that he was a famous man until the day came when a great ceremony was organized in his honor. (quoted in Ellenberger, 1970, p. 593)

Mild-mannered and unsophisticated in his mannerisms and tastes, Adler presented himself to the outside world as "a short, sturdy man who could not be called handsome. He had a large, round head, a massive forehead, and a wide mouth" (Ellenberger, 1970, p. 594). Even in middle age he failed to cut an impressive figure. His devoted biographer and follower, Phyllis Bottome, had expected to meet a "Socratic genius" when she finally arranged a face-to-face meeting with Adler; instead she described meeting "a very ordinary 57-year-old man who simply possessed a deep and abiding interest in the lives of ordinary people" (1962, p. 138).

I like thinking about Adler and his young wife living together as intellectual and sexual equals, harboring bohemian fantasies while living their mundane lives in a pleasant but boring middle-class suburb of Vienna. Adler's wife's close friend was the wife of the famed Marxist revolutionary Trotsky, who lived in Vienna from 1907 until the early days of the Russian Revolution. I can imagine the excitement generated as the Adlers and the Trotskys and their friends talked about overthrowing the old order and establishing a world with economic justice. Men and women, tailors and knife throwers, revolutionaries and psychiatrists would share a common inheritance of peace, justice, and "continuous social revolution." The common people would be educated about their role as parents through vast networks of government-supported "child guidance clinics." Fear, ignorance, superstition, and sexual inequality would be abolished. Every child would receive the same encouragement that Alfred had received from his father. Every child would grow up to know the true meaning of courage.

Adler's Theory: The Integrated, Meaningful Life

Before we review the elements of Adlerian psychotherapy, you need to understand something of the theoretical structure it is based on. Adler's grand, comprehensive theory is his own creation. It is based on a combination of what he learned from his medical patients about triumphing over adversity and from his personal experience growing up.

Adler's theory owes little, if anything, to Freudian constructs and principles. Adler minimized the importance of both sexual motives and the unconscious in the structure of human character. As Freud's psychoanalysis was a study of instinctual life, Adler's was a study of social life. About the only fundamental thing the two agreed on is the overwhelming importance of a child's early experiences as powerful determinants of adult personality.

Albert Einstein once wrote to Freud that his theory was "beautiful" in its scientific logic. Adler's theory is not beautiful in this sense. It is a practical, sensible, and even obvious statement about what it means to be a human being living in a complex and difficult world. It is based on an analysis of how we each become a unique individual.

Four Principles

Four principles support the structure of Adler's theory. Freud's followers have always tended to dismiss these principles as "mere common sense." But in trying to understand human beings, one could rely on much worse than "mere" common sense.

The Quest for Meaning and Significance. The first principle of Adler's theory is based on Charles Darwin's principles of evolution and the philosopher Herbert Spencer's philosophy of evolutionary "progress."

Strictly speaking, Darwinians don't believe in "progress". Instead, they recognize that as conditions in the world change there is a "natural selection" of those organismic variants best adapted to that particular set of conditions. There is no "direction" in such an evolutionary process. Life is constantly evolving, but a true Darwinian does not see life as perfecting itself to some state of ultimate completion.

Spencer, on the other hand, was more a figure of the Enlightenment. He believed that human nature and human society are constantly evolving toward something better:

> Sentient beings have progressed from low to high types, under the law that the superior shall profit by their superiority, and the inferior shall suffer from their inferiority. Conformity to this law has been and still is, needful, not only for the continuance of life, but for the increase of happiness. (Spencer, 1907, p. 170)

Adler fully incorporated Spencer's notion of social evolution into his thinking about psychology. He came to believe that evolution is guided toward an ultimate perfection—that people aren't just existing but evolving toward a more perfect and just human community. Both Aristotle and St. Thomas Aquinas had endorsed such a *teleological* view—that life has existential purpose—and Adler believed that the correctness of such a view is implicit in everything people do to improve themselves and the future lives of their children.

Adler was not an especially religious person. He had been raised and married a Jew but had converted to Protestantism as a young man and even had his children baptized. But I don't think his teleology was an essentially religious idea. I think he believed that human beings really are capable of evolving as higher and higher forms of life, intellectually and emotionally. Adler's confidence in perfection was surely strongly influenced by the writing of Marx and Engels—that a new human being would abolish injustice, exploitation, and the exercise of will to overpower others.

Adler believed that the existential purpose of human beings is to find meaning and significance in their lives. He didn't believe the sex drive is the overshelming motive that Freud considered it. Sex, in Adler's theory, serves only a reproductive function at a biological level and a power function at the social level. Sex as a motive cannot account for the great hopes of common men and women.

Instead, Adler believed, humans are bound to find their ultimate and true teleology expressed in their social relationships. At an earlier evolutionary stage, perhaps, they had been guided by the aggressive drive, which ensured survival under the life-or-death law of the jungle. But, Adler argued, as we evolved away from that state, we developed a social-interest motive, an inherent capacity for *fellow feeling,* which is a biological drive characteristically found in the most highly evolved members of the human species.

Before we leave this point (which I expect you will find rather abstract and hard to pin down at first reading), I need to add that Adler felt the capacity for fellow feeling is the leading edge of human evolution. It therefore exists more as potential than as reality in most people. He felt it is important, therefore, that education, government, medicine, and religion work in consort to awaken this latent motive in the species, most especially in children.

Parenthood is the highest calling of any human being, Adler argued, for given to parents is the supreme opportunity to awaken the social-interest motive in their children. All parents have both the opportunity and the responsibility to better all humanity by increasing the number of "awakened" people in society who will gladly work together for the common good.

Did you ever have a parent, teacher, or coach who told you that you weren't working up to your "full potential"? What did that person actually mean? Adler would have meant that most of us are not living up to our full potential as members of the species, that we are inherently capable of the fullest sort of human connection with others. Furthermore, we will always feel an ontological emptiness—an existential void—until we fully develop this special human capacity within ourselves. Our salvation, according to Adler, lies ultimately in learning to love one another. Selfishness is a lonely evolutionary backwater, a dead end where no human being can find true fulfillment, significance, meaning, or self-actualization.

The Inferiority Complex. The second foundational component of Adler's theory is the *inferiority complex,* "The fundamental law of life is to overcome one's deficiencies" (Adler, 1933, p. 48). Adler declared that to be a human being is to be constantly aware of one's insignificance and inherent weakness. Incessant striving to overcome this inherent inferiority is the fundamental motive of human striving; "a sense of worth of the self shall not be allowed to diminish" (Adler, 1968, p. 100).

Adler perceived that we are born into the world feeling incomplete, weak, and helpless. These feelings can be based on physical reality or psychological reality, but either way they are inevitable. Feelings of physical inferiority can be caused by any "organ weakness," such as weak eyesight, shortness of stature, childhood illnesses, or a lack of physical coordination. Feelings of psychological inferiority come from sibling rivalries, feeling weak and powerless around one's father, and recognizing one's inferior status in the oedipal situation. In addition, Adler was significantly ahead of his time in recognizing how the social injustices surrounding gender role expectations instill feelings of inferiority within a child.

Children embark on a lifelong struggle to develop their personality in a way that optimally compensates for their physical and psychological inferiorities. Just as the circus people compensated for their organic weaknesses by exhibiting their extraordinary body strength and unusual physical skills, we all develop the external aspects of our personalities to compensate for our own perceived weaknesses and inferiorities.

Often a patient's physical health history provides insight into the key aspects of his or her inferiority complex. Adler believed that physical health breaks down at precisely those points where environmental demands exact their greatest toll. Children with weak stomachs might, therefore, develop ulcers as adults. But by learning to strengthen their stomachs, such children may also grow up to be surgeons or nurses—capable of performing tasks the rest of us might not have a "strong enough stomach" to accomplish.

As a 4-year-old I developed a frustrating stutter. Adler would not be surprised to learn that I chose to become a professional talker, as a therapist and a teacher, to compensate for this developmental "weakness." I am sure that at times my patients and my students wish I had grown up with analogously weak hearing.

It is important to note that the striving generated by the inferiority complex is essentially a negative striving. Unlike the social-interest motive, the inferiority complex does not lead toward self-actualization and growth. Rather it leads toward compensation, striving for superiority to establish our own security. The inferiority motive, therefore, often leads people in directions directly opposite those that would bring them the greatest evolutionary significance. My human nature often contradicts the goals of my human teleology; doing what I hope will make me invulnerable actually makes me less fully human. This conflict is at the root of all psychical disturbances in general and the neuroses in particular.

The Organization of Mental Life. Adler's third important point is the centrality of "complexes" that define human personalities. These complexes become the creative but *neurotic fictions* of our striving to overcome our deficiencies. The inferiority complex is at the center of all the other complexes. But in most of us, these inferiority feelings are masked by the ways we cover them up or compensate for them.

Inherent here is a point that Adler shared to a certain extent with Freud: What appears at the surface of a person's personality may in fact betray its mirror opposite at the level of the unconscious. Thus for an Adlerian, a young woman diagnosed with anorexia nervosa (pathological refusal to eat) may be expressing a truly vast hunger (for love as well as for food), but because the direct expression of this need would expose her weakness to others, she develops the neurotic fiction that she has no appetite.

The *masculine protest* is the prototype of the neurotic fiction. Girls who feel that their femininity makes them weak and vulnerable may adopt a "masculinity complex" to compensate for this fear. Similarly, boys who fear that their masculinity is not strong enough may become schoolyard bullies to hide their feared weakness. My acquaintance who is constantly on guard against closeted homosexual men seems to be saying to the world that the very last thing you could accuse him of is confusion about his sexual preference or doubts about his attractiveness to women.

What is characteristic of people who develop these exaggerated neurotic fictions is that at some basic level they suffer from discouragement. They don't believe in the adequacy of a well-regulated compensatory system. They don't wear just a little makeup to conceal a blemish; they become beauty queens and dictators of fashion. They can't be satisfied with doing well on a test; they have to challenge the professor over every last point they lost.

The problem, of course, is that these "deeply discouraged" people seek significance in their lives (the first motive) by aggressively seeking the "fictitious triumph" of social power over people. Social power, they unconsciously reason, will successfully conceal their true insecurities (the second motive). From Adler's perspective, these people are trying to avoid exercising genuine social interest because that level of fellow feeling makes them feel vulnerable and inferior to others.

The result is massive self-deception. The beauty queen comes to think of herself as better than anyone else but also feels terribly alone and despised. The bruising, insensitive jock finds himself unable to self-disclose to anyone. And the effeminate homosexual man consigns himself to a social ghetto, depriving himself of the nonsexual yet intimate companionship of other men.

There are literally dozens of complexes. Some of the more obvious ones:

- *Inferiority complex.* He cannot be expected to solve problems or take responsibility like ordinary persons.
- *Electra/Oedipus complex.* She can't find any man as good and wonderful as Daddy was. He can't break the apron strings that tie him to his pampering mother.
- *Redeemer complex.* She knows the one true way and cannot sleep until you are converted, saved, and redeemed. But then once you are, she is off to save the next sinner.
- *Proof complex.* He doesn't or can't believe anything until every bit of evidence is presented six times. (It's not much fun to fall in love with this one; his insecurities are always your fault.)
- *Leader complex.* This person always thinks it's her ball or party or idea. If you don't let her be the star, center of attention, or chair, she won't participate.
- *"No" complex.* Everything is wrong. He'll do just the opposite of anything you suggest.

The Prototype as the Basis of the Self. One's childhood *prototype* is the basis of the specific complex that emerges in the adult personality. The essence of Adler's fourth point is that the individual's "style of life" (some Adlerian writers refer to lifestyle) is her or his philosopher's stone.

Adler was greatly influenced by the philosophy of Hans Vaihinger, who published *The Philosophy of "As If"* in 1911. Vaihinger wrote that we each create the world we live in by the assumptions we make about that world. These creative fictions are the product of both conscious and unconscious experience and are in part a reflection of our natural temperament.

If you agree with Will Rogers that you've never met a person you didn't like, you will live your life "as if" every new person you meet will be your friend. If you perceive college to be an excruciating punishment visited upon you by your unloving parents, you probably will experience college as a painful and unproductive waste of time. If you believe that life has a mysterious creative power, Adler believed, you will live your life giving full expression to "that power which expresses itself in the desire to develop, to strive, and to achieve—even to compensate for defeats in one direction by striving for success in another" (Adler, 1929, p. 1).

The neurotic, however, has usually begun life with a negative "as if," which leads him or her to adopt a style of life, or prototype, consistent with that negative preconception. Adler gave the following example of this point:

> Perhaps I can illustrate this by an anecdote of three children taken to the zoo for the first time. As they stood before the lion's cage, one of them shrank behind the mother's skirts and said, "I want to go home." The second child stood where he was, very pale and trembling and said, "I'm not a bit frightened." The third glared at the lion and fiercely asked his mother, "Shall I spit at it?" The three children really felt inferior, but each expressed his feelings in his own way, consistent with his style of life. (1931, p. 50)

The interplay of temperament and social learning leads a child to become the "creative artist" of his or her own personality. As a child I sculpted a somewhat shy and careful style of relating to the world, whereas my wife's prototype was verbal and, for lack of a better word, bossy. When first introduced to my kindergarten class, I headed for the reading corner and hoped nobody would notice me. My wife took on kindergarten by absorbing, monitoring, and attempting to enforce the rules of the classroom. In grade school I spent a lot of my time buried in biographies of famous people; she organized the neighborhood children into make-believe classrooms. We both became teachers, but we arrived there by entirely opposite prototypes.

The Triumph of Fellow Feeling

All that now remains is to integrate the concept of the prototype, or style of life, into the rest of the model. Recall that we are working with two motives. The first motive—the drive for meaning through social interest—needs to be awakened in most of us, because we are not sufficiently evolved as members of the species. The second motive, our essential feelings of helplessness and inferiority, is worked out according to a ritualized plan, our characteristic way of responding to the world. This working out is accomplished through our experience with our prototype or style of life.

When the plan is productive—which is to say, when the prototype resolves our inferiority feelings by increasing our fellow feeling—we are on the right track and can realistically hope to live happy and productive lives. But when the plan does not make us prosocial, we do not develop the inherent satisfaction that comes from awakened social feeling. In this event, our feelings of inferiority intensify, which causes us to defensively reinforce the protective shield of our prototype, which exaggerates our behavior and in time creates a neurotic complex, which further prevents us from developing genuine human relationships with our families and associates.

A neurotic system is one in which the style of life becomes so rigid and self-protective that the possibility of enriching life through genuine human interest is drastically diminished. Our "triumphs" become more and more fictive. Our neuroses deepen as concerns about power, motivated by insecurity, become the sole motive operating in our lives. We become more and more isolated as our "as if" picture of the world becomes more threatening, less nurturing, and more stagnant.

The harm in this situation is that our social-interest motive may never be fully awakened, and thus we may never experience any real fellow feeling. The result is either suicide or madness, both topics of intense interest to Adler.

But the real problem is less the feelings of inferiority that we experience than the lifestyle choices that we make (witness the circus people and Adler himself). Please recall that the greatest harm that can be done to a child is discouragement and that the great gift Adler received from his hapless father was encouragement. Encouragement is the key to a productive lifestyle choice. My encouragement came from people who valued reading and ideas; my wife's, from people who valued propriety and discipline. If children were encouraged by the right sorts of models, all would be well. Hence the establishment of child guidance clinics by Adlerians throughout Western Europe and North America in the 1920s, 1930s, and 1940s.

Three Great Wrongs: Abuse, Neglect, and Pampering

Poor parental models—drunken fathers or depressed mothers, for example—are not capable of inspiring their children to truly productive prototypes. Discouragement due to poor models of adult behavior is often found in the case histories of seriously disturbed children. But the seeds of neurosis are also sewn in conventional middle-class families by the two most common errors of parents: pampering and neglect.

The ill effects of pampering are a subject of great interest in Adler's writings. At one point he goes so far as to say that a lot of Freud's psychoanalytic concepts were the neurotic conclusions of a "pampered tyrant" obsessed with having other people meet his every need. The pampered child is never held responsible for his own actions, never has the satisfaction of "doing" for himself. The pampered child makes choices only to please the self, without concern for how these choices will affect other people. Such a child never overcomes the deepest feelings of inferiority and helplessness (think of how truly frightening it must be for the pampered freshman living away from home for the first time to have lost the instant support of family and friends) but also never experiences any of the joy that comes with making life a bit better for someone else.

The opposite of pampering, neglect, is at least as destructive as pampering in the formation of a developing child's prototype. Neglected children live in perpetual fear of being abandoned and thus reason that they must coerce all the love and attention they can to survive. Neglected children may have an especially difficult time recognizing their inherent capacity for fellow feeling. Because they are often left alone with intense feelings of rage, anger, and helplessness, they may find it difficult to comprehend and experience even tentatively positive feelings. Such children, and I suspect we see this all too often among highly stereotypical, "masculine" men, all too often grow to adulthood emotionally and sensually inhibited.

The Importance of Birth Order

A final determinant of style of life is a child's birth position in the family. Adler believed that this factor is especially salient in first-born children, who struggle with their psychological demotion in the household when a second child is born: "They are admirers of the past and pessimistic about the future" (Adler, 1931, p. 147).

Second-born children have the best of both worlds, with an older sibling to look up to and a younger one to look after—unless the first-born child is a girl and the second-born a boy, a family constellation that can trigger a form of masculine protest in both children.

But Adler observed that the youngest child in a family is at greatest risk:

> The reason for this generally lies in the way in which all the family spoils them. A spoiled child can never be independent. He loses courage to succeed by his own effort. Youngest children are always ambitious; but the most ambitious children of all are the lazy children. Laziness is a sign of ambition joined with discouragement; ambition so high that the individual sees no hope of realizing it. (Adler, 1931, p. 151)

Only children, in contrast, "are often very sweet and affectionate, and later in life they may develop charming manners in order to appeal to others, as they may train themselves in this way, both in early life and in later" (Adler, 1929, pp. 111–112). If you are one of these "sweet and affectionate" only children, don't get too cocky. Adler went on to say that only children often come to very bad ends because of all that superficial charm. His view was that the best results usually obtain when children are raised in large families.

A Therapy Based on Helping Others

Adlerian psychotherapy follows directly from the theory I have sketched here. Neurotics are perceived to be the victims of profound discouragement, generally as a result of pampering or neglect during the period in childhood when the prototype was being established. The therapeutic challenge is to find creative ways to open the patient's style of life to modification so that his or her social-interest motive is more likely to be awakened. In this way the person will discover more immediately the rewards of a life of service to others.

> When scrutinized, the neurotic will be found to be an individual placed in a test situation who is attempting to solve his problems in the interest of his own personal ambition rather than in the interest of the common welfare. (Adler, 1932, p. 91)

Adler usually asked his patients to begin therapy by relating to him the most memorable story, event, or dream of their childhood. He argued that the keys to the prototype and to the patient's unique sources of inferiority feelings would always be found in such early recollections. As therapy unfolded, often by analyzing the unconscious corrective suggestions embedded in dreams, Adler would guide the patient to explore the "goals, concepts, and notions" that colored, guided, and shaped her or his life.

Like a modern-day cognitive therapist (see Chapter 14) Adler engaged his patients in mental exercises to show them they could create whatever feelings they wished by constructing and reconstructing the "as if" world of every experience.

One Adlerian technique I've used many times in therapy is to ask the client to write out a "future autobiography," starting from today. (It is safe to assume that I've already heard a recounting of the past.) The client and I then go over the story to see what patterns of perception and motivation she plans to continue into the future, which old ones she plans to discard, and which new ones she imagines introducing. The future autobiography is therefore much like dream work, but in forward motion. Dreams solve the problems of the past; a future autobiography "solves" the problems of the future.

However therapy proceeds, the goal is to teach the person about the potential emotional and psychological rewards that come with awakening the social-interest motive. The patient generally needs to abandon a neurotic fixation, a complex of self-protective strategies that have been in place since early childhood. This task requires the patient to have an enormous amount of trust in both the therapist and the world.

The transference relationship—the powerful emotional connection between the client and the therapist—helps the client find the courage and encouragement to change and to face inferiority feelings head-on. If transference takes place, the client and the therapist can confront together what Adler called the three great problems of life. The client must find the courage to lay aside the selfishness manifest in her or his illness in order to embrace human responsibilities in

Occupation
Love and marriage
Society

Adler realized fully well, and often taught, that "cooperation requires courage." He also made his patients a promise: "You can be cured in 14 days if you follow this prescription: Try to think every day how you can please someone."

Adler's Enduring Influence on the Talking Cure

Adler's influence on the developing fields of psychology and social work was incalculable. Unfortunately, his influence on the development of the thinking of second-generation psychoanalysts (see Chapter 10) has never been recognized because of his apostasy from the psychoanalytic movement.

Adler was the first of the great psychoanalysts to arrive in the United States in the face of the escalating Nazi campaign against Jews in the 1930s. His work was well received in the New World and would eventually prove to be highly influential in the humanistic psychology movement, which is covered in Part III of this book.

The more psychologists learn about child development and the long-term consequences of infantile temperament, the more convincing Adler's speculations about style of life become. The more experience we gain with cognitive therapy, the more respect we have for Adler's recognition of the tremendous emotional consequences of his psychology of "as if." And the more appreciation we gain for the role of gender in shaping our lives, the more we recognize what a great prophet we had in the scrawny little merchant's son from Vienna.

My feeling is that Adler's ideas make the most sense after an immersion in the founding Enlightenment ideas of psychoanalysis. Although there is debate within psychodynamic circles about the necessity of abreaction (the release of pent-up affect associated with repressed memories; see Grünbaum, 1983), there is considerable agreement that psychoanalysis is at root a hermeneutic experience. That is, for many psychodynamic therapists, the "cure" comes in the understanding of self—the notion of self as text, which was mentioned in Chapter 7.

Adler, however, explicitly rejected the therapeutic encounter directed only toward a hermeneutic understanding of self, whether abreacted or contemplated in tranquility. For an Adlerian, no account of human life is complete without a consideration of fundamental human values. A contemporary psychologist, Hans Strupp (1980), although not identified as an Adlerian, wrote eloquently on this theme. Strupp called on psychologists to recognize the overwhelming importance of "essential values" communicated by the therapist in a therapeutic relationship. For Strupp, psychotherapy is incomplete without recognition that "the ideals of brotherly love and human relatedness . . . are coequal to knowledge (reason, truth, *logos*) and reduction of suffering" (p. 398).

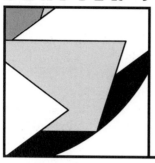

CHAPTER 9

Carl Jung's "Analytical Psychology"

The Marriage of the Sun and the Moon

The correspondence between Carl Jung and Sigmund Freud took place during the years both men were forming their theoretical and therapeutic orientations. The correspondence reveals how similar they were, as well as how profoundly they came to differ over time. The correspondence also tells us much about their relationship as colleagues and as friends. Eventually, these two great intellects and powerful personalities had a cataclysmic falling out over the issue of the spiritual core within the human psyche. But this break provided Jung the freedom to explore and to develop his own ideas about psychology and psychotherapy.

Jung developed what he called "analytical psychology" to differentiate it clearly from Freud's theory of psychoanalysis. Jung's theory is based on commonalities among the psychology of all peoples who have ever lived. Rituals and rites, myths and legends communicate the archetypal symbols and values of each society—and thus of all humankind. Jung's theory of opposites is very similar to many of the core ideas in Eastern philosophy and religion.

Jung's psychology is about the possibilities inherent in the human psyche to produce transformative change—from existence as a separate individual to the archetypal experience of the Universal. These are ideas common to Christianity, Buddhism, and many other religions.

The Freud/Jung Correspondence

Carl Jung (pronounced "Yung") maintained a 6-year correspondence (1906–1913) with his early mentor, Sigmund Freud. (The excerpts here are from Freud and Jung, 1974.) The letters document Jung's intellectual journey from early fascination with Freud's theory of the unconscious to his independence. The break between the two men was emotionally catastrophic. The substance of their differences involved Jung's fascination with the spiritual component of the human psyche, which Freud dismissed as Jung's "spook complex." At a personal level, Jung's relationship with Freud was probably doomed from the outset. What else could come of a collaboration between men of such genius who brought such a measure of passionate intensity to their friendship?

When we read these letters, we are reading the "official" intellectual and personal history of the relationship between Jung and Freud. Well-educated people of their era maintained active correspondences that they expected to be understood as a permanent record of their lives and associations. The correspondence thus gives us a revealing glimpse into the "adolescence" of the talking cure, as the emerging movement of psychoanalysis grew in fame and importance throughout Europe.

A Worthy Disciple

This was the first letter in the series, written to Jung by Freud:*

11 April 1906, Vienna
Dear Colleague,
Many thanks for sending me your *Diagnostic Association Studies,* which in my impatience I had already acquired. Of course your latest paper, "Psychoanalysis and Association Experiments," pleased me most, because in it you argue on the strength of your own experience that everything I have said about the hitherto unexplored fields of our discipline are true. I am confident that you will often be in a position to back me up, but I shall gladly also accept correction.

Yours Sincerely, *Dr. Freud*

5 October 1906, Zurich
Dear Professor Freud,
Please accept my sincere thanks for the present you kindly sent me. This collection of your various short papers should be most welcome to anyone who wishes to familiarize himself quickly and thoroughly with your mode of thought. It is to be hoped that your scientific following will continue to increase in the future in spite of the attacks which [the

---

*This and all following quotations from W. McGuire (Ed.), *The Freud/Jung Letters: The Correspondence between Sigmund Freud and C. G. Jung.* Copyright © 1974 by Princeton University Press. Reprinted by permission of Princeton University Press.

German neurologist] Aschaffenburg, amidst the plaudits of the pundits, has made on your theory—one might almost say on you personally. . . . What I can appreciate, and what has helped us here in our psychopathological work, are your psychological views, whereas I am still pretty far from understanding the therapy and the genesis of hysteria because our material on hysteria is rather meager. That is to say that your therapy seems to me to depend not merely on the affects released by abreaction but also on certain personal rapports, and it seems to me that though the genesis of hysteria is predominately, it is not exclusively sexual. I take the same view of your sexual theory. . . . I hope to send you soon a little book of mine, in which I approach demential praecox [schizophrenia] and its psychology from your standpoint. In it I have also published the case that first drew Bleuler's attention to the existence of your principles, though at the time with vigorous resistance on his part. But as you know, Bleuler is now completely converted. With many thanks,

Very truly yours, *C. G. Jung*

7 October 1906, Vienna
Dear Colleague,
Your letter gave me great pleasure. I am especially grateful to learn that you have converted Bleuler. Your writings have long led me to suspect that your appreciation of my psychology does not extend to all my views on hysteria and the problem of sexuality, but I venture to hope that in the course of the years you will come much closer to me than you now think possible. . . . [Y]ou more than anyone must know how consummately the sexual factor hides and, once discovered, how helpful it can be to our understanding and therapy. I continue to hope that this aspect of my investigations will prove to be the most significant.

. . . Like so many of our pundits [Aschaffenburg] is motivated chiefly by an inclination to repress sexuality, that troublesome factor so unwelcome in good society. Here we have two warring worlds and soon it will be obvious to all which is on the decline and which is ascendant. Even so I know I have a long struggle ahead of me, and in view of my age (50) I hardly expect to see the end of it. But my followers will, I hope, and I also venture to hope that all those who are able to overcome their own inner resistance to the truth will wish to count themselves among my followers and will cast of the last vestiges of pusillanimity in their thinking.

Yours very sincerely, *Dr. Freud*
PS My "transference" ought completely to fill the gap in the mechanism of cure (your "personal rapport").

23 October, 1906, Zurich
Dear Professor Freud,
By the same post I am taking the liberty of sending you another offprint containing some of my researches on psychoanalysis. I don't think you would find that the "sexual" standpoint I have adopted is too reserved. The critics will come down on it accordingly.

As you have noted, it is possible that my reservations about your far-reaching views are due to a lack of experience. But don't you think that a number of borderline phenomena might be considered more appropriately in terms of the other basic drive, *hunger:* for instance, eating, sucking (predominately hunger), kissing (predominately sexuality)? Two complexes existing at the same time are always bound to coalesce psychologically, so that one of them invariably contains constellated aspects of the other. Perhaps you mean no more than this; in that case I have misunderstood you and would be entirely of your opinion. Even so, however, one feels alarmed by the positivism of your presentation. . . . .

Very truly yours, *C. G. Jung*

27 October 1906, Vienna
Dear Colleague,
Many thanks for your new analysis. You certainly did not show too much reserve, and the "transference," the chief proof that the drive underlying the whole process is sexual in nature, seems to have become very clear to you. . . .

I have no theoretical objection to according equal importance to the other basic drive, if only it would assert itself unmistakably in the psychoneuroses. . . . I own that these are knotty questions that still require thorough investigation. For the present I content myself with pointing out what is glaringly evident, that is, the role of sexuality. . . .

I am glad to hear that your Russian girl [Jung's new patient] is a student; uneducated persons are at present too inaccessible for our purposes. . . . [Freud then explicated his recently published theory of anal eroticism and its link to certain combinations of character traits.] [Such people] are neat, stingy, and obstinate, traits which are in a manner of speaking the sublimations of anal eroticism. Cases like [the Russian student's are] based on repressed perversions [and] can be analyzed very satisfactorily. . . .

Sincerest regards

Yours, *Dr. Freud*

On March 3, 1907, nearly a year after the initial correspondence, Jung and his family traveled to Vienna for a week of socializing and intensive meetings. Jung attended one of the famous Wednesday evening sessions of Freud's psychoanalytic circle, and afterward Jung and Freud retired to Freud's study for their famous 13-hour meeting, which left both men emotionally exhausted but intellectually elated. Freud had finally found the one man with the intelligence, courage, vision, and drive to continue the psychoanalytic movement after the master himself had passed from the scene.

Later that month, Jung wrote Freud from Zurich to say that he was beginning to come around to Freud's view that masturbation is "the essence" of schizophrenia. But Jung continued to express concern that Freud's adamancy about his theory of sexuality was preventing Jung's colleagues in Switzerland from taking psychoanalysis seriously. Jung asked if Freud would be willing to find "a less offensive collective term" for "libidinal manifestations." He told Freud that he was going to begin a study to document the sexual "wish-dreams" of his schizophrenic patients, to show the world the data supporting Freud's theory. He assured Freud that, unlike others of Freud's followers, he was not just *jurat in verb magistri* ("swearing to the word of the master") but was rather an active scientific colleague. Jung concluded his letter with this confession:

> I am no longer plagued by doubts as to the rightness of your theory. The last shreds were dispelled by my stay in Vienna [and] I hope my work for your cause will show you the depths of my gratitude and veneration. . . . A visit from you would be seventh heaven for me personally; the few hours I was permitted to spend with you were all too fleeting. . . .
>
> Yours gratefully, *Jung*

The Jungs and the Freuds became as close as family over the next 2 years. The men visited each other as frequently as they could, vacationed together, and maintained a lively correspondence about the subject and the politics of psychoanalysis. The Jungs visited the Freuds in Vienna again in March 1909. The two men once again attended the Wednesday evening circle and again retired to Freud's study to continue their discussions.

The "Spook Complex"

Jung had finally decided to tell Freud about his lifelong interest in the paranormal. In Freud's study, Jung probably broached the subject by talking about how many of his schizophrenic patients suffered under the delusion of being possessed by devils and evil spirits. Jung brought the conversation around to parapsychology and to precognition and expressed his fascination with the metaphysics of all occult phenomena.

Freud became very upset. He demanded that Jung stop talking about "nonsense" immediately.

There was a silence, and then a loud sound like a pistol shot came from the bookshelves beside the two men's chairs.

> We both started up in alarm, fearing the [bookcase] was going to topple over on us. I said to Freud: "There, that is an example of a so-called catalytic exteriorization phenomenon."
>
> "Oh come," he exclaimed. "That is sheer bosh."
>
> "It is not, " I replied. "You are mistaken, Herr Professor. And to prove my point I now predict that in a moment there will be another such loud report!" Sure enough, no sooner had I said the words than the same detonation went off in the bookcase.
>
> To this day I do not know what gave me this certainty. But I knew beyond all doubt that the report would come again. Freud only stared at me. I do not know what was in his mind, or what his look meant. In any case this incident aroused his mistrust of me,

and I had the feeling that I had done something against him. I never afterward discussed the incident with him. (Jung, 1965, pp. 155–156)

For Freud, of course, the entire incident was most unsettling. He demanded that Jung stop his "spookery" at once. He said that he had been through this sort of thing with Wilhelm Fleiss (whose numerology had predicted Freud's early death, as you may remember), and he wouldn't put up with it from Jung.

On April 2, 1909, Jung wrote to Freud about the incident. He told Freud that he had talked over the entire affair with his wife (not something that would please Freud) and that, as a result,

I had the feeling that under it all there must be some quite special complex, a universal one having to do with the prospective tendencies in man. If there is a "psychanalysis" [sic] there must also be a "psychosynthesis" which creates future events according to the same laws. (I see I am writing rather as if I had a flight of ideas.)

Jung's Declaration of Independence

A "flight of ideas," indeed. Jung had just had his first brush with the insights that were to occupy him for the rest of his life. As if he unconsciously knew that he had to resolve his own oedipal relationship with his "papa" Freud before he could give birth to his own intellectual masterpiece, Jung continued in his letter to Freud:

That last evening with you has, most happily, freed me inwardly from the oppressive sense of your paternal authority. My unconscious celebrated this impression with a great dream which has preoccupied me for some days and which I have just finished analyzing. I hope I am now rid of all unnecessary encumbrances. Your cause must and will prosper, so my pregnancy fantasies tell me, which luckily you caught in the end.

16 April 1909
Dear Friend,
I hope this letter doesn't reach you for a while. I'm sure you see what I mean. I simply prefer to write now while the feelings aroused by your letter are still fresh. . . .

It is strange that on the very same evening when I formally adopted you as eldest son and anointed you—*in paribus infidelium* [in the lands of the unbelievers]—as my successor and crown prince, you should have divested me of my paternal dignity, which divesting seems to have given you as much pleasure as I, on the contrary, derived from the investiture of your person. Now I am afraid of falling back into the father role with you if I tell you about how I feel about the poltergeist business. . . . My credulity, or at least my willingness to believe, vanished with the magic of your personal presence; once again, for some inward reasons that I can't put my finger on, it strikes me as quite unlikely that such phenomena should exist; I confront the despiritualized furniture as the poet confronted undeified Nature after the gods of Greece had passed away. Accordingly, I put my fatherly horned-rimmed spectacles on again and warn my dear son to keep a cool head, for it is better not to understand something than make such great sacrifices to understanding. I also shake my wise head over psychosynthesis and think: Yes, that's how the young people are, the only places they really enjoy visiting are those they can visit without us, to which we with our short breath and weary legs cannot follow them. . . .

Consequently, I shall receive further news of your investigations of the spook complex with the interest one accords to a charming delusion in which one does not oneself participate.

With kind regards to you, your wife, and children.

Yours, *Freud*

With their father/son relationship cooling off, if not in fact becoming frosty, Freud and Jung resumed their correspondence. But their relationship was doomed by their intellectual and philosophical differences. At first they focused on their common "enemies," which resulted in Freud's orders on November 25, 1910, for Jung to "purge the Zurich Society" of dissenters, to "throw them out mercilessly." But this endeavor could not long distract them from their differences.

In November 1911, Emma Jung made several secret efforts to reconcile her husband with the "father *imago*," which actually Freud was to them both. She boldly attempted to psychoanalyze their differences as a case of Freud treating his "spiritual son" in the style he had adopted for dealing with his own children. Freud replied with great annoyance and asked Emma to keep her "amiable carpings" to herself.

Meanwhile Freud, "rather tired after battle and victory," had forced Alfred Adler and his associates to resign from the Psychoanalytic Society. Freud had begun devoting his efforts to establishing loyalty to the literal interpretation of his writings. And he was growing increasingly concerned about the directions that Jung's work was taking. On November 14, 1911, Freud reproached Jung for Jung's writings on the psychology of religion. Later Freud suggested that Jung's differences with him were the result of unresolved countertransference feelings aroused in Jung by work with his women patients.

By March 1912 Jung was becoming increasingly frustrated, as president of the Psychoanalytic Society, at having to clear every detail of his work with Freud. He quoted Friedrich Nietzsche's *Also Sprach Zarathustra* (*Thus Spake Zarathustra*):

One repays a teacher badly if one remains only a pupil.
And why, then, should you not pluck at my laurels?
You respect me; but how if one day your respect should tumble?
Take care that a falling statue does not strike you dead!
You had not yet sought yourselves when you found me.
Thus do all believers—.
Now I bid you lose me and find yourselves; and only when you have denied me will I
   return to you. (1961, p. 103)

Freud replied by asking Jung:

Do you think I am looking for someone else capable of being at once my friend, my helper and my heir, or that I expect to find another so soon? . . . Rest assured of my affective cathexis, and continue to think of me in friendship, even if you do not write often.

Heresy

In late summer 1912 Jung sailed for New York, where he had been invited to give a series of lectures at Fordham University. Although he titled the lectures "The Theory of Psychoanalysis," Jung made a great effort to distinguish his ideas about psychoanalysis from Freud's in these lectures and in several lengthy newspaper interviews. Jung's heresy was pointed at the very heart of Freud's psychoanalysis, as Jung later acknowledged:

When I was working on my book about the libido and approaching the end of the chapter "The Sacrifice," I knew in advance that its publication would cost me my friendship with Freud. For I planned to set down in it my own conception of incest, the decisive transformation of the concept of libido, and various other ideas in which I differed with Freud. To me incest signified a personal complication only in the rarest cases. Usually incest has a highly religious aspect, for which reason the incest theme plays a decisive part in almost all cosmologies and in numerous myths. But Freud clung to the literal interpretation of it and could not grasp the spiritual significance of incest as a symbol. I knew that he would never be able to accept any of my ideas on the subject.

. . . For two months I was unable to touch my pen, so tormented was I by the conflict. Should I keep my thoughts to myself, or should I risk the loss of so important a friendship? At last I resolved to go ahead with the writing—and it did indeed cost me Freud's friendship. (1965, p. 167)

Poor Freud! In early November 1912 he wrote to welcome his "son" home from the United States, telling him, "I am eagerly looking forward to an offprint of your [New York] lectures."

Jung by now knew the end was at hand. He wrote to Freud requesting an urgent meeting as soon as Jung could get to Vienna. But Freud had meanwhile written a letter (which has evidently been lost) expressing himself on the subject of Jung's heresy, a letter that Jung had to answer.

15 November 1912, Zurich

Dear Professor Freud,

Your letter, just arrived, has evoked in me a Psychoanalytic attitude which seems to me to be the only right one at the moment. I shall continue to go my own way undaunted. I shall take leave of [the society's] journal because I refuse to go on working with [it.] Only when granted freedom do people give of their best. We should not forget that the history of human truths, is also the history of human errors. So let us give the well-meant error its rightful place.

Whether my liberalism is compatible with the further conduct of the Association's affairs is a question to be discussed by the Association itself at the next Congress. [Was he planning another Adler-style "him or me" confrontation?]

Adler's letter [offering reconciliation between his new Society for Free Psychoanalysis and Freud's Viennese Psychoanalytic Society] is stupid chatter and can be safely ignored. We aren't children here. If Adler ever says anything sensible or worth listening to I shall take note of it, even though I don't think much of him as a person. As in my work heretofore, so now and in the future I shall keep away from petty complexes and do unflinchingly what I hold to be true and right.

With best regards,

Most sincerely yours, *Jung*

If Jung had expected Freud to be the one who would turn their estrangement into silence, he was disappointed. Freud reacted to Jung's letter with great personal anguish, even collapsing at a meeting in Munich when Jung's name was mentioned in passing. But he wrote only encouraging letters back to Jung, obviously hoping Jung would retract sufficiently to allow them to discuss their differences.

An Oedipal Drama

Jung either couldn't or wouldn't compromise. He sent Freud what Jung called a "secret letter":

18 December 1912, Zurich

Dear Professor Freud,

May I say a few words to you in earnest? I admit the ambivalence of my feelings towards you, but am inclined to take an honest and absolutely straight forward view of the situation. If you doubt my word, so much the worse for you. I would, however, point out that your technique of treating your pupils like patients is a *blunder*. In that way you produce either slavish sons or impudent puppies (Adler-Stekel and the whole insolent gang now throwing their weight about in Vienna). I am objective enough to see through your little trick. You go around sniffing out all the symptomatic actions in your vicinity, thus reducing everyone to the level of sons and daughters who blushingly admit the existence of their faults. Meanwhile you remain on top as the father, sitting pretty. For sheer obsequiousness nobody dares to pluck the prophet by the beard and inquire for once what you would say to a patient with a tendency to analyze the analyst instead of himself. You would ask him: *"Who's* got the neurosis?"

You see, my dear Professor, so long as you hand out this stuff I don't give a damn about my symptomatic actions; they shrink to nothing in comparison with the formidable beam in my brother Freud's eye. I am not in the least neurotic—touch wood! I have submitted *lege artis et tout humblement* to analysis and am much the better for it. You know, of course, how far a patient gets with self-analysis: *not* out of his neurosis—just like you. If ever you should rid yourself entirely of your complexes and stop playing the father to your sons and instead of aiming continually at their weak spots take a good look at your own for a change, then I will mend my ways and at one stroke uproot the vice of being in two minds about you. Do you *love neurotics* enough to be always at one with yourself? But perhaps you *hate* neurotics. In that case how can you expect your efforts to treat your patients leniently and lovingly *not* to be accompanied by somewhat mixed feelings? Adler and Stekel were taken in by your little tricks and reacted with childish insolence. I shall continue to stand by you publicly while maintaining my own views, but privately shall start telling you in my letters what I really think of you. I consider this procedure only decent.

No doubt you will be outraged by this peculiar token of friendship, but it may do you good all the same.

With best regards,

Most sincerely yours, *Jung*

Freud could no longer avoid the inevitable.

3 January 1912, Vienna
Dear Mr. President,
Dear Doctor,
[The letter begins by covering some business matters of the International Psychoanalytic Association.]

Otherwise your letter can not be answered. It creates a situation that would be difficult to deal with in a personal talk and totally impossible in correspondence. It is a convention among us analysts that none of us need feel ashamed of his own bit of neurosis. But one while behaving abnormally keeps shouting that he is normal gives ground for the suspicion that he lacks insight into his illness. Accordingly, I propose that we abandon our personal relations entirely. I shall lose nothing by it, for my only emotional tie with you has long been a thin thread—the lingering effect of past disappointments—and you have everything to gain, in view of the remark you recently made in Munich, to the effect that an intimate relationship with a man inhibited your scientific freedom. I therefore say, take your full freedom and spare me your supposed "tokens of friendship." . . .

Regards,

Yours sincerely, *Freud*

6 January 1913, Zurich
Dear Professor Freud,
I accede to your wish that we abandon our personal relations, for I never thrust my friendship on anyone. You yourself are the best judge of what this moment means to you. "The rest is silence."

Yours sincerely, *Jung*

These were the last letters the two men exchanged.

Origins of Analytical Psychology

Carl Gustaf Jung (1875–1961) went on to create a brilliant and radically different school of psychoanalysis, called analytical psychology to distinguish it from his predecessor's psychoanalytic psychology. The origins of this new theory, which differed from Freud's even in its earliest stages (as can be clearly seen in the first letters in their correspondence), lay in the depths of Jung's unconscious mind, in his early research into spiritualism, and in his careful observations of his schizophrenic patients.

Freud had discovered that he could unlock the secrets of his own unconscious mind by uncovering the hidden and forgotten meanings of his dreams. Between 1897 and 1899 he was deeply involved in what was the world's first psychoanalysis—his self-psychoanalysis. Freud wrote that he had been required to summon great courage to become the archaeologist of his own mind. But he, unlike Jung, had not had to confront his own madness in the process.

A terrible pressure built up inside Jung's psyche during the final months of his relationship with Freud. I believe the pressure of the barely contained energy that in his New York lectures Jung had called libido finally compelled Jung to write that extraordinary December 18, 1912, letter to Freud. Jung's desperate, compelling need to explore the full depths and context of his unconscious mind was, I believe, held in check only by his formal obligations to Freud, to the psychoanalytic movement, and to exploration of the sexual aspects of neuroses.

Jung's break with Freud was motivated by powerful emotional conflicts with deeply unconscious roots in the psyches of both men. The sad irony is that the "son," Jung, severed the relationship with the "father," which was for Freud the ultimate act of oedipal betrayal. Freud carried the emotional wound that Jung had inflicted for the rest of his life. I am sure, however, that if Freud were reading this over my shoulder, he would hasten to point out that although Oedipus murdered his father, the tragedy was that Oedipus spent the rest of his life blinded by the consequences of the deed.

With Jung's explosive release—the symbolic, abreactive "killing of the father-imago"—Jung plunged into a 5-year confrontation with his unconscious, with madness, with his own soul, and ultimately with God. Or perhaps he just went insane. Whether you accept the antivitalist insanity interpretation or the vastly more poetic and Romantic notion of an individual's redemptive journey into hell, there is little room to doubt the power and brilliance of the theory that emerged from this tumultuous period of Jung's life.

An Unlikely Family History

Jung's background differed in several important respects from that of the other early members of Freud's circle. The most notable difference may have been financial; Jung came from a patrician upper-middle-class family. Jung was Swiss; Josef Breuer, Freud, Adler, and practically all the others were Austrian. And nothing in Jung's early experience or in his later life led him to adopt the sorts of antivitalist loyalties that were deeply shared by virtually all Freud's closest circle.

Jung was also the first Christian "convert" to psychoanalysis, which at that time was becoming widely known in Germany as a "Jewish psychology." In fact, in their early correspondence Freud wrote that the reason a point in his theory eluded Jung was that Jung did not have Freud's background in Jewish mysticism. (The connection between psychoanalytic theory and Jewish mysticism has received attention from several contemporary scholars—for example, Bakan, 1958/1990; Halligan & Shea, 1992; Kakar, 1991; and Parsons, 1993.) What Freud may not have known about his young disciple is that Jung had grown up in a very religious family with its own mystical religious tradition. A Latin phrase attributed to the 15th-century Dutch theologian-philosopher Erasmus, *Vocatus atque no vocus deus aderit* ("invoked or not invoked, the god will be present"), was such an important principle in Jung's life that he had it carved in stone over the front door of his house (Alexander & Selesnick, 1966, p. 235).

Jung's family background was also quite different from Freud's or Adler's. In fact, it was probably his family background that gave Jung the unique view of the psyche that colored every aspect of his analytical writings. Although Jung's family were all fairly conventional Swiss Reformed Church Protestants, there was a strong tradition of Romantic mysticism and even spiritualism on both sides of his family of birth.

Father's Side of the Family. As a young man, Jung's paternal grandfather was part of a large circle of young literary and political radicals in the circle of the Romantic poet Johann Goethe. In fact, Goethe was rumored to have been Carl Jung's great-grandfather, an assertion that has not been verified. In any case, Carl's grandfather became a physician and a professor. Widowed at an early age, he took as a second wife a young tavern waitress after a proposal of marriage to a proper lady of the town was rejected. When his second wife died, he married a third time. He eventually fathered 13 children, the youngest of whom would become Carl Jung's father.

Grandfather Jung was described by everyone who knew him as a man of irresistible charm. He devoted his later life to the causes of Freemasonry and the residential care of retarded children. Contemporary accounts of his passing remarked on the death of "a legend in his own time," according to Ellenberger (1970). Grandfather Jung, in Adlerian terms, surely had much to do with the "concerned physician" prototype the grandson adopted in his choice to become a physician and to work with the mentally ill.

Grandfather Jung's youngest child, Carl's father, inherited much of his father's Romantic charm but none of the family wealth. He is described by historians as an impractical dreamer who was suited for little but the life of a village parson. Everyone described him as quiet, unassuming, and perhaps even a little boring. Nevertheless, he was considered an "inspired preacher to peasants." But he evidently was plagued by religious doubts most of his life. His distinct preference for pondering himself instead of the big questions of theology and life were to have a major impact on the personality and interests of his first-born child, Carl.

Mother's Side of the Family. Carl Jung's mother was descended from a long line of strong-willed, interesting, but decidedly eccentric folks. She was, like her husband, also the youngest of the 13 children in her family. Her father, Samuel Preiswerk, was a distinguished theologian, Zionist, and Protestant minister.

As was the case with Grandfather Jung, the Reverend Preiswerk's much-beloved first wife died at an early age. The Reverend Preiswerk's second marriage was not to a barmaid, however, but to a woman who possessed the gift of second sight and other spiritualist endowments. This union evidently caused some bad karma in the spirit world, because Grandfather Preiswerk always insisted that his little daughter Emilie sit behind him while he wrote his sermons so that the jealous spirit of his deceased first wife would not interfere.

Emilie was to become Carl Jung's mother. She was described by townspeople as "fat, ugly, authoritarian, and haughty" (Ellenberger, 1970, p. 662). That, at least, was the way she appeared by day. When Jung remembered his childhood, he remembered that at twilight a second personality would emerge in his mother:

> There was an enormous difference between my mother's two personalities. That was why as a child I often had anxiety dreams about her. By day she was a loving mother, but at night she seemed uncanny. Then she was like one of those seers who is at the same time a strange animal, like a priestess in a bear's cave. Archaic and ruthless; ruthless as truth and nature. At such moments she was the embodiment of what I have called "natural mind." (1965, p. 50)

From this experience Jung first got the idea of the essential duality of the psyche, the fundamental law of opposites that Jung came to believe was common to all people.

Cousin Helene. Young Carl entered medical school at the University of Basel in 1895. He pursued largely literary interests in Schopenhauer (see the introductory quote in Chapter 7) and Nietzsche, the semimystical writings of Emanuel Swedenborg (who also fascinated William James's father—see Chapter 11), as well as the psychiatric writings of Franz Anton Mesmer (see Chapter 3). To earn his medical degree, Jung conducted research using one of his cousins as a subject. She was another of Samuel Preiswerk's grandchildren, the 15-year-old Helene Preiswerk.

Cousin Helene became Jung's Anna O., the prototypical case containing almost all the elements that would later be fit together to make up his finished theory.

> According to Jung's account, the young lady first experimented with turning tables, in July 1899, and at the beginning of August she began to manifest mediumistic somnambulism. She first incarnated the spirit of her grandfather Samuel Preiswerk, and witnesses

admired how accurately she reproduced his pastoral tone, although she had never known him. . . . Helene also personified a number of deceased members of her family and acquaintances, and displayed a remarkable talent for acting. It was surprising how during these sessions she spoke perfect High German instead of her customary Basel dialect. It was not clear to what extent she remembered what she had said during her somnambulic state when the sessions were over, but she always maintained that it was truly the spirits of the dead who spoke through her mouth. She attracted respect and admiration from several relatives and friends who would come to ask her for advice. About one month later she fell into semi-somnambulic states, in which she remained aware of her surroundings but kept a close communication with spirits. In that condition she said her name was Ivenes, spoke in a quiet, dignified tone, and showed no trace of her usual unstable and giddy character. (Ellenberger, 1970, p. 689)*

In September Helene, or Ivenes, reportedly "magnetized" herself and talked in a made-up language of Italian and French:

Ivenes said that she journeyed to the planet Mars, saw its canals and flying machines, and visited the inhabitants of the stars and the spirit world. She was instructed by clear spirits and she herself instructed black spirits. The controlling spirit remained that of her grandfather, Reverend Samuel Preiswerk, with his edifying speeches. Other spirits could be classified into two groups. Some were rather dour and others exuberant . . . characteristics [which] corresponded with the two aspects of the young medium's personality, between which she constantly oscillated. These personifications were gradually replaced by revelations. The medium poured out an extraordinary abundance of details about her own previous lives. She had been the Seeress of Prevorst, and before that a young woman seduced by Goethe—and this allegedly made her Jung's great-grandmother. In the fifteenth century she had been the Countess of Thierfelesenburg, in the thirteenth century she had been Madame de Velours, who had been burned as a witch, and earlier still a Christian martyr under Nero in Rome. . . .

In March 1900 she began to describe the structure of the mystic world with the aid of seven circles: the primary force in the central circle, matter in the second, light and darkness in the third, and so on. Once these revelations were exhausted it seemed that the medium's inspiration declined. [But] six months later she showed her audience "apports," that is, objects allegedly brought to the sessions by spirits. (Ellenberger, 1970, pp. 689–690)

Unfortunately, Helene's grasp had exceeded her reach, and it was discovered that the objects she had caused to be materialized had actually appeared with the considerable real-world assistance of the household servants. A system of wires linked various objects hidden about the room to the medium's table.

Helene quickly lost interest in the whole episode and was sent to Paris by her concerned family so she could learn the art of dressmaking. In later life she reportedly had no memory of any of the events that occurred during her strange adolescent interlude. She became an accomplished dressmaker in Basel but died of tuberculosis while still very young.

I confess that I am attracted to this story because of an ancient scandal in my own family. As a child I had an elderly aunt whose husband had amassed a fortune in antiques and art from the East India trade in the "old days." My first memory of Aunt Elizabeth was when she and Uncle Robert arrived at our house one day unannounced. Aunt Elizabeth asked each of the children to kiss our Uncle Robert goodbye. We asked where the kindly old gent was going, and Aunt Elizabeth replied, "The spirit world is calling him home." Uncle Robert looked perfectly fine to us kids, but we all dutifully kissed him goodbye. The next thing I knew, Uncle Robert was dead—buried in a solid teak casket with gold fittings, according to family legend.

The scandalous thing was that, over the next 5 years, operating on instructions from Uncle Robert's spirit—brought to her through a young and, the family added, "slick" Boston medium—Aunt Elizabeth gave away every possession of value and sold her home for a dollar to the young medium's spiritualist group. In the process, the spirit also commanded that I be given some Indian arrowheads that Uncle Robert had found in his garden. This gift from the spirit kingdom probably explains why I am to this day less alarmed about reports of activity in the spirit world than are many of my less well-endowed colleagues.

Scientific Study of the Human Soul

Jung began his work as a physician at the prestigious Burgholzli sanitarium in December 1900, largely on the basis of the high praise lavished on his dissertation research, whose subject was his cousin Helene/Ivenes. You may recall that this was the famed institution to which Anna O. had been taken after the failure of Josef Breuer's hypnotic treatments. The chief physician at the sanitarium when Jung arrived was Eugen Bleuler, the world's greatest expert on schizophrenia and a staunch advocate of what I described in Chapter 2 as moral therapy. However, Bleuler insisted that it was not a kind of therapy but simply humane respect for human life. It is also interesting to note that in 1902 Jung spent a sabbatical leave in Paris studying the therapeutics associated with hypnosis. His teacher was none other than Pierre Janet, whom we last encountered in Chapter 4.

Bleuler and Jung shared an intense interest in research into the nature of madness. Freud considered the great Bleuler an important early "convert" to psychoanalysis, but Bleuler proved only marginally interested in Freud's sexual etiology hypothesis of mental illness. Bleuler doubted that it would generalize to patients with problems other than hysterical neuroses. When Bleuler resisted too firmly, the result was Freud's order to "purge the ranks" in his November 1910 letter to Jung.

To his credit, Bleuler gave Jung free rein to conduct his mental association experiments with the sanitarium's schizophrenic patients. Jung undertook these studies with the stated ambition to establish a psychology based on "the scientific study of the human soul." He regarded all the productions or manifestations of the broken minds of the truly insane as the fundamental "psychological reality" of their mental life.

Jung came to understand that all the bizarre manifestations of personality shown in the behavior and especially in the hallucinations and drawings of schizophrenics were to be taken as "the split-off contents of the unconscious" mind. He also recognized that these "elements of mind" were commonly manifested in the split-off personalities of multiple-personality patients. Today we recognize that multiple-personality disorder and schizophrenia are completely different, but in Jung's time they were lumped together as dementia praecox.

A Question of Motives. Psychotherapy with a Jungian analyst has few completely distinctive features. Employing free association and dream analysis, working closely with memory fragments, and trying to discover the symbolic significance of seemingly random life events—the hallmarks of Jungian analysis—are also common features of virtually all psychoanalysis. In Jungian therapy the relationship between the analyst and the patient is less rigidly defined than it is with a Freudian analyst, but it is still a formal encounter between a patient and a healer. The differences between Freudian and Jungian analysis are profound, however, in terms of what is presumed to be happening over the course of therapy and what fundamental motives are assumed to be moving the therapy along.

Recall that for Freud dreams and associations lead back to some sort of psychic trauma. By abreacting this trauma within the context of the therapeutic "transference" relationship, the energies bound up in keeping the memory safely repressed are released—and with them the force binding the neurotic symptoms together. The patient leaves therapy when the force that has brought her or him there is dissipated. Unless the here-and-now environment triggers another psychic episode, the patient lives life no more troubled than anyone else in society.

This Freudian approach has a curious mixture of scholarly and curative motives. The psychotherapy patient becomes a scholar of the self. This person, over time, comes to accept and live with the truth about his or her existence, and this truth comes to be understood as the substance of true human freedom. Conscious awareness of the truth of one's own experience is the essence of the cure. Achieving an ability to know, comprehend, and live with the truth permits one to more satisfactorily discharge the demands of the biological (sexual and aggressive) drives.

From an Adlerian perspective, the scholarly motive is of minimal importance. What is central is the ethical motive. Adler perceived that human beings fundamentally long for power but with appropriate guidance can transform that longing into the quest for perfection. In Adlerian psychotherapy, the equivalent of discovering the truth about oneself is correcting one's selfish and infantile, neurotic lifestyle. By becoming more ethical, in Adler's system, you are "cured."

In Jungian psychotherapy, the ethical and scholarly motives are foremost; the curative motive is deemphasized. Was Cousin Helene "sick"? Was my Aunt Elizabeth mentally ill for giving away her fortune and treasures? From a Jungian perspective, I think not. Freud described human beings as "polymorphously perverse." I think Jung would have said that human beings are "polymorphously creative." The difference is essential. Both Freud and Jung were scholars of the human condition. But Freud was a scholar of the sick and perverse; Jung was a scholar of the spiritual and transcendent. Jung perceived human beings as constantly striving, very much as Freud and Adler had. Jung, however, uniquely perceived that we strive primarily toward wholeness, integration, the supreme self-knowledge that allows us to resolve our own fate.

Vitalism Revisited. Are you patiently waiting to get away from all this conjecture about the unconscious and the "deep" meaning of things? If so, you will be happy to know that we will soon get to some good, old-fashioned behaviorism. But perhaps you are being won over, ever so gradually, by some of these psychoanalysts.

If you haven't been scared off by Jung's vitalism, are you ready for psychology to become the "science of the human soul"? Do you have the sense of wonder and tolerance for the unknown and the unknowable that is required of one who seeks to become a student of the metaphysical? Or are you willing to leave all metaphysical inquiry in the hands of the churches, the priests, and the holy people of the world?

"Whoever wishes to know about the human mind will learn, nothing, or almost nothing, from experimental psychology," said Jung (1912/1972, p. 244). If you fancy that you can somehow escape the psychic realities of the metaphysical by hiding in the rat laboratory or measuring attitude change in a social psychology experiment, "if," in Jung's words, "you fancy that nothing metaphysical ever happens to you, you forget one metaphysical happening: your own death" (1897, quoted in Ellenberger, 1970, p. 688).

The Psychology of Archetypes

As is psychoanalytic theory, Jung's theory is based on the demands and the transformations of human energy systems. When Jung gave his New York lectures, he retained the Freudian term *libido* to refer to that energy. Jung totally transformed the meaning of that term, however. Libido, according to Jung, always appears in crystallized, coherent form. Those forms are what Jung called *archetypes*, universal human symbols passed in the DNA from one generation to the next, from the earliest forms of organic life to the child being born at this very minute. Every human being possesses an intuitive, instinctive knowledge of these archetypes.

This unconscious knowledge of the immaterial, the transcendent, and the sacred is revealed in dreams, myths, and sacred rituals. This knowledge is outside the boundaries of time and space; it is eternal and limitless. This knowledge is the essence of the human soul.

Jung's Concept of Libido. In its raw, unconcealed, and untutored form, libido is visible in the ravings and hallucinations of the insane. An insane person is one who has lost the ability to reintegrate libido into ordinary consciousness.

A person's "nosological type," according to Jung, could be assessed by observing the direction of the flow of that person's libido. An *introvert* withdraws his or her libido from the world and appears apathetic to the outside observer. When this withdrawal from the world becomes extreme, the person appears out of touch with reality and "in a world of his or her own." Persons with schizophrenia represent an extreme of the introverted type. Hysterics, on the other hand, represent the extreme of people who have "lost themselves." An *extrovert* can be seen to have an "exaggerated emotivity." The only pleasure such as person seems able to grasp is that derived from outside the person.

Jung first aired these views at the 1913 meeting of the International Psychoanalytic Association in Munich, at which he was reelected as president:

> These two opposite directions of libidinal flow were assumed to be psychic mechanisms encountered in normal persons as well as in mental patients; . . . they also appear as in the differences between various schools of psychoanalysis. Jung considered Freud's insistence on "empirical facts" [Freud's positivism and antivitalism] and on the concept of the libido gaining pleasure from the environment as an expression of Freud's extroverted attitude. Adler, on the other hand, who emphasized the internal guiding fictions, was expressing his own exaggerated introverted tendencies. In the concluding sentence of the paper Jung spoke of his own plans for elaborating a *balanced analytical psychology* *"which would pay equal attention to the two types of mentality."* (Alexander & Selesnick, 1966, p. 243)

By then Jung knew that his association with Freud, and with his fellow psychoanalysts, was tenuous. Perhaps the introversion/extroversion theory was part of the intellectual process Jung went through to separate himself from Freud and his movement.

The Collective Unconscious. The part of Jung's libido theory that has received the most attention over the years is his assertion that libido is universally apparent and universally shared among all humans. The prime example is the existence of the concept of "God" in all cultures and all times. As Jung said, "If I didn't know that God exists, I would surely have to invent Him." Or as Epictetus said: "I am a rational being, and I therefore have to praise God. That is my calling and I follow it." Knowledge of "God" can be interpreted as a universal human instinct that lies deep within the psyche.

Jung called the region of mind that contains this universal source of mental energy the *collective unconscious*. Specific manifestations of the collective unconscious are influenced by culture. Thus the actual image that appears in a dream or in a myth derives its form from the dreamer's or the storyteller's conscious experience. But the essence of the form has been determined by the human gene pool.

I recently came across a detailed study of Canadian folklore based on one of the Old Woman archetypes. This archetype evidently goes back hundreds of years and has even found its way into some Christian rituals in remote sections of Newfoundland. Let me give you a taste of it in the hope that it will encourage you to think further about archetypal images in your own life. The report is in the words of a 62-year-old woman who had lived in Newfoundland all her life:

Yes, the people . . . did speak of having nightmares. Usually they said "I was hagged last night." To my knowledge this was experienced most often in the nighttime, in the person's home and it always came in human form.

I saw only one actual person who experienced the hag. It was the year 1915 and it concerns three people: Robert ——, John——, and Jean ——. Robert was the Salvation Army school teacher and John was just an ordinary workman.

Whatever your personal picture of God, of "grandmother," or of the Evil One may be, which is to say that whatever exact form the crystallized libido takes in your unconscious mind, it is the same instinct and powered by the same energy as the god/grandmother/devil in the mind of an Ogala Sioux or in the dreams of one of Pharaoh's slaves. Robert was trying to date Jean who was John's steady girlfriend. About a month after this had been going on Robert began to be hagged. Every night when he went to bed, it was as if someone was pressing across his chest—it was as if he was being strangled. Robert became so sick that the people he boarded with thought he was going to die. But one night an old man suggested that Robert place a piece of board directly across his chest with an opened up pocket knife held between his hands. It was hoped that when the hag came to lie across his chest, the hag would be killed. However, in the morning when Robert got up he found that the knife was sticking into the piece of board. Only for the board Robert would have been killed. Perhaps because the hag thought he [*sic*] had killed Robert that it never came back again. Robert knew that John was the person who was hagging him. He put it down to jealousy on John's part. Both men were about the same age, between eighteen and twenty years old. In this case of hagging it was male against male.

Robert told the people that he stayed with the hag was human—he could hear it coming and could recognize it but when it came he couldn't speak—he could only make throaty noises. The hag just walked in or appeared while Robert was sleeping but he woke up while he was being hagged. Robert said that he was always lying on his back and usually he was under stress. The hag was brought about by a curse. It always affected his throat most and took his breath away.

The way to call a hag, Robert later learned, was to say the Lord's Prayer backwards in the name of the devil. The only way to avoid the hag was by drawing blood or using the word of God and keeping the light on in the bedroom. Although Robert was hagged he always spoke freely about the whole thing whenever anyone asked him. (Hufford, 1982, pp. 3–4)

Dozens more accounts of the Old Hag and hagging are documented in David Hufford's book, *The Terror That Comes in the Night* (1982). Most remarkable, from a Jungian perspective, is that the Old Hag appears in the folk stories of other groups of people all along the Atlantic coast of North America. The tradition of the Old Hag is still current among some members of isolated communities of African Americans in out-of-the-way corners and on some of the small islands off the Carolinas. For those of you with an empiricist bent, Hufford's book is full of data tables documenting (in excellent Jungian fashion, although Jung receives only passing mention in a footnote in *The Terror That Comes in the Night*) the characteristics of the Old Hag and those who have encountered her.

The Power of Symbols. Jung's theory states that humans are utterly dependent on symbols to transform psychic energy (libido) into constructs with value and meaning. Established religions draw much of their power from their proprietary interest in these symbols. The Catholic Mass, according to Jung, is a celebration of a psychological and psychic union with God—precisely because the Mass orchestrates dozens if not hundreds of the most powerful and therefore most sacred symbols recognized by human beings:

> From a psychological point of view [the Mass] can be translated as follows: Christ lived a concrete, personal, and unique life which, in all its essential features, had at the same time an archetypal character. This character can be recognized from the numerous connections of the biographical details with worldwide myth-motifs. . . . Since the life of Christ is archetypal to a high degree, it represents to just that degree the life of the archetype. But since the archetype is the unconscious precondition for every human life, its life, when revealed, also reveals the hidden, unconscious ground-life of every individual. That is to say, what happens in the life of Christ happens always and everywhere. In the Christian archetype all lives of this kind are prefigured and are expressed over and over again for once and for all. And in it, too, the question that concerns us here of God's death is anticipated in perfect form. Christ himself is the typical dying and self-transforming God. (Jung, 1983, pp. 247–248)

Even if you aren't Catholic (or Christian), you may accept the belief that you possess a soul. The idea of the soul is itself an archetype when considered from a Jungian perspective. What you think about as or have learned to call your soul is, in actuality, your culture's verbal convention for referring to an idea about your existence that is universally human. The religious or spiritual practices you may associate with tending to your soul are ways your culture has derived to pass this archetypal knowledge along to its members. In Jung's view, your awareness of that part of your existence you call your soul is one of the *transforming archetypes,* a mental instinct or a crystallization of libido that links you to all other human beings, to the cosmos, and ultimately to God.

If this line of thought is a little hard to grasp all at once, take heart. It's possible that it is simply an elaborately rich delusion and not worth your mental energies. On the other hand, maybe it does begin to explain something profound within each of us. My students tend to split right down the middle on this issue.

You can read hundreds of fascinating books on the collective unconscious, and you could spend the rest of your life trying to comprehend it. I suggest Robert Pirsig's *Zen and the Art of Motorcycle Maintenance* (1974) as a starting point. Pirsig takes you on a Jungian voyage, a voyage between reality and insanity, the sacred and the profane. It's an awesome trip. It is entirely possible, however, to understand the complexity (but perhaps not the wonder) in Jung's system without ever buying into the collective unconscious and "the psychology of the soul." But these ideas are worth a ponder, when you get some time.

A Caution: Flirting With Fascism. It is appropriate at this point to offer a serious caution about Jungian analysis. It is true that "on the whole Jung's psychology has found more followers among speculative philosophers, poets, and religionists than in medical psychiatry" (Alexander & Selesnick, 1966, p. 244). But his views have also been attractive, for a variety of reasons, to fascists. In the 1930s and 1940s, Jung's theory was used by the Nazi Party to provide "scientific" evidence for the superiority of the Aryan race. Early in the 1930s, Jung became a Nazi sympathizer and even accepted the presidency of the Nazi New German Society of Psychotherapy.

Alexander and Selesnick (1966) speculated that Jung was motivated by opportunism more than racism and National Socialism, but Jung did claim that his psychology revealed the inferiority of "Jewish theory." He branded both Freud and Adler, as well as their followers, "not only sinfully stupid but criminal" (p. 408).

Jung's "racial" view of the unconscious permitted him to attack on fraudulently "scientific" grounds a "genetically inferior Jewish race," which is "capable quite consciously even in the most friendly and tolerant environment to indulge in their own vices [a wicked piece of race-baiting based on Nazi propaganda about alleged Judaic religious practices]" (p. 408). What may be even more bizarre is that Jung explicitly linked Jews with women in their inherent inferiority and tendency toward amoral treachery. He then attacked psychoanalysis in particular as a "Jewish psychology," which he described as a "soulless materialistic movement" dedicated to "treat[ing patients] reductively, and attribut[ing] to them ulterior motives and to suspect behind their natural purity an unnatural dirt" (p. 409). Jung meanwhile extolled the psychic characteristic of his fascist German benefactors, proclaiming them to be a youthfully barbaric race of intuitive geniuses.

After the German defeat in 1944, there was some talk of putting Jung on trial as a war criminal. Eventually the Allies were persuaded that Jung had abandoned his fascist teachings and had retreated to his native neutral Switzerland before the Nazi campaign of genocide.

I point all this out to you to encourage you to think carefully about the notions of "race" and "genetics" embedded in Jung's theory. The wonderful brilliance and creativity manifested in Jung's writing, or in any writing for that matter, should not cause us to accept uncritically ideas with powerful potential for supporting the evils of racism.

Analytical Psychotherapy

Now, as Freud might have said, I shall reveal to you the workings of Jung's "analytical psychotherapy." Kaufmann (1989) summarized analytical psychotherapy as "an attempt to create, by means of a symbolic approach, a dialectical relationship between consciousness and the unconscious" (p. 119). *Symbolic approach* means that the analysis examines dreams, fantasies, drawings, religious phenomena, hallucinations, sculpture, myths, and early memories. *Dialectical relationship* means a creative, meaningful, logical link. And the term *unconscious* refers both to the individual psyche and to the collective unconscious.

Jungian analysis, therefore, involves the revelation to conscious awareness the content and meaning of the unconscious, through the interpretation of symbolic products of the unconscious mind.

Kaufmann added: "The psyche is seen as a self-regulating system whose function is purposive, with an internally imposed direction toward a life of fuller awareness" (p. 119). In fact, in Jung's scheme, all human behavior is both purposive and prospective—that is, directed toward the future. Thus his form of psychotherapy has, as did Adler's, a teleological component. But the purpose of the dialogue between consciousness and unconsciousness is distinctively Jungian, "a life of fuller awareness."

Levels of Human Awareness

In Jungian therapy, the development of genuine awareness is progressive, occurring in five sequential stages. Some writers have described it as the "onion" model: Unraveling the realities of the psyche is like dissecting an onion, one layer at a time. This is an acceptable way to think about the next few pages, but it is seriously flawed in one respect. When you have finished dissecting an onion, you discover that each layer was just like every other layer. And when you get to the nucleus of an onion, there's nothing left. In contrast, in analytic psychotherapy each layer is symmetric with, but very different from, every other layer. When you get to the center you find . . . I want to say you find God, but that is probably misleading. So let's say that you encounter the eternal or the divine.

Instead of thinking of it as an onion, I much prefer thinking of analytical psychotherapy as somewhat like a Native American vision quest, a journey of self-exploration in search of the truth that will give life its direction, meaning, and significance.

Level One: The Problem of the Persona. At the outermost layer of our experience we project to the world (and to ourselves) a complex array of masks. These masks are the social roles we play, the "me" that is in various relationships, the quirks and bumps of our ways of relating to the world—the outward manifestations of our "personality." Probably 75% of the therapy that takes place in the college counseling service I work in revolves around problems of persona.

We all, to one degree or another, live with the paradoxical feeling that we are not really what we seem to be. How many of us feel that our best friends, spouse or lover, parents, and colleagues really know the person we are inside? For that matter, how many of us really know ourselves? How often do we take off the "mask" of social convention without immediately putting on a second or a third mask in exchange?

Resolution of who we truly are as individuals requires establishing our ethical significance through a process of self-discovery and self-examination. This process is accomplished by establishing a continuous and unimpeded flow of perception between inner and outer reality, by becoming more genuine in our relationships with others and thus with ourselves. Jung, perhaps more for the sake of appearing conciliatory than as a genuine piece of serious advice, told a prospective patient that spending some time in Adlerian psychotherapy would be an excellent way to accomplish the necessary life tasks at this stage.

If you don't resolve the challenge presented by your persona, you cannot move to the next stage. Jung had several techniques for getting patients "unstuck." He once invited one of his patients, a distinguished military leader, to dine with him before their session. When the general arrived, he found that the table had been set with a simple meal consisting of the basic rations that would be served a raw recruit in the Prussian army. On another occasion Jung reportedly sent a very noble and arrogant lady to his kitchen to help the maids clean the luncheon dishes before he would consent to begin their session. I hope you can imagine how such unexpected "counter" role playing might have helped these clients see past their masks so therapy could proceed.

Level Two: The Psychoanalytic Stage. After the ethical/persona level of psychotherapy has been completed, it is time to move to the psychoanalytic stage, which is basically the Freudian system recapitulated. Jung did not think the sexual motive is the universal source for every neurotic manifestation, but he did not deny that sexual motives are important at this stage.

For most patients, the psychoanalytic stage has two phases. In the first phase they uncover, in the standard Freudian fashion, their "pathogenic secret." For my young patient Luke (in Chapter 7) that pathogenic secret was his secret rage at his father and, more importantly, his mother for the way he had been treated as a child.

In one of Jung's more celebrated cases, the patient's pathogenic secret was that she had done nothing to prevent her children from drinking contaminated water. As a result, her much-loved infant daughter had died of typhoid fever, precipitating a psychotic depression in the mother. Through the psychoanalytic techniques of dream analysis and word association, Jung discovered that "she was a murderess" (1965, pp. 115–116) unconsciously motivated to "undo" her marriage to her husband after discovering that her former lover, "the son of a wealthy industrialist," had expressed dismay that she had not married him. (Unfortunately, the "wealthy son" had not revealed his feelings towards her when they might have made a difference.) The "unconscious or only half conscious" motive behind the poisoning of the children was prompted by the unconscious wish to be reunited with a man she had loved before she married her husband.

In North America in the 1990s it would appear that many people's pathogenic secret has to do with having been sexually molested or abused as children. The media are filled with accusations and confessions to that effect.

I once treated a depressed young man for several months before he "revealed" his pathogenic secret: His father was an alcoholic. How was that a secret? He knew about Dad but all the rest of the family were in a conspiracy of total denial of Dad's problem.

The pathogenic secret is revealed in most cases by the cathartic, abreactive method, but Jung did not believe that transference was anything but an artifact of the strange relationships between Freudians and their patients. Jung worked directly with his patients, expressed himself freely in front of them, and expected his patients to do the same.

Jung raised the interesting question of what the therapist was to do with the knowledge revealed in the course of analytic detective work with the patient's unconscious. Here is what he wrote about the woman who murdered her daughter:

> I was confronted with the problem: Should I speak openly with her or not? Should I undertake the major operation? I was faced with a conflict of duties altogether without precedent in my experience. I had a difficult question of conscience to answer, and had to settle the matter with myself alone. If I had asked my colleagues they would probably have warned me, "For heaven's sake don't tell the woman any such thing. That will only make her still crazier." To my mind, the effect might well be the reverse. . . .
>
> Nevertheless, I decided to take a chance on a therapy whose outcome was uncertain. I told her everything I had discovered through the association test. It can easily be imagined how difficult it was for me to do this. To accuse a person point-blank of murder is no small matter. And it was tragic for the patient to have to listen to it and accept it. But the result was that in two weeks it proved possible to discharge her, and she was never again institutionalized. (1965, p. 116)

After resolution of the pathogenic secret, there is sometimes a transferencelike quality to the second phase of the psychoanalytic stage. In this phase the patient has her or his first interaction with the *shadow archetype*. The shadow is, essentially, the contents of our personal unconscious. It is disturbing to apprehend because it is the mirror opposite of our ordinary conscious awareness of ourselves.

A quick technical note before we move on: The shadow archetype always appears as a same-sex image.

This probably is the most confusing aspect of Jung's theory for first-time readers. Try this exercise to discover something about your own shadow archetype: Make a list of four or five things that are the most distinctive and clear-cut aspects of your personality. Take your list and meditate on it. Dream about it. Talk to your best and dearest friend about it. What you should discover is that each of these traits coexists in you with an equally strong reverse trait. The rich man dreams of beggars; the fat man dreams of starving refugees in Somalia. The shy, unassuming girl harbors a secret feeling that she has twice the personality of her more popular peers; the virginal maiden has dreams that would shock a sailor. Each and every part of us has an equal and opposite part in our personal unconscious. And the resolution of these opposites is the very essence of Level Two; it must be done before we can continue our quest.

When you try to interpret a same-sex dream image in a Jungian context, always begin by flipping it 180 degrees. When you reverse the image that way, you should find something "just like me" at the core. The shadow archetype is simply trying to lead you toward a resolution of some aspect of your personality that has become muscle-bound, inflexible, or one-sided. To be able to continue on your journey, you need to deal with this imbalance in your personality. You need to try to center yourself a bit more carefully. Perhaps you need to study some Zen, write some poetry, or take a small child for a walk.

Level Three: The Threshold Stage. The shadow archetype is the first fundamental mental instinct we encounter in analytical psychotherapy. It is the first crystallized messenger from the collective unconscious. You can enjoy getting to know her (if you are female) and even appreciate the ironic sense of humor she will demonstrate as she shows you yourself in your dreams. When you have established a good self-correcting relationship with your shadow, you are ready to enter the next phase of your journey.

As the name suggests, the threshold stage brings you right to the edge of a whole new awareness of being alive. You have accepted and resolved the principal messages from your shadow. Now you need to meet your opposite-sex archetype: *animus* for women, *anima* for men. You need at this stage to resolve the false dichotomy between men and women, male and female, that has been established by culture and civilization.

When it comes to thinking about gender, most of us are horribly one-sided. We tend to discount or ignore the opposite sex's point of view. Even more, we tend to fear and distrust people who aren't fairly obvious and clear about their femaleness or maleness. But androgyny is the very center of the puzzle we must solve if we wish to continue on this journey. The animus/anima puzzle is the central paradox of all life: We are opposites, yet we are one.

One aspect of life is yin, the other is yang; but neither makes any sense or is complete without the other. In ancient Chinese philosophy, yin is feminine; it is the moon. Yin is the world of creation, receptivity, intuition, and nature. It is dark and exists in shadows and metaphors. It is unconscious knowing; it is collective and nurturing. Yang is driving energy, possession, logic, strength, and aggression. Yang is sun; it is phallic and wants to penetrate the dark. Yin is the dark fertile earth; yang is the bright hot heavens.

From his encounter with his own anima, Jung said that he had learned an important lesson:

Treat [your anima] as a person, if you like as a patient or a goddess, but above all treat her as something that does exist. . . . [Y]ou must talk to this person in order to see what she is about and to learn what her thoughts and character are. (1973, p. 461)

The anima/animus experience is the first glimpse many of us have of the truth of these words: "There are things in the psyche which I do not produce, but which produce themselves and have their own life" (Jung, 1965, p. 183).

As you are probably aware, this aspect of Jung's theory has become a potent force behind the self-discovery aspect of the men's movement in the United States, through the work of the poet Robert Bly and the writer Sam Keen.

Every man carries within him the eternal image of woman, not the image of this or that particular woman, but a definite feminine image. This image is fundamentally uncon- scious, an hereditary factor of primordial origin engraved in the living organic system of the man, an imprint or "archetype" of all the ancestral experiences of the female, a de- posit, as it were, of all the impressions ever made by woman—in short, an inherited system of psychic adaptation. Even if no women existed, it would still be possible, at any given time, to deduce from this unconscious image exactly how a woman would have to be constituted psychically. . . . Since this image is unconscious, it is always unconsciously projected upon the person of the beloved, and is one of the chief reasons for a passion- ate attraction or aversion. (Jung, 1931/1954a, p. 198)

Every man reading this book would at least recognize the suggestion that he "get in touch with his feminine side" now and again; and women readers probably find the demands of the animus not only reasonable but important from time to time in their lives. But few may be ready to accept the central idea behind the Jungian con- cept of the animus/anima: The union of the sun and the moon, the yin and the yang, is the fundamental law of psychic life. The experience of union, or complete oneness with creation, requires the union of all apparent opposites. We see in this aspect of Jung's theory the tremendous impact of Eastern philosophical and religious teach- ings on the development of his thinking. As you will see in Part IV of *Talking Cures*, the notion of extinguishing the tensions caused by discriminative thinking is at the very heart of Japanese psychotherapies.

I fear, however, that for most Westerners the task Jung proposes is very challeng- ing. Keep in mind that most of Jung's patients were in late middle age, a time in life when these concepts may meet with less rigorous resistance from a Western-trained intellect.

Level Four: The Religious Problem. The fourth stage of analysis deals with recogniz- ing and understanding the purposiveness of life. The patient (who by this stage is less a patient seeking treatment than a pilgrim on a sacred journey) enters this stage of the quest by encountering "the religious problem."

The religious problem, in my experience, is something that most students understand intuitively but that few have ever confronted face to face. It appears when—in the process of study, reflection, meditation, and analysis—one encounters "an autonomous force . . . that persistently pushes us to achieve wholeness . . . constantly trying to launch us on a process of fulfilling our truest self, thereby finding our own wholeness and particular meaning in life" (Kaufmann, 1989, p. 120).

This confrontation is a "religious problem" in several respects:

- It challenges and soundly defeats any latent antivitalist thoughts we might have been keeping in reserve. We are forced to confront a will that exists within our psyches and that has the same power as our sex drive or our need for love and companionship. But it is not reducible to the status of a biological drive; it is a window into something vastly greater and more awesome than our strongest biological drives.
- The answers available to us about this "force" in established religions and religious doctrines are not adequate to the task of explaining it. It is an essential mystery. Although it is the core of all religions and religious teachings, ultimately it cannot be expressed in words or rituals.
- It may well be blasphemous. How does one look at God? How does one address Creation? How does one presume to know the Great Spirit? The Judeo-Christian tradition has some specific and stern teachings on this subject. The subject has also fascinated writers for centuries. My favorite encounter with this problem is found in Fyodor Dostoyevsky's (1912) story about the Grand Inquisitor, which raises the question whether human beings can continue to live if they acquire direct knowledge of God.

Perhaps you can imagine how confronting the religious problem could lead a person to the brink of madness and perhaps even push him or her over the edge. Reflect on those experiences you may have had that brought you closest to the universal. I can think of five or six such "transcendental" moments in my own life: the first recognition of grown-up passionate love, the birth of our son, the awesome beauty of Utah's high desert. For many of my students, those moments have come, for example, during prayer or religious revival, in connection with athletic performances, and at the moment before impact when they knew they were going to be in an automobile accident.

This phase of analytic psychotherapy is a time of great discovery and even conversion. Jung frequently advised his patients to attend a Roman Catholic High Mass prior to coming to their sessions with him. The Mass would prime their collective unconscious by flooding it with archetypal symbols—especially the "personifying archetypes" of God, Jesus, the Virgin Mary, and the Holy Spirit and the "transforming archetypes" of the cross, the mandala, and the quaternity. In essence, Catholic High Mass and all other powerful spiritual rituals "contain" the sacred—that is, they become sacred by incorporating the most powerful archetypal symbols. You might say that organized religions are the custodians of the most powerful archetypes—and thus hold the keys to human destiny in their symbols, myths, and rituals.

In point of fact, for Jung all religions are "psychotherapeutic systems" (Jung, 1935/1968, p. 181). He commonly encouraged his patients to embrace religion, and especially Catholicism, "with my blessing!" as a part and a consequence of having gone through analysis with him—even though the majority of his patients were not raised in the Catholic faith.

Level Five: Self-Actualization. At the fifth level of progression, the questing person must totally transform the self, abandon the old ego, and accept an entirely new *universal personality*. This process has been described under a number of different names. In psychology we tend to call it by the hopelessly inadequate term *self-actualization*. In other traditions it is known as the attainment of Buddahood, sainthood, or immortality—depending on the religious tradition. The pilgrim is called on to shed everything that has gone before—called as in the Bible Jonah was called— to experience a total transcendence.

At this point Jung's theory becomes almost entirely theological and thus beyond the scope of this book and this author. Jung told us that at this stage the barriers to cosmic understanding fall away, the veil is lifted, "everything falls into place, the cogs mesh, and the thing really seems to be a machine which in a moment would run of itself"—leaving one with a sense of wonder and "delight." (This idea is discussed at length in Jung, 1917/1953, Part II.) It seems rather obvious that Jung actually had this experience during his 6-year self-analysis and that his theory came largely from that transcendent experience. In Zen Buddhism, we would call it satori.

A Patient's Dream

Let me conclude this chapter with a dream fragment presented by a patient approaching the end of his analytical psychotherapy:

> It is a warm summery day. I find a cocoon hanging on a vine and pick it up. The covering is a delicate green color. Its transparency allows me to see the orange wings of the butterfly inside and I realize that it is a monarch butterfly. I cup my hands together to provide warmth for the cocoon, hoping that the warmth from my hands will help it emerge sooner. Then I realize it won't help. I must simply wait for it to emerge by itself. (Kaufmann, 1989, p. 148)

Oh, by the way: The Greek word for butterfly is *psyche*.

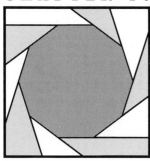

CHAPTER 10

Ego Psychology:
Anna Freud, Erik Erikson,
Karen Horney, and
Erich Fromm

Let a Hundred Flowers Bloom,
Let a Thousand Thoughts Contend

If you have a memory for recent Chinese history, you will recall that the preceding words were first uttered by Mao Tse-Tung during a brief period of ideological openness in China just prior to the Cultural Revolution. Much like Mao, Sigmund Freud led his revolutionary followers on a long march to overthrow the established order and to replace the traditions of the past with an entirely new vision of a brave and glorious future built on a scientific foundation. Both men held their movements together by insisting on ideological purity within the ranks. But in so doing each left his movement without a clear successor, because any deviation from the received doctrine could be regarded as heretical and as reason for shunning anyone who might have the vision to lead.

In 1923 Freud was diagnosed with the cancer that would end his life 16 years later. He continued his leadership of the psychoanalytic movement but became increasingly dependent on his daughter Anna to continue his life's work. His overbearing presence no longer an inhibiting factor, his followers were free to develop their own ideas about psychoanalysis and the talking cure. This chapter is about the alternatives developed by four of Freud's direct descendants, all of whom eventually won loyal followers of their own. Psychoanalysis was like a tree, and Freud had been the roots and trunk. Now the tree was growing, and branches were sprouting in every direction.

Anna Freud, Sigmund's daughter, developed a psychoanalytic view of the developing child and an analytic method, play therapy, for working with them.

Erik Erikson, one of Anna Freud's students, extended her work into a concern for lifelong psychological development. He also extended our thinking about the importance of the psychological maturity and genuineness of the therapist.

Karen Horney's contribution was to extend psychoanalytic theory to the psyches of women. Horney's theory of psychoanalysis was more interpersonally focused than any of the prior developments in the field. She understood life as a struggle for self-control and self-assertion and the quest to discover a "real self." She was very interested in the psychological relationships between men and women.

Erich Fromm extended psychoanalysis to encompass a more sociological view of the human condition. Fromm stressed highly evolved social needs, which place human beings at the mercy of the societies in which they live. It is the drive to satisfy these uniquely human needs that gives life its meaning and significance. Fromm's writing was profoundly influenced by the rise of fascism in Europe during the 1930s and 1940s.

The Rise of Psychoanalytic Ego Psychology

This chapter briefly traces the development of four of Sigmund Freud's heirs and successors, primarily through their work in the United States in the 1940s and 1950s. As you read about them, keep in mind the vast political, social, and economic changes that swept the Western world between 1930 and 1950: the world wide economic collapse of the 1930s, the rise of fascism in Europe, the emigration of practically all the next generation of psychoanalysts to the United States throughout the 1930s, a long and brutal world war, and the eventual triumph of democracy. All these changes had a profound impact on the development of psychoanalytic thinking in the post-Freudian era.

At the beginning of this era, psychoanalysis was a highly intellectual and almost exclusively bourgeois enterprise; its concerns were those of private individuals living in a competitive, materialistic society. But during these two decades, largely because of the increasing importance of North American values and experience, psychoanalysis came to reconsider Freud's views of women, to rethink some of his assumptions about the dominant influence of sexual and aggressive instincts, and to adopt a much broader view of the nature of repression. As the social historian Philippe Aries (1985) observed, psychoanalysis arose largely as a consequence of the sexual confusion created in Europe in the 19th century when lusty peasant sexuality confronted the secret sexuality of the refined bourgeoisie. What was the role of psychoanalysis to be in an age when sexuality had lost much of its shock value?

In Freud's day the typical psychoanalytic client was a young middle-class woman whose inner conflicts and inhibitions had culminated in what one of my own clients once called a "tidy, quiet nervous breakdown." But in the New World, where people were much freer to express themselves, especially sexually, hysterias became virtually unknown. In their place men and women experienced anxiety, when they were no longer able to cope with the demands of the outside world. Their breakdowns were not "tidy"; a full-blown anxiety attack doesn't look much like a conversion hysteria.

Freud had perceived the task of the analyst as breaking through the defense mechanisms that prevent the ego from harnessing the sexual and aggressive powers of the instinctually driven id. The new analysts were concerned with the development and enhancement of the ego itself. These new "ego psychologists" even came to write about the "functional autonomy of the ego"—a simple enough sounding concept, but one that threatened to move psychoanalysis completely beyond it biological foundations.

> In short, one of the main clinical and theoretical contributions of psychoanalytic ego psychology was to soften and modulate the sweeping claim of Freudian instinct theory that virtually all behavior was energized by, directly or indirectly, overtly or covertly, in the service of, [biological] drive gratification. Following the theoretical emendations of ego psychology, there was now room in psychoanalytic theory for behavior and functions relatively autonomous of the vicissitudes of drive. At the same time . . . because patients can be unaware of both their wishes and their defense mechanisms against them, a central focus of interpretation is on the patient's defensive strategies. (Eagle & Wolitzky, 1992, pp. 114–115)

The oedipal conflict was no longer understood as a purely sexual and aggressive source of human conflict and confusion. It could now be understood in the vocabulary of social psychology. It could be addressed in terms of envy and frustration, of feelings of desertion and longing, of basic security and the capacity to trust, of the ability to give and receive love.

Psychoanalysts had to adapt to these changes to retain their relevance in the modern age. But in doing so they broke psychoanalytic theory into a hundred pieces—or perhaps a hundred flowers.

Some Fundamental Assumptions of Ego Psychology

The primary Freudian insight retained by these modern ego psychologists was the conviction that our adult lives are played out under the terms laid down in our earliest childhood. For the analyst, the words of the poet William Wordsworth, "The child is the father of the man," are quite literally true. The neurotic symptoms and maladaptive personality traits of the adult are in reality "pathological compromises" (Eagle & Wolitzky, 1992) stemming from the child's thwarted and conflicted needs to be loved, nurtured, and recognized. In psychoanalysis, the patient's unconscious "works" on these problems by projecting them out of the past and into the ongoing relationship with the analyst.

When I was working with young Luke (introduced in Chapter 7), he became convinced for a while that "nothing I do is ever good enough for you." In fact, I had never evaluated or judged any of his actions. Eventually he came to see that it was not I with whom he was having a desperate argument but rather those emotional forces in his life (in this case, his parents) who had never allowed him to feel praiseworthy and thus also worthy of being loved.

In Luke's transference with me, he was working out the problems he had encountered as a child. From the ego psychologist's perspective, these issues were not so much his sexual and aggressive feelings but his ability to renounce "regressive longings to merge and to cling to infantile dependence" in order to foster appropriately adult "urges towards greater autonomy and individuation" (Eagle & Wolitzky, 1992, p. 118).

Under Freud the goal of therapy was the corrective and restorative emotional release of the libido, which had been dammed up behind a wall of repression. For "neo-Freudians," therapy was more likely to be regarded as helping the patient "reduce the harshness of the . . . superego, [thus allowing] the patient opportunity to form a new identification" of "self" (Eagle & Wolitzky, 1992, p. 117), which will be more conducive to growth and change. Psychoanalysis thus became a procedure in which contact with a wise and insightful healer helps a person overcome arrested psychological development by giving up childhood's legacy of counterproductive, self-protective symptoms and strategies.

The best examples I can think of to illustrate these principles come from what Freud might have called the psychopathologies of everyday life. If you were to sit down for a serious heart-to-heart chat with an older, wiser person who both knows you well and gets to observe you regularly in day-to-day life, what might this person tell you about yourself that you don't want to know or think about?

We may perform miracles at school or at work and remain optimistic, productive, cheerful, and thoroughly competent in everything we do—until we run into an authority figure. Then we may become overly emotional, irrational, and even a little paranoid.

Or we may be competent and successful until we look in the mirror—where we inevitably see a fat, unattractive person whom nobody could respect or love.

I've worked with men who couldn't bear the thought of having a female boss or a homosexual co-worker. I know people who invest all their self-worth in their salary or grade-point average. I know a student who permits himself to sign up only for courses with a reputation for being ungodly difficult—whether he is interested in the topic or not. If I get a single crappy, nasty, or vindictive comment on my end-of-semester course evaluations, I completely lose sight of the 50 evaluations that told me I provided students with an important and productive learning experience.

Experiences like these don't make a compelling case for the idea that sexual and aggressive drives are the engines of human feeling and action. Thus we are almost inevitably drawn to the view that our emotional and psychological difficulties today are the consequences of our early lessons about the world and our place in it.

Object Relations. In the developing child, the emerging self is pitted against a series of not-me "objects" with which he or she must interact to fulfill the most fundamental instinctual needs. The challenge for the child is to learn to negotiate with this outside world without trading away satisfaction of such fundamental needs as love, security, and esteem for individual autonomy and a sense of self.

The ego psychologists focused on *object relations,* on how the patient learned as a child to compromise between security and independence. As the patient seeks to grow into a successful adult, he or she must develop a strong sense of personal identity (Kernberg, 1976). This personal identity must integrate the many different aspects of the self that have emerged in relation to the thousands of other "objects" with which the individual has had to negotiate.

Ego Defenses. A healthy identity, according to Kohut (1971), is one that encompasses an autonomous self with adequate reserves of self-confidence and self-esteem. When this developmental challenge has been met, the individual possesses the ability to successfully meet his or her own needs while participating in the life of the community. This challenge is essentially lifelong, however. From time to time we all encounter situations in which our sense of self is not adequate, in which we may not believe that we have the capacity to meet the demands being placed before us.

At such times we react to the world much as we learned to react when we were under the intimate care of our parents. Our ego's weakness is manifested in various defensive maneuvers we employ to protect ourselves from being overwhelmed, rejected, or denied nurturance. The compromises we have struck with the world may come unglued, and we may slip into a terror of insignificance and isolation. During times like this, we can be very much at the mercy of the world around us. We may appear to those closest to us to have lost sight of who we are and what we have come to stand for. This situation calls for a corrective restructuring of the self system:

> Although it could be illustrated in half a dozen different expressions, the centrality of the deficiency/defense assumptions is particularly apparent in the self psychology of the late Heinz Kohut. For Kohut, the nucleus of psychopathology lay in structural defects and deficiencies in the self. Defensive and compensatory practices were said to drive and lead the person in two directions: the guilt-ridden pursuit of pleasure; and the "tragic" (albeit creative) attempt to move "beyond the pleasure principle" and to manifest the patterns of a core or "nuclear" self. A "tension arc" is said to connect these bipolar aspects of the self, with the person being "driven" by pleasure-seeking ambitions and simultaneously "led" by their ideals. (Mahoney, 1991, p. 237)

Sometimes our ego defenses become so intrusive and our insight into them so limited that we must seek some form of therapy to get at the truth of our own motivation and experience. I met such a person several years ago.

Case Study: Gail and the Problem With No Name

Gail was a 31-year-old bank employee who had recently been promoted to the position of assistant vice president and head of the consumer loan department. She was the youngest person to be so recognized in the history of her firm. She was talented, popular, assertive, and self-confident—at work.

At home she was a completely different person. Gail had three children, each of whom had been tracked in the "gifted" classes in elementary school, and a husband who told her several times a day that she was the greatest wife-partner-mother-person he had ever known. Her kids were well adjusted, well behaved, and affectionate. Her husband was loving, supportive, and actively involved with his family.

In spite of all this good news, Gail sometimes would get in her car at the end of the work day and cry her eyes out at the prospect of having to return home. She dreaded weekends and holidays when she had to be away from her work and home with her family.

Like a lot of middle-class people Gail came for therapy because she thought she was about to lose her mind. She feared herself headed for a major breakdown and was worried about the consequences of psychiatric hospitalization for her family and her career. But while she told me all this, over her lunch hour, she remained Gail the Power Banker. I heard but really could not "see" her story. I knew she was telling me the truth, but it seemed to be the truth about someone wholly different from the highly successful and composed person sitting in front of me.

We ran through the obvious possibilities: She was in love with someone else? No. She resented the demands that her husband and family put on her? No. She was sexually unhappy? Perhaps unfulfilled sexually by men? No! Money problems? Problems at work? Biologically based depression? A crummy house or unpleasant neighborhood? Wanted to be alone, needed more privacy? No, no, no, no, no. Gail honestly didn't know what was bothering her. She may even have been scared a bit that she flunked my 20-questions examination.

I saw Gail with her kids—no clues there. I saw her with her husband, Dan—no clues there. Except that I observed she was very tense and ill at ease in Dan's presence, not at all as confident and "in charge" as she had been during our initial meeting, when she and I had been alone together.

I saw the husband alone. Dan was at least as baffled as Gail and as baffled as I was becoming.

Meanwhile, Gail and I were having a good professional relationship, especially considering that I hadn't done a darned thing for her. The relationship was good enough that she started to have some very vivid dreams on the nights before and after our sessions. The dreams were often frightening in both their intensity and imagery, and they frequently involved something horrible happening to Dan. Gail was always an innocent but helpless bystander as Dan fell off a cliff, was gunned down in the yard, choked on Sunday dinner, or developed a fatal disease. Combining these dreadful images with her apparent discomfort when she and Dan had been in my office together, I thought we might be getting on to something.

The Tyranny of Perfection. I began to believe that Gail's life had some terribly big "shoulds" in it and that somehow a major "should" or two had gotten out of whack. I recalled a passage from the neo-Freudian analyst Karen Horney and mentally tried it on Gail for size:

> The neurotic tries to actualize [her] idealized self with regard to the *outside world:* in achievements, in the glory of success, or power or triumph. [The neurotic] tries to assert the exceptional rights to which [her] uniqueness entitles [her] whenever, and in whatever ways, [she] can. . . . And whenever [she] falls palpably short of being [her] idealized self, [her] claims enable [her] to make factors outside [her]self responsible for such "failures." . . .
>
> Many reactions of despondence, irritability, or fear occurring during analysis are less a response to the patient's having discovered a disturbing problem in [her]self (as the analyst tends to assume) than to [her] feeling impotent to remove it right away. (1951, pp. 64, 71–72)

I was intrigued by two possibilities. One, Gail had substituted the "safe" image of her husband for herself in her death dreams; it was really she who was supposed to die, but her unconscious had converted Gail to Dan in the dream image. Two, some very real problem in Gail's life might be solved if Dan just one day dropped stone-cold dead. Either hypothesis would fit the behavior I had witnessed and the story I had heard. Either would also perhaps fit what Horney said about "the tyranny of the should." What's your guess, gentle reader?

By now I was beginning to be convinced that the problem was somehow more related to the marriage than to the nearly perfect kids or the more than perfect job. That concept—perfection—kept coming back to me. Gail was the perfect banker and the perfect mother. Was she also the perfect wife?

I tried switching the ideas around in my head. Gail had a perfect job, perfect kids, and a perfect house. But did Gail have a perfect spouse?

I pursued a literal interpretation of the dreams. I asked Gail to tell me how her life would change if her dreams came true. Oh, it would be just terrible. So sad. Destroy the children's happiness. Leave her all alone. She'd never remarry. Last thing in the whole world she'd want. Would hope that she would die first, so she would never have to go through it.

Yes, but dreams are often perverse wishes. What problems would Dan solve by disappearing? I didn't ask Gail who would be pleased but where the silver lining would be in such a tragic scenario.

Gail began talking to me cautiously, even intellectually. Well, because Dan didn't have a college degree and didn't have a really great job and because her job was now paying her extremely well, losing Dan would be sort of insignificant economically.

One positive outcome might be that the children would become a lot closer to their maternal grandparents. They disapproved of Dan and hadn't gone to the wedding. Gail had been 3 months pregnant at the time, which her parents had guessed; but the real issue was Dan's lack of education, his unsuitability for her in terms of social-class background.

Gradually Gail revealed to me, and to herself, the story of the painful choice she had made between her family and Dan a dozen years earlier. Maybe she wouldn't have made that choice if she hadn't been pregnant; but then again, maybe she allowed herself to become pregnant to take the choice out of her hands.

Gail loved Dan. But at some level she was also ashamed of him. She often feared he would say or do something in front of others that would reveal his working-class background. She was even afraid he might say something really stupid when he came to talk with me. And now how much more complicated Gail and Dan's life together was becoming. The children of a man who had never read a book in his life were in classes for gifted children. Wait until they get older. Wait until they reject Dan's side of the family and embrace the shame that their father worked in a factory—all while their mother rose to the top of her profession.

The Unconscious Secret. We can look at what happened to Gail from a dynamic perspective: As increasingly desperate and fearful threats to her long-term security began to dominate her unconscious mind, she had to find more effective ways to ward off and compartmentalize her anxiety. By the time I saw her for the first time she had lost all contact with the roots of her problem. As Anna Freud, one of the pioneers among the ego analysts, put it:

> So long as the defenses set up by a person's ego are intact, the analytic observer is faced by a blank; as soon as they break down, for example, when repression fails and unconscious material returns, a mass of information about inner processes becomes available. (A. Freud, 1968, p. 125)

Gail's unconscious mind had evidently accepted the invitation presented by the therapeutic situation and produced the series of revealing dreams. But her unconscious denial of any such massive imperfection as resenting her loving husband's social class and educational background prevented her from recognizing the causes of her own considerable emotional problem.

In time we were able to trace the origins of Gail's perfectionism and denial to her parents' highly puritanical world view. She was able to see how she had "programmed" herself for success and power, both to protect her fragile ego from their harsh criticism and to make them accepting and proud of her.

Her rebellious act—sleeping with and becoming pregnant by a kind and gentle young working-class man—had opened up a new world for her. She discovered how to communicate emotions and how to express and receive love. She also found out that it was acceptable to have fun once in a while.

Her present crisis had evidently been precipitated by her recent promotion. She generally saw the proper and severe senior management of the bank as having many of the same values as her father. In our sessions she remembered that her very first thought when she received the letter announcing her promotion was that she had to make sure that neither her new bosses nor, perhaps more importantly, the people now working under her would ever get to know her husband.

About the time we were finishing working through these issues, it was time for me to leave the clinic. I suggested that my leaving was a good opportunity for Gail and Dan to try some couples therapy. I ventured the observation that Gail had probably failed to hide from Dan, as fully as she thought, her contempt for his educational and occupational status. What was, perhaps, "her" problem was now in fact "their" problem; and because they both wanted to keep their marriage together, it was important for them to do some serious work on their relationship.

I never heard how Gail's story finally turned out, but I did learn that my suspicions about Dan's awareness were well founded and that his concerns about the marriage were ready to be addressed in counseling.

Anna Freud

The development of a talking cure with explicit emphasis on the development and functioning of ego, as opposed to instinct, became the life work of Sigmund Freud's youngest child, Anna (1895–1982). From most accounts, she grew to adulthood in a relatively unhappy home (see Roazen, 1971, for the most complete biographical treatment of Anna Freud's life.)

Sigmund Freud had evidently lost all intellectual interest and almost all emotional interest in his wife by the time Anna reached young adulthood. One suspects that no spouse in history could have competed with the intensely loyal followers Freud gathered around him as the psychoanalytic movement solidified its position of importance in European psychiatry throughout the 1920s.

Yet Freud never truly allowed himself to yield the reins of power to an outsider, no matter how loyal, devoted, and eager such a follower might be. The ultimate control that Freud wielded over his disciples was each new member's "training analysis." Freud had begun the tradition by psychoanalyzing himself during the closing years of the 19th century. To be psychoanalyzed directly by the master was the one key to psychoanalytic perfection that eluded Freud's most ambitious followers; you may recall from Chapter 9 that it became a point of intense contention between Carl Jung and Freud as their relationship and collaboration began to fall apart.

Thus it was no small decision on Freud's part to accept his daughter Anna into analysis when the girl was barely out of her teens. From those days until the end of her life, Anna had room for only one man in her life, and that man was her father.

Gradually the older Freud cemented that tie in the two most powerful ways he possibly could—by ensuring that Anna would not leave home to pursue an "independent" education and by subjecting her innermost emotional and intellectual life to a complete psychoanalysis. Anna Freud's biographer commented as follows:

> Freud's motives may have been the very best, but medically and humanly the situation was bizarre. As her analyst, he would inevitably mobilize her feeling of overvaluation, while at the same time invading the privacy of her soul; he added new transference emotions to their relationship, without the possibility of ever really dissolving them. A genius who was also naturally an immense figure in his daughter's life, as her analyst he tied her permanently to him. (Roazen, 1971, p. 440)

Monte (1991) speculated on the impact this strange and powerful father/daughter alliance had on the future course of psychoanalysis:

> With no formal academic training or credentials in medicine or psychology, Anna Freud was nevertheless committed to psychoanalysis by the strongest of bonds: She was engaged in intellectual and emotional self-exploration with the founder of psychoanalysis, her own father, who had to function in the acutely contradictory roles of professional and paternal intimate. (p. 171)

The Drama of Succession

In 1920 Freud signified to the rest of Vienna's Psychoanalytic Society, his most trusted inner circle of psychoanalytic followers, the place he accorded his daughter by conferring on her one of his legendary rings (see Chapter 16 for the story of Wilhelm Reich's receipt of a similar ring). Anna would now be able to address the inner circle, pronounce clinical judgments, and most importantly, interpret her father's word to the believers.

This period also marked the turning point in Freud's private life. In 1923 his cancer was diagnosed, and Anna became the stricken leader's most intimate companion, nurse, and confidant as the disease took its course. She was with him through numerous devastating surgeries and trips to hospitals for radiation treatments. She became his official voice as she read his papers to conferences he was too sick to address. Freud called Anna his "faithful Antigone" (Monte, 1991), after the daughter of the dying, blind Oedipus in Sophocles' play *Antigone*.

Anna gradually took over the day-to-day affairs of her father's movement and, it would seem, increasingly subsumed her own identity to faithfully represent her father in all things. As *The New York Times* noted in her obituary on October 10, 1982, Anna "had her father's ability, though on a smaller scale, to rally others or, more to the point, to generate disciples when she needed them." It was Anna Freud who had to negotiate with the Gestapo when the Freud family and library were seized during the Nazi occupation of Vienna in 1938, and it was Anna who relocated her dying father and aged mother to safety in London, where he died in 1939.

Anna Freud devoted most of her independent thinking to the psychoanalytic study of children. One wonders if she ever fully appreciated the importance of the changes she introduced into the orthodoxy of psychoanalysis. However, from the fact that Freud openly encouraged more doctrinaire analysts (Melanie Klein, foremost among them) to publicly dispute Anna's work, we may surmise that the weakened but still determined father suffered great conflict over his daughter's deviations. And we can be certain that Anna Freud recognized she was "transgressing the strict confines of the psychoanalytic technique and situation, and had created [a new] field of direct observation, in its own way" (A. Freud, 1971, p. 139).

The Psychoanalytic Study of Children

Through her study of children, Anna Freud came to recognize that the development of the ego is the primary task of children, that ego development is not secondary to the mastery of sexual and aggressive impulses as children mature. She also came to recognize the ego's efforts to protect itself from the powerful forces with which it contends. She never questioned the power of the id or her father's assertion that the ego serves its "master" by transforming the id's demands into socially acceptable behavior. But she considered the ego a semiautonomous component of the psyche, uniquely motivated to achieve independence, continuous growth and development, and a firmly constituted view of social reality.

Perhaps most importantly, Anna Freud offered an interpretation of human behavior much freer of the pessimistic struggle against human nature that her father had proclaimed. Into her old age, she wrote about "man's struggle against himself," but she saw that struggle as occurring within a developmental context. Instead of being a struggle against society or instinct, the ultimate task of a child's life is to find the strength and courage required to develop the self fully. Healthy children struggle to achieve emotional self-reliance out of their initial dependency: from being passively cared for to being active and autonomous in self-care; from being engaged in self-stimulating play to engaging in meaningful work; from selfishness to true companionship; from moral control based on the threat of punishment to self-regulatory ego and superego schemata.

Anna Freud's therapeutic work with institutionalized and hospitalized children marked the beginnings of extending the talking cure to children. Previous approaches had treated children as "miniature adults," especially cognitively (Glen, 1978). Anna Freud understood, however, that children's thinking requires much more creative analysis on the part of the therapist who wants to find out what their real motives and fears are. She let children talk about their fantasies and their dreams within the context of a carefully established "treatment alliance" (see Langs, 1976). Trust plays much the same role as transference plays in therapy with adults.

Anna Freud observed that children have little apparent ability to communicate in the verbal retelling of their mental productions. In fact, she didn't believe that children are capable of any reasonably full and direct expression of their unconscious emotional lives. The only way to access a child's unconscious, she believed, is to observe that child at play. All a child's unconscious fears and motives are projected in play. Because of Freud's pioneering work during the 1930s with interpreting the dynamics of children's play behaviors, psychodynamic play therapy became the main method for studying the psychic development of children and the central focus of most psychodynamic therapeutic work with young children.

Erik Erikson

Erik Erikson (1902–1994), a student and analysand of Anna Freud in Vienna in the late 1920s, became fascinated with the insights emerging from psychoanalysts' work with children. Erikson's first book, *Childhood and Society,* published in 1950, was based on his psychoanalytic interpretation of the patterns of psychological development he observed in children from different cultures. Ironically, however, Erikson's fascination with the psychic content of children's lives, and especially their play, ultimately led him to abandon his formal training in psychoanalysis.

As was the case with his mentor, Anna Freud, Erikson had virtually no formal education or medical training. A native of Germany, in his younger days he was an artist. Later he was brought into the psychoanalytic circle as the head teacher for the private school the analysts had decided to establish for their children. He was, therefore, somewhat less committed to the painstaking scholarship that characterized much of the writing of his contemporaries. But Erikson excelled at careful observation, a skill he had perfected as an artist.

In 1933, at the age of 31, Erikson was one of the first European-trained psychoanalysts to take up permanent residence in the United States. Over the ensuing years, Erikson strove to develop a psychology that faithfully brought order to the complex data he observed in the human behavior all around him. At first Erikson "really thought I was merely providing new illustrations for what I had learned from Sigmund and Anna Freud. I realized only gradually that any original observation already implies a change in the theory" (quoted in Evans, 1969, p. 13). Perhaps because of the dramatic shift in perspective brought about by the move from Vienna to New York, these "new illustrations" Erikson encountered in his clinical work with his American patients were to have a profound impact on the future of psychoanalysis.

Erikson came to question one of the most treasured assumptions of the Freudian orthodoxy. He argued that culture defines the individual by providing a dynamic context within which the individual grows to maturity. The orthodox view that Freud had espoused in *Civilization and Its Discontents* (1930/1961), that the interests of society and of the individual are inevitably at war with each other and that neurosis is the "cost" of civilization, was almost completely displaced by the view that each human life is played out in a complex and unique "psychohistory" within which is forged that individual's unique identity.

From this perspective, as Monte (1991) observed, the ego serves the function of integrating and stabilizing developmental changes in the growing and maturing person. This adaptive, problem-solving hub of our identity is challenged at regular developmental stages by a culture organized around mechanisms and rituals that reward the acquisition of certain character structures. Those structures are the ones that support and reinforce the community's purposes.

The Theory of Epigenetic Development

What most people who have taken an introductory psychology course remember about Erikson is his famous eight-stage "epigenetic theory of development." It postulates that, in the lifelong process of ego development, all human beings are "tested" in various ways by "moments of decision between progress and regression, integration and retardation" (Erikson, 1963, p. 270). This extensive program of developmental sequences is not, as Sigmund Freud argued, resolved within the first 50 or 60 months of life but instead takes a lifetime.

The reason the stages are called *epigenetic* is that Erikson believed each one has to be functionally resolved before the person can advance to the next stage. The success I will experience in the stage I am in now will be determined by the success, or lack thereof, my ego experienced in passing through the earlier stages. Think of life as being like a train that passes through a number of stations on its way to its final destination. At each station the train takes on additional coaches, some with more passengers and in better condition than others. Then the train moves to the next station, more or less on schedule.

The lifelong impact of our experiences at each stage is determined by the ratio of positive to negative outcomes encountered during crises. These crises are embedded in the age-related developmental tasks we confront every day: leaving Mom and Dad to go to elementary school; deciding which hairstyle best reflects our personality; finding a meaningful career and establishing our own family; fearing death or anticipating a richly textured old age.

These are the stages of life, and the developmental tasks at each stage, as Erikson (1959) saw them:

- In *infancy;* trust versus mistrust during the oral stage; autonomy versus shame and doubt during the anal stage
- In *childhood;* initiative versus guilt during the phallic stage; industry versus inferiority during the latency stage
- In *adolescence;* identity versus confusion during the early years of the genital stage

■ In *adulthood;* intimacy versus isolation during the full genital stage; generativity versus stagnation during the working years; ego integrity versus despair during old age

Dealing with questions of intimacy versus isolation is often of paramount importance during the college years. Your success in developing mature and lasting interpersonal relationships while you are in college significantly shapes the way you enter into other relationships for the rest of your life. You will achieve a balance between complete openness to others and complete self-sufficiency as you grow through this stage of your development. And this balance will in large measure be uniquely determined for you by the products of your "personality," which have been established by the way you experienced each of your previous stages of development. In other words, your current (or most recent) romantic relationship or close friendship is a significant reflection of how trusting, autonomous, initiating, and genuine you have become as a result of your earlier psychological development. Moreover, the style of interdependence and intimacy you adopt as a result of your personal development in your twenties will probably have a profound impact on the sort of person you will become in your forties.

The Acquisition of Life "Virtues"

A person's relative success at each stage of development leaves a character marker, or "virtue," that becomes a relatively permanent part of that person's overall identity. Each virtue reflects the successful integration of the psychosocial growth process with the person's psychosexual development. In developmental order, the epigenetic virtues are hope, will, purpose, competence, fidelity, love, care, and wisdom.

Erikson would say that for most college students the virtue that should be emerging is the ability to love. Love is manifested in the person's ability to be genuine and to share the self without excessive self-defense. This is the developmentally ideal resolution of the conflict between intimacy and isolation. Success in this critical phase of human development is foreshadowed by the successful establishment of hope, will, purpose, competence, and fidelity to identity in earlier stages of development. This process creates a blueprint for the enduring strengths and weaknesses of character that are exposed in times of great stress or personal challenge.

Psychotherapeutics: Focus on the Therapist

In the method and function of psychotherapy he espoused, Erikson remained fairly orthodox. He believed in using free association with adults and in analyzing the symbols and rituals used by children during free play. The goal of therapy, he believed, is to make the unconscious conscious—which will, one hopes, enable the patient to achieve insights that can be used to restore a fuller level of stage-appropriate functioning to the person's intellectual and emotional life.

One interesting aspect of his theory is that Erikson considered countertransference more important than transference in the therapeutic interaction. His notion, which seems quite sound to me, was that therapists who are "stuck" or impeded in their own ego development will have a very difficult time giving freely and wholly of themselves in a therapeutic session. As he wrote:

> [The therapist must] develop as a practitioner, and as a person, even as the patient is cured as a patient, and as a person. It is an experience which enables the cured patient to develop and to transmit to home and neighborhood an attitude toward health, which is one of the most essential ingredients of an ethical outlook. (1964, pp. 236–237)

An article in *The Behavior Therapist* by Spencer and Hemmer (1993) spoke directly to this point. They asked whether therapists who have negative emotional and political views toward gay male and lesbian clients can provide these clients with meaningful and effective therapeutic services. Noting that only 5% of therapists in a 1991 American Psychological Association survey "reported a gay-affirmative orientation to therapy," Spencer and Hemmer suggested that "therapists [must] continue to confront their own fear and avoidance behaviors as needed so that their treatment interventions can be more efficacious and appropriate to their gay and lesbian clients" (p. 96).

A therapist whose own psychosocial development and identity is flawed in such a way as to result in even an unconscious resentment of gay men and lesbians, members of ethnic or racial groups, and the like would, in Erikson's terms, simply be "role playing" at being a therapist. Such a therapist would be unlikely to afford clients the sort of authentic human encounter that either of them would find meaningful or therapeutic. Employing the metaphor of the actor acting without integrity on the stage, Erikson said of this sort of encounter:

> But what if role-playing becomes an aim in itself, is rewarded with success and status, and seduces the person to repress what core-identity is potential in him? Even an actor is convincing in many roles only if and when there is in him an actor's core identity—and craftsmanship. (1974, p. 107)

The result is "unwise pretense" and a breaking of the "golden rule of therapy," which is that the therapist must be committed to being and becoming a whole person. The therapist must be able to communicate freely and without the distortion of countertransference based on the therapist's own irrational agenda and legacy of flawed ego development.

Erikson's impact on the development of the talking cure was specifically this point. The therapist must be aware that both the client and the therapist are working their way through their separate tasks of ego development. Yes, the client needs to recover the sense of hope or trust or identity that she or he was prevented from developing at the appropriate time in childhood. But the therapist must also be aware of her or his own psychodevelopmental agenda and less than optimal virtues.

The parties to the therapeutic meeting influence each other, impinging on points of weakness and issues of current identity. Each can help promote the growth and wholeness of the other—but only by recognizing the other as distinct and separate. Then both parties can experience the sort of significant human relationship in which it is possible to find the meaning of one's unique identity. From this discovery arises the opportunity for personal growth and further individuation for the patient and therapist.

Once again I find myself thinking, "Well, surely my reader already knows that!" But this concept was an important moment in the history of the talking cure, because it broke the mold of the impassive, emotionally anonymous patriarch as healer and giver of life. Erikson made psychoanalysis human, and he did so in a way that makes sense to psychologists from a wide variety of perspectives (as I hope I have shown you by illustrating the point with a quote from a behavior therapy publication). Monte (1991) observed that "Erikson's theory is probably the most widely read, taught, and written about theory in contemporary psychology" (p. 291).

In his focus on human experience as a lifelong process of testing, interpreting, and integrating knowledge about the self and the world, Erikson gave us the first postmodern interpretation of the human development process. It is yet another "salvationist" talking cure (see Chapters 19 and 24), but at least it celebrates and affirms life and offers hope that we can find meaning and significance in the life we began leading a second ago.

Karen Horney

In discussing the case of Gail a little earlier, I described the frustration of my early nonproductive sessions with her. Eventually I thought about her situation within the context of Karen Horney's ideas, which seemed to be the key. Horney (1885–1952) was one of the pioneering neo-Freudians and one of the first women psychoanalysts. Horney's work, especially as it is found in *Feminine Psychology* (1967), takes a major step toward further reducing the phallocentric, anatomy-is-destiny formulation of mental life that characterized the thinking of the original circle of male intellectuals who surrounded Sigmund Freud in the early years of the psychoanalytic movement.

A Psychodynamic Focus on Gender

Horney's contribution to the development of the talking cure is essentially twofold. Her most important contribution was probably to rewrite psychoanalytic theory so that it became much more responsive to issues of gender in clinical analysis and in treatment with both men and women. She reasoned, for example, that what Freud had called "penis envy" was in reality a manifestation of women's resentment that they are often treated as second-class citizens in the home and in society. What women want, she argued, was not a penis but a greater share of the esteem, power, and privilege accorded to the half of the human race who have a penis.

She observed that girls tend to blame not only themselves but also their mothers for their biologically determined social inferiority. This "tormenting sense of inferiority" inevitably leads to women's suppression of their femininity, or "denial of the vagina" (Horney, 1967, pp. 147ff) and a "flight from womanhood" (1967, pp. 54ff). Consequently, any assertion of a woman's true nature—which of course is a combination of masculine and feminine traits—leads to the experience of anxiety and dread.

"Dread of Woman."   Men are equally disadvantaged by the sexism in society, according to Horney (1967). Men's *dread of woman* was a consistent theme in her writing about sex and psychopathology. Horney stressed that the culture's vast overvaluation of the male role forces men to assume awesome responsibilities and leads them to dread anything in themselves that reminds them at all of the qualities associated with women. Thus men become anxious when they encounter in themselves "something uncanny, unfamiliar, and mysterious"; this fear leads them to regard their own instinctual homosexual feelings with great alarm and confusion.

From this perspective, Freud's assertion "Anatomy is destiny" takes on a wholly new meaning. Because anatomical sex is socially operationalized as gender, because gender is the basis for cultural expectations from which our esteem flows, and because each gender perceives that like itself the opposite gender achieves esteem only at the expense of its opposite number, distrust and an "atmosphere of understandable suspiciousness" between the sexes has become a way of life.

Men and women try to overcome this state of affairs by coming together in a state of "overvalued romantic love," hoping that erotic attraction will expunge at the personal level what has poisoned us at the social and cultural level. But of course we bring the outside world's politics with us into our romantic relationships. Horney noted that in analysis men reveal unconscious fear and distrust of the "magical influence" that women hold over their penises and come to fear the "mysterious being" who may be secretly judging them as inadequately masculine.

Neurotic Fictions.   Women, on the other hand, often desire erotic intimacy with men in the neurotic hope that they can possess a measure of the magical power ascribed to the male genitals. Women overvaluate love in the hope that a passionate commitment to their man will eliminate their lingering resentments over the inferior status accorded them in life. Love becomes the vehicle for "living through the other." This *neurotic fiction* is another reason why so many marriages fail.

The question is how psychoanalysis helps to the relieve these problems. Horney's answer:

> How can analytical insights contribute to diminish the distrust between the sexes?
> There is no uniform answer to this problem. The fear of the power of the affects and

the difficulty in controlling them in a love relationship, the resulting conflict between surrender and self-preservation, between the I and the Thou, is an entirely comprehensible, unmitigatable, and as it were, normal phenomenon. The same thing applies in essence to our readiness for distrust, which stems from unresolved childhood conflicts. These childhood conflicts, however, can vary greatly in intensity, and will leave behind traces of variable depth. Analysis not only can help in individual cases to improve the relationship with the opposite sex, but it can also attempt to improve the psychological conditions of childhood and forestall excessive conflicts. This, of course, is our hope for the future. In the momentous struggle for power, analysis can fulfill an important function by uncovering the real motives of this struggle. This uncovering will not eliminate the motives, but it may help to create a better chance for fighting the struggle on its own ground instead of relegating it to peripheral issues. (1967, p. 118)

Basic Anxiety

Horney's second major contribution to the talking cure was to develop a theoretical context within which basic anxiety could be addressed as a problem in its own right. She began with the position that Erikson also developed, that human nature is constructive and is therefore strongly influenced by culture. Also like Erikson, she saw culture as providing the essential framework within which each individual seeks to develop his or her unique potentialities. Pathology occurs when this innate progressive force is constrained, distorted, or blocked by countervailing social forces.

Pampering and Neglect Revisited. Examples of countervailing social forces seem somewhat Adlerian (see Chapter 8) in that they begin in infancy. Parental pampering, neglect, humiliation, derision, inconsistency, blind adoration, blatant sexism, partiality to siblings, brutality, and perfectionism create in the child an almost magical set of rules that the child attempts to follow in order to feel a full sense of belonging and safety within the family constellation. The child looks to these rules as a way of warding off her or his terror of abandonment for not being good enough. Because the child cannot live up to the vast array of rules she or he has put in place, the child lives with an apprehensiveness and insecurity that Horney called *basic anxiety*.

Central to the experience of basic anxiety is a tendency to seek and hold on to anything that makes the child feel safe. Eventually the strategies the child adopts to secure this safety become powerfully reassuring in their own right. Horney referred to these strategies as "strategic necessities." The three basic strategies are present to varying degrees in most people but are seen in exaggerated form in the self-protective manipulations of neurotic people (see Horney, 1950, for a full discussion):

- *Helplessness.* Neurotically moving toward people in a desire to secure protection and security through total compliance with their actual or imagined wishes

- *Aggressiveness.* Neurotically moving against people in the hope of dominating and thus gaining mastery over them
- *Detachment.* Neurotically moving away from people as a way of avoiding being further hurt or abandoned

Eventually, among those who have been seriously derailed during childhood, these neurotic strategies become neurotic compulsions that serve no adaptive function in the person's life. But they do come to dominate that person's life. They may even become a facade, an alienated false self, that paradoxically the individual may come to regard as a "despised real self" (Monte, 1991, p. 584). Such a person might say, "Of course, I have to be this way only because of the crappy, hostile, unloving, and unpredictable world that you have set up for me. If it were not for you, I would be just fine." However, this kind of "fine" is unrealistic and is only part of a fantasy of what the ideal self might be.

Hostility and Alienation. At this point in a person's life, Horney believed, basic anxiety becomes coupled with basic hostility. The result is the person's *alienation* from who he or she really is. This is how the process works: I become simultaneously afraid to break through all the rules I have set up to make myself feel safe from the way you treat me and terribly, terribly angry that you have made me so anxious. I come to believe that I am actually a much more wonderful person than anyone could possibly know, come to feel profoundly disappointed that nobody acknowledges my wonderfulness, and soon completely lose sight of who and what I really am, what I am actually doing in the world, and how the way I am being treated is largely a consequence of the crazy ways I am behaving. I begin to live in a profoundly neurotic reality constructed around my expectations for myself, which arise from my expectations for how you will treat me. I create elaborate sets of rules about what I should like, should feel, and should wish (Horney, 1950).

Soon these neurotic regulations create a straitjacket that separates me further and further from the reality of experiencing either you or myself:

> In other words, the tyranny of the shoulds drives [me] frantically to be something that [I] am or could be. And in [my] imagination [I] am different—so different, indeed, that the real self fades and pales still more. Neurotic claims, in terms of self, mean the abandoning of the reservoir of spontaneous energies. Instead of making [my] own efforts, for instance with regard to human relations [I] neurotic[ally] insist that others should adjust to [me]. (Horney, 1951, p. 159)

The Aims of Psychotherapy

For Horney, "the goal of psychotherapy was to provide the individual with the means to free the real self, to accept its character, and to allow it full and spontaneous expression without the curtailment of learned defensiveness" (1946, quoted in Monte,

1991, p. 583). But how is this agenda to be accomplished? The neurotic views the efforts of the therapist as extremely dangerous. The therapist, after all, is challenging and seeking to pull apart that singular bit of armor that protects, unifies, and distinguishes the self.

Here Horney once again borrowed from Alfred Adler. She recognized that preservation of the neurotic's fictive self is his or her crowning neurotic triumph. Any threat to this reality is also a threat to the neurotic's most fundamental sense of safety, his or her "protective structure."

Therapeutic progress occurs only one step at a time. Gradually the therapist and the client work through every neurotic impulse, as each one appears in the therapeutic relationship. Transference, according to Horney, was Freud's greatest discovery (Ewen, 1988, p. 176); through the transference process, the patient reveals habitual tendencies to move toward, against, and away from relationships. As these tendencies become apparent, the patient can hold them up to scrutiny and analysis. The patient gradually learns a way of interacting with others that reveals bits and pieces of the true self. With personal growth comes a gradual release from the tyranny of shoulds that have been constructed over a lifetime. Gradually the neurotic need to be a flawless human being becomes a less controlling force in the patient's choices and relationships. (See Chapter 14 for alternative strategies for dealing with this problem.)

Ultimately, psychotherapy should help a person accept adult responsibility for his or her "real" self. The person begins to experience the world as a much more rewarding and worthwhile place. The "actual" self comes into contact with a world that, by and large, treats the person fairly objectively most of the time. In this nonneurotic reality, the person discovers a reservoir of what Americans call will and Horney called "inner-independence," accompanied by greater spontaneity of feelings and a quality Horney called "wholeheartedness."

I believe that what Horney hoped her patients would achieve is the experience some existential therapists have called "life-as-it-is-ness." As Horney stated, "It does not lie within the power of the analyst to turn the patient into a flawless human being. He can only help him to become free to strive toward an approximation of these ideals" (1945, p. 243). The true aim of analysis is thus not to render life devoid of risks and conflicts but to enable an individual to eventually solve problems himself or herself (Horney, 1939, p. 305).

Horney's Unique Contribution

Horney's ability to write so cogently about gender and the fundamental conflicts that invade the relationships between men and women are unique in the history of psychoanalysis. That she had been raised in northern Germany by an emotionally strong mother who physically protected Karen from a sometimes abusive father probably explains how she came to be one of the few women to graduate from medical school in Europe at the turn of the century and how she could hold her own in the enclave of male privilege that psychoanalysis was in her day. Her biographer wrote,

> Karen's ambivalent feelings towards her father, her dependency upon her mother and her struggle to free herself from this dependency, her longstanding resentment at playing a secondary role to her brother, the conflict within herself between the roles of assertive professional woman and the compliant childbearing homemaker—all those had to be confronted. (Rubins, 1978, p. 38)

The independence of thought Horney articulated as a young analyst probably came as quite a shock to her mentors.

Horney emigrated to the United States in 1932. Her views on women, her extremely liberal attitudes about sex, and her departure from Freudian orthodoxy about anxiety made her anathema to both the Chicago and New York psychoanalytic establishments. She eventually established her own American Institute for Psychoanalysis, which for a short time welcomed psychoanalysts from a wide variety of schools and positions. Eventually, however, this venture collapsed as a casualty of the battle by psychiatrists (of which she was one) to prevent nonphysician analysts, like Erich Fromm and Erik Erikson, from practicing psychotherapy in the United States.

It was perhaps her tough, creative spirit that made Horney's psychoanalysis so directly relevent to the social and emotional political issues that defined the emotional disorders most frequently afflicting Americans at mid-century. Horney herself wrote, eloquently and enigmatically, "Does not the real work begin *after* the analysis? The analysis shows one her enemies but one must battle them afterwards, day by day" (Horney's diary, quoted in Rubins, 1978, p. 39).

Erich Fromm

One of the newly immigrated analysts most profoundly influenced by Horney and her American Institute for Psychoanalysis was Erich Fromm (1900–1980), a Berlin-trained analyst with a Ph.D. in sociology. He arrived in Chicago in 1933, about the same time as Horney. Fromm went on to develop a psychoanalytically based theory that more fully examined the problem of alienation from one's own nature, which Horney had first addressed in her work on the tyranny of shoulds.

Fromm's ideas have influenced my thinking to such an extent that I want to delay discussing them in detail until Chapter 19, where I will present some of my own ideas about the talking cure. But it is appropriate to conclude this chapter with a brief look at this "hundredth flower" blooming in the intellectual hothouse that was psychoanalysis in the United States during the reign of the neo-Freudian ego analysts.

In some sense, Erich Fromm is the most important intellectual figure in this book. His writing constructed the first bridge between the lofty intellectual ideals and theories of Sigmund Freud and the realities confronting ordinary men and women in the modern age. Fromm addressed the emotional and psychological needs of people who, day by day, try to live their lives as creatively and humanely as possible given the social, economic, and political forces that oppose them in the world.

Fromm believed that the talking cure could not only liberate human beings from their personal histories but could also show them how the full exercise of their psychological, emotional, and spiritual freedom could make them free in the world as well.

The key to understanding this aspect of Fromm (which I will not return to in Chapter 19) is to recognize his horror as a German teenager at the vicious nationalism of his teachers and neighbors in the period leading up to World War I. Later, during the 1930s and 1940s, he was also profoundly affected by the rise of fascism and anti-Semitism in Germany.

Fromm was particularly inspired by one of his high school teachers, who had been "a voice of sanity and realism in the midst of insane hatred." His teacher's example caused Fromm to start pondering the great question of his life: "How is it possible?" (Fromm, 1962, p. 7). How is it possible that one man could find the courage and the self-assurance to stand so firmly against the madness that had enveloped everyone else around him?

Fromm broadened his question during the war to include behavior of both extremes (Monte, 1991). How is it possible that some people can be sufficiently brave to stand against the screaming mob and to advocate reason in a time of violence and hate? And how is it possible for the ordinary people who are your neighbors, your schoolfriends, and your teachers to become transformed into demoniacal killers?

> My main interest was clearly mapped out. I wanted to understand the laws that govern the life of the individual man, and the laws of society—that is, of men in their social existence. I tried to see the lasting truth in Freud's concepts as against those assumptions which were in need of revision. I tried to do the same with Marx's theory, and finally I tried to arrive at a synthesis which followed from the understanding and the criticism of both thinkers. (Fromm, 1962, p. 9)

From this lifelong quest for understanding came a series of books that aspired to unravel the mysteries of humankind's most basic and most important needs. Fromm postulated that human being's are driven by both their instinctual, animal needs, as Sigmund Freud had described, and their distinctly human needs.

The Human Quest for Fulfillment

The quest for fulfillment of these human needs allows us to rise above our basic animal nature. We can seize the day and lead our lives productively, in the pursuit of love, creativity, community, genuine individuality, reason, and significance.

But living such a life arouses our most basic fears as well. What if I decide to declare my love for you and you accept that love, only to manipulate and humiliate me?

What if I accept membership in your community but then discover that our only bond is our mutual distrust and dislike of everyone outside our community? What if I fail in my acts of creation and have to confront my own emptiness? What if I declare my uniqueness to the world and then discover that everyone rejects me for not fitting in? What is the honor accorded to the person who teaches reason in a classroom gone mad with nationalistic or racial hatred?

To choose to be human is to dare to be separate—to dare to exercise freedom. Meanwhile, all of economics and politics and education invites us to sell out, to conform, to fit in, to enjoy the rewards of the system. How difficult it is to refuse to alienate ourselves from who and what we truly are and truly believe! How painful a choice it is to forgo the protective anonymity of conformity!

A few years ago, I taught a course about the politics and sociology of being male. Sixteen students and I spent the semester trying to come to terms with the non-obvious assumptions we had made about the world and about ourselves because we were all men. (Women would have called this process "consciousness raising," but because we were all men, we called it "education.") We pondered the complexities of all the standard topics of "men's studies": competition, intimacy, sports, sex, parents, parenting, career, marriage, and stress.

We also talked at length about our reactions to homosexuality and to homosexually oriented men and women. Virtually everyone in the seminar came to discover a reservoir of emotionally based homophobia in himself. Almost everyone recognized that this homophobia had at least some roots in what one person called "the fear of the hidden possibilities in the self." We met with some openly gay male students and tried to understand the experience of being gay in our society and on our campus. At the end of these discussions, I asked the students to read Fromm's *The Art of Loving* (1956) and to try thinking about homosexuality and homophobia from Fromm's perspective.

As the fates would have it, 2 years later homosexuality became a major civil rights issue on our campus. By a further quirk of fate, 8 of the 30 or so student senators who were to vote on the issue were alumni of my seminar. The gay student organization lost the vote in a landslide. None of my 8 former students voted to support their homosexual fellow students at any of three different meetings on the issue.

Over the course of the next semester, I was able to ask most of my 8 former students why they had voted as they had. Every man I spoke to said that in his heart and mind he had agreed with the proposed civil rights petition from the gay students. But each had feared that voting in accord with his conscience would bring a torrent of social disapproval, a stigma as perhaps "latently" homosexual, and a reputation as a disloyal member of the fraternity, club, or team that had elected him to the senate.

This is precisely what Fromm was writing about: How is it possible that every single man from my class could vote against his own conscience? How is it possible that each of them fell prey to mass hysteria on an important civil rights issue? On the other hand, how is it possible that a minority of 10 or 12 students time after time stood up for their convictions and voted for this legislation in the face of such massive social pressure to vote against it? Questions like these pervade the writings of Erich Fromm.

Fromm's Vision for the Talking Cure

With the advent of Fromm's "interpersonal school of psychotherapy" (May & Yalom, 1989), a distinctly North American psychoanalysis came of age. It was capable of addressing (if not necessarily answering or resolving) the important issues that keep modern men and women from feeling alive and free. It was a vision of psychoanalysis true to the Enlightenment vision of human beings: left alone by government, conducting their lives according to the principles of reason, justice, and personal freedom.

Fromm gave psychoanalysis a new aim, a goal that transcended the vision of the magnetists and the mesmerists to "cure the sick":

> The psychoanalyst is not only concerned with the readjustment of the neurotic individual to his given society. His task must be also to recognize that the individual's ideal of normalcy may contradict the aim of the full realization of himself as a human being. It is the belief of the progressive forces in society that such a realization is possible, that the interests of society and of the individual need not be antagonistic forever. (Fromm, 1944, p. 384)

P.S.: Two years later, an entirely different student senate, none of whose members had received the benefits of my seminar, overwhelmingly reversed itself and granted full recognition of the rights of gay and lesbian people on our campus. My only question is, Was this turnabout, as Fromm might have put it, a "return to a full vigorous expression of humanness," a happy unfolding of an essentially progressive history? Or was it perhaps a result of the fact that I was safely ensconced off campus on sabbatical, writing this book?

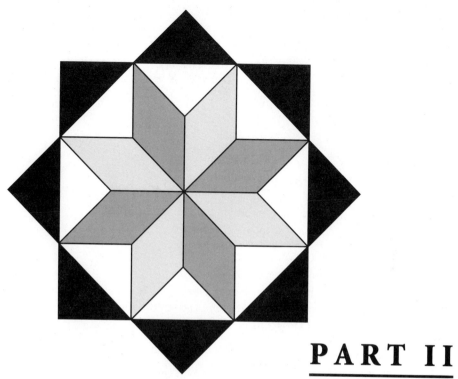

PART II
Psychotherapy in America: From Walden Pond to Walden Two

I went to the woods because I wished to live life deliberately, to front only the essential facts of life, and see if I could not learn what it had to teach, and not, when I came to die, discover that I had not lived. I did not wish to live what was not life, living is so dear; nor did I wish to practice resignation, unless it was quite necessary. I wanted to live deep and suck out all the marrow of life, to live life so sturdily, and Spartan-like as to put to rout all that was not life, to cut a broad swath and shave close, to drive life into a corner, and reduce it to its lowest terms, and, if it proved to be mean, why then to get the whole and genuine meanness of it, and publish its meanness to the world; or if it were sublime, to know it by experience, and be able to give a true account of it in my next excursion.

HENRY DAVID THOREAU

ON A TREE FALLEN ACROSS THE ROAD
(TO HEAR US TALK)*
The tree the tempest with a crush of wood
Throws down in front of us is not to bar
Our passage to our journey's end for good,
But just to ask us who we think we are

Insisting always on our own way so.
She likes to halt us in our runner tracks,
And make us get down in a foot of snow
Debating what to do without an ax.

And yet she knows obstruction is in vain:
We will not be put off the final goal
We have it hidden in us to attain,
Not though we have to seize earth by the pole

And, tired of aimless circling in one place,
Steer straight off after something into space.

ROBERT FROST

SONG OF MYSELF

1
I CELEBRATE myself, and sing myself,
And what I assume you shall assume,
For every atom belonging to me as good belongs to you.
I loafe and invite my soul,
I lean and loafe at my ease observing a spear of summer grass.

My tongue, every atom of my blood, form'd from this soil, this air,
Born here of parents born here from parents the same, and their parents the same,
I, now thirty-seven years old in perfect health begin,
Hoping to cease not till death.

Creeds and schools in abeyance,
Retiring back a while sufficed at what they are, but never forgotten,
I harbor for good or bad, I permit to speak at every hazard,
Nature without check with original energy.

WALT WHITMAN

---

*From *The Poetry of Robert Frost,* edited by Edward Connery Lathem. Copyright © 1951 by Robert Frost. Copyright 1923 © 1969 by Henry Holt and Co., Inc. Reprinted by permission of Henry Holt and Co., Inc.

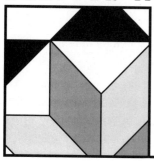

CHAPTER 11

William James and American Psychology

A Psychology of Use

The early history of the talking cure in North America comprises three principal traditions, all rooted in a spiritual understanding of madness. The indigenous peoples of North America (the folks who "discovered Columbus") accepted that madness was visited on people by evil spirits as punishment for breaking taboos. The Puritans accepted the idea of witchcraft and possession by devils and enforced their beliefs with the death penalty. Black slaves, brought here from Africa, retained much of their African cosmology and relied on spiritualist healers to treat emotional suffering.

The post-Enlightenment talking cures developed by Jean-Martin Charcot and Pierre Janet in France and by Sigmund Freud, Alfred Adler, and Carl Jung in central Europe were brought to North America. But the new discipline of psychology was developing along its own lines in 19th-century North America. To understand that development we must first understand the social and political climate shaping the emerging American character. Americans of that era were a practical people, given more to the metaphysical virtues of common sense than to any theories of the unconscious. Psychology was studied under the name moral philosophy, as an extension of religious teachings rather than an independent science. Like middle-class Europeans, however, Main Street Americans tended to subscribe to the full litany of Victorian virtues. Masturbation and nonreproductive sexual practices were considered the cause of many physical and psychological disorders.

William James, a professor at Harvard University with interests in both biology and philosophy, became "the father of American psychology"—although he strictly rejected the idea that his view of psychology had anything to do with the teachings previously associated with that name. He consistently viewed himself as a moral philosopher. James became the champion of the metaphysical notion of free will. Free will and individualism thus became deeply embedded in North American psychological thought. Sigmund Freud called American psychology "a vast mistake." Nevertheless, James's belief in free will and the power of the individual to heroically shape his or her own destiny profoundly affected the development of a North American talking cure.

Early North American Views of Madness

The earliest recorded practices associated with treating mental and emotional disorders in North America were those of the million or so individuals whose ancestors had lived throughout North America for more than 10,000 years before the first Europeans arrived. Native peoples recognized a wide variety of psychological disorders, including hysteria, depression, and hallucinations. They usually viewed madness as caused by possession by evil spirits.

The Native American Perspective: Alienation From Self

These groups commonly adopted what we would consider today an almost humanistic-existentialist view of emotional suffering. Various tribal groups, for example, referred to madness as "soul loss" and "being lost to oneself." Native peoples thus appear to have widely understood the core of mental illness as self-alienation (Gamwell & Tomes, 1995).

Indian cosmology recognized that the spirit world contains both good and evil spirits and that the lives of human beings are continuously influenced by interactions with these spirits. Madness could be understood either as a punishment inflicted on a person who had broken a moral law, such as an incest taboo, or as the result of powerful witchcraft practiced by a rival or an enemy.

An afflicted person would consult with a shaman, a man or a woman who had demonstrated significant powers to mediate between the spirit world and human beings. Often shamans were also *berdaches,* a pejorative French term used by European trappers and explorers to describe members of Native American tribes, usually male, who lived as members of the opposite sex. (See Callender & Kochems, 1987, for a fascinating review of the anthropological literature on the *berdaches.*)

Shamans regularly invoked supernatural aid in treating the mentally afflicted. They first would try to determine the cause of the illness through divination and dream analysis. If the illness stemmed from breaking a taboo, the curing ceremony included some form of confession, followed by rituals of atonement and purification. If witchcraft was suspected, the shaman used special rituals to counteract the witch's malevolent powers. (Gamwell & Tomes, 1995, p. 15)

If the disorder was psychosomatic, the shaman might perform a ritual designed to encourage the patient's abreactive discharge of pent-up emotion. As in any modern group-centered culture, these pent-up feelings were often anger, jealousy, and other "individualistic" expressions of self. These rituals seem to have let group members blow off steam in socially sanctioned ways that did not threaten the cohesiveness of the group.

More serious disorders were taken as signs of more serious interventions by the inhabitants of the spirit world. The Iroquois had highly specialized medicine societies for treatment of the mentally ill. Their Corn Husk society kept the rituals for stopping bad dreams and hallucinations; the Otter society controlled rites to cure nervous tremors (Gamwell & Tomes, 1995). The Navajo conducted the Night Way ceremony for the treatment of severely disordered persons, who were described as "acting like moths." This ceremony, which lasted a week or longer, invoked the spirits of the mountains to heal the afflicted. It involved both sacred chanting and elaborate "sand paintings," which reproduced the sacred, secret visual symbols required for healing. (Carl Jung was fascinated by this use of ritual and symbol and made extensive studies of archetypical images in Native American healing ceremonies.) While a medicine man or "singer" performed the *yeibichai,* or "talking gods," chant, the afflicted person sat in the middle of each successive sand painting as it was constructed and absorbed the power of its healing symbols and figures (Gamwell & Tomes, 1995, p. 13).

Madness in Colonial Massachusetts

The European colonists who settled in North America in the 17th century brought Old World Christian views of madness with them. There were numerous instances in the English colonies of mentally ill persons being found guilty of witchcraft. In 1691–92 more than 100 girls and women were tried for witchcraft in Salem, Massachusetts; 19 of them were executed. Their symptoms, by the way, included outbursts of strong emotion, including anger, visual and auditory hallucinations, and writhing limbs. We now believe that they were, in fact, victims of accidental poisoning by stored grain that had gotten wet and grown a fungus that is hallucinogenic when eaten. But this explanation did not come in time to save a West Indian slave girl named Tituba from confessing under torture to her dark alliance with the devil.

The spiritual leader of the Massachusetts colonists, Cotton Mather (1663–1728) went so far as to claim that Satan caused the frequent cases of melancholia observed to afflict Christian preachers in the colony. He also believed that the evil temper and unpleasant disposition of his third wife, "Lydia," was caused by satanic possession— some 25 years after the infamous Salem witch trials (Gamwell & Tomes, 1995).

African American Healing Rituals

The other group of early Americans we need to consider are the African slaves who had been brought in bondage to the colonies from western Africa. They too had a well-established cosmology for understanding madness, generally believing that emotional disorders are the consequence of sorcery and magic. A syncretic African American cosmology emerged from the blended traditions of various ethnic groups—Bantu, Yoruba, Ibo, and Hausa—who had been imprisoned together by slave traders.

As in Native American society, some members of the African American community were recognized as having special powers for healing and for intervening between the spirit world and life on earth. The healing process required identifying, through divination or dreams, the evil source of illness. Specialists in magic—known as conjurers, hoodoos, voodoo priests, and rootmen—were among the most feared and respected members of the slave community (Gamwell & Tomes, 1995).

Of special note are the rituals used to cure slaves suffering from the ill effects of (necessarily) suppressed rage. Powerless people needed symbolic ways to express their most powerful feelings—and perhaps some symbolic vehicle for revenge against their tormentors. The great African American writer Zora Neale Hurston, writing in 1935, documented one interesting account of this double-edged talking cure among slaves, the story of Old Dave. He was a powerful conjurer on a southern plantation. Old Dave got his revenge on his cruel master by conjuring insanity into the planter's wife and children and thus breaking the man's spirit.

19th-Century North American Psychology

> Enlightenment is man's release from his self-incurred tutelage. . . . Have courage to use your own reason! (Immanuel Kant, 1724–1804)

> I despise philosophy, and renounce its guidance—let my soul dwell with Common Sense. (Thomas Reid, 1710–1796)

> Nature and Nature's Laws lay hid in Night: God said, Let Newton be: and all was Light. (Alexander Pope, 1688–1744)

Competing Visions of Truth

If you were a Caucasian male from a good Christian family that believed in the value of a college education and were lucky enough to find yourself in a pretty good North American college—and you had been born 150 years ago—you might well have found yourself in a required moral philosophy seminar, engaged in lively debate on the relative merits of the views expressed in the preceding three quotations.

If you'd read Charles Darwin and Thomas Jefferson, you might have been the class skeptic, full of optimistic belief in science and reason. You would have championed the radical social ideas of John Locke and John Stuart Mill. You were almost certainly an abolitionist in the slavery debate, and you might even have held some radical views about the liberation of women. You probably would have wondered why so very few of your peers and teachers had Immanuel Kant's necessary "courage to use your own reason" and the willingness to challenge and question the world as it exists. We can imagine you as a chemistry or botany major with an interest in law or medicine. There wouldn't have been much at college that you would have truly enjoyed, but then you weren't exactly the sort of young man the college founders had had in mind when they had knelt in the snow to establish the place.

If, on the other hand, you had come to college, like most of your classmates, to prepare yourself for assuming a suitable moral place in society—perhaps as a teacher or a minister—your sympathies would surely have been touched by the work of the Scottish moral philosopher Thomas Reid. You would have been profoundly troubled by the moral softness of your radically relativist peers, who rejected the primacy of divine law in regulating the affairs of men. For you, Darwin's catalogued discoveries were further evidence of the majesty of creation, signs of God's blueprints for the universe. You would have accepted as a fundamental truth, revealed by scripture, the distinct division between the human being's essential nature and that of the other animals of God's creation. You would have regarded the discovery of the laws of the human mind as the unveiling of the divine. Both the mystery uncovered by science and those human faculties employed to comprehend the mystery would have fit into this schema. There was, you would have understood, a profoundly moral metaphysics to be discovered in psychology, which was the study of God's most perfect creation. But with it came an awesome responsibility to put what had been learned to proper Christian use.

And then you might have been among those who would have preferred Alexander Pope's approach. His cleverly ambiguous couplet at the beginning of the section implies that you clearly have no sense of the urgency and gravity of this debate. And you are welcome, sir, to engage yourself with nonscientific studies. Preferably elsewhere.

And I? I must undergo the most radical transformation of all. For to be the professor in this class, I must become a member of the clergy, preferably an elder of the church and probably the college's president. The metaphysics of knowledge is a serious business. It has led many a young man dangerously away from the truth. Science in the hands of one who is morally unprepared or ill equipped to harness its energies can lead young minds to ruin. Science is the essence of mental discipline; it requires a strong mind and an iron will if one is not to be led astray by pretty discourse and fallacious argument. But science is first and foremost an uncompromising moral business. A teacher's occupation is to lead young men toward the Christian righteousness that follows from behaving in accordance with the Plan for our destinies.

As the professor, I would be struck cold with fear and loathing of those who discourse on a "reasoned" science. They would have your uncle an ape! They would replace the magnificence of culture with the brutality of the jungle; they would have survival as paramount and redemption but dogma. Worse! They would drown out the eternal passions of the human heart with recourse to mathematics and to laws regulating the movement of stones and markets.

Preachers and Teachers for the Frontier

My college in Indiana was founded in 1832 by a small group of devout New England Presbyterians to furnish the burgeoning frontier with an ample supply of Christian "preachers and teachers" with these sorts of views. In part the founders wanted to save the souls of the heathen Indians, but in larger part they wanted to ensure that the western territories would be controlled by like-minded Christian citizens who could keep the country from falling into immigrant Catholic hands. "Our Christian way of life" was their cause, and education was one of their principal instruments.

From as early as 1836 until as late as 1914, psychology courses at my college were taught as moral philosophy. They were taught by professors of the English Bible, and usually the college president, as a graduation requirement for all seniors. This approach to instruction probably marks the beginning of the battle that continues to this day over the teaching of "politically correct" ideas in colleges and universities.

The course at our college changed names several times over the years: Mental Philosophy from the 1830s through the mid-1860s; Metaphysics through the mid-1880s; Moral Philosophy and Mental Science through 1895. By the turn of the century, the course was taught as Physiological Psychology; interestingly, however, the Bible was still the primary textbook, supplemented by the marginally more secular *The Philosophy of the Human Mind,* written by Thomas Reid's devoted student and follower, Dugald Stewart.

This program of study, called either Scottish Psychology or Faculty Psychology, investigated the nature of "human faculties." Its stated purpose was to show students how to engage in self-improvement in accordance with divine plan. Despite the up-to-date emphasis on the physiology of the human nervous system, the college catalog from 1896 is at pains to make clear that

> physiological [psychology] and general psychology [the Scottish psychology based on divinely inspired "faculties"] are carefully arranged in relation to each other, so as to be mutually supplementary. In both subjects individual attention will be given to all members of the class who are *expected* to present their personal difficulties for consideration. A seminary will be held weekly in connection with these courses. [italics added]

With American psychology firmly established within American higher education as a 19th-century adjunct to religious fundamentalism (Leahey, 1992), we can only imagine what sort of agonies "the boys" went through in trying to decide which "personal difficulties" they would present to the college president in their psychology class. What we can be sure of is that each successive president took his moral responsibilities with utmost gravity as he strove to show his lads how to apply "the method of the science and the laws of mental action together with a philosophical treatment of the nature of judgment and reason."

Sigmund Freud and Carl Jung both lectured extensively in the United States in the early years of the new century, but I've seen little evidence that anything they had to say made its way into the mainstream of North American psychotherapy until well after World War I. Then the immigration of many hundred European-trained psychoanalysts brought the practice of "depth psychology" to New York and Chicago. William James, "the father of American psychology," found Freud's theories the result of "a man's obsession with fixed ideas" and "could make nothing" of Freud's interpretation of dream life (Erikson, 1968, p. 150). Is it any wonder that early in the 20th century Freud described the state of North American psychology to his followers as "a mistake. A vast mistake, but a mistake nonetheless"?

Moral Therapy: The Rise of the "Rest Cure"

Recall from Chapter 4 that the prevailing school of treatment of the insane in the United States throughout the 19th century was moral therapy, and you will begin to see why I have chosen this somewhat parochial route to introducing the development of the talking cure in the United States. Prior to 1900 there had been very little change in treatment of the mentally ill since the days of Benjamin Rush during the War of Independence. Treatments for emotional disorders were far less scientifically credible than they were in Europe and were strictly limited to medical and paramedical procedures.

"Just Plain Common Sense"

Rest cures were commonly advocated in the 19th century for persons who were anxious or depressed. It was deemed especially important that the afflicted person not exercise thinking powers more than several times a day. This prohibition even extended to reading materials; anyone who would, in a state of nervous exhaustion, take on anything more stimulating than a book of "most-loved sermons" or insipid light "garden" verse would, of course, have only himself or herself to blame if the condition worsened. Bland diets were also much in fashion in treating nervous disorders. Spicy and exotic foods were widely perceived to excite the nervous system, especially in persons of delicacy and breeding, to the point of complete exhaustion—as would riding in trains, playing card games, dancing, and listening to modern music.

All these prescriptions were in the service of, in the words of the great Scottish psychologist Reid, "just plain common sense." As you may have started to figure out, the metaphysics of common sense as applied to abnormal psychology was in reality the study of the psychopathology of immorality. What did spicy food, the tango, and romantic fiction have to do with nervous exhaustion? The answer was obvious to therapists in Reid's mold: They all excite the sexual nervous system. And a sexual nervous system in a state of perpetual excitation, unless one is a gypsy or of Mediterranean descent (or African, although African Americans were essentially invisible to these men of science), will cause one to weaken gradually until weakness becomes madness and, if left untreated, death.

These Victorian Americans were a dreadfully dreary lot when it came to anything sexual. But they had perfectly worked out the essence of Scottish psychology: Temperance, abstinence, and prudery were proper for good Christians, in accordance with the laws of the psyche as God himself created it. I'm not sure that the early American physiologists believed much in the power of "sexual toxins," as the Victorian physicians of Europe had, but these good Christian men certainly believed that sexual exhaustion was the greatest menace to emotional and social health.

Madness and the Solitary Vice

The greatest crime against our essential human nature, they thought, was masturbation. This "solitary vice" not only led its victims to dissipate precious bodily fluids, depleting the essence of vitality, but also stole pleasure, which would surely lead any Christian man or woman to ruin (Christians being so much more refined and advanced, neurologically speaking, than all those who are darker-skinned and less biologically "advanced").

One physician-psychologist, Mary Melendy, advised in her book *Maiden, Wife, and Mother: How to Attain Health—Beauty—Happiness* (1903) that mothers have a special obligation to protect their sons from falling into the abyss of solitary vice. Melendy cautioned:

> Teach him that these [sexual] organs are given as a sacred trust, that in maturer years he may be the means of giving life to those who shall live forever.
>
> Impress upon him that if these organs are abused, or if they are put to any use besides that for which God made them—and He did not intend they should be used at all until man is fully grown—they will bring disease and ruin upon those who abuse and disobey those laws which God has made to govern them.
>
> If he has ever learned to handle his sexual organs, or to touch them in any way except to keep them clean, not to do it again. If he does, he will not grow up happy, healthy and strong.
>
> Teach him that when he handles or excites the sexual organs, all parts of the body suffer, because they are connected by nerves that run throughout the system, this is why it is called "self-abuse." The whole body is abused when this part of the body is handled or excited in any manner whatever.

Teach them to shun all children who indulge this loathsome habit, or all children who talk about these things. The sin is terrible, and is, in fact worse than lying or stealing! For, although these are wicked and will ruin their soul, yet this habit of self-abuse will ruin both soul and body.

If the sexual organs are handled it brings too much blood to these parts, and this produces a diseased condition; it also causes disease in other organs of the body, because they are left with a less amount of blood than they ought to have. The sexual organs, too, are very closely connected with the spine and the brain by means of the nerves, and if they are handled, or if you keep thinking about them, these nerves get excited and become exhausted, and this makes the back ache, the brain heavy and the whole body weak.

It lays the foundation for consumption, paralysis, and heart disease. It weakens the memory, makes a boy careless, negligent and listless.

It even makes many lose their minds; others, when grown, commit suicide. (pp. 32–33)

Moralizing Therapy: Sex and Madness

The explicit connection of madness with masturbation and other sexual excesses was as much an article of faith to the early North American psychologists as it was to Freud and his peers. One had only to go to the asylums, to see the demented people constantly stimulating themselves into further levels of hopeless depravity, to witness the effects of masturbation. Other sexual practices, almost as common, had equally devastating consequences. Among these was the suicidally dangerous practice of coitus interruptus, or "withdrawal," nearly every teenager's old but notoriously unreliable friend.

As early as 1832, sex manuals for young men were cautioning against the dangers associated with withdrawal. Let's develop the argument as a good Victorian Scottish psychologist would. First, the Bible clearly states that it is forbidden to spill one's seed:

Then Judah told Onan to sleep with his brother's wife, to do his duty as the husband's brother and raise up issue for his brother. But Onan knew that the issue would not be his; so whenever he slept with his brother's wife, he spilled his seed upon the ground so as not to raise up issue for his brother. What he did was wicked in the LORD'S sight, and the LORD took his life. (Genesis 38:8–11, Oxford New English Bible)

As psychologists, we must use our God-given faculty of common sense to figure out the "psychology" embedded in this scriptural teaching. Here's how it goes: When a man initiates his wife in the practices of the marital bed and then engages in the disputed practice of coitus interruptus, his wife is left in a state of great nervous excitation, from which there is no natural release. This condition causes the wife much aggravation and leaves her in a state of nervous arousal, which can lead her to experience mood swings, nervousness, and unfeminine sharpness of tongue. To put this situation right, the wife will, perhaps even unconsciously, begin planning ways to resolve her dilemma. She may exaggerate her femininity or introduce certain exotic spices in the main meal of the day as a way of rekindling desire in her husband, so that he might "finish the job," so to speak.

Should the husband succumb to this temptation while also amending his practice of coitus interruptus, he can put all to rights. But what if he repeats his old withdrawal habit? If his wife is a strong-willed woman but ignorant of psychology, she may persist in her behavior, which will cause her to develop a vast array of nervous symptoms (and we are advised by our colleagues in Vienna and Paris that the account will usually be given up to hysteria). Meanwhile, her husband may fall into a state of weakness from which he may never fully recover.

If you are saying to yourself, "Well, if it has to happen to me, that's the way I choose to be carried off," you have clearly missed the point of the story. The moral lesson is that mental well-being and emotional strength are the result of a proper education in the Bible and psychology and of the strengthening of the will. However, as some of you already know, when it comes to matters of strengthening the will within the sexual domain, most men are totally inept. Despite all the 19th-century manuals exhorting boys and men away from self-stimulation and "unnatural" sexual practices such as coitus interruptus, and toward a life of Christian self-restraint and Christian virtue with their wives, the message for the most part fell on deaf ears.

The Cult of Pure Womanhood

So moral philosophy turned its attention to women and urged them to become the keepers of their family's well-being. North American psychologists, even in the earliest years of the discipline, wrote long and frequent articles for women's magazines and published advice books about how to "maintain a Christian household." Wives were advised about the dangers of wasting a man's strength through sexual dissipation, and they were vested with the moral authority to keep the menace of sexually induced nervous and emotional illness at bay.

By the mid-1880s this movement had coalesced politically with the Women's Christian Temperance Union, which aimed to prevent child beating and wife abuse by advocating strict temperance. Thus there emerged a powerful middle-class women's movement called the "cult of pure womanhood."

The power of this movement was such that the locus of moral power in the American family shifted dramatically from the traditional Judeo-Christian all-powerful patriarch. In the patriarch's place stood that paragon of moral strength and religious rectitude, Mother—the head of a scientifically managed Christian household.

The practical force of this movement is demonstrated in the fact that by 1900 the life expectancy of women in the United States actually exceeded that of men for the first time in history, as the birth rate dropped precipitously. The Christian family was becoming the "psychologically correct" family that Reid and his followers had proclaimed a century earlier. But there is no evidence that this movement away from sexual intercourse did much to decrease the prevalence or frequency of the allegedly ruinous practice of masturbation.

William James

Enter now a truly remarkable, one-of-a-kind young man who was destined to dethrone the Scottish psychologists at the very peak of their powers. William James (1842–1910) was born in a hotel in New York City into a family of extraordinary gifts, talents, and idiosyncracies.

A Family of Legend

As a member of the established upper crust of New England society, William's father (William Sr.) had tried unsuccessfully to take his rightful place as a member of the Presbyterian clergy. He discovered little room in the seminary for free-thinking young men of independent wealth and distinctly transcendental views, however.

William Jr., his younger brother Henry, and their baby sister Alice became one of the most famous and prolific literary families in American history. Ralph Waldo Emerson came to their house for elegant dinners and for a place to stay when he was in New York on lecture tours. Henry David Thoreau, with his "mountainous inward self-esteem and harmless and beautiful force of outward demeanor" (Lewis, 1991, p. 64), became a frequent guest at the Jameses' table.

The James family were "at home" to everyone who was progressive, challenging, and modern. Their lives were at the center of everything that was "the wonder of Boston" in the years before and during the American Civil War. They were an elegant and established family of "modern gentlemen," although not one of them ever enjoyed the unquestioned approval of the upper crust of New England society.

It was in the James family tradition to read and debate every idea of the day and to become intellectually independent critics. The children were expected to join in lively conversation with all manner of visiting dignitaries and the leading lights of the literary and civic scene. Some spectators considered the lot of them "sinners for all eternity; damaged goods" (Lewis, 1991).

In and Out of School. Most remarkable, perhaps, was the singular lack of formal education enjoyed by any of the James children. Henry Sr., seeing that the forces of small-minded reaction controlled every educational venue, decided to educate his children with private tutors while they traveled throughout the world.

At age 16, young William spent a short time in a public high school in France, where he discovered a fascination for science, especially scientific investigations that involved ingesting mind-altering substances. But within a year the young man was enrolled in art school in Geneva, Switzerland. In Switzerland, in due course, he developed a fascination with anatomy, a central aspect of his formal training as a painter. Art school was soon abandoned, however, in favor of an apprenticeship with a prominent landscape painter in Newport, Rhode Island.

It wasn't long before William began to think more seriously about science. At age 19, therefore, his father arranged for him to enter Harvard University's Lawrence Scientific School, where William proposed to begin studying chemistry. His first teacher at Harvard was Professor Charles William Eliot. Eliot was drawn to the young freshman's charm and originality but concluded that William "was not wholly devoted to his work as a chemist," largely because he enjoyed exercising his widely "excursive mind" (Lewis, 1991).

By age 21, William had withdrawn from Harvard and was living at home with little to keep him occupied. So it must have been some relief to his parents when he announced a year later his intention to become a physician. Papa arranged (through Professor Eliot) for William to enroll in classes at the Harvard Medical School, where he rediscovered his fascination with anatomy but also discovered that medical education was "all so much humbug."

At Sea With Louis Agassiz. The ever-patient Professor Eliot then arranged for William to meet the famed antievolution Swiss naturalist Louis Agassiz, who was new to the Harvard faculty and in the process of organizing an expedition to the Amazon. Agassiz was determined to resolve the apparent discrepancies between biblical accounts of Creation and the fossil record by demonstrating that "all biological species are immutable and rigidly separate divine creations." Agassiz believed that a properly researched fossil record would fully support his theory. Such a fossil record had not been recovered, Agassiz believed, because a period of massive glaciation had erased the critical evidence.

Agassiz was looking for young, adventurous scientists who could pay their own way on an expedition to uncover this missing fossil record. So in 1865 William set sail for Amazonia in search of the lost fossil records in the glacial deposits of the Amazon's delta. As the expedition sailed down the Atlantic coast out of Boston, they could see the fires still burning from the battles of the Civil War. They sailed past the port of the city of Charleston while it was still in flames.

William spent the entire voyage seasick: "The sailing was entirely a matter of hideous moist gales that whiten all the waves with foam." Once they reached shore, he fell ill with a smallpoxlike illness (probably varioloid), which rendered him temporarily blind and deeply depressed. From his experience with Agassiz, William wrote to his parents, he had earned a great lesson: "I am cut out for a speculative, not an active life" (Lewis, 1991, pp. 173–177).

Returning to Harvard at the earliest opportunity, William believed that his health was permanently ruined. He suffered still from depression, but in addition he experienced back pain, eyestrain, insomnia, and acute digestive difficulties. He became deeply suicidal during the long Boston winter that followed, and it was agreed that a change of scenery was very much in order.

In Germany With Hermann Helmholtz. In 1867 William enrolled as a student of physiology at the University of Berlin, where he undertook preliminary studies in the newly developing field of experimental neurology. William, excited by what he saw in Berlin, wrote home that surely "it is time for psychology to become a science!"

Upon hearing that the work being conducted by Hermann Helmholtz and Wilhelm Wundt ("the father of experimental psychology") was exclusively devoted to developing an experimentally based psychology, William decided to join them. So after only a few weeks in Berlin, he packed his bags for Heidelberg, with an eye toward continuing his studies in neurology and neuroanatomy. Less than a week later, however, he was booking passage back home to Boston. His "blue despair" made any other course of action impossible.

The tolerance of William's family to his complaints was quite remarkable for the time. However, they were already acquainted with psychological problems. Both his father and his father's sister had suffered from lifelong nervous imbalances, and his own sister Alice spent most of her life as a neurasthenic psychiatric invalid.

With Medical Degree in Hand. The family arranged for William to be awarded the M.D. degree in 1869 after he submitted a very minimal research paper and passed a 90-minute exam on anatomy. His comment on the few weeks he spent preparing for the exam was typical of his attitude toward rote learning: "Oh, how much drudgery, and of what an unpleasant kind it is." His depression was growing more and more profound, however, and he reached a suicidal low in the winter of 1870.

Erik Erikson (see Chapter 10) characterized William James's ordeal as a classic example of late-adolescence "identity crisis," brought on by the young man's failure to resolve the oedipal crisis. From a psychodynamic perspective, William's problems were essentially caused by the overbearing influence of Henry Sr. in the lives of his children. The interference was rooted in the father's

> combination of infirmity, inclination, and influence [which made] his family life a tyranny of liberalism and a school in utopianism in which every choice was made from the freest and most universal point of view and, above all, was to be discussed with Father. (Erikson, 1968, p. 151)

The Issue of Free Will

Much has been written about William James's "decision" during that terrible winter of 1870 to change his condition by a sheer act of will. At the depths of his depression, he declared that his salvation could only lie within the exercise of his will. At that point he declared the famous dictum:

My first act of free will shall be to believe in free will. . . . I will abstain from the mere speculation and contemplative Grubelei in which my nature takes most delight, and voluntarily cultivate the feeling of moral freedom by reading books favorable to it, as well as by acting. . . . Hitherto when I have felt like taking a free initiative, like daring to act originally, without carefully waiting for contemplation of the external world to determine all for me, suicide seemed the most manly form to put my daring into; now, I will go a step further with my will, not only act with it but believe as well; believe in my individual reality and creative power. My belief to be sure *can't* be optimistic—but I will posit life (the real, the good) in the self-governing *resistance* of the ego to the world. Life shall be in doing and suffering and creating. (1870, quoted in Lewis, 1991, pp. 204–205)

A Life of Action. What most writers have overlooked is that James had decided to exercise his "free will" in order to abandon his self-imposed life of "speculation" and to replace it with a devotion to "action and belief in my individual reality and creative power." It is also commonly overlooked that all of this "decision" and "commitment" and harnessing of will in truth didn't do him a whit of good. He ended the year 1870 writing that he was incapable of anything but "morbid shrinking from intellectual conversation" and telling his friends that he was "long since dead and buried" as an intellectual and social person.

Professor Eliot, now President Eliot, once again came to the young man's rescue. This time Eliot offered James a part-time job teaching comparative physiology at Harvard. Although James remained more or less depressed for the rest of his life, teaching did seem to be the turning point that the 30-year-old had been searching for. Teaching the young men of Harvard, "dealing with men instead of my own mind, and having diversion from those introspective studies which had bred a sort of philosophical hypochondria in me" provided the first glimmer of hope that James could lead a normal life.

Despite the fact that his classes were wildly popular, at the end of the first year of teaching James suffered a massive nervous breakdown. He wrote that he was possessed of "a horrible fear of my own existence. I became a mass of quivering fear. After this the universe was changed for me forever." He resolved to "abandon" mental science in favor of comparative anatomy. President Eliot accepted his statement that he "could never again face teaching" and appointed James the director of Harvard's Museum of Comparative Anatomy (Lewis, 1991).

Marriage. In the end, if any one thing "saved" James from the insane depression that haunted him, it was his marriage in 1876, when he was 34 years old. He wrote, "I found in marriage a repose I had never known before." At this juncture he was able to resume his teaching and to begin serious work on his long-promised and eagerly awaited textbook of psychology.

There is, perhaps, a direct connection among James's marriage, his recovery from depression, his focus on the importance of will, and the consolidation of his own views on the dangers of masturbation. It was all subsumed under the phrase "the moral business" within James's journals.

"The Moral Business."   The term had been coined by Henry Sr. to describe his own nervous difficulties and those that afflicted his children. There is no question that morality was perceived by the Jameses as bearing a profound and central relationship to the haunting tragedy of the family's "morbid psychology"—nervousness, hysteria, and even madness.

William James's theory of psychology was first and foremost, and for all his life remained, a matter of moral strengthening, or moral will power:

> "The moral business" was William's way, under the influence of Henry Senior, of referring to the whole question of the active will . . . and the affirming ego; . . . we can virtually equate will and ego and identity and even manhood in William's mental workings. The elder James, in William's idiom, had decisively thrown the moral business overboard after [William's nervous breakdown in 1844, when the elder Henry] had decreed the "absolute decease of my moral or voluntary power," and the surrender of his being to the vitalizing love of God. William did indeed perceive the choice for him as plain as could be: should he follow the example of his father and give up once and for all any attempt to energize and exert his will; or quite to the contrary should he make the active will the very center of his life's effort, with all else contributory to that? Until that time, [William wrote in his diary,] he had not hitherto given any real trial to "the moral interest" but had deployed it chiefly to hold in check certain bad habits, tendencies to "moral degradation" (another allusion, probably, to auto-eroticism). (Lewis, 1991, p. 201)

A Return to Moral Philosophy

By 1878 William James was in a peculiar situation. He had earned a medical degree, had lectured in physiology and anatomy, and he had taught the first-ever laboratory in psychology in the United States. He was even about to see Harvard University award its first Ph.D. in psychology. But James thought of himself almost exclusively as a philosopher. In 1877 President Eliot had been persuaded, probably with the encouragement of the biology faculty at Harvard, to list James's graduate and undergraduate psychology courses as offerings in the philosophy department. And in 1880 James managed to have his title changed from assistant professor of physiology to assistant professor of philosophy. He then began teaching a series of exceptionally popular courses on "mental science."

The result of these administrative changes was political crisis among the faculty at Harvard University. Psychology was widely considered a branch of moral philosophy and physiology at this time, but moral philosophy did not extend to include the heretical, morally relativistic teachings of Kant and other post-Enlightenment philosophers. Nevertheless, James's moral philosophy advocated such liberal causes as women's rights, vivisection (the use of animals in research), and German experimentalism. He perversely attacked theologically based prescriptions for human behavior, imperialist U.S. foreign policy, and creationist science. Having William James teach psychology was practically blasphemy!

James assigned the pious psychological textbooks of the day to his students, but he then audaciously used those books as devices to launch pointed ridicule at "faculty psychology" and the "common sense" view, still being faithfully taught by his colleagues in the philosophy department. No wonder James later scornfully declared, "I never had any philosophic instruction, the first lecture on psychology I ever heard being the first I ever gave" (quoted in Erikson, 1968, p. 152).

A North American Psychology

James's fascination and even obsession with "the moral business" was at the very center of the beginnings of North American psychology and psychotherapy and remains so to this day. James evidently believed that only the exercise of his will kept him from descending into the depths of utter madness. The following passage conveys the horror that James felt as he recognized his own vulnerability to depression whenever he failed to keep rigid control over his mental processes:

> Whilst in [a] state of philosophical pessimism and general depression of spirits about my prospects . . . suddenly there fell upon me without warning, just as if it came out of the darkness, a horrible fear of my own existence. Simultaneously there arose in my mind the image of an epileptic patient whom I had seen in the asylum, a black-haired youth with greenish skin, entirely idiotic, who used to sit all day on one of the benches, or rather shelves against the wall, with his knees drawn up against his chin, and the coarse grey undershirt which was his only garment, drawn over them inclosing his entire figure. He sat there like a sort of sculptured Egyptian cat or Peruvian mummy, moving nothing but his black eyes and looking absolutely non-human. This image and my fears entered into a species of combination with each other. *That shape am I,* I felt, potentially. Nothing that I possess can defend me against that fate, if the hour for it should strike for me as it struck for him. There was such a horror of him, and such a perception of my own merely momentary discrepancy from him, that it was as if something hereto solid within my breast gave way entirely and I became a mass of quivering fear. (1902, quoted in Lewis, 1991, p. 202)

A Psychology of the Will

For anyone who took James's view at all seriously, it would simply be axiomatic that freedom from insanity is primarily a matter of freedom of will. Mental health can be seen as equivalent to moral freedom; both are enjoyed by people who can think about and do what they firmly believe in. If they can harness their ideas to human action, they can transform the world into whatever they will it to be. The human mind thus possesses a "simultaneous theater of possibilities," which will be made to conform to the truth that the willful mind declares.

It is essential to keep in mind that, for James, the exercise of will is a powerful moral force. For him there was no "debate" about free will; its existence was not just a "fact" but a human imperative: *"The question of fact in the free-will controversy is thus extremely simple.* It relates solely to the amount of effort of attention or consent which we can at any time put forth" (James, 1890, vol. 2, p. 571).

> It is a *moral* postulate about the Universe, the postulate that *what ought to be can be, and that bad acts cannot be fated, but that good ones must be possible in their place*. . . . Freedom's first deed should be to affirm itself. (James, 1890, vol. 2, p. 573)

Heroic Mind. Only by becoming self-governing, by developing what James unabashedly called a *heroic mind* (1890, vol. 2, p. 578) can we successfully resist the destructive, eroding influence of the world (including perhaps "the loutish passive faces of students with their wearying fighting over grades") and emerge triumphant over existence itself.

> Thus not only our morality but our religion, so far as the latter is deliberate, depend on the effort which we can make. *"Will you or won't you have it so?"* is the most probing question we are ever asked; we are asked it every hour of the day, and about the largest as well as the smallest, the most theoretical as well as the most practical things. . . . What wonder if the effort demanded by them be the measure of our worth as men! What wonder if the amount which we accord of it be the one strictly underived and original contribution which we make to the world! (James, 1890, vol. 2, p. 579)

James was clearly not practicing "medicine," and even his defenders saw that his "pragmatic" school of philosophy, in the words of his assistant Hugo Munsterberg, could be considered original only "by a person completely ignorant of the writings of Immanuel Kant." It certainly wasn't Germanic science that James included in his famous textbook, and as you can see, it certainly didn't look anything like the psychoanalysis concurrently coming out of Europe. James's theory was however, salted with quite a bit of Charcot here and there (James had visited Charcot at the Salpêtrière in 1882).

The totality of the work was something completely new and distinctively North American. James had taken the "flux of the human condition" and turned it into a literary, even a poetic, subject according to George Santayana, one of his students at the turn of the century. James's work was full of recognition of the essentially creative, spiritual nature of humankind. And yet it was written with an antivitalist materialism at its core—that the experience of the divine is a creation of the human mind, a position also developed by Jung in his writings about universal archetypes.

A Promotion of Sorts. Meanwhile President Eliot had the practical problem of what to do with his old friend. Where would James "fit" at Harvard University? In 1889 President Eliot advised James that at the next commencement he would be appointed the first Alford Professor of Psychology at Harvard University. James is reputed to have replied, "Do it, and I shall blow my brains out in front of everyone at the first mention of my name." Such was James's admiration for the other Harvard professors who called themselves psychologists. In the end, however, President Eliot prevailed, and James did not carry through his threat.

By 1892, however, James had managed to work his way back into the philosophy department. Even though he had been responsible for establishing the first laboratory dedicated to experimental psychology in the United States, James all but abandoned his colleagues and students in the new discipline of experimental psychology. After a few almost desultory years as the premier U.S. psychologist, the exceptionally reluctant George Washington of the American Psychological Association, James had managed to get back to his first love, which was writing and teaching about philosophy.

Pragmatism

In his final works, James attempted to establish pragmatism as a formal school of philosophy, distinct from both Kant's neoplatonic constructionism and rationalism's idealistic, nonutilitarian commitment to some remote, exalted, and exhaustive final truth. James attempted to systematize his thinking about the essential "zest in life," which a fully alive and willful person experiences but which, James felt, other philosophers had missed in their accounts of the human condition. He wanted to identify that which "warms our hearts and makes us feel ourselves a match for life."

His conclusion was that this transcendental essence cannot be explained by a natural science, such as psychology. He observed that, although we can feel fully human and alive only if we strike our claim for independence and free will, all of science must necessarily and logically deny the existence of any sort of free will within the organism.

Pragmatists, said James, were members of the "party of hope." Psychology, that new branch of moral philosophy, was in reality little more than

> a string of raw facts; a little gossip and wrangle about opinions; a little classification and generalization on the mere descriptive level; a strong prejudice that we *have* states of mind, and that our brain conditions them: but not a single law in the sense in which physics shows us laws, not a single proposition from which any consequence can causally be deducted. . . . This is no science, it is only the hope of a science. The matter of a science is with us. (James, 1992a, "Briefer Course," final paragraph, p. 433)

Pragmatism became, in a sense, a metaphysics of thinking—a study of how ideas are transformed into actions through the application of human intentionality. James wrote that the exercise of will can be maintained by constant practice and habit but that the initial exercise of will requires creative living and, above all, risk taking.

James came to believe in heroism as a primary psychological construct. He saw that our average, humdrum lives—in his childhood friend Thoreau's words, lives of "quiet desperation"—extinguish our sense of what it is to be alive and intentional. Such "heroism" was certainly an important aspect of James's own life. After a couple of weeks of boring lectures at the Chautauqua Institute in upstate New York in 1899, for example, he wrote of his ever-growing need for "something primordial and savage to set the balance straight again"—not the mind-set of your average 57-year-old academic. He saw the struggle to be human as the struggle to exercise one's humanity, to engage in "the everlasting battle of the powers of light with those of darkness."

James's Impact on the Talking Cure

North American psychotherapy, in my view, still reflects the heroic view of the human condition that James established. How often have I stayed awake thinking of ways to challenge some utterly defeated client to "raise the standard of the heroic self" against "the arrayed powers of darkness"? One must reassert one's will, regardless of the severity of the prior circumstances that have smashed it down. One must embrace the "uncertified possibilities of the moment" in a universe with unlimited possibilities. This is "heroism reduced to its bare chance, yet ever and anon snatching victory from the jaws of death."

As you read in ensuing chapters about the development of characteristically North American approaches to the talking cure, I hope you will have the opportunity to observe that none of them make the least sense without these granite foundations that James established. James was not particularly interested in developing psychotherapies (he wrote rather disdainfully about his own "mind-cure doctress"), but like his soulmates Henry David Thoreau, Walt Whitman, and Robert Frost, James celebrated human will and the triumph of intentionality over doubt, weakness, and timidity. Like his father's old pal Ralph Waldo Emerson, James gave no real credibility to "the dark, the foul, the base" (Lewis, 1991, p. 560)—the disorders of the human spirit—in the prospect of "marching cheerfully forth to face the dangers" of being.

A century earlier, Jefferson had proclaimed the American creed: "All men are created equal and endowed by their creator with certain inalienable rights, among them being life, liberty, and the pursuit of happiness." The only things truly sacred in this life are embracing the opportunities and living life to its fullest by plunging forward into the river of experience—the flood of simultaneous possibilities.

To do James full justice, I must end this chapter on a note of humility. He said that human beings are to the universe what pet dogs are to drawing rooms—at best only tangentially aware of and part of the wider realities of life. Although we can feel and perhaps even be strengthened by the moral power of pragmatism, at the same time we must remember also that analogy of the dog in the drawing room. James tells us that if we surrender our will to the blowing winds of the universe, we will lose all sense of who and what we are. But at the same time, he is not completely advocating the nihilistic, extreme self-reliance of pragmatic anarchy.

James isn't simply calling on us each to "do our own thing," although that notion was one derivation of the North American school (see the discussion of Gestalt therapy in Chapter 16). James described a "radical pragmatist [as] a *happy-go-lucky anarchist sort of creature*" (Leahey, 1992, p. 279), the opposite of a robotized, automaton sort of person. James called us to join the ranks of the "tough-minded." He urged us to become people who seize the day, *"Carpe diem,"* in order to possibly find salvation. Pragmatism challenges each of us to know ourselves well enough to control, as best we can, our own destiny.

Because of James's influence, the North American talking cure became a "talking challenge"—a bungee jump into the abyss of human possibilities, a plunge into the river of human experience.

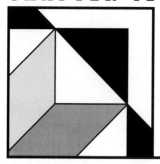

CHAPTER 12

The Radical Behaviorisms of John Watson and B. F. Skinner

Pragmatism Triumphant

Free will, heroism, individuality, and the power of the self were all elements of North American psychology when John B. Watson began his work in the early years of the 20th century. Watson gave European psychotherapy a sharp slap in the face with his mechanistic ideas about human behavior. As "the father of behaviorism," Watson is most remembered for his work with the infantile origins of the fear response. His famous case study on the acquisition and generalization of fear has been the subject of countless introductory psychology lectures. Has anyone never heard of the case of Little Albert? Watson proved that he could condition "neurotic" fears in otherwise normal infants.

One of Watson's students, Mary Cover Jones, worked on eliminating both natural and acquired fears. Her work with the infant Peter showed some of the effects and early applications of behaviorism as a conditioning "cure."

The effects of applied behaviorism were visible to Watson even in his own family. He raised his two sons according to his behavioristic philosophy and methods, with tragic results.

A generation later, B. F. Skinner took behaviorism to new heights with his work in what became known as radical behaviorism. Skinner published a large number of empirical and philosophical works, many arguing the superiority of behaviorism over humanistic, cognitive, and psychodynamic psychology in establishing a scientific understanding of human behavior.

Magnetism Revisited

Say, friend, are you feeling tense? Repressed? Overworked? Do your friends tell you that you are humorless, effete, overintellectualized? Are you drained from general exhaustion? Do you find yourself frustrated, cut off, deprived of honest physical labor? Has the "sanctuary" of your college room or apartment become a prison? Do you long for the freedom of the outdoors and the joy of self-improvement?

If so, you are the prototype of the Victorian middle-class American at the end of the 19th century (Cushman, 1992). Products of a society that valued restraint, unemotional and logical analysis, quantification, and moderation in all things, many North Americans of this era yearned for something that would enliven them spiritually, give their lives meaning, purpose, and direction. Where was that "zest" that William James had written about? How could one achieve the vividness of daily life enjoyed by the Romantic poets? What was it that makes a life worth living? Where was the core of life to be found?

The first North American secular psychotherapies offered an answer: animal magnetism. As Edmund Shaftesbury (1925) taught in his book *Universal Magnetism,*

> *Magnetism is universal.* This is the first principle. Much of the mystery of existence may be accounted for when we come to recognize the fact that the forces of nature obey the great law of magnetism; although man is powerless to explain the reason or the origin of this law. (p. 12)

Shaftesbury offered his readers "The Majestic Home Training Course Embracing All Human Powers," in eight handsome leather-bound volumes. It included courses on personal magnetism, control of others through magnetism, mental mastery of life through magnetism, "keys to the deepest mysteries of existence," the laws of secret magnetic control over others, and "future seeing and destiny." And my personal copy of *Universal Magnetism* includes a special limited-time offer for *"Sexual Magnetism: Private Studies for Male and Female,* formerly $25.00, now only $7.00!"

In case readers were tempted to take Shaftesbury's ideas a bit lightly, they were advised that a certain young woman "recently hypnotized herself to get rid of certain misfortunes that haunted her, and went crazy. The doctors said that, had she developed magnetism, she would have expelled the first condition, and avoided the last" (p. 5), They were also told of a young man who "suffered the kind of irritability that brings on insanity" as a result of careless habits, which caused him to lose the power of his natural magnetism. "One of the brightest young men we have ever met, he lost all of his magnetism, all his good nature, all his self-control, and, finally, all his mind by allowing this habit to grow on him little by little" (p. 119).

A Spiritualist Account

Does any of Shaftesbury's theory sound familiar? It should, for it is nothing less than the Americanized version of Franz Anton Mesmer's theories, introduced to the United States in 1836 by Mesmer's disciple Charles Poyen. Here it became mixed with a large dose of masturbation phobia. Magnetic therapies were the vogue for treating a range of psychiatric symptoms, including listlessness, convulsions, physical weakness, and moral confusion (Cushman, 1992).

What is critical to your understanding of this early therapeutic movement is to recall that magnetism was both scientific and spiritual; it fused ethical and moral concerns with scientific methodologies. Magnetism presaged what Reiff (1966) called "the triumph of the therapeutic" by harnessing people's faith to relieve them of the burdens of secular life.

> The major underlying tenet in all these theories was a belief in the accessibility and availability of the realm of the spirit in a nontraditional and experiential setting. They featured a secular universalism and a valorization of self-expression that was rooted in the larger Romantic and Counter-Enlightenment movements in Europe. Characteristic of this universal vision was Anton Mesmer's statement: "There is only one illness, and one cure." Poyen used hypnotic trance to help patients get in touch with a generalized non-denominational spirituality (i.e., animal magnetism) that dwells within every individual. After contact with this source of spiritual energy, patients felt invigorated, renewed, and transformed. Mesmerism and its heirs emphasized alternative states of consciousness, exotic American naivete and optimism, and a secular anti-intellectual spiritualism. (Cushman, 1992, p. 31)

What was both "modern" and uniquely North American about these essentially spiritualist therapies was that they were not in any sense religious. To the contrary, they were keenly "scientific." They relied on an implicit faith in the power of the self. Fully two-thirds of *Universal Magnetism* is devoted to issues of "developing the will," "cultivating definiteness of purpose," and "harnessing one's personal powers."

One can imagine Walt Whitman and James finding the whole business quite compelling, as indeed they actually did. Pragmatism was a philosophical ideal for James, and it was a moral standard for bourgeois North American culture. The magnetists' "talking cures" were entirely consistent with the pragmatic ideal: They promised practical results—to make clients more popular, secure, successful, and even charming. As Shaftesbury observed,

> No better ambition can be found in life than the desire to rule the drawing-room; . . . brilliancy and merit, when magnetic, may lead the salon, even if wealth and ancestry are lacking. . . . For you, then, to be socially magnetic, the first step is to decree by act of your will that these charms shall be yours. (1925, p. 332)

The Power of the Self

Democratic, optimistic, backed by science, no strings attached—with the new talking cure you could "be all that you can be." But you would have no one to blame but yourself if you fell short of the mark. Whether you chose mesmerism, phrenology, spiritualism, the positive thinking of Mary Baker Eddy (the founder of Christian Science), or magnetism, the North American doctrine was essentially the same. The self, which was the focus, was perceived to have four foundations.

Self-Reliance. The first foundation is self-reliance, the almost unfathomable construct of "apolitical interiority" (Cushman, 1992, p. 32). This North American doctrine made no room for "excuses" based on race or creed or sex. Whatever ills confront us as individuals, their cause and their solution are not to be found in economic and sociological theorizing. Theorists like Karl Marx, Friedrich Engels, and Max Weber were talking to Europeans, not to the downtrodden masses of Boston and Buffalo. Whatever is missing in our lives must be recovered by each of us individually. We need to be refocused materially and reawakened spiritually in order to glorify and actualize God's plan.

Willpower. Second, James propounded with remarkable clarity, the solution to our problems lies in developing the willpower to focus and direct our thinking. This Zen-like approach to self-regulation and control was at the very core of all these early secular therapies; you will see in the next few chapters that this assumption remains at the center of the modern cognitive therapies. Imagine, if you will, trying to explain to Sigmund Freud that a person who learns to control her or his conscious thought processes can eliminate emotional distress. I am almost certain that he would shake his aged head and mutter, "A vast mistake, but a mistake nonetheless."

Having been reared in a Yankee household where "mind over matter" was the golden rule of getting along with others, and where going to a doctor or a hospital was a public admission of moral weakness and lassitude, I can assure you that a child can learn a great deal of mental self-control, given the right environment.

Virtue and Self-Reward. The third foundational concept of the North American doctrine is that the development of self brings with it the right to enjoy our own reward. Because virtue is a matter of individual self-control, which is a matter of mental discipline and spiritual resourcefulness, then virtue is in fact its own reward. But the virtuous are not simply satisfied and happy with the knowledge of their own virtue. Far from it. When North Americans say that virtue is its own reward, I believe they mean to say that the virtuous have earned every last penny of the rewards that come to them, that virtue certifies the right of ownership to those rewards that the virtuous have won. (And God help the feckless politician who confesses a desire to tax away a portion of the result!)

In this view, then, psychological well-being is a matter of personal secular salvation. Persons with that well-being do well in the world; they are socially and materially well off. If I had had the $7 to spare for the Sex Magnetism Home Training Course, I would surely have discovered that magnetically powerful men attract magnetically powerful women and vice versa; undoubtedly they produce magnetically powerful little tots, who end up in magnetically significant colleges and universities, where they commingle with equally highly charged persons.

Character. Fourth, we must consider the issue of personality. A central article of faith in North American psychotherapies has been that each person possesses a true, genuine self and that psychological well-being requires discovering and reaffirming that self—a process that requires renouncing the false, socially conforming self (Cushman, 1992). Some people refer to this true self as the person's "true nature," which usually is some aspect of the self that the person has demonstrated since childhood and that probably has some essential reflection in the personality of one or both parents. This North American view of self is nothing like the sexual, aggressive, selfish, and conflicted self construed by Freud. For North American "therapists," the self is a striving, competitive, problem-solving, goal-directed achiever. The self is a manager of others. It seeks both spiritual enlightenment and material gratification without awareness of any possible contradiction between those ends.

"Character," on the other hand, is something like moral integrity. North American therapists at the turn of the century believed that character has to be instilled in the self, "through self-discipline, thrift, hard work, cleanliness, and religious instruction" (Cushman, 1992, p. 35). Character is what keeps the self from falling into pleasurable vice, degeneracy, and low company.

The problem with pleasure (or at least its pursuit), in the minds of the early North American psychologists, is that it depletes the energy necessary to do that which has to be done. Persons who give into pleasure lose their drive, their competitive edge. They lack resolve and ambition; they cannot harness their resources to ensure success for themselves and their families. Poor people might be pitied, but they must never be encouraged in their sloth. Charity, that most self-righteous gift, must be reserved for those willing to pull themselves up by their own bootstraps and reassert their wills on the world of commerce. If this new science of psychology had anything to offer the nation, it was a way to restore people to a state of productivity, optimism, and resourceful energy.

John B. Watson

This is the context we must keep in mind when we read the following assertion, made in 1924 by the most prominent North American psychologist of his day, John B. Watson (1878–1958):

Give me a dozen healthy infants, well-formed, and my own specified world to bring them up in and I'll guarantee to take any one at random and train him to become any type of specialist I might select—doctor, lawyer, artist, merchant-chief and, yes, even beggar-man and thief, regardless of his talents, penchants, tendencies, abilities, vocations, and race of his ancestors. (p. 104)

Watson, "the father of American behaviorism," was in my opinion also James's heir apparent—although it is true that James would hardly have recognized his ideas on pragmatic philosophy for the transformations they underwent. But with the emergence of Watson, we have the first modern, distinctly North American natural science faithful to both the American myth that "all men are created equal" and the American obsession with perfection, achievement, and mastery.

James's psychology was founded on what he called "naive realism," the idea that in developing a natural science of psychology, "What you see is what you get." James referred to this doctrine as the "stable reality" that was his "strongest moral and intellectual craving." Like the devout but perhaps fatally concrete-thinking Thomas Reid, James demanded that psychology make sense. Like Immanuel Kant, however, James also reckoned that the power of reason must be used to test and find the limits of "common sense." This new North American science of psychology had to rest on testable, verifiable assertions that could be put to practical use.

Unfortunately, few of James's ideas actually accomplished his goal, and most of his work on pragmatism was, in effect, autobiographical testimony to the redemptive power of will, determination, and personal courage. The lessons that common people could learn from James were not far different from the lessons they could learn from Mary Baker Eddy or in any of the dozens of "power of positive thinking," self-help manuals of the day, including those of the magnetic school.

A Newtonian View of Psychology

Watson was different. He envisioned a Newtonian natural science of psychology that would remove all the mystical machinery obscuring cause and effect in human affairs and would leave human beings fully responsible for controlling and directing their own fate. Watson saw that it was possible to create that "bright and shining city on a hill" that the early Puritans had envisioned for the New World, and he saw that it was possible through the application of science.

Watson's *behaviorism* thus developed free of artificial constraints imposed by religion, ideology, or sentiment. Behaviorism didn't care where you were born, what the race (or IQ) of your ancestors was, or what environmental opportunity or handicap your parents had known.

Behaviorism also celebrated the triumph of evolutionary biology. Here is the manifesto Watson declared in 1913:

Psychology as a behaviorist views it is a purely objective branch of natural science. Its theoretical goal is the prediction and control of behavior. Introspection forms no essential part of its methods, nor is the scientific value of its data dependent upon the readiness with which they lend themselves to interpretation in terms of consciousness. The behaviorist, in his efforts to get a unitary scheme of animal response, recognizes no dividing line between animal and brute. The behavior of man, with all of its refinement and complexity, forms only a part of the behaviorist's total scheme of investigation. (p. 158)

In this statement, Watson rejected everything essential to the psychology that had developed from experimental and introspective research in German universities over the preceding 40 to 50 years. Behaviorism rejected all mentalism in favor of a strictly empirical materialism. It rejected any anthropomorphic assumptions about the unique qualities of human "mind" in favor of a strictly mechanistic view of the organism and even rejected the notion of free will in favor of a strict scientific determinism. Human beings were completely and absolutely entities in a universe operating under the laws of Newtonian physics. The behaviorist's task was to identify those laws, so that they might be implemented for the common good of all people and of society as a whole.

Watson's conceptual tools were extremely limited. He possessed the notion of the "conditional reflex," from the Russian physiologist Ivan Pavlov, which accounts for the learned reactions of the glands and smooth muscles and which essentially accounts for all emotional reactions. And Watson had the "law of effect," discovered by one of James's students, Edward Thorndike, in his work measuring the intelligence of cats:

Of several responses made to the same situation, those which are accompanied or closely followed by satisfaction of the animal will, other things being equal, be more firmly connected with the situation, so that, when it recurs, they will be more likely to recur; those which are accompanied or closely followed by discomfort to the animal will, other things being equal, have their connections with that situation weakened, so that, when it recurs, they will be less likely to occur. (Thorndike, 1911, p. 244)

The law of effect accounts for the changes in behavior that occur as a result of what we know as operant and instrumental learning—essentially, any learning that does not involve associative reflex conditioning of the glands and smooth muscles.

Psychology as the Behavior of Organisms

To understand Watson fully, it is important to recognize that he began his studies at the University of Chicago. He was interested in animal psychology and a student of "the father of instinct theory," Lloyd Morgan. Pressed to defend his study of animal psychology when human psychology was still in its infancy, Watson noted the implicit assumption that the laws governing the production of behavior were discontinuous between the species. However, when the leading psychologists of the day (between 1911 and 1914) fell to explaining animal behavior in terms of primitive humanlike consciousness, Watson considered their ideas "absurd."

In 1913 Watson published his manifesto, and the next year he published a book, *Behavior: An Introduction to Comparative Psychology,* that set forth in detail the rationale for using animal subjects to study psychology. He cited the advantages of careful experimental control over extraneous variables, precise knowledge of hereditary conditions, and the freedom to develop procedures ethically unacceptable with human subjects.

The psychological community was ready to receive his message. In 1915, at the age of 35, Watson was elected president of the American Psychological Association. Behaviorism had triumphed over both mentalism and introspection. Psychology would become a hands-on, essentially nontheoretical, entirely practical branch of applied natural science. It would be applied to every aspect of human life, including child-rearing, business organization, the assessment of people for military service, advertising, and the problems of the mentally and emotionally ill.

Watson had a special passion about issues of mental health. Perhaps because he had himself suffered a severe breakdown as a young man and had not found meaningful help when he turned to psychoanalysis, he came to believe that psychoanalysis had "substituted demonology for science" (Watson, 1926, quoted in Leahey, 1992, p. 360). In his later writings, Watson went to great lengths to explain that behaviorism held the only acceptable answers to what were at that time called "mental diseases."

In a classic explanation of Watsonian behaviorism, the experimental animal psychologist gets right to the point: Mental diseases are nothing more than

> sickness of personality, or behavior illnesses, behavior disturbances, or habit conflicts. . . . When the psychopathologist tries to tell me about a "schiz" or a "homicidal mania" or an "hysterical" attack I have the feeling, which has grown stronger with the years, that he doesn't know what he is talking about. And I think the reason he doesn't know what he is talking about is that he has always approached his patients from the point of the view of the *mind* rather than from that of the way the whole body behaves and the genetic reasons for the behavior. (Watson, 1924, p. 27)

Watson's Imaginary Dog. Watson presented a "case study" of so-called mental disease in an animal to demonstrate how misleading and impractical the concept of mind is in considering disordered behavior:

> Without taking anyone into my counsel suppose I once trained a dog so that he would walk away from nicely-ground, fresh hamburg steak and would eat only decayed fish. . . . I trained him (by use of electric shock) to avoid smelling the female dog in the usual

canine way—he would circle around her but come no closer than ten feet. . . . Again, by letting him play only with male puppies and dogs and punishing him when he tried to mount a female, I made a homosexual of him. . . . Instead of licking my hands and becoming lively and playful when I go to him in the morning, he hides and cowers, whines, and shows his teeth. Instead of going after rats and other small animals in the way of hunting, he runs away from them, and shows the most pronounced fears. He sleeps in the ash can—he fouls his own bed, he urinates every half hour and anywhere. Instead of smelling every tree trunk, he growls and fights and paws the earth but will not come within two feet of the tree. He sleeps only two hours per day and sleeps these two hours leaning up against a wall rather than lying down with head and rump touching. He is thin and emaciated because he will eat not fats. He salivates constantly (because I have conditioned him to salivate to hundreds of objects).

Then I take him to the dog psychopathologist. His physiological reflexes are normal. No organic lesions are found anywhere. The dog, so the psychopathologist claims, is mentally sick, actually insane. . . . The psychopathologist says I must commit the dog to an institution for the care of insane dogs; that if he is not restrained he will jump from a ten-story building, or walk into a fire without hesitation. (1924, p. 27)

Watson had actually done none of these things. His use of this imaginary example is as if Freud had made his case by saying, "Imagine that the father now threatens to castrate the child in punishment for the child's incestuous fantasies towards the mother." Although Watson was a great pioneering scientist, his example is almost that absurd. At worst, it sounds like the lab report of a mad scientist demonstrating his evil power.

Watson didn't see the irony in his making science by hypothetical example. In fact, he continued in this same piece to develop a hypothetical cure for the hypothetical dog, by hypothetically using the law of effect and Pavlovian conditioning to remove the "symptoms" one by one, until the dog was just as normal as you please. He then wrote,

Yes, I admit the exaggeration, but I am after elementals here. I am pleading for simplicity and ruggedness in the building stones of our science of behavior. I am trying to show by this homely illustration *that you can by conditioning not only build the behavior complications, patterns and conflicts in diseased personalities, but also by the same process lay the foundations for the onset of actual organic changes which result finally in infections and lesions*—all without introducing the concepts of the mind-body relation ("influence of mind over body") or even without leaving the realm of natural science. In other words, as behaviorists, even in "mental diseases" we deal with the same material and the same laws that the neurologists and physiologists deal with. (Watson, 1924, p. 28)

Watson's central point, as strangely made as it may seem, was that human beings are nothing more than raw potential, ready to be "whipped into shape," to become "any kind of social or asocial being on order."

Nowhere was Watson more definite and prescriptive in his views than with respect to the rearing of children. He believed that the home—and for all practical purposes, the mother—is responsible for whatever good or ill comes to a child. He believed that every mother should be required to take lessons in scientific child-rearing. And what child-rearing it would be:

> There is a sensible way of treating children. Treat them as though they were young adults. Dress them, bathe them with care and circumspection. Let your behavior always be objective and kindly firm. Never hug and kiss them, never let them sit in your lap. If you must, kiss them once on the forehead when they say good night. Shake hands with them in the morning. . . . Try it out. . . . You will be utterly ashamed of the mawkish, sentimental way you have been handling it. . . .
>
> In conclusion won't you then remember when you are tempted to pet your child that mother love is a dangerous instrument? An instrument which may inflict a never healing wound, a wound which may make infancy unhappy, adolescence a nightmare, an instrument which may wreck your adult son or daughter's vocational future and their chances for marital happiness. (Watson, 1928, quoted in Leahey, 1992, p. 361)

The Legend of Little Albert. Surely, however, Watson remains most remembered for the classic series of *in vivo* experiments that began with conditioning a highly generalized fear in the 11-month-old infant Albert B. in 1920 (Watson & Rayner, 1920). Here is a sample of what Watson said about selecting the subject of his most famous "experiment":

> We were rather loath at first to conduct experiments in this field, but the need was so great that we finally decided to attempt to build up fears in the infant and later to study practical methods for removing them. We chose as our first subject Albert B., an infant weighing twenty-one pounds, at eleven months of age. Albert was the son of one of the wet nurses in the Harriet Lane Hospital. He had lived his whole life in the hospital. He was a wonderfully "good" baby. In all the months we worked with him we never saw him cry until after our experiments were made! (Watson, 1924, pp. 158–159)

I suspect that every reader of this book remembers Little Albert from an introductory psychology course. You will recall that the point of the study was to demonstrate how the infant's initial attraction to a furry little animal could be transformed into a terrified fear. It began by pairing Albert's initial orientation to a white rat with the loud striking of a steel bar behind the baby's head:

1. White rat suddenly taken from basket and presented to Albert. He began to reach for the rat with left hand. Just as his hand touched the animal the bar was struck immediately behind his head. The infant jumped violently and fell forward, burying his face in the mattress. He did not cry, however.
2. Just as the right hand touched the rat the bar was again struck. Again the infant jumped violently, fell forward and began to whimper. In order not to disturb the child too seriously no further tests were given for one week. (Watson & Rayner, 1920, p. 4)

Albert did not cry when he was shown the rat a week later. But after five trials in which the rat was presented to Albert as the bar was clanged over his head, the rat alone produced the fully conditioned fear and avoidance response. Thereafter:

> The instant the rat was shown the baby began to cry. Almost instantly he turned sharply to the left, fell over on his left side, raised himself on all fours and began to crawl away so rapidly that he was caught with difficulty before reaching the edge of the table. (Watson & Rayner, 1920, p. 5)

Albert's conditioned fear persisted for five days and generalized to a rabbit, a dog, a fur coat, cotton wool, and even a Santa Claus mask. Each of the secondary stimuli produced a noticeable but weakened emotional reaction from the child.

Watson and his colleague, Rosalie Rayner, demonstrated that both the conditioned fear and the generalized conditioned fears were entirely stable and resistant to extinction for several weeks after a "freshening session" with the steel bar to each of the test stimuli. They also demonstrated that the conditioned reaction was not confined to the original testing situation. Curiously, however, Albert did not appear to have developed a conditioned fear reaction to the presence of either Watson or Rayner, who after all were also part of the stimulus array when the steel bar was struck.

At this point Albert's mother demonstrated enough belated good sense to remove him from the experiment, so he was rescued from making any further contributions to science.

Contrary to many published accounts, Watson did have a "therapeutic" plan for the baby Albert, which included

1. Constantly confronting the child with those stimuli which called out the response in hopes that habituation would come in to play
2. By trying to "recondition" by showing objects calling out fear responses (visual) and simultaneously stimulating the erogenous zones (tactile) [progressing from the lips to the nipples and, only as a last resort, to the sex organs]
3. By trying to "recondition" by feeding the subject candy or other food just as the animal is shown
4. By building up "constructive" activities around the object by imitation and by putting the hand through motions of manipulation. (Watson & Rayner, 1920, pp. 12–13)

Little Peter's Therapy. What may be less well remembered, because it is less often reported, is that in a followup study published in 1924, Watson's graduate student Mary Cover Jones extended the principles demonstrated in the case of Albert. Jones's subject was a 3-year-old child named Peter, who inexplicably demonstrated intense fear reactions to a variety of furry stimulus objects, including rabbits, cotton balls, and fur coats. Jones demonstrated, in what was in reality the first published case of the efficacy of behavior therapy, how Peter's fear could be systematically deconditioned by repeatedly exposing the child to the feared stimulus. Jones paired the gradual approach of a caged rabbit with the positively reinforcing activity of Peter's eating his favorite foods.

Jones worked with 70 different children in her landmark study, from as young as 3 months to as old as 7 years of age, all "maintained in an institution for the temporary care of children." The institution was a place where primarily middle-class children were placed for short-term intervals, usually while the mother was temporarily unable to care for her children. As part of her observation of these children, Jones

> attempted to find those who would show a marked degree of fear under conditions normally evoking positive (pleasant) or mildly negative (unpleasant) responses. A wide variety of situations were presented in a fairly standardized way to all of the children: such as being left alone, being in a dark room, being with other children who showed fear, the sudden presentation of a snake, a white rat, a rabbit, a frog, false faces [masks], loud sounds, etc. This procedure served to expose fear trends if they were already present; it was not designed as a conditioning process, but merely as a method of revealing prior conditionings. In the majority of the children tested, our standard situations failed to arouse observable negative responses. (M. C. Jones, 1924, p. 383)

Once the fears had been demonstrated, various therapeutic procedures were instituted to attempt their elimination. These methods included the following:

- *Elimination through disuse.* Time simply passed without further exposure to the feared stimulus. Fears did not disappear under these conditions. In fact, Jones reported that the initial degree of fear persisted, sometimes for months.
- *Verbal appeal.* This method was of no use whatsoever, except in the case of one 4-year-old girl who was "talked out" of her fear of a white rabbit.
- *Negative adaptation.* This method required repeatedly exposing the child to his or her feared stimulus "without reeducative measures." This method worked for some children, but "from our experience in general, it would appear that repeated exposure . . . is more likely to produce a summation effect than an adaptation."

In addition, the methods of *repression* (peer ridicule and scolding), *distraction* (introduction of a distracting stimulus along with the feared stimulus), and *social imitation* (nonfearful models approaching the feared object) were all compared with the method of *direct conditioning*, which had been used with Little Peter.

Jones's conclusions were straightforward:

> In our study of methods for removing fear responses, we found unqualified success with only two. By the method of direct conditioning we associated the fear-object with a craving-object, and replaced the fear by a positive response. By the method of social imitation we allowed the subjects to share, under controlled conditions, the social activity of a group of children especially chosen with a view to prestige effect [sic]. [All other] methods proved sometimes effective but were not to be relied upon unless used in combination with other methods. (1924, p. 390)

Postscript to a Behaviorist's Life

This history of the early years of behavioral approaches to psychotherapy would not be complete without a postscript. Watson's impact on the future of psychology was profound. He truly was the founder of behavioral psychology as it is currently practiced around the world. But both he and his ideas were profoundly flawed. As most psychologists know, Watson lost his professorship at Johns Hopkins University when his wife discovered him having an affair with Rosalie Rayner, his student and research colleague. John and Rosalie married after the subsequent divorce and produced two sons. John Watson decreed that the boys be raised scientifically, and Rayner complied. Rayner died unexpectedly when the boys were both preteens, and they were subsequently sent away to boarding schools. Watson more or less lost interest in them.

Both sons grew to manhood with deep emotional scars. Both became professional men, but both were plagued with intense depressions. One son, a psychiatrist, committed suicide. The other son, James, attributed his survival to an extended period in psychoanalysis, which enabled him to overcome the effects of the strange and brutal childhoods he and his brother had endured. Some years later, James wrote of his father, the great John Watson:

> I have some unhappy thoughts about . . . the effects of behavioristic principles on my being raised into an adult. . . . In many ways I adored [my father] as an individual and as a character. He was bright; he was charming; he was masculine, witty, and reflective. But he was also conversely unresponsive, emotionally uncommunicative, unable to express and cope with any feelings of emotion of his own, and determined unwittingly to deprive, I think, my brother and me of any kind of emotional foundation. He was very rigid in carrying out his fundamental philosophies as a behaviorist. (James Watson, 1987, quoted in Fancher, 1990, p. 303)

In his "Damn the torpedoes: Full speed ahead!" approach to the human condition, Watson fit rather well, I think, James's picture of the pragmatist as a "happy-go-lucky anarchist." Much of Watson's psychology was inspired by his belief that everything else in psychology was either mere speculation or irrelevant, arcane, pseudoscientific babble. Watson had not gone so far as to reaffirm common sense as the foundation of psychology, but he did rest his entire approach on only two phenomena: the reflex arc and the law of effect.

B. F. Skinner

After the mid-1920s, it remained for others to work out the details of psychology as a behaviorist sees it. That task fell predominantly to Burrhus Frederick Skinner (1904–1990), a longtime member of the Harvard University faculty and the founder of the North American psychological school of radical behaviorism. What distinguishes *radical behaviorism* from the various other behaviorisms that emerged in Watson's wake is its insistence that as a comprehensive approach to understanding, predicting, and thus controlling behavior, absolutely nothing in the human condition is outside its domain.

Skinner recognized and took on the challenge that William James had pondered in his writings about the will: Although everything we perceive convinces us that we have free will, in fact science denies that we have any. In Skinner's view, a convincingly complete science of human behavior had to posit that 100% of our behavior, including such "private events" as thinking, feeling, and conceptualizing, is determined and thus potentially fully knowable.

One of the leading self-described "liberal behaviorists" of the present day, Michael Mahoney (see Chapter 14), wrote the following mouthful, which if fully analyzed can serve as a concise summary of Skinner's position:

> The [radical] behaviorists' preoccupation with unmediated functionalism [unmediated by cognition, what James would have called free will] is itself an expression of multiple ideological legacies, the most formative having been *evolutionism, associationism, determinism, operationism, pragmatism, positivism,* and *objectivism*. . . . What is noteworthy here . . . is the fact that orthodox behaviorists have continued to adhere to perspectives long since abandoned by their originators. (1989, p. 1373; italics added)

Mahoney is in effect saying that Skinner developed the ideas first put forth by James and revolutionized by Watson into a perfect system of completely objective, deterministic, Newtonian science—only to have "science" itself abandon this sort of thinking as unworkable, illogical, and in the end unscientific.

In 1987 Skinner published a paper with the title "Whatever Happened to Psychology as the Science of Behavior?" in which he expressed his frustration:

> For more than half a century the experimental analysis of behavior as a function of experimental variables and the use of that analysis in the interpretation and modification of behavior in the world at large have reached into every field of traditional psychology. Yet they have not *become* psychology, and the question is, Why not? (p. 782)

Obstacles to a Science of Human Behavior

The answer Skinner himself gave is that "three obstacles [have stood] in the path of the science of human behavior": humanistic psychology (see Chapter 15); cognitive psychology, or the study of human thinking and problem-solving processes (see Chapter 14); and psychotherapy.

Psychotherapies are a problem, or an obstacle, for radical behaviorism because they rely on

> the use of reports of feelings and states of mind [for which there is] no justification for their use in theory making. The temptation, however, is great. Psychoanalysts, for

example, specialize in feelings. Instead of investigating [objectively] the early lives of their patients or watching them with their families, friends, or business associates, they ask them what has happened and how they feel about it. It is not surprising that they should then construct theories in terms of memories, feelings, and states of mind or that they should say that an analysis of behavior in terms of environmental events lacks "depth." (Skinner, 1987, p. 783)

In a striking concession, Skinner conceded, however, that

behavior modification [in contrast with psychotherapy] is more often preventive than remedial. In both instruction and therapy, current reinforcers (often contrived) are arranged to strengthen behavior that student and client will find useful *in the future.* . . . It is not enough to *advise* people how to behave in ways that will make a future possible; they must be given effective reasons for behaving in those ways, and that means effective contingencies of reinforcement now. (Skinner, 1987, p. 785)

A Behaviorist Talking Cure?

Let me confess, here and now, that I am and for more than 20 years have been one of the 3,500 members of the Association for the Advancement of Behavior Therapy. Before I left graduate school, I had read literally every psychological work that Skinner had written. I was and am a behaviorist—and a therapist. And sometimes I am additionally a psychotherapist.

How is this possible? If psychotherapy is an "obstacle" to the development of the natural science of human behavior, how could any therapist be a behaviorist or any behaviorist a therapist? (To answer the more embarrassing question, no, I have never owned a dog of any breed that was under the consistent behavioral control of any force other than the content of her own little doggy "mind" and canine "will".)

But I certainly don't want to make light of the question. Should Skinnerian-based radical behaviorism be included in a book with the title *Talking Cures*? The answer is a resounding but carefully delineated yes. Let me give an example from my own practice.

Case Study: Rob's Phobia.   Rob (that's his real name, because he wanted desperately to have his "cure" documented in this book) was an ordinary, brighter-than-most-people college senior. He had somewhat reluctantly decided around November of his last year in college that he should probably begin thinking seriously about his future.

Rob's major adviser, the sort of caring teacher–mentor–role model that parents hope their offspring will get hooked up with in college, took the young man under his wing. He studied Rob's transcript for a while, then took out a piece of paper and wrote the names of six major research universities. "There," he said. "At least two or three of these will take you. Have a good life." Thus Rob became a candidate for admission to a Ph.D. program in his chosen field. The circle had been completed, and the faculty member had discharged his obligation to have himself replicated as many times as possible during his life as a professor.

Rob was a very successful applicant. He was accepted by four of the six graduate programs and was offered a great deal of money by two of them. That's when he came to see me. Both schools that had offered Rob generous fellowships were in major urban areas. Both had inner-city campuses; both departments were located in high-rise buildings. Rob was in a state of near-panic.

The problem was that Rob had a deathly, terrifying fear of elevators. He hadn't been in an elevator since he was 8 years old, the year he had become separated from his mother in a crowded elevator in a large department store. He had spent several terrified minutes riding up and down in a crowded, rapidly moving closet, the whole time screaming at the top of his lungs, as he remembered it.

The fear had incubated for the next 14 years (although it had not generalized to, say, escalators or airplanes). At the point I met him, even looking at a set of closed elevator doors caused him to break out in a cold sweat. But right now what was causing him to sweat was the prospect of either turning down all his offers for graduate school or spending the next 5 years climbing 20 or 30 flights of stairs several times a day while praying that nobody would discover his secret.

I sat Rob down and took his history. "Unremarkable," I noted in my most official penmanship. I explained Pavlov, Little Albert, Little Peter, and the law of effect to this future world-class academic humanist. I proposed relaxation training, to which he immediately agreed. I set forth a list of approximately 20 subgoals having to do with elevators. I began with his doing some research on the history of elevators in the United States and ended with his riding the tallest people-carrying elevator in our town—six floors! I suggested that we would later take a field trip to find even taller buildings to conquer.

Note that we did not discuss Rob's attitudes toward his mother, his phallic associations with elevators, his feelings about "rising above" the status of his father, or any of that great psychodynamic stuff. Rob was to practice relaxation four times a day and to attempt one elevator-relevant *in vivo* stimulus from the list (in order) every two days. But he was never to go any further on the list than he felt entirely comfortable with. If he felt he was backsliding, he was supposed to call me for a booster session at once. Otherwise, we would meet weekly to practice relaxation and assess his progress.

That was a Wednesday. On Friday Rob appeared at my office to say that he had been watching the books go up and down on the small freight elevator in the library without experiencing any anxiety whatsoever. He was happy and somewhat relieved.

On Monday Rob again appeared at my office, this time to say that he would not need to keep his Wednesday appointment. Over the weekend he had driven to Chicago and delivered himself to the Sears Tower, then the second tallest building in the world. Practicing his relaxation techniques all the time, he had ridden up and down in the Sears Tower elevator five times. By the end of that exercise, he had rid himself of any anxiety whatsoever.

I looked at him with mock disgust and said, "Big deal. I bet you didn't dare take the ride to the housewares floor at Marshall Field's!"

So the answer to my question is yes, of course there is room for behavior therapy in this book on talking cures. In fact, behavior therapy techniques have become so well established and have been disseminated so widely that virtually every mental-health practitioner I know uses behavior therapy routinely, with virtually every patient who comes for help. Behavior therapy is practical, efficient, inexpensive, extremely effective, and highly ethical, and it provides satisfying long-term, long-lasting results. A vast array of problems can be addressed by its method of careful environmental analysis and its systematic approach to changing the antecedents and the consequences of behavior.

Lingering Questions. But we still need to address two questions. The first is, when is behavior therapy effective? The answer in general is that it is effective when addressing a problem that has been the subject of a great deal of behavioral research of precisely the sort that Skinner advocated. For example, as we come to understand the conditions that maintain posttraumatic stress disorder or obsessive-compulsive disorder, we learn more and more effective strategies for rearranging the environment of the person who suffers from it.

Another answer to the question of when to use behavior therapy is that we can rely on it to the degree that we can decipher, understand, and control the environmental factors (including the internal biochemical stimuli) that maintain problem behaviors.

In my experience it is also the case, as you saw with Rob, that behavior therapy is effective with people who ask for help in strengthening their Jamesian wills. At least 75% of the successful behavioral therapy I have ever done, seen, or read about can be reinterpreted as strategies for developing and strengthening will. In Chapter 13 I will suggest an interpretation of this observation in terms of "personal effectance" feelings and motives; but for right now I would just like to enjoy the rich irony of turning behavior therapy back to its roots in North American pragmatism. Anything that shores up and reinforces a patient's will is surely worth pursuing.

The second lingering question is how to approach or explain those situations or clients for which or for whom behavior therapy is not effective. For that matter, how do you explain the innumerable cases where clients' lives are profoundly changed in a therapy with almost no evident behavioral engineering? For an answer, is it necessary to go back to questions of mind and consciousness, hypotheses about unconscious motives, and speculations about the role of intelligence in mediating emotion?

Skinner addressed this question quite forcefully: "Questions of this sort should never have been asked. Psychology should confine itself to its accessible subject matter and leave the rest of the story of human behavior to physiology" (1987, p. 785). But is the answer really that simple? What if Rob had been unwilling or unable to practice relaxation or to trust my advice enough to go to the library to watch the books on the freight elevator?

I am willing to grant Skinner that my treatment of Rob was "scientific." But I am not willing to say that what happened in the emotional therapeutic relationship between Luke and me (described in Chapter 7) shouldn't have happened to a self-respecting "psychologist." A lot of my clinical work isn't very "scientific," but I think I remain very much the "scientist" in my observations of how psychotherapy is progressing. I don't think my concern about my clients is an obstacle to helping them—any more than my insistence on objectivity, pragmatism, and soft-core positivism is.

Dare I say it—that I suspect love has cured far more psychopathological problems than science? Mahoney said it for me, in proper academic prose: "In other words, anti-philosophical empiricists are commonly the victims of the most anti-scientific of all philosophies, namely the positivism and subjective idealism of Berkeley and Hume, *who aimed above all else to restrict the scope and importance of science*" (1989, p. 1374).

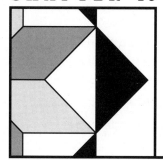

CHAPTER 13

The Behavioral Revolution in Psychotherapy

The Construction of Heaven on Earth

By the 1920s, psychology had firmly established itself in North America as a modern natural science. The power of psychology was so well established in the public mind that it was even held partially responsible for the Great Depression of the 1930s.

Throughout the 1930s and 1940s, however, large numbers of European psychologists, coming to the United States to escape fascism and World War II, began to challenge the intellectual and philosophical bases of American psychology. Academic, behavioristic psychology had to make room for the new field of clinical psychology. In return, displaced behaviorists began to question the scientific legitimacy and utility of psychodynamic psychology. At Yale University, John Dollard and Neal Miller attempted to fashion a behavioral analog to Sigmund Freud's psychoanalytic theory. Other behaviorists— such as Joseph Wolpe, Hans Eysenck, and Albert Bandura—began to develop a clinical psychology based exclusively on the scientifically verifiable principles of conditioning and learning.

The struggle between the older psychodynamic constructions of European psychology and the more practical and experimentally based American "behavior therapies" occupied the attention of most clinical psychologists in North America through the 1960s. The most outspoken advocate for the North American approach was B. F. Skinner. He wrote extensively against humanistic, cognitive, and psychodynamic psychology, which he considered to be creating obstacles to the progress of a "science of human behavior."

The behaviorists' commitment to the scientific method, reliance on testable models of behavior based on empirical research, and rejection of the "disease" model of mental illness in favor of a "symptom" model established behavior therapy on the cutting edge of psychotherapeutic progress. In this chapter, the case study of Martin shows the effectiveness of behavior therapy in treating a complex psychological disorder. Recent advances in behavior therapy, such as acceptance and commitment therapy, reflect the continuing intellectual development of the behavioral approach.

Behaviorism as the "Party of Hope"

> Much remains to be done, and it will be done more rapidly when the role of the environment takes its proper place in competition with the apparent evidences of an inner life. As Diderot put it, nearly 200 years ago, "Unfortunately it is easier and shorter to consult oneself than it is to consult nature." . . .
>
> And so I return to the role that has been assigned to me as a kind of twentieth-century Calvin, calling on you to forsake the primrose path of total individualism, of self-actualization, self-adoration, and self-love, and to return instead to the construction of that heaven on earth which is, I believe, within the reach of the methods of science. I wish to testify that, once you are used to it, the way is not so steep or thorny after all. (Skinner, 1975, p. 49)

I chose the subtitle for this chapter, "The Construction of Heaven on Earth," to bring home a point: Since the 1920s, psychology in North America has concerned itself with something far grander than "just" developing a natural science of behavior. It has also attempted to create and perfect William James's "psychology of use" as a means of perfecting the human condition.

The practical benefits of psychology had been demonstrated as early as 1893, when Hugo Munsterberg, William James's young and iconoclastic assistant at Harvard University, set up the world's first industrial psychology exhibit: At the Chicago World's Fair, visitors could test their reaction times as "motormen" in a simulated streetcar apparatus. By the 1930s, psychology was widely and popularly viewed in North America as essential to business management, education, immigration, advertising, testing for feeblemindedness, and treatment of madness. Psychotherapy was still an exotic and unproven enterprise, but the idea of educational counseling, child guidance clinics, and university counseling centers was well established. Psychologists were offering the public "scientific" advice about every aspect of life.

James had claimed at the turn of the century that pragmatists were "the party of hope." As the 1920s, this title had been won by the young progressive psychologists, many of them women, who were turning to behavioral psychology to provide answers to society's most vexing problems (Benjamin, 1993).

Much as the faculty psychologists of Thomas Reid's day promised that psychology would disclose how to "awaken, elevate, and control the imagination; arrange with skill the treasures which memory gathers, rousing and guiding the power of genius," psychologists of John B. Watson's persuasion promised to help people raise their children, manage their business, select their friends, and develop their personal habits to maximum advantage. As one newspaper columnist advised his readers, "You cannot achieve [happiness and effectiveness] in the fullest measure without the knowledge of your own mind and personality that the psychologists have given us" (Wiggam, 1928, quoted in Benjamin, 1993, p. 165).

Psychologists had become so influential by the 1930s, however, that a *New York Times* editorial blamed the field of psychology for the devastation brought on by the great economic depression. Although psychologists had been a fount of easy answers in the abundant 1920s, they seemed to have little of substance to offer to a nation facing "serious economic and morale problems" (Benjamin, 1993, p. 165). And by 1940, the scientific, academic form of psychology that had once been praised so widely was losing ground to psychoanalysis. By this time, almost as many psychiatrists were in practice in North America as psychologists were in the American Psychological Association. The psychiatrists operated on a purely physical and medical model of mental illness, which accepted at face value the analogy between physical and psychological "disease."

Psychoanalysis Comes to the United States

Since Watson's day there had been relatively few advances in translating findings from scientific psychology's laboratories to applications for human problems. Most psychological research investigated experimentally induced neuroses in animals (especially cats). What little interest existed in North America in the talking cure remained almost entirely in the domain of the European-trained psychoanalysts.

By 1936 clinical and applied psychologists were becoming increasingly concerned about the economic viability of their profession. In addition to the devastating effects of the depression on North American colleges and universities, these psychologists confronted two other significant challenges. Their first and most obvious concern was the dramatic growth of psychoanalysis in the United States. As more European-trained intellectuals and psychoanalysts came to the United States fleeing Nazi persecution, interest in experimental psychology in general and North American behaviorism in particular began to wane.

For its part, the psychoanalytic movement decided to cast its lot with medicine. Consequently, even highly regarded Ph.D. psychologists who were not also physicians were soon frozen out of the practice of psychoanalysis in the United States— despite the fact that Sigmund Freud himself had clearly and unambiguously expressed his belief, in *The Question of Lay Analysis* (1926/1959a), that a medical degree was not essential to the practice of psychoanalysis. This trend intensified as the economic depression deepened.

Freud was alarmed by the medicalization of the talking cure that was taking place in North America and stated in very clear terms that he regarded psychoanalysis as a research-based discipline, as a part of the science of psychology. The essential qualification for becoming a psychoanalyst, he reminded his followers, is the special training and personal psychoanalysis necessary for all candidates, including physicians.

Not only did Freud's North American followers ignore his specific instructions, which he addressed directly to them on this issue, but after his death in 1939, most of the nonmedical analysts practicing in the United States were deposed from positions of leadership in the movement, including even those who had been trained by Freud himself (Vandenbos, Cummings, & Deleon, 1992, p. 74). Thus "psychotherapy" had become almost completely medicalized in the United States by mid-century. This development dramatically changed the political and intellectual dynamics of psychoanalysis and relegated psychiatry to a tenuous niche in the hierarchical structure of North American medicine for a good many years thereafter.

Immigrant Psychologists Challenge Behaviorism

The second big challenge that North American psychology confronted in the 1930s stemmed from the massive migration of European intellectuals to the United States. Fascism made it impossible for them to work in their native countries in Central and Eastern Europe. Among these new immigrants were psychologists who had been trained in and were still active in schools of psychology such as Gestalt psychology. Not only did these schools not reject mentalism, but they actually embraced the ideas of mind, phenomenology, and motivation.

Among these new Americans were Kurt Lewin (pronounced "Levine"), who arrived from Berlin in 1933 and went on to become the founder of contemporary social psychology. Max Wertheimer, Wolfgang Köhler, and Kurt Koffka became part of the "university in exile" at the New School for Social Research in New York City and pioneered an experientially based psychology that directly challenged the reductionism of North American behaviorism. Psychology was also profoundly influenced by Kurt Goldstein, a German psychologist whose focus on "holism" brought Gestalt concepts into the mainstream of contemporary neurology.

These pressures on old-line, mainstream North American psychology led the American Psychological Association (APA) for the first time in its history to take seriously a number of issues beyond the immediate domain of the academic community. In 1935 a call went out to the 2000 or so APA members soliciting support for a new, progressive, and socially active organization, the Society for the Psychological Study of Social Issues. Its purpose was

> to encourage research upon those psychological problems most vitally related to modern social, economic and political policies [and] to help the public and its representatives

to understand and to use in the formation of social policies, contributions from the scientific investigation of human behavior. (Krech & Cartwright, 1956, p. 471)

More than one in six APA members responded to the appeal by joining the new organization. (The Federal Bureau of Investigation opened a secret file on the new, and probably subversively "pink," organization.) Thus mainstream psychology in the United States was given a second chance to make a contribution to "heaven on earth."

Dollard and Miller Test the Science of Psychoanalysis

It is indicative of the tremendous influence psychoanalysis exerted in intellectual circles in the United States in the late 1930s that a major new direction in academic psychology came to be the translation of Freudian principles into the natural-science language of behaviorism. In a major research effort conducted at Yale University in the 1940s, John Dollard and Neal Miller attempted to restate Freudian "laws" as testable hypotheses in the vocabulary of stimuli, responses, and reinforcement. They hoped that the rigorous empirical testing experimental psychology would refine and clarify analytic doctrine so it could become a true behavioral science.

Dollard and Miller (1950) soon discovered, however, that even the most basic Freudian concepts defied translation into the concrete language of experimental psychology. It was as if they were trying to program a computer to write lyric romantic poetry. The result would not only insult and displace the poets, it would also fruitlessly divert the energies and skills of the computer programmers. As the noted historian of behavior therapy, Terrence Wilson, commented, "Translat[ing] psychodynamic therapies into the language of . . . learning theory [had] little consequence for any clinical innovation because [Dollard and Miller] were merely reinterpreting psychotherapy as it was, rather than advocating different concepts and procedures" (1989, p. 247).

Keep in mind that Dollard and Miller had proposed to demonstrate the worth of the behavioral approach by showing that it was methodologically sophisticated and powerful enough to operationalize psychodynamic constructs. They had not really proposed to subject psychodynamic constructs to rigorous behavioral investigation. Their form of psychology was, in effect, too unpopular in the 1940s to have had anyone take such a suggestion seriously.

Fishman and Franks (1992) described the absolute supremacy of psychoanalysis during the 1940s as follows:

> The only available and acceptable form of psychotherapy was based upon psychoanalytic premises actualized under the leadership of a physician. Psychopharmacology had relatively little to contribute and the only nonmedical influence of positive significance stemmed from the ministrations of social workers. Psychologists, having little of practical value to offer, began to question the utility of spending three or four undergraduate years studying a body of knowledge which stressed the methodology of the behavioral

scientist only to find that graduate training in clinical psychology and its eventual application rested upon the goodwill and psychodynamic tutelage of the physician.

Given this set of circumstances, it was understandable that it was a disease model of mental illness which prevailed. Disorders of behavior were regarded as diseases for which an "etiology" had to be found, leading to some form of "treatment." Hence the stress on "diagnosis," "patient," "therapy," and "cure." The treatment of psychiatric disturbance remained fundamentally a medical problem in which the nonmedical psychologist was, at best, a useful ancillary worker. (p. 166)

Psychology or Medicine?

Scientific psychology's challenge to this medicalized, quasipsychoanalytic status quo came from two sources in the 1950s, neither of whom was American.

Joseph Wolpe

In 1958 a South African psychiatrist, Joseph Wolpe, published *Psychotherapy by Reciprocal Inhibition.* In it he reinterpreted anxiety disorders in terms of the straightforward principles of Pavlovian conditioning and proposed that such disorders could be eliminated through a process of *deconditioning,* which he called "systematic desensitization." In effect, Mary Cover Jones's research with Little Peter in 1926 had finally gained recognition in the psychiatric literature.

Systematic desensitization was the first scientifically viable, behaviorally based "talking cure" ever developed. At last there was a therapeutic alternative to the standard psychodynamic practice of uncovering the deep historical roots of nervous pathology. And it was a treatment based on the fundamental laws of human behavior.

Wolpe considered anxiety—defined as "a persistent response of the autonomic nervous system acquired through the process of classical conditioning" (Wilson, 1989, p. 247)—to be at the root of all neurotic reactions. Anxiety aroused at a pathological level by specific stimuli could be deconditioned by systematically blocking its emergence and counterconditioning emotional responses incompatible with anxiety to the same stimuli. Relaxation proved to be the most widely useful counterconditionable emotional response, but Wolpe also demonstrated that sexual arousal and assertiveness could also be effectively learned as counterconditioned responses to block anxiety. (I can't resist imagining James receiving reports of this "development" from his philosopher's throne in heaven and wondering why psychologists needed an additional 50 years to figure this out. How is a counterconditioned response any different from James's exercise of the will?)

What made Wolpe's book so revolutionary was his claim that 90% of his counterconditioned patients were either "cured" or "markedly improved." Freudians didn't even talk about cures. Their "transformations of hysterical misery into common, everyday unhappiness" took years and years of intensive psychoanalysis. Wolpe's methods took no more than a handful of sessions over the course of several weeks. If his results could be replicated, a revolution would be at hand.

Hans Eysenck

The widely awaited evidence came from a group of psychologists at the Maudsley Hospital at London University in England under the direction of Hans Eysenck. In 1961 Eysenck published *The Handbook of Abnormal Psychology: An Experimental Approach.* He followed it up in 1964 with a collection of case studies based on the application of this new "behavior therapy." The Maudsley group was not content, however, simply to demonstrate the effectiveness of applying experimental psychology to clinical treatments. They extended the careful work of behavioral analysis to the very heart of the clinical enterprise and in the process raised fundamental questions about the reliability, validity, and general utility of the medical approach to understanding and treating emotional and psychological disturbances.

This second major attack on the medical model of psychotherapy had actually appeared in scientific circles before the publication of Wolpe's book. In 1952 Eysenck had published a paper titled "The Effects of Psychotherapy: An Evaluation." Eysenck's logic and method were remarkably straightforward. He based his analysis on several published studies, including one on the effects of "hospitalization" on the recovery rate of neurotic patients and another on the recovery of neurotic patients who had filed disability insurance claims and received only general medical care for their condition. Eysenck reported that approximately two-thirds of severely neurotic patients appeared to recover within approximately 2 years without any psychotherapy. (Remember that modern tranquilizers had not yet been introduced into treatment programs at the time of this research.)

Eysenck's question was obvious: Could proponents of mainstream psychotherapy demonstrate a significantly higher success rate to justify their activities? He researched the answer to his question in 24 published psychotherapy outcome studies, which included followup data on 8,053 patients. Most of these patients (7,293) had received what Eysenck labeled "eclectic treatment," meaning any treatment other than psychoanalysis. The remaining 760 patients had received psychoanalysis.

Sixty-four percent of the "eclectic treatment" patients were rated as either cured, much improved, or improved. The same was true of only 44% of the psychoanalytic patients. When psychoanalysts protested that Eysenck's figures were misleading because of the very high dropout rates in psychoanalysis, he recalculated the figures excluding everyone who do not finish treatment. The revised entry for psychoanalysis was 64%, the same rate as for eclectic treatment and essentially the same as the success rate for no-treatment state hospital patients and disability-claim patients.

Eysenck concluded:

> The data fail to prove that psychotherapy, Freudian or otherwise, facilitates the recovery of neurotic patients. Roughly two-thirds of a group of neurotic patients will recover or

improve to a marked extent within about two years of the onset of their illness, whether they are treated by means of psychotherapy or not. This figure appears to be remarkably stable from one investigation to another, regardless of type of patient treated, standard of recovery employed, or method of therapy used. From the point of view of the neurotic, these figures are encouraging; from the point of view of the psychotherapist, they can hardly be called very favorable to his claims. (1952, p. 321)

Eysenck ended his article by suggesting that including the methods of traditional psychotherapies in the curriculum of clinical psychologists was "premature."

In followup studies over the next 15 years, Eysenck was able to replicate his findings again and again, quite often in well-controlled studies. Among the many findings he reported:

- Clinician judgments of improvement bear little relation to client self-reports, and neither is a good predictor of actual behavior.
- Patients assigned to "waiting list" control groups often do better while waiting for therapy than do people actually receiving treatment.
- When people do experience positive outcomes from therapy, there is no advantage to having received that treatment from a trained professional. The cure rates achieved by housewife "therapists" and undergraduate "therapists" were as good as and often better than the rates for experienced and in-training therapists.

In 1966 Eysenck summarized the results of his research into the effectiveness of the talking cure:

The writer must admit to being somewhat surprised at the uniformly negative results issuing from all his work. In advancing his rather challenging conclusion in the 1952 report, the main motive was stimulating better and more worthwhile research in this important and somewhat neglected field; there was an underlying belief that while results to date had not disproved the null hypothesis [there are no differences between conditions], improved methods of research would undoubtedly do so. Such a belief does not seem to be tenable any longer in this easy optimistic form, and it rather seems that psychologists and psychiatrists will have to acknowledge the fact that current psychotherapeutic procedures have not lived up to the hopes which greeted their emergence fifty years ago. (p. 40)

The Behavioral Revolution

This was precisely the historical moment when I entered the scene as an eager young undergraduate psychology major and almost-charter-member of the Association for the Advancement of Behavior Therapy. Out with the old superstitions! In with psychology as a natural science, rededicated to finding ways to help human beings lead happy and productive lives!

Albert Bandura's Social Learning Theory

We were immediately caught up in the next wave of developments, which were advanced by Albert Bandura and his colleagues at Stanford University. In 1969 Bandura published *Principles of Behavior Modification,* which became the bible of my graduate-school years. Bandura advanced the notion of "social learning theory" to supplement the canon. He demonstrated in hundreds of different experiments (all of which at one time I could recite from memory) that human beings learn to acquire, modify, inhibit, and disinhibit their behavior through the process of observation. Bandura did not minimize the importance of the law of effect, of B. F. Skinner's research on the patterning of reinforcement, or of Pavlovian conditioning in controlling emotional responses. But he did advocate the view that the individual and her or his environment interact.

In the classic experiment of its kind, Billy, the rotten-child confederate of the experimenter, enters the experimental playroom, evidently unaware of the fact that he can be observed through the one-way glass. Billy then either plays constructively according to the stated rules or transgresses by playing with forbidden objects or by aggressively striking the large plastic, inflatable Bobo doll standing in the room. After a while, the "teacher" reappears in the room and either "reinforces" Billy for being a good boy (whether he was or not) or punishes him for disobeying the rules that have been established for the playroom.

The children who are the real subjects in this experiment begin their participation by watching a videotape of Billy's behavior in the playroom, complete with the positive or negative consequence the teacher administers when she returns at the end of the play session. Now the real subjects are allowed to play in the room on their own while being observed through the one-way mirror. Will they play with the forbidden objects? Will they pummel the Bobo doll? Of course, what they do depends on what they saw in the videotape.

But here's the important thing: When a child observed Billy breaking the rules and beating up the Bobo doll and getting punished for doing so, the forbidden toys and the Bobo doll were perfectly safe in the experimental session. The child-subjects learned the lesson by watching Billy's consequences.

They also learned exactly what they saw Billy do—and the reinforcement contingency that went with the behavior. The children who witnessed both the act and then the punishment could almost perfectly perform the forbidden behavior on request.

Learning Without Reflexes or Reinforcers

If you had a brother or sister, or went to school, or lived with other organisms of any sort while growing up, you probably already know what Bandura discovered in his experiments. But you have to remember that when psychologists are really good at what they are doing, they "know" virtually nothing before they conduct their observations.

The dilemma confronting scientific psychology following Bandura's research was how to explain the acquisition of a novel set of behaviors (playing with specifically forbidden toys, hitting the Bobo doll in specific ways) through observation alone and when the observed behavior had not been "reinforced"—had, in fact, been punished. Neither Pavlovian conditioning nor Skinnerian contingency management could offer much of an explanation. Yet clearly, vast amounts of our emotional, social, and motor behavior are learned through observing other people's actions and the consequences they receive for these actions.

Bandura offered a very Watsonian explanation: that the "modeling" effect is verbally mediated—that behavior is acquired, stored, and retrieved by thinking about it. That explanation probably doesn't shock you as deeply as it shocked the loyal radical behaviorists who read it when Bandura first suggested the idea. I remember painfully clearly my Skinnerian graduate-school adviser demanding of his students that we account for the behavior in question without reference to "covert mental events," namely thinking. Soon, however, we too were talking about "expectancies" and "values," "symbolic processes" (language), and "self-regulatory mechanisms" (deciding what you are going to do on the basis of what you have figured out about the contingencies of reinforcement operating in the environment).

My bride and I avoided the challenge by opting for somewhat more limited dissertations. Brenda gave behavior therapy to phobic rodents (no verbal mediators there, presumably), and I conducted Pavlovian research on anticipatory stress reactions to "painful electric shocks." (Before you protest too profoundly, I wish to point out that the procedure required me to shock myself several times a day but each male college student subject only once and then only very briefly.) Before we left the wonderful world of radical behaviorism, we did conduct some research demonstrating that rats can learn to press a bar and can acquire fairly sophisticated cue discriminations by observing "sophisticated" rats in an adjoining box. I guess we kept trying to prove to Bandura that you don't have to be able to think to be a good experimental subject.

In truth, orthodox radical behaviorism never had much of a chance with me. Even when I was learning to conduct systematic desensitization, I was convinced that it was roughly 90% talking cure and 10% Pavlov. The magical experience of watching our infant son turn into a walking, talking, problem-solving creature, with a temperament and a personality that was uniquely him from the first day we brought him home from the hospital, made me agree with Skinner that in the play behavior of children are enough data to found any number of completely independent (and contradictory?) "systems" of psychology (see Benjamin, 1993). I won't even mention the perversely antibehaviorist personalities of every family pet I have ever owned or known.

The Boundaries of Behavior Therapy

Behavior therapy is still in the process of sorting itself out intellectually and epistemologically. It continues, in some significant measure, to promote itself by showing how ineffective competing schools of psychotherapy are rather than by doing the difficult and painstaking work of developing itself as a natural science. And it has more than its share of dogma, doctrines, and territories. Its success in the 1980s in demonstrating that all psychiatrically classified disorders will yield to behavioristic deconstruction has not been accompanied by success in demonstrating that its cure rates are vastly superior to those of waiting-list and placebo control groups.

In the meantime, psychiatry—which is still fundamentally psychodynamic in its orientation—has again performed a classic end run around behavior therapy. Now our clients come to us full of "medicines." Persons diagnosed with obsessive-compulsive disorder report to behavior therapy while taking antidepressants. Self-destructive undergraduates are advised to take Ritalin to ease their pain. Even a President of the United States, George Bush, was given powerful tranquilizers to "help" him get to sleep.

Today when I express absolutely no interest in joining the crusade to force doctors to grant medication privileges to Ph.D. psychologists, I am regarded as a hopelessly naive academic oblivious to the disastrous economic consequences of my righteous fundamentalism. Yet I am hardly alone in regretting that as behavior therapists become more concerned with "professionalism"—that is, making sure that a piece of the "managed health care revenues" pie is earmarked for behavior therapists—those conceptual, scholarly, and scientific issues that gave rise to behavior therapy in the first place are losing ground (Fishman & Franks, 1992, p. 189).

On a more optimistic note, behavior therapists do seem to be increasingly aware of and respectful toward the contributions of researchers within and beyond academic psychology. An emerging view of behavior that stresses the interaction of life-span developmental, biological and embryological, social, cultural, gender, class, and environmental variables in a holistic, naturalistic, and nonreductionist context offers exciting possibilities for the future. Behavior therapists still have the potential to become the "happy-go-lucky anarchists" and pragmatists that James envisioned, while developing their art within the boundaries of established and demonstrated science:

> In the 1990s, the principles of behavior therapy are applicable to all types of disorders, individual situations, and settings. Biofeedback, behavioral medicine, community and environmental psychology are increasingly part of the behavior therapy scene. However, it has to be recognized that expansion is not necessarily synonymous with success. Thus, although behavior therapy may be regarded as a treatment of choice for autism, for example, in no way can it be regarded as a cure. The strength of behavior therapy lies not in its demonstration of therapeutic success, gratifying as that may be, but in the uniqueness of its approach. Appropriately investigated failure can be as valuable as success. (Fishman & Franks, 1992, p. 189)

A Behaviorist's Catechism

A number of lists of the distinguishing features of behavior therapy have been published. All share three common features:

- A commitment to the scientific method in investigating disorders, developing intervention strategies, and assessing the effectiveness of treatments
- Reliance on models of behavior and behavior change based on the principles of learning derived from empirical research
- Rejection of the disease or quasidisease model of human behavior in favor of a psychological interpretation, in which "symptom" behavior is indicative of problems of living

I am tempted to assert that behavior therapists are different from their less behavioral colleagues less in terms of what they do with clients than in terms of how they conceptualize client difficulties. Regardless of the techniques a client and I agree to apply to a problem, my general orientation to the therapeutic situation is what really marks me as a behavior therapist.

O'Leary and Wilson (1987) derived nine "core" assumptions that describe the belief system of most behavior therapists:

1. Most abnormal behavior is acquired and maintained according to the same principles as normal behavior.
2. Most abnormal behavior can be modified through the application of social learning principles.
3. Assessment is continuous and focuses on the current determinants of behavior [versus the global person-personality labeling approach typical of traditional psychological and psychodynamic assessment].
4. People are best described by what they think, feel, and do *in specific life situations.*
5. Treatment methods are precisely specified, replicable, and objectively evaluated [and modified as necessary to meet the demands of the situation].
6. Treatment outcome is evaluated in terms of the initial induction of behavior change, its generalization to the real life setting, and its maintenance over time.
7. Treatment strategies are individually tailored to different problems in different individuals.
8. Behavior therapy is broadly applicable to a full range of clinical disorders and educational problems.
9. Behavior therapy is a humanistic approach in which treatment goals and methods are mutually contracted, rather than arbitrarily imposed. (p. 12; italics added)

Case Study: Martin, the Man Who Was Falling Apart

You will recall from Chapter 12 that Rob's elevator phobia was treated successfully with behavior therapy. Behavior therapists love to treat clients with phobias because phobias nearly always reveal us to be the powerful healing scientist-practitioners we claim to be. I would venture to say that any untreated phobic person within driving distance of a university that trains psychology graduate students in behavior therapy either lives in complete seclusion or is part of an untreated control group.

But what of more complicated emotional disorders? I am here to prove that behavior therapy works for them too. The case of Martin will be my vehicle. I should warn you that behavior therapists are the case study maniacs of psychology. We surely publish more case studies than everyone else in clinical psychology combined; this propensity must have something to do with being happy-go-lucky anarchists. At any rate, here is my favorite behavior therapy cure, heretofore unpublished.

Martin (not his real name) was referred to the local storefront mental health center by a psychologist-colleague in private practice. I was the on-call therapist that Friday afternoon and was able to assure my colleague that we could take Martin off her hands without delay—a professional courtesy to a colleague who felt the patient should be seen and hospitalized before the weekend. So I alerted the attending physician at the hospital to save me a bed before the weekend rush began and waited to fill out the necessary paperwork with Martin and his family.

I had been advised by the therapist that Martin was an incurable schizophrenic with a severe personality disorder. Apparently his condition had been deteriorating over the previous several weeks, but my colleague didn't clarify whether she was talking about his mental condition, his physical condition, or his financial condition. As far as I could figure, all three were in pretty rough shape. Martin's hospitalization would be at the expense of the taxpayers of the state of Indiana, because he had exhausted all his private medical insurance coverage and Social Security disability benefits.

Hysteria Revisited

I expected someone pretty messed up but was scarcely prepared for Martin's entrance. He was in a wheelchair, wrapped in enough blankets to keep him warm in an arctic blizzard, and when he raised his head to look at me, he passed out cold.

Instead of frantically reaching for the phone to call 9-1-1, the receptionist gave his wheelchair a little push so as to be able to close my office door. "Wait!" I choked out. "How did he get here?" This receptionist had met and talked with more mental patients than I ever had; nothing our patients did phased her. (I only wish the same could have been said about the rest of the staff—including me.) So the receptionist looked at me and, as she closed the door, said, "He's a walk-in, of course. Didn't you get the message?"

Martin had walked the seven blocks and several flights of stairs (with his blankets) from his therapist's office to our office. The wheelchair, evidently, was ours; he'd found it in the waiting room.

Martin regained consciousness. He answered my questions in a whisper, but he was totally cooperative. He was ready to be committed to the state hospital; he understood that once he signed himself in there was no guarantee about how soon he might be out again. He only asked that I call his wife at work to tell her where he had gone.

I asked Martin to help me fill out a "symptom checklist," a form I had invented on the spot. We generated a list of 57 discrete symptoms. The most interesting of these were "freezing blood," "multiple brain strokes," "breathing paralysis," "heart stoppage," and "blindness." I expressed my deepest concern, as well as regret that I wasn't a "real" doctor.

"It wouldn't matter if you were," Martin replied. "The doctors all think I'm insane. *That's* why I have to go to the hospital."

"But the mental hospital can't cure frozen blood and heart stoppage! You need to go to the Mayo Clinic or someplace! Don't you know that most of the doctors up at that hospital are only there because they were no good with *real* sicknesses?"

Martin stared at me. He moaned. His eyes rolled up inside his head. His legs started to vibrate. He tried to answer, but only choking noises came out.

"Blood freezing?" I asked.

Martin nodded yes.

"Awesome" was stupidly all I could think to say.

And then the strangest thing happened. Martin started to laugh. Which made me laugh. And then we were both laughing. And then it was all over.

"When was the last time you laughed?" I asked.

"A long time. A long, long time. I can't remember when." He was almost crying now.

"Well, that's probably the most important thing anyone's told me all week," I replied.

Almost immediately after I said this, Martin started to hyperventilate. I grabbed my lunch bag out of the trash, bunched it up in front of his face, and shoved his head down between his knees.

"Don't do that. Please," I said. "If you pass out in here, we're both going to look bad."

"Then you *do* believe me?"

"Martin, I believe everything. I also believe you are going to walk out of this office today a cured man. Now let's get serious."

Martin, a married, 26-year-old, Caucasian male high school graduate, was probably the most obviously "messed up" patient I had ever met on an outpatient basis. Yet in many respects he was psychologically as "healthy" as I was. He had a very respectable intelligence, he didn't use any mind-altering chemicals, and he wasn't any more depressed than you might expect a person to be who was locking himself up in a state mental hospital. He had a skilled trade for a profession, had a loving and attractive wife, had never been in trouble with the law, and could still laugh at himself. Best of all, he was in perfect physical health, although he was as skinny as a rail and had no upper-body strength to speak of.

A hundred years ago, his name might have been Anna O. or Alice James. His diagnosis would have been hysteria or neurasthenia. Martin simply called it "nerve problems." My official diagnosis was "somatization disorder," also known as Briquet's syndrome:

> Recurrent, multiple somatic complaints for which medical attention is sought but which have no apparent physical cause are the basis of this diagnosis. Common complaints include headaches, fatigue, allergies, abdominal, back and chest pains, genitourinary symptoms, and palpitations. . . . Hospitalization and even surgery are common. Patients are given to histrionics, presenting their complaints in a dramatic exaggerated fashion or as part of a long and complicated medical history. Many believe that they have been ailing all their lives. (Davison & Neale, 1982, p. 181)

A Behavioral Solution

My strategy was to turn Martin into a happy-go-lucky anarchist sort of fellow. I had two objectives. One was to persuade him that he was 100% in control of his own body, that he could make his symptoms appear, intensify, diminish, disappear, and then reappear—completely at will. My second objective was to get him to discover the "reinforcement contingencies" that were operating in his life and the way his "illness" served and disserved himself and others.

Body Control. In pursuit of the first objective, I had Martin "practice" making his blood freeze. Martin produced some world-class goosebumps on command. He then made them go away. He practiced making himself go blind, then recovering his sight—at first only to tunnel vision but then back to full sight. I had him "stop" his heart (he could bring his pulse down to about 38 beats per minute in about 30 seconds) and then speed it up to 140 beats per minute or better. I had him practice having seizures, both with and without skeletal rigidity. I told him I would spare him headaches, nausea, and dizziness but assured him that if he doubted his power to bring these states on, he could practice them at home.

We alternated all these strange manifestations with a new physical response, which he took to like a duck to water: progressive muscle relaxation. Within 15 minutes and four or five trials, Martin had learned how to turn his body into a relaxed pool of physical ease. I would give him a stress cue: "You can feel your blood starting to freeze." Then after 15 seconds or so, I would turn that suggestion into one of deep relaxation.

Martin was a genius at this form of treatment, of course. He had spent a lifetime perfecting complete and near-total control over his autonomic nervous system. He was a Yogi mystic, although in reverse. Yogis can make themselves well and whole; Martin had learned to break himself into a thousand pieces and make each piece sick at will. But he had done all this without a trace of conscious awareness. He just thought his body did these things on its own. He did not experience any sense of personal control with these strange bodily systems.

If I had shocked Martin by making him laugh, I nearly sent him into a state of panic with my next venture. Because he had asked me to call his wife (to tell her we were admitting Martin to the hospital), I did so about 45 minutes into our session. I asked Anna to come to the office because I had something to show her.

Fifteen minutes later a pretty woman of 24 was shown into my office. She was scared half out of her mind—absolutely certain, as she told me later, that I wanted her to sign the papers to have her husband locked up. Instead, I wanted her to see what Martin had learned in my office. I put him through his entire routine—freezing, relaxing, paralysis, relaxing, seizures, relaxing, blindness, relaxing.

She was dumbfounded. First of all, she couldn't believe that anyone could do the things Martin could do simply by focusing his will. Second, she couldn't believe that it was her husband showing off, laughing, and acting like a normal 26-year-old guy.

We had one penultimate piece of business to take care of. "Sex?" I asked her. "Can he have sex?"

"Oh, no," she replied. "He finds sex much too painful. We haven't had sex in more than a year."

"Martin?" I asked. "I'm not sure," he replied.

I looked at the pretty woman sitting in front of me. "I am," I said. "After all, it's a whole lot easier than making your blood freeze."

I then gave them a crash course in sensate focus exercises, which is nonintercourse-centered sexual pleasuring, and assigned Martin the role of pleasure giver. I recommended that on leaving my office they check into an inexpensive motel outside of town to work on their "homework."

Reinforcement Contingencies. That prescription introduced Phase Two of the program. I asked Anna to tell me about the "contingencies of reinforcement" operating in their lives. She told me that their marriage was controlled and dominated by Martin's mother and grandmother, two powerful women committed to the view that Martin was an invalid and too sick to do anything for himself.

Anna recited the ways in which over the previous 4 years Martin's life had been more and more tightly controlled by his mother and grandmother. How they had attacked Anna in the cruelest terms for daring to take Martin out for a walk the previous autumn. How living together as husband and wife in the same house with Martin's family had been a constant nightmare for her and, as it seemed, the emotional death of the man she had married 5 years earlier.

Martin agreed with everything Anna said and filled in the blanks about what happened when Anna left the house in the morning to go to work. He swore that he had truly believed he had gone insane and was incapable of exerting any control over his own body, let alone the horrible situation with his mother and grandmother. By this time Anna and Martin were both in tears. To my romantic, happy-go-lucky-anarchist's eyes, they were clearly at least as much in love as they were scared about what all this new understanding meant for the future.

I promised to see them both on a regular basis, individually and as a couple. I asked them to give me complete control over their plans, to agree completely to whatever I asked them to do.

The very first instruction was to go and check into that motel within the next hour. And the second was for Anna to call her mother-in-law to tell her that Martin was under the care of Dr. Bankart at the Treatment Center and that she didn't know when they'd be home again. And then she was to hang up, without giving a phone number or address.

Heroic Rebellion

The first session lasted a little less than 2 hours. My plan from then on was to antici-pate the contingencies they would encounter as Martin attempted to get his life back in order and as they attempted to restart their life together as husband and wife. One of the first things I did was assign Martin to a workout program at the local YMCA, so he could get his physical strength back. After a month they had found the resources to rent their own modest place to live, and my job got easier and easier. To my delight, as well as theirs, the sexual problem took care of itself almost immediately.

The other exciting thing that happened was that Martin gained an ally in his fa-ther, who had given up on Martin years before. But when Martin's father recognized what the young man was trying to accomplish, he told his wife and mother-in-law to "back off and give the kids a break." He also managed, without his wife finding out, to secure some part-time paid work for Martin until he could fully get back on his feet again.

Unexpected contingencies came from Martin's siblings, who took the heat from the two matriarchs for his "rebellion," and from Anna's mother, who had been si-lently waiting for Anna to get herself out of the marriage. Anna's mother was the least enthusiastic supporter of the overall treatment plan, excepting of course Martin's mother and grandmother. In the end, we realized that we could not count on her to support the couple's independence and Martin's wellness. Anna's mother became less emotionally supportive of her daughter as Anna grew more committed to her mar-riage with Martin.

Martin discovered that his awareness of bodily sensations was much, much more acute than other people experience. He had to learn to ignore a lot of messages that his body was giving him. He had to learn that feeling a chill isn't equivalent to hav-ing your blood freeze and that sometimes the best thing for a slight headache is to take an aspirin and divert your attention to relaxation or some external stimulus, such as music or television. He came to understand that he was prone to try escap-ing anything unpleasant by losing himself to a sort of nonreflective self-hypnosis.

Anna and Martin had to learn as a couple how to work with that problem; Anna had to balance between firmly enforcing reality and just giving up on her husband's self-imposed "absences." They had a lot of things to undo because of their four miserable years of estrangement while living with Martin's family.

Two years later, I received a call at my college office. It was Anna. She wanted to know if I could come to Martin Jr.'s christening in a couple of weeks. It'd be a distinct pleasure, I told her.

ACT Therapy

Steven Hayes and his colleagues at the University of Nevada at Reno have been working on the development of what they call acceptance and commitment therapy (ACT, pronounced "act"), which is a comprehensive Skinnerian approach for working with clients like Rob and Martin. The goal of their research is to develop a multistage "in-depth psychotherapy" based on the principles of radical behaviorism (Kohlenberg, Hayes, & Tsai, 1993). The basic idea behind ACT is that clients have to learn how to regain effective control over their own behavior—in most cases by learning how to undermine and ultimately unlearn their own defensive, emotional avoidance reactions to aversive stimuli in the service of important goals and values.

Acceptance

In many instances, Hayes and his colleagues argue, clients have lost a sense of self-control. They have mistakenly concluded that because they cannot control the perturbing thoughts, immediate sensations, invoked memories, and powerful emotions that occur in response to aversive stimuli, they are therefore powerless in those situations. Clients devote all their energies to "not feeling bad," "making bad thoughts go away," and "feeling safe." However, as any good Zen master knows, all these unpleasant "events" are of no real or permanent consequence. The unpleasant feelings, memories, thoughts, and sensations may be automatic, but they are not necessarily in control of our actions.

What we usually think of as heroic behavior provides a useful proof to this assertion. When the hero plunges into the frigid river to rescue the drowning child, the hero's initial emotions, thoughts, fears, sensations, and so forth are no different from yours or mine. The hero wants to go on living as much as anyone else. But for the hero, the automatic fears evoked by the situation are overridden by the more compelling and immediate demand for effective action.

Hayes and Wilson (1993) wrote about this phenomenon as "the successful creation of meaning" and related it to effective psychotherapy. For the hero, the meaning of the child in the roiling river is that the child needs to be rescued, and this meaning takes precedence over the fears, thoughts, and self-protective impulses that the situation also "means." For Rob, elevators initially meant panic, embarrassment, dread, and extreme psychological discomfort. In the initial stages of counseling, however, Rob also realized that elevators placed an unacceptable (and in this case irrational) limitation on his ability to function as a normal human being. Rob needed to realize that although his elevator fears were quite powerful, they were also an old, unwanted, and unnecessary aspect of his life. He also needed to accept that he could not wish or force them away but that he had the capacity to commit himself to behaving "heroically" in elevator-relevant situations.

Commitment

The commitment aspect of ACT is the recognition that as human beings we all have the capacity to act out of a sense of mission, purpose, or intention. The key problem sometimes is that we do not clearly understand what our mission is. For the hero, it is unambiguously to rescue the drowning child. For Rob it was to ride elevators. For Martin it was to live a mature and productive life with his wife (or as Freud put it, to love and to work). Rob and Martin both had to decide to behave heroically in situations where they had previously been behaving out of fear and avoidance.

Here is a somewhat simple-minded way to experiment with ACT at home in your spare time. Begin by identifying some unpleasant and unnecessarily limiting aspect of your own life that you would like to change. Figure out why you have not yet done anything effective to change it. Identify your own escape and avoidance patterns in this situation, and then write them out as a logical proposition: "I want to do (or think or say) X, but if I do, I will end up feeling bad. So I just can't (or won't) do it." Do you recognize the avoidance pattern in this statement? You end up not doing, thinking, or feeling what you want as a way to avoid feeling something unpleasant (afraid, depressed, guilty, embarrassed).

Now make one small but profound grammatical change in your statement. Change *but* to *and:* "I want to do (or think or say) X, and when I do, I will feel some unpleasant consequences. These simply exist; they are part of the situation." This simple semantic shift alone can make an enormous difference in how I regulate my own life. Routinely changing all the "but" excuses in my day-to-day life makes me vastly better able to assess my priorities and makes me a more creative problem solver.

To complete the ACT sequence, however, we must now add the commitment factor, the principle or value that your avoidance violates or blocks: "I want to tell her the truth, and when I do it will make me feel ashamed and guilty. Yet for me, being truthful is the most important thing between two people in a relationship."

Therapy

ACT thus happens in two stages. The first, and probably the longest, stage is a behavioral analysis of why the person is not behaving as he or she wishes to. In other words, the therapist helps the client explore all the contours of his or her emotional avoidance and excuse system. In the second stage, the therapist asks the client to identify and act on the fundamental ideas that give life its depth and meaning. The client must accept the fact of the unpleasantness, which is always the short-term consequence of confronting instead of avoiding unpleasant situations, and must then commit to acting in the name of his or her ideals and values.

What I would especially like you to notice is that ACT is in perfect accordance with the principles of radical behaviorism. Although it uses "verbal behavior" to cue and direct intentional actions, it does not attempt to modify or manipulate such "private events" as attitudes and beliefs. Nor does it rely on any hypothetical "cognitive restructuring" as the vehicle for therapeutic change. As Hayes wrote, "Rather than trying to change private events, ACT attempts to recontextualize them" (Kohlenberg et al., 1993, p. 584).

A Defense of Behavior Therapy

Despite the interesting range of applications of the principles of radical behaviorism that have appeared in case studies, many otherwise well-educated people seem to continue to hold bizarre and fairly rigid beliefs about behavior therapy. It is often depicted in the media and in popular fiction as some sort of coercive manipulation of people by amoral robot programmers. If these sorts of "therapists" exist, I have never met one, and I am absolutely certain that they have no kinship with any genuine well-trained behavior therapist.

I would like to leave you with an entirely different image of behavior therapy. My image is drawn from Ursula Leguin's 1969 science fiction novel, *The Left Hand of Darkness*. In this passage the book's narrator is explaining why he traveled alone from a vastly more advanced civilization on a far-off planet for the sole purpose of helping his warring hosts make peace with each other:

> It was for your sake that I came alone, so obviously alone, so vulnerable, that I could in myself pose no threat, change no balance: not an invasion but a mere messenger-boy. But there is more to it than that. Alone, I can not change your world. But I can be changed by it. Alone, I must listen, as well as speak. Alone, the relationship I finally make, if I make one, is not impersonal and not only political: it is individual, it is personal, it is both more and less than political. Not We and They; not I and It; but I and Thou. (p. 245)

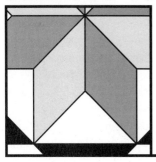

CHAPTER 14

Cognitive (Behavioral) Psychotherapy

Second Thoughts

As William James would have been quick to see, the ways we think about and perceive our selves and the world affect the ways we behave and feel. That these ways of thinking and perceiving can be systematically altered is the basic assumption of cognitive behavior therapy. Albert Bandura's work with children instigated interest in cognitive theories of behavior in the 20th century, but such theories had been around since the days of the classical Greek philosophers.

Modern cognitive behavior therapy was largely developed on the foundations of behaviorism and behavior modification. Donald Meichenbaum developed some of the earliest demonstrations of a cognitive component in behavior modification in his work with hyperactive children. Albert Ellis developed rational emotive behavior therapy, a much more confrontational form of cognitive therapy that assumes people's maladaptive behaviors are rooted in a system of irrational ideas. Aaron Beck's cognitive-restructuring therapy, widely used in the treatment of depressive and anxiety disorders, is based on the observation that anxious and depressed people have actively constructed maladaptive representations of their world.

Although cognitive behavior therapy evolved from the approaches developed in behavior therapy, its reliance on changing cognitions in order to create therapeutic change is open to question. B. F. Skinner himself raised the issue:

> BEHAVIORISM, with an accent on the last syllable, is not the scientific study of behavior but a philosophy of science concerned with the subject matter and methods of psychology. If psychology is a science of mental life—of the mind, of conscious experience—then it must develop and defend a special methodology, which it has not yet done successfully. (1964, p. 79)

Mind, Self, and Behavior

Behavior therapists have successfully developed a wide range of therapeutic interventions for the treatment of anxiety-based disorders. These treatments have proved to be especially effective in working with patients with somatoform disorders, like Martin (introduced in Chapter 13). These are psychological disorders manifested in physical complaints for which no organic basis can be found, such as somatization disorder, hysteria, and hypochondriasis.

Generally, consistent with Joseph Wolpe's original paradigm, behavior therapy interventions for these disorders target either reducing the underlying anxiety or making it worthwhile for the patient to give up his or her symptoms. In the last chapter I showed you how a combination of humor, relaxation techniques, and behavioral practice helped Martin regain mastery over his feelings of helplessness and his fear that he was going insane. Once Martin discovered that he could consciously control what his body was doing, he was able to recover quite rapidly the behaviors he needed to live a productive, normal life.

In a published example of therapeutic intervention targeted at making it worthwhile for a patient to give up symptoms, a therapist reported on his work with a man who had relinquished his job because of pain and weakness in his legs and attacks of giddiness (Liebson, 1967). The therapist helped the patient return to full-time work by persuading his family to refrain from reinforcing him for his idleness and by arranging for the man to receive a pay increase if he succeeded in getting himself to work.

B. F. Skinner would have been pleased. So would have John Calvin, Thomas Reid, all the Republican Party members of my family, and the collective membership of the Association for the Advancement of Behavior Therapy. But then Gerald Davison and John Neale, two distinguished pioneering behavior therapists, added:

> An important consideration with any such operant tactic . . . is to make it possible for the patient not to lose face when parting with the disorder; that is the therapist should appreciate the possibility that the patient will feel humiliated at becoming better through treatment that does not deal with the "medical" problem. (1982, p. 188)

The careful reader might be curious to know how Davison and Neale can talk like that and still regard themselves as self-respecting behavior therapists. Isn't this just the sort of thing that Skinner (1975) was objecting to as "the primrose path of dalliance"? Once we start talking seriously about "saving face" and "feeling humiliated," haven't we abandoned Skinner's "steep and thorny way to a science of behavior"?

The answer is that nobody really knows. What was radical about Skinner's radical behaviorism, after all, was its firm commitment to exclude nothing from analysis that was important in the human experience. Surely a patient's expressed, or even implicit, concern for saving face is part of her or his reality—something that a good radical behaviorist could not in good practice ignore. It was largely my concern for their "saving face" that caused me to send Martin and Anna to the "treatment center" at the Days Inn for a weekend. When I made that recommendation, had I stepped beyond the bounds of a scientific commitment to Martin's well-being? Does it matter whether I did or not?

My conclusion is that it does matter. I want to argue fiercely with Skinner, who wrote in the last paper he published, a month before his death, that "cognitive science is the creation science of psychology, as it struggles to maintain the position of a mind or self" (1990, p. 1209). I don't believe I as a therapist can do my job properly if I ignore questions of "mind" and "self," and I see no reason to believe that those questions cannot be addressed in a rigorous, scientific, objective fashion.

Skinner claimed (p. 1210) that behavior analysts accept "the fact that they [have] little to gain from the study of a creative mind." But I can see little else that is worth studying. True, I observed Martin's "sick" behavior, but more importantly I made him laugh and discovered his darkest fears (madness), his most private hope (normality), and his greatest asset (his love for Anna). Am I then a lapsed believer, a heretic, lost in the land of the unbelievers, as Freud accused Jung of being?

Plenty of psychologists would say yes. But far more would beg to differ. Many of these would call themselves cognitive behavior therapists, a term I usually use to identify myself when pressed to define my own specific place in the constellation of psychologists. This chapter is devoted to an exploration of the main ideas of cognitive behavior therapy. But if you are a radical behaviorist, you may drop the middle term and simply call it cognitive therapy.

In this chapter I will introduce the work of an assortment of cognitive therapists, each of whom would tell you that he is engaged in behavior therapy. It is an open question whether the behavior therapy movement will eventually close ranks to exclude cognitively oriented "creation science" therapies or whether the "cognitive revolution" will take the reins of behavior therapy from the Pavlovian conditioners and Skinnerian behavior modifiers.

A Cognitive (Behavioral) Approach to the Talking Cure

The best place to begin the study of cognitive therapy is with the work of Albert Bandura and his development of social learning theory in the late 1960s. Bandura's assertion that observational learning is a powerful determinant of behavior, as you saw in Chapter 13, reintroduced a "mediational variable," or an inner observer-learner, into scientific psychology.

Bandura demonstrated rather conclusively that the mechanism or mode of observational learning is verbal, and he demonstrated repeatedly that even small children learn through observation not only complex behaviors but also the rules that govern the performance of those behaviors. Bandura also observed that children are capable of complex modifications of these performance rules to optimize the outcomes of their interactions with the socializing community. In other words, kids are quite clever at the way they observe, modify, and display complex social and instrumental behaviors. And some kids, of course, are much more skillful at observational learning than are other kids.

Self-Regulation

Very skillful children become masterful manipulators of their environment. They learn quickly how to adapt their behavior to changing situational demands and become quite adept at self-regulation and self-directed behavior change. These children may stand in marked contrast to their less skillful peers in their ability to get along with others, focus their attention, and complete complex tasks—especially if one compares them with children who have been diagnosed with attention deficit disorder or hyperactivity.

From a behavioral perspective, the fascinating thing about complex cognitive behavior is that it goes on continuously. It is not cued by specific stimuli that signal opportunities for reinforcement or trigger conditioned reflexes from previous experience. Some psychologists, such as Walter Mischel at Stanford University (see Mischel, 1973), have gone so far as to suggest that what we commonly think of as "personality" is the unique pattern of ways in which each of us attends to, interprets, codes, categorizes, and regulates our interactions with the environment. It is a constant, ongoing process of adaptation and discovery. Adapting to this constantly changing flow of information between the self and the environment is the very essence of social learning and thus the central subject matter of social learning theory.

Within the context of social learning theory, we can think of psychotherapy as a specialized, educationally rich, structured situation in which social learning occurs. Contrast the theoretical framework constructed by psychodynamic theory. In traditional relationship-focused psychodynamic therapy, the patient's unconscious engages the persona or, better, the *imago* of the analyst. Within the context of the transference relationship, emotionally corrective learning experiences ensue. The client learns new truths about herself or himself by testing old ideas in a therapeutically constructed relationship and thus comes to know herself or himself in new and constructive ways.

In behavior therapy, however, the client explicitly develops new self-awareness in relation not only to the therapist but also in occupational, family, romantic, and social settings. These lessons are subject to behavioral analysis in a discussion between the client and the therapist or perhaps within a therapeutic group. Ideally, the client formulates hypotheses about the contingencies operating in her or his world and tests those hypotheses by altering behavior in various ways to see if the resulting outcomes are more favorable or less aversive. Presumably, those changes in self-presentation that result in more positive outcomes are thus "reinforced" and become strengthened—that is, more likely to occur in the future. Old ways of thinking, perceiving, organizing, behaving, and relating simultaneously grow weaker or less likely as more rewarding behaviors take their place.

Self-Efficacy

Bandura reasoned that this process takes place in all human interactions. As a result of their ongoing interactions, people develop generalized expectancies of what their outcomes will be in a wide variety of situations and of their ability to exert control over these outcomes. These generalized expectancies of personal effectiveness, which Bandura (1977) called *self-efficacy*, become the primary mediators between, or the connection between, environmental stimuli and the organism's subsequent response.

Soong's Problem With Shyness. Imagine that a person named Soong is shy. She will expect interactions with strangers to be rather painful and will come to have a rather low expectation for self-efficacy when she has to interact with people she doesn't know. In other words, she will come to believe that she cannot, or does not know how to, behave in this social situation in a way that will enhance her positive outcomes and minimize her negative outcomes. By analyzing the situational determinants of Soong's feelings of shyness, we can determine how generalized her feelings of low self-efficacy have come to be.

If I am counseling Soong about this problem and ask her if she is shy with her brothers and sisters, she will probably look at me as if I came from a different planet. She will tell me that interactions with her brothers and sisters are completely different. In short, she has the same high expectation of self-efficacy when dealing with family members that most other people have in our culture. Soong is only "shy," or lacking in feelings of self-efficacy, when she is in situations characterized by the presence of strangers—and then only when she knows that she may be expected to engage an unfamiliar person in conversation.

With a little therapeutic luck, Soong may even tell me that her shyness is greatest in a specific stimulus situation, such as with a mixed-sex group of college-age strangers. Perhaps her shyness is somewhat less intense when talking with strangers who are teachers and less yet with strangers where she works.

As a cognitive behavior therapist, I would probably ask Soong to explain why she feels relatively secure and confident talking with strangers at work. Is her level of comfort there a property of the setting or the people in the setting, or is she perhaps "a different person" when she is slaving away for some ungrateful capitalist boss? Whatever her reply, I would reinterpret it in terms of her expectancies of success and her feelings of self-efficacy in that particular setting. I would point out to her that the social behaviors she exhibits at work—smiling, making eye contact, asking and answering questions, offering assistance, and the like—are precisely the same behaviors she would have to use at a psychology majors' picnic on campus.

So what's the big deal? Soong will tell me that I don't understand the problem, that the situations are very different, that she can't and hasn't ever been able to handle social situations, and that work isn't a social situation. I will ask her how work is different. Strangers are strangers, aren't they? Isn't Soong still Soong in both places? Does she have a split personality that I should know about?

Eventually Soong will fall into my therapeutic trap and tell me that when she is in the work situation she feels quite secure and confident. I will temporarily ignore the fact that in other social situations Soong feels completely helpless, because we both already know that she always feels absolutely rotten in social settings. More importantly, at this point "negative" information is irrelevant to coming up with an effective intervention that will help her solve her problem.

The relevant question is why she feels secure, comfortable, and efficacious at work. Soong will almost certainly claim initially that she doesn't know, that knowing answers like that is my job. But I'll continue to press her for an answer: How does Soong know she is safe, competent, and effective at work? Soong's answer eventually will be that when she is in the work setting she believes, and therefore she expects, that she can control and master her environment and bring about desired outcomes for her customers, her fellow employees, her supervisor, and herself.

In Bandura's terms, Soong is able to function effectively and without anxiety in her work environment because in that environment she experiences feelings of self-efficacy. Self-efficacy mechanisms are considered the cornerstones of effective self-presentation and self-management in virtually all cognitive behavior therapies. In somewhat more technical terms, "self-efficacy is viewed as a common cognitive mechanism which mediates the effects of all psychological change procedures, that is, these procedures are postulated to be effective because they create and strengthen a client's expectations of personal efficacy" (Fishman & Franks, 1992, p. 170).

Rob Revisited. Let's go back to the case of Rob, the student who was afraid of elevators. Ordinary behavior therapy would explain that Rob's traumatic experience, getting separated from his mother on a crowded elevator, created a conditioned fear that over the years generalized to all elevators. Furthermore, it would say that the Pavlovian reflex association between elevators and anxiety was gradually lessened through systematic deconditioning, by gradually pairing relaxation with increasingly salient and threatening elevator stimuli.

Had Rob been a "good" (passive and obedient) client, that explanation would suffice. But Rob was a "bad" client. Rob didn't do what he was told; he started out following instructions, but after a couple of days he went off to Chicago to cure himself. In technical terms, Rob gave himself a series of "flooding" trials, extinguishing the conditioned fear response to stimuli by "flooding" his nervous system.

A cognitive explanation for what transpired is that by having Rob practice relaxation, we established a weak but highly generalizable feeling of self-efficacy about his own elevator-relevant arousal level. After a dozen or so sessions of practicing relaxation, Rob (like most but unfortunately not all clients) discovered that he could reliably cause himself to relax at will. Then, standing in front of the freight elevator at the library and giving himself the pretty obvious self-efficacy message—"I can watch this tiny elevator go up and down without falling apart; in fact, I can even watch it and make myself relax"—Rob gave himself a new message. That message probably went something like this: "I could spend the next couple of months going around to increasingly large elevators and making myself relax until I get to the point where I can be like the other 260 million people in this country and ride on an elevator without wetting my pants. Or I can simply find the biggest elevator within 200 miles and conquer the thing."

If you want to know whether you are more of a behavior therapist or a cognitive behavior therapist, ask yourself whether you think Rob successfully deconditioned himself to elevators or whether you think he just realized while standing in that library watching the books go up and down that he was able to overcome his childhood fear of elevators. I prefer the self-efficacy explanation, but I also think that all our talk about systematic desensitization and relaxation and Ivan Pavlov probably helped Rob come to the new perception of himself as a person who could ride elevators without undue anxiety and discomfort. I doubt that many of us can manufacture self-efficacy out of pure will power in those areas of our lives where we have years and years of experience at being feckless, inept, helpless, and unsuccessful.

Six Assumptions of Most Cognitive Therapies

With this introduction to cognitive (behavioral) therapy, we can take a somewhat broader approach to our topic. Kendall and Bemis (1983) suggested that cognitive behavior therapy makes six distinctive assumptions:

- Humans respond primarily to their cognitive interpretations of reality rather than to the objective features of that reality.
- Most human learning is cognitively based.
- Thoughts, feelings, and behaviors are causally interrelated, largely in a circular fashion.
- Attitudes, expectancies, attributions, categories, and other cognitive activities form the basis for most behavior—normal, pathological, and therapeutic.
- Cognitive processes can be translated into testable behavioral formulations about the way reality is constructed.
- The task of the cognitive behavior therapist is to act as diagnostician, educator, technical consultant, assessor, gadfly, coach, and mentor in order to enable the client to design learning experiences that may ameliorate dysfunctional cognitions and the behavioral and emotional patterns that accompany them.

Aaron Beck, one of the leading proponents of the cognitive approach, wrote the following "overview," which states these assumptions in narrative form. Note, however, that Beck assigned the causal role to cognition, whereas Kendall and Bemis (1983) and I take the position that thoughts, feelings, and behaviors all create, and in turn reinforce, one another:

> Cognitive therapy is based on a theory of personality which maintains that how one thinks largely determines how one feels and behaves. The therapy is a collaborative process of empirical investigation, reality testing, and problem solving between therapist and patient. The patient's maladaptive interpretations and conclusions are treated as testable hypotheses. Behavioral experiments and verbal procedures are used to examine alternative explanations and to generate contradictory evidence that supports more adaptive beliefs and leads to therapeutic change. (Beck & Weishaar, 1989, p. 285)

Manipulation Versus Persuasion

In the early days of behavior therapy (the 1960s and 1970s), it was synonymous in many people's minds with behavior modification. "Behavior mod," a widely used term with negative connotations for most people, was associated with the application of positive and negative reinforcement, token economies, timeouts, and positive punishment imposed by some training agent on "clients" whose behavior was deemed in need of coerced, permanent change.

From Behavior Modification to Behavior Therapy

Most behavior modification programs were carried out in institutional settings, such as mental hospitals, prisons, classrooms, sheltered workshops, and even industrial facilities. Most of us who were trained in these procedures were also asked on occasion to design a behavior modification program for a desperate parent who, as we used to say in graduate school, needed someone to "fix my rotten kid." In general, the psychologists involved in these efforts were not perceived as conducting therapy as much as they were charged with "managing" clients and with maintaining social order within institutions where the "real" work was carried out by psychiatrists (Ayllon, 1989, cited in Glass & Arnkoff, 1992, p. 596).

To the general public, the work of behavior modification "engineers" probably looked and sounded a lot like the procedures depicted in the frightening, futuristic 1971 movie *A Clockwork Orange*. This film, which still cannot legally be shown in Great Britain, depicted mad behavioral scientists torturing the film's violent main character in order to modify his behavior "scientifically." By 1974 reaction to the widespread application of behavior modification procedures had become so intense that the U.S. Law Enforcement Administration announced that federal funds could no longer be used to support behavior modification programs in prisons.

Of course, behavior modification principles in the hands of incompetent, sadistic, or malicious persons are dangerous to the basic human rights of people under their control. But the same could be said for any aversive means of control, from guns and nightsticks in the hands of prison guards to public humiliations, physical punishments, and detention in the hands of high school assistant principals.

The frustrating thing was that behavior modification programs were often cut or eliminated to satisfy local political constituencies, even in the face of evidence that they were highly effective in changing behavior in desired directions and highly cost-efficient. For example, a highly effective, low-cost behavior modification project was abandoned in the state of Illinois, even though all the severely regressed schizophrenic patients in the program became able to function in the community on much lower dosages of medication (Paul & Lentz, 1977).

The image of the crazed robot-making, behavior-modifying Dr. Frankenstein is so well entrenched in the public mind that even the prestigious *New York Times Book Review,* which certainly ought to know better, began a review of a behavior modification book on toilet training with the exclamation "Surely this is a book about poodles, not about children!"

Criticism of the behavior modification approach also came from within the ranks of the Association for the Advancement of Behavior Therapy (AABT). One of the most heated debates was whether behavioral psychologists ought to apply their technology with persons who wanted to change their sexual orientation, a prospect that was at least minimally possible. Gerald Davison was a pioneer in describing effective behavior modification procedures for changing the erotic orientation of violent sex offenders. The procedure, called orgasmic reconditioning, gradually changed the masturbation fantasies of sadistic men toward more conventional, consensual fantasies and images.

There were good reasons to think that these procedures could also be applied to increase heterosexual arousal in men who were "ego-dystonically" (that is, unhappily) homosexual—a category of diagnosis psychiatrists added to the diagnostic manuals in 1973, when the American Psychiatric Association voted very narrowly that homosexuality per se was no longer a psychiatric disorder. Davison championed and in time won full endorsement for the proposition that the diagnosis of ego-dystonic sexual orientation made little sense, because it was exclusively applied to homosexual persons but never to heterosexual ones—although both homosexual and heterosexual persons may have precisely the same symptoms and dissatisfactions.

Davison (1978) didn't question the potential "success" of using orgasmic reconditioning procedures to change sexual orientation. But he did write,

> What are we really saying to our clients when, on the one hand, we assure them that they are not abnormal and on the other hand, present them with an array of techniques, some of them painful, which are aimed at eliminating that set of feelings and behavior that we have just told them is okay? (1976, p. 161)

Davison was convinced that such quasitherapeutic interventions were unethical, and as president of AABT in 1976 he was forceful in persuading the membership to adopt a policy consistent with his position. I would note, however, that the most famous sex researchers in the United States, William Masters and Virginia Johnson, continue to offer sexual orientation reassignment therapy in their clinic.

By the end of the 1970s, "behavior modification" had evolved into "behavior therapy." The essence of that change was a major shift in emphasis away from the mad-scientist model to a model of therapeutic change predicated on self-control. This new interest in issues associated with self-control—such as self-monitoring, self-assessment, self-evaluation, self-reinforcement, self-efficacy, and self-directed change—kicked the "cognitive revolution" into high gear. I will spend the remainder of this chapter looking at several of the "self-talking" cures that emerged as part of this movement.

From Behavior Therapy to Cognitive Therapy

One of the more clearcut examples of the transition from behavior modification to behavior therapy to cognitive therapy is the work of the Canadian psychologist Donald Meichenbaum. Meichenbaum had been working with schizophrenic adults and hyperactive children in a traditional behavior modification setting. He gradually became aware that these patients often gained greater mastery over their own behavior—that is, greater self-control—by coaching themselves, covertly speaking the instructions they had been given by their behavior modifiers.

Self-Instructional Training. Meichenbaum called this approach to self-control *SIT,* short for *self-instructional training.* The basic idea is to carefully appraise a stressful or difficult situation and then prepare a set of instructions, including relaxation and guided imagery, to "walk and talk" one's self through the situation. Meichenbaum has also applied this approach to stress inoculation training.

In one demonstration of how SIT works, Meichenbaum "deputized" a group of elementary schoolchildren who had been diagnosed as hyperactive. Each child was given a sheriff's badge with a tiny microphone built into it. The children were instructed to "radio in to base" with their plans for achieving assigned tasks. What the children learned was to slow down, articulate a plan for their actions, and then carry out those actions according to that plan.

You probably use SIT when learning a new skill or following complicated directions. I drive my wife within striking distance of insanity by using SIT, in a normal conversational voice, when I am cooking from a complicated recipe, assembling some piece of furniture or gadget, or best of all, following written instructions to find someone's house. SIT is a great way to accomplish difficult or complex tasks without increasing my arousal level. On the down side, I tend not to internalize or memorize instructions when I use SIT. Likewise, several researchers have reported that SIT has not resulted in the expected maintenance and generalization of behavior change (see, for example, Arnkoff & Glass, 1992, p. 664). My Japanese colleagues tell me, however, that SIT is a very popular approach to stress reduction among Japanese counselors and therapists.

Meichenbaum's self-instructional training can be extended to a wide variety of self-coaching situations. Meichenbaum (1977) reported that it is useful therapy for people who must live with chronic pain. SIT also has direct applications for sports psychology. I can recall Michael Mahoney (see Chapter 13) explaining that the most successful athletes (among a group of athletes with equivalent skill levels) can be identified through a simple assessment of their cognitive expectancies for the actual competition. Less successful athletes give themselves punishing and negative self-instructional training, associated with the difficulties they will encounter and the mistakes they have to try not to repeat. Successful athletes give themselves positive self-instructions concerning the details of the things they need to do at each stage of the event.

In counseling I have found that this strategy works extremely well with students who have examination anxiety problems. A negative self-instructional style is characterized by statements like "Oh no, a question on cell structure. I never do well on questions like this, and this subject must be at least 25% of the exam." I try to get them to tell themselves things like "OK, cell structures. What four things do I remember about cell structure? How can I apply what I know to this question?" Students who learn this technique usually increase their performance on an examination by at least one standard deviation.

The same strategy can be applied to self-reinforcement and self-punishment. Most people are terrible at administering contingent positive reinforcement to themselves for gradually working their way through a complex or difficult task. I sometimes think people must hold the secret view that self-reinforcement is a shameful practice akin to other notoriously forbidden forms of self-pleasuring, so few people do it well. But these same people are often able to administer all sorts of nasty self-punishments, like calling themselves bad names and sabotaging their own work through procrastination, carelessness, and overblown self-effacing humility.

Case Study: Sarah, Rebel Without a Clue. Sarah provides a good example of poor self-reinforcement and all-too-effective self-punishment. She was a ninth-semester senior. Sarah needed an extra semester to graduate because her grades as a freshman and a sophomore were so poor that she had had to change her major several times. Her older sister Beth had soared through the same undergraduate program a couple of years earlier, one of those people who receive every award the place offers.

Sarah, to her horror, had eventually drifted into exactly the same major and minor as Beth and even had the same professors and classes that Beth had taken. For reasons that defied my understanding, she also joined Beth's old sorority. My job, as her counselor during this precarious ninth semester, was to coach Sarah through the final weeks of exams and papers that would lead to her graduation.

Sarah's thinking was a cognitive disaster area. At least 95% of her cognitions were self-punishing. She told herself 50 times a day that she was "lazy," "no good at anything," "a disappointment to her parents," "retarded," and (my favorite) "a rebel without a clue."

We completely reorganized Sarah's cognitive closet. I demanded that she think exclusively in terms of meeting, one by one, the 200 or so discrete goals we had determined she needed to meet in order to graduate. We drew up a rigorous schedule she had to follow. Every time she met one of her goals on time, she could reinforce herself by thinking about graduation and the plans she had for the time when she would be free from academics. When Sarah completed a major goal, such as turning in a paper on time, she could spend an hour or two with her best friends, a group of fellow students known more for their willingness to ponder the mysteries of the universe than for their dedication to studying for the graduate-placement exams. They, in turn, agreed to support Sarah's self-management system by not welcoming her to their conversation unless she could report the accomplishment of a scheduled task.

The armory of negative cognitions about self were all discarded and replaced by just one. Sarah was extremely close to her grandmother, a warm and nurturing archetype of what a grandmother is supposed to be. It seemed to Sarah that Granny liked and even admired the feckless Sarah even more than she liked and admired the successful Beth. I had Sarah put a framed photo of Granny on her desk. Whenever Sarah messed up by not following through on an assigned task, she had to spend 2 minutes looking at the picture of her grandmother and imagining calling her up to tell her that, because Sarah hadn't bothered to finish her philosophy paper (or whatever the current task was), there was no point in Granny flying up from Florida for Sarah's graduation.

It worked—not brilliantly but enough to get the "clueless rebel" to graduate. We estimated that Sarah had increased her working hours by several hundred percent. More importantly, perhaps, she learned to stop running herself down every time she hit an obstacle or ran out of motivation. Further proof of her success were the visits I received from a number of her friends, who came to me for help with similar issues of procrastination and avoidance.

Rational Emotive Behavior Therapy

In my work with Sarah, I think I was still being a behavior therapist, even though I wasn't really administering any of the contingencies; even though the behavior being modified was really a set of highly private self-statements; and even though my deepest sympathies more likely lie with "clueless rebels" than with future lawyers, MBAs, and proctologists.

But now we turn to some cognitive therapies in which therapeutic change is less clearly a genuinely behavioral phenomenon. Some old-guard behavior therapy types would contend that these approaches have little or nothing to do with systematically altering behavior and thus are not really behavior therapies. They would argue that these attitudinally based talking cures might more accurately be thought of as psychotherapy by logical persuasion.

These cognitive therapies trace their philosophical roots to the writings of the Stoics, especially the Greek Stoic philosopher Epictetus, who was born in 55 c.e. Epictetus wrote that what disturbs people is not "things, but the view that people take of things." In short, as Alfred Adler (1912) said (see Chapter 8), "We are self-determined by the meaning we give to our experiences. *Omnia ex opinione suspensa sunt* [Everything depends on opinion]."

Basic Tenets of REBT

The best-known approach derived from this perspective, rational emotive therapy (RET), was developed by psychologist Albert Ellis in the 1950s. In 1993 he changed RET to rational emotive behavior therapy, so I will use the letters *REBT* throughout this discussion.

REBT has eight basic propositions (Ellis, 1989, pp. 197–200):

- People are born with the potential to be rational as well as irrational. People think about their own thinking and can learn from their mistakes. But they also learn to repeat their old mistakes and to be superstitious, perfectionistic, and grandiose.
- People's tendency toward irrational thinking, self-damaging habituations, wishful thinking, and intolerance is frequently exacerbated by their culture and their family group.
- Humans tend to perceive, think, emote, and behave simultaneously—which means that changing their behavior usually requires the use of perceptual-cognitive, emotive-evocative, and behavioristic-reeducative methods.
- Psychotherapy should be highly cognitive, active, directive, and homework-assigning and should be relatively brief.
- REBT therapists do not rely on "warm" relationships as the mechanism for therapeutic change. Instead, they often deliberately use "hardheaded methods of convincing clients they had darned well better resort to more self-discipline."
- REBT therapists use role playing, assertion training, desensitization, humor, operant conditioning, suggestion, support, and many other "tricks" to get their point across. The usual goal of REBT is not merely to eliminate clients' presenting symptoms but to help rid them of other symptoms as well and, more importantly, to modify their underlying symptom-creating propensities.

- REBT holds that serious emotional problems stem directly from magical, empirically unvalidatable thinking. If disturbance-creating ideas are vigorously disputed by logical-empirical thinking, they can be eliminated or minimized and will ultimately cease to recur.
- The "real" cause of emotional upsets is not the things that happen to people but their unrealistic interpretations of unpleasant events as a consequence of their unrealistic beliefs about the world. People have to accept the necessity of changing their "crooked way of thinking" if they wish to live more satisfying lives. This change can only be accomplished by repeatedly rethinking irrational beliefs and repeatedly taking corrective actions designed to undo them.

The Rational Element. As you can probably see, REBT is not just a therapeutic conversation with a caring professional person. It is an all-out assault on "crooked thinking." Reading or listening to Ellis can be a pure delight. Every therapeutic encounter is a crusade against the irrational nonsense that most of us picked up from adults as children. It is an assault against what Karen Horney (Chapter 10) called "the tyranny of shoulds." Ellis much more graphically called it "musterbation."

Ellis nailed people for "thinking and talking like Moses"—laying down commandments that they and all other people must follow if they are to be spared great emotional catastrophes. Ellis is sort of a one-man refutation of all of the sloppy, sentimental, love-slob, self-pitying lyrics of the entire country-and-western song industry. "So you left me for my best friend and stole my dog too," Ellis would say. "Well, sure, it would be preferable if I had my dog back, and it is certainly inconvenient and uncomfortable to have you gone, but it is not a catastrophe, it is not simply awful, and in fact I can get me a new dog and probably a less screwed-up lover besides."

The Emotive Element. The aspect of REBT that may not be perfectly obvious, even to people who have read a fair amount of Ellis (and he is one of the most prolific and widely read therapists alive today) is the *E* in *REBT*. The emotive element, I think, is the key to successful application of REBT.

If we go back to the case of Sarah, which I used to illustrate a cognitive behavior approach, we can see some elements that are precisely right for an REBT interpretation. Because Sarah didn't perform at the same high level as Beth, and because school was therefore harder for Sarah than it had been for Beth, she felt that life was basically unfair to her. "Life must always be fair" is one of Ellis's favorite screwed-up ideas about the world. (Another of my favorites is "Not being loved by every person whom I decide that I love is simply a catastrophe that I cannot live with.")

Sarah was also a world-class procrastinator. Like everyone with this condition, she held to the belief that if a piece of work wasn't absolutely perfect, she couldn't turn it in. By definition, most of everything we do is imperfect, so it followed that Sarah was never going to turn in anything on time. Everything she turned in had to be coerced from her, and thus the quality was logically "beyond" her personal control.

These issues are all perfectly irrational material for REBT. But the question a REBT therapist would have had to ask is what was the emotional core of Sarah's irrational belief system. Sarah was a relatively unemotional person who associated with a group of equally unemotional, Type B people whose sole meaningful activity was staying up all night to ponder the mysteries of the universe. As close as I could get to this emotional core was asking Sarah whether her grandmother supported all the negative things Sarah had to say about herself. Of course, Granny absolutely did not.

A very real and very important emotional agenda did underlie Sarah's problems at school. But the question was whether we could uncover and address that agenda in time. I judged that we couldn't; thus we could not really engage in the REBT process. Had Sarah gone to Ellis, I think that her emotional agenda would have become apparent in the face of Ellis's confrontational style. But like Joseph Breuer, who was reluctant to engage his patients in discussion of sexual questions, I find that this sort of confrontation "is not to my taste." Fortunately, my less confrontational, more purely cognitive strategy proved to be effective enough to reunite Sarah and her grandmother at Sarah's graduation.

Case Study: Flo's Terrible Pain

The key to successful REBT is discovering the powerful emotional roots of powerful irrational ideas and then connecting the two. How many times have you said, or heard a friend say, "I know this is crazy, but I believe . . ."? When REBT works, there is almost always a direct confrontation between the emotional and the rational, an emotional abreaction—as Freud would say—that allows reason to replace unreason, ego to replace id.

Flo was a 47-year-old African American woman referred to me by a neurologist who had been unsuccessful in treating Flo for debilitating headache pain. The presenting problems were frequent and severe headaches, over which Flo exhibited no control, and the increasing probability that Flo was becoming psychologically and physically dependent on powerful painkillers as a way of coping with the pain.

Flo considered being sent to a (relatively) young white male psychologist—who was really a college professor—less than overwhelming evidence that her neurologist was competent and caring. There is in fact a considerable body of evidence that African Americans are skeptical to downright suspicious of talking cures and are highly unlikely to complete psychotherapy that proceeds from a confessional model (Ridley, 1984).

So Flo was probably somewhat relieved when I began our session by focusing directly on the subjects of pain control, medications, and headache management. I gave her some very basic exercises to try that are often effective in reducing pain intensity, counseled her about the miraculous power of Excedrin and its generic equivalents, and produced a complete ten-step at-home program to learn how to predict and control headaches. Her pain at the start of the session had been a 9 on a

10-point pain scale and a 3.5 when the hour was up. I confirmed that she should consider this pain reduction a major accomplishment and that the Excedrin would reduce the 3.5 level to something completely manageable.

Two follow-up appointments went very well, and Flo was beginning to demonstrate that she could control both the pain and the headaches far more than she had imagined. She hadn't been to or called the doctor or the emergency room even once in three weeks.

But the next session was a disaster. Flo refused to "trick herself" anymore with "behavior modification." She had abandoned everything we practiced and demanded "real" therapy. I wanted to know what had changed, and she told me a long story about going to a church meeting, where she had told her Bible study class about her therapy. Both her minister and her sister had denounced psychology, "behavior modification," and the mental health clinic itself.

When I probed, I discovered an REBT treasure of "crooked thinking," "musterbation," and profound self-condemnation. Flo had been persuaded that her headaches were punishment for the sins she had committed as a wife and a mother. They were what she deserved for being a bad daughter, a neglectful sister, and a "fallen" Christian. My therapy was a trick because it led her to turn her back on her disgrace as a member of the community. She was, she explained, and always had been, the "black sheep" of the entire family—for breaking away from the church as an adolescent, getting pregnant as a teenager, marrying the "wrong" man, and not being able to control her adolescent children. (Flo also held down three jobs and had a son at the local university, but none of that seemed to matter as much as her previous sins.)

My point is that in Flo's case the irrational beliefs and painful headaches were linked to a powerful emotional agenda. They were so powerful as to lead her to abandon a very effective therapy for a very serious psychophysiological disorder.

Flo and I made a pact. Therapy would focus on all these philosophical and emotional issues, and she would resume the headache work to stop punishing herself. After a few sessions, during which I realized that I could not effectively address all the issues Flo was dealing with, I referred her to a family counselor in our clinic who felt that she understood the background issues better than I did. I urged Flo to continue her headache "behavior modification." As a sort of going-away gift, Flo told me that she had joined the choir of a different church. This "good news" was somewhat diminished by the revelation that the new church was that of her husband's family, who were equally negative toward Flo.

REBT Today

Two recent developments in REBT should be mentioned. The first is that, as mentioned above, in 1993 Ellis decided to change the name of his therapy to rational emotive behavior therapy. Ellis took this step to emphasize unambiguously the direct link between what we believe and what we do. In Ellis's words, "RE[B]T theory states that humans rarely change and keep disbelieving a profound self-defeating belief unless they often *act* against it" (1993, p. 258).

> Actually, RE[B]T has always been one of the most behaviorally oriented of the cognitive-behavior therapies. In addition to employing [Joseph Wolpe's] systematic desensitization and showing clients how to use imaginal methods of exposing themselves to phobias and anxiety producing situations it favors in vivo desensitization or exposure and often encourages people to deliberately stay in obnoxious situations—e.g., a poor marriage or a bad job—until they change their disturbed thoughts and feelings and then decide whether it is best for them to flee from these situations. (1993, p. 258)

The other new development in REBT is its extension into the field of addictions and substance abuse. Ellis's analysis of the primary therapeutic challenge confronting persons who persist in abusing such substances as alcohol, nicotine, and tranquilizers is that people consume their substance of choice to escape and avoid feeling bad. The important change-oriented therapeutic issue, Ellis claims, is not how crummy and worthless the client feels after abusing but what a "Big Baby" the client is. Whenever the client begins to feel bad, he or she takes the substance with the self-justification that "I just can't stand it."

"Of course you can stand it," challenges the REBT therapist. "Are you so fragile, so precious, and so special that you don't have to tolerate pain, loss, frustration, and discomfort—just like the rest of us? There's no room for Big Babies in the USA (unconditional self-acceptance)!"

After completing a training workshop on using this approach with substance-abusing clients, I have had the opportunity to try it out on a number of undergraduates referred to me for treatment. My preliminary data are very encouraging. But Ellis has not yet had the opportunity to present any long-term followup data from clients treated exclusively with REBT. I can also report a reasonably successful application of the Big Baby/REBT principle in the treatment of one student-client who was unable to overcome the lingering emotional effects of a broken love affair.

Case Study: Charlie's Broken Heart

Every time Charlie felt "just miserable," he made an emotionally devastating move to try to win back his former girlfriend. In my analysis, his Big Baby behavior was a consequence of his belief that he just couldn't bear the thought that She of the Ultimate Perfection didn't, wouldn't, and maybe never did love him truly and forever. Losing her was a catastrophe he could not be expected to bear.

Since they had broken up more than a year ago, Charlie's devastation had become almost a chronic obsession. In addition to making himself miserable, alienating all his friends, frustrating his family, annoying the heck out of She of the Ultimate Perfection, and making my therapeutic interventions look pretty worthless, Charlie's acting like a Big Baby around the clock began to cause him to miss classes, fail to write papers, and mess up on exams.

I am happy to report that an almost complete remission of symptoms occurred in less than three weeks of an intensive course of REBT. The first major therapeutic breakthrough came in response to my ironic observation: "Gee, Charlie, that's a total bummer. I mean, here you are 20 years old, and chances are you are never going to have sex again—in your whole life!" Charlie wasn't that bizarrely irrational. But my observation revealed him to be stuck between a rock and a hard place. He could falsely agree with me on an absurd but pitiful assumption, or he could counter some of his own despair with a wee bit of reality testing. Just because somebody dumps you, you don't have to live the rest of your life celibate!

As our REBT therapy progressed, we focused exclusively on Charlie's implicit beliefs about what a great tragedy it was that he was feeling bad. I confronted him with the ontological fact that he could indeed "stand it." Furthermore, I pointed out, it was much less clear whether everyone around and close to Charlie could stand him much longer if he continued to act like a Big Baby.

I said Charlie experienced an "almost complete remission" because a month after we completed therapy, She of the Ultimate Perfection decided she wanted to resume the relationship with Charlie. At last report, Charlie had broken off with her, explaining that he was having trouble dealing with his beloved's dependency needs. True story.

The Nature of Persuasion

REBT offers a very basic and straightforward analysis of life's painful dilemmas. I'm not sure that I have ever successfully persuaded anyone to change a deeply held irrational belief, but I am sure that I have managed to get people to question some of the assumptions they make in their lives that strike me as particularly wacky or dysfunctional. I'll confess that when I run into something in my own life that seems to be evidence of some irrational belief, I tend to turn toward Gestalt approaches (see Chapter 16). But Ellis's Institute for Rational Living has more sensible and important things to say about sex and sexual attitudes than anything else I have ever read.

As mentioned in Chapter 13, Steven Hayes and his colleagues are working on many of the same issues as they develop acceptance and commitment therapy that Ellis has identified in the development of REBT. Hayes has also found in patients and substance-abusing clients what Ellis calls the Big Baby syndrome; people just can't stand feeling bad.

Hayes, however, disagrees with Ellis that the solution lies in confronting irrational beliefs and attacking them head-on. In fact, Hayes told me he doesn't much believe in trying to change people's deeply held beliefs in the therapeutic process. Instead, Hayes and his colleagues focus on a thorough and deep exploration of the client's most important values. Hayes believes that if people can come to see the relationship between their behavior and their most deeply held values more clearly, their behavior is very likely to change to support these values.

For example, an unemployed and divorced client who was dependent on multiple chemicals, when asked what the most important thing in the world to him was, replied: "My relationship with my son." This "value" became the central focus of therapeutic attention in ACT. It was essential that the client's substance-abusing behavior change if he was to enjoy any hope of a meaningful relationship with his child. Where this therapy really hits home, in my view, is that when the client then says, "But I'm a Big Baby, and I can't stand not having a drink or shooting up some dope to make my pain and my loneliness go away," the therapist confronts him with the contradiction between giving in to the whining, self-destructive demands of the Big Baby and living up to the ideals established for the sake of salvaging a relationship with a child.

Cognitive-Restructuring Therapy

Another approach that may or may not be considered a branch of "behavior" therapy involves Aaron Beck's search at the University of Pennsylvania for a talking cure for depression. It is surely the most important research in this area in the United States today. Beck's work has also been extended with significant success to the treatment of anxiety disorders and relationship problems and is a promising approach to the treatment of agoraphobia, paranoia, anorexia nervosa, and obsessive-compulsive disorder.

As was also the case with Ellis, Beck came to cognitive therapy from psychoanalysis. He had become more and more frustrated with using traditional psychotherapies to treat depressed patients. Psychodynamic theory tends to see the depressed person as engaged in a process of self-punishment—a process Flo exhibited with striking clarity. But Beck didn't find that interpretation of depressive thinking very accurate or very useful.

Flawed Beliefs

Rather, Beck argued, depressed people exhibit deeply flawed "cognitive schemata"— they tend to see the glass half empty and the world a harsh and negative place. They aren't necessarily making irrational belief statements, as Ellis described, but they are interpreting everything that they see and that happens to them in a negative and self-defeating light. As Arnkoff and Glass (1992) stated,

> Depressed persons make a fundamental cognitive error in seeing the world as more negative than is warranted. This depressive "schema" or cognitive structure that organizes information, contains a negative cognitive triad consisting of a negative view of one's self, one's world, and one's future. (p. 662)

The patient/therapist relationship is critical to the success of cognitive therapy. Patients have to be able to speak their mind clearly and without censoring their cognitive processes. The therapist must be able to hear accurately what clients are saying and then must be able to give feedback about the "errors" that she or he hears. The therapist's principal job is to hypothesize about patients' core organizing beliefs and to explore ways that patients might put those core beliefs to the test.

According to Beck, depressed people fall into the demoralizing trap of always making the most negative inferences about their experience. They do so because they have structured their experience around a distinctive set of "cognitive distortions," systematic errors in reasoning, that become particularly salient during times of distress. Ellis has a "dirty dozen" of specific self-statements that make life nasty and unrewarding; Beck et. al. (1979) lists six common distortions that a cognitive therapist should listen for in patients' descriptions of life:

- *Arbitrary inference.* "A poor grade on an exam in a course where I am otherwise doing quite well shows that I don't belong in college and probably was accepted to this palace of higher education by mistake."
- *Selective abstraction.* "My wife must be getting ready to leave me; she laughed harder at Greg's joke than she did at mine, and she's heard his dumb joke a dozen times."
- *Overgeneralization.* "Harvard University Press isn't interested in publishing this book. Publishers are all so unaware of the important issues. Why did I ever bother to write this book?"
- *Magnification and minimization.* This distortion has a sensitization/denial dimension. The patient either makes mountains out of molehills, catastrophizing some event, or disregards some important piece of information that would contradict the reality he or she has set up. Undergraduates do both of these in bad (poorly communicative) relationships all the time.
- *Personalization.* "I saw my therapist at McDonald's the other day. He refused even to look up to see me. I hate feeling rejected!"
- *Dichotomous thinking.* "If I don't file my tax return by the April 15 deadline, what's the point of ever filing it?"

Note, please, that we all engage in these distortions from time to time. The cognitive therapist is concerned with which of these we use, and with what result, when we are emotionally challenged. My own cognitive distortions tend to revolve around questions of cosmic "fairness." What would make this fact clinically significant for Beck would be if, during some difficult period in my life, I became convinced that I was being treated unfairly, started using some combination of the above "distortions," and became increasingly depressed by that perception of unfairness.

My REBT therapist would want to know why I need to believe that life is fair. Why do I need to fall apart when I find out that there are people in the world who don't play fair?

But my cognitive therapist would want to hear me talk about the evidence I found for being treated unfairly. If I felt that I was a victim of discrimination on the basis of my age, race, sexual orientation, or personal beliefs, my therapist would ask me to recite the evidence I had for believing that to be the case. She would then work closely with me to show how I could test the validity of my perceptions and beliefs and what "automatic thoughts" I might be having about people's rejection and unfair treatment of me.

The Challenge of Change

As a talking-cure practitioner, I am a reasonably effective cognitive behavior therapist. I can keep track of the cognitive distortions my clients are making, and I can help them open up to competing interpretations of reality. But I'm never quite sure how to get them to change their mind.

I hope you will remember Luke, the source of my initiation into the mysteries of transference, who was introduced in Chapter 7. My initial diagnosis of Luke was that he was and for a long time had been severely depressed. As a young and adventurous behavior therapist, I was eager to try out some cognitive techniques on Luke. So one day, while he was going on about how rotten and ugly life was, I challenged him to test his hypothesis that he couldn't think of anything that made life worth living. It was a magnificent fall afternoon: bright sun, crisp air, maple trees at the peak of their color.

I called our maintenance office to ask if I could borrow a pickup truck for a couple of hours, bundled gloomy Luke into the passenger's seat, and took off for a tour of some backroads through a nearby state park. When we returned I felt like a combination of Henry David Thoreau, Walt Whitman, and Robert Frost all rolled into one fine cognitive behavior therapist.

"So, Luke," I said. "What did you think of that?"

"You know," he replied, "I've lived in Indiana all my life. But I never recognized before today how damned flat it really is."

Conclusion? I guess you can lead a person to a cognition, but you can't make him think it.

PART III
Psychology on Trial

It is a capital mistake to theorize before one has data. Insensibly one begins to twist the facts to suit theories, instead of the theories to fit the facts.

ARTHUR CONAN DOYLE AS SHERLOCK HOLMES, *A SCANDAL IN BOHEMIA*

You have spent your life making molehills out of mountains—that's what you are guilty of. When man was tragic, you made him trivial. When he was picaresque, you called him picayune. When he suffered passively, you described him as simpering; and when he drummed up enough courage to act, you called it stimulus and response. Man had passion; and when you were pompous and lecturing to your class you called it "the satisfaction of basic needs," and when you were relaxed and looking at your secretary you called it "release of tension." You made man over into the image of your childhood Erector Set or Sunday School maxims—both equally horrendous . . . *nimis simplicando*! What do you plead, guilty or not guilty?

ROLLO MAY AS SAINT PETER

CHAPTER 15

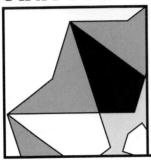

Humanistic Psychotherapy: Mary Calkins, Gordon Allport, and Carl Rogers

First Things First: Discovering the Person

After World War II, North American psychology and psychotherapy began to develop a renewed interest in William James's ideals of individualism and development of the self. This school of thought, known as humanistic psychology, identified itself as the "third force" in American psychology, alongside behaviorism and psychoanalysis.

Mary Whiton Calkins, one of James's early students, was one of the first proponents of a purely individual psychology. Although never granted a Ph.D., because she was a woman, Calkins devoted her life to studying psychology as James had done—as a philosophy of human existence.

Gordon Allport, best known for his work with personality traits, was another critically important figure in the development of humanistic psychology. Allport resisted the separation of the fundamental insights of religion from the knowledge base of psychology (but he never proposed that any particular religious ideas were necessary for a psychological understanding of human beings). Consistent with this perspective, Allport developed the idea of the proprium, *the innermost part of the self, as the experiential core of human existence. Is this the soul?*

Carl Rogers, founder of the humanistic psychology movement, became one of the best-known psychologists of our age. Rogers's concept of unconditional positive regard has been accepted by all schools of psychotherapy as central to the establishment of an authentic therapeutic relationship. Humanistic psychology is enormously popular in the United States and around the world; however, the therapy that Rogers proposed is much more challenging than is commonly perceived. To perform Rogers's client-centered therapy effectively, the therapist must have extraordinary interpersonal skills and be able to maintain complete focus on the here-and-now experience of every client he or she encounters. This can be a very challenging task, as well as an enlightening one.

Mary Calkins: The Beginnings of a Psychology of Self

> I ceased to be a teacher. It wasn't easy. It happened rather gradually, but as I came to trust students, I found they did incredible things in their communication with each other, in their learning of content material in the course, in blossoming out as growing human beings. Most of all they gave me courage to be myself more freely, and this led to profound interaction. They told me their feelings, they raised questions I had never thought about. I began to sparkle with emerging ideas that were new and exciting to me, but also, I found, to them. . . . I changed at that point from being a teacher and evaluator, to being a facilitator of learning—a very different occupation. (Rogers, 1983, p. 26)

As I am writing this book, I am surrounded by tall stacks of research materials—a pile of histories of psychology, a pile of biographies, a pile of social histories, a stack of books on philosophy. Judging by only what I read in these books, I would perceive that every important figure in the history of the talking cure was a white male. (As someone said a decade or so ago, "In psychology, even the rats are white, and male.")

If the politics of a thing were its ultimate reality, we would probably concede the point and move on. Fortunately, however, by exercising our Jamesian wills, we can uncover the contributions that women have made to the history of the talking cure, just as we can gain an appreciation for the feminist critique and reformulation of the therapeutic enterprise (see Chapter 18). In Chapter 12 I documented the contributions of Rosalie Rayner and Mary Cover Jones (Little Albert and Little Peter, respectively) to the development of behavior therapies in John B. Watson's time.

Another woman worthy of mention is Mary Whiton Calkins (1863–1930), who in 1890 began graduate study in psychology at Harvard University under William James. James's old mentor, who was then president of Harvard, Charles Eliot, vigorously resisted having a woman intrude into the all-male bastion. James called this policy "flagitious," an "excellent but now little-used word, meaning 'shamefully wicked; vile and scandalous,' [which] deserves to be revived" (Fancher, p. 264n).

As usual in his dealings with President Eliot, James won the day—but only after a fashion. Calkins was allowed to continue her research at Harvard without benefit of formal registration. She completed all the requirements for the Ph.D., and James testified that her work was "much the most brilliant examination for the Ph.D. that we have ever had at Harvard." Scholars around the world, including Sigmund Freud himself, concurred that Calkins was "surely one of the strongest professors of psychology in the country." She was included in 1903 on a list of the 50 most important

American psychologists and became president of the American Psychological Association in 1905 and president of the American Philosophical Association in 1918. Nevertheless, Harvard University did not condone graduate education for women and refused to award her the degree. The university had an obsolete principle to maintain.

Eventually the pious gentlemen of the Harvard Corporation offered to grant Calkins a Ph.D. through Radcliffe College, the undergraduate college for women begun in 1894. Calkins, however, had the good sense to refuse to accept what would have been an honorary degree—and a sham one at that, because she had had no previous contact with Radcliffe College.

The Experience of Self

Calkins's contribution to the development of psychotherapy was, regardless of the small-minded campus politics of the time, extraordinarily important. She introduced into modern psychology the idea of a *self*. Today, we can hardly imagine a selfless psychology, but Calkins wrote in 1910 that she possessed an "ever strengthening conviction that psychology is most naturally, consistently, and effectively treated as a study of conscious selves in relation to other selves and to external objects—in a word, to their environment, personal and impersonal" (quoted in Furumoto, 1991, p. 60). This was a perplexing and profoundly challenging idea to the psychologists of her day.

Calkins proposed that psychology reconcern itself with conscious experience and that it become the science wherein human beings seriously and holistically study their own experience—"the study of conscious, experiencing, functioning beings, that is of persons, or selves" (Calkins, 1912, p. 43). No wonder Harvard found her heretical!

Calkins's (1930) idea of self has five elements:

- "A totality, a one of many characters"
- "A unique being in the sense that I am I and you are you"
- "An identical being—I the adult self and my ten-year-old self are the same self"
- "A changing being—I the adult self differ from that ten-year-old"
- "A being related in a distinctive fashion both to itself and its experiences, and to environing objects personal and impersonal" (p. 45)

The meaning of the first four elements ought to be self-evident. The fifth point suggests something that was revolutionary and new to psychology in 1910: "Objects" in the world possess both universal aspects and phenomenologically experienced representations of those aspects. In Chapter 1, I invited you to eat a bowl of rice with me. You knew what a bowl of rice is, but you may not have been prepared for my invitation to regard eating a bowl of rice as a symbolic act, a revelatory act, and ultimately an intimate act. In Calkins's sense, my offering you a bowl of rice, in the form of this book, requires you to experience the personal significance that my self attaches to the act of offering it to you.

Calkins referred to the meaning-imparting function of self as *attitude*. Her use of the term was so far ahead of its time that it is very current today. Examples of this usage include my contention that I am not paid to argue about grades with students with "attitudes." Harvard University overseers of the 1800s and early 1900s couldn't deal with women professionals because of unconscious "attitudes" rooted in men's definition of themselves as superior selves.

Calkins herself gave a more delicate and charming interpretation of *attitude*. She said that her "receptive experience" of clouds includes their "fleecy whiteness," their "charm or pleasantness," her "wishes and fantasies" triggered by gazing at the sky, and the compulsions that she sees in clouds—for example, to run home and close the windows before a storm.

Calkins well knew that the dour titans of psychology would not look favorably on the notion that human beings "construct" an infinitely varied reality from their often common experience. She wrote—I think perhaps as defiant as she was demure—that she feared her views would be judged "non-essential and dull. . . . Yet anyone who, without bias, will study the material of psychology by the use of [this system of psychology] will discover them for what they are—not impositions on experience but descriptions of it" (1930, p. 48).

Calkins's Contribution to the Talking Cure

Psychology, for Calkins, was the study of how conscious experience is shaped. She wrote:

> With each year I live, with each book I read, with each observation I initiate or confirm, I am more deeply convinced that psychology should be conceived as the science of the self, or person, as related to its environment physical and social. (1930, quoted in Furumoto, 1991, p. 64)

This notion inspired a dramatic change in the way psychologists perceive the person. As Fancher (1990) pointed out, "Calkins saw the self as an active, guiding, and purposive agency present in all states of consciousness, and requiring to be included in any complete introspective report" (p. 267).

It is true that when Watson and behaviorism came along, they obscured the ideas of Calkins and every other introspectionist. The New World embraced scientific psychology and forgot Calkins for more than half a century. (See Madigan and O'Hara, 1992, for an interesting rediscovery of Calkins's early scientific work on the properties of human memory.) However, she struck a spark that kept the humanistic lights of North American psychology lit until the dominance of radical behaviorism faded.

Calkins's legacy was the idea that humans possess hearts and minds as well as re-flexes and neural circuits; she recognized that each of us exists with the special cre-ation of being that we call our self. She held the hope that psychology would not turn its back on this fundamental truth, but when she saw that it had, like her mentor James she turned to the study of philosophy. Others would come later to celebrate her vision.

Gordon Allport

I was not born in Indiana, but I have been a Hoosier longer than I have been any-thing else and considerably longer than 99% of my native-born Hoosier students. Thus I dedicate the next few pages to my favorite Hoosier psychologist, Gordon W. Allport (1897–1967).

Allport was born in the tiny village of Montezuma, Indiana, just a few miles from my house. The third son of a country doctor, he was raised, in his own words, with "plain Protestant piety and hard work." He was also raised with a classic midwestern belief that, "if every person worked as hard as he could and took only the minimum financial return required by his family's needs, then there would be just enough wealth to go around" (Allport, 1967, pp. 4, 5). All an Allport, or any upstanding Hoo-sier boy for that matter, needed to get along in life was a strong character, a sharp competitive edge, a gregarious nature, an aptitude for science and logic, a love of ath-letics, manual dexterity, some small but clever artistic or musical skill, and an appro-priate interest in society and social position.

Gordon's oldest brother Floyd possessed all these qualities and more. But in a small rural community, when you are the baby brother of the town's greatest hot-shot superstar, you do the best you can. Norman Rockwell's picture of the perfect American boyhood doesn't seem to make much room for the class intellectual—"the guy who swallowed a dictionary," as Gordon was called in his high school yearbook. Unlike his brother, he wasn't very sociable or athletic; instead, he was a little more sensitive and aware than a lot of the other kids.

This is the kid who hangs around the library while his older brothers are cited in the local paper every week with their scholarships, athletic successes, and inspira-tional talks to the Rotary Club and the local chapter of the Daughters of the Ameri-can Revolution. Gordon eventually followed Floyd to Harvard, but even there, Gor-don was overshadowed by his older brother. The only sign of Gordon's future contribution to the talking cure was that he was a hardworking, enthusiastic psychol-ogy major who wanted to "find out what makes people tick" and who really believed that every individual ought to "perform at the highest level of which one is capable, [once] one is given full freedom to do so" (Allport, 1967, p. 5).

Allport was the sort of small-town intellectual with "callow forwardness" who could think it would make perfect sense, as a young college graduate who happened to be passing through Vienna, to call on Dr. Sigmund Freud. Allport's idealism was shattered when Freud mocked his effort at conversation and sent him packing as if he were the intruding nuisance of a small boy. That instance of humiliation provided Allport with a lesson about the dangers of psychology that shaped the rest of his life.

Allport returned to Harvard and stayed there. He received the Ph.D. in 1922 and in essence continued the work that Calkins had begun a quarter century earlier. He never became a clinician or, as far as I know, developed any real interest in psychotherapy. But he did develop and extend psychology's view of the individual as a unique self. In doing so, he laid the foundations of the humanistic psychology that would be built following the end of World War II.

The Process of Becoming a Person

Most people remember Allport for his work on *traits*. He was interested in discovering how major and minor traits—determined by a mixture of social, biological, and psychological forces—define the self. For our purposes, however, Allport's more valuable contribution was his vision of the organism as a complete and dynamic whole, a unique and fully integrated expression of a person. Each life, he believed, can be understood only as a dynamic unity directed toward self-enhancement, growth, and appreciation of the limitless opportunities for self-expression and actualization of potential.

This is a process-oriented view of human behavior. But unlike Freud's view of the process as tied to the past and locked in conflict, Allport's view stresses *becoming*. He recognized that every life is a work in progress.

The Nomothetic View Versus the Idiographic View. Moreover, Allport believed that a life can only be understood *idiographically*, or in its unique set of particulars. In contrast, most North American psychologists of Allport's era were developing *nomothetic*, or "central tendency"–based, views of organisms, coded as laws of behavior. Allport argued that the only "laws" of any importance were those applicable in a specific situation at a specific time in a specific individual's life situation.

Let me try to illustrate this point with a nonclinical example from my own recent experience. My college requires all graduating seniors to pass two days of written comprehensive examinations in their major subject. This ancient tradition frightens students, reassures faculty, and makes alumni believe that we still hold our students to very high standards.

But what is a "comprehensive" examination? Everyone seems to assume a normative (that is, nomothetic) view. Some departments set a minimum score that students must achieve on a standardized, multiple-choice national exam. This strategy assures a high level of "objectivity," but nobody is quite sure what any given score really means. The 25 or so different departments end up with at least 25 or so different "norms" about what constitutes a passing performance. Ultimately, regardless of how objective the content of any exam is, the decision about what constitutes passing or "passing with distinction" and so forth is a function of the persuasive power of individual faculty members within individual departments.

These exams work wonderfully to identify the very top students who know everything (and who could be readily identified without an examination). They also do a dandy job of finding the one or two students every year who have learned practically nothing during their 4 years of college. The exams also provide a relatively good normative measure of central tendency by which we can compare students from year to year. Recent psychology graduates, for example, have had a mean score on the exam several points higher than graduates in past years, and recent performances have been somewhat less variable than in the past. But these exams tell us next to nothing about the students in the vast middle because we have no idiographic data (except individual scores) to give our nomothetic judgments any meaning.

A few years ago I volunteered to be in charge of my department's comprehensive examination process. I persuaded my colleagues to call the test "morphogenic comprehensive examinations in psychology." (*Morphogenic* is another word for *idiographic;* I didn't want anything that sounded like *idiot* or *idiotic* attached to my grand idea.) The exam itself was unchanged. But now students were also required to write an autobiographical essay in which they described the intellectual route they had taken in becoming a graduating psychology major. In these autobiographical statements students were supposed to describe how their coursework and research activities had influenced their thinking about psychology, to identify the ideas they had encountered that had influenced them the most, and in general to chart the course of their development as young psychologists.

The central Allportian idea was that the department could read each student's exam papers within the context of her or his individual experience as a young scholar. The evaluation of each student's exam would then be based not on some meaningless score or statistical norm but rather on our analysis of what could reasonably be expected of a person with a particular set of academic experiences and interests.

It was a near-perfect scheme. My colleagues at other colleges loved the idea and wanted me to send them information about the process. But our students hated it because of the extra work, and my colleagues hated it because they couldn't figure out how to grade the examinations "fairly." Our college administrators hated the idea because it was so unlike what every other department in the college was doing.

The "morphogenic" exam was abandoned after a 2-year trial, primarily because I had not recognized that most students do not experience or process their education morphogenically. They don't learn the material for their own enrichment and enlightenment, their own becoming. They learn it for the "curve" and for the peculiar demands of each professor. And then, just as countless generations of students have before them, they try their mightiest to wipe all the material out of their memory banks after the final exam, to make room for the next semester's brainful of unintegrated ideas and concepts.

And so my department went back to a system in which everything is relative to "the average," average being the apparent standard of undergraduate education in North America. And everyone is, on average, once again happy. As James noted more than a century ago, the primary prerequisite for most college education is a vast capacity for boredom.

The "Cumulative Record" of a Life. As far as I can see, the only psychologists who would have fully understood the point that Allport and I were trying to make would have been the strict Skinnerians of the 1950s, who were interested in the effects of specific patterns of reinforcement on the specific behavior recorded from individual organisms. Like Allport, they had little interest in knowing, for example, that the average rat presses the average bar an average of so many times in an average of so many minutes, resulting in an average of so-many reinforcers per unit of time. What they judged to be important was how slight changes in the environment—"schedules of reinforcement"—can increase or decrease the behavior of an organism. Those observations have meaning only in a "cumulative record" of the individual organism's behavior. In fact, Skinner published a collection of his own most important work in the 1950s in a book with the title *Cumulative Record* (Skinner, 1961).

So too was Allport interested in the "cumulative record" of a person's life. But for Allport the key to understanding the organism is not simply a thorough understanding of its history. The Skinnerian concept of control is the ability to use the organism's history to predict the effects of various environmental influences on behavior. Allport wanted to go beyond control, to discover the unifying principles that define a unique life.

Proprium: The Core of the Self

Allport described the self as "the me as felt and known" (1961, p. 127). The self, he believed, is the central organizing scheme of our personality, the key to our inner nature. Allport called this essential core of the self the *proprium*. If you would feel comfortable thinking of this innermost part of yourself as your soul, you are more than welcome to do so.

Some of my superiors at the college accused me of trying to invade the private minds of our students with the morphogenic comprehensive examination. Apparently, our culture is deeply disquieted by anyone's wanting to "know" other people beyond the nomothetic level. Recall what Calkins said 80 years ago:

> With each year I live, with each book I read, with each observation I initiate or confirm, I am more deeply convinced that psychology should be conceived as the science of

the self, or person, as related to its environment physical and social. (1930, quoted in Furumoto, 1991, p. 64)

An Exercise in Idealism. The psychology Allport left us highlighted the most treasured values of small-town North American life. He cherished individualism, but not the repellent egoism of the 1980s. He idealized the communitarian values of an earlier age, when every member of the community made a meaningful social contribution. And only in the process of becoming who you really and truly are, he believed, can you be maximally productive—and, perhaps, minimally screwed up. The same ideas are prominently championed in B. F. Skinner's utopian novel based on the principles of behaviorism, *Walden Two* (1948).

When I was an undergraduate, I participated as a subject in a longitudinal research project. I was asked to describe my moods several times a day and to record what I was thinking and what was motivating me. The researchers were primarily interested in mood and personality, but their methods were thoroughly Allportian because of the focus on day-to-day life. Here is a segment of their write-up of the collected data:

> The happy men possessed self-esteem and confidence. They were successful and satisfied in interpersonal relations. They showed ego-strength and a gratifying sense of identity. Their lives had organization, purpose, and the necessary mastery of themselves to attain their goals. The less happy men were pessimistic in their expectations and lower in self-esteem and self-confidence. More unsuccessful with their interpersonal relations, with evidence of isolation, anxiety, and guilt, they showed little sense of satisfying ego-identity. They felt inferior in their academic performance and their lives lacked continuity and purpose. (Ricks & Wessman, 1966, p. 15)

Allport hoped psychology would develop the "stencil of values" (Allport, 1955) that would help the unhappy, those like some of the young men in the study, become and thus feel happier, more like the happy men described in the study.

Part of Allport's vision was "democratic ideals," which make it possible to lead one's life openly and creatively and thus make life worth living. Allport (1955) described democratic ideals as "a measure of rationality, a portion of freedom, a generic conscience, propriate ideals, and unique value" (p. 100).

These ideals can be found by looking within, to our own special sense of being in the world. However, Allport worried about what he saw as an increasing trend among North Americans to turn their backs on the full measure of their humanity. Perhaps, he wrote, Americans are losing what the theologian Paul Tillich (1952) described as

> the courage to be as a part in the progress of the group to which one belongs, of his nation, of all mankind [as] expressed in all specifically American philosophies: pragmatism, process philosophy, the ethics of growth, progressive education, crusading democracy. (quoted in Allport, 1955, p. 81)

Allport believed that psychology has a crucial role to play in helping us recover the idealism of our small-town Jeffersonian roots—to "provide the forward intention that enables [each person] at each stage of his becoming to relate himself meaningfully to the totality of Being" (1955, p. 96).

An Abiding Respect for Individuals. If Allport's ideas sound a lot like what you learned in Sunday school, they probably are. Allport didn't think that religion and psychology pursue different ends or different visions of human experience and fulfillment. For Allport, the *proprium* is the soul, although he never insisted that we adopt that notion as doctrine. As Schultz (1977) pointed out:

> Allport's prescription for a mature healthy person seems to be a distillation of the basic truths philosophers and theologians have been preaching for centuries. It seems obvious that it is healthy to have a firm self-image and self-identity, to feel a sense of self-esteem, to be able to give love openly and unconditionally, to feel emotionally secure, and to have goals and a sense of purpose that give meaning to life. (p. 22)

As unexceptionable as these ideals may seem, you can see how revolutionary they were when integrated into a psychology dominated by Watsonian behaviorism. Only a few years before, psychologists had serenely advocated against touching, holding, or expressing affection for one's own children. Calkins and Allport challenged the Calvinist roots of the North American experience—challenging us to throw away our hair shirt knitted of original sin and a struggle against nature and to don instead the warm and fuzzy sweater of family, community, and respect for individuality.

Allport was not really an applied psychologist, although he had organized his students to do some pioneering social work with newly arrived immigrants in Boston. He remained all his life the introspective, bookish fellow he had been back home in Indiana. His was an academic, ivory-tower psychology, based on years of conversation with the "best and the brightest"—upper-middle-class, achievement-oriented, white males of the sort who were sent to Harvard and destined to become people of significance. When Allport retired from teaching, his former students showed their respect and admiration by presenting him with a beautifully bound collection of their professional papers. The book bore this inscription: "From his students—in appreciation of his respect for their individuality."

Carl Rogers

It was another midwesterner, Carl R. Rogers (1902–1987), who translated the writings of Calkins and Allport into a talking cure. Rogers worked continuously from 1940 until his death to develop the field of humanistic psychology. I had the opportunity on several occasions to see Rogers in person and to hear him talk about psychotherapy. These were pivotal events in my own development as a therapist.

Person-centered, nondirective psychotherapy is the one talking cure I feel myself temperamentally unable to do with any real skill. Yet, curiously, every supervisor and observing student who has seen me at work tells me that I have integrated a great many Rogerian techniques into my therapeutic style. I hope they mean that I communicate at least a small measure of the unconditional respect and affection for my clients that were the hallmark of Rogers as a person and as a therapist.

A Declaration of Independence

The fourth of six children, Rogers described his rural northern Illinois parents as highly practical, down-to-earth, fundamentalist Christians who were "absolute masters of repressive control" over both themselves and their children. The Rogers family shunned all forms of contact with the outside world, and the children were raised to be contemptuous of intellectuals. His mother's most cherished Biblical verses were "Come out from among them and be ye separate" (II Corinthians 6:17) and "All our righteousness are as filthy rags" (Isaiah 64:6). Rogers noted some years later:

> I think the attitude toward other persons outside our large family can be summed up schematically in this way: Other persons behave in dubious ways which we do not approve in our family. Many of them play cards, go to the movies, smoke, dance, drink, and engage in other activities—some unmentionable. So the best thing to do is to be tolerant of them, since they may not know better, and to keep away from any close communication with them and live your life within the family. (1973, p. 3)

Sin and wickedness besieged the Rogers family. Young Carl entered adolescence with

> the realization by now that I was peculiar, a loner, with very little place or opportunity for a place in the world of persons. I was socially incompetent in any but superficial contacts. My fantasies during this period were definitely bizarre, and probably would be classed as schizoid by a diagnostician, but fortunately I never came in contact with a psychologist. (Rogers, 1973, p. 4)

Ironically, Rogers's style of therapy turned out to be the opposite of everything he learned during his childhood. His upbringing, he explained in an autobiographical note, contradicted virtually every element of the profound humanism that has become synonymous with the worldview known to us today as "Rogerian."

Rogers appears to have become Rogers (as Allport might have put it) on the proverbial slow boat to China. In 1922, the 20-year-old undergraduate set off with a group of fellow students to attend a conference in China for the World Student Christian Federation. China was a very popular destination for devout young missionaries following the ill-fated Boxer Rebellion, a period when China was politically vulnerable to foreign incursions of all sorts.

Unlike Allport, that other idealistic young midwestern American undergraduate, Rogers experienced a profound transformation in his thinking as home grew more distant. As the earnest young missionaries slowly steamed their way across the Pacific Ocean, Rogers found himself staying up night after night to talk and debate theology. He found himself increasingly unable to support a conservative religious ideology as he thought more about the truths implicit in his own experience of life.

Rogers returned to the United States a transformed human being. He announced his "theological independence" to his parents and declared his intention to marry his childhood sweetheart. Far more heretical was his decision to move to New York City to enroll as a divinity student at the shockingly radical (to his fundamentalist parents) Union Theological Seminary.

I can vividly imagine what must have happened back home on the farm when this shocking news arrived. With the wisdom of a shrewd undergraduate, Rogers had decided to send news of his change in plans by mail—from China. By the time the inevitable explosion occurred, his decision was a fait accompli, and he was not to be moved away from his plan:

> Since we did not have the benefit of airmail it took two months for a reply to arrive. Thus I kept pouring out on paper all my new feelings and ideas and thoughts with no notion of the consternation that this was causing in my family. By the time their reactions caught up with me, the rift in outlook was firmly established. Thus, with a minimum of pain I broke the intellectual religious ties with my home. (Rogers, 1967, p. 351)

After attending the seminary in New York for a few months, Rogers discovered quite abruptly that he had "thought myself out of religion" altogether. In time he found himself drawn to an alternative way of understanding the world and soon applied to begin graduate work in psychology at the Teachers College of Columbia University, a hotbed of radical behavioristic thinking in the 1920s. At Columbia his first serious psychological and intellectual challenge was to separate himself from a doctrinal religious perspective.

A Therapy Forged From Grim Realities

At Columbia, Rogers became a great admirer of none other than John B. Watson (see Chapter 12). He decided that behavioral psychology offered him an ideal opportunity to earn a living helping others yet to remain outside the influence and doctrines of organized religion.

Rogers's clinical training took place at an Adlerian institution, the Rochester, New York, Guidance Center. There he worked as the chief therapist and director of the Child Study Department. These were good years for Rogers: "I wasn't connected with a university, no one was looking over my shoulder from any particular treatment orientation," and "nobody gave a damn how you proceeded, but hoped you could be of some assistance" (Rogers, 1970, pp. 514–515).

Rogers stayed in Rochester until 1940 and wrote a textbook on child psychotherapy, which contained the germ of the nondirective approach he would pioneer over the next few years. From Rochester he assumed a professorship at Ohio State University, where he founded the counseling psychology program and developed a model program for the training of mental health professionals. His approach to psychotherapy was published as a book in 1942 under the title *Counseling and Psychotherapy*.

The new book made Rogers a well-regarded national figure and gained him the invitation in 1945 to establish the Student Counseling Center at the University of Chicago. His new position gave him the opportunity to develop the practice of nondirective psychotherapy, as well as a long-awaited opportunity to put his ideas to work at an administrative level. However, as at Rochester, he was forced into some bitterly intense turf wars with psychiatrists, who were fighting determinedly to prevent all psychologists from practicing psychotherapy.

Lobotomies. In those years, surgical interventions were all the vogue in institutional psychiatry. In 1942 an article was published in *Time* magazine describing the newest technique for performing prefrontal lobotomies:

> After drilling a small hole in the temple on each side of the skull, the surgeon then inserts a dull knife into the brain, makes a fan shaped incision through the prefrontal lobe, then downward a few minutes later. He then repeats the incision on the other side of the brain. . . . The patient is given only local anesthetic at the temples—the brain itself is insensitive—and the doctors encourage him [*sic*] to talk, sing, recite poems or prayers. When his replies to questions show that his mind is thoroughly disoriented, the doctors know that they have cut deep enough into the brain. (quoted in Dawes, 1994, p. 48)

Hold that image in your head, gentle reader. Hear the singing, talking, praying, and poetry-reciting voices of the 228 lobotomized patients reported on in a 1952 *Time* story: 151 were later judged "improved," and 73 were "the same or worse." And 4 died from the procedure (Dawes, 1994). Now go out and rent a videotape of *One Flew Over the Cuckoo's Nest*. This was the psychiatric climate Rogers worked in during the years he developed his own approach to psychotherapy.

Rogers later reflected that the pitched battles he fought with the psychiatrists had been the fiercest struggles of his life. He had fought them, he said, with the battle cry "Don't tread on me!" (1980, pp. 54–55).

"Trust, Listen, Encourage, Foster." In drastic contrast to the prevailing treatments of the day, the essence of Rogers's approach at this time was to *trust* his clients, his colleagues, his students, and his staff and coworkers. His method was to *listen* carefully to what people said, to *encourage* them to proceed according to their best intentions, and to *foster* a democratic atmosphere at every level of human interaction.

In 1957 Rogers moved to the University of Wisconsin in Madison for a joint appointment in psychology and psychiatry. The appointment was a victorious resolution of his dispute with organized medicine and an opportunity to work with seriously impaired schizophrenic patients. However, although life was good for Rogers in Madison, the situation violated everything he believed about the development and education of his students. Thus, he left Madison in 1963 to found his own training and research center, the Western Behavioral Science Institute in La Jolla, California, where the humanist thinktank, The Center for the Studies of the Person, is still located.

After leaving Wisconsin, Rogers attempted unsuccessfully to get the *American Psychologist* to publish his manifesto on graduate education: "Current Assumptions in Graduate Education." In this document Rogers charged graduate schools with "doing an unintelligent, ineffectual, and wasteful job of preparing psychologists, to the detriment of our discipline and society" (Rogers, 1969, p. 170). The unpublished paper spread throughout the graduate student underworld of the late 1960s. When I read my copy, I understood why Rogers was never mentioned in any of our graduate courses.

By the late 1960s Rogers was widely recognized among young radical psychologists as a kindred spirit. Although by then in his late sixties, he seemed to graduate students to be a fellow revolutionary. Like them, he was determined to change the world through the unfettered exercise of focused will and intellect. That a world-famous clinical psychologist would resign from a prestigious place like the University of Wisconsin because of the way his students were treated and consequently find himself censored and shunned by the establishment at the American Psychological Association was clear vindication of every rebellious thought and impulse so many others felt. These were the times that shaped my emerging identity as a professional psychologist.

"Persons or Science?"

Meanwhile, the "theory" that Rogers was developing continued to evolve and mature. Early in his career, he had focused on being nondirective, allowing the client's inner impetus "toward growth, health, and adjustment" (Rogers, 1942, p. 29) guide the counseling relationship. Nondirective therapy focused less on the intellect and more on feelings than had any other therapy ever articulated. Psychotherapeutic sessions focused on the here and now and defied Freudian prescriptions about the importance of uncovering the past with an emotionally neutral therapist-analyst.

In a fascinating essay published in 1955 under the title "Persons or Science?" Rogers argued that such an approach was not only humanely significant and therapeutically effective but scientifically viable as well. He urged humanistic psychologists to embrace the scientific method and to abandon any notion that science is incompatible with "objective knowledge of the basic principles by which individuals may achieve more constructive social behavior which is natural to their organismic process of becoming" (p. 277).

In the essay Rogers articulated two principles about the nature of humanistic psychotherapy:

> (a) There are many . . . persons who are relatively open to their experience and hence likely to be socially constructive. (b) Both the subjective experience of psychotherapy and the scientific findings regarding it indicate that individuals are motivated to change, and may be helped to change, in the direction of greater openness to experience, and hence in the direction of behavior which is enhancing of self and society. (1955, p. 277)

The nondirective therapeutic relationship is the very model of human caring, understanding, and acceptance. The role of the therapist is to help the individual client learn to "relate himself successfully to another person in a more adult fashion" (Rogers, 1942, p. 30), primarily by gaining greater self-awareness and self-acceptance through the clarification of feelings:

> Effective counseling consists of a definitively structured, permissive, relationship which allows the client to gain an understanding of himself to a degree which enables him to take positive steps in the light of his new orientation. (Rogers, 1942, p. 18)

In 1989 a Japanese clinical psychologist in Tokyo reverently showed me the preceding quotation in a Japanese psychology textbook and declared that these were the finest words ever written by a non-Japanese psychologist. In fact, if you want to skip the chapters on psychotherapy in Japan at the end of the book, just read that quote to yourself over and over again as a mantra until enlightenment takes over your mind.

A Crisis of Conscience

While Rogers was still working at the University of Chicago, he became clinically involved with a deeply disturbed young woman whose emotional and psychological disorganization was stronger than Rogers's capacity for a therapeutic and compassionate relationship. In a process probably very similar to the one I described myself going through with young Luke in Chapter 7, Rogers lost track of his own self and began to vacillate erratically between warm permissiveness on the one hand and cool professional distance on the other (Monte, 1991, p. 700). The result was an emotional and intellectual chaos that threatened to overwhelm both the client and the therapist. Rogers wrote:

> I stubbornly felt that I *should* be able to help her and permitted the contacts to continue long after they had ceased to be therapeutic, and involved only suffering for me. I recognized that many of her insights were sounder than mine, and this destroyed my confidence in myself, and I somehow gave up *my* self in the relationship. (1967, p. 367)

Rogers had the good sense to put himself into therapy at that point. As he himself pointed out, he was fortunate that by then he could turn to therapists who had been soundly and humanely trained and who could offer him genuine help during this difficult time. Rogers became a consumer of his own medicine, and he later judged it to have saved his life.

As Rogers reflected on what had gone wrong in his work with the young woman, it seemed to him that perhaps she had experienced his counseling as too overwhelming to her fragile ego. It was possible that too much acceptance and too much freedom in the therapeutic relationship had been one of the causes of the breakdown of the therapy (and the therapist as well?). In 1951 the language Rogers used to describe his therapeutic method changed from *nondirective* to *client-centered*—a distinction that took the emphasis off technique and placed it squarely on the psychological realities apparent in the therapeutic relationship.

The Essence of Rogers's Talking Cure

Instead of focusing on acceptance and trust and openness as *techniques*, Rogers began to focus on *empathic understanding* of the client and *interpersonal communication* of that understanding back to the client. In 1957 Rogers published a definitive statement of the "theory of therapy, personality and interpersonal relationships as developed in the client-centered framework" (Rogers, 1957/1992, n. 1). The title of the article is more than compelling: "The Necessary and Sufficient Conditions of Therapeutic Personality Change." In it Rogers argued:

> For constructive personality change to occur, it is necessary that these conditions exist and continue over a period of time:
>
> 1. Two persons are in psychological contact.
> 2. The first, whom we shall term the client, is in a state of incongruence, being vulnerable or anxious.
> 3. The second person, who we shall term the therapist, is congruent or integrated in the relationship.
> 4. The therapist experiences unconditional positive regard for the client.
> 5. The therapist experiences an empathic understanding of the client's internal frame of reference and endeavors to communicate this experience to the client.
> 6. The communication to the client of the therapist's empathic understanding and unconditional positive regard is to a minimal degree achieved. (1957/1992, p. 827)

With their talking cure developing under this set of necessary and sufficient conditions, humanistic psychotherapists began to develop a phenomenological understanding of the other. The true art of humanistic psychology involved combining this phenomenological understanding with introspective "subjective knowing" and empirical "objective knowing." The resulting knowledge of the self and of others made possible what Rogers called "a science of the person," which

> will attempt to face up to *all* of the realities in the psychological realm. . . . [I]t will throw open the whole range of human experiencing to satisfying study. It will explore

the private worlds of inner personal meanings, in an effort to discover lawful and orderly relationship there. (Rogers, 1964, p. 119)

Psychological Contact. A final development of Rogers's approach to therapy came during the University of Wisconsin period, when he added an "experiential" element to client-centered therapy. The key was "the mutual expression of feelings" by both the client and the therapist. This formulation became increasingly necessary as Rogers extended his approach to different kinds of populations, including institutionalized schizophrenics and entrenched educational bureaucrats. Because neither group was known for being especially good at understanding others or putting feelings into words, humanistic psychotherapists needed nonverbal ways of expressing acceptance, empathy, and understanding of the client's perspective.

The talking cure was now, sometimes at least, the nonverbal cure. Emotional connectedness and human acceptance could be conveyed through facial expression, touching, and any other immediately expressed form of human communication. The success of this method depends on the establishment of "psychological contact" between the vulnerable, "incongruent" client and an "integrated, congruent therapist" who clearly communicates unconditional positive regard, empathic understanding, and emotional congruence (Rogers, 1957/1992).

Perhaps you can see why I do not claim to be a skilled Rogerian therapist: It's difficult to remain so perfectly supportive for any length of time. I am flattered by the observation that I at least appear to be doing some of these things. But I can assure you that I am not so "integrated and congruent" that I can dispense altogether with my relaxation tapes and structured cognitive homework assignments.

Perhaps the magnitude of the challenge is why I am astounded when, in the oral part of the comprehensive examination with senior psychology majors at our college, after a faculty member from some other department asks what school of psychology the student identifies with, the student says, "The humanistic psychology of Carl Rogers." This is the answer nearly 100% of the time. It makes me want to leap up and clobber the students over the head with a rubber chicken. Not only have they no idea what they are talking about; they also have never seen or heard anyone behave toward anyone else in a Rogerian fashion. For them, like most people, *Rogerian* means sympathetic and nonjudgmental listening—the sort of thing you might do if your best friend is feeling terrible for having just dumped her latest boyfriend.

I can only hope that you will reflect on the extraordinary task facing Rogerian therapists: to experience and communicate unconditional positive regard to every person they counsel for every minute of the session; to empathically and phenomenologically know what the client is feeling and expressing at all times, even in contradiction to what the client is saying; "to perceive as sensitively and accurately as possible all of the perceptual field as it is being experienced by the client" (Rogers,

1951, p. 4); and all the while to remain genuine and authentic in relation to that person. I could barely do all these things with my son when he was 18 months old.

Let me conclude this section with just three observations:

- Rogers really could do all these things. Watching him was almost a sacred experience for me. His interactions with clients were like small miracles of compassionate understanding and communication.
- I have been able to do these things some of the time with a great many clients but with many different results. Sometimes we have achieved a moment of triumph and breakthrough; at other times I have scared the client back into his or her shell. Several times this technique has caused clients to develop an intense romantic attachment to me.
- If I ever met anyone who claimed to operate this way, I would fire, not hire, and maybe even run away from such a person in a nanosecond. These skills are, after all, precisely the skills of the seasoned psychopath—a topic to which we will return in Chapter 18.

I think most true followers of Rogers's client-centered therapy have little problem with my third point. Nor, I think, would Rogers, although he would probably make me feel so good about saying it that I would want to retract it.

Humanistic Orientation. In reality, there are very few humanistic psychotherapists among psychiatrists, psychologists, social workers, and counselors. Norcross and Prochaska (1988) surveyed practicing psychologists about their theoretical orientations and discovered that even those who claimed to be humanistically oriented were quick to add a hyphenated *cognitive* to the label. In fact, if pressed, I would probably admit myself to being a humanistic-cognitive-behavioral-existential-feminist-Zen therapist, which would mean basically that I refuse to answer your question. (One of my favorite students likes to answer the frequently asked question from his peers "What is your sexual orientation?" with the Zen-like answer "Monogamous." My imaginary answer is of the same ilk.) Norcross and Prochaska reported that the only professional group at all likely to claim a humanistic orientation (56%) is social workers, who seem to perceive themselves as a little bit of just about everything: 78% of them also claim to be dynamic, 51% are also behavioral, and 49% also say they are cognitive.

Humanistic psychotherapy is probably more a philosophical orientation than a theoretical orientation these days, a way of saying that you deliberately try not to be a fascist in the consulting room and that you make the client share responsibility for how the sessions go.

A true person-centered therapist today probably does 95% of her or his work in groups and does not get overly involved in the moment-to-moment expressions of "psychological contact." There is a vast literature on therapeutic groups, and for

Rogers, therapeutic groups represented the ultimate fruition of his theory and approach (Rogers, 1970). If you go back to my description of what is supposed to happen in a therapeutic "encounter" you will readily see why. If you are interested in reading about some of the dangers and pitfalls in poorly managed humanistic therapy groups, please read *After the Turn On, What?* edited by Houts and Serber (1972).

The Interview With Gloria. To get a feel for Rogerian psychotherapy, you have to read a lot of Rogers; and a lot of Rogers is verbatim transcripts of interactions between Rogers and his clients. Audiotapes are also available, as are a limited number of videotapes, which are all the more impressive because so much of the communication is nonverbal.

My favorite videotape features a 30-year-old client, Gloria, who is interviewed in turn by Albert Ellis (see Chapter 14), Fritz Perls (see Chapter 16), and then by Rogers (1965). Gloria is obviously confused and troubled by a problem with her 9-year-old daughter, "Pammy." Gloria isn't sure how she should respond to Pammy's curiosity about Gloria's sexual relationships with men since her divorce from Pammy's father. Ellis has a New York, in-your-face style and is exquisitely rational. Perls has a similarly no-nonsense approach and is quite confrontational. They are every bit as "authentic" as Rogers, but other than that you would think they came from different planets.

The Rogers/Gloria interview begins with Rogers preparing himself to meet Gloria for the first time. He asks: "Can I be real?" (Will I bring genuineness, congruence, and transparency of self to this meeting?) "Will I find myself spontaneously prizing this person?" (Will I communicate a feeling of acceptance, caring, and nonpossessive love?) And finally, "Will I understand this person?" (What does it feel like to be her?)

For approximately the next 20 minutes, Rogers and Gloria discuss primarily the problems Gloria has had in accepting herself and in accepting responsibility for her feelings. "I don't like the responsibility," she says; Rogers replies, "It's an awfully risky thing being alive." In Rogers's eyes, this encounter is an opportunity for Gloria to explore her most human feelings and her most important attitudes toward herself. Rogers asserts his trust that "if I am more real, then she will be more real" and Gloria will begin to find greater self-knowledge and self-acceptance. And gradually, as Gloria moves the locus of her thinking and judging from outside herself to a set of inner values and beliefs, she will become more spontaneous, feel more whole, and become more tentative in her perceptions.

As Rogers sums up his approach, he says:

> It is because I find value and reward in human relationships that I enter into a relationship known as therapeutic, where feelings and cognition merge into one unitary experience which is lived rather than examined, in which awareness is nonreflective, and where I am participant rather than observer. (1955, p. 277)

A Functional Analysis of Client-Centered Therapy

A common misconception about Rogerian psychotherapy is that it is little more than being an "active listener." In fact, engaging a client on Rogers's terms is something like the attentional focus required in Zen (see Chapters 21 and 22), except that the therapist's attention is directed toward the entire array of information that we share, as senders and as receivers, within any intimate relationship. I am continually surprised by how cognitive a lot of Rogers's work with clients is. Although the "content" of the conversation may be feelings and emotions, Rogers seems most clearly to be aiming for the client to achieve a much clearer understanding of what is happening inside her or him.

In 1966 a psychologist, Charles Truax, published an interesting functional analysis of what actually transpires between the client and the therapist in Rogerian counseling sessions. Truax had been involved with Rogers's therapeutic work with schizophrenic patients in Wisconsin, and his main research interest was identifying the "effective ingredients" in the patient/therapist relationship (Truax, 1963). For the 1966 report, Truax analyzed excerpts from a single, long-term, successful therapeutic relationship that Rogers had recorded at the University of Chicago Counseling Center. Truax sought evidence of Rogers's use of empathy, warmth, and directiveness in working with a client.

Five clinical psychologists independently rated a sample of 40 TPT (therapist/patient/therapist) interactions along nine patient scales and three therapist scales. The three therapist scales were essentially three classes of reinforcers: empathic understanding, acceptance, and directiveness.

Tactical Acceptance. The results demonstrated that Rogers tended to display empathy and warmth tactically. That is, his communication of empathy and warmth were administered to the client discriminatively. When the client was focusing clearly on his self and his feelings, displaying insight, keeping an orientation on his presenting difficulties, and "expressing himself in a style similar to that of the therapist," he was "reinforced" by the interest, warmth, and positive regard of the therapist. When he strayed away from clarity, however, Rogers responded to him with an increase in directiveness and a reduction in both therapist empathy and unconditional acceptance (Truax, 1966, p. 5).

When we read this study in graduate school, we were supposed to conclude that all effective therapy is a matter of differential reinforcement of the patient by the therapist. Revisiting these data 30 years later, however, I see something quite different. Rogers was genuinely self-perceptive in 1955 when he said, "Feelings and cognition merge into one unitary experience which is lived rather than examined, in which awareness is nonreflective, and where I am participant rather than observer" (p. 277). The cartoon character Barney loves you unconditionally and makes you part of his big happy family, and PBS's Mr. Rogers likes you "just the way you are." But for most adults, Forrest Gump notwithstanding, real life is a tad more complicated. The "uniform conditions which are globally facilitative of personal growth and integration" (Truax, 1966, p. 7) are applied in humanistic psychotherapy by a fully engaged participant in the dynamic interpersonal transaction between the therapist and the client. From any theoretical perspective, the therapist must discriminate in some way between the adaptive and the maladaptive interpersonal and verbal behaviors of the client. Otherwise, the therapist would simply be some kind of empathy-acceptance automaton or, in the words that conclude Truax's report, no more than a "reinforcing machine" and the client a "talking pigeon" (Truax, 1966, p. 8).

Proof. With so few real client-centered therapists in the United States (I am told they are fairly common in Japan), it is difficult if not impossible to evaluate scientifically the value of this approach to therapy. Practically every psychotherapy outcome study uses a "nondirective feedback" control group to show that Brand X therapy works better than "just" relating to people. But I've never seen anyone successfully challenge Rogers's data on the success of his methods, which is all drawn from testimonials of former clients.

One client (Gloria, in fact) even asked Rogers and his wife if she could think of them as her "parents in spirit."

> We each replied that we would be pleased and honored to have that status in her life. Her warm feelings for us were reciprocated. . . . I am awed by the fact that this fifteen-year association [Gloria had died shortly before this was written] grew out of the quality of the relationship we formed on one thirty-minute period in which we truly met as persons. It is good to know that even one half-hour can make a difference in a life. (Raskin & Rogers, 1989, pp. 188–189)

Case Study: Two Guys in Indiana

Perhaps the best I can do to give you the emotional flavor of Rogers's approach is to share with you something of my ongoing relationship with an undergraduate I'll call Sam. Sam came to see me several years ago because he felt that he needed someone to talk to, "in order to get his head straight." He had important questions about his relationships with a wide variety of people, including his divorced mother and father, each of whom resented his relationship with the other parent; his step-parents; his full, half, and step siblings; and his girlfriend of long standing, with whom the relationship didn't seem to be going anywhere. He was also concerned about his career choices, which seemed at odds with what everyone else wanted him to do; his choice of majors; his intolerance of disturbing antisocial behavior on the part of some of his friends at school; his growing distance from old high school friends, who had once been closer than his family; his consumption of alcohol; and above all a nagging, disturbing, depressing feeling of guilt that hung over him in almost every relationship he had.

Sam recounted how he had started attending various self-help groups to clarify some of these issues. He sometimes went with other people, and sometimes he went alone; but he always came away from these sessions feeling both resentful of their message that he was pretty screwed up and powerless and vaguely guilty that he resented the advice of caring, good people who seemed to want to help him so much.

Of late, a pressing issue was whether he had to admit to the totality of his powerlessness to become fully "normal." Was he just another macho male who couldn't accept the deep and pervasive truth about himself and his superficial existence in the world? Or had he fallen into the middle of a rather uninteresting soap opera that this season was focusing on the life of Sam, the mild-mannered undergraduate?

Something strong and nonverbal communicated between us during the first few minutes of our first session. Sam was obviously trying to size me up, and I was trying to figure out if he was another one of these guys who come into counseling to get some narcissistic "permission" to continue in a self-indulgent, self-destructive lifestyle. My associate, who had made the appointment, told me she sensed that "Sam is a pretty unusual guy; there's a lot going on there." Talking with Sam, even somewhat superficially in our initial meeting, I got the feeling I knew what she meant. Maybe it was the coincidence that Sam had been born at almost the same moment in history when my own son had been born. But I would have bet the Rogers family farm that something extraordinary had taken place.

Opening Up With "Tactical" Self-Disclosure

Suddenly in our first session, on a creative, precognitive, intuitive impulse, I started self-disclosing. I told Sam about my own dysfunctional family background, my own parents' messy and hateful divorce, my own ambivalence about the judgment of my friends, and my own questions about whether I could pass muster with some of those self-help groups Sam had encountered. I told Sam I thought I knew something of what he was feeling, and I tried to express, to share, to communicate my ideas not about what he was feeling but about what talking to Sam made me feel right there, at that moment in my life.

As I have told you, I am not much of a Rogerian. At the time I was simply following a strong intuition that had bubbled up inside me. As first sessions go, it was quite a session.

But I wondered if I would ever see Sam again. He may well have thought that I was even crazier than he feared he might be. We hadn't gotten to any of the relationship issues he wanted to talk about. "We" had spent almost the whole session talking about feelings; I say "we," because maybe it was just I who talked about feelings.

That night I dreamed some extraordinarily vivid and inspired dreams. I woke feeling that something very significant had happened within my unconscious mind, something that caused a whole lot of reorganization in my thinking and perceiving. If I had exploited my own needs in that initial conference with Sam, it had at least done me a world of good. I also woke up from those dreams "knowing" some things about Sam that now seemed obvious but that I hadn't any awareness of the previous day.

Two days later Sam dropped by "to see if I was busy," which fortunately I was not. This time I asked him to do all the talking, and I think I even apologized for talking too much during our first session. It was a very good and very productive and very businesslike session between a bright, motivated, and highly insightful client and a very responsible and caring therapist. I think he was just as proud of "us" at the end of the session as I was. This felt a bit like world-class therapy, directed toward something less than catastrophic problems in living. But it was a very satisfying business for both of us.

Then the devil made me do it again. As Sam was getting ready to leave, I had to ask the big question: "Sam, when you were here last time it was a very important time for me, for reasons I don't fully understand. But there was one thing that puzzled me—no, in retrospect, it totally shook my confidence. When I was talking about what it was like growing up in an alcoholic family—surrounded by denial on all sides—I somehow felt that I was talking about something that I needed to talk about, that it was the key to a bond between us, that it was enormously important that we talk about it. Frankly, Sam, as I was talking about it, I had to really concentrate on holding back some very strong feelings. But—and this really bothers me—despite everything my counselor's intuition was telling me, you didn't seem at all moved by what was going on. Did I read that right?"

A huge tear rolled out of Sam's right eye. "I went back to my room after our session," he said, "and cried like a baby for almost 2 hours. It was the biggest and best cry I've had since I was 9 years old."

"Why the stone face in here?"

"Why did you have to hold back those 'very strong feelings'?" he asked.

"Guy stuff," I replied.

"Yeah, guy stuff. And I'm suffocating on it. The reason you didn't see anything is that it took every ounce of my guy training to hold it back—to keep a stone face—to protect myself from showing a stranger, another guy, what I was feeling. And it was way too strong to trust anyone with it."

"Wow! I am a great therapist after all! Can you come back on Monday so we can really talk?"

Learning From Experience

In the weeks that ensued, Sam and I discovered an ease of communicating, verbally and nonverbally, that was both extraordinary and completely natural. I came to know him through stories of his childhood. I foresaw (somewhat regretfully) that his longstanding but dependency-based relationship with his lover would not survive his growth and new self-assurance. I foresaw that he would be able to forge a new relationship with his father and that it would be at the cost of his childhood's intimacy with his mother. I saw his learning, in Rogers's words, to actualize "the vast resources of self-understanding and for altering . . . self-concepts, and behavior towards others" that result in "increased self-esteem and greater openness to experience" (Raskin & Rogers, 1989, p. 189).

Over the space of roughly one semester, Sam made enormous progress in resolving many of the questions that had brought him to counseling. He is getting ready to go to graduate school and is looking forward to the future with confidence and self-assurance. We keep in touch, once a month or so, though not as client and therapist.

I used to be surprised and disconcerted that Rogers never used the word *love* in his professional work, but I don't feel that way anymore. Sam and I don't "love" each other; I'm not sure we are what you would call "friends" either. We are two men who discovered a powerful bond, an emotional connection, and that bond changed and transformed both our lives in very powerful and very productive ways.

And all I brought to the relationship were empathy, caring, genuineness, unconditional nonpossessive regard, and congruence between what I was thinking and feeling and what I was communicating.

I can't help but compare my relationship with Sam to my relationship with Luke (see Chapter 7). Apart from being somewhat older when I met Sam, was I the same person in both situations? Sam was certainly less globally disturbed and significantly less self-destructive than Luke, but I wonder now how much of Luke's disturbance was actually brought out by my wanting to play the game both ways, like Rogers in Chicago—warm and empathic when it was safe but methodological and self-protective when the interpersonal and emotional going got rough. I wonder what might not have happened if I hadn't asked Sam "How come?" at the end of our second session.

Perhaps the connection we made was just coincidence. Or perhaps I'm still capable of learning something about my profession—and myself.

CHAPTER 16

Challenges to the Existing Order: Wilhelm Reich and Fritz Perls

And Now for Something Completely Different

The middle years of the twentieth century were a time of great social change around the world. Upheaval resulting from World War II caused global political and economic unrest, and in the United States, anticommunism became a sort of secular religion. As we have seen, where there is social change, there will likely be new developments in the field of psychology.

William Reich escaped the turmoil of war-stricken Europe to find himself a victim of an anticommunist crusade in North America. In attempting to forge theoretical and political links between psychoanalysis and communism, he was ultimately judged apostate by both movements. He spent his life challenging the established social order and ended up dying in a federal prison cell in the United States. Reich's revolutionary ideas about the biological link between sexual freedom and physical and mental health are what made him such a dangerous figure to the established order. From an early age he had experienced sexuality as a powerful physical and emotional force. These experiences were the basis for his grand theory of human liberation based on the accumulation of vital life energy: the orgone.

Frederick (Fritz) Perls, a former student of Reich's, also rode a wave of European unrest and social chaos. Perls, however, escaped to South Africa before coming to North America in 1946. An early meeting with Sigmund Freud shaped the rest of Perls's life. Perls developed Gestalt therapy, a talking cure based on confronting life in the here and now and living in complete accord with the principle of self-regulation. Perls's confrontational style demanded that his patients "Be Here Now!" The Gestalt therapy "prayer" reflects this celebration of the individual as a part of the human situation.

Three Great Revolutions

My life is revolution—from within and from without—or it's comedy! If I could only find someone who has the correct diagnosis! (Reich, 1988, p. 116)

Evolution

While writing this book I have been reading the biography of Charles Darwin by Desmond and Moore (1991). They painted a detailed picture of the vast social upheaval in France and England resulting from the disruptions of the French Revolution. One of the most important changes in the social structure of Europe, and especially England, was the breakup of the entrenched power of the established church. Prior to the Enlightenment, church authorities had controlled and regulated every aspect of life at practically every rung of the social order. This power began to crumble, however, as Enlightenment ideas about the inherent nobility of common people and assumptions about scientific truth challenged the conventional wisdom and established authority at every turn.

Darwin was as much a product of the emerging field of evolutionary biology as he was its greatest contributor. (Desmond & Moore, 1991). Darwin suffered considerable torment, in no small measure because evolutionary doctrine was profoundly subversive and revolutionary in its day. I doubt that many of us can imagine living in a society where the superrich rule by divine authority, the middle classes are guided by scripture, and the poor are carted off to prison or even death if they offer their own opinions too vociferously.

When Darwin's theory of evolution knocked human beings off the celestial platform of special creation and revealed us to be the products of a competitive struggle where the only ultimate morality was survival of the fittest, what was left to hold on to? What would be science's next assault on human decency and social order? Anarchy! Women's rights! Universal suffrage! Premarital sex! Where would it all end? If religion and tradition failed to provide a meaningful guide to self-understanding, did we have to appeal to the laws of the jungle to comprehend the human situation?

Marxism

By the early years of the 20th century, there were two loud and clear answers to these questions. One was Marxism, which offered a utopian vision of the natural evolution of society. The factory worker and peasant would proclaim the dictatorship of the proletariat. Like Lev Tolstoy, we would all throw down our books and papers and go joyfully to join our brothers and sisters in the fields to bring in the harvest. According to Karl Marx, in a fully evolved society of universal equality (much as Gordon Allport's Hoosier dad had foretold), each person would contribute to the common good to the best of his or her ability and take only the minimum required to satisfy his or her own needs.

The closest we ever got to Marx's ideal was, I suppose, the Russian Revolution, and it proved to be no more true to a humanitarian vision of utopia than actual life in Montezuma, Indiana. Marxism offers a beautiful vision of the future, however. I hope we can sympathize with the young radical students at the turn of the century who, like Alfred Adler and his wife (see Chapter 8), dreamed of taking part in a worldwide struggle that would radically transform bourgeois society to create social and economic justice and a true community of all men and women.

Psychoanalysis

The other great revolution, of course, was psychoanalysis. This revolution was quieter, completely peaceful, and in some ways vastly more subversive than Marxism. The police and the military could, after all, control the mob and protect the means of production. Revolutionaries and anarchists could be tracked down and thrown in jail. But this "Jewish psychology," as it came to be known throughout fascist Europe, threatened the day's most fundamental assumptions about human nature. It questioned the legitimacy of religion, the supremacy of the state, and the sanctity of the family. Some even said it championed free love and regarded children as sexual creatures. Marxism attacked the profit motive, but psychoanalysis attacked innocence and purity. It was, in the eyes of many members of the established order, a "gutter religion" whose views of human nature were even more repugnant than the teachings of the evolutionists.

The irony, of course, was that Sigmund Freud, very much like Darwin, was only as "revolutionary" as his scientific findings compelled him to be. His renunciation of religion as nothing more than the product of mass hysteria due to the suppression of biological needs was indeed radical stuff. But nobody would accuse the early analysts of being free thinkers, let alone "happy-go-lucky anarchists." Rather, we could say Freud proposed a secular religion that replaced the psychic fantasy of God with a commitment to "Progress Through Science."

But even that challenge was limited. Freud's views on homosexuality, women's rights, the plight of the masses, and the importance of a strongly controlled central political authority all were carefully crafted to preserve the status quo. Freud supported an "orderly" world, and he was no more able to tolerate dissent close to home—in his family or among his followers—than among the "rabble" outside his door. In Freud's view, North American democracy, with its relative social disorder, was a massive mistake. In such a society, from where would come the moral power to control the powerful sexual and aggressive passions that constantly seek expression in our daily lives?

Another problem arose within psychoanalysis itself. As a doctrine, it was so tightly controlled intellectually yet so fluid in its construction that it was difficult to define at any given time. Was it for or against free love and open sexual expression? Was Carl Jung the heir apparent or another betraying apostate? Was psychoanalysis a medical doctrine for treating the mentally ill? Or was it a brilliant philosophical view of humanity but of little practical value, because most people "as yet remain beyond its reach" intellectually and culturally?

More importantly, was psychoanalysis a science? If so, then why couldn't it permit free and independent inquiry? Why did it require an elaborate initiation ritual before anyone could be recognized as capable of contributing to its development? Why was it ruthlessly controlled by one person who maintained exclusive rights to pass it on to his chosen followers?

Wilhelm Reich: Therapy as Liberation

Enter at this point in our history Wilhelm Reich (1897–1957), a German-Ukrainian bourgeois Jew. As a 25-year-old graduate of the University of Vienna medical school, he was accepted into Vienna's Psychoanalytic Society in 1922 as its youngest-ever member. Reich was not only young; he was brilliant, rash, visionary, and revolutionary. At last, perhaps Freud thought, he had found the "son," the heir apparent, he had been searching for since the early days with Josef Breuer, Wilhelm Fleiss, Alfred Adler, Carl Jung, and the rest of that traitorous bunch.

Sigmund Freud's Heir

Within 2 years of meeting the young Reich, Freud announced to his followers that he had decided to appoint the 27-year-old newcomer as director of the Seminar for Psychoanalytic Therapy. Because this organization controlled who could and could not become a psychoanalyst, Freud's decision was tantamount to announcing his intention to hand over to Reich the keys to the empire.

That certainly was what Reich assumed. So in 1927, when he approached Freud for a blessing or anointment or public sign, he had no apparent reason to question that Freud would assent. But when the moment arrived Freud refused, as he had refused all the others except, in 1918, his own daughter, Anna. Like the others in the inner sanctum, Reich could join in the fellowship that came with wearing the master's sacred ring (Dyer, 1983), but he could not be analyzed by Freud himself.

Such was the power of Freud's rejection of yet another of his almost-adopted sons that Reich fell ill and had to be hospitalized. During his hospitalization in Switzerland, Reich ruminated on his position and on his own psyche. He was, first of all, a physician. But as a close second he was a social visionary, a revolutionary thinker, and a mover and shaker. He was a man of powerful convictions and unwavering intentions. Wasn't that the reason Freud had made him gatekeeper for the entire movement? Or was Freud's real purpose to force Reich to choose between his social and political convictions and his professional identity as a psychoanalyst?

When Reich returned to Vienna, he resolved to put things right by following two courses of action. First, he announced to his fellow analysts that he had joined the Communist Party and was dedicating himself both to its egalitarian ideals and to its total opposition to fascism. Second, as the movement's chief training analyst, he would insist on a literal interpretation of Freud's doctrine of the sexual etiology of neuroses; the neuroses were unambiguously to be regarded as rooted in sexual dissatisfactions. It must follow, Reich demanded, that the ultimate resolution of neurotic disorders could only be achieved by liberating neurotic patients' sexual yearnings. Marxism would liberate humankind from economic tyranny, and psychoanalysis would liberate it from the oppression of the sexual instincts.

To give you just a small idea of Reich's approach to sexuality, consider the following bits of personal history from his autobiography. (Warning: Those prone to hysterical weakness are advised to read this section sitting down.)

> One of our farmhands had a son approximately twenty years old who was a complete idiot. All day long he would lie in the sun in front of the house, wearing only a shirt, and play with his genitals while mumbling unintelligible sounds. I enjoyed watching him play with himself and, through this, experienced highly pleasurable sensations. I can not say whether or not my later intense pleasure in masturbating, which lasted for so many years, is rooted here. It is quite probably, however, due to the intensity of my sensations while watching the idiot and his performance. But this is not to say that I wouldn't have succumbed to masturbation apart from this incident. (1988, p. 13)

> At approximately eleven and a half, I had intercourse for the first time. It was with a cook who had been hired from someone in town. She was the first to teach me the thrusting motion necessary for ejaculation and at that time it occurred so quickly and unexpectedly that I was frightened and thought it was an accident. From then on, I had intercourse almost every day for years—it was always in the afternoon, when my parents were napping. (p. 25)

Reich also recounted how as a boy he watched nightly as his mother made passionate love with his tutor. This sordid relationship was eventually discovered by the boy's father and resulted in his mother's suicide when he was 14.

Exile in the Wilderness

Such insights into one's own being perhaps ought to have been consistent, in principle, with Freud's notions of recovering the lost details of one's childhood sexual history. But Freud would have no part of them. In response to Reich's self-declared insurgency within the psychoanalytic movement, Freud exiled Reich to Berlin in 1930. Yet another son had broken with the father over the theory of sexuality. But ironically, this son was lost for trying to push the theory beyond anything Freud could endorse: "Where and how is the patient to express his natural sexuality when it has been liberated from repression? Freud neither alluded to nor, as it later turned out, even tolerated this question" (Reich, 1973, p. 152).

Reich was expelled from the International Psychoanalytic Association in 1934. This must have come as a particularly hard blow considering that the German Communist Party had expelled him for similar reasons during the previous year. Reich had tried to introduce radical theoretical notions into the great salvationist megatheories of his day—communism and psychoanalysis—only to discover that neither had any tolerance for his views of human liberation. The analysts could not give up their essentially bourgeois sensibilities and professional men's insistence on decorum and propriety; the communists were not interested in anything but a dogmatic, class-based analysis of human oppression. In Reich's view, both organizations were more committed to the preservation of doctrinal discipline and a received ideology than they were in removing the chains of oppression from common people.

Beyond all these frustrations and disappointments, by this time Reich was being hounded by the Nazis in Germany. They, too, were suspicious of his revolutionary social views. Worse in Nazi eyes was the fact that Reich was a Jewish intellectual. He fled to Denmark, where he was divorced from his analyst wife. After only a year he was expelled from Denmark; then he was expelled from Sweden and ultimately from Norway, where he was divorced from his second wife.

Reich ultimately found refuge in New York at the New School for Social Research (the "university in exile"—see Chapter 8) in 1939. Ominously, however, the United States had imprisoned Margaret Sanger in 1917 for her crusading efforts to provide contraceptive information for women, had exiled the anarchist Emma Goldman for stating her political views in public, and was growing deeply paranoid of international communism. J. Edgar Hoover must have been napping when Reich's immigration papers were approved.

Once in the United States, Reich married again and began to develop a comprehensive psychotherapeutic theory. The essence of that theory was in many ways the logical extension of Freud's earlier writings. In fact, Reich's theory is probably more purely "Freudian" than anything Freud wrote after about 1928.

A Comprehensive Theory of Human Sexuality

At the center of Reich's theory is a total repudiation of the mind/body dichotomy, which had plagued Freud from as early in his work as "The Project for a Scientific Psychology" (see Chapter 6). For Reich, the mind and the body are inseparable. The key to their integration is not the sexual instinct per se but the neuropsychological function of the orgasm. Reich advocated that physical health and mental health are one and the same and that both depend on "complete and repeated genital gratification" (1973, p. 96). The sex drive is in fact the drive for life, the longing for orgasm nothing less than "striving to reach out beyond the narrow sack of one's own organism" (Reich, 1961, p. 348).

To be free of physical and mental obstruction, one must be able to express freely all sexual and emotional feelings. The repression of these feelings dams libido—quite literally sexual energy—resulting in physical and emotional loss of function and even paralysis. Reich believed that therapy, whether for the body or the mind, is a matter of removing all impediments to the full discharge of life energy—which he meant to be understood as the full capacity for sexual orgasm.

Over time Reich extended his notions of sexual energy to a universal source of energy found in all living things. This cosmic energy Reich called *orgone*. He came to believe that orgone is the basic building block of all life on the planet. Orgone took on an alchemic quality as the fundamental stuff of all physical and mental health, character, self-expression, and creativity. "In an ultimate sense, in self-awareness and in the striving for the perfection of knowledge and full integration of one's bio-functions, *the cosmic orgone energy becomes aware of itself*" (Reich, 1961, p. 52).

The oppression of sexuality, Reich argued, is the key to the control that government and class systems exert on the masses. By keeping people sexually oppressed, the ruling classes keep people from experiencing their own natural powers—which can, however, be released and revealed to them through the process of therapy. By freeing the bound-up, inhibited, and strangulated orgone energy inside each of us, Reichian therapy would make us more aware, powerful, and self-affirming. We could then escape our emotional and physical paralysis, as well as the control of the ruling classes and their lackeys in government and industry. Or, as I like to tell my students, anyone with a really great sex life—who experiences mind-blowing, earth-shattering orgasms on a regular basis—will not, indeed cannot, get into a neurotic tangle over something as trivial as grades and the social nonsense endemic to any campus.

One important clarification is necessary at this juncture. Reich's theory was not a call for superficial, promiscuous sexual encounters. In fact, Reich argued that meaningless, unemotional sex is a symptom of deeply neurotic and manipulative tendencies. In such encounters we may pleasurably exploit each other sexually but rarely, if ever, express ourselves fully, openly, and mutually. Thus sex is ideally a physical and emotional act—it is, in short, making love. But, Reich observed,

> I say on the basis of ample sexual experience that only in a few cases in our civilization is the sexual act based on love. The intervening rage, hatred, sadistic emotions, and contempt are part and parcel of the love life of modern man. (quoted in Rycroft, 1971, p. 81)

Psychotherapy for the Total Organism

Reading this quote, I think of Luke's sexual promiscuity as, in fact, he flirted with suicide. I think of the dozens and dozens of college students I have counseled who have never engaged in sex when they and their lover were completely sober. I think of the dozens and dozens of married couples I have counseled who invest more energy and more of their true selves into a business deal or a dinner party than in expressing their deepest sexual self to their mate. To be truthful, as a typical middle-class American, I wonder about my own orgiastic potency, my own "capacity to surrender to the flow of biological energy, free of any inhibitions; the capacity to discharge completely the dammed up sexual excitation through involuntary, pleasurable convulsions of the body" (Reich, 1973, p. 102).

I hope I have you on the edge of your seat hoping to find out how to achieve such glory. Just imagine telling your boss or your least-favorite professor or dean, "I just had a cosmic, mind-blowing, totally freeing orgasm with my lover, so I won't be feeling the need to come to work or attend your boring class today. See you later—maybe." For reasons I'll get to in a minute, this level of liberation is a little difficult. But basically, especially if your problem is a physical or psychosomatic one, therapy begins with some Reichian, orgone-enriched psychotherapy.

Character Armor. You will begin therapy by undergoing a thorough physical exam. Your therapist will take special note of your "character armor." A Reichian therapist will want to gain a clinical impression of where your inhibited life energies are stored up: in your voice, in your gaze, in some part of your body. He or she will take note of the defensive way you hold your head, play with your fingers, breathe hesitatingly, slouch in your chair, jiggle your leg when you talk. He or she may ask you to exaggerate and hold some peculiar physical mannerism or facial expression and may ask what memories came to mind when you were doing it. The analyst also will assess how you came to select your particular physical complaint—headaches, stomachaches, lower back pain, numbness of the extremities—in terms of your overall life story and especially in terms of the self-control strategies you learned as a child.

For at least half the session, your talking cure will involve nonverbal communication in the form of "body talk." The therapist will attack your body armor, the somatic rigidity that is the result of years of practiced inhibition, the physical straitjacket you put on each day to reinforce the emotional and sexual straitjacket society requires you to wear. Therapeutic techniques might include massage, exercise, dance or movement, or any number of yoga or Zen practices (see Chapters 21 to 23).

The key concept in Reich's thinking is that your body is a perfect reflection of your psychic history—that your body is bound by the straitjacket of the aches and pains of common, everyday unhappiness; that you are the physical representation of your entire history of hurts and disappointments, your lost loves, the blocked and interrupted impulses of your childhood.

The Release of Pleasure. There is a deep yearning in your aching muscles and tired organs—a yearning to recover the passion of youth, to experience explosive and releasing pleasure, to be free of the restrictions that have been strapped on your back for so long that they now feel like just another part of your body.

The cure is to awaken your psychic awareness by awakening your sexual nature. Your sexual nature is in turn awakened through expressive movement, which releases bound-up energy and creates a transformative change in your ability to experience reality. Under such circumstances, and with an equally charged partner, sex can be a transformative and liberating experience. People in full possession of their sexual nature can never be controlled against their will. They become truly free, liberated, and autonomous.

An astonishing account of Reichian therapy is found in a book written by the actor Orson Bean (1971), titled *Me and the Orgone*. It describes the author's tremendous emotional release while undergoing a course of treatment with Dr. Elsworth Baker. During what sounds like some major massage in an early phase of treatment, the following interaction takes place:

"Stick your finger down your throat," said Baker.

"What?" I said.

"Gag yourself."

"But I'll throw up all over your bed."

"If you want to you can," he said. "Just keep breathing while you do it."

I lay there breathing deeply and stuck my finger down my throat and gagged. Then I did it again.

"Keep breathing," said Baker. My lower lip began to tremble like a little kid's, tears began to run down my face and I began to bawl. I sobbed for five minutes as if my heart would break. Finally the crying subsided.

"Did anything occur to you?" asked Baker.

"I thought about my mother and how much I loved her and how I felt like I could never reach her and I just felt hopeless and heartbroken," I said. "I felt like I was able to feel these things deeply for the first time since I was little, and it's such a relief to be able to cry and it isn't a lot of crap, I was just scared."

"Yes," he said. "It's frightening. You have a lot of anger to get out, a lot of hate and rage and then a lot of longing and a lot of love. Okay."

And I got up and dressed and left. (quoted in Frager & Fadiman, 1984, p. 192)

A Brief Encounter of the Massage Kind. My own story with this phenomenon can't compare in intensity but is perhaps worth sharing, as it does perhaps suggest something you could try on your own if circumstances permit.

Once while attending a banquet at the end of a long and tiring day, I became aware of a terribly stiff and painful neck. I mentioned it to my seating companion, who happened to be a very old friend and a person about as old as my mother. My friend, Roberta, patted my hand and asked if I knew that she had just completed a training course in therapeutic massage and was planning to become a licensed therapeutic masseuse. When she asked if I would let her try to relieve my stiff neck, I said I would be delighted to.

Suddenly she was standing behind my chair and giving my aching muscles a good kneading. I was initially in pain. Then I was in ecstasy. Then I was ready to thank her and resume paying attention to the after-dinner speeches. Then I just gave way.

Roberta continued to do something to my neck, but I wasn't sure what it was. I felt that I was floating about 3 feet off the floor. Inexplicably my eyes filled with tears, and I was overcome with the most amazing feeling of love and tenderness for my old friend. When I turned my head to look at her, she smiled and sat down next to me again.

After I had regained my composure, I offered the observation. "I guess that's not the same kind of massage they offer in the trailers behind the truck stops on the turnpike, eh?"

Roberta smiled a conspiratorial little smile and said, "I guess that wasn't the kind of stiff neck you get from sitting behind a steering wheel all day, eh?"

A Secret Legacy

As you have seen in both the struggle Rogers endured with organized psychiatry in North America and Freud's unsuccessful attempt to keep psychoanalysis free from control by the U.S. medical establishment, psychiatric authority was no more progressive and adventurous at its core than were any of the systems Reich had encountered in Europe in the 1930s. Reich's ideas proved too radical for his conservative and highly orthodox colleagues in New York. He was refused recognition even among the supposedly more open-minded psychiatrists in Chicago, the "liberal" center for psychoanalysis in North America (see Chapter 10). So Reich formed his own organization, the Orgone Institute, where he carried on his research and teaching.

His next phase was to be his last. Reich came to believe that orgone energy could be accumulated, stored, and then therapeutically infused into orgone-deficient life systems. He invented and eventually marketed orgone accumulators, which he claimed could be used in the treatment of a wide variety of illnesses, including epilepsy, hypertension, asthma, heart disease, and cancer.

In 1954 the U.S. Food and Drug Administration (FDA) filed an injunction against Reich to prohibit the distribution and use of orgone accumulators. Reich refused to comply and was duly arrested, tried, and convicted of contempt of court. He was sentenced to federal prison, where he died of heart disease. Reich thus became, in some sense, the first genuine martyr in the history of psychotherapy.

The government of the United States was in near-hysteria in the mid-1950s. Communists, anarchists, and subversives were feared to be undermining our entire way of life, and federal agencies took these threats with deadly seriousness. After Reich was imprisoned, the FDA seized and destroyed all his private papers, publications, and research notes. They also destroyed all his orgone accumulators.

After Reich's death in 1957 it was revealed, however, that Reich had managed to find a hiding place for his most important papers and discoveries. His followers disclosed that these had been buried in a "time capsule," which would not be opened until 100 years after his death, in 2057. The remaining surviving pieces from Reich's laboratory are now on display in the Orgone Museum in the little town of Rangely in northern Maine, where Reich had fled hoping to escape persecution by government authorities.

Every once in a while you can still find an old orgone accumulator at a garage sale or in a junk shop (many thousands were sold through mail order in the 1950s). Unfortunately, all the alleged orgone accumulators I've seen were nothing but a box containing an ultraviolet lamp—which may or may not have been authentic products of Reich's Rangely laboratory.

Clearly, at least by the time of his imprisonment, Reich was no longer involved with science, at least as most of us would understand it. He had passed beyond the range of a textbook on talking cures, and had entered another dimension altogether. In some sense his work is truly visionary, however. He managed to reconnect the body and the psyche in a way that makes complete sense from a non-Western perspective like yoga but that challenges the Western legacy of thinking that, although the body belongs to nature, the mind—the soul—belongs to God.

It's fun to read Reich's ideas, and he makes great sense after you have great sex. It is also very easy to dismiss him as a nut, an extreme liberationist. But at worst, Reich was an incurable romantic. The part of me that is tired of all our modern, post-Enlightenment reliance on "better living through chemistry" is glad for his having been here. Here's a conundrum for you to test on yourself: Your kids will have to be raised either by John Watson or Wilhelm Reich. Which would you choose?

Fritz Perls: Gestalt Therapy

Reich's short tenure as the Vienna Psychoanalytic Society's training analyst had a profound effect on the future of the talking cure. He influenced the thinking of the generation of young European intellectuals who studied psychoanalysis in the 1920s and early 1930s. As these men and women then fled Nazi persecution in Europe, they disseminated the form of psychoanalysis they had learned from Reich all over the world. One of these people was Frederick S. Perls, known to all as Fritz. Perls was born in Berlin in 1893, served as a medic in World War I, became a psychoanalyst after the war, and was trained and analyzed by Reich in 1927.

As hard as it would be to believe later on, Perls began his psychiatry career as a rather conventional figure. With the rise of anti-Semitism in Germany, he initially moved his successful practice to Holland. When forced by the German invasion of Holland to move again, he relocated to South Africa, where he and his wife enjoyed extraordinary success as the continent's only officially certified psychoanalysts.

Theory of Unfinished Situations

In 1936, as a highly successful psychiatric practitioner, Perls sailed his private yacht 4000 miles from South Africa to Germany to deliver a paper to the Psychoanalytic Congress in Czechoslovakia and to meet privately with Freud. Perls eagerly awaited an opportunity to discuss his psychoanalytic ideas with the great man himself.

It is reported that Perls first had a meeting with his former mentor, Reich, who by that time was apostate in the movement. Perls reported that Reich "sat apart from us, and hardly recognized me. [He] sat there for a long interval, staring, and brooding" (Perls, 1969b). Perls went from this disappointing encounter directly to the audience with Freud.

Perls thought he would begin by humoring the old man with the story of how he had sailed to the meeting all the way from Johannesburg. Perls said, "I came from South Africa to give a paper and to see you." Freud stood in the doorway to his room listening for a few seconds, then closed his eyes and said, "Well, when are you going back?" Perls reacted to this insult with rage. He vowed, much as Allport had done under similar circumstances a decade earlier (see Chapter 15), "I'll show you—you can't do this to me" (Perls, 1969b).

Thirty-three years later, Perls recalled this incident with renewed force. It remained "one of the four main unfinished situations in my life [along with not being able to sing well, make a parachute jump, and go skin diving] to have a man-to-man encounter with Freud and to show him the mistakes he made" (Perls, 1969b). Freud could have this effect on people.

The encounter left Perls a very different man. When he got back to South Africa, he renounced everything about his "old" life and declared, in words that sound almost identical to those spoken by William James a half century earlier, that henceforth "I had to take all responsibility for my existence myself." As a part of this newly found conviction, Perls rejected

all the trimmings of a square respectable citizen: family, house, servants, making more money than I needed. . . . I just extracted myself through my spite and rebelliousness. . . . The dammed-up and unexpressed doubts about the Freudian system spread and engulfed me. I became a skeptic, nearly a nihilist—a negator of everything. . . . True, I accepted then much of Zen, [but] in a cold, intellectual way. (Perls, 1969b)

In 1946 Perls emigrated from South Africa to the United States, establishing the Institute for Gestalt Therapy in New York City in 1952. From New York he moved to Big Sur, California, and to the Esalen Institute in the 1960s and finally to Vancouver, British Columbia, where he founded a Gestalt kibbutz (commune). There he died in 1970.

Origins of Gestalt Therapy

Gestalt *theory* was first described in the 19th century in Germany as a reaction to the pedantic elementalism that was becoming immensely popular in physical science. The essence of Gestalt theory is that the whole of an array of elements is more than the sum of its constituent parts, that the whole object has a meaning and reality that cannot be understood by breaking it into its molecular or atomic components. According to Perls, "A gestalt is an irreducible phenomenon. It is an essence that is there and that disappears if the whole is broken up into its components" (1969a).

Perls's Gestalt therapy bears little if any relation to Gestalt *psychology,* which was a specialized branch of experimental psychology concerned with how complex stimuli acquire meaning and function. Gestalt psychology had its origins late in the 19th century but largely died out after World War II.

For Perls, Gestalt *therapy* was something of his own invention, a dramatic intellectual break with his past. (From here on, the term *gestalt* will apply only to Gestalt therapy.) It was, he claimed, "the end of all that Freudian crap" (1969b, p. 1). However, a surprising amount of psychoanalytic theory remains in Gestalt therapy. Much of that theory is a more or less direct recasting of Freudian concepts and terminology (see Frager & Fadiman, 1984, pp. 220–221n).

The emphasis in Gestalt therapy, however, is on the present moment, the here and now, and that present-centeredness influences every moment of the therapeutic environment. The past may well have shaped our present lives, but we can smash that mold with courage and with our will. We can confront and overcome the toxic residue of the past in our lives. But to do so, we must confront our essential human nature head on and without blinking.

It is important in thinking about Gestalt therapy to remember to take it as a whole. It seeks to describe the ways we have become fragmented and alienated from our true selves. We cannot understand our true selves by thinking elementally about our own existence; we must strive to grasp the gestalt that is life itself. So too the theory behind Gestalt therapy must be grasped as a coherent, dynamic whole—no matter how fragmented the telling makes it appear.

Unfinished Situations and Resentments. Human beings are plagued by the psychic injuries they have experienced in the past, especially in childhood, as interruptions of their basic quest for gratification and fulfillment. Each of these injuries creates an "unfinished situation." The dynamic totality of these unfinished situations becomes every individual's psychic agenda. Psychic agendas force many people to look backward, to try always to resolve the problems of yesterday in the context of today's events and relationships.

The primary law governing human affairs is that every organism tends toward wholeness and completion. But we also tend to project our incompleteness into the future, which makes us feel insecure and anxious. Thus the unfinished situations in our lives become the source of long-term dysfunctions in living and relating to others.

What Freud called the "repetition compulsion" is in reality the press of unfinished situations to gain access to consciousness and thus resolution in the here and now. These unfinished situations are organized into a "hierarchy of importance," which serves as an artificial or "external" source of regulation in our lives. Because this essentially neurotic regulation is in opposition to genuine self-regulation, we experience it with great conflict and resentment.

Defense Mechanisms. We can temporarily escape resentment by engaging in behavior that conforms to four generic "neurotic styles":

- *Projection.* I understand and perceive my own impulses as someone else's responsibility and fault. When I should say *I,* instead I say *you* or *it.* This is the "blame game." I am not responsible for who and what I am. I use the excuse that I am controlled by the way my mother raised me or the expectations my boss has for me or the bad things people have done to me. I don't regard myself as the agent of my own satisfaction.
- *Introjection.* I ignore what I am really feeling and what I really want in order to feel and think the way I have been taught. What I experience as "me" is really packaged junk that is part of someone else's agenda. Someone else's impulses, wishes, and resentments become mine. I take in whole what I am told and let it govern me without ever "owning" it or "digesting" it. I feel constantly torn by the world of arbitrary "ought," "must," and "should" because these ideas and urges aren't coming from anywhere inside me. I don't really know what I believe because I don't have any genuine self-regulatory powers.
- *Retroflection.* I live in the past, full of regret and resentment. I explain my life by saying "If only . . ." I seem pathologically unaware that this is a new day and that I am actively responsible for creating the world I live in. I perceive myself as a determined object, not as a decision-making self.
- *Deflection/confluence.* These are reciprocal neurotic styles. I avoid accepting responsibility for myself either by not letting the truth sink in and make itself obvious (deflection) or by just "going with the flow" and absorbing the motions of the surrounding environment (confluence). By conforming and avoiding reflection, I never have to deal with the realities of the here and now.

A Therapy of "Being Here Now"

The therapeutic alternative to these neurotic styles is to accept reality as it is right now. Gestalt therapy has the aim of helping the client admit his or her impulses to consciousness in order to deal with them as a fully conscious, responsible adult. Perls referred to this process as allowing unfinished situations into the "zone of awareness," which can be achieved only when you "lose your mind and come to your senses."

Self-awareness may cause some temporary discomfort, or even pain, but it is only when you become fully aware of yourself that you can also become aware of the powerful forces of self-regulation operating within you. This organismic self-regulation is the essence of authenticity, of living your life fully awake and fully open to the potential of every moment, of living life without regret, guilt, or cowardice. It is the essence of "being here now."

Rogers and Perls. This theme is similar to one developed by Rogers (see Chapter 15) that I have delayed explaining until now. Both Rogers and Perls anchored their theories with the assumption that human beings are fully capable of near-perfect self-direction and self-regulation. This very old and distinctly North American idea sees society and civilization as fundamentally corrupting. Human perfection happens as a matter of course when a person is living in a state of nature (to which the Protestants added a state of grace), but in our interactions with society we become corrupted and lose touch with our basic inner nature.

For Rogers this "contamination" (not a word Rogers used, but a good Zen word that fits all the cases we want to review) comes from the *conditions of worth* that other people impose on us; these conditions are embedded within the Skinnerian "contingencies of reinforcement" to which we are all subject. Rogers argued that the child is unable to recognize these alien standards because they are associated with his or her only reliable source of love and social esteem. In Rogers's parents' household, for example, the children internalized the repressive, coercive means of control taught in the name of Christian fundamentalism. The Rogers children all developed psychosomatic illnesses because their internal, organismic self-regulatory mechanisms were totally unreliable guides to behaving in a way that would produce the love and esteem they needed from their parents. Even as an elderly man, Rogers said that he felt a twinge of guilt and neurotic anxiety every time he opened a soda—that was how profoundly he had introjected his parents' ideas about the sinful wickedness of even the most simple pleasures.

Rogers believed that an unconditionally positive therapeutic environment could short-circuit this wretched state of affairs. If the therapist or the therapeutic group remained absolutely and unconditionally positive—regardless of what I was thinking, feeling, saying, or doing—I would of necessity find some alternative system of behavioral regulation. Of course, Rogers believed that the best alternative source of regulation is self-regulation.

Reich and Perls. Reich probably would have had little quarrel with Rogers's statement of the problem but would argue that Rogers didn't go far enough with the remedy. Reich believed that external regulation is accomplished through deliberate class exploitation and oppression. He wrote in *The Mass Psychology of Fascism* (1970) that "every social order produces in the masses of its members that structure which it needs to achieve its aims" (p. 23).

For Reich, our sexuality is the key to our liberation. But it is also the key to our enslavement. If the family, the educational system, the church, and the government can effectively prevent us from ever fully experiencing our libido, our life energy, we will remain "people in trouble" forever.

Reich would probably not be impressed by a Rogerian therapy session unless it generated genuine, powerful human feelings—which indeed is how many experiential group encounters turn out. As one of my more psychopathic clients once advised me about his own group experiences, "T-groups are great places to go to get laid."

Perls openly regretted that his mentor, Reich, had gone into the orgone business, "an invention of Reich's fantasy which . . . had gone astray" and that turned Reich "away from his genius, only to eclipse himself as a 'mad scientist' " (1969a). Perls was impressed by Reich's notions of self-regulation but almost completely rejected Reich's idea that the loss of self-regulation is caused by sinister external forces. He called Reich's theories "mildly paranoid" and insisted that the psyche is fully capable on its own of creating the interruptions that make a person externally regulated. Perls even argued, from a classically Freudian perspective, that the energies released through the therapeutic encounter can be reintegrated and harnessed by the self—a process that would not be possible if, as Reich maintained, those energies were external to the self.

The Gestalt Prayer. We are left with a question: How does Gestalt psychotherapy help the individual become self-regulating again? Here, I think, Perls showed us the true genius of the talking cure. Perls believed that the conflicts manifest in the unconscious must be brought out of the past—out of the "demilitarized zone" of fantasy, dream, and memory—and into the here and now. The therapeutic session must become a living theater of the mind where dreams and impulses are lived out, usually symbolically but always immediately and fully. As awareness bursts into consciousness, the person must become the reality of what she or he is experiencing. The empty chair next to the client becomes the mother who withheld love; the foam bat placed in the client's hands becomes the sword with which she or he can "stab" the betraying father in the heart; the dream symbol is unlocked and its power unleashed to reveal the unfinished situations that prevent us from experiencing life here and now.

Therapy is about brushing aside the veils of illusion, usually by breaking through what Perls called the "explosive layer" of personality. Reich would have called it the "orgasmic layer," so that the great awakening would be a cathartic experience allowing the client to seize control over his or her own life.

Gestalt therapy is not about reason taming instincts or about unconditional positive regard or about the development of will. It is not even about the pursuit of happiness. "Happiness? That's what Disneyland is for," Perls said. Nor is it about freeing the masses from economic exploitation or about learning to live with humiliation and disappointment. Gestalt therapy is about being fully alive, being fully in touch with one's feelings, being expressive, accepting, and responsible. It is about accepting anger as well as joy, victory as well as defeat, isolation as well as connection. It is about being aware of life. It is about living the Gestalt prayer:

I do my thing and you do your thing.
I am not in this world to live up to your expectations
And you are not in this world to live up to mine.
You are you and I am I,
And if by chance we find each other, it's beautiful.
If not, it can't be helped. (Perls, 1969b, p. 4)

A Libertarian View

Perls, like Reich, presented us with at least as many problems as he solved. How are we to take Gestalt therapy? Is it a completely new therapy, or is it a colorfully repackaged version of psychoanalysis? Prior to the wretched excesses of our society during the Reagan years, I was fond of Perls and resonated to his in-your-face individualism. But the more I thought about it, the more troubled I became by the Gestalt prayer. My unease broke through to conviction one day when I saw it printed on a T-shirt for sale in a radical bookstore in Philadelphia. Underneath the prayer was printed the likeness of Adolf Hitler. Is it enough to get people to "do their own thing"? What if "their thing" is antisocial or inhumane?

There is an apocryphal story about Perls that contains a strand of metaphorical truth, whether or not it is literally true. Perls was very outspoken about what he thought and felt, as he probably more or less had to be. That quality is at the center of his description of a self-regulating person. He would walk away from people who bored him by saying, "I never asked to be introduced to you" (Shepard, 1975, p. 9). He would exclaim to complaining patients that he didn't understand why they insisted on coming to him to whine about their problems with everyone else. One day a woman in therapy with Perls was complaining bitterly about her husband, how cruelly he treated her and how much abuse she took from him every day. Perls replied, "Look, why don't you go home and deal with your problem with your husband, and then come back and get some therapy for yourself?" The woman got up, so the story goes, went home, blew her husband's head off with a shotgun, and then came back to finish her therapy session.

This story, like the T-shirt in Philadelphia, reflects a serious problem. Any therapy that posits each person in isolation from everyone else could be misconstrued as recommending a total lack of regard for others. I understand that Perls lived on a commune, had rejected materialism, and probably believed that the organismically self-regulating person enjoys warm and satisfying relationships with others. But from where I stand today, I am not sure that individual authenticity in and of itself makes a complete person and that "awareness per se—and by itself" is the point of my therapeutic work.

Still, Perls offered at the very least a thought-provoking and outrageously unorthodox way of talking about our problems. He is a great tonic for those of us who become too rigid in thinking about psychotherapy, seeing it only in terms of elemental changes in discrete behaviors.

A Gestalt Exercise. I want to end this chapter on an upbeat note, by telling you of a Gestalt technique that I frequently use in my classes with senior students and sometimes with my more rule-oriented, oversocialized, emotionally constricted patients. If you fit either of these categories, you are welcome to join in.

First, tear a piece of paper into narrow strips (if this step takes you more than 5 minutes, please go back to Chapter 14 and reread the section on perfectionism and rational emotive therapy.) Now write on each strip either your chief resentments or the rules and "musts" that you, as Moses, impose on yourself as an employee, spouse, student, and so on. But stick to one modality, please.

Read to yourself what you have written. (For more fun, do this exercise in a group and read your strips to each other.) You should have four to six major life interrupters in front of you. If you have written something other than a blood-pressure-escalating resentment or a truly authoritarian rule, try again.

Now put the pieces of paper in a plastic garbage bag, and seal it with a twist tie. Make sure the pieces of paper are all in there.

Good. You now have your own unique, customized, tailor-made "disappearing dis-it bag." Don't panic! You can make your dis-it bag reappear whenever you want to torture yourself. But *first* give yourself an opportunity to experience life without playing what Perls called the "self-torture game."

Take a minute to reflect on what you have just done. How will your life be different (not necessarily *better*—this isn't great sex—or *happier*—this isn't Disneyland) if you decide to leave those symbolic interruptions in the bag? Who will stop talking to you? Who will congratulate you? What will be easier? What will be harder? Finally, how do the answers to these questions change your awareness of the way you have constructed your life?

Mutiny of the Happy-Go-Lucky Anarchists. I would estimate that approximately half the people who have done this exercise get absolutely nothing out of it. But a number of the rest have used it in some very interesting ways. It seems to offer them an opportunity to become more self-aware, to become a bit more self-responsible and self-regulating, to think more clearly about their present situation.

Do you remember my friend Sarah, the "rebel without a clue" in Chapter 14? This exercise got her to think and gave her some help in determining her priorities. A lot of her friends took to carrying folded plastic bags in their notebooks, which they would flash to me when we passed on campus. They were a secret society of students who had put all sorts of cultural treasures in their illegal and unauthorized dis-it bags. One young man even brought his bag to his oral comprehensive examination in my department—dangerously close to insurrection. Mutiny rears its happy-go-lucky anarchist's head! Heaven forbid that the deans should find out; my little exercise could be grounds for my immediate dismissal.

Now where did I leave that bag . . . ?

CHAPTER 17

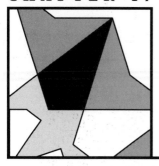

Existential Psychotherapy: R. D. Laing, Viktor Frankl, and Rollo May

A Psychology of Humans Being

Although existential psychotherapy cannot be precisely distinguished from other forms of psychotherapy in terms of technique, it can and does separate itself in terms of focus and aim. Existential therapists do not try to help their patients adapt to the social, political, and cultural realities around them. Instead, they attempt to guide patients toward discovery of the "authentic" self. This self is the essence of one's being, of existence, and of all wishes and dreams. Unfortunately, however, the authentic and genuine self must always coexist within established social, political, and cultural realities—a fact that causes ontological anxiety.

For existential therapists such as R. D. Laing, normality in today's world is like being a half-crazed creature in a mad world. Laing hoped that his patients could break through their madness to discover their true selves and live courageously outside the constraints of social, political, and cultural expectations.

Viktor Frankl urged his patients to experience the true self. His logotherapy attempts to help us to encounter and understand the meaning of our existence. His experience in the Nazi concentration camps showed Frankl that people without purpose soon perish. For Frankl, the ultimate quest is to discover the meaning in and of life.

Rollo May's existential psychology focuses on issues of self-integration, authentic being, and rediscovery of the living person who has become disoriented and lost amid the dehumanizing effects of modern culture. The existentialist hero is the antihero, who resists the madness of the surrounding world. The key to living, May believed, is achieving authentic "being in the world." To do so, one must experience life from the core of the self, without filters or excuses.

The Talking Cure and the Power of Entrenched Authority

The mainstream of American psychology is far from the objective science that it purports to be. As a scientific enterprise, it is woven from the political, economic, and moral threads of mainstream society. Rather than pursuing the value-free search for truth and understanding in order to help solve human problems, much of psychology is merely the handmaiden of the status-quo and of society's prevailing values. . . .

This apparent apathy toward the human situation is the result of either the psychologists' willful avoidance (e.g., the purists who play "scientist" in their laboratory of glittering gadgets) or their inability to translate their concern into meaningful, intelligent, professional behavior. Because mainstream psychology is embedded in the dominant political, economic, and religious ideologies, professional psychologists have upheld these ideologies rather than examining their impact on the lives of others. Thus, many researchers simply have not looked at the meaningful problems while many others who have looked were unable to see beyond their own social ideologies. (Braginsky, 1985, pp. 880–881)

As you can be see in Braginsky's quote, and as you will see in Chapter 18, which is a feminist critique of the traditional talking cures, I am by no means alone in criticizing well-established approaches to psychotherapy. Often they ignore, or actually work against, the best interests of patients. In fact, some would argue that this criticism could be extended to every talking cure described in this book (Szasz, 1970, 1974). Let me give you some examples:

- When Albert Bandura (1969) told us that "cure" is usually achieved when the patient declares full and final acceptance of the insights of the therapist, wasn't he really telling us that cure is a matter of getting the patient back in line with whatever dominant cultural ideologies the therapist endorses?
- How often do psychotherapists work to persuade the victims of emotional and sexual abuse that they must "work through" and "own" their conflicted feelings toward their mother or father and thereby assume emotional responsibility for the wrong done to them as a child?
- How many times do behavior therapists offer to "fix" problem behaviors—like loving persons of the "wrong" gender or fearing humiliation and failure—without questioning the assumptions underlying clients' wishes to be "normal" and "well-adjusted"?
- How many Rogerian therapists unconditionally accept and support their clients without taking any responsibility for the clients' helplessness in the world to which they return? Whose responsibility is it to prepare clients for the reality that those "conditions of worth" that have been so painfully overcome in the therapeutic group are going to fight back, perhaps with a vengeance, at the earliest opportunity?

■ Ask any therapist who works with kids or young adults: What's the first thing the kids want to do as soon as they are even minimally functional again? They want to run right back into the chaos of the dysfunctional home situation or marriage that was the source of the problems. What are the human and professional responsibilities of a therapist in such a situation? Who is the therapist's client? Where are the therapist's loyalties invested?

A Window Into Culture

A few years ago, a Tokyo daily newspaper ran a letter in its "Readers Lifeline" advice column from Mrs. A, a 35-year-old working mother of three kids. She had just discovered that her husband had been involved in a long-term homosexual relationship. When hubby decided that he was tired of the affair, he tried to back out of it. But his illicit lover then demanded 5 million yen (about $50,000) as the price of ending the relationship. The husband agreed and then asked his wife for the money from her savings. The wife appealed to "Lifeline" for help. She wrote:

> I got very upset. It is so opportunistic of my husband to betray our family and then ask me to live with him. I have confidence I can raise the children if my husband and I divorce. But I do not know if it is really good for the children.

The newspaper replied with the following advice:

1. This sounds like an American problem, not a Japanese one.
2. Since you have children, you must be normal; so your case is not hopeless.
3. Your husband was probably drunk when he had sex with this man, so it doesn't really mean anything about his character.
4. You must sit down and negotiate with this young man; he is asking for way too much money.
5. If your husband goes with men because of some sexual problem, then he should see a psychiatrist.

The assumptions made by the newspaper writer are so obvious and foreign to we who are not Japanese that we can all become instant social critics. Clearly the advice columnist is a genuine "handmaiden to society." She went so far as to deny that a "real" Japanese family would even have such a problem and was satisfied that the wife is blameless because she has done her duty by bearing children. If the husband is homosexual, then that is a medical problem. The problem is reduced to one of selfish greed on the aggrieved lover's part.

My students can "deconstruct" this problem in a flash, becoming intrepid anthropologists of a culture they know little about. They find the newspaper's advice bizarre and inhuman and question every single assumption it made.

But then I give them a case about an American man who is having problems at work and at home, is drinking too much, has huge financial problems, and is pondering suicide after having an unhappy affair with someone in his neighborhood.

(Half the class learns that the affair is with a man, half that it is with a woman.)* All my students want to know more about the poor guy's sex life, and they find it absolutely unfair that I object. Moreover, the half of the class that learns about the "affair with a man in the neighborhood" always explains the patient's despair exclusively in terms of "latent homosexuality." Most students fall into my trap even when I give them this case after they have had a chance to talk about the "weird Japanese assumptions" operating in the case of Mr. and Mrs. A.

Enforcement of the Tacit

How can a group of young people, more or less just out of high school, already be thinking in such doctrinaire fashion? I'll concede that I have confronted them with the one variable (homosexuality) that scares them all to death. But does it alone account for the instant reductionism that takes place in my classroom? Few of them—most likely none—ask me about the intellectual, spiritual, or even emotional life of the suicidal patient. This is a perplexing response from undergraduates, a species of human being that stays up all night debating whether God exists and whether She is all-knowing, whether a person can love two people equally at the same time, whether you can get into medical school with a B average. Even these young, intelligent people, who in some ways are at the summit of their innocence and idealism, even these folks have no real clue about how to approach the central questions of the human dilemma. How can we expect more from hardened professional psychotherapists, a species whose members have sold their souls to 5 or 6 years of graduate school, internship, and research in the name of career success?

So what do we say to the suicidal American suburbanite? Did I mention that he has AIDS? Well, maybe he doesn't. Did I suggest that his father abused him as a child? That his daughter was raped at a high school dance? That he works for his wife's father and hates his job? That he believes in life after death? That he doesn't?

Or how do we address the Tokyo housewife's dilemma? She either dumps her philandering husband, or she produces the money and takes him back. What more is there to know? What more can we do? What sort of talking cure do we want to suggest to her and her distressed family?

Should we send her to Albert Ellis to straighten out her crooked thinking? Send her to Carl Rogers for unconditional positive regard? Send her to Carl Jung to help her sort out her pathogenic secret? Where does the answer lie?

The Therapist's Responsibility

The answer probably lies in trying to understand what makes the Tokyo housewife's life worthwhile—in her heart and mind. Wouldn't we want to know what her deepest commitments are? I would want to know why she thinks an anonymous newspaper columnist knows what she should and shouldn't do.

---

*This exercise has been adaped from Davison and Friedman (1981).

The existential psychotherapist Rollo May, I think, would ask us to consider not the choice that confronts a person but the dilemma that choice creates. William Shakespeare, I believe, phrased that dilemma as well as anyone who has ever lived. The dilemma that confronted Hamlet confronts all of us at some point in our lives. Are we to surrender to the abyss or to endure the slings and arrows of continued existence? Is it more noble to put an end to our troubles or to abandon all self-doubt and throw ourselves into the middle of our troubles?

Of what possible use is a psychotherapist at such a juncture? Can you imagine the farce a modern-day Shakespeare could write by imagining Hamlet taking his troubles to a repressed-memory "therapist"? In fact, unless your therapist is a medical doctor, you can't even get a Valium or Prozac prescription. Thomas Szasz said once that the function of the therapist is to make sure that if you are going to jump out of the window from the 14th floor of the building, you at least wait until the sidewalk is cleared so you won't harm anyone else with your actions.

Is that really the extent of the therapist's responsibility? When I treat my student-clients for substance abuse, I generally tell them that if they want to save their own lives I will work with them day and night and every day of the year until they get clean. But I will not ask them to get clean for me, for their mothers, for Jesus—not for anybody. I will turn them over to the authorities if I find out they have been threatening the lives of others by driving drunk. But I probably won't call their roommate if I find them passed out on a sidewalk. It might be my job to clear the sidewalk under the jumper or to have the drunk driver arrested to prevent harm to someone else, but it's not my job to rescue clients or to make them want to save themselves. Mrs. A in Tokyo has to understand that it is a matter of supreme indifference to any newspaper columnist whether Mrs. A stays with her husband or doesn't.

The real question is whether anyone regards Mrs. A's choices with anything but supreme indifference. I'm not saying that it doesn't matter whether my student kills herself with booze or cocaine or whether Mrs. A. pays off the blackmailer. I'm sure it matters a lot—to them. But I am saying that I am indifferent—unless Mrs. A. is my mother or the alcoholic sophomore is my daughter. But even then, whether my daughter lives or dies or my mother divorces should not depend on whether their actions change the conditions of my life for better or worse. I'd be honored if they took my needs into consideration but amazed if that were the only data they needed. How could I tell the patient in the window of the 14th floor not to jump? Would I say that her death might cause someone else psychological pain? In the first place, how could I know that it would? Second, even if it would, the student may well be angry enough to believe that the other person richly deserves such retribution.

The Dilemma of Human Freedom

What we are talking about here, I believe, is the issue of freedom. If Mrs. A. were actually my client, I hope she would make her decision only after coming to grips with the realities of her own existential freedom. May (1967) observed:

At the beginning of therapy, thus, [patients] present the picture of a *lack* of freedom. The progress of therapy can be gauged in terms of the patient's capacity to experience the fact he is the one who *has* this world [I might say *choice* in place of *world*] and can be aware of it and move in it. . . . The progress of therapy can be measured in terms of the progress of the "consciousness of freedom." (p. 174)

Perhaps the reason I like May so much is that he gives me, as a psychologist, something meaningful to do, while I wait for patients to make their choices. I can "reveal" all sorts of deep and wonderful psychological insights. I can help them find meaning in their dreams, observe their behavior in a variety of settings, and offer my hypotheses. I can, as I did in the case of Sam (Chapter 15) even make them cry— push them to feel something other than numbness. As an existentialist I can be in- tellectual, philosophical, and scholarly about my clients' dilemmas and explain all sorts of things to them about the world. I can show them a tenderness of feeling and a respect of person that they may never have experienced from another person, let alone another male person.

This process, which may seem directionless, has an effect:

What is exceedingly interesting here is that the patient moves *toward* freedom and responsibility in his living as he becomes more conscious of the *deterministic* experi- ences [and contingencies of reinforcement, I would hasten to add] in his life. That is, as he explores and assimilates how he was rejected or overprotected or hated as a child, how his repressed bodily needs drive him, how his personal history as a member of a minority group, let us say, conditions his development, and even as he becomes more conscious of his being a member of Western culture at a particular traumatic moment in the historical development of that society, he finds his margin of freedom likewise en- larged. As he becomes more conscious of the infinite deterministic forces in his life, he becomes more free. (May, 1967, p. 175)

This is a philosophical paradox—and a relatively old one. Benedict de Spinoza (1632–1677), a Dutch philosopher, said, "Freedom is the recognition of determin- ism." B. F. Skinner, a U.S. behaviorist, said over and over again, "I want people to feel free, freer than they have ever felt before" and went on to write a utopian novel, *Walden Two,* based on those principles (1948), and a book titled *Beyond Freedom and Dignity* (1971). From Spinoza to Skinner, those who have been most insistent that human beings are controlled by nature have also been the strongest advocates that:

We feel we are free, but that is only an illusion. If we properly understood the causes of human behavior and thinking, we would see we are not free. . . . Thus wisdom is rational self-control, rather than a futile effort to control nature, or God. (Leahey, 1992, p. 105)

I am not proposing that existential psychotherapy is just another form of behav- iorism or another product of the Enlightenment (although it includes elements of both). What I am suggesting is that within the context of existential psychology pa- tients can discover that "freedom is a quality of action of the centered self" (May,

1967, p. 176). Their freedom does not depend on what a flaky husband or a black-mailer decides, not on what religion or family decides, not even necessarily on what common sense or morality decides.

We experience freedom when we operate from the center of our self, that part of the self that May called "consciousness, the experience of self acting from its center." It is derived from

> the individual's neuromuscular apparatus, his past genetic experience, his dreams, and the infinite host of other more or less deterministic aspects of his experience as a living organism . . . related in their various ways to this centered act and . . . only understood ["understandable" too, perhaps?] in this relationship. (May, 1967, p. 177)

The therapist knows this paradox by training and perhaps even from experience, and the client may or may not have some intuitive knowledge of this fundamental truth.

The Challenge of Regaining Your Mind and Coming to Your Senses

The real challenge for both therapist and client is not simply to recognize the paradox but to reach this state of consciousness, this level of self-awareness. Is the therapist's "unconditional positive regard" sufficient? Can self-awareness be achieved by confronting the emotional anchors of "crooked thinking"? By confronting the client's anima? By allowing all the client's neurotic emotional realities to "transfer" to the relationship with the therapist? By consigning all resentments and self-doubts to a "dis-it bag"? By carefully analyzing the untested and illogical assumptions in the client's personal logic system? By the client's getting in touch with his or her body, sensuality, and fundamental sexual and aggression instincts?

The answer here has to be a very Japanese one: *tabun*, the all-purpose "perhaps," which maintains harmony and doesn't interfere with the natural course of events. The minute I come down from my philosopher's throne to prescribe an answer—to say perhaps, "Well, that Perls fellow is certainly out to lunch" or "Behaviorism might work for poodles, but never for humans"—then someone is sure to trot out a client who just turned her entire life around by talking to an empty chair or learning how to manage her children more effectively with positive reinforcement. And the minute I endorse a particular perspective, some eager doctoral student is going to publish a dissertation showing that a personal-grooming control group effected greater and more permanent symptom relief than the group treated with the method I've decided to stake my reputation on. So the answer must be equivocal.

Let me suggest that there is no one way to bring all the people to consciousness all the time. Virtually any crazy idea I come up with might, given enough time and enough trials, prove effective for somebody. The "science" of psychotherapy can be used to discover how to maximize the probability that a particular intervention will produce a desired result in a specified client population most efficiently, and that "theory," to the degree that we need it, can be used to help us explain the result after we have obtained it.

A central feature common to all existential approaches to the talking cure is that these dilemmas are recognized as part of the human condition. I am probably more "existential" in my approach than most therapists would admit to being, although I couldn't tell you how I got there or which approach I use most consistently or with what result. Maybe existentialism is really just every therapist's stealth guidance system, used to focus attention on the targeted client and her or his "symptoms." Or perhaps existentialism is the most profoundly human part of every encounter we have with another person. I wonder how often I reveal my true self as a therapist, let alone as a person, when people come to me to be "cured."

There are several "schools" of existential psychotherapy, and we should look at several of them for their own sake. I invite you to join me in a sort of cook's tour of the philosophical kitchens where talking-cure existentialists cook up consciousness, will, and action for the resolution of life's problems and dilemmas. I hope you find something to your taste.

R. D. Laing

Let's begin with the Scottish psychiatrist R. D. Laing (1927–1989), whose existential viewpoint was the product of both working with severely disturbed schizophrenic patients and growing up in a dysfunctional family. Like Perls, Laing's writings combine autobiography, prose, poetry, accounts of dreams, and verbatim reports of what his patients said.

In his semiautobiographical *The Facts of Life* (1976), Laing described his own coming into the world as follows:

> My parents and I lived in a three-room flat.
> My mother and I slept in one room in separate beds,
>   and my father slept in another room.
> According to both of them, all sexual activity had ceased
>   between them irrevocably before I was conceived.
>
> My mother and father still swear they do not know how
>   I was conceived.
>   But there is a birthmark on his right knee and one
>   on mine.
>   A fact against immaculate conception. (p. 8)*

---

*From *The Facts of Life,* by R. D. Laing. Copyright © 1976 by R. D. Laing. Reprinted by permission of Pantheon Books, a division of Random House, Inc.

Laing's immediate family was not only bizarre, as the poem so vividly communicates, but also quite large and chaotic. He recalled his childhood confusion about the world of adults:

> From as far back as I can remember, I tried to figure out what was going on between these people. If I believed one, I couldn't believe anyone else. Especially at the time when my mother, my mother's mother, and my mother's younger sister were all part of the same household—from ten months to eighteen months—I could not believe all of them, one of them, or none of them. (p. 4)

Laing's own experience led him to conclude that the family is often the progenitor of madness, that madness "is a prudent, sagacious, and cunning measure artfully contrived to make an insane situation liveable" (Monte, 1991, p. 463).

> The family's function is to repress Eros; to induce a false consciousness of security; to deny death by avoiding life; to cut off transcendence; to believe in God, not to experience the Void; to create, in-short, one-dimensional man; to promote respect, conformity, obedience; to con children out of play; to induce a fear of failure; to promote a respect for work; to promote a respect for "respectability." (Laing, 1967, p. 65)

Little wonder, then, that in Laing's view the role of the therapist is to lead the patient to recover a full sense of self, to accept that

> true sanity entails in one way or another the dissolution of the normal ego, that false self competently adjusted to our alienated social reality; the emergence of the "inner" archetypal mediators of divine power, and through this death, rebirth and the eventual reestablishment of a new kind of ego functioning, the ego now being the servant of the divine, no longer its betrayer. (Laing, 1967, pp. 144–145)

Many colleagues fiercely resist my enthusiasm for Laing. They quite rightly view schizophrenia as a tragic and shattering brain disease, not a poetic form of self-expression in a crazed world, as Laing regarded it. Furthermore, they reject the notion (as I do) that families have much if anything to do with the creation of schizophrenia—except perhaps for the transmission of a genetic predisposition for the disorder.

It is probably better not to think about genuine organic madness and Laing in the same frame. But consider Laing's claims about normalcy with an open mind. There is some truth in Laing's assertion that normalcy is, in existential reality, a form of alienation—"a product of repression, denial, splitting, projection, introjection, and other forms of destructive action on experience" (Laing, 1967, p. 27).

Existential Exercise: Breaking the Code

I recommend the following Laing-like exercise to my students who are disturbed by Laing's attack on family and normalcy: Think of one really stupid rule that everyone in your family is expected to abide by. Don't choose a functional rule, like "Don't discharge semiautomatic weapons in the house" or "Don't raise the topic of welfare mothers around Uncle Willie." For the experiment to work, the rule should be one of those iron-clad laws of civilization that you might imagine young Carl Rogers growing up with in a fundamentalist, rural midwestern household. A perfect example that one of my students hit upon was "Men should always wear socks." Then, the next time you are nestled in the bosom of your family, break that rule, and exhibit no concern whatsoever for the fact that you have broken it.

I guarantee that you will receive an eye-opening lesson. Laing perceived that "man cut off from his own mind, cut off equally from his own body—[is] a half crazed creature in a mad world" (1967, p. 27). And he noted the family's role:

> Long before a thermonuclear war can come about, we have had to lay waste to our own sanity. We begin with the children. It is imperative to catch them in time. Without the most thorough and rapid brainwashing their dirty minds would see through our dirty tricks. By the time the new human being is fifteen or so, we are left with a being like ourselves, a half-crazed creature more or less adjusted to a mad world. This is normality in our present age. (1967, p. 58)

My sockless friend not only discovered that his singular act of rebellion overshadowed everything else that happened that weekend at home, he also discovered that it was the source of family conversation for years thereafter. "Just imagine, not wearing socks!" Just imagine if he had declared himself to be madly in love with his male college roommate!

The Interpersonal Perception Method

Laing developed an elaborate "theory" of human behavior and psychotherapy derived from his personal and clinical experience. It is a blend of existentialism, psychoanalysis, phenomenology, and family systems theory. The key element is the IPM, or "interpersonal perception method," which can be used to capture the *metaperspectives* infusing all our interactions.

The best introduction to IPM is Laing's book of metarelationship poetry, called *Knots* (1970). Here's a sample:

> How clever has one to be to be stupid?
> The others told her she was stupid. So she made
> herself stupid in order not to see how stupid
> they were to think she was stupid,
> because it was bad to think they were stupid.
> She preferred to be stupid and good,
> rather than bad and clever.
>
> It is bad to be stupid: she needs to be clever
> to be so good and stupid.

It is bad to be clever, because this shows
how stupid they were
to tell her how stupid she was. (p. 23)*

As an existential therapist, Laing worked to establish a living connection with the patient's true "embodied" self, who that person truly is and what that person is truly experiencing. Laing did everything in his power to reach the inner person, however frightened and battered and brutalized that person had become. His technique was "simply" to express an intense interest in understanding exactly what the patient was experiencing at the moment of the encounter. He and the patient became two people encountering each other in the chaos of the cosmos.

Case Demonstration: Homeless in Phoenix

I once had the opportunity to observe Laing at work in person. The setting was a huge convention hall divided into curtained-off "theaters"; at the center of each was a large raised platform looking something like a boxing ring. Chairs and microphones were set up on each platform for the performers. Each of the larger theaters could hold 500 to 600 spectators. It was a week-long affair, attended by several thousand professional psychologists, psychiatrists, social workers, counselors, and graduate students. All of the living "great names" from the world of psychotherapy were there, and the program listed times when each of these masters would be holding panel discussions and lectures on their work and demonstrating their therapeutic techniques.

I vividly remember the therapy demonstration conducted by Rogers. As every other therapist had done, he began by clarifying a few principles, establishing a few ground rules, and asking for volunteers. A number of hands went up. I don't remember exactly how he made his selection, but his method was careful, thoughtful, and very Rogerian. A 40-something woman who identified herself as a therapist was chosen, and she joined Rogers on the stage. What followed was an impressive demonstration of Rogers at the height of his powers. Within no more than 5 minutes, the formerly composed and thoroughly professional woman was in tears and sharing her most private and important feelings with Rogers and his 700 students of the day. At the end of the session, the client, obviously much restored, expressed her gratitude for the tremendous difference Rogers had made in her life—formerly just professionally but now personally too. The crowd reacted with reverential awe and thunderous applause. It was a powerful learning experience for me and also touched me very personally. What power Rogers had; what humanity he possessed.

My exposure to Laing was completely different. Where Rogers had been calm, almost serene, and profoundly gentle, Laing was disheveled, sort of lost, and, it seemed,

---

*From *Knots,* by R. D. Laing. Copyright © 1970 by R. D. Laing. Reprinted by permission of Pantheon Books, a division of Random House, Inc.

more than a little nervous. He had just come from Tucson, Arizona, which he kept pronouncing as "Tuck-son," which caused everyone else to laugh. I'm not sure he understood the joke, but he went along with the crowd in "good sport" fashion. My reaction to the man was that he was either a little drunk or quite ill or was himself just a little schizophrenic. Some things he said seemed a bit incoherent, and his Scottish accent was thick enough to mask a lot of his words in the vastness of the hall.

The next day, more out of curiosity than anything else, I went to see Laing's therapy demonstration. It started late—quite late. Laing had "gone away" but was expected back "soon." A lot of people started to lose interest and wander off to competing sessions.

Eventually Laing showed up. He was accompanied by a middle-aged, very poorly dressed, and very unkempt woman. Laing asked her to sit down and introduce herself to us. She was schizophrenic! Laing had been gone to find a "patient" for his demonstration. The patient told us that she lived in the Phoenix bus station, where Laing had found her. I suspect that, like me, many of my peers in the audience had never been so close to a homeless "bag lady" before. The nervousness and unevenness that I had seen in Laing the day before were completely gone. I began to sense that from his perspective we were gone. For the next half hour, he "encountered" his new patient with an attitude of genuine fascination.

Here is the interesting part: At the beginning of the interview the patient was quite crazy. It was painfully obvious that she was a victim of "dumping" by some state mental health agency—a chronically mentally ill person unceremoniously pushed out onto the street to fend for herself. Somehow she had found her way to the Phoenix bus station, and that was now the only reality she had. As the half hour went on, however, a miraculous transformation seemed to come over both of them. Their voices grew more conversational and more intimate. He was talking with her the way I might be able to talk to a client I had known for months. And she was telling him her private story in a most unschizophrenic manner. Her life unfolded before us as she told Laing about her experience as a chronically mentally ill, homeless person.

The last thing I remember is Laing asking her to explain why she had chosen to come with him that day (it was cold, blowing, and snowing in Phoenix), instead of staying with her possessions in the security of her corner of the bus station. She explained in a beautifully soft and expressive voice that she hoped her participation would give "all those doctors out there" a chance to see that homeless people and mentally ill people are human beings too and that she hoped maybe they could learn something from her that would help them better treat the people they met in their work.

Within the next couple of years both Rogers and Laing died. I learned a lot from both, but I still haven't figured out if they were telling me different things or if in reality they were telling me the same thing and I was too dense to understand. But I am pretty sure that I became an existentialist at that conference.

Viktor Frankl

I have mentioned that existentialism doesn't have very many, if any, techniques that distinguish it from other therapies. What really unifies existential approaches is their insistence that clients operate under the most fully free conditions they can muster in their specific life situation.

I also looked briefly at the paradox that existentialists recognize, which is that freedom is often realized only after one has come face to face with the reality of how thoroughly the shape of the world is determined by others. The classic example is the people who cannot recognize that they have any authentic choices left in life until they discover the one glaring exception: the choice to continue life or to end it. I believe it was the philosopher Friedrich Nietzsche who said that the idea of suicide has saved a great many lives. Until we face nonbeing squarely we cannot choose to be alive and fully human.

Viktor Frankl was 37 years old in 1942 when he discovered this paradox on his own. Frankl was the only member of his family and one of the few members of his community to survive the mass extermination of the Jews under Adolf Hitler. In the process of moving from his position as chief of neurology at one of Vienna's most important teaching hospitals to his position as inmate number 119,104, Frankl discovered that survival in a world gone utterly mad may depend on nothing more than finding and preserving the meaning of life.

Frankl's work is preserved in a very powerful book, *Man's Search for Meaning*, which was originally published in 1962 and has been released in a fourth edition. In it Frankl showed that until a person confronts the terrifying reality that "mankind has nothing to lose except his ridiculously naked life," he or she may have no true knowledge of what it means to be fully alive, fully human, and fully committed to preserving freedom.

The Quest for Meaning in Life

For Frankl, the only way we stay alive—in the existential sense of that term—is by finding meaning in our lives. He believed meaning isn't something that just "happens" to us as a result of living but a human attribute that requires a process of active discovery. Meaning is derived from "the will to meaning" and is exercised to discover the "meaning of life." Only when we are well engaged in the quest for the meaning of our existence do we discover the freedom to rise above circumstances and fate, to articulate within ourselves our sense of personal responsibility for others and for our own existence. Only then do we recognize that immersion in something valued beyond ourselves is the ultimate salvation of our whole being.

Noogenic Neurosis. Without cultivating the "creative, attitudinal, and experiential *values*" essential for the experience and expression of freedom, we are doomed. If we are without such values and locked in prison, lost in a blizzard, or devastated by disease, we will perish. If we are without such values and simply average, everyday people, we will lead lives of despair and meaningless emptiness.

Frankl described the condition of living without meaningful values, spirituality, or responsibility as *noogenic neurosis*. Persons with such a condition lead lives that are empty, meaningless, purposeless, aimless, and lost. Reflecting on his experience in the concentration camps, Frankl (1962) wrote, "Woe to him who saw no more sense in his life, no aim, no purpose, and therefore no point in carrying on. He was soon lost" (p. 76).

Existential Neurosis. Existential emptiness can also be a sort of mental disorder, which Maddi (1967) called *existential neurosis*. People showing signs of this disorder are unable to exert will and seek fulfillment. They reveal a

> meaningless or chronic inability to believe in truth, importance, usefulness, or interest value of any of the things one is engaged in or can imagine doing. [Remember Luke's "I never recognized until today how flat Indiana really is"?]
>
> [Their] most characteristic [emotional] features . . . are blandness and boredom, punctuated by periods of depression which become less frequent as the disorder is prolonged.
>
> . . . If there is any activity shown, it is in the direction of ensuring minimal expenditure of effort and decision making. (Maddi, 1967, p. 313)

Davison and Neale (1982) further described existential neurosis in terms of a "premorbid" personality. People experiencing existential neurosis feel "a great sense of emptiness and a lack of fulfillment, *in spite of the fact that they may be extremely effective in satisfying society's demands in every possible way*" (p. 60).

Frankl was not at all sure that people who have reached such a state are well served by institutionalized psychotherapies. Especially suspect are therapists with a Skinnerian orientation, who take away even more of the client's sense of control, and traditional psychodynamic therapists, who remain essentially anonymous to their patients.

Logotherapy

Frankl accused psychoanalysis of creating an unreal world of masks and mirrors. He feared that many psychoanalysts don't trust anything as real (a mistake one would not make with Wilhelm Reich, at any rate). Thus they play at the game of uncovering layer upon layer of meaning without ever acknowledging the truth of the person underneath all the layers.

> What is needed, I would say, is an unmasking of the unmasker! Although in some cases the unmasking may be right, the tendency to unmask must be able to stop in front of

that which is genuine in man; else it reveals the unmasking psychologist's own tendency to devaluate. (Frankl, 1959, p. 161)

Frankl's existential *logotherapy* is directed at renewing a sense of purpose, meaning, and intention, in filling what Frankl called "the existential vacuum." Logotherapy stresses

- *Engaging in creative and productive activity.* Pursuing physical, intellectual, and service-oriented work; "giving to the world"
- *Becoming receptive to raw experience.* Surrendering one's self to the power of beauty in nature and in art; opening one's self to intense sensory experience, the "greatness of the moment"
- *Developing a set of values.* Living one's life intentionally, with dignity, courage, and acceptance of the inevitable; transcending one's self

Frankl's interpretation of what makes a life worth living is somewhat like traveling to a distant point by train. The object is much less to arrive than to travel hopefully, to experience the journey fully. Frankl was not asking us to achieve anything, even something as high-minded as self-actualization. To the contrary, he wanted us to be rid of a focus on self, whether it be self-preservation or self-actualization. People preoccupied with self, he argued, have

lost sight of their meaning and purpose in the world. When they have missed the target (their task and meaning) and thereby frustrated their will to meaning, they become intent only upon their selves. To be psychologically healthy is to move beyond the focus on the self, to transcend it, to absorb it in one's meaning and purpose. Then the self will be spontaneously and naturally filled and actualized. (Schultz, 1977, p. 115)

Two Journeys Out of Hell

Frankl wanted psychotherapy to serve us by challenging us to extract meaning from our existence—to become survivors in the same way that he was a survivor. If you are intrigued by this view, start by reading Frankl's books firsthand for yourself. Then I encourage you to read both Alex Haley's *Autobiography of Malcolm X* (1965) and Elie Wiesel's *Night* (1960).

When you read about Malcolm X, ask yourself how Frankl's views would explain the transformations he experienced. Malcolm X started as a streetwise hoodlum but developed a vision of leading African Americans out of the despair and ruin to which they had fallen prey.

When you read Wiesel's book, ask whether Frankl's experience in the death camps was anything like the experience of the much younger Wiesel. I don't find much to support Frankl in *Night*, but I encourage you to see for yourself.

Rollo May

A third approach to an existential talking cure is the one that has guided the creation of this book from the early beginning. Rollo May, who died in 1994, was born in a small town in Ohio in 1909. He graduated from Oberlin College, where he was interested in the humanities and nurtured by the progressive social and political atmosphere that still prevails in the Oberlin community. May is the only psychotherapist I know of who published a book of his own art, *My Quest for Beauty* (1985). In this work he revealed that during a turbulent period in early adulthood only his ability to perceive and appreciate "beauty" kept him alive.

May studied psychology in graduate school but found his studies "naive and simplistic [and lacking] exactly what made life most rich and exciting." He "longed for some community in which one could ask questions about the meaning of despair, suicide and normal anxiety" (May, 1973, p. 2).

May spent the next academic year (1932–33) studying and working with Alfred Adler (see Chapter 8) in Vienna. He came away from that experience knowing where he wanted to take his life but not sure how to get there. Graduate schools in the United States were too behavioristic and experimental. So he tried the Union Theological Seminary, the same school Rogers had headed for after his graduation from college. There May became friends with the existentialist-theologian Paul Tillich, whose influence is apparent in all May's writing.

May combined work in religion with some teaching for a while in the 1930s, and he wrote a book on counseling, which was heavily influenced by his experience working with Adler in a child guidance clinic. Meanwhile he had gone back to graduate school (The Teachers College at the University of Columbia, once again the same choice as Rogers's). At graduate school he divided his time between fighting tuberculosis, a fight he just barely won, and completing a Ph.D. in clinical psychology.

The juxtaposition of life-threatening illness and graduate study in psychology seems very natural to many of us who have survived it. Many of May's later ideas about human strength, endurance, and triumph came from the experience:

> The disease occurred not simply because I was overworked, or ran athwart some T.B. bugs, but because I was trying to be something I wasn't. I was living as a "great extrovert," running here and there, doing three jobs at once, and leaving undeveloped and unused the side of me which would contemplate, would read and think and "invite my soul" [Walt Whitman again] rather than rushing and working at full speed. The disease comes as an opportunity to rediscover the lost functions of myself. It is as though the disease were nature's way of saying, "You must be your whole self. To the extent that you do not, you will be ill; and you will become well only to the extent that you do become yourself. (May, 1953, p. 95)

The Whole, Integrated, Authentic Self

May's existential psychology focuses primarily on issues of self-integration, authentic being, and rediscovery of the living person who has become disoriented and lost amid the dehumanizing effects of modern culture. The existentialist hero is the antihero, the person who resists the madness of the surrounding world. But isn't such a person the perfect example of madness, "unadjusted" to life as it really is? Another way to look at this question is to ask, "What is the cost of being 'normal,' of being well-adjusted, of 'fitting' so nicely into the machinery of the university or the corporation?"

Psychic Castration. May suggested that the cost of being "normal" is a sort of "psychic castration":

> Patient after patient I have seen (especially patients from Madison Avenue) chooses to be castrated, that is, to give up his power [May explicitly stated that this dilemma is common to both men and women, despite his use of the male pronoun and metaphor], in order not to be ostracized. The real threat is not to be accepted, to be thrown out of the group, to be left solitary and alone. . . . One's own meaning becomes meaningless because it is borrowed from somebody else's meaning. (1967, p. 120)

One of my favorite television comedy series was BBC's *Fawlty Towers*, in which John Cleese plays Basil Fawlty, a half-mad hotel keeper at a down-at-the-heels resort in England. In one episode, Basil's wife gives him an order to do something or other around the hotel and reinforces her demand with the warning, "And Basil, you know what I will do to you, don't you, if you don't do as I ask." "Certainly, my dearest," replies Cleese. "But you'll have to sew them back on first."

Dasein. May told us that we all share Basil Fawlty's situation to some extent. We are all faced with the choice between being perceived as utterly mad and submitting to castrating authority. In existential terms, we are all confronted by an ongoing and inescapable *ontological dilemma*, a dilemma of our being.

On the one hand, we all yearn for an active, aware, and authentic state of "being in the world." In German, the precise term for this state is *dasein* (literally "Being There"):

> *Dasein* indicates that man is the being who is *there* and implies also that he *has* a "there" in the sense that he can know he is there and not just any place, but the particular "there" that is mine, the particular point *in time* as well as space of my existence at this given moment. Man is the being who can be conscious of, and therefore responsible for, his existence. (May, 1958, p. 41)

On the other hand, we feel that the person who stands before God and the cosmos as a triumphant human being is on the edge of catastrophe. Such a person risks the possibility of not only being struck down by the gods but also being totally isolated from the rest of humanity. This is the fate of Oedipus, the king who defied conventional wisdom and piety and demanded to know the truth held by the gods. This sort of defiance may inspire the individualistic, self-sufficient admirers of Ayn Rand, but it scares me half to death.

Ontological Anxiety and Guilt.   Our fundamental, existential human choice, according to May, is always between ontological anxiety and ontological guilt. *Ontological anxiety* haunts us when "we go where no man has gone before" and stand alone in the world as a distinct being. We are condemned to the crushing experience of *ontological guilt* when we try to avoid anxiety by "going with the flow," living a life of unauthentic, shallow conformity.

As Fritz Perls (Chapter 16) noted, we can distract ourselves from this painful dilemma by filling our lives with mindless resentments and details—details that Perls called "chickenshit, bullshit, and elephantshit" (so we wouldn't let size alone impress us overmuch or forget what we and the animals all have in common). But eventually the noise quiets, the babble ceases, the brain clicks out of autopilot. We start to sense and feel and at last begin to know something. At such times we have no place to hide from ourselves. So what do we do? Open another bottle of cheap wine? Go in search of a one-night stand? Develop a secret plan for starting a war? Or do we do something more creative and productive?

May said that if modern psychotherapy serves any function at all it should be to provide a meaningful and reliable resource for those existential moments. He placed the dilemmas of human experience at the center of the therapeutic enterprise. He wanted the talking cure to provide "a situation in which the patient's sense of identity, significance and responsibility may be discovered and developed [through] the deepening and widening of consciousness" (May, 1967, pp. 211, 220).

Love and Will in May's Talking Cure

If we're talking about consciousness, we're only a half step beyond William James and Mary Calkins. Maybe less than half a step, because the other thing that May wanted therapists to develop in clients is will, which he redefined as commitment to a definition of self as the responsible agent for one's own existence:

> [James's exercise of freedom by willing himself to be free reveals that] we have the power to throw our weight on this possibility. . . . We say in effect, "Let this be the reality for me." The fiat "Be it so!" is James's leap; it is his statement of commitment. He knew that in an act of will a man was doing something more than what met the eye; he was creating, forming something which had never existed before. There is risk in such a decision, such a fiat, but it remains our one contribution to the world which is original and underived. (May, 1969, p. 269)

Many people coming to therapy are convinced that they have no will. If I am lucky, they insist on the point so vociferously that I am able to turn the tables on them and show them that they are challenging me with at least as much will as I am sending their way in return.

The Value of Wishing. Usually I start any discussion of will by talking with my clients for a session or two about wishes. Almost all of use are capable of wishing for something, even when we are in the pits of a depression.

I can always get clients who say they don't have anything to wish for to tell me that there are things they must *not* wish for. And sooner or later, most folks admit that they have never really stopped wishing for love, for a different body, for power or money, for a second, or third or fourth or fifth, chance at something (most of us are remarkably good at blowing genuine opportunities when they are presented to us).

Like May (1969), I believe that wishing is mixed up with feeling and that once I get someone's wish list, that person can't pretend to be a zombie anymore. For certain, clients' wish lists are usually confused and illogical: "I wish I could lose weight, then X would love me the way I always needed to be loved, so then I wouldn't have to overeat." This statement is, of course, several different wishes, which are all jumbled together with a lot of "crooked thinking" connecting them in a self-defeating spiral of despair. But as a therapist, once I have perceived a wish, I can be certain that I have connected with a feeling. And once I've connected to a feeling, I can become focused, with the will of a terrier-therapist.

If you can connect a wish with a feeling and somebody can help you clarify that wish, making it comprehensible and realistic, then you are only a half stroke away from your first act of will. Once you connect the power of the wish with the power of the feeling, you can make a decision: to fulfill your wish. A person committed to a course of action that could fulfill a wish is experiencing an act of will.

Decisions and Choices. The odd thing is that often, once the will is harnessed, you will discover that the wish was trivial or unworthy—at which point, of course, you can abandon the wish. In many cases, wishing is the dress rehearsal for the "big show," which is living as a "willing" person in a world full of complex and confusing choices. The question then becomes how you harness this will. How do you rescue your being from the forces competing for your existential power? I believe this is the question that captured Sigmund Freud's energies.

We can make the question more complicated than even Freud imagined: If authentic living requires the active affirmation of freedom through the exercise of will, but if will is at the same time leading us in many different and largely contradictory directions as it chases after a thousand different wishes, then isn't will both the problem and the answer to the problem?

We might answer this question the way Jung challenged the positivist antivitalists of his day, by revising his quote about the metaphysics of death to suit our own purposes: "If you fancy you have no control over your will, you forget the willfulness of one fact—the fact that you continue your own life."

You are alive. Thus you face the ultimate wish of your own existence. If you have nothing inside you to harness and make sense of your will, then why do you choose to live? Why then do you fear nonbeing? Aren't all your wishes ultimately an expression of your *dasein*? Or perhaps you have read too much Freud. In that case, are you afraid of what lies in the darkest and deepest parts of your being?

You may be resisting the idea that all wishes should be brought to light: "Thousands and thousands of people end their own lives every year! Surely psychotherapy must recognize that some wishes are terribly destructive and must not be encouraged. Surely powerful wishes must be censored and regulated and subjected to executive approval if civilization is to survive. The alternative is to live in wish-ridden anarchy!" (The possibility of happy-go-lucky anarchy is many therapists' existentialist fantasy.)

Perhaps the answer is that existential therapists can use the possibility of suicide and other disapproved wishes the way forest rangers use controlled burns to stop forest fires. Perhaps had therapists confronted suicide victims and rape perpetrators with a challenge to their own beings—shown them that the choice to live or to take a chance with love is just as authentic and ultimately more courageous than the choice to die or to seize sexual gratification violently—perhaps the course of human events would have been different. This view suggests that choice, and perhaps only the fact of choice, illuminates the lives of those who despair. Perhaps, then, it is unfair to accuse psychotherapists of oversimplifying the human condition.

A Psychological Consideration of the Power of Evil

The thinking of many existentialists is further complicated by the concept of the *diamonic* as another facet of will. This is a rather elaborate concept, which I simplify at the cost of losing much of its elegance, especially in May's writing. The diamonic is "any natural function which has the power to take over the whole person" (May, 1969, p. 121). Anger and rage are diamonics, or at least they can be. So are love and eros, as Reich understood. AIDS can be a diamonic. Think of diamonic as the passions in your life, like the rage the poet conjures not to go gently into that good night.

As members of society, we are all taught something of the disruptive danger of the diamonic when it takes us outside the range of normal interaction with others. The diamonic is a phenomenon of utmost concern in societies like Japan, where any idiosyncratically expressed passion may disturb the *wa,* or harmony, of the group. Many of us in Western culture also fear the diamonic—and experience the energy that derives from it with considerable anxiety.

The first example of how the will derives from the diamonic is drawn from this chapter: The diamonic that was fascism when it hurled Frankl into the Holocaust (see also Erich Fromm's 1941 *Escape From Freedom*) became the opportunity for the imprisoned psychiatrist to come to terms with his life, to find meaning through his suffering.

The undergraduate pondering suicide at the betrayal of the only important and profound diamonic love he or she (but *he* is statistically more likely) has ever known can be nurtured in therapy to preserve and celebrate that part of the self that had been unknown.

The victim of AIDS can resign from life or become a modern-day angel of death—or confront the diamonic, determined to make any remaining days a testament to his or her worth as a human being.

The loyal wife betrayed by divorce after years of married existence can become a victim of her anger and despair or can "show the son of a bitch" that "living well is the best revenge" (see Chapter 18).

May (1969) described the transformative power of the diamonic as follows:

> We . . . see that the diamonic begins as impersonal. I am pushed by the clamor of gonads and temper. The second stage consists of a deepening and widening of consciousness by which I make my diamonic urges *personal*. I transform this sexual appetite into the motivation to make love to, and to be loved by, the woman I desire and choose. But we do not stop there. . . . The diamonic pushes us toward the logos [the underlying meaning or significance]. The more I come to terms with my diamonic tendencies, the more I will find myself conceiving and living by a universal structure of reality. This movement towards the logos is *trans*personal. Thus we move from an impersonal through a personal to a transpersonal dimension of consciousness. (p. 176)

Life as It Is

The person confronted by the diamonic is, to say the least, fully alive. Edgar Allen Poe once wrote that there are only four events of importance in a person's life: birth, marriage, death, and the terror in between. Or as a student scribbled on a wall in the basement of our library, "The great thing about being scared shitless is that you are never bored."

The existential therapist joins with clients to bring them into full awareness of every aspect of their situation, terrifying or otherwise. The purpose is to cause clients to wake up to the realities of existence, to realize "This is it! There is no other life than the one I am leading right now."

Neurotics try to avoid threats to being by becoming only marginally aware of the facts of that being: "If I close my eyes, the bear or dean or bank or results of my work won't be able to get me!" The task of the therapist is to provide the inspiration to get these people to take their hands from their eyes and open their beings to the possible.

Existential psychotherapy requires both the therapist and clients to encounter life as it is, without filters or excuses. For May, genuine self-affirmation requires personal courage, self-consciousness, uncontaminated awareness, participation in community, perceptual and phenomenological centeredness, and a willingness to encounter the unknown (Monte, 1991, pp. 489–496). It is precisely these attributes that clients come to therapy to acquire or, sometimes, recover. From the existential perspective, the therapist is a leader or a guide. Clients are pilgrims. Life itself is a sacred quest.

CHAPTER 18

Toward a Feminist Psychotherapy

Talking Back

The history of the talking cure has to a great extent been a history of the way powerful men have understood and reacted to the emotional and psychological distress of women. In recent years women have begun "talking back" to their therapists, and they have increasingly refused to be the passive recipients of cures designed to help them fit in and be quiet.

Ida Bauer, whom Sigmund Freud called Dora in his published case study, was an angry young woman caught up in a sordid family story of marital infidelity and paraphilic lust. Freud's inability to comprehend that Dora's psychological misery was rooted not in her psyche but in her world seems hard to believe a hundred years later. The assumption that women's emotional and psychological problems are rooted in the female psyche is one of the most unfortunate of Freud's legacies. The good news, however, is that Dora confronted the adults who had destroyed her peace of mind and achieved a self-cure, one of the first documented cases of symptom resolution through personal empowerment.

There are two main streams of feminist thought in psychotherapy today. In the first, feminist therapists like Nancy Chodorow have tried to rewrite psychoanalytic theory to make it reflect the experience of women. They have tried to create a psychodynamic understanding of women that does not use men as the standard and that recognizes the powerful bond between women and their mothers. Other psychologists in this tradition, such as Karen Horney and Carol Gilligan, have focused on the developmental patterns unique to women.

Others, however, have challenged the value of any "therapy" based on the assumption that women's distress is rooted in the female psyche. One study showed that sexist bias against women is so pervasive in our society that clinical judgments of women, even those made by seasoned therapists,

are fatally flawed (Broverman et al., 1970). The study showed that psychothera-
pists tend to use only one model of a healthy mature adult—and that model is
masculine.

Feminist social critic Mary Daly has criticized all established psychotherapies
as phallocentric and as closed to locating women's problems in society. Psycholo-
gists Edna Rawlings and Diane Carter, building on this idea in the 1970s, de-
scribed a genuinely nonsexist therapy. Ultimately, however, nonsexist therapy did
not appear to speak to the specific needs of women. By 1980, Lucia Gilbert was
able to describe the basic components of a "feminist therapy," which operates
fundamentally on an empowerment model.

A truly separate feminist psychotherapy does not yet exist, for no unifying
theory or specific methodology uniquely defines a feminist approach. There are,
however, three guiding principles that distinguish feminist psychotherapy from
more traditional alternatives: that which oppresses the client must be changed; the
therapist/client relationship is between two competent adults; and the goal of
therapy is the empowerment of the person seeking help. (Empowerment is a theme
continued in Chapter 19.)

> Psychotherapy is clearly a political enterprise. Ideas such as an individual's distress can
> be ameliorated by particular mental interventions, or that one can explore the truth of
> inner life, or that psychotherapy helps the individual understand her or himself, are not
> neutral. The very subject of psychotherapy—the individual—develops within a social con-
> text and is only understandable within with reference to the specifics of that context.
> Thus how we construct an understanding of the development of the individual, mental
> distress, psychological symptoms or therapy as a mechanism of change, intimately
> reflects an understanding of how the world works. (Bloom, Eichenbaum, & Orbach,
> 1982, p. 7)

Case Study: Ida Bauer Meets Sigmund Freud

At the age of 47, Philipp Bauer was a troubled man. He had suffered off and on from
syphilis for more than 20 years. During this time, he had also infected his wife with
gonorrhea. Now his pretty young mistress's husband was growing increasingly im-
patient; and to top it all off, his daughter, Ida, was becoming unmanageable. He
called on his neighbor and confidant to talk about his problems. The doctor was very
compassionate and exceptionally wise. The physician agreed to try to talk with the
girl—to see what could be done to set things straight.

But Ida was a stubborn and strong-willed adolescent. The doctor could see immediately that the girl's condition had become significantly worse over the past months. The electrical treatments had evidently been an utter failure. Ida could barely speak above a whisper, and her annoying dry cough was persistent and loud. It would have been obvious to a first-year medical student that the hysteria was deepening into a pervasive and debilitating melancholia.

After his examination of the girl, the doctor summoned the father to come in haste. If there was any hope of reversing the progress of her disease, treatment must begin at once—an hour a day, six days a week. It would take a year, maybe longer. Almost certainly longer. Fascinating case.

Never before had the doctor, Sigmund Freud, seen a girl so dissipated from masturbation. He explained the medical facts to the worried father:

> Hysterical symptoms hardly ever appear so long as children are masturbating, but only afterwards, when a period of abstinence has set in; they form a substitute for masturbatory satisfaction, the desire for which continues to persist in the unconscious until another more normal satisfaction appears. (Decker, 1991, p. 105)

The only genuinely satisfactory resolution would be for the girl to marry—and even then, her only hope would be to find a much older and more experienced husband who could satisfy her smoldering sexual instincts. With men in a situation like this, there were other remedies—a mistress or a professional, a prostitute—but marriage was the only alternative for a woman or, in this case, a girl of 17.

There was also the possibility of trying the "talking cure," the new psychoanalysis. Freud explained that it had proved useful in some of his colleague Josef Breuer's work, especially with highly unstable and strong-minded girls like Ida. Analysis had almost completely replaced electrical treatments in Freud's own work with young women. It might help.

But the girl was fiercely resistant. She was sick of doctors. She had been ill for years and years, and no physician had helped a bit. She hated them all. The so-called "doctors" had almost killed her when they misdiagnosed her appendicitis as a false pregnancy and left her to suffer in unspeakable agony for days on end. But the father insisted. He warned darkly of asylums and involuntary treatments; there were ways to make rebellious young women listen to reason, terrible ways. And so shortly before her 18th birthday in the year 1900, Ida Bauer entered psychoanalytic treatment, and the history books, as the famous "Dora." (All the historical details of this story are drawn from Decker, 1991.)

A Victorian "Gentlemen's Agreement"

Dora discovered her father's long-term affair with "Frau K.," the young but sickly wife of a neighbor and family friend in Vienna, at the age of 12. She became fascinated with her father's mistress and began spending a lot of time around the K. household—ostensibly to help in the care of the young K. children. But in reality,

Dora was most interested in watching over the barely concealed comings and goings of her father while Herr K. was out of town on business.

The affair became more or less public knowledge 2 years later, when the families decided to take a mountain vacation together. The emboldened lovers took adjoining single rooms in the hotel, away from the rest of their families. From the lovers' perspective, Dora must have been even more of a problem than either of their apparently indifferent spouses.

The day came, however, when Frau K. suggested to her lover that her husband was beginning to show signs of distress over the affair. But, and this was a delicate subject, she had noticed that her husband was quite smitten with the girl, Dora.

That was when Dora's father had his brilliant idea. He arranged over the next several days under various guises for the girl to be left in the sole charge of Herr K. in the hotel. He thought of his actions as a sort of "returning of the favor" among gentlemen, a small gesture of understanding between Victorian men.

At first the naive Dora appreciated the attention and returned the flattering comments and glances of her family's friend. However, when her would-be lover escalated his attentions, attempting to kiss and fondle the girl, Dora flatly refused her suitor.

Dora's hysterical symptoms began to appear at this time. They were at the outset clearly patterned after her mother's own complex of painful symptoms, which resulted from the chronic and inadequately treated gonorrhea she had contracted from her husband, Dora's father. Dora and her mother spent many weeks in the "cleansing waters" of the thermal springs in the Bavarian countryside, "treating" their matching gynecological symptoms. These treatments had become, according to Freud, "the ruling passion" of the rejected wife's life, her passive revenge, a symptom of her "vaginal aggression."

In due time, Freud even went so far as to accuse the mother of having caused a large measure of Dora's illness as a result of her own obsessive-compulsive cleaning rituals. Eventually the family quarters became so thoroughly sanitary that Dora's father was no longer allowed into his own sitting room, even to fetch his cigars. If she permitted her husband the full run of the house, Dora's mother claimed, he would contaminate the perfectly cleaned and preserved rooms. Freud described his patient's mother's condition as "a housewife's psychosis." In Freud's words, "she cleaned the house and its utensils . . . to such an extent as to make it almost impossible to use or enjoy them."

Meanwhile, Dora continued to fend off the increasingly amorous intentions of Herr K. In the process she became increasingly mired in hysterical symptoms—to the point that she was treated unsuccessfully by a whole series of neurologists, including Freud, for her cough, aphonia, headaches, and shortness of breath. All this had occurred, by the way, by the time Dora was 15 years old.

In late 1900, through the material revealed in Dora's dreams and free associations in the psychoanalytic sessions, Freud evidently came to understand and to believe the story the girl had been telling him from the start. It was, after all, not an unusual story, and her hysterical symptoms seemed to accord with accounts of her encounters with Herr K. If she would accept the true nature of her symptoms and let her fantasies come to terms with reason, perhaps in time her case could be successfully resolved.

In what is now revered as one of Freud's earliest clinical psychoanalytic interpretations, he explained to Dora that the psychological reality of her cough stemmed from her unconscious wish to "become" Frau K. and thus to become her father's true lover. The cough was her unconscious repulsion caused by her unconscious wish to observe her father's mistress (and thus Dora herself) perform fellatio on him.

The Therapeutic Value of Anger

Can we even imagine the dilemma Dora found herself in as a middle-class teenage girl coming of age in Vienna in 1900? From the outside, she and her mother appeared to be "the identified patients." They were the ones who were nervous, weak, and sick. Meanwhile, as only some inside the family could see, Dora was not only being constantly thrown into the middle of the erotic escapades of her father and his lover but also being subjected to Herr K.'s attempted seductions at every turn. And now her physician was telling her that her symptoms were due to *her* impure thoughts and actions.

Dora became intensely angry. Psychoanalytic lore has it that this was Freud's first case in which a patient displayed "negative transference" (as Chapter 7 explained, the patient's unconscious projection of a historically rooted negative emotional agenda onto the relationship with the therapist.) But my guess is that the girl was just plain angry—furious, in fact.

Dora finally resolved to put the matter to Freud directly: "You may tell my father to break off his relationship with Frau K. Also, tell him to order Herr K. to keep away from me." Seventy-five years later, feminist therapists would understand Dora's assertive expression as the first step on the royal road to her recovery.

Freud responded, however, by marveling at the "shrewdness" of the girl's father for having had the good sense to bring a girl with such troubled thoughts to see him. Freud perceived that Dora's real problem was the hysterical fear she experienced when her sexuality was aroused by Herr K.'s "courting"—especially, Freud reasoned, because she had not resolved any of the sexual feelings for her father that had been aroused by watching her father make love to his mistress. Dora and Freud evidently lived on different planets.

All this transpired at the same time in Freud's life when he was working tirelessly to lay down the foundational principles that would establish psychoanalysis as a revolutionary scientific movement. Clearly his need to find cases that perfectly fit his theoretical breakthroughs was his paramount interest. He had previously grossly distorted the facts in the case of Katharina by masking the fact that Katharina was a victim of paternal incest, and he was in the process of making an equally distorting analysis in the case of Fraulein Elisabeth von R., whom he described as being very similar to Dora. When it came to his young women patients, it appears that Freud, in today's parlance, "just didn't get it."

Meanwhile, Dora was growing increasingly suicidal, and her father was growing increasingly alarmed that something dreadful was going to happen. All this time, of course, Herr K. kept pressing his case for his "right" to the girl as a sexual companion.

Finally, after three months of continuous treatment, Dora gave up on ever being able to make her physician pay any attention to what she was telling him. In December 1900 Dora notified Dr. Freud that she would not be consulting with him any longer.

When Freud received the news, he perceived that Dora had abandoned therapy because of the transference to her physician of "the cruel impulses and revengeful motives" she harbored toward her father and Herr K. Ernest Jones, Freud's English biographer, went a step further. In telling the story of Dora in 1955, Jones added in his notes that the girl's desertion of Freud revealed her to be "a disagreeable creature who consistently put revenge before love; [which was the same] motive that led her to break off treatment prematurely" (p. 256).

What neither Jones nor Freud revealed to us is that Dora's case had a somewhat happy conclusion. Her depression deepened in January after her sessions with Freud were terminated. Her father was furious with her and with Freud for "giving up" on treatment. But Freud, in turn, blamed the father for not forcing the girl to come to treatment and remained convinced that Dora's sexual fantasies and unfulfilled wishes, kindled by masturbation and ignited by Herr K.'s attentions, were at the root of her problem. But over the winter, Ida, as we should now call her once again, seems to have worked hard at pulling herself together. Her symptoms gradually diminished, and she regained some of her strength.

Then in May, Ida attended the K. family's funeral for their 9-year-old daughter. For some reason, perhaps because of the emotion brought on by the death of the young girl, with whom she had been very close for several years, Ida decided to seize the moment. She demanded that both Herr and Frau K. admit what they were doing to each other and to her. The grieving parents broke down and in front of everyone admitted to the truth of all Ida said. Ida returned home and confronted her father, demanding that he too acknowledge the truth.

The result of these events was a dramatic reduction in Ida's hysterical symptoms. In Ida's untutored hands, the talking cure had at least briefly become the "confrontive cure," and its healing power had been significant.

A Final Encounter

In reading this case, you have to wonder at the power of the human spirit—especially in this tragically self-destructive 17-year-old woman, who even at age 15 had seemed to Freud "a girl of intelligent and engaging looks [and] intellectual precocity."

The next news we have of her is really quite remarkable. Two years later, when Ida was 19, she quite suddenly began to suffer from strong neurological pain in her right cheek. On April 1 she apparently decided on her own to consult with none other than Dr. Freud about the problem. Regarding her visit a neurotic trap, Freud refused to see her. He wrote that he was not taken in by her decision to pay him a call on All Fools' Day! He recognized, he said, that this was Dora's "cruel way" to remind him of the "slap in the face" she had delivered both to Herr K. and to him. Freud took care to inform us that instead of playing into her neurotic game, he sent word that he had decided to "forgive her" for her treatment of him 15 months earlier. And that, finally, was the last time Dora darkened the door of Freud's consulting room and his psyche.

Explorations of Women's Psychological Pain

One might have expected Freud's publication of this case and his other abortive attempts to treat women with the psychoanalytic method to have ended the short, unhappy history of this variation of the talking cure. Instead, Dora became a seminal teaching case of the "dark continent" of women's sexuality and the mysterious nature of the unconscious lives of women. Freud used Dora to begin exploring the power of transference relationships in effecting nervous cures. But he never seems to have looked back with any insight either into his own motives and methods or into the true nature of Dora's case.

Freud's Psychoanalytic Method

However critically we may look on Freud's lack of empathy with his female hysterical patients, we would have to agree that he was still light-years ahead of his time in many respects. In his day, the standard recommended medical treatments for hysterical "fits" included suffocation, beatings with wet towels, ridicule, public humiliation, and showers with icy water. Here is an excerpt from a lecture of Dr. L. C. Grey, a distinguished professor of medicine, to a class in the late 1880s on how to achieve "victory" over resistant hysterical women:

> Do not flatter yourselves . . . that you will gain an easy victory [over the hysterical patient]. On the contrary, you must expect to have your temper, your ingenuity, your nerves tested to a degree that cannot be surpassed even by the greatest surgical operations. I maintain that the man who has the nerve and the tact to conquer some of these grave cases of hysteria has the nerve and the tact that will make him equal to the great emergencies of life. Your patient must be taught day by day . . . by steady resolute, iron-willed determination and tact—the combination which the French . . . call "the iron hand beneath the velvet glove." (1888, quoted in Smith-Rosenberg, 1972, p. 675)

Another View of Hysteria. Dora, as it now appears to us, presented a classic case of a young woman's "flight into madness" as a means of coping with the impossible demands placed on her by her family and her culture. In her review of the phenomenon of hysteria among 18th-century women, Smith-Rosenberg (1972) attributed hysteria to sex roles and sex role conflict in a society and in a time when

> the ideal female . . . was expected to be gentle and refined, sensitive and loving. She was the guardian of religion and spokeswoman for morality. Hers was the task of guiding the more worldly and more frequently tempted male past the maelstroms of atheism and uncontrolled sexuality. . . . The stereotype of the middle class woman as emotional, pious, passive, and nurturant was to become increasingly rigid throughout the nineteenth century. (pp. 655–656)

The Victorian woman was, in short, the "weaker sex," yet she was expected to resolve the enormous paradoxes involved in existing as a woman:

> There were enormous discontinuities and inconsistencies between such ideals of female socialization and the real world in which the . . . woman had to live. The first relates to a dichotomy between the ideal woman and the ideal mother. The ideal woman was emotional, dependent and gentle—a born follower. The ideal mother, then and now, was expected to be strong, self-reliant, protective, an efficient caretaker in relation to children and home. . . . The discontinuity between the child and adult female roles, along with the failure to develop substantial ego strengths, crossed class and geographic barriers—as did hysteria itself. (pp. 656–657, 659)

Psychoanalysis, then, should be understood as a major breakthrough in the treatment of hysteria. Yet the theory of psychoanalysis seems to stand resolutely in the way of any genuinely compelling understanding of women's madness. As Smith-Rosenberg (1972) noted, psychoanalysts have long been frustrated by their inability to establish "satisfying and stable" clinical relationships with their hysterical patients and have insisted on locating the roots of hysteria deeply within the flawed psyches of women, whom they regard as "excessively ambivalent [in] preoedipal relation with . . . mother [which results in] complications of oedipal development and resolution" (p. 653).

What was required was recognition that madness could have its roots in the world beyond the control of the individual patient. We might consider this a rather obvious and even fundamental perception, but such a reconsideration of psychiatric dogma wouldn't come for almost a century after Dora, as feminists began to "deconstruct the canon" of psychoanalysis. They stated the obvious: "What Dora need[ed] most [was] confirmation of the truthfulness of her perceptions and thus confirmation of herself. But the stereotypes are there: women are not listened to [Dora's mother was never even interviewed], women are not to be believed [Papa, Frau K., and Herr K. denied their conspiracy until the fateful encounter at the funeral], women are like children" (Hare-Mustin, 1983, p. 593).

Freud's blindness to the human dilemmas and existential challenges that confront women are all the more tragic or shocking when one considers how perceptive and insightful he was about men's problems. At best he was a lifelong victim of his age and his middle-class Jewish assumptions about women's place. In 1883 he expressed his protective biases in writing to his beloved Martha Bernays, the woman he so passionately yearned for and eagerly courted:

> I dare say we agree that housekeeping and the care and education of children claim the whole person [of a woman] and practically rule out any profession. . . . It seems a completely unrealistic notion to send women into the struggle for existence in the same way as men. Am I to think of my delicate sweet girl as a competitor? After all, the encounter could only end by my telling her . . . that I love her, and that I will make every effort to get her out of the competitive role into the quiet, undisturbed activity of the home. . . . [T]he position of woman cannot be other than it is: to be an adored sweetheart in youth, and a beloved wife in maturity. (1883/1960, pp. 75–76)

"Was Will Das Weib?" The possibility also exists that something more roundly misogynic was going on in Freud's psyche. In 1925 (1964a) he wrote,

> I cannot escape the notion (though I hesitate to give it expression) that for women the level of what is ethically normal is different for what it is in men. . . . We must not allow ourselves to be deflected from such conclusions by the denials of the feminists, who are anxious to force us to regard the two sexes equal in position and worth. (p. 258)

And in 1933 (1964b): "Envy and jealousy play an even greater part in the mental life of women than of men" (p. 125). Freud's general assessment of women was published in *Civilization and Its Discontents:*

> Women soon come into opposition to civilization and display their retarding and restraining influence—those very women who, in the beginning, laid the foundations of civilization by the claims of their love . . . find [themselves] forced into the background by the claims of civilization and . . . adopt a hostile attitude towards it. (1930/1961, p. 56)

Not too surprisingly, then, Freud summed up his lifelong frustration and love/hate relationship with women with a cry of despair. At the end of his life, in a conversation with Princess Marie Bonaparte, a psychoanalyst whom he had personally trained, Freud exclaimed, "*Was will das Weib?*" (Gay, 1989, p. 670). Indeed, what does woman want?

Mitchell (1974) made what a reviewer called "a brave and important" stab at reconciling feminism and psychoanalysis:

> The greater part of the feminist movement has identified Freud as the enemy. It is held that psychoanalysis claims women are inferior and that they can achieve true femininity only as wives and mothers. Psychoanalysis is seen as a justification for the status-quo,

bourgeois and patriarchal, and Freud in his own person exemplifies these qualities. I would agree that popularized Freudianism must answer to this description; but the argument of this book is that a rejection of psychoanalysis and of Freud's works is fatal for feminism. However it may have been used, psychoanalysis is not a recommendation *for* a patriarchal society, but an analysis *of* one. If we are interested in understanding and challenging the oppression of women, we cannot afford to neglect it. (p. xiii)

But orthodox psychoanalysis may be so locked into the assumption that "anatomy is destiny" that it will never be able to answer Freud's question about women's psychological needs.

Hare-Mustin (1983) concluded after her reevaluation of the case of Dora and the psychoanalytic perspective on women that "some women's problems in living may actually be a result of social, economic, ethical, or legal conditions, but they have been misidentified or erroneously regarded as psychiatric disturbances subject to intervention by psychotherapy or clinical treatment" (p. 593). Perhaps there is more to the female psyche than penis envy.

What would you say to a man who summed up his insights into the experience of menopause with the following "observation"?

It is a well known fact, and one that has given much ground for complaint, that after women have lost their genital function their character often undergoes a peculiar alteration. They become quarrelsome, vexatious, and overbearing, petty, and stingy; that is to say, they exhibit typically sadistic and anal-erotic traits which they did not possess earlier, during their period of womanliness. Writers of comedy and satirists have in all ages directed their invectives against the "old dragon" into which the charming girl, the loving wife and the tender mother have been transformed. We can see that this alteration of character corresponds to a regression of the sexual life to the pregenital sadistic and anal-erotic stage, in which we have discovered the disposition to obsessional neurosis. (Freud, 1913/1958b, pp. 323–324)

Perhaps Freud was right to be suspicious of the reasons Dora chose to visit him on April 1, 1902—All Fools' Day.

Nancy Chodorow's Feminist Analysis

I am not suggesting that psychoanalysts are incapable of treating female patients. Rather, I am trying to demonstrate that the intellectual and ethical foundations on which they do so are seriously flawed by a deep and pervasive misogyny. Any number of later psychoanalytic revisionists, including most importantly in this context Karen Horney (see Chapter 10), attempted fundamental revisions of the psychoanalytic understanding of the feminine psyche. But as long as the problems women face were considered a product of their deviation from the male standard, how could any talking cure for women be truly therapeutic?

A Revised Psychoanalysis. In contemporary psychology, Nancy Chodorow (1989) has done a brilliant job of reconstructing psychodynamic theory to bypass Freud's misogynic thinking. Chodorow's feminist approach to psychoanalysis focuses on psychic experiences central to the development of women, and she is willing to attribute male oppression of women to masculine sexual socialization. The following lengthy excerpt will give you a feel for the specifics of Chodorow's argument:

> Freudian theory does not just oppress women. Rather, Freud gives us a theory concerning how people—women and men—become gendered and sexed, how femininity and masculinity develop, how sexual inequality is reproduced. . . . Freud tells us how nature becomes culture and how this culture comes to appear as and to be experienced as "second nature"—appears as natural. Psychoanalytic theory helps to demonstrate how sexual inequality and the social organization of gender are reproduced. It demonstrates that this reproduction happens in central ways via transformations in consciousness in the psyche, and not only via social and cultural institutions. It demonstrates that this reproduction is an unintended product of the structure of the sex-gender system itself—of a family division of labor in which women mother, of a sexual system founded on heterosexual norm [sic], of a culture that assumes and transmits sexual inequality. Freud, or psychoanalysis, tells us how people become heterosexual in their family development (how the originally matrisexual girl comes to be heterosexual rather than lesbian); how a family structure in which women mother [sic] produces in men (and in women, to some extent) a psychology and ideology of male dominance, masculine superiority, and the devaluation of women and things feminine; how women develop maternal capabilities through their relationship to their own mother. Thus, psychoanalysis demonstrates the internal mechanisms of the socio-cultural organization of gender and sexuality and confirms the early feminist argument that the "personal is political." It argues for the rootedness and basic-ness of psychological forms of inequality and oppression.
>
> But psychoanalysis does not stop at this demonstration. Freud suggests that these processes do not happen so smoothly, that this reproduction of gender and sexuality is rife with contradictions and strains. People develop conflicting desires, discontents, neuroses. Psychoanalysis begins from psychic conflict; this is what Freud was first trying to explain. . . . Male dominance on a psychological level is a masculine defense and a major psychic cost to men, built on fears and insecurity; it is not straightforward power. Psychoanalysis demonstrates against theories of over-socialization and total domination, a lack of total socialization. It demonstrates discontent, resistance, and an undercutting of sexual modes and the institutions of sexual inequality.
>
> Psychoanalysis is also a theory that people actively appropriate and respond to their life environment and experiences, make something of these psychologically, and, therefore, presumably can act to change them. (1989, pp. 176–177)

A Theory About Women. Chodorow has very successfully avoided the old psychoanalytic "male as standard" problem. But her revised psychoanalysis still produces a psychology of women bound by assumptions of the universal inevitability of patriarchy. In her formulation,

> issues of diversity associated with ethnic, racial, sexual, and class identity are inadequately addressed. Mothering and parenting are often defined in narrow, culturally particularistic [and patriarchal] ways, which may lead to racist, ethnocentric, or classist interpretations of the family. Furthermore, feminist psychoanalytic therapists only infrequently explore social change solutions or methods for altering the mothering patterns that are presumed to support and perpetuate patriarchy. (Enns, 1993, pp. 29–30)

Chodorow's approach reminds me a bit of the strategy adopted by a young wife I once knew who was angry that her husband always wanted to be the center of attention in social settings but could talk intelligently about only one topic, baseball. The wife's strategy was, every time he brought up baseball, to turn the conversation to a team in which her husband had no interest. Although this ploy was effective in demonstrating to their mutual friends that she was not totally dominated by his interests, it was ineffective in revealing what was really on her mind. In analogous fashion, Chodorow has refocused psychoanalysis on something other than the penis, but we have yet to learn directly from her what is really on Everywoman's mind.

Although feminist psychoanalysis may well be the theoretical model of greatest interest to feminist psychotherapists, the majority of whom were trained in the phallocentric tradition of psychodynamic psychology (Enns, 1993), even feminist psychotherapy often remains a theory *about* women. Furthermore, as Rigby-Weinberg (1986) wrote, Chodorow and other "object-relations" theorists (see Chapter 10) continue to "conceptualize women's distress as intrapsychic in origin, resulting in the same practice of "blaming the victim" of social subordination and economic discrimination" (p. 192). Nowhere in the traditional therapeutic framework are therapists and their clients invited to engage in the process of "identifying and changing the personal and cultural meanings associated with maleness and femaleness" (Kaschak, 1992, p. 211), which many would argue is the prerequisite for restoring a person's control over his or her own mind, body, and heart.

Consistent with the historical traditions of orthodox psychoanalysis, the feminist variety continues to describe women as more or less passive objects who need to be rescued by all-powerful, puzzle-solving therapist-healers:

> Psychoanalytic theory radically challenges our understanding of ourselves as whole, autonomous individuals, then seeks to reconstruct that wholeness and autonomy. It poses two solutions to this goal in its metapsychology and attempts them in its therapeutic technique and understanding. [Chodorow focuses on the mother-daughter bond as the primary psychic source in women's lives.] But the therapeutic setting can, finally, produce knowledge and self-knowledge of a relational self. And psychoanalysis can only know the self in the analytic situation; anything else is underground speculation. (Chodorow, 1989, p. 162)

Psychology's Unconscious Bias

You may recall from Chapters 12 and 15 that the talking-cure industry in the United States before the behavioral revolution (and the development of its humanistic alternative) was both fully medicalized and overwhelmingly psychodynamic. Quite naturally, then, many North American psychotherapists had the same androcentric assumptions and biases about women that the Old World talking cures had institutionalized in orthodox psychoanalysis.

This issue was not addressed by clinical researchers until fairly recently. Striking evidence of traditional therapy's bias against women was first revealed in a report published in 1970 in *The Journal of Consulting and Clinical Psychology* by Broverman, Broverman, Clarkson, Rosenkrantz, and Vogel. They asked a mixed-sex group of 79 psychiatrists, clinical psychologists, and social workers to fill in a bipolar adjective checklist representing therapeutic ideals of mental health along 122 dimensions. Examples of the attributes: "very aggressive–not very aggressive," "very emotional–not very emotional," "feelings very easily hurt–feelings not very easily hurt," "very logical–very illogical." Each clinician was asked to check one pole for each attribute.

The participants in the study were divided into three mutually exclusive groups. One group was asked to rate "a mature, healthy, socially competent male"; a second group rated "a mature, healthy, socially competent female"; and a third group rated "a mature, healthy, socially competent adult."

The results revealed striking consistency of judgment among all three classes of professional therapists. From a radical feminist–existential perspective, these "handmaidens to society" (Braginsky, 1985) had learned their lessons exceedingly well, regardless of the precise nature of their professional training.

A second interesting point is that there were no differences between the 46 male therapists and 33 female therapists. The ideology of the talking cure was safe in the hands of Papa Freud's sons—and his daughters.

For these therapists, two kinds of people exist on the planet: adults (male) and women. In other words, one can be either a mature, healthy, socially competent female or a mature, healthy, socially competent adult. But one cannot be both. One unidentified feminist concluded from these data that, from the perspective of the mental health profession in the United States, "a normal healthy woman is a crazy human being" (Hyde, 1991, p. 321). Ida Bauer had discerned that perspective for herself as far back as 1900.

Hare-Mustin (1983) concluded her review of the Dora case with the hope that "as women's half-known lives become better known, the old myths, traditional expectations, inadequate and inappropriate treatment, and conformity to sex role stereotypes will no longer be accepted as the basis for the psychotherapy of women" (p. 599). She might well have added, seconding what Carl Rogers (1973) said of his own experience in growing up in a schizoid world, that most women should be grateful they had not come into contact with a psychotherapist. A fundamental supposition of mainstream North American clinical psychology at mid-century was that "feminism, at its core, is a deep illness" (Donovan, 1985, p. 104).

A Gendered Psychology

The Broverman et al. (1970) study was the opening shot of a decade-long battle between feminist revisionists and the entrenched establishment in North American psychotherapy. Meanwhile, research relevant to the debate was coming from experimental psychology. Throughout the decade of the 1970s, gender variables became the focus of increasing numbers of empirical investigations. A new "psychology of gender" emerged at the convergence between developmental psychology's intense interest in the construction of gender and social psychology's growing interest in the construction and enforcement of gender stereotypes. Almost overnight, psychologists were required to deal with gender as a primary variable of interest in applications for research funds. Affirmative action programs demanded that women faculty be added to graduate programs in clinical and experimental psychology. Women were attracted to the discipline in record numbers, and by the early 1980s the number of Ph.D.s awarded to women in psychology exceeded the number granted to men.

It seemed as if North American psychology was about to be transformed into a discipline that could study the lives of mature, healthy, socially competent adult men and women. In 1980 Annette Brodsky, one of the leaders in the emerging women's movement in psychology, wrote:

> I think we can be encouraged by the distance we have traveled in the last decade. Certainly there are still incidents of gross sexism and ignorance of women's unique problems, and large segments of the therapist population are unwilling to admit they may have any biases, much less be educated on how to remediate them. It only seems that we are losing ground every time we see a throwback to the rampant sexism of the fifties and sixties. (p. 341)

To make her point about how far psychology had come in just a decade, Brodsky quoted a passage about women from a 1967 journal article:

> Having obtained many rights, they are dissatisfied with not having more. . . . Indeed there are definite advantages to their present status. There is also some biological evidence supporting their present status. They have not been trained for equal status and responsibility. They seem naturally adapted to their less free, less responsible, more serving role. They are in danger of losing what makes them unique and lovable if they gain equal status. (O'Donovan, 1967, quoted in Brodsky, 1980, p. 342)

Resistance From the Center of Power

By 1995, judging from the total absence of references to feminism in the tables of contents of a half dozen or more brand-new abnormal psychology textbooks sitting on my desk, the feminist revolution of psychology had either been thoroughly transformative and successful or been coopted by the conservative "counterrevolution" of the 1980s (Rigby-Weinberg, 1986). My best guess is that reality is a bit of both, with a heavy weight toward the latter.

Institutionalized psychology continues to resist considering the experience of women, however distinct from the experience of men, as equal in value and importance. The level of resistance can't be overstated. Among the newly minted psychologists we have interviewed for positions in our department over the past several years, it is painfully clear that the (white) male still firmly controls the standards for defining "normalcy." Those few people who study women appear to expend far more of their energies trying to explain why and how women differ from men than why and how populations of women differ.

Scholarship on women and women's experience has become dangerously ghettoized within women's studies programs, of incidental interest to mainstream clinical psychologists. In 1993 I did a computer search on the topic of feminist psychotherapy and found ten articles published within the last decade in North American psychology journals. Nine of the articles were published in the feminist journal *Women and Therapy*. This finding does not indicate to me that the establishment is "mainstreaming" feminist issues into the clinical psychology curriculum.

I would be willing to predict that over the next decade the American Psychological Association (APA) will invest vastly more of its resources in getting legislation passed to allow clinical psychologists to prescribe drugs than in making sure that candidates for licensure demonstrate a thorough knowledge of the latest scholarship on the psychology of women. And yet the APA supposedly committed itself to the study of women back in 1977.

The Task Force on Sex Bias in Psychotherapy

For a short, glorious while in the 1970s, the prospect of a gender-based transformation of clinical psychology looked not only possible but likely. In 1975 the APA published a report from a task force, whose members were both men and women, set up to investigate sex bias and sex-role stereotyping in the practice of psychotherapy. The report was based on a survey of women psychotherapists who belonged to APA.

The task force identified four general areas in which sex bias and sex-role stereotyping occur in psychotherapeutic interactions:

- *Fostering of traditional gender roles.* The survey addressed especially practices promoting emotional and psychological well-being based on being attractive and subservient to men. Here is how one "patient" described her experience in therapy:

I was eighteen when I started therapy for the second time. I went to a woman for two years, twice a week. She was constantly trying to get me to admit that what I really wanted was to get married and have babies and lead a "secure" life; she was very preoccupied with how I dressed, and just like my mother, would scold me if my clothes were not clean, or if I wore my hair down; told me that it would be a really good sign if I started to wear makeup and get my hair done in a beauty parlor (like her, dyed blond and sprayed); when I told her that I like to wear pants she told me that I had a confusion of sex roles. (Chesler, 1972, p. 255)

- *Therapist bias in expectations and devaluation of women.* Under this category I would include ignorance of the basic psychology and biology of women, unwillingness or disability to recognize that many women need to be given instruction and encouragement in assertive behavior, the telling of sexist jokes and the use of sexist language, and imposition of a lower standard of excellence and self-actualization in evaluating the choices that have to be made by women. The most blatant example of this form of sexist bias I ever witnessed was in a group therapy program for battered women, conducted by a Ph.D. psychologist within a public mental health center. The central focus of this group was Bible reading and prayer, directed toward "helping battered women find the spiritual strength and guidance to be better wives and mothers."
- *Sexist use of psychoanalytic concepts.* I assume this point does not require further elaboration.
- *Therapist response to women as sex objects.* This category includes the seduction of female clients. Abusive sexual behavior is approximately 20 times more likely when the therapist is male and the patient is female than in any other combination. Even though this practice has been unequivocally prohibited by the codes of ethical conduct that govern all professional psychotherapy (see, for example, APA, 1977), it occurs with discouraging regularity. In a 1975 survey, 5.6% of male psychologists admitted to the practice, and 80% of those who had done it once were repeat offenders (Holroyd & Brodsky, 1977). Various reports since then make it clear that 10% or more of all women who enter psychotherapy have to contend with sexual demands from their "therapists"; I would bet my own money that the 10% figure is a very low estimate. And it does not include the probability of sexual aggression against women who are institutionalized in mental hospitals. Such incidents are rarely punished: Between 1979 and 1985 in the state of New York, disciplinary action was taken against sexually abusive psychologists and social workers a grand total of 2 times (Cliadakis, 1989). The reader interested in a comprehensive review of this literature should read Akamatsu, 1988; Kuchan, 1989; and Schoener, 1989.

Male therapists' motives for becoming sexually involved with their female patients were the subject of an interesting report by Holroyd and Brodsky in 1977. One brave but benighted dinosaur justified having sexual intercourse with his patients on the grounds that "the use of sexual energy, up to and including actual intercourse between therapist and client, can have considerable healing effect for the client." But most of the offending therapists admitted that their motives were purely selfish. Ninety percent of these offenders described themselves as "vulnerable, needy, and lonely," and more than half (55%) claimed to be "frightened by intimacy."

What I find most telling about these reports is that 70% of the offenders "maintained a dominant role" with their patients, and 60% even said they had sex with their patients while maintaining "a father role." It is worth noting that one hears precisely the same system of self-justification when listening to the stories of career pedophiles and pederasts. Ninety-five percent of these offending therapists self-reported that they would "never do it again"; but as we have seen, 80% of sexually abusive therapists were repeat offenders.

Before leaving this point I feel compelled to share one further anecdote from a conversation I had with Brodsky in April, 1993. I called her to ask why the 1975 APA task force's report on sex bias took the weak-kneed stand on therapist/client sex that "further investigation of the ethical and therapeutic issues regarding sexual intimacy within psychotherapy" was necessary before that behavior could be prohibited by ethical standards. (Such a prohibition was finally adopted in 1977.) Brodsky's answer was that this was the one and only subject that the members of the task force were divided over and about which they could not reach consensus. The majority of the task force could not force the minority to renounce this last vestige of male sexual privilege in "the helping profession." The notion, popular in Freud's day, that the prescription for most of women's emotional problems is "Rx: Application of a healthy penis; dose to be repeated" serves the male therapist's ego and emotional needs too well to be abandoned without a struggle. I often think of this as the "myth of the magnetized member." I can assure you that the practice continues to this day.

Chemical Therapies

To the task force's list of sex bias and sex-role stereotyping in psychotherapeutic interactions I would add at least one other feminist grievance: an overreliance on medication for the treatment of women's psychological problems. Up to now, at least, psychologists have not been culpable of this abuse—only psychiatrists. In the United States, women receive 73% of all mood-altering drugs and 80% of all prescribed psychiatric drugs. By some estimates, more than half of all the women in the United States will have a psychotropic medication prescribed in response to emotional or psychological distress at least once in their lifetime.

Women who consult physicians are actually somewhat less likely than their male counterparts to receive psychotherapy for emotional problems, either with or without medication. Men, who represent roughly a third of those seeking help for emotional and psychological difficulties, actually account for 42% of visits to physicians' offices for face-to-face consultations. Only 44% of depressed women in one survey received anything but drugs for their treatment, and most of these women were not referred to a psychiatrist (or psychologist) for further evaluation (see, for example, Hyde, 1991, p. 312).

If you want a vivid depiction of the situation, pick up any commercial medical publication. In 98% of the advertisements for psychotropic medications, the physician is male; in 78% of the ads, the patient is female. See if these facts don't cause you to agree that substituting the words *wide-awake women* for *ghetto residents* in the following quotation, from a psychiatrist writing about therapeutic practices among racial and ethnic minorities, makes perfect sense:

> To many ghetto residents it seems that the liberal psychiatrist is a forceful agent of repression . . . who functions as an insidious agent of colonial forces whose primary purpose is to counsel or tranquilize the oppressed into a state of apathy and submissiveness. (Halleck, 1971, p. 98)

The Myth of Anatomy as Destiny

Traditional talking cures have at their heart the mission of helping people adjust to the world as it is. For women, this adjustment has meant learning how to adapt to our society's expectations about gender roles. (See Lerner's *The Creation of Patriarchy,* 1986, for a full historical account of this phenomenon.) Looked at in this light, the talking cure as it has been traditionally applied to women has simply been one additional "brainwashing device to keep women passive" (Donovan, 1985, p. 104).

The woman (or man, for that matter) who cannot or will not accept the necessity of bending to the social role prescribed by anatomy is often perceived to be suffering from some essential biological, moral, or social flaw. This deficit of character may be attributed to anything from masturbation to hormonal imbalance to witchcraft. For a long time, the most progressive opinion has suggested that the "flaw" is due to some early traumatic learning experience from which the "unfortunate victim" has yet to recover.

Throughout the history of thinking about madness and emotional disorder, the model of sanity and self-regulation has been the heterosexual, majority-group male. Women who are either too similar to the ideal (men) or too radically dissimilar are regarded as deeply troubled and flawed creatures in need of paternalistic supervision. The institutionalization of these differences has ranged from the absurd notion common in 1920s medical textbooks that "all women are basically hysterical by nature" to the modern equivalent, which states that it is normal for women of a certain age to behave once a month with cognitive, emotional, affective, and behavioral instability. (As a feminist colleague once remarked, it never occurs to men to say that once a month women become much more like men but that for the rest of the month they are really quite superior to men in their temperamental stability and emotional sensitivity.)

Implicit belief in the inherent superiority of masculinity and masculine models of thought, feeling, and behavior has been quite naturally extended to our thinking about the talking cure. The masculine model of psychotherapy informs us that therapeutic relationships must be "scientific," "value-free," and "cerebral" and must produce clinically dispassionate explorations of this or that "dark continent" (to quote Freud) of women's experience. In this worldview, psychotherapy is a product of deductive and positivist science—a male enclave to which an appropriately qualified woman may gain acceptance, at least in the more progressive (or law-abiding) institutions, if she is sufficiently subservient to the dominant male ethos.

What these young "men" of science learn in graduate school is "discipline," "technique," and "scientific theory," which will guide their healing ministrations to the less fortunate. Learning the labels is all-important; making "diagnoses" is an essential skill. The closer in temperament, training, and disposition a young psychology major is to a future engineer, cancer researcher, or computer programmer, the more likely that student is to be successfully trained as an "APA-approved" Ph.D. psychologist. It's a wonder we don't yet require them all to take testosterone supplements and attend interpersonal communication skills workshops featuring action-packed Arnold Schwarzenegger movies.

Mind Gynecology

If you think I am being hard on the profession, read Mary Daly's book *GYN/ECOLOGY* (1978), which makes my critique look soft-headed. Daly referred to all professional and semiprofessional talking-cure therapists as "mind gynecologists" (a term coined by Freud). She accused psychotherapists of every stripe of specializing in "killing the human spirit,"—of engaging in mind-destroying "deep boundary violation" (p. 257).

Daly compared the spread of psychoanalysis and psychotherapy to the spread of Christianity:

> The proliferation of therapies, which are like shadows, distorted reflections and resurrections of each other, [have] the effect of including everyone not only as a patient but as mini-therapist [which bears] an ominous resemblance to the proliferation of christian [*sic*] churches and sects, and to the consequent witnessing by "born-again" laity . . . [who] seduce more and more into membership. (pp. 275–276)

Daly argued that this "seduction" created in women a powerful feeling of "disease," flooding consciousness with a psychobabble which invades the ears of Everywoman, informing her in a thousand tongues of her Sickness and Need for Help. This invasion continues unchecked because it fixes women's attention in the wrong direction, fragmenting and privatizing perception of problems, which can be transcended only if understood in the context of the sexual caste system. (p. 276)

Daly rejected outright any attempt at compromise, such as feminist therapy. She believed that therapeutic language is fatally contaminated, that dependency is too integrated into the therapeutic process, that all therapy relegates the "Self [to] becom[ing] a spectator of her own frozen, caricatured history . . . filed away, misfiled, in file-cabinets with inaccurate categories" (p. 283). "Only Journeying breaks the cycle," Daly declared, and "in journeying/process, therapy is not the priority" (p. 287).

Journeying, as feminist therapists use the term, is a process of self-discovery and self-empowerment. It "begins with a woman telling her own story" (Kaschak, 1992, p. 216) and "returning her own vision to each woman. . . . Seeing is believing and knowing for oneself, often for the first time. [It] involves naming not just the unnamed but the unnameable, speaking not just for the unspoken but for the unspeakable" (p. 225).

What is essential, from a feminist perspective, is to depathologize women's experience, which is often the opposite of what goes on in traditional psychotherapy:

Women who have been seduced, brow-beaten, and mind-raped by individual therapists or by gangs of mini-therapists in marathon encounter sessions should reconsider the meaning of "normality" in such a setting. A clue is to be found in the fact that whereas only a few decades ago anyone was stigmatized who was discovered going to a therapist, today the stigma is inflicted on any woman who does *not* go to a therapist. Any institution which could so rapidly reverse its status, gaining power and prestige in the most "advanced" nation of a patriarchal planet, clearly must be serving the interests of patriarchy. (Daly, 1978, p. 287)

A Feminist Talking Cure

Now I can hear a thoughtful reader saying, "Just hold on there for one second. I haven't struggled through 18 chapters of this book only to be told that the whole history of the talking cure is part of an antifemale, penis-worshiping plot!" You are certainly entitled to hold that opinion if you have come with me this far. But I'm not sure what sort of ammunition I can give you to refute what Daly was saying. Back in the 1970s, we thought we could develop a set of psychotherapeutic principles consistent with feminist values, but that assumption has since been questioned.

Starting Point: Nonsexist Psychotherapy

In 1977 Edna Rawlings and Dianne Carter published *Psychotherapy for Women,* a first attempt to sort out some of the issues raised in this chapter. Rawlings and Carter found Daly to be an articulate champion. They began by agreeing with Daly that "the values structure and goals of sexist therapy are destructive to women [and] that clients in therapy move closer to the values of their therapists." Sexist therapy, therefore, does destroy the feminist self and replaces it with a definition of self that is "demeaning, powerless, and negatively valued" (p. 49). But they were concerned, as well they might be, that substituting one ideology (feminism) for another (even if that be sexism and patriarchy) really doesn't address the issue of therapists' dehumanizing control over the values and worldviews of their clients and patients.

Assumptions of Nonsexist Psychotherapy. Rawlings and Carter therefore proposed some "values or assumptions" for a nonideological *nonsexist psychotherapy* (1977, p. 52):

- Therapists are aware of their own values and take active measures to ensure that they remain aware of the pervasiveness of sexual values and the ways in which these unconscious ideologies have shaped the values and expectations of both the client and the therapist. This is, essentially, a commitment to ongoing self-examination to make sure that one's awareness of the prevalence of sexist thinking is not diminished over time.
- Sex-role behavior prescriptions are not used in the process of helping clients determine "what they want for and from themselves." This point is explicitly applied to working with clients whose sexual orientation is homosexual.
- Sex-role nonconformity is not labeled as pathological. Therapists encourage people "to be able to work out behavioral styles and assignment of tasks which gives . . . them satisfaction."
- "Marriage is not regarded as any better an outcome of therapy for a female than for a male."
- "Females are expected to be as autonomous and assertive as males; males are expected to be as expressive and tender as females."
- "Theories of behaviors based on anatomical differences are rejected."

These principles are radical, revolutionary, and contrary to accepted practice, but they are also quite sensible. I have yet to encounter anyone who could seriously challenge any but the last one. Even there, in my experience, the overgeneralizations that men have greater upper-body strength than women do and that women have greater pain tolerance than men do are rarely, if ever, involved in perpetuating emotional or psychological distress.

A somewhat larger problem arises, however, in light of the current literature on psychological sex differences across a variety of dimensions. The prescription for nonsexist therapy offered by Rawlings and Carter perhaps ought to be amended to take into account sex differences in moral reasoning (Gilligan, 1982); differences in the relative importance men and women attach to the values of communion and agency (Bakan, 1966); and psychological differences in perceptual, attributional, and expressive styles, developmental sequences, and attitudes toward issues such as love and procreation. Ignoring these differences is not nonsexist; it is ignorant.

Cultural Values. I find an additional difficulty in such an open-ended, albeit nonsexist, approach to therapy. I frequently detect in myself and among my liberal friends, for example, a tendency to attach the label *humanistic* to all the values we judge to be virtuous and righteous but the label *sexist* (or patriarchal) to those values with which we most seriously disagree. This tendency can cause enormous problems when trying to communicate with people from different ethnic groups and nationalities.

If I am talking about teen pregnancy rates among African Americans in U.S. ghettos or alcoholism rates among Native Americans on reservations or the attitudes of Japanese women toward "career versus the role of mother," I find that my commitment to an ideological dichotomy between humanistic, nonsexist values and patriarchal sexism may prevent me from getting beyond, and may actually blind me to, my equally biasing middle-class and Eurocentric values. I am, moreover, quite sure that I bring this blindness with me into the counseling situation. Therefore, being committed to a nonsexist ideology would rarely make me a better therapist than anyone else, especially if that other person had spent time studying the culture of the ghetto teenager, life on the reservation, or the realities of life in contemporary Japan.

I was therefore somewhat relieved to read that Rawlings no longer feels she can wholeheartedly endorse nonsexist therapy: "In spite of my earlier endorsement of nonsexist therapy, I would not take that position today" (1993, p. 90). However, Rawlings's reasons for rejecting her earlier position are clearly more in accord with the arguments put forward by Daly than with the more culturally based objections I have just raised:

> The sexism in so-called nonsexist brands of psychotherapy may be less blatant, but any approach to psychotherapy that conceptualizes women's social problems as personal pathology and promotes "cures" for women's distress primarily through individual personal change strengthens the patriarchal status quo. (p. 90)

Empowerment for Social Change

It is appropriate at this point to turn our attention to the more fundamentally radical concept of *feminist psychotherapy*. In 1977, after introducing the values and assumptions behind nonsexist therapy, Rawlings and Carter set forth some ideas for a feminist transformation of the talking cure. They emphasized that such an ideological approach should be undertaken only under carefully delineated conditions—not, for example, with "traditional female clients for whom the tenets of feminism are threatening" (pp. 50–51) but primarily with those clients "who are dissatisfied with the constriction of the culturally defined role for women and are seeking alternatives" (p. 51). They also suggested that these principles could be used for conducting support groups, teaching classes in women's studies, writing books, and communicating with other therapists. They observed, in addition, that therapists might elect to introduce elements of feminist therapy into their work with relatively traditional women clients "as [their] consciousness develops" during the course of nonsexist therapy.

Rawlings and Carter argued that feminist psychotherapy incorporates the principles of nonsexist therapy. But it then extends to notions of social protest and progressive social change. Their analysis is essentially a manifesto of feminist thinking, applied to the lives of the individual therapists and clients in the process of psychotherapy.

Gilbert (1980) seems to have been the last person to publish a serious critique of the ideas that Rawlings and Carter put forward in 1977. Gilbert found two overriding principles in feminist psychotherapy that distinguish it from both traditional and nonsexist approaches to psychotherapy. In the discussion that follows, I have included under each point a diverse collection of perspectives from the literature of feminist therapy.

The Personal Is Political. The first of Gilbert's principles for feminist psychotherapy: That which oppresses and limits you is part of the "system" and thus must be changed. This point has four components:

- You have to learn to distinguish between the internal and the external. You have been socialized to believe many things about yourself and your world that you know to be untrue. You must validate this knowledge within yourself and not let it go. Don't accept a psychological explanation for life's difficulties when the more profound answer can be found in politics, economics, and sociology. This point speaks to the "dual consciousness" that Brown and Gilligan (1992) and many others have recognized in the lives of women and girls, the "it" in "the problem with no name," which Betty Friedan described in *The Feminine Mystique* in 1963. The realities of modern life create tremendous stressors on women's bodies and psyches. However, any woman who begins to believe that the stress she is experiencing is being caused by her mind is confusing cause and effect. The fact is that the sources of greatest concern for most women are practical and largely political. These include, in approximate order of importance in the experience of healthy women who are "making it," physical health, management of personal time, career success, social relations, love relations, and parent/child relations (from both directions).
- Female experience can be validated through therapy; in therapy you can come to see and accept that you are not crazy. But your world may be. The "three C's"

of mental health are *commitment* to a set of goals, values, and ideals that are distinctly yours; *control* over your own body, life situation, and choices; and *challenge* to make a difference, set an example, juggle diverse roles, and take charge of your own life. Effective therapy should help you find and hold onto all three C's.

- Therapy is about exploring attitudes and values. Both parties to the therapy must explore and proclaim their attitudes and values concerning women and confront the discrepancies that are thus revealed. Most important to the therapy are the values and attitudes that control your private system for gaining and maintaining self-esteem.

- The goal of therapy is change rather than adjustment. Come to therapy prepared to take charge of your life. Learn how to become more assertive, independent, self-responsible, and effective; accept responsibility for taking charge of yourself.

The Therapist/Client Relationship Is Egalitarian. This second principle means that the therapist is a person, just like you. Take the therapeutic couch to the secondhand store. No, the doctor will not write a prescription for raising your children, managing your sex life, or resolving the conflict between the two.

Gilbert offered a number of subpoints under this second principle, but I want to emphasize two. First is that the therapist becomes a real, living person to the client, a fellow human being looking for the answers to life's dilemmas. (See, for example, Greenspan, 1986, for a thoughtful analysis of how the feminist therapist's self-disclosure is used to further clients' personal growth.) Furthermore, as Albert Ellis (Chapter 14) said, every client needs to come to the realization that all human beings, even feminist therapists, from time to time think and act like "fallible f—— -up human beings—just like everyone else." Lerman, in a paper presented at the APA convention in 1974, said this about therapist/patient relationships:

> The therapist by being who she is can serve as a model for the kind of woman who knows herself and her psychological boundaries, who relates in a human female way and can express her own gentleness along with her own definitiveness. Not least, she can share with the client in a very important way about what it means to be a woman in this society. There is a potential bond arising out of a communality of experiences. (pp. 8–9)

Isn't that what Ellis and I just said? Well, actually, no. We didn't make any assumptions about the therapist's gender. But Lerman is not necessarily being careless with pronouns. Some fundamental issues within the ideology of feminist psychotherapy raise the question of whether men can ever participate in feminist therapy either as clients or as therapists.

Gilbert's second subpoint about the egalitarian relationship between therapist and client is that "the process of assuming power in one's life may bring up feelings of anger, and dealing with anger is essential to feminist therapy" (1980, p. 249). This point is derived from Gestalt therapy (Chapter 16), in much the same way that the first subpoint was derived from rational emotive behavior therapy (see Chapter 14).

In Gestalt therapy, what is important is that you are feeling something and that you have the right, freedom, opportunity, and maybe even obligation to express yourself. These objectives are, in essence, at the heart of becoming more assertive. In feminist therapy you are in a room with a person who wants you to discover the power in yourself and wants you to learn to express yourself without worrying about the established order. Ultimately, feminist therapy concerns itself with the client's personal empowerment—personal, political, economic, and social self-assertion and self-expression (see Worell & Remer, 1992).

As Howard (1986), among others, has outlined, feminist therapy addresses therapeutic issues embedded in the real world—such as employment, sexual assault, sexual orientation, eating disorders, incest, rape, abuse, battering, and the stress associated with being a person of color. Feminist therapy is perhaps the only place in psychology where one will find issues related to physical appearance and women's control over their own bodies (Kaschak, 1992). It is one of the few approaches to therapy that recognizes and addresses the special problems confronted by lesbians.

Feminist therapy has its roots less in the mother-blaming world of clinical training (Rigby-Weinberg, 1986) than in the consciousness-raising groups of the early 1970s. In fact, some feminist therapists have predicted that consciousness-raising groups might one day replace psychotherapy. Doesn't that notion take us back— back to the 1970s and back to the mesmerists magnetizing trees in villages to provide free therapy for all.

Feminist Psychotherapists as an Endangered Species

As I write this book, it is unclear whether something clearly identified as "feminist psychotherapy" really exists as an alternative to traditional forms of psychotherapy. Note, for example, the dearth of "theory" in this chapter. The closest one could come to a solid theory to support feminist psychotherapy is probably the work of Alfred Adler (see Chapter 8), which has indeed been explored for its implications for feminist psychotherapy by Rigby-Weinberg (1986).

As far as I can tell from reviewing the mainstream psychological literature, the feminist psychotherapy "movement" lost its momentum sometime in the mid-1980s. For example, in Freedheim's massive *History of Psychotherapy,* published in 1992 by the American Psychological Association, the word *feminist* is mentioned in the index only nine times—and then always in conjunction with some other mainstream therapeutic modality, such as "feminist thought in family therapy." Feminist psychotherapy, if it is mentioned at all these days, is often considered one among several minor competing "theoretical orientations" that influence contemporary psychology (Norcross & Freedheim, 1992, p. 885; see also Enns, 1993). In Freedheim's history, Freud gets 37 listings in the index (and a great many pages), but Edna Rawlings gets none, and Dianne Carter is mentioned only as her work contributes to family systems theory.

Worell and Remer's *Feminist Perspectives in Psychotherapy,* also published in 1992, offers somewhat more cause for optimism about feminist psychotherapy. But even this book is more about "applying feminist principles to the lives of other women" (p. xvii) than about presenting a unified, coherent, comprehensive model for therapeutic change.

Although thousands of feminists call themselves therapists, the chances are that you won't be able to find a "feminist therapist" when and if you need one. Alas, most clinical training in North America is still based on "a model for healthy development [which] is still a male model leaving little girls living with wounds and a life of yearning" (Bloom et al, 1982, p. 10). In the eyes of many feminists the problem with mainstream clinical psychology is that it remains predicated on the *essentialist* assumption that "anatomy is destiny" and the *psychodynamic* assumption that the root of unhappiness is within the psyche. If you hold to the position that no therapist who holds an essentialist intrapsychic view of psychopathology can really be called a feminist psychotherapist, you might never meet a therapist who would qualify. So, if you meet someone who claims to be a "feminist therapist," my advice is to look for a hyphen. There is a world of difference between a feminist therapist and a feminist-therapist.

Feminist Therapy as a Value System

Ultimately, as Rigby-Weinberg (1986) explained, *feminist psychotherapy* is a description of a therapist's value system. No set of psychological theories or therapeutic techniques is uniquely "feminist." But there are some underground, subversive, happy-go-lucky-anarchist feminist therapists lurking about out there. If you are very lucky, you might find one who is willing to begin your free, no-obligation get-acquainted session by talking about her (or his, but not necessarily your) basic assumptions, values, and attitudes, especially as those relate to the issues that have brought you to the threshold of therapy.

Once you have begun your discussions with such a person, you should hear a speech that goes something like this: "My view of the reason that people come to talk with me is that they have grown deeply discouraged with the progress they are making with their lives. They probably think of themselves as 'sick,' but my job is to show them that the only sick thing about them is that they have internalized and swallowed whole a set of attitudes, values, and assumptions about life that don't fit them or their circumstances very well. What I offer these people in addition to genuine care and concern and an absolute guarantee of professional integrity is a promise that I will do everything in my power to respect and to try to understand their perceptions of reality—both inside and outside their own skin. My goal is always to try to establish egalitarian relationships with the people who come to me for help with the problems they are having in being able to lead their lives with intentionality, dignity, and authority. Where I differ with them I will let them know, and I will give them the reasons for the views I have. From my perspective, we are all probably at least a little crazy, and some of that craziness is what makes each of us unique and interesting. But it is also the case that some of our craziness comes from the world trying to force us to live and be in ways that are not authentic to us. The real question is whether we feel that we exercise sufficient control over our own life while engaged in the complicated process of being and becoming a fully actualized human. In my experience, what this means is that we all need to work more diligently on retaining a sense of our own identity as a member of a very confusing and often difficult society. If you need support, guidance, and encouragement to take charge of your own life, to make the changes that you feel you need to make, while at the same time keeping all those balls in the air that we all seem to be juggling, I think you have come to the right place."

CHAPTER 19

The Metaphysics of the Talking Cure

Soliloquy

Rollo May once wrote that consciousness is "the experience of the self acting from its center." Whatever truth we can know about our self can only be found at the center of being.

> We dance round in a ring and suppose,
> But the Secret sits in the middle and knows.
> (Frost, 1967, p. 495)*

Unfortunately, we do not dwell at the center of our being. We live in the world at a time when the challenge to discover the truth at the center has largely fallen to psychology.

Where does the future of this psychology lie? North American psychology has always been focused on the metaphysics of everyday life, and there has always been a utopian feel to it. But in its zeal to perfect the human condition, psychology has often been perceived as a handmaiden to the existing social order, the "partially mad" social, political, and cultural status quo. The psychotherapist's ultimate responsibility, however, is to awaken the client's consciousness of the self. The ultimate expression of this self, I will argue in this chapter, is in "having the world truthfully," using all the powers of being (love and will, biology and intellect, solitude and passion) to experience the world and the self fully, free from distortion and repression. Psychotherapy in this context becomes the psychology of liberation and empowerment.

---

*"The Secret Sits" from *The Poetry of Robert Frost,* edited by Edward Connery Lathem. Copyright © 1942 by Robert Frost. Copyright © 1970 by Lesley Frost Ballantine. Copyright © 1969 by Henry Holt and Co., Inc. Reprinted by permission of Henry Holt and Co., Inc.

As conceived by feminist psychotherapists, empowerment gives every client a renewed sense of trust in her or his own powers of perception, reason, and action. Thus empowered, each of us can come to know ourself and the world more truthfully and thus be more truly free. The result is a sort of intellectual and metaphysical enlightenment. In short, North American psychology has come full circle, returning to the metaphysics and moral philosophy championed by its founder, William James.

The Sin of Oversimplification

The first voice speaks:

> Freedom not only requires us to bear responsibility for our life choices but also posits that change requires an act of will. Though *will* is a concept therapists seldom use explicitly, we nonetheless devote much effort to influencing a patient's will. We endlessly clarify and interpret, assuming (and it is a secular leap of faith, lacking convincing empirical support) that understanding will invariably beget change. When years of interpretation have failed to generate change, we may begin to make direct appeals to will: "Effort, too, is needed. You have to try, you know. There's a time for thinking and analyzing. But there's also a time for action." And when direct exhortation fails, the therapist is reduced . . . to employing any known means by which one person can influence another. Thus I may advise, argue, badger, cajole, goad, implore, or simply endure, hoping that the patient's neurotic world view will crumble away from sheer fatigue. (Yalom, 1989, p. 9)

The second voice speaks:

> First, psychologists violate the public good and the trust placed in them by the public at large. Second, they do a disservice to their presumptive beneficiaries by providing inappropriate solutions to misconstrued problems. If psychologists continue to encourage society to avoid confronting its real problems, then meaningful solutions and necessary reforms cannot occur. Finally, by serving as handmaidens to the social order, psychologists degrade their profession and destroy all that it has the potential to become. (Braginsky, 1985, p. 890)

A third voice speaks:

> The counseling service? Oh sure, I've heard of it. But I've never gone there, of course. I prefer to solve my own problems. But, you know, I suppose I'd go there if I ever completely lost my mind. (student response to interview on campus perceptions of the student counseling service)

A Plea of Not Guilty

Talking cures, *Talking Cures*—a stroke of genius, self-justifying psychobabble, or a reasonable but blunt instrument? How do I plead? I'll admit that I am often guilty as charged on the "handmaiden" count mentioned by Braginsky. But I am sure psychotherapists don't oversimplify the human condition (as Rollo May charged—*Nimis simplicando*—in the guise of Saint Peter) any more than physicians, preachers, or politicians do. And where else could that college kid get help if he ever completely lost his mind?

So I'll enter a plea of not guilty, and my defense will be simple. I will look at the computers of the "technopsychologists" and their postmodern, poststructuralist, deconstructed models of analysis and their "wet mind" metaphors of cognitive neuroscience, and I will say: "Let she who is without insult to the human soul cast the first aspersion. I rest my case."

Some expect the impossible of psychology. They ask not just for a philosophy but for a complete technology as well. Perhaps B. F. Skinner was the only honest psychologist introduced in this whole book. He never claimed he could read the human mind or heart. Like a true tinkerer, he offered us "helpful hints" to make our lives more efficient and less chaotic. He didn't presume to speak to the issue of what we would do with the time saved or what we might accomplish with the increase in order and emotional stability he gave us. Skinner simply gave us some ways to gain a greater sense of control, a greater "feeling of freedom," as he put it, in a world where we know and control very little and experience very little freedom.

We can agree, perhaps, that the great leap forward the talking cure made when it came to North America changed the focus of our thinking away from the past and toward the future. With naive optimism embedded in New World idealism, North American psychotherapists were able to express their faith in that "bright and shining city on a hill" where human beings could grow to perfection and become everything that they had the potential to become.

Psychotherapists have largely turned away from the pessimistic biological determinism of Sigmund Freud's assertion that "anatomy is destiny." They accepted the wisdom of nature, which teaches that even on a cold day in April, everything is still possible; when the conditions become just right, all of creation will bloom. Life itself lacks only the inspiration of the warm days of summer to come to fruition. As Carl Rogers helped us to see, although we may have temporarily lost the skills, we have not lost the fundamental capacity to exercise "a sensitive ability to hear, a deep satisfaction in being heard; an ability to be more real, which in turn brings forth more realness from others; and consequently a greater freedom to give and receive love" (1980, p. 26). Love can make us whole, free us from the tyranny of the past.

In North America, we accept a definition of psychology that perceives human beings in terms of wholeness, purpose, connection, and the future. We accept as an article of faith that:

the mentally healthy person is the productive and unalienated person; the person who related himself to the world lovingly, and who uses his reason to grasp reality objectively; who experiences himself as a unique individual entity, and at the same time feels one with his fellow man; who is not subject to irrational authority, and accepts willingly the rational authority of conscience and reason; who is in the process of being born as long as he is alive, and considers the gift of life the most precious chance he has. (Fromm, 1955, p. 241)

Nevertheless, we Americans have a dreadful problem when it comes to practicing these truths and living these ideals. We distinctly dislike facing realities that are unpleasant. We want to ignore our talking cures' disregard for the social, cultural, economic, political, and personal realities of sexism, racism, homophobia—and all the other varieties of human ignorance, hate, and indifference. As Rogers understood, psychotherapists are clearly not immune to this problem:

Particularly striking [in the analysis of the content of therapeutic sessions] was the almost common observation that the client-centered process of therapy somehow avoided the expected and usual patient expressions of negative, hostile, or aggressive feelings. The implicit suggestion is clear that the client-centered therapist for some reason seemed less open to receiving negative, hostile or aggressive feelings. Is it that the therapists have little respect for, or understanding of their own negative, hostile or aggressive feelings and are thus unable to adequately perceive those feelings in the patient? (quoted in May, 1967, p. 18)

Individualism: A False Refuge?

What we seem to substitute for truth telling in these "negative" situations is a therapeutic call for individualism. This appeal to individualism is perhaps most clearly heard in the writings of existential psychotherapists. May, for example, pointed to the therapeutic significance of individual consciousness, defining it as "the experience of the self acting from its center" (1967, p. 177). This form of consciousness defines the personal as primary—and from the perspective of both Marxism and people outside our culture, may well support the view that our culture fosters personal selfishness and social alienation. Even more importantly, perhaps, an outside observer may conclude that as psychotherapists we Americans train ourselves and our clients to disregard the social, economic, and political realities of oppression in order to focus on the possibilities for transcendence that exist within the self.

Many North American psychotherapists seem to believe that human beings can get away with using "self-actualization" as a sophisticated form of psychological denial. American psychology seems to say: "Never mind what happened to you. Don't pay any attention to what is happening to the rest. Be or do or give your personal best, and you can become anything you choose to be." If you are willing to accept a little technical help from John Watson (his "own specified world to bring [you] up in"), perhaps there are no practical limits to your becoming whatever you will.

Some critics claim that the talking cure makes a state religion out of isolated, selfish individualism:

> The therapeutic self . . . is defined by its own wants and satisfactions, coordinated by cost-benefit calculation. Its social virtues are largely limited to empathic communication, truth-telling, and equitable negotiation. . . . Therapy helps us translate our experience of this society into personal meanings, and then back into social action. In its quest to reunify the self, the therapeutic attitude distances us from social roles, relationships, and practices; and from their attendant measures of authority, duty, and virtue. Yet therapy itself is a tightly regulated and carefully balanced relationship. It etches the social contract into our intimacy. It echoes in our hearts the "go along to get along" idea of procedurally regulated cooperation with others for the sake of the utilities with which to purchase our private pleasures. (Bellah, Sullivan, Swindler, & Tipton, 1985, p. 127)

I spent more than half my professional life believing that the ultimate goal of psychotherapy is to help clients overcome, remove, and resolve their emotional and psychological impediments to "becoming." I believed that helping them establish and recognize basic competencies in their lives would make them more likely to discover their "authentic" selves. I accepted on faith the idea that any psychotherapy that helps people more competently be the unique individuals they are would lead them to know and accept who they are. And that knowledge would free them from whatever forces were keeping them from becoming self-actualized in everyday life. My talking cure, I once insisted, is no handmaiden to society; it is a proclaimer and a celebrator of the courageous, authentic self.

Of what conceivable value are talking cures if they don't lead to a more direct, immediate, and vital experience of an autonomous, authentic self? In North American humanism, it is not enough to define mental health in terms of the absence of mental illness:

> From the standpoint of normative humanism we must arrive at a different concept of mental health; the very person who is considered healthy in the categories of an alienated world, from the humanistic standpoint appears as the sickest one—although not in terms of individual sickness, but of the socially patterned defect. Mental health, in the humanistic sense, is characterized by the ability to love and to create, by the emergence from the incestuous ties to family and nature, by a sense of identity based on one's experience of self as the subject and object of one's own powers, by the grasp of reality inside and outside of ourselves, that is by the development of objectivity and reason. The aim of life is to live it intensely, to be fully born, to be fully awake. To emerge from the ideas of infantile grandiosity into the conviction of one's real though limited strength;

to be able to accept the paradox that every one of us is the most important thing there is in the universe—and at the same time not more important than a blade of grass. To be able to love life, and yet to accept death without terror; to tolerate uncertainty about the most important questions with which life confronts us—and yet to have faith in our thought and feeling, inasmuch as they are truly ours. To be able to be alone, and at the same time one with a loved person, with every brother on this earth, with all that is alive; to follow the voice of our conscience, the voice that calls us to ourselves, yet not to indulge in self hate when the voice of conscience was not loud enough to be heard and followed. The mentally healthy person is the person who lives by love, reason, and faith, who respects life, his own and that of his fellow man. (Fromm, 1955, p. 180)

Over the past decade or so, however, I have begun to recognize an ironic contradiction in my carefully constructed worldview. A fundamental doubt began to develop during my first extended stay in Japan. There I began to question the value of my passionate commitment to rugged individualism—and to question whether North American psychology was all the wonderful things I held it to be.

An Expatriate's Tale

For a time my family and I lived in the center of Tokyo. We were not Japanese, and thus for all practical purposes we were invisible. It was the rugged individualist's ultimate test. Our 14 million neighbors didn't even believe in individualism—I mean they believed that it existed, but they believed it was a sort of cultural pathology, the product of bad mothering. They thought that complete individuals could have no historical or emotional center. For them, individualism was isolation, and isolation was the central pathology of selfishness. The Japanese cannot imagine anything much sadder than growing up selfish.

We traveled to a town in the mountains in western Japan so small that its name does not appear on any national maps. It is the Lake Woebegone of Shimane Prefecture—"the little town that time forgot and the ages can't improve." We had a wonderful stay, made great friends, ate mountains of wonderful food, drank gallons of locally made sake, and took restorative moonlit baths in outdoor thermal pools.

One day, however, we noticed something very peculiar about this magical little place so far off the beaten track. Every single car in the town was white. Every single car on every new and used car lot was white. Even the pickup trucks were all white. We asked our hosts why. I knew that if I gave way to my fantasy of moving there, the first thing I would do would be to buy a screaming red Toyota to establish my individualism. These Japanese were just too conformist for my tastes. Our host, Mr. Ashida, chuckled at my question. He imagined that in the United States everyone tried very hard to have a car that was different from everyone else's. Yes, everyone owning a white car did make figuring out which car was yours in the supermarket parking lot a bit of a challenge. "But Bankart-sensei," he said, "we Japanese people like to enjoy our privacy. When we all drive white cars, nobody knows the private business of anyone else."

Privacy! How can the citizenry of a country like Japan, who feel sorry for people who live with the stigma of individualism, value privacy? Privacy was something that I had never once discussed with any of my clients or patients.

The *Honne* of the Ashida Family. These people so value privacy that they refuse to give any outward sign of their identity through the color of their automobile, the style of their clothing, or even the way they wear their hair. Yet over the course of a few days, the Ashida family extracted from me and my family the most intimate details of our "private" life. Imagine a dinner party where your host asks how much you weigh. Why do you wear a beard? What is your "plan" for your children? Do the people you work with respect you?

What was happening, I now realize, was that we were being accepted "inside"; we were becoming part of the *honne,* the inside world, of the Ashida family. They were being a little rude in their questions, but time was short and we had no go-betweens to fill them in on who we were and what we were really all about. For the first time, we were experiencing intimacy with a Japanese family. The Ashidas were about to become our son's "host family" for several weeks, and the family had decided to extend their kinship to his parents as well.

It was an exhilarating experience to have finally "cracked" Japanese society (even at the cost of finding out that with just a bit more effort around the rice pot I could have qualified, in size at least, as a sumo wrestler), but it was also deeply puzzling. Everywhere we went in Japan, and especially in our Tokyo neighborhood, we were living the ideal of North American individualism. Actually, we had no choice. We looked different, we talked and even laughed different, we dressed different, our roles within our family were radically different, and even the things we bought in the grocery store were different. We were certainly not conforming to any known norms of Japanese society. Everything about us was a product of our difference. We were a celebration of American individualism, like it or not.

What we learned from being adopted by the Ashida family was that in the rest of Japan, as perhaps in most of the rest of the world, we were also *separate.* By drawing us in to the *honne* of their family (if only to a degree), the Ashidas permitted us to comprehend how alone and separate we were everywhere else. Living in someone else's culture had given us the opportunity to distinguish among different aspects of our ontology: In Japan we could experience the ultimate flowering of our individualism, the ultimate loss of our privacy (we were forever on display in Japan), and now, in stark relief, the feeling of acceptance and belonging within a tight-knit family.

I gradually began to realize that if I were to move to this magical place, my first act would be to sell the bright red, flashy car that we in fact do own, in favor of buying a nice white sedan just like everyone else's. I would want to protect my privacy almost as much as I would want to submerge my individualism. I would fear that everyone in the village would criticize my friends the Ashidas for encouraging a "selfish" foreigner to intrude on the network of their community. Only by abandoning my American individualism would my new friends come to know and accept the *honne* of who I really am and who I aspire to become, as an individual.

Three Lessons Learned Abroad. I returned home to the United States inspired to try to understand the conundrum that our Japanese sojourn had left me with. I was impressed by the fact that Fromm's definition of mental health is as applicable in a small town in Japan as it is in New York or Chicago or Tokyo,—or Montezuma, Indiana:

> Mental health . . . is characterized by the ability to love and to create, by the emergence from the incestuous ties to family and nature, by a sense of identity based on one's experience of self as the subject and object of one's own powers, by the grasp of reality inside and outside of ourselves, that is by the development of objectivity and reason. (1955, p. 180)

I was also impressed by my Japanese colleagues' reports that of all the North American psychotherapies, only Rogers's seemed to work well and gain acceptance in Japan. Japanese therapists, too, seemed to believe that "a sensitive ability to hear, a deep satisfaction in being heard; an ability to be more real, which in turn brings forth more realness from others; and consequently a greater freedom to give and receive love" is essential to the therapeutic process.

The third thing that impressed me was that I had heard all this before—and often. But where? Who had challenged most consistently my old, traditional thinking about "will" and "ego autonomy" and "individualism"? It was a person who had written:

> I am constantly frustrated at finding that for the most part psychological theory is a theory of men and not women. I do not find my own experiences recognized, much less validated or explained in the traditional literature. I find that what has been a quest to understand human beings has been a self-examination by men, and to borrow a term from Freud, a narcissistic examination at that. This, I believe, is a tragedy for at least half the human race whose psyches remain invisible; enshrined by men as the "other" half, the unwhole half, the half without a penis. (Bankart, 1978)

It was a feminist. It was my partner and co-therapist, my colleague from graduate school, and my companion at countless faculty dinner parties. It was Brenda Bankart, who had repeatedly pointed me toward the literature of the psychology of women. But at that point I hadn't figured out how to make that literature part of my innermost therapeutic dialogue.

Research on Communal College Men

We were doing some longitudinal research on male adolescent development patterns at the time. We had reported several distinctive patterns of emergent masculine agency in the lives of successful high school men (B. M. Bankart, C. P. Bankart, & Franklin, 1988). But some men didn't fit the pattern. Some young men seemed indifferent to being viewed as agentic, masterful operators. They seemed to have different values. We were curious about the nature of this difference.

Mark Vincent and I conducted a study of male college freshmen to investigate how the self-perceptions and worldviews of young men high in "instrumental agency" differed from those of an identical group of young men who were high on the personality dimension of "communion" (C. P. Bankart & Vincent, 1988). Bakan (1966) defined these concepts as follows:

> I have adopted the terms "agency" and "communion" to characterize two fundamental modalities in the existence of living forms, agency for the existence of the organism as an individual, and communion for the participation of the individual in some larger organism of which the individual is a part. Agency manifests itself in self-protection, self-assertion, and self-expansion; communion manifests itself in the sense of being at one with other organisms. . . . Agency manifests itself in . . . the urge to master; communion in non-contractual cooperation. (pp. 13–14)

The results of our study were interesting in a number of ways. First, we were among the first to publish data showing that communion is not the exclusive preserve of women; significant numbers of men in our sample viewed the world through "communal" lenses. The assumption that only women are communal, common in the literature of gender-based personality differences, is wrong. Any effort to write about men in purely agentic terms will fail to describe a significant minority of young men in the United States. The data also suggested that women do not necessarily enjoy a "moral superiority" to men, if communalism is assumed to be one of the things that make women superior (a common formulation in what Pollitt, 1992, has called "difference feminism").

Our data also showed that communal men describe themselves in very different terms than do agentic men. Communal men endorse such self-descriptions as *loyal, sensitive, sincere, sympathetic, caring, understanding, thoughtful, gentle, compassionate,* and *warm.* Agentic men prefer to describe themselves with words like *aggressive, dominant, determined, persuasive, skilled at leading others, self-reliant, industrious, ambitious, persistent,* and *competitive.* However, the differences between the men within each group far outweighed the differences between the two groups in objective measures related to accomplishment, success, and achievement motive.

The most puzzling difference to emerge between the communal and agentic young men was in the only demographic difference we could find between the groups. Communal youngsters came from rural communities and small towns, and agentic youngsters came from urban and suburban communities. Why these differences in background were so clearly discriminative in the developing personalities of these men remains a bit of a mystery.

The Disappearing Sample

An even greater mystery was that when we went back to our sample a few weeks later to conduct some further research, the communal students had disappeared. When we then went back to collect some followup data from some of our communal subjects, we discovered that several of them had left our college and that a large proportion of the rest had become clients of the counseling service. We tried to locate a fresh batch of communal subjects at the end of the school year, but we couldn't find any.

It appears that communal young men, at our college anyway, go underground within a few weeks of coming on campus. They come to feel that they don't "fit" in the highly competitive and individualistic classrooms, fraternities, and dormitories on our campus.

I discovered one of our original communal subjects living all alone in a small, barely furnished apartment off campus; he'd been there since Christmas vacation. He was dropping his pre-med studies, in which he had been very successful, in favor of a major in poetry and philosophy. He told me that his former fraternity brothers said he couldn't "hack it." But his interpretation was that the cost to his personhood in the pre-med classes and in the fraternity had been too high. He felt himself becoming someone he didn't want to become; he felt in danger of losing touch with the part of himself most central to his identity as a human being. His words were almost identical to the words that Brenda had used in talking about Sigmund Freud. He found that in science classrooms and at fraternity gatherings he too could not "find my own experiences recognized, much less validated or explained." He too felt that he was "other," "invisible," and "unwhole." For a communal person, this sort of emotional and psychic exile was almost unbearably painful and alienating.

As I went through my records, comparing counseling lists with the sign-up sheets from our study, I saw the pattern recurring time and time again. The instrumental, agentic, individualistic students, who were not necessarily any better or brighter, were generally "successful" in the college community. The more sensitive, connected, emotionally aware, communal students were experiencing crisis after crisis as their invisible minority status brought them to the margins of the community's ideals.

The Ideal of Normalcy: Erich Fromm Revisited

Apart from the chilling consequences this form of self-selection has on the ranks of physicians (or psychotherapists, for that matter), it seems extraordinarily important to me as a practitioner of the talking cure. I had tried earlier to make sense of what I observed and experienced in Japan with the literature of the psychology of women and to assimilate it all into a sort of meta-analysis of the beliefs and values that shaped who and what I was as a therapist. The cornerstone of my analysis was an assertion made by Erich Fromm that had guided my therapeutic thinking for 20 years:

> The psychoanalyst is not only concerned with the readjustment of the neurotic individual to his given society. His task must also be to recognize that the individual's ideal of normalcy may contradict the aim of the full realization of himself as a human being. It is the belief of the progressive forces in society that such a realization is possible, that the interests of society and of the individual need not be antagonistic forever. Psychoanalysis, if it does not lose sight of the human problem, has an important contribution to make in this direction. This contribution by which it transcends the field of a medical specialty was part of the vision which Freud had. (1944, p. 384)

This credo had "worked" for me as a therapist in the past because I had not lived in a collectivist culture, had not fully understood what some of the feminist therapists were saying, and had perhaps been insensitive to the communal themes in the lives of so many of my clients. My traditional, individualistic, agentic American clients had merely needed to harness their will, I assumed, to change their "crooked thinking," and to buy into my interpretation of their situation in order to be cured.

But now I tried changing Fromm's ideas as follows (my changes are italicized):

> The *psychotherapist* is not only concerned with the readjustment of the *discouraged* individual to his *or her* given society. *The* task must also be to recognize that the *society's* ideal of normalcy may contradict the aim of the full realization of *self* as a human being. It is the belief of the progressive forces in society that such a realization is possible, that the interests of society and of the individual need not be antagonistic forever. *Psychotherapists,* if [they do] not lose sight of the human problem, [have] an important contribution to make in this direction. This contribution *means, of course, that psychotherapy is completely irrelevant to any known or existing* field of a medical specialty, *an observation that* was part of the vision which Freud had.

The critical change is in the second sentence. Fromm wanted to change the "individual's ideal of normalcy" (a goal I once embraced with all the agentic power I could muster). But as a therapist, a committed humanist, and a person who has listened to my longtime partner, I now need to question "society's ideal of normalcy," which does not recognize the existence of many of my exiled student-clients.

To be fair to Fromm, most of his patients were victims of their own desperate need to conform and belong. Fromm's "ideals of normalcy" were the ideals of the postwar United States, where everyone was supposed to fall perfectly into place in society. The irony is that the ideals which I am questioning are those of agentic individualism, which were introduced by therapists to provide an alternative to what Fromm called "automaton conformity."

The ideals of normalcy have driven a great many of my clients to something akin to schizoid uniqueness. They represent the American dream gone mad in a hallucination of materialism. Their mantra has become "I do my thing, and you do your thing; and you can believe that my 'thing' is bigger, more powerful, and more determined than anyone else's 'thing.'"

A Psychology of Empowerment

If talking cures are going to advance into the next century, psychotherapy is going to have to undergo another revolution equal in magnitude to the emergence of psychoanalysis out of magnetism and neurology, the evolution of cognitive therapy out of pragmatism and conditioned reflexes, and the challenge to strict determinism articulated by "third force" humanistic and existential psychologists. The model for this transformation may well be feminist psychotherapy, if hard-headed, empirically oriented feminists are involved in guiding that movement into the future.

If we need to give the new talking cure a name, let that name be *empowerment therapy*. This term first appeared in the literature of feminist therapies (see Worell & Remer, 1992) as a way of talking about shifting psychotherapy away from a "salvationist" or "adjustment" model toward an effectance-based model oriented toward changing social structures and systems as well as changing people. Some critics of this approach are uncomfortable because it lacks standing with "postmodern philosophy, psychoanalysis, Marxism, and deconstructionism" (Fischer, 1993). However, empowerment therapy's forthrightness in confronting the realities of living, as opposed to theories about the realities of living, is its greatest asset.

The 28% Solution

The New York Times reported in 1993 on a National Institute of Mental Health survey of 20,000 men and women from households selected to represent the entire population (Goleman, 1993). The survey found that 28% of the people in the United States are in current need of some form of psychotherapy. All the theories in the world about why so many human beings are in such a mess are useless unless they help us respond to the challenge. Heterosexual therapists are going to have to work with gay and lesbian and bisexual clients, young therapists with the elderly, Jews with Muslims, Boston Brahmins with Haitian refugees, fundamentalist Christians with Jews and atheists, women therapists with Asian and Hispanic men, lonely and vulnerable male therapists with strong and resourceful women. And we are all going to have to be able to work with our most at-risk populations: persons with AIDS and young African American males.

No one therapeutic technique can be applied to all these potential clients. No one theory or process will address all their concerns equally well. For reasons of temperament and training, no single therapist can employ successfully more than a subset of different approaches to psychotherapy. But all therapists can accept as their professional duty the empowerment of every single person who shares his or her life with them as a client or a patient.

I agree with my feminist colleagues who believe that we must cease being the handmaidens of society and recognize the social, political, and economic sources of suffering and oppression. But I disagree with the radical assertion that everything personal is *only* political. I reject the necessity of telling every client that we are each fine "just the way we are" and that the world around us will have to change. Some of us are not fine just the way we are, and the world won't change, at least not in time and not enough.

In Maya Angelou's poem *On the Pulse of Morning,* she exclaims:

Women, children, men,
Take it into the palms of your hands
Mold it into the shape of your most
Private need. Sculpt it into
The image of your most public self.
Lift up your hearts
Each new hour holds new chances
For new beginnings.
Do not be wedded forever
To fear, yoked eternally
To brutishness

The horizon leans forward,
Offering you space to place new steps of
    change.*

Talking cures have a role to play in that process, and it is a role therapists will have to fill creatively and hopefully if we are to prove our worth to society. I don't believe Angelou would have all that change come from the outside, from political force. The forces of change must include "courage," as she calls it, to

Have the grace to look up and out
And into your sister's eyes and into
Your brother's face.

Thus change requires some sort of internal transformation too. Angelou challenges us to look to the new morning "with hope," and that hope must come from deep within ourselves.

---

*From *On the Pulse of Morning,* by Maya Angelou. Copyright © 1993 by Maya Angelou. Reprinted by permission of Random House, Inc.

The Basic Ontological Choice: Autopoiesis or Regression

The psychology of empowerment is, or at least can be, the creative engine of human hope, and psychologists can continue to be members of William James's "party of hope." If they do, then the therapeutic relationship will remain at the heart of the transformation of hysterical, tyrannical, irrational, existential misery to an active quest for wisdom, enlightenment, and knowing—which is the direct, immediate, and spontaneous grasping of truth.

Michael Mahoney calls this transformative process *autopoiesis* (Mahoney, 1991). This process, in Mahoney's view, involves an ontological choice. One choice can be called *regression.* We regress when we fall back on familiar but unproductive, outmoded, or inadequate organizational schemas and structures to stabilize reality. This strategy is by definition conservative. It uses denial and overgeneralization to survive. It is closed to new possibilities and to new perceptions. It moves glacially over time, slowly restricting itself further and further and becoming increasingly unable to assimilate new information or to resolve the discrepancies that arise from outmoded classification schemes. An example of regression is when a bigoted politician is confronted by a decorated and courageous war veteran testifying before Congress who is at the same time an African American, a Japanese American, a woman, or a homosexual. The complex and complicated real world does not compute for regressive processors. Overwhelmed by the pace of change, they become fearful and rage at those who challenge the certainties that they have organized their world around. They feel that "the world is going to hell"; they are victims of entropy.

The alternative ontological choice is the one Mahoney sees as being explored within the relative safety of psychotherapy. Those whose selves are organized autopoietically are continually creating and trying new structures to see if they solve the problems of the moment more satisfactorily than the existing structures. The naturalist Steven Jay Gould (1989) and evolutionary biologists refer to this process in evolution as "punctuated equilibrium." As long as my current structures are stable and coherent and can provide meaningful context for all of the new information they are receiving, then those structures are doing their job. But as they become strained and unstable, then autopoiesis leads me to search for new ways of understanding. These new constructions create the possibility of higher levels of awareness, understanding, and integration of the world.

Let's look at an example of autopoiesis. Most heterosexual American teenagers (especially males) grow up with terribly hostile attitudes toward male homosexuals. Male homosexuals are, in fact, the most hated minority group in the United States, according to most studies of long-term prejudice in our society. Some teenagers, however, eventually encounter a friend, a relative, or a respected teacher or coach who lets them know that he is gay. These teens then either have to be autopoietic— to rethink and reexamine all they have been taught and have believed about homosexuals and thereby change their cognitive, behavioral, and emotional structures concerning gay men—to accommodate the new information that a person they care about and respect is also gay. Or they have to engage in a regressive strategy rejecting the old friend, denying the truth they have just learned, or becoming acutely paranoid that homosexuals are everywhere and that nobody is to be trusted.

Now project a homophobic teen into the U.S. military in the 1990s and confront him with the possibility that his platoon leader, sergeant, or commanding officer is gay. How will he react? The man who is open to autopoiesis is able to accept the change in his situation. But the regressive person finds himself in an unbearable, uncomfortable, untenable situation. The autopoietic person remains able to function and maintain his being in the world; the regressive person further restricts his world and finds himself increasingly isolated from the mainstream.

Therapy as a Safe Place for Taking Stock

For Mahoney, psychotherapy is a refuge where individuals can safely address their own state of being in relation to the changes taking place around and within them. Mahoney's metaphor is exploration; he believes a good therapeutic relationship makes it possible for clients to engage in safe self-exploration. Within psychotherapy, clients may ask "what if" questions and explore the *range of meanings* that can be assigned to any given event in their lives.

In Chapter 10 I told of asking Gail to tell me the "what ifs" about her dreams of her husband dropping dead. Gail's unconscious mind was clearly exploring a radical solution to a problem her conscious mind could not fathom. Her restrictive upper-middle-class background made it difficult for her to reconcile sharing her life with someone who did not meet her parents' standards. Gail's emotional breakdown was the cost she had to pay for her regressive style of organizing her domestic and family affairs. Interestingly, Gail was simultaneously autopoietic in her professional life, an area where her family had left her alone to make her own decisions according to her own needs and values.

I can quite successfully conceptualize almost all the problems clients bring to me in terms of autopoiesis and regression. What works best, in most cases, is to find a situation in clients' lives where they have been dynamically autopoietic. If they take those situations as models for the problems they are currently facing, I can usually get them to discover the parameters of their own solutions, without butting into their private affairs and decisions. Let me illustrate with a fairly dramatic case study.

Case Study: Carlos's Dilemma

Carlos was referred to me by an alarmed faculty member to whom Carlos had revealed that he was going to "go ahead with his plan" to kill himself. As soon as I met Carlos, I knew that he was deadly serious about his threat. He put up no resistance to meeting with me nor to telling me, quite calmly, how and when he intended to do the deed. He had set a date to end his life, and he knew that nobody could stop him. He did agree, however, to let me try to earn my imaginary fee by dissuading him from going forward with his plan. He also agreed to do nothing to harm himself as long as he was in therapy and to call me immediately if anything changed. This is the standard contract that therapists strike with suicidal clients. What the clients get from it is a small bit of insurance that they won't kill themselves impetuously or by accident and the feeling that they are dealing with a therapist who is at least as nutty as they are.

The clinker in this case was that Carlos would not tell me his reasons for suicide. He had a lame excuse or two, but they were totally unconvincing to either of us. Carlos was a macho "tough guy," and I could not break through his heavily armored shell to anything remotely personal or emotional. But I did manage to annoy him sufficiently that he exploded at me a couple of times, always on the same topic—that I "didn't know shit about Hispanic culture."

"For instance?" I taunted. "I don't know that all you guys are supposed to be these big macho studs, but you are all scared to death of your mothers?"

My taunt was nonsense, but I thought it might break through his shell. It did. Carlos exploded in fury at me. When he was 11 years old, his older brother had shot him—had meant to kill him too! Carlos's problem had nothing to do with his mother. I was a jerk. What did I know about having a 38-caliber bullet removed from a lung?

Was Carlos trying to finish the job his brother had started? Silence. Very, very, very long silence.

"Why did your brother try to kill you?" I asked, quietly. I was hoping against hope that I hadn't totally destroyed our relationship. At the very least, I couldn't let him leave the office until we had recommitted ourselves to the no-suicide-without-a-call contract.

Silence.

"You *are* trying to finish it. I think I can see that now. Please. Tell me, please, why a nice Hispanic boy would want to kill his 11-year-old brother with a gun."

"I was reading."

"Reading? Shooting is a pretty stiff penalty for being a pencilhead."

"Not so much reading. Looking."

"Pictures?"

"Of guys."

"You mean to tell me that you are going to assassinate yourself for being gay?"

"I have to. If my father finds out, he will either kill me or himself or both of us. I'm going to save him the decision and the consequences."

So we talked. We talked for a long, long time. The conversation was eerie, though, because we might have been talking about football scores or Madonna's after-tax income. His homosexuality was a fact. His family's shame should they ever find out about his homosexuality was a fact. The necessity of killing himself was a fact.

In Mahoney's terms, I had to create a "scaffold" for Carlos to stand on, something to make his search for a solution safe and stable. But he himself had to make the journey, mostly alone. My views on the subject were already well known; I was almost notorious for my position on civil and human rights for gays and lesbians. Still, I was useless to him except that I knew something of the power contained within the struggle he was going through.

Carlos had to find some way to survive the "shame" of his sexual orientation. Prayer had failed; screwing women had failed; being a tough guy had actually backfired—it had brought him to the attention of several gay men who were attracted to tough guys. Nothing had given him the excuse he needed to live.

The solution happened so slowly that I almost didn't recognize it when I finally saw it. Carlos had two major victories under his belt. First, he had survived the bullet, and he was now extremely close to his older brother. For some perhaps wonderful reason, his brother now accepted Carlos's homosexuality and even consented to hang out in gay bars once and a while when Carlos went home for vacations. Carlos wasn't sure if this companionship was a sign of brotherly love or just a way to make sure that Carlos didn't get picked up by anyone that his big brother thought was a sissy. But both brothers had accepted reality in a creative way. Second, Carlos had survived in college as a member of an ethnic minority group. In his words, he had survived "4 years of nonstop listening to somebody else's music." I reminded him that he had also survived 4 years of being darkly closeted in a place where homophobia was rampant.

Slowly, Carlos built a new foundation for himself out of these previous "autopoietic" episodes in his life: from gunshot survivor to brother, from ethnic and sexual minority to graduating senior. Almost nobody he knew had survived either "insult," but Carlos had survived both.

After graduation Carlos went to graduate school, where he met and fell in love with a fellow student. He stayed in therapy for a long time and has only minimal contact with his parents. He "protects" his father from knowing the truth, but his lover finds it hard to believe that Carlos's father hasn't figured out something from the number of times he and Carlos's father have talked on the phone. Maybe Carlos underestimates the generative, autopoietic power in his father's life. But at any rate, Carlos is a survivor.

Human Freedom: Having the World Truthfully

Whatever the procedures a therapist selects, they ought to help create opportunities for greater choice. Autopoiesis is simply a fancy way of referring to the process that took Carlos from having a choice only of where, when, and how to commit suicide to having a whole range of choices in his life. Therapy, not the therapist, made those choices possible. I was clever or lucky enough to find a way to give

Carlos the opportunity, but he was able to seize it, to create some alternative versions of reality, to see some connections and some parallels that he was blind to before he essayed the talking cure.

Keeping Carlos in mind, I want to devote the remainder of this chapter to an exploration of the issues involved in using psychotherapy as a forum in which clients can create choices and thus experience empowerment.

The Concept of Freedom

Richard Williams, in a 1992 *American Psychologist* article, confronted the question of how psychology can help people understand and make choices. Williams began with a version of the same dilemma that confronted William James (see Chapter 11): Although we all believe that we exercise free will and choice, all of science, and especially behavioral psychology, seems to deny even the possibility of choice. This dilemma, noted Williams,

> assumes a dualism between mind and world or between agent as perceiver and the world as grounds for perception. This dualism is deeply rooted in the modern tradition. . . . It is one of the basic but unacknowledged assumptions that underlie traditional psychology. The solution to the problem . . . requires a rethinking about and, ultimately, an overcoming of this dualism. (pp. 755–756, n. 3)

The solution, Williams suggested lies in rethinking the concept of freedom. Psychological analysis ought ultimately to create knowledge of the self and of the world, which creates the perception of freedom. Freedom, in this context, becomes a rather more elegant and useful heuristic than the concept of will, which has popped up at regular intervals throughout this book. Instead of thinking of freedom as some existential property of some autonomous agent, Williams recommended that we consider it the state of a relationship between an actor and the world. When Carlos first talked with me, his "freedom" was trivial. He was free to kill himself today or tomorrow or after graduation. But he was not free to decide not to kill himself. As a consequence of therapy, Carlos was considerably freer—that is, he existed in the world with a number of options to choose between. In Williams's terms, Carlos left therapy with a much greater awareness of the range of options available to him; he was much closer to "having the world truthfully" (1992, p. 757).

Psychotherapy, then, is a matter of finding a process that helps people move forward "to regain a truthful involvement with the world" (Williams, 1992, p. 758). The person who lives truthfully is truly empowered to take or to not take whatever steps he or she judges to be morally and socially correct—independent, I would hope, of the therapist's own views of the morally or socially correct choice. Let me summarize the case as Williams put it: "Take the case of a man deciding whether to leave his long-term marriage to pursue an involvement with another woman." The behaviorists would argue that such a man is never truly free, because "he will do whatever is necessitated by his reinforcement history, his biological status, or the causal power of some abstraction such as exchange theory. And because his act is necessitated, it is worthy of neither blame nor praise" (p. 758).

However, "from the perspective that holds that freedom is living truthfully, the decision about whether this man is free or not is not so easy to make." Williams said that we would need to engage the man in a conversation about the "nature of his desire" both to abandon his current marriage and to be with the other woman. We would need to know "whether his constructive world is a truthful one, whether he is involved truthfully in either relationship. If not he is not free, because he does not have the truth of the matter. He is responding to what is not" (p. 758).

Furthermore, if he is not encountering the person of his wife and the person of his would-be lover truthfully—that is, "if [their] identities and relationships are not as he perceives them, if they run deeper and involve him morally in ways he does not suspect"—"then he is falsely in the world and, thus, not free" (1992, p. 758).

In parallel, we might argue that through therapy Carlos came to identify and confirm his relationship with his brother "truthfully." But we can now also strongly suspect that the same could not be said for his relationship with his father, which appears to be a very ritualized relationship.

Williams noted:

> In summary we might be moved to conclude that the man is free only insofar as he is involved truthfully in the world and that he will continue to be free only if he continues truthfully. This truth is a moral truth. It stretches far beyond this hypothetical man or any person who feels him or her self faced with a choice. It stretches to our very being and our understanding of who we are and who we will be. The understanding as well as the exercise of agency demands our best moral efforts as psychologists and as human beings. . . .
>
> If psychology is going to come to grips with agency and, thus, with humanity it must be a psychology of the moral and the social rather than of the individual and the necessary. (1992, pp. 758–759)

An Inescapable Metaphysics

We have now come full circle to metaphysics and moral philosophy. But did you really think there was ever another way? Not, I fear, within the talking cure. As a therapist you may prescribe all the tranquilizers and antidepressants under the sun. You may hypnotize the oppressed, and you may chant your incantations until you are blue in the face. You may listen to confessions until the cows come home. You may theorize about social injustice, sexual instincts, and patriarchy until you have filled a library with your conjectures. But until you confront the truth, you will not be free. Until you are moral, you will never be able to make an honest choice. Until you experience the humanity of one of your fellow creatures, and she or he experiences

PART IV

Non-Western Approaches to Psychotherapy: The Tao Is Silence

Be dutiful at home, brotherly in public; be discreet and trustworthy, love all people, and draw near to humanity. If you have extra energy as you do that, then study literature.

CONFUCIUS

A way can be a guide, but not a fixed path;
names can be given, but not permanent labels.
Nonbeing is called the beginning of heaven and earth;
being is called the mother of all things.
Always passionless, thereby observe the subtle;
ever intent, thereby observe the apparent.
These two come from the same source but differ in name;
both are considered mysteries.
The mystery of mysteries
is the gateway of marvels.

TAO-TE CHING

Those who know others are wise,
those who know themselves are enlightened

TAO-TE CHING

CHAPTER 20

A Brief Introduction to Eastern Philosophies

Embracing Silence

Remember the bowl of rice, that sacred grain of the East, introduced in Chapter 1? Do you remember its texture, size, and stickiness? How it was cooked and what it tasted like? Can't you remember? Then your senses must be absorbed elsewhere. You need to remedy that.

Deautomatization is the key to recovering awareness. It requires destruction of the illusions of ordinary consciousness, reawakening of the senses, correction of the imbalance, and direct confrontation with confusion, or as Carl Jung might say, the shadow. Aldous Huxley called this process the awakening of the "mind at large."

The philosophies underlying this supposition are two powerful streams found throughout traditional Asian art, literature, and society: Confucianism and Taoism. According to these philosophies, the mind becomes clouded and loses its innate innocence as the person becomes more involved with and caught up in the surrounding world. Confucianism offers the person a broad structure of ritual, duty, and respect for living a properly ordered professional life; Taoism offers escape from the restrictions of Confucianism into the realm of beauty and simple, natural pleasures. In Taoism, balancing opposing forces is the key to living humanely. Therefore, a balance between the rigors of Confucianism and the simple pleasures of Taoism make for a harmonious life both within oneself and in the world at large.

For Westerners, these ideas may sound terribly abstract. However, they are generally comparable to many of the theories described in this book. The perfect balance can be compared perhaps to self-actualization or to the realization of the center self. Self-actualization may not be fully equivalent to achieving perfect Taoist balance, but it can give some clue as to the potential significance of achieving balance. Achieving this balance is the province of the third great stream in Asian philosophy, Zen Buddhism—defined here as the art of seeing into the nature of one's being.

The Expansion of Consciousness

When you study Buddhism you should have a general house cleaning of the mind.
(S. Suzuki, 1970, p. 110)

The English writer Aldous Huxley (1954) proposed that one of the primary functions of the human brain is to regulate the amount of information we have to process in our ordinary waking consciousness. The metaphor he employed is the reducing valve. In his view, the business of the brain is to keep us from becoming overwhelmed and confused by the flood of sensory information from the environment and the memories of past associations that prevent us from focusing on immediate survival-based demands.

Language and linguistic systems are the principal mechanisms of this reducing valve. As we are socialized into our linguistic community, our language becomes the creator of our realities. Events and discriminations that lie outside our linguistic competence by and large do not exist for us; our language filters information, producing a restricted level of consciousness and awareness.

You probably already know the classic example—that Eskimo language recognizes more than two dozen kinds of snow—but thousands and thousands of other examples exist as well. When I went to Japan for the first time, rice was rice was rice. Now, however, having lived in Japan for a considerable period, not only am I more aware of the dozens of kinds of rice that the Japanese grow and consume, I am able to some degree to judge the quality of individual servings of rice. I know what perfect sushi rice should look like, smell like, stick together like, and taste like. I would never use Chinese long-grain rice in sushi, nor would I ever confuse the horrible stuff called rice that is served in college cafeterias with the sacred grain planted and harvested every year by the Japanese royal family. This is precisely how my English mother-in-law feels about tea, my spouse about ballpoint pens, and the unbelievably intense guy sitting next to me on the plane about (I am not making this up) the tomatoes that go into ketchup. Specialized vocabularies open our minds to specialized perceptions and highly encoded memories.

A true teacher, by my definition, is one who leaves a student with a sense of wonder at how much more fascinating and even compelling the world is after the lesson than it was before. When I was a kid I loved forests and trees. I knew every different kind of tree in New England (or thought I did). I loved my expertise in woody plants to the point that, when I took one of those vocational inventories in the fifth grade that are used to track some children (at 10 years old) into college and some into business or the trades, I was "tracked" to become a tree surgeon. At a much later point in my life my friend Julie, a professional botanist, invited me on a walk through a state park near her home. "Oh boy, trees! Acres and acres of trees," thought I. But Julie never looked up, and we never went through the "acres and acres of trees." Instead we looked down. We searched through a dozen square centimeters of the forest floor. Julie spent an hour or so, as my teacher, unclogging the reducing valve that was my tree-centered awareness of forest biology and ecology. She shared her awareness of the world of ferns, lichens, mosses, flowering plants, grasses, and fungi with such an intimate enthusiasm that it forever changed the way I walk through a woods.

The Japanese would say that Julie was a true *sensei*, a word that we know from dumb martial arts movies but that nevertheless is one of the most important words in the Japanese language. A *sensei* is a master at unclogging and expanding the reducing valves that control our awareness of ourselves and the world around us.

Mind at Large

Huxley would say that a *sensei* is a person who enables us to recover our *mind at large*, or the potential within each of us to come into touch with the infinite range of simultaneous possibilities that exist in "other worlds"—including the other world of my rice bowl and Julie's tiny patch of forest floor.

> As Mind at Large seeps past the no longer watertight [reducing] valve, all kinds of biologically useless things start to happen. In some cases there may be extra-sensory perceptions. Other persons discover a world of visionary beauty. To others again is revealed the glory, the infinite value and meaningfulness of naked existence, of the given, unconceptualized event. In [this] final stage of egolessness there is an "obscure knowledge" that All is in all—that All is actually each. This is as near, I take it, as a finite mind can ever come to "perceiving everything that is happening everywhere in the universe." (Huxley, 1954, p. 26)

You may have been wondering how long I would try to lull you into a false feeling of intellectual security with my homey stories about bowls of rice and walks in the forest before sneaking in all sorts of nonlinear, non-Western stuff—like "All is in all" and the rest of the "sixties agenda," as some of my more linearly minded students sometimes call it. Some students have objected to these ideas as "un-Christian" and others as "un-American," but in reality these ideas are universal across time, cultures, religions, and nationalities.

What these troubling ideas seek to challenge is strict materialism—the "common sense" of a Thomas Reid, who would argue that the only things worth learning in psychology are common sense, and "I already know those." People with a strictly materialist point of view usually come to Japan to learn "how the Japanese do things" in order to go back to their home country to "beat the Japanese at their own game." One of my students, an economics major, once rather truthfully admitted, when asked to explain to a television reporter why she chose to spend a year studying in Japan, "I came here primarily from an economic motive." But, my student learned, "the Japanese don't make any sense when they talk about economics; they only talk about philosophy." The industrialist is frustrated to discover that Japanese "management technology" can't be imposed from the top down; it requires more change from management than from employees. And my poor materialist psychology student shrugs off what she or he learns as of no "practical value," because there is no technique to apply, no statistic to calculate, not even a theory to test.

What they don't understand is that the mind at large really isn't "un" anything, especially un-American or un-Christian. It is a different way of conceptualizing boundaries and understanding one's place in the universe. It does, however, involve a fundamental redefinition of self and a fundamental reconsideration of what the words *talk* and *cure* mean when applied to the process of changing one's life. Consider what William James had to say on this topic:

> Looking back, then, . . . we see that the mind is at every stage a theater of simultaneous possibilities. Consciousness consists in the comparison of these with each other, the selection of some, and the suppression of the rest by the reinforcing and inhibiting agency of attention [the psychological aspect of Huxley's reducing valve]. . . . The mind, in short, works on the data it receives very much as a sculptor works on his block of stone. In a sense the statue stood there from eternity. But there were a thousand different ones beside it, and the sculptor alone is to thank for having extricated this one from the rest. Just so the world of each of us, however different our several views of it may be, all lay embedded in the primordial chaos of sensations, which gave the mere *matter*, to the thought of all of us indifferently. We may, if we like, by our reasoning, unwind things back to that black and jointless continuity of space and moving clouds of swarming atoms which science calls the only real world. But all the while the world *we* feel and live in will be that which our ancestors and we, by slowly cumulative strokes of choice, have extricated out of, like sculptors, by simply rejecting certain portions of the given stuff. Other sculptors, other statues from the same stone! Other minds, other worlds from the same monotonous and inexpressive chaos! My world is but one in a million alike embedded, alike real to those who may abstract them. (1890, p. 290)

Deautomatization: Developing Awareness

Of course, the goal of a book about the evolution of the talking cure is to extend these general ideas about expanded consciousness and "mind at large" to a set of propositions about what human beings can do to restore their sense of emotional well-being and stability. Perhaps the reason I like Michael Mahoney's ideas so much (see Chapter 19) is that they help me accomplish this goal. He conceptualized the troubled psyche as one in which "regressive" strategies of dealing with the world have so constricted the mind's reducing valve that life has become unbearable and the dynamic world—that theater of simultaneous possibilities—has become unimaginable. Mahoney (1991) challenged psychology to find ways to support people's efforts to "open up" and to "expand their awareness and their consciousness" in order to establish new cognitive structures that will support them in their day-to-day lives.

A term I find especially helpful in thinking about these issues is *deautomatization,* which was developed in the 1960s by Arthur Deikman (1966). He argued that the long and rich mystical traditions found within all religious practices arose from the efforts of believers to seek direct experience of God. Deautomatization requires us to destroy the illusion of "ordinary consciousness," to seek a holistic reawakening of the senses, and to directly confront confusion and shadow.

Deikman (1966) quoted from a 14th-century Christian text "If ever thou shalt see [God] or feel him as it may be here, it must always be in this cloud and in this darkness. . . . Smite upon that thick cloud of unknowing with a sharp dart of longing love" (pp. 324–325). How many of us caught up in the pain of a love affair that either was not connecting or was slowly coming apart have wanted to "smite that thick cloud of unknowing with a sharp dart of longing love"? As a therapist, how many times have I driven myself to distraction trying to smite the "dark cloud of unknowing" that prevented the client and me from joining to fight whatever demons were eating away at the client's emotional well-being and creative life force? How many times in my own life, when confronted with crushing disappointment or hopeless emotional confusion, have I tried to dream, talk, analyze, reason, bargain, pray, meditate, bully, or seduce myself through that thick cloud of unknowing?

The Spirituality of the Psyche. What I am introducing here is a concept rarely encountered in Western psychology. It sometimes makes the religiously faithful angry with me and principled skeptics suspicious. It is what the Dutch psychoanalyst J. H. Van Den Berg (1971) referred to as the "spirituality aspect of the psyche." It is the part of our subconscious mental life that—rather than being concerned with sex, aggression, and the social needs of the ego—is involved with our ideals, reflections, philosophy, and awareness of mortality. This part of the psyche has largely been lost, Van Den Berg argued, in an age when we all suffer from "anomic dislocation," a loss of contact with our central identities as spiritual beings.

Erich Fromm argued in *The Sane Society* (1955) that prior to the industrial age, human beings were never lonely. Fromm maintained, from a fairly orthodox Marxist perspective, that prior to the industrial revolution human beings lived in highly cooperative and communal societies where they experienced an immediate connection between their labor and the quality of their lives.

Van Den Berg didn't dispute Fromm's ideas, but he added that prior to the modern era everyone was able to believe directly and immediately in the "vitality of God." People were spiritually vitalized; they had something to believe in fully and ultimately. But now we have a sanitized, organized, packaged, and deconsecrated God, if we have one at all. We have lost contact with the "vital" in our daily lives. As Friedrich Nietzsche said, quoting his famous "madman" in *Thus Spake Zarathustra,* God is dead: "Where has God gone? I shall tell you. *We have killed him*—you and I. We are all his murderers. . . . What are the churches now if they are not the tombs and sepulchers of God?" (1961, p. 42).

What does Van Den Berg make of Nietsche's conclusion?

Here is what I really want to say: Whoever lives in a society which is not characterized by an anomic dislocation of the sector of spirituality, that is, whoever lives in a society which has not been secularized, will never be truly alone, no matter how much he may feel abandoned by other human beings. He will be with the sector [of the psyche concerned with] spirituality, as well as with the impenetrable core of this sector. He will be with God. *He will never be lonely.* He can be alone in the sense that there are no other living persons in his vicinity. But he will not be distressed by this. In the past this last assumption was held to be completely true. People used to live more separate lives; they were more to themselves, more on their own. That did not distress them. It distressed them so little that there were even people who out on their own free will would lock themselves up in a cell, and stay there for years and years to meditate, to sing, to write, to live. Who would do such a thing these days? Most people would simply go mad if they tried. It is hardly ever done these days. If done at all, it forms an exception. (1971, p. 356)

As you might expect, with any topic this rich in human meaning and experience, William James also had something to say. He wrote of deautomatization:

This overcoming of the usual barriers between the individual and the Absolute is the great mystic achievement. In mystic states we both become one with the Absolute and we become aware of our oneness. This is the everlasting and triumphant mystical tradition, hardly altered by differences in clime or creed. In Hinduism, in Neoplatonism, in Sufism, in Christian mysticism, in Whitmanism, we find the same recurring note, so that there is about mystical utterance an eternal unanimity which ought to make a critic stop and think, and which brings it about that the mystical classics have, as has been said, neither birthday nor native land. Perpetually telling of the unity of man with God, their speech antedates languages, and they do not grow old. (1929, p. 410)

Transforming Archetypes. If you cast your mind back to Chapter 9, you will probably recognize that these ideas are not fundamentally different from those articulated by the Swiss psychiatrist Carl Jung. But Jung carried the discussion forward by a millennium or two:

What one could almost call a systematic blindness is simply the effect of the prejudice that the deity is *outside* man. Although this prejudice is not solely Christian, there are certain religions which do not share it at all. On the contrary they insist, as do certain Christian mystics, upon the essential identity of God and man. . . . The application of the comparative method indubitably shows the quaternity [a transforming archetype] as being a more or less direct representation of the God manifested in his creation. We might, therefore, conclude that the symbol, spontaneously produced in the dreams of the modern people, means the same thing—*the God within*. (1938, p. 72)

If we were still living in a medieval setting where there was not much doubt about the ultimate things and where every history of the world began with Genesis, we could easily brush aside the cosmic significance of dreams and the like. Unfortunately, we live in a "modern" setting, where all ultimate things are doubtful, where there is a prehistory of enormous extension, and where people are fully aware of the fact that if there is any numinous experience at all, it is the experience of the psyche. . . . One could even define religious experience as that kind of experience which is characterized by the highest appreciation, no matter what its contents are. (p. 75)

The Experience of Mind at Large

What these various views have in common is a shared notion of an energizing, arousing, and directional motivation inherent in all human beings. Van Den Berg, Fromm, James, and to a somewhat lesser extent Jung (but especially when he wrote about evangelical Protestantism) asserted that when a society becomes desecrated, when spirituality becomes a purely private and secular endeavor, the human psyche is devastated.

What a curious profession—this talking cure—our human psychic drama spawned. At this point, you may well believe it almost bizarre that this collage of antivitalist, will-mongering, happy-go-lucky anarchist, feel-good, social engineers of the "party of hope" that you have been reading about would be the "handmaidens" chosen by the ruling order to minister to the needs of the spiritually deprived. But here we are. When people decide they don't want to take their problems to the drug companies or harness their problems in the pursuit of power and wealth, here we are, ready to serve the masses with our (in)famous 50-minute hour.

Of course there are alternatives. Huxley (1954) was one of the first to suggest the possibility of expanding consciousness through "hypnosis, spiritual exercises, or by means of drugs." But he concluded that

through these permanent or temporary by-passes there flows, not indeed the perception "of everything that is happening everywhere in the universe," but [at least] something more than, and above all something different from, the carefully selected utilitarian material which our narrowed, individual minds regard as complete, or at least sufficient, picture of reality. (p. 23)

Can we say what it is that consciousness pilgrims are seeking? As Deikman (1966, p. 329) reminds us, the poet William Wordsworth (1904, p. 353) wrote about it like this:

> There was a time when meadow, grove, and stream
> The earth and every common sight,
> To me did seem
> Apparelled in celestial light,
> The glory and the freshness of a dream.

But mind at large demands something more than childhood memories of objects bathed in celestial light. It demands presence in the light. It requires integration as both knower and known. It accepts no substitute for being in the world. It will not be fooled by partial truths and secondhand experience. Is there anything more boring than hearing of someone else's dream? Is there anything more empty than telling a dream to someone else?

Mind at large requires destruction of the illusion created by repeated experience, a tearing away of the veils that separate us from presence, the reawakening of the senses, the dishabituation of our nervous systems from the droning patterns and the lies of everyday life. It demands an awakening from the deep sleep in which we walk through our everyday lives, a sobering up of what is known in the Buddhist tradition as the "drunken monkey" of our perceptual system—our befuddled brain responding to only fragments of sensory information, one "loud" stimulus at a time.

Moments of Unusual Consciousness

When I ask my students to remember moments in their own lives that have somehow exemplified expanded consciousness or mind at large, their experiences usually fall into four categories:

- *Extreme positive emotion.* Scoring the winning point in an important game. Being formally united with other members of a group, such as a fraternity or sorority. Recognizing the "self" in another, as in "coming out" for the first time. Receiving a best-ever report card or performing artistically at the height of one's powers.
- *Perfect human connection.* Having a sexual experience that transcends every other physical and emotional experience in one's life. Saving someone's life. Giving birth to or participating in the birth of a wanted child. Watching a perfect sunrise or hearing a perfect silence in nature.
- *Dread or shock.* Realizing you are about to be in an accident. Waking up from surgery. Finding out you have AIDS or some other incurable disease. Recognizing that a perfect love has been shattered or a relationship has ended. Having your best friend tell you that he or she is homosexual.
- *"Religious" conversion.* Taking a drug "trip" to someplace you have never been before. Achieving a breakthrough in psychotherapy. Waking up with the solution to a vexing or perplexing problem in your head. Making a decision to give up a harmful drug or a degrading personal habit.

According to Deikman (1966), all these experiences tend to share a set of features related to the discovery of mind at large:

- *Feelings of intense realness.* This feature is the opposite of depersonalization or derealization. It is not a property of the sensations themselves, nor is it an intellectual conclusion you come to. Deikman described it as an experience wherein "stimuli of the inner world become invested in the feeling of reality ordinarily bestowed on objects. Through what might be termed 'reality transfer' *thoughts and images become real*" (p. 333).
- *Unusual modes of perception.* Colors become clearer, tastes become more distinguishable and fuller, sounds are more true, weight and motion become more apparent, and the invisible may become perceived. People may, for example, become acutely aware of their own breathing or heartbeat; they may actually notice the force of gravity or the illumination produced by the energy invested in a painting or a musical composition.
- *Feelings of being at one with something or someone else.* Some people experience union with God or with all humankind or all living things or with one other person. For example, here is a gay man's experience of such union in the act of sexual intercourse:

  After the act is completed what I remember most vividly and savor long afterward was the union, the tenderness, and the language which was established between my partner and myself. Just being inside a man makes us a unit and for that one moment . . . we are a complete "ONE" emotionally as well as physically. (Hite, 1981, quoted in Sprecher & McKinney, 1993, p. 83)

- *Ineffability.* The experience cannot be translated adequately into words. I suppose one reason we honor our poets, artists, and musicians so highly, is that they at least try to communicate some of the ineffable to us. Try to remember the first time you, totally sober, made or declared love to a perfect other person, even if the moment was brief. Could you ever put that experience into words? If you have experienced a moment of deep religious connection with whatever you consider to be divine, could you explain what you felt to anyone else?
- *Trans-sensate phenomena.* This feature is what we refer to when we say that Saint So-and-so came face to face with God. It is the ultimate mystical experience. In Zen Buddhism it is called satori. I will come back to this point later, when we explore the tenets of Zen more closely, but for now perhaps an anecdote will suffice. When Professor Huston Smith of the Massachusetts Institute of Technology was talking with the Zen master Shunryu Suzuki shortly before Suzuki's death, Smith asked why Suzuki had not written more extensively about the experience of satori. Suzuki's wife teased, "It's because he hasn't had it!" "Shhh!" replied the old master. "Don't tell him!" Smith recalled this memory with the final lines of a poem written to honor Suzuki-sensei:

Walking with you in Buddha's gentle rain
Our robes are soaked through,
But on the lotus leaves
Not a drop remains.
(Smith, 1970, p. 10)

Well, I can write and you can read and we can talk about these matters forever. But as long as we are trying to think like Westerners, this explanation is going to be more like reading a book about your parents' sex life than like falling in love for the first time. As that clever old English Quaker, William Penn (1644–1718), wrote a long time ago: "More true knowledge comes from meditation than by reading; for much reading is an oppression of the mind; and extinguishes the natural candle, which is the reason for so many senseless scholars in the world."

The rest of this chapter is devoted to a discussion of Asian philosophy. I hope I have persuaded you that we have a lot to learn from several thousand years of wisdom developed within cultures where God is not dead and where the spiritual sector of the psyche is of paramount importance. Let me conclude this section, then, with a bit of Sufi wisdom, a gentle reminder that there are many things in life we cannot learn from dissection and elemental analysis:

Show a man too many camels' bones,
and show them to him too often,
and he will lose his ability to recognize a camel
when he sees a live one.

A Cross-Cultural Note on the Nature of Causation

So far, this book has presented an awful lot of camel bones. European and North American approaches to psychotherapy are all so elemental, reductionistic, and positivist—so "scientific"—that they have littered the emotional and psychic landscape with a vast array of camel bones. In contrast, Asian approaches to understanding the world, including human beings, follow a very different pattern, and it is not necessarily a pattern with which very many Westerners feel completely comfortable.

I don't think that most psychologists in Japan credit "science," at least as we think about it in the West, with providing much useful information about the nature of human beings. The East does not focus on life in objective, rational, analytical terms; it does not see the source of human behavior and motivation in elemental and alien terms. The Japanese language, for example, is rich in terms describing a person's heart. Japanese psychologists talk about nervousness as a disturbance of the stability of the organism, not as a condition alien to the health of the person.

When I lived in Japan, I observed that when Japanese news programs cover a story about someone who has just run amok, the reporters don't interview terrorized witnesses to provide an "action-cam" account of events. The producers accept as obvious that any number of accounts of the actual events are possible and that none of them have a superior claim to accuracy. So the program reports the facts: "Joe Tanaka, 27, of Shinjuku ward, Tokyo, was arrested by local police Monday for the stabbing of a prostitute in a bar at 12:14 A.M." The news anchor then turns to the reporters in the field for interviews with Tanaka's former teachers and his childhood neighbors. What Japanese viewers want to know is where this crazy behavior came from. How does it make sense? What signs did Tanaka-san give as a child that he was "this sort of a person"?

As Westerners we are distinctly uncomfortable with questions like this. We want to know what drove Tanaka to act as he did. We don't ask, as a Japanese person would, "Was Tanaka often selfish and moody as a child?" In the West we tend to see the eruption of criminal behavior as a sign that the person is sick, that he or she is damaged in some way: Tanaka has cracked under the pressure of living with the unnatural constraints of civilization.

The Japanese, however, tend to see the eruption of bizarre behavior as a sign that the integrity of the system is at risk. A mother or perhaps a teacher has failed to bring the miscreant securely into the web of relations and connections with other people; Tanaka has escaped the secure and reassuring network of civilization.

This difference in fundamental assumptions about life is profound and results in very important differences in "treatment" orientations, as you will see in the next three chapters. In the East (although I speak specifically of Japan, many of my points may be generalized to other Asian cultures as well), human conduct is perceived to be regulated by such concepts as duty, honor, and obligation.

The Teachings of Confucius and the Tao

Few people have had as profound an impact on history and civilization itself as K'ung Fu-Tzu (551–479 B.C.E.). Confucius, as he is known in the West, may have been the first "moral philosopher" in the Chinese tradition. It is impossible to understand Chinese, Japanese, Korean, or other East Asian cultures without understanding Confucian teachings.

> If we were to characterize in one word the Chinese way of life for the last two thousand years, the word would be "Confucian." No other individual in Chinese history has so deeply influenced the life and thought of his people . . . as a molder of the Chinese mind and character. . . . Confucianism since the time of its general acceptance has been more than a creed to be professed or rejected; it has become an inseparable part of the society and thought of the nation as a whole, of what it means to be a Chinese.
> (De Bary, Chan, & Watson, 1960, p. 15)

Confucius' writings are a guide to a perfectly ordered life, achieved by aligning oneself with the natural moral order of the universe. According to Confucius, the source of this order can be discovered in the wisdom of the ancient sage-kings of legend, who conducted their lives in accordance with the will of heaven. The ancients "had embodied the humanity and perfect virtue . . . and their deeds and their reigns represented all that was wise and good in Chinese history and society" (De Bary et al., 1960, p. 17).

The Confucian world is one of perfect order and peace, where each person has a place and a function in society. The highest calling in life is that of the gentleman-scholar, who lives his life with dignity, humility, optimism, and good sense. "Unless men individually embraced the idea of *jen*—humanity, benevolence, or perfect virtue—there was no hope that society could be spared the evil, cruelty, and violence that was destroying it" (De Bary et al., 1960, p. 16). *Jen* is sometimes translated as "love." It is "the supreme excellence in men or perfect virtue" (p. 26); it is the essence of humanity.

When we read Confucius' guidance on how "good people" are to conduct themselves, it is almost like listening to James's moral philosophy:

> Cultivated people have nine thoughts. When they look, they think of how to see clearly. When they listen, they think of how to hear keenly. In regard to their appearance, they think of how to be warm. In their demeanor, they think of how to be respectful. In their speech, they think of how to be truthful. In their work, they think of how to be serious. When in doubt, they think of how to pose questions. When angry they think of trouble. When they see gain to be had, they think of justice. (Confucius 16:10, quoted in Cleary, 1992, p. 93)*

The Qualities of a Virtuous Person

The most important principle in Confucian teachings is that every human being must accept responsibility for performing his or her duties without prompting or supervision and with a minimum of disruption. The essence of virtue is to know and to fulfill one's obligations, as defined by one's position in the family, the community, and the state. A virtuous person can stand alone without fear and can leave society without distress. The integrity implicit in such conduct will prevent that person from becoming either a fool or a tool. Such a person is above backbiting and painful slander and serves only the cause of justice. The virtuous person is guided by loyalty and faithfulness to what is right and stays away from the company of those who do not behave with integrity, loyalty, and faithfulness.

Persons who are exemplars of Confucian teaching have three qualities of particular interest to us: "They are humane and therefore do not worry, they are not con-

---

*This and all following quotations from *The Essential Tao*, translated and presented by Thomas Cleary. Copyright © 1991 by Thomas Cleary. Reprinted by permission of HarperCollins Publishers, Inc.

fused, and they are brave and unafraid" (Cleary, 1992, p. 99). They accomplish this psychologically wholesome state of being by living their lives in accord with practical wisdom, which is derived from the laws of metaphysics that give the world order and meaning.

The Teachings of the Yellow Emperor

The writings of the philosophers Lao-tzu and Chuang-tzu (attributed to the mythical Yellow Emperor) appeared two centuries after Confucius. They gave us Taoism, the other fundamental doctrine of classical Chinese thought.

De Bary et al. (1960) described the Tao (pronounced "Dow"), also known as the Way, as the perfect complement to the sometimes heavy-handed teachings of Confucius:

> In many ways the doctrines of Confucianism and Taoism complement each other running side by side like two powerful streams through all later Chinese thought and literature, appealing simultaneously to two sides of the Chinese character. To the solemn, rather pompous gravity and burden of social responsibility of Confucianism, Taoism opposes a carefree flight from respectability and the conventional duties of society; in place of the stubborn Confucian concern for things human and mundane it holds out a vision of other, transcendental worlds of the spirit. Where the Confucian philosophers are often prosaic and dull, moralistic and common-sensical, the early Taoist writings are all wit and paradox, mysticism and poetic vision. (p. 48)

De Bary et al. asked us to imagine the hard-working Confucian scholar–bureaucrat–family man and responsible citizen escaping to his Taoist shaded garden or mountain retreat, where he perhaps gets a little drunk on plum wine while reading poetry and enjoying the quiet beauty of nature. This idea is perhaps the equivalent of meeting your venerable, esteemed psychology professor at a Pearl Jam concert or while he is walking his dog through the park on a snowy afternoon.

The *Tao-Te Ching* (also known as the *Lao-tzu*, after the ideal ruler whose book of advice the *Tao-Te Ching* is supposed to be) describes "the perfect individual, the sage, who comprehends the principle of the Tao and orders his own life and actions in accord with it, humbling himself, pursuing a course of quietude and passivity, free from desire and strife" (De Bary et al., 1960, p. 50). Although mental health per se is not the focus of the Tao, we can safely infer that the anxious, depressed, or psychosomatically ill person is one who has lost sight of how to live life without strife and coercion. He or she has lost sight of the natural, the basic, and the spontaneous. In modern language, you could say that he or she is a person grown discouraged about the ability to fulfill his or her duties and yet live in harmony.

The solution lies in helping that person recover the intuitive ability to follow the Way. Sages "always consider it good to save beings, so that there are no wasted beings."

Thus a psychotherapist's function is to save patients from a life mired in detail and wasted in Confucian ritual; to wake them from their "dream" of being separate and disconnected from what the Tao calls "mystic virtue."

In the Tao, this idea is reflected in a concern for the soul—which is likened to water, the universal requirement of all life and a force that always follows its own nature. As Chuang-tzu said, "Leaders find their model in Nature; Nature finds its model in the Way; the Way finds its model in spontaneity" (Cleary, 1991, p. 167). Living truthfully is fluid and unimpeded by doubt or guessing; it does not encounter opposition because it is one with the natural rhythms of the universe. Even emperors and queens are ruled by the vastness of the Tao, as are peasants and common laborers.

When the Tao is violated, when the individual fails to live a life guided by mystic virtue, then the natural harmony of the universe is disturbed. The "cure" therefore lies in the recovery of virtue. Virtue can be restored by cultivating the essential aspects of a worthy person: "*inward honesty,* by being a companion of Nature; *outward tact* by living courteously in the service of others; and *companionship with the ancients,* by living in accord with tradition" (Chuang-tzu, ch. 4, quoted in Cleary, 1991, p. 86).

So far the Tao sounds, albeit metaphorically, somewhat like a behavioral prescription. A Chinese John Watson wouldn't have too much difficulty "conditioning" these principles, if he could more clearly define what it means to be a "companion of nature." But the Tao recognizes that virtue does not belong to the person who merely internalizes Karen Horney's "tyranny of shoulds" or becomes one of Albert Ellis's "musterbators." As Chuang-tzu says to his disciple, who is eager to run off to organize his life in accord with the Tao:

> How? How would that do? Too many governing principles, and unsure besides. Although this way of yours is not progressive, still it keeps you from being charged with a crime; but that's all. How can it be enough to effect reform? You are still following your own inclinations. (Chuang-tzu, ch. 4, quoted in Cleary, 1991, p. 87)

Chuang-tzu tells his disciple to fast but also warns him that it won't be easy. The disciple is now totally perplexed. His family is so poor that they "fast" all the time. It is their way of life. In fact, he tells the sage, it has been months since he has drunk wine or eaten meat. Should he assume that his consciousness is about to explode from the virtue of such long and intense poverty?

Chuang-tzu dismisses this sort of fasting as merely "religious" practice. It has no value in directing a serious person to the Tao. The disciple must commit himself to mental fasting if he is serious about his quest. To resolve the disciple's confusion, Chuang-tzu explains mental fasting:

> You unify your will: hear with the mind instead of with the ears; hear with energy instead of the mind. Hearing stops at the ears, the mind stops at contact, but energy is that which is empty and responsive to others. The Way gathers in emptiness; emptiness is mental fasting. (ch. 4, quoted in Cleary, 1991, p. 87)

"Wait!" cries the disciple. "The reason I have not been able to master this is that I consider myself really me. If I could master this, 'I' would not exist. Could that be called emptiness?"

Chuang-tzu now gets to make the speech he's been eager to make all along. Here is the essence of the "cure" in this mental fast, this embrace of silence:

> That's all there is to it. I tell you, you can go into that corral without being moved by repute. If you are heard, then speak; if not then stop. Let there be no dogma, no drastic measures; remain constant and abide by necessity. Then you'll be close.
>
> It is easy to obliterate tracks, hard not to walk on the ground. It is easy to use false-hoods in working for people; it is hard to use falsehood in working for Nature.
>
> I have heard of flying with wings; I have never heard of flying without wings. I have heard of knowing with knowledge; I have never heard of knowing without knowledge.
>
> But if one does not stay here, that is called galloping even while sitting.
>
> If you have your ears and eyes penetrate inwardly, and are detached from concep-tual knowledge, then even if ghosts and spirits come after you they will stop; how much the more will people! (ch. 4, quoted in Cleary, 1991, pp. 87–88)

If you are sitting down, staring at that passage, and getting ready to hurl this book, you have already grasped what the Tao means by "galloping while sitting." If you are beginning to get a glimmer of the sage's deep message, then perhaps you are learning about "flying without wings." Perhaps most importantly, if you are truly coming to know yourself (but not in the Western sense of knowing yourself as a separate, private skin bag), then you are coming to know that the ghosts and spirits can't harm you.

Case Study: Vivian's Odyssey

If you can do this with little difficulty, then you are more fortunate than my old friend Vivian, whom I first met 18 years ago. The Vivian who came into my clinic office was a profoundly depressed and acutely self-destructive woman in her mid-twenties who showed almost all the signs of becoming acutely psychotic. One thing was very clear from her psychiatric history: If there was a way a person could screw up her life and every relationship in it, Vivian had found it and done it. In fact, she was one of those rare unfortunate people who I felt might be better off if she just let herself drift into psychosis rather than stay in "this world" fighting the horrors of her own existence.

In those days we didn't know very much about posttraumatic stress disorder (our involvement in the Vietnam War had just ended), and we didn't recognize that emo-tional and sexual abuse could produce a psychiatric profile equivalent to that expe-rienced by someone who has survived hand-to-hand combat in trench warfare. To-day, I hope, every social worker, psychologist, psychiatrist, and addictions worker would recognize the true nature of Vivian's situation within the first half hour of treatment. But then we just thought that Vivian was a tragically disturbed person, with more symptoms and more self-defeating behavior patterns than any six people should have to bear.

I became Vivian's therapist (her previous therapist had left the clinic for a different position) during a period when she was in and out of the hospital on a regular basis. What I found most distressing about working with Vivian was that I never knew when I said good-bye to her after a session whether she would stay alive until our next session. Ultimately, I felt we had no choice but to recommend Vivian to a state mental hospital, where she might be kept alive long enough to gain some substantial help with her problems.

She remained a patient within the state mental health system for almost 2 years, first as an inpatient and then in a halfway house. Eventually, with the help of a lot of psychotherapy and the support and encouragement of the hospital staff, Vivian grew strong enough to return home and resume life with her family.

Vivian and I have remained friends over the course of the many years since her initial hospitalization. We get together to talk several times a year, not as therapist and patient but as student and teacher. For Vivian has taught me what it means to be a survivor. Through coming to know Vivian's life story, I have learned something about the depths of depravity to which human beings can sink and the terrible cruelty and harm that even "normal" parents can inflict. Vivian seems to credit me with having been a transformative force in her life, but all I ever did was listen to her with compassion and treat her with decency and respect. Let there be no mistake in what I am saying here: In this relationship it is I who am the student and Vivian who is the teacher.

Vivian is a survivor of incest. As a child she had been repeatedly and brutally victimized by everyone in her family. From as far back in her childhood as she can remember, her father cruelly and sadistically abused her. Her mother not only more or less consciously let it all happen but then neurotically blamed Vivian for letting it happen. Vivian adapted to this insane world by blocking the truth of her life from her consciousness. Eventually this blocking led to a total paralysis of her will; she became globally dysfunctional. The ghosts and spirits of her childhood overtook her and robbed Vivian of her sanity.

Meanwhile, Vivian's parents remained pillars of their community and church. Vivian's bitter knowledge of the truth about her family therefore posed a threat that her mother and father, and evidently her grandparents as well, lived in fear of every day of their lives. They despised Vivian for her very survival. They wished she would just disappear, like a piece of trash or a stray animal. Vivian grew up aware at some level that her existence threatened the family's emotional security, economic well-being, and social position in the community.

Vivian survived, almost perished, and ultimately triumphed primarily because underneath her near-psychosis she remained an exceptionally intelligent, perceptive, and aware person. Given enough time and the emotional refuge of the state hospital, Vivian proved herself exceptionally able to engage with her therapists in the intellectual and ethical self-examination at the heart of the talking cure. She was especially well equipped to translate what was happening to her emotionally and spiritually into language, to share her experiences with her therapists, and thus to give them the greatest possible advantage in trying to help her come to terms with her problems.

It is instructive that Vivian gradually liberated herself from her past by finding the courage and the integrity to follow the Tao's prescription to "have your ears and eyes penetrate inwardly, and . . . detach from conceptual knowledge, then even if ghosts and spirits come after you they will stop; how much the more will people!"

There is also an essential connection between Vivian and Confucius. Vivian's intuitive grasp of the rigorous ethical demands of her self as wife, mother, and member of her community saved her from destroying her own life. She worked her way back from madness by engaging the same ethical intelligence that had prevented her from minimizing the evil that had been done to her. She knew that any passive acceptance of "cure" would exonerate the evil in the lives of people who had done their utmost to destroy her. She had to confront the "ghosts and shadows" from her past with the full powers of her being. Her intelligence demanded that the solutions she derived meet the highest standards of moral truth.

Vivian was too ethical and too smart to let a little Prozac or a little Valium or even a little Thorazine block out the horror of the reality she had experienced. Every aspect of premature "normality" added to the lie; every self-destructive impulse was a bright light shining on the hypocrisy and the deception that her family projected to the community. Her madness became her ticket for the journey into that Taoist "white room" with its "auspicious signs" celebrated in a traditional Zen poem:

> For those who gaze into space,
> the empty room produces white light;
> auspicious signs hover in stillness.

Day after day and night after night, as Vivian lay in the hospital slowly working out the conditions of her survival, the ghosts and spirits came after her, just as the Tao had foretold. Whatever peace Vivian could find had to be negotiated with these demons and with the terrible emotional pain with which she had lived every day of her life since age 9. As Lao-tzu put it in the *Tao-Te Ching:*

> Those who know do not say;
> those who say do not know.
> Close the senses,
> shut the doors;
> blunt the sharpness,
> resolve the complications;
> harmonize the light,
> assimilate to the world.
> (56: 1–8, quoted in Cleary, 1991, p. 43)

One day fairly recently, I was supposed to meet Vivian for coffee and one of our several-times-a-year conversations about how her life was changing. I was eager to hear the latest news about her children, whom Vivian had miraculously raised to become extraordinarily independent and successful young adults. But instead I received a call that Vivian was in the hospital, having collapsed at work a short while before.

I went to the hospital and learned that Vivian had received a phone call at work telling her that her father had just a few minutes earlier committed suicide. This was, of course, the just ending that Vivian had so desperately hoped for, for so many years. It was also her utterly feared nightmare; suicide was the old man's ultimate act of emotional terrorism.

But now Vivian is face to face with the question, What does the death of one's tormentor accomplish? Is it the so-wished-for end of the lifelong fear and loathing? Or is it the transformation of the demon from confrontable, despised corporal being to elusive, haunting, eternal ghost? If the latter, how does one ever exorcise that ghost from one's consciousness?

The end of Vivian's "mental fast" is not immediately in view. But she knows that she is a survivor and that she would not be alive today if she had not learned over the course of many painful years how to "unify her will, hear with her mind, remain consistent and abide by necessity," as Lao-tzu counseled. Since beginning therapy so many years ago, Vivian has learned something about speaking only when she is heard and stopping when she is not. She has learned that it is difficult "not to walk on the ground," but she has also learned that her survival depends on not invoking "falsehoods in working for Nature." It has been a privilege to know her, to share some of her journey with her.

Zen Buddhism's Consuming Fires

Vivian, I think, would have an intuitive understanding of a poem written by the 12th-century Zen monk Mumon Ekai:

> Hundreds of flowers in spring, the moon in autumn,
> A cool breeze in summer, and snow in winter;
> If there is no vain cloud in your mind
> For you it is a good season.
> (Shibayama, 1974, p. 140)

For Vivian, "good seasons" are hard to know. The brutal treatment she received at the hands of those she innocently believed were supposed to love and protect her left her with the emotional scars of a "contaminated mind." The process of overcoming her fear has been the process of freeing herself from the greed and anger with which she learned to protect and guard herself. Her greed was for attention and affection, which as a young woman she tragically took wherever she could find it, regardless of its cost or quality. Her anger was perversely directed at her own being. Her life was controlled by a cruel and savage passion: to feel power, to gain revenge, to be vindicated. To survive.

There was no conscious room in Vivian's teenage life for the Tao. Or perhaps she had invented her own Tao, a self-destructive Tao of hate and self-loathing. Vivian's corrupted Tao (her diamonic, in the language of Chapter 17) knew the pleasures of no seasons. The only goals it recognized were greed and craving, as Vivian compulsively overate and went through periods of self-destructive promiscuity; hate and aversion, as Vivian despised and feared everything in her life except her children; and delusion and ignorance, as Vivian knew virtually nothing of her self but found refuge in steadily deepening mental illness.

In Zen Buddhism, which we might think of as the "how-to" handbook of Eastern philosophy, greed, hate, and delusion and their psychological aspects—craving, aversion, and ignorance—are called the *three consuming fires*. Zen directs its followers to spiritual-psychological practices that will extinguish those fires and in turn expand consciousness to a universal level of awareness. In practicing Zen, greed becomes compassion for all living things. Love is born out of hate and becomes universal. Delusion gives way to wisdom, which unlocks the secrets of the universe.

Human will, which in Zen becomes understood as something like conviction, is the ultimate transformation of character. It comes with the simultaneous realization of all three of these enlightened attributes: wisdom, compassion, and love. If you could talk with Vivian, you would see a person who is in the process of discovering and strengthening her will in precisely this way.

We learn in Zen that wisdom, compassion, and love are the essential keys to living life at peace and thus experiencing joy. By opening ourselves to the mystic virtue of the Tao, we discover that "lying, stealing, sexual misconduct, killing, and taking mind-clouding intoxicants" are symptoms of misplaced mind—mind poisoned by affective contamination, by the sorrows of life.

In practicing Zen, we grasp the vision of the great 17th-century poet, Basho. Basho traveled all over northern Japan writing *haiku*, 17-syllable poems that reveal the beauty and the wonder of the world, perceived simply as it is. One of my favorite Basho poems directs the passerby to pay attention to a common roadside weed, the *nazunna* flower:

When I look carefully
I see the nazunna blooming
By the hedge!
(D. T. Suzuki, 1960, p.1)

Now, to have fun with the will and wisdom of this poem, replace *the nazunna* with the name of whomever you love the most. See if Basho hasn't captured the essence of what we aspire to when we say we love someone. If this exercise works for you, I think you have just gained a glimmer of the Tao of love.

The Zen Prescription

Zen, at least as we tend to think of it in the West, is more remedial than simply taking a moment to watch your beloved "bloom." It is much more fundamentally involved in the process of salvation. It is prescriptive; it tells you how to quit messing up your life. It illuminates the way for you to discover the Tao in your own life.

In essence, Zen is very simple; it asks you to behave as if you already had the Tao in the center of your mind and your heart. It is manifestly obvious, and it is all around us. As Shibayama (1974) told us, Zen is a matter of neither "practice" nor pure metaphysics. Zen simply is. As Shibayama put it, "Ordinary mind is Tao" (p. 40).

He explained with an ancient teaching story called a *koan*. I have to admit that an awful lot of rubbish has been written about *koans*. For some people Zen is nothing but a series of little paradoxical stories, long pointless jokes without punch lines. But the true *koan* is a lesson wrapped in a paradox. You can't "learn" a *koan* like you can learn a mathematical formula. A *koan* is like a *nazunna* flower: you have to look carefully to observe it quietly blooming by a hedge. Shibayama's *koan* is a classic lesson in Zen thinking:

> Joshu once asked Nansen [Joshu is the eternal student, Nansen the eternal *sensei*], "What is Tao?" Nansen answered, "Ordinary mind is Tao." "Then should we direct ourselves toward it or not?" asked Joshu. "If you try to direct yourself toward it, you go away from it," answered Nansen. Joshu continued, "If we do not try, how can we know that it is Tao?" Nansen replied, "Tao does not belong to knowing or not knowing. Knowing is illusion: not-knowing is blankness. If you really attain to Tao of no-doubt, it is like the great void, so vast and boundless. How, then, can there be right and wrong in the Tao?" At these words, Joshu was suddenly enlightened. (1974, p. 140)

The 17th-century Zen poet Bunan put the same thought in a slightly different way:

> While alive
> Be a dead man,
> Thoroughly dead;
> And act as you will,
> And all is good.

This is one of the hardest ideas in Zen Buddhism for many Westerners to grasp. It is perhaps like one of those "Chinese finger puzzle" woven tubes that you can buy in a joke store, the kind you stick your index fingers into from either end. The harder you then try to pull your fingers out of the tube, the tighter it grips your flesh. The only solution to the puzzle is to relax your grip. Your fingers will be automatically freed.

So too in Zen. It is the essence of letting go, of surrendering to mind at large. Zen is natural, uncontaminated, untrammeled, receptive mind. Zen is trust in the benevolent power of all our natural psychological processes.

If you are like some of my students and cannot imagine what on earth I am talking about, solve this homegrown *koan* for me: I am going to give you a precious and extraordinarily beautiful butterfly to appreciate as you will. Hold out your hand for it. What will you do once it lands ever so lightly on the tip of your finger?

Character: Zen's Inner Light

Every Zen-practicing psychologist I have asked has agreed with the observation that for most Westerners the key to understanding Zen is understanding that its essence is character. Character is the Western way of describing the existence of Tao within you. It is a way of grappling with the dilemma of what you are going to do with that butterfly sitting on your hand. Do you kill it to make sure it won't ever fly away? Do you try to grab it with your other hand to affirm your ownership of it? Do you run to the biology library to dissect it? If you are a person of "character," you simply open your hand to it and appreciate it for the brief moment it is there.

How then do you compensate for the butterfly's "loss" when it flies away? Do you regret its impermanence? How can you be "cured" of the need to possess and thus to destroy that which you are freely given? How can you escape the inevitable sorrow that follows after any intense joy?

Zen is not a cure. It does not offer you an escape. It is not an adjustment, nor is it compromise. Rather it is about liberation; it is about the transformation of self from object to subject. It is appreciation for the world that is given to you and that is unfolding all around you. It is about the recovery of the spiritual in life; it is about learning how to live life by "looking carefully."

Zen is inescapably about acknowledging and meeting the obligations attendant upon living in a world full of human suffering. As a wise old monk in northern Japan told me, it is about waking up the side of consciousness that exists but perhaps only on the dark side of the moon.

The monk and his disciple, whom he affectionately called Moonrocket on account of the novice's eager desire to enlighten the unconscious part of his own existence, shared their simple lunch of vegetables and thick noodles with me and asked me to share a Zen message with my students. The words belong to the *sensei* (1981); Moonrocket did the translation:

> When the student of Zen sits correctly for a half hour or an hour, for that period the clouds and the mists will clear and the original light will shine through. As proof of this we find that restless people become calmer, narrow-minded people become more broad and tolerant, rough-minded people become gentler, and weak and feeble people gain strength.
>
> We might say that the function of any religion in human life is, broadly, to solve the problems of life and fate. Fate is drawn from our karma. Karma means all our thoughts, words, and deeds.

To take a simple example, we all know how the facial expressions of people differ. People who think good thoughts and do good deeds have bright and gentle faces, while those who think bad thoughts and bad deeds have dark and cold faces. These facial expressions are the result of our words and deeds over a certain period.

If a man pursues a good karma, his destiny will improve; if he neglects it, it will worsen. Karma and destiny exist in a relation of cause and effect.

Why is it that men have fallen into this state of irreconcilable strife? Where does the cause lie?

I would answer without hesitation that it is because man has not faithfully followed the teachings of the Buddha and Christ. The Buddha taught charity. Christ taught love.

"Come to Your Senses!"

D. T. Suzuki was the Zen master most responsible for the integration of Zen teachings into mainstream Western psychotherapies. Suzuki summed up his perspective with brilliant clarity. "Zen," Suzuki-sensei wrote, "is the art of seeing into the nature of one's being" (1953, p. 3, quoted in Fromm, 1960, p. 114)

In the context of this chapter and this book, Zen is a set of practices (which we will explore in the next chapter) designed to bring us "alive," to bring us into a state of being where we can disregard the reducing valve of past experience and experience the expansive healing power of mind at large.

Like many Japanese intellectuals, Suzuki saw Westerners, or at least the rooms full of psychotherapists and psychoanalysts to whom he addressed his remarks, as largely and even tragically lacking the courage or the character to confront the bewilderment of conscious beings. He saw us fleeing to the linear certainties of "diagnosis and treatment" as a way of avoiding the essential mysteries of life. Basically, he was asking whether we have the courage and the character to live life without the isolating, insulating protection of our professional theories, concepts, and techniques.

He had a valid point. We therapists encourage people to gobble up mountains of Prozac and Valium. Our discourse does little to discourage suicide, abortion, and addictions of all sorts. We observe members of our society, from the very richest to the poorest and most despairing, destroying their lives for the stimulating "fix" of cocaine and the numbing relief of heroin or alcohol. Surely we are masters of avoiding something. Could it be bewilderment?

As therapists, aren't we sucked in by the idea that we can respond to our clients' problems ever more hygienically and dispassionately, by appealing to science and technology? Don't we believe that progress is an impersonal force, totally outside ourselves? At some level, don't most Western therapists believe, along with Albert Ellis and Sigmund Freud, that the answers to our problems lie in strengthening our analytical abilities, even at the expense of our spirituality, our consciousness, and the development of mind at large?

The Zen master, perhaps rightfully, accuses us of turning our backs on and fleeing simple human bewilderment. But he also knows that as human beings we all embrace bewilderment too. Isn't love totally bewildering? Isn't surviving a freakish accident? Isn't beholding your own child? Isn't confronting God or nature or the cosmos or whatever you call it? Isn't the fact of your own death ultimately bewildering?

D. T. Suzuki encouraged us to be of strong character and courageous resolve: "O Followers of the Way, difficult it is to be really true to oneself! The Buddha-dharma is deep, obscure, and unfathomable, but when it is understood, how easy it is!' (1960, p. 39).

It is time, gentle reader, to lose your mind—and come to your senses. In Zen you can bypass the reducing valve that forces you to perceive everything with the analytical, discriminative, differential, inductive, scientific, conceptual, impersonal, organizing, self-assertive thinking of the lion and the eagle. In Zen you can get beyond the useless habit of having a defensible opinion on just about everything, the compulsion to separate a thing into parts, to dissect it, conceptualize it, and thus pretend to understand it.

Come to your senses! Engage the world with your synthetic, totalizing, integrative, nondiscriminative mind. Open yourself to the intuitive, affective, subjective, deductive. Don't be afraid of the nonsystematic, nondiscursive, and spiritual knower inside your head. Stop acting like James's dog in the parlor. Raise your consciousness to embrace the definitively human by celebrating your "original nature."

CHAPTER 21

Therapeutic Implications of Zen Buddhism

On the Care and Feeding of Natural Mind

Thus far we have contented ourselves with a relatively Eurocentric view of the talking cure. When speaking of "cures" from other areas of the world, we have regarded them less as psychology than as philosophy or religion. Recall, however, that European and North American psychotherapies also have intellectual origins in philosophy and religion, and existential therapeutic approaches may have even come full circle. William James, Alfred Adler, Carl Jung, Gordon Allport, and others would remind us that religion, philosophy, and psychotherapy are all reflections of the human condition and thus essentially inseparable.

This chapter focuses on a non-Western approach, Zen Buddhism, that has ancient roots in Japanese culture. The basic teachings of Zen speak to the development of "character" as the way to integrate the physical, emotional, and psychological aspects of being. The development of character requires rigorous training and focused practice. For the student of Zen, the goal is to develop and integrate the human faculties of ethics, wisdom, and love. If we accept the existentialist formulation that wisdom and love are the components of will, Zen produces a psychology that in many ways is the perfect synthesis of the European and North American talking-cure traditions.

The aim of Zen is enlightenment: the immediate, unreflected grasp of reality, without affective contamination and intellectualization, the realization of the relation of myself to the Universe. This new experience is a repetition of the pre-intellectual, immediate grasp of the child, but on a new level, that of the full development of man's reason, objectivity, individuality. While the child's experience, that of immediacy and oneness, lies before the experience of alienation and the subject-object split, the enlightenment experience lies after it. (Fromm, 1960, p. 135)

In Chapter 20 we looked at some of the philosophical foundations underpinning non-Western and largely Chinese and Japanese approaches to studying and understanding human experience. In this chapter we will explore some of the psychological applications of one element of this tradition, Zen Buddhism. This "talking cure" is unusually quiet.

The Doctrine of the Unborn

An early Freudian, Franz Alexander, spoke of meditation as a "regression to the conditions of intrauterine life." I'm not sure how Alexander, or anyone else, could know what intrauterine life was like, but this phrase is a helpful starting point for our discussion of Zen-based therapies, providing we take Alexander's words metaphorically.

In Buddhism, as in the Judeo-Christian tradition, human beings are perceived as losing native-born innocence through the process of growing up. D. T. Suzuki (1960) referred to the "doctrine of the Unborn," the loss of an innocent and instinctive unconscious through the process of "training" in everyday living. Over time, we tend to stop hearing the songbirds out our kitchen window, we don't see the *nazunna* blooming by the roadside, we miss the thousand subtle ways that our worlds change hour to hour. All these perceptions are in the experience of the unborn, but they are obliterated in daily life by what Ornstein (1977) called "ordinary consciousness."

Yet it is a central assumption in Zen that our capacity to know and appreciate the world is never truly lost. It exists in a realm not exposed to awareness. D. T. Suzuki called this zone of mind the "cosmic unconscious," that aspect of human experience that in Zen is considered "the fountainhead of all creative possibilities" (Suzuki, 1949, p. 19, quoted in Fromm, 1960, p. 133).

The purpose of Zen training is to recover our childlike awareness of the world around us and to incorporate that awareness into our daily lives. D. T. Suzuki said that the ability to incorporate "all the conscious experiences . . . gone through since infancy" into one's "whole being" is the key element of genuine emotional and psychological maturity (quoted in Fromm, 1960, p. 133). The classic example of this phenomenon in practice is the hero of countless Japanese legends, movies, and television programs, Musashi, the Zen swordsman. Musashi's "sword is wielded as if it had a soul in itself," because he has mastered the discipline required to become one with every motion he makes: "As soon as [the swordsman] takes up the sword his technical proficiency, together with his consciousness of the entire situation, recede into the background and his trained unconscious begins to play its part to the fullest extent" (D. T. Suzuki, 1960, p. 19).

Similar mental discipline comes into play in all the traditional Zen arts, from flower arranging to poetry writing, the tea ceremony, and the fine art of making love.

(We will consider a range of such Zen practices in Chapter 23.) In every Zen practice a rigorous discipline must be adopted, less to acquire the specific skills required than to recover the innocent natural mind, the cosmic consciousness of the unborn. The goal is to execute the skill in perfect harmony with the circumstance and situation: "The sword is yielded as if it had a soul in itself."

Practice and discipline are necessary to overcome the loss of perfect innocence. Think of the number of times you have walked into an examination, full of every bit of information necessary to prevail over the tested material, when suddenly a fourth or more of the things you "know" are obliterated by anxiety, distractions in the room, bodily sensations, a confusion among terms. What you needed was not necessarily greater mastery of the content of the course, the book and the lectures, but greater mastery over yourself—your attention processes, arousal level, self-consciousness.

D. T. Suzuki would say that in this situation your sense domain has been invaded by intellect and that you have lost the "naivete of sense experience." As he explained:

> When we smile, it is not just smiling: something more is added. We do not eat as we did in our infancy; eating is mixed with intellection. And as we all realize this invasion by the intellect or the mixing with intellect, simple biological deeds are contaminated by ego-centric interest. This means that there is now an intruder into the unconscious, which can no longer directly or immediately move into the field of consciousness. (1960, pp. 19–20)

Klesha: Contaminated Mind

We can say that our difficulties in our taking such tests are due to our ordinary conscious mind losing the "answers" we knew by heart 30 minutes ago; our thinking has been "contaminated" by anxiety about our grade or our reputation as a scholar. Similarly, our smile may be contaminated by self-consciousness: Is it appropriate, is it polite, are our teeth "whiter than white"? Our answers on an exam, our response to entertainment, our reaction to the taste and aroma of food may be contaminated by the training we have received as adult members of the community. Our conscious mind becomes contaminated by "intellection," and our thoughts become clouded and confused by *klesha*, the Sanskrit word meaning affective contamination:

> The mature man is now asked by Zen to cleanse himself of this affective contamination and also to free himself of the intellectual conscious interference if he wishes to realize a life of freedom and spontaneity where such disturbing feelings as fear, anxiety, or insecurity have no room to assail him. When this liberation takes place, we have the "trained" unconscious operating in the field of consciousness. And we know what it is [to be] "Unborn," what . . . "everyday mind" is. (D. T. Suzuki, 1960, p. 20)

Klesha, contamination by the passions, is very much the problem confronted by most psychotherapy patients. Klesha is making unnecessary errors on an examination because of the emotional "baggage" we bring into the exam room with us. It is the failure to communicate clearly and simply from the heart because we are busy maintaining safe emotional distance. It is contamination by greed—greed for possessions, for fame, for affection. It is the isolation we impose on ourselves through narcissistic self-glorification and the illusion of individualistic omnipotence.

In Erich Fromm's terms (1960, p. 131), *klesha* is being unaware of one's own reality and of the reality of the world in its full depth and without veils. We can begin thinking about the aims of Zen in terms of the language used by Fromm in the passage at the beginning of this chapter. We need to go back to the world as we saw it before we all became contaminated with intellection and passion—back to the "immediate grasp of the child . . . *before* the experience of alienation and the subject-object split." In Western terms, we need to find some way to overcome the limitations we impose on reality when we think of ourselves as isolated, complete individuals. Fromm saw the goals of Zen as consistent with the "true aims of all great humanistic religions: overcoming the limitations of an egotistical self, achieving love, objectivity, and humility, and respecting life so that the aim of life is living itself, and man becomes what he potentially is" (1960, p. 80).

Natural Mind

What we potentially are, of course, is "natural mind." The care and feeding of natural mind requires above all else overcoming the illusion of separateness. Belief in separateness is entirely the product of intellection that has been fatally contaminated by affect. A cornerstone of Zen thinking is that every ounce of energy I invest in my ego is an ounce of energy that I cannot invest in my self, in being fully alive. Let me see if I can convince you of this point with two widely different examples. They both illustrate how investment in a separate, individual ego prevents the expression of self.

Example One. D. T. Suzuki (1960) told the story of a child, an art student, and a student of Zen who are each given a pad of paper, a box of crayons, and a patch of ground under a tree. Each is asked to draw a picture of a dragon. The child draws what his imagination tells him a dragon must look like. If he is a fortunate child, he will not have been given special "enrichment" classes in art. If he has been neither pampered nor neglected nor abused, he will be free to search his fantasy life to produce an image that satisfies his inner definition of what a dragon should look like if he ever met one.

The art student will probably complain that he doesn't know what a dragon is supposed to look like. Or if he has seen a picture of a dragon in a book, he will replicate its general shape; if he is especially self-confident, he will make it his own by incorporating into the drawing special artistic touches that are his signature. Unless he is a particularly gifted or particularly inept artist, his dragon will probably follow established guidelines for what people in his culture think dragons are supposed to look like.

In stark contrast to the child and the art student, the student of Zen will first go through the process of "becoming" the dragon. She will draw the dragon from the inside out. She will draw herself as a dragon—assuming of course, she draws anything at all.

Example Two. A man passing through a village saw the young student Masato searching for something on the ground.

"What have you lost, my friend?" he asked.

"My key," said Masato. So they both went down on their knees and looked for it.

After a time it was growing dark. They had made no progress, so the passerby asked, "Let's stop for a minute now; and see if you can't remember where you were when you dropped it."

"Oh, I dropped it over there, in my house," replied Masato.

"Then why are we looking out here?"

"Ah, because there is more light here than inside my own house" (adapted from Shah, 1966).

The Aim of Zen

The aim of Zen is to cast light inside the house, in the rooms where the key to knowledge has been mislaid. The solutions to the dilemmas of human life lie within the deeply transformative powers of self-awareness. By recovering a childlike sensitivity to the inner and outer world, the followers of Zen perceive the world freshly, free from the blinders and the distractions of ingrained mental habits, and rediscover will, intention, and the ability to focus consciousness.

Practitioners of Zen, by losing their mind and coming to their senses, experience existential freedom. A sense of complete security and fearlessness is part of the recovery of natural mind, the natural appreciation of the world as it is. This ontological consciousness is the pure experience of what William James called the transcendental self and Carl Jung wrote about as the metaphysical self. Zen practice is designed to awaken sleepwalking students, to permit them to see the world anew with newly found equilibrium, uniformity of self, equanimity, and tranquility.

In Japan this consciousness is akin to seeing the first fleeting cherry blossom of spring or a glimpse of Mount Fuji towering above the clouds. For many North Americans it is perhaps a fleeting moment of perfect communication between lovers or the temporary glow of sunrise over a desert canyon. It is always a perfectly ordinary moment made extraordinary by the clarity of perception that the self brings to the moment. It always transcends desire; it obliterates fear. It removes the veil of ignorance from knowing. In Fromm's psychoanalytic language, it is *"making the unconscious conscious transform[ing] the mere idea of the universality of man into the living experience of this universality; it is the experiential realization of humanism"* (1960, p. 107). It is, in D. T. Suzuki's words, the birth of the "naked true man of no rank who goes in and out of your facial gates." Suzuki illustrated his point with a *koan*:

> One day Rinzai Gigen (died 867) gave this sermon: "There is the true man of no rank in the mass of naked flesh, who goes in and out from your facial gates [that is, your sense organs]. Those who have not yet testified [to the fact], look, look!"
> A monk came forward and asked, "Who is this true man of no rank?"
> Rinzai came down from his chair and, taking hold of the monk by the throat, said, "Speak, speak!"
> The monk hesitated.
> Rinzai let go his hold and said, "What a worthless dried up stick of dirt this is!"
> (adapted from Suzuki, 1960, p. 52)

Vivian's Battle With *Klesha*

In Chapter 20 I told you something about Vivian, the woman whose sanity and even life were nearly destroyed by her family's unrelenting abuse. I tried to reconceptualize what had happened inside Vivian from a Zen perspective, suggesting that the brutality she had grown up with had scarred her natural mind with the three consuming fires of greed, hate, and delusion. To protect herself from being utterly vandalized, Vivian had developed the delusion that she could keep herself safe by greedily satisfying all her cravings. In Zen terms, she suffered the delusion that she could somehow escape her fate by blocking every authentic impulse and giving full rein to every contrived impulse she ever experienced.

Of course, what Vivian discovered was that one cannot escape one's fate. Lying, stealing, cheating, and becoming intoxicated are the natural outlets for the clouded, angry, vengeful mind, but they never resolve life's dilemmas because they always leave the mind more agitated, more anxious, and more trapped. (Fromm's *The Anatomy of Human Destructiveness*, 1973, explores these issues in significant detail.) The only resolution for a life lived as compensation, as was so strikingly clear in Vivian when I first saw her in therapy, is madness or suicide.

In retrospect, Vivian and I can now see that only one aspect of Vivian's life back then gave her a glimmer of the "naked true man of no rank" who resided within her tortured soul. I suppose Jung would have called it the mother archetype. Vivian could never have deserted her children to the cruel and exploitative world from which she felt only she could protect them. With her children, Vivian knew she was more than a separate, separated ego enclosed in a bag of skin. When it came to protecting her children—filling a promise that they would not grow up abused and full of self-hatred—Vivian abandoned her delusions and her steel-armored self-absorption. As a mother, she knew, she had to live her life, not be a passive pawn in other people's games. (And indeed, to her intense horror, her parents never relented from trying to gain custody of her children during the entire period of her hospitalization.)

I am certainly not saying that caring for children is the existential answer to the ontological dilemmas confronting women or any other class of people. But Vivian found in her children something to fight for and to commit herself to. Vivian survived her ordeal initially only because she was able to focus her life forces on her responsibilities and being as a mother. Her relationship with her children gave her the only authentic existential moments of her entire life; her powerful maternal feelings made it imperative that she survive her madness. My interpretation of Vivian's survival is that her love for her children was so great that she was able to "extinguish the passions" of her madness in its service and thereby forge a connection between her basic human nature and the creative therapeutic process. As Moonrocket and his master told me (see Chapter 20), "the clouds and the mists will clear, and the original light will shine through."

Are these concepts too abstract to be applied robustly to our Western talking cure? I imagine that for a great many patients, and for a majority of the therapists cut from the scientist-practitioner mold, the emphasis in Zen on transformation of character would be unfathomable. On the other hand, a significant minority of psychotherapists believe that

> the most important lesson psychiatry can learn from Zen is its teaching about the original nature of man. To tap the individual's full potential for intuitive insight and for appropriate action. The advantages of such an intuitional approach would be obvious. Learning through the process of self-discovery would reduce resistance to change, while enhancing the person's self-esteem, and his capacity for independence. He would be constantly reminded that whatever progress he is making is largely due to his own effort.
>
> What applies to effective psychotherapy pertains equally well to the ultimate goal of Zen discipline, which is to cultivate the ability to think, feel, and act with a degree of objectivity, spontaneity, freedom, and compassion. A Zen master described such a person as "One who eats when he is hungry, and drinks when he is thirsty." (Dai, 1981, p. 24)

The Role of the *Sensei*

Before we turn to the "practical" or application aspect of Zen, there is one further contribution of Zen to modern psychotherapy that deserves mention: the special relationship between the *sensei* or master and the student or disciple. It is easy to overlook this aspect of Zen because teachers of Zen do not try to make themselves the center of the lesson or of the student's attention. There is no room in Zen for the towering, controlling, directing, authoritative ego of a Sigmund Freud, the reassuring redemptive understanding of a Carl Rogers, the intrusive insistence of an Albert Ellis, or the rude, rambunctious antics of a Fritz Perls. The Zen master does not set up environments and assume creative control over people's destinies, as a John Watson or a B. F. Skinner does. The Zen master provides a much more rigorous training environment than the genteel comfort of the consulting room.

In Zen training, the *sensei* is completely as one with the student. Everything the student does and says reveals a measure of the student's progress to the master. There is a compassionate quality to the instruction that is not contaminated by age or status differences, by the intrusion of intellect, or by the fires of ego.

My Encounter

My most vivid encounter with this concept of the *sensei* may sound somewhat trivial, but I believe it is very telling. A few years ago I attended an academic conference in Japan on Zen applications to physical and mental health. We convened at several universities, where we gave and listened to addresses on various applications of Zen practice (some of these addresses will be reported in Chapter 23). After one morning session, several of us adjourned to a nearby Zen temple for some meditation practice. It was a beautiful 18th-century wooden building, still in active use as a Zen training center.

The abbot of the temple welcomed us and gave us a few simple instructions so we might unobtrusively join his community in meditation. It was late July, and the temperature outside was in the mid-90s and not much cooler inside.

We were each shown to a small raised wooden platform where we were to spend an hour or so in tranquil reflection. As I got deeper and deeper into my meditation, I began to feel lighter and lighter and, quite remarkably, cooler and cooler. Almost before I knew it, the training *sensei* was ringing his bell, indicating that the hour was up. I pivoted around to look into the center of the room, feeling wonderfully refreshed (even though I had lost all feeling in my lotus-position-locked legs). And what did I see: The gentle old abbot had been standing behind me with a large folding fan—fanning me, with a wonderful slight smile on his face. He had evidently stood there in complete silence for the better part of an hour, fanning this quite obviously overheated American professor. So much for my egolessness. I had actually imagined that I had gone so far with my meditation that I was able to transcend the discomfort of the Tokyo climate in July. In reality it was a quiet act of kindness, not an aspect of my enlightenment, that made my hour so rewarding.

The realization of that fact probably had more of an impact on my natural mind than any other aspect of the week's events. The abbot's concern for me became the enlightening aspect of the day's meditation; it brought me into connection with him in a very simple but extraordinarily intimate way. The old monk's unspoken act of kindness filled me with *samadhi*, the Sanskrit word for equanimity and tranquility.

Fromm addressed the transformative function that Zen can have on the person and the process of psychotherapy:

> Zen, different as it is in its method from psychoanalysis, can sharpen the focus, throw new light on the nature of insight, and heighten the sense of what it is to see, what it is to be creative, what it is to overcome the affective contaminations and false intellectualizations which are the necessary results of experience of the subject-object split.
>
> It is this very radicalism with respect to intellectualization, authority, and the delusion of the ego, in its emphasis on the aim of well being, Zen thought will deepen and widen the horizon of the psychoanalyst and help him to arrive at a more radical concept of the grasp of reality as the ultimate aim of full, conscious awareness. (1960, p. 140)

Mu!

D. T. Suzuki's Zen master is more likely to grab the headstrong novice by the throat or to slap the student soundly with a stick (in formal Zen training the stick is used to slap students back into full awareness as their mind starts to wander or they fall asleep) than to silently wave a fan over the student. But Suzuki also clearly stated that the relationship between the *sensei* and the student is essential to the student's education and awakening:

> I cannot help adding another word or two here. An interpersonal relationship is sometimes spoken of in connection with the koan exercise when the master asks a question and the pupil takes it up in his interview with his master. Especially when the master stands rigidly and irrevocably against the pupil's intellectual approach, the pupil, failing to find what to make of the situation, feels as if he were utterly depending on the master's helping hand to pick him up. In Zen this kind of relationship between master and pupil is rejected as not conducive to the enlightenment experience on the part of the pupil. For it is the koan *"Mu!,"* symbolizing the ultimate reality itself, and not the master, that will rise out of the pupil's unconscious. It is the koan *"Mu!"* that makes master knock down pupil, who, when awakened, in turn slaps master's face. There is no Self in its limited finite phase in this wrestlers-like encounter. It is most important that this be unmistakably understood in the study of Zen. (1960, p. 58)

A Zen Primer

Zen is more than a theory. It is a way of life directed by a strict and rigorous philosophy. It is the essence of compassion for human suffering, but it is not the sort of kind and egalitarian doctrine that many North Americans favor. It teaches us about the nature of the universe not for knowledge's sake but in order to show us how to strengthen our character and resolve in the face of adversity.

Ultimately, if we accept the formulation that wisdom and love are the components of will, Zen produces a psychology that is the perfect synthesis of the European and North American talking-cure legacies. In fact, I would venture the hypothesis that Zen meditation could be an adjunct to Western psychotherapies of all stripes—as likely to be employed as a device for accessing the unconscious by an orthodox Freudian as a means of inducing deep relaxation in strict conditioning therapy.

Four Noble Truths and the Noble Eightfold Path

Zen transcends all these approaches by its insistence on a strict code of conduct, which was laid down many centuries ago in India, in the teachings of the Venerable Siddhartha Gautama, the Buddha, in the sixth century B.C.E. At the core of his teachings are the "four noble truths":

- *All life is suffering.* Dissatisfaction is inescapably part of human ignorance.
- *All suffering stems from desire.* Our minds are unbalanced by our cravings.
- *Elimination of desire removes all suffering.* Craving must be replaced with acceptance. "The hungry man eats; the thirsty man drinks."
- *Elimination of desire comes from following the "noble eightfold path."* Life lived in perfect moderation is the ideal state of being.

The four noble truths thus open the door to the noble eightfold path, eight precepts for ethically correct living:

- *Right understanding* of the nature of cause and effect and of human beings' place in the universe. Sometimes this precept is stated as "right view" or "right belief."
- *Right thought,* also sometimes described as "right intention."
- *Right speech,* or not telling lies, gossip, or slander; cultivating ways of using speech to increase harmony among living things.
- *Right conduct,* which is honorable and peaceful. For Buddhists, right conduct involves demonstrating love and compassion for all living things.
- *Right livelihood,* making sure that one's occupation does not result in or bring harm to others.
- *Right effort,* which is a direct reference to the exercise of will.
- *Right mindfulness,* which includes a well-disciplined consciousness and control over bodily sensations and functions.
- *Right concentration,* which includes disciplined attention and leads to the practice of meditation.

Three Domains. Overall, this teaching can be divided into three essential domains. To master this life and gain peace of mind, a person must

- Engage in ethical conduct, which includes speech, actions, and conduct
- Engage in mental discipline, which includes effort, mindfulness, and concentration—giving rigorous training to consciousness
- Strive to develop universal wisdom, or *prajna:*

> There is no corresponding English word, in fact no European word for [*prajna*], for European people have no experience specifically equivalent to *prajna*. Prajna is the experience a man has when he feels in its most fundamental sense the infinite totality of things, that is, psychologically speaking, when the finite ego, breaking its hard crust, refers itself to the infinite which envelops everything that is finite and limited and therefore transitory. We may take this experience as being somewhat akin to a totalistic intuition of something that transcends all our particularized, specified experiences. (D. T. Suzuki, 1960, p. 74)

When we conceptualize Zen as a non-Western equivalent of our talking cures, we need to keep these three fundamental goals in mind.

Ethical Standards. Has the patient been living according to the highest ethical standards? Does the person's occupation permit her or him to conduct life with integrity and to engage in humane interaction with others? Is she or he refraining from lying, stealing, engaging in sexual misconduct, killing, taking mind-clouding drugs? Is she or he free from behavior controlled by greed, anger, and aversion? If I am working with a student who I know is cheating or anyone who is violating the vows of marriage or being cruel to her or his children, "therapy" cannot proceed without addressing these ethical issues. If my client harbors racist, misogynic, or homophobic attitudes, can that person ever be "cured" if those attitudes are never examined and changed? In a similar vein, wasn't Alfred Adler (see Chapter 8) essentially correct to insist that his patients develop "fellow feeling" and "social interest"?

Can therapeutic ethics be defined only in terms of avoiding doing harm? I should be surprised if the ethical systems of my clients were not a central focus of my therapy; I would have to question whether I was really doing the job I was paid to do.

Case Study: My Problem With Leo

I once had to dismiss a client from counseling on account of his ethics. I was working with an undergraduate, "Leo," who was increasingly troubled by a relatively serious case of academic performance anxiety with an accompanying sleep disorder. The problem was one of long standing and was becoming more and more serious as Leo approached upper-level work in his major.

We undertook various behavioral and analytic strategies for understanding his problem. The sessions seemed to be heading in the direction of rational emotive behavior therapy (see Chapter 14), because Leo's anxiety was well rooted in his dogmatic beliefs about the necessity of always being perfect—or at least always being perceived as a person who was perfect.

Meanwhile, I was also involved with a very young-looking freshman who had been the subject of a great deal of emotional, verbal, and physical abuse as a pledge in a fraternity. One of my jobs is to prompt students in these situations to work assertively to put an end to such harassment or to bring it to the disciplinary attention of the college administration. The beginning stages of intervention involve educating the victim about college policy on fraternity hazing and harassment and then asking him to identify the person within the fraternity who holds official responsibility for seeing that the policy is respected and adhered to. The freshman did the research I assigned him and came back to report that the very person who had responsibility for enforcement of the college hazing policy was, in fact, the most offensive and aggressive member of the organization—yet another case of putting the fox in charge of the chicken coop.

Well, as you have probably guessed, the culprit in all this was my other client, Leo. A quick check with my advising network confirmed that indeed Leo was the house bully. Every student in the organization who was younger than Leo despised and feared him; most everyone else in the house thought he was a class-A jerk. But not a soul was willing to stand against Leo or even to put pressure on him to resign his elective office in the fraternity.

I knew I couldn't continue to work with Leo if it meant pretending that I didn't know the harm he was doing to his fellow students. His character had to be part of the treatment focus, or we would get nowhere in counseling. But I also had to protect the identity of the freshman who had come to me for help.

I was at an impasse until the dean's office finally got word of the situation and decided—in their usual tepid and cautious fashion—that they had to take action. By this time about six freshmen from the fraternity were talking about leaving school. Once the dean's office intervened, their investigation revealed that Leo was at the center of the problem. They "strongly recommended" that the house deal with the problem within its own disciplinary framework.

The fraternity chapter made three decisions. They punished the freshmen for "revealing fraternity secrets." They voted to stop all "official" forms of harassment, "even though it is a lot of fun for everyone." And they told Leo if he wanted to stay in his office, he would have to talk with the counseling service about his "attitude."

Perhaps those wiser than I could have made this situation work, but evidently I wasn't clever enough to tie it all up in a package. Leo demanded from me a letter to the fraternity saying that he was seriously involved in counseling and was therefore in compliance with their demands. But the catch was, he refused to discuss in our sessions his behavior toward the freshmen.

So I refused. In fact, I demanded that Leo acknowledge the connection between his unethical behavior in his fraternity and his original presenting problems. I may even have suggested that anyone who treats other people the way Leo treated them deserved to be anxious and to lose some sleep. I couldn't work with him on one issue without at the same time addressing the rest of his life.

Leo's answer was to walk defiantly out of my office, never to return. In time he graduated, but he never spoke to me again. About half the freshmen resigned from the fraternity. About six of the upperclassmen, who felt utterly betrayed by the cowardice of their fraternity and the callowness of the college administration, eventually became individual clients in counseling as they developed the need to renegotiate their relationship with both organizations. Leo never resigned, nor was he removed from his office.

Two Types of Meditation

Getting back to Zen, I would argue strongly that the emphasis on ethics and character—as these are reflected in thought, word, and deed—are essential to the therapeutic enterprise. But what of Zen's second main point, mental discipline?

There are two principal approaches to developing mental discipline in Zen; both are forms of meditation, but one is alleged to be more "advanced" or "mature" than the other. I would prefer to say that one becomes applicable after some extended practice with the other. At any rate, they both have the same aim: to strengthen character by disciplining consciousness, to put us back in control of our own minds, to light a candle of inner awareness so that we can look for the key, or as Emerson said, to make us able to live in the present, above time.

Concentration Meditation. *Concentration meditation* is the practice that most Westerners associate with Zen. When it takes the form of *zazen,* it involves sitting (or alternatively standing or lying) perfectly still in a carefully prescribed manner. The person who is meditating "concentrates" on a *mantra,* a sound or a phrase that can be repeated in one's mind; "ooohmmmm" is the generic mantra, but expensive boutique mantras are also available from any number of mountebanks (keep in mind that in Zen you often get what you don't pay for). Or you can substitute a *koan* for the mantra. My favorite beginner's *koan* is "Can God create a rock so big that she can't lift it?" A slightly more advanced *koan* is "Is love ever selfless?" From my experience, almost any idea derived purely from Gestalt therapy (see Chapter 16) can be used as a *koan.* The only central property of the *koan* is that it must defy solution by any form of analytical, reductive, or deductive mental process.

When I engage in concentration meditation, I prefer either focusing on my breathing—which I try to visualize, according to the season, as either hot or cold—or imagining a light glowing from my abdomen, which slowly grows and diffuses throughout my entire body. Students beginning sitting *zazen* are frequently told to "count" their breaths and to try to maintain a dual consciousness between awareness of their breathing and awareness of the counting. Kapleau (1965) suggested that students may also be asked to "follow the inhalations and exhalations of the breath with the mind's eye only, again in a natural rhythm and without strain" (p. 11). But he was quick to add that these early forms of exercise of the conscious mind, this *zazen*, are not to be confused with the practice of meditation itself.

Awareness Meditation. *Zazen* should be thought of as training the consciousness in the discipline it will need when the time comes to move on to *awareness meditation*. *Zazen* prepares the mind for awareness meditation:

> The uniqueness of zazen is this: that the mind is freed from bondage to *all* thought forms, visions, objects, and imaginings, however sacred or elevating, and brought to a state of absolute emptiness, from which alone it may one day perceive its own true nature, or the nature of the universe. (Kapleau, 1965, p. 12)

Zazen involves "intense inner struggle to gain control over the mind and then to use it, like a silent missile, to penetrate the barrier of the five senses and the discursive intellect. It demands determination, courage, and energy" (Kapleau, 1965, p. 12).

> With the body and mind consolidated, focused, and energized, the emotions respond with increased sensitivity and purity, and volition exerts itself with greater strength of purpose. No longer are we dominated by intellect at the expense of feeling, nor driven by the emotions unchecked by reason or will. Eventually zazen leads to a transformation of personality and character. Dryness, rigidity, and self-centeredness give way to flowing warmth, resiliency, and compassion, while self-indulgence and fear are transmuted into self-mastery and courage. (Kapleau, 1965, p. 13)

Honesty requires me to confess that *zazen* is as far as I have ever gone with meditation practice, and I am not sure I have practiced it with the seriousness of purpose and strict discipline required to experience more than a glimmer of what Kapleau described. For me the Buddha is always a chubby, smiling, serene, and all-encompassing figure who would find it very peculiar if I ever became seriously disciplined about *zazen* or any other personal practice. I'm not suggesting that I am just another hippie psychologist, just that I take the teachings about moderation quite seriously and therefore could not in fairness consider myself a serious student of *zazen* practice.

I am more of a follower of the Soto sect of Zen. Soto sect members often describe themselves as "just sitting," which is a pretty wonderful mode to be in now and again, if you can master the art of it. My client Leo would have been better off by light-years had he had any idea of how to "just sit"; but the technique is something that my friend Sam, introduced back in Chapter 15, has a good start on. Someday, I hope in my heart, Vivian and I will be able to go watch the eagles soar over Sugar Creek and "just sit."

The U.S. poet Robert Frost (1967) had a similar thought: "We dance round in a ring and suppose, / But the secret sits in the middle and knows" (p. 495). As did Ralph Waldo Emerson:

These roses under my window make no reference to former roses or to better ones. They are for what they are; they exist with God today. There is no time to them. There is simply the rose; it is perfect in every moment of its existence . . . but man postpones and remembers. He can not be happy and strong until he too, lives with nature in the present, above time. (quoted in Naranjo, 1970, p. 69)

Satori

The truly serious student of Zen eventually moves from *zazen* to awareness meditation. This is the "advanced" form of meditation where one fills one's consciousness with "sacred" images and symbols. These images include the individuating and transforming archetypes that Jung wrote about extensively, which I mentioned in passing in Chapter 9. Anyone who has not experienced this level of consciousness may not fully comprehend the meaning or significance of this experience, but usually it is what people have in mind when they speak and write about *satori*, or enlightenment. Curiously, one rarely hears satori mentioned in Zen circles in Japan, but in the West scholars treat it as more or less the main organizing principle in all meditative practices.

Probably the most serious error you can make when thinking about satori is to think of it as a destination or a state of being to be achieved or attained, which is how you will hear most Westerners speak of it. In fact, however, it is not even an experience that occurs in stages—another great Western psychological principle ("I'm at the esteem stage, but I hope soon to be at the self-actualization stage"), which seems to me a lot like junior high school boys competing with each other for size or distance.

Satori can be thought of as simply one of the different levels of awareness that a person may experience in life. In Japanese these levels, not stages, are described in a series of three *kenshos* (Kennett, 1977):

1. At the first level one experiences a burst of insight and clarity, suddenly seeing the "immaculacy of nothingness." I have often wondered if this is what some Christians experience when they have a "born-again" experience. I think, oddly enough, that quite a few people in the West experience this feeling in moments of utter despair. I once experienced this level of *kensho*, or something like it, several times during a summer I spent as the sole occupant of the summit of Mt. Moosilauke in New Hampshire (I was a hermit–park ranger–ecoterrorist one summer while in college) and then again when camping with a very close friend in the wilderness of the high desert in Utah.

2. The Zen masters teach that such experiences can be experienced more deeply and profoundly as one continues meditation and training. In time one may reach the second level of *kensho*, which we can think of as a sort of "career-*kensho*"; you experience it when *kensho* becomes a regular part of your everyday life. The famous D. T. Suzuki, whom I have quoted at length in this chapter,

once characterized this experience as "a million little moments that make one dance" (quoted in Kennett, 1977, p. 5).

3. The third level of *kensho* is essentially immortality, or achieving Buddahood. As a self-declared "simple country head doctor," I am not about to try to tell you what immortality is, let alone what Buddahood is. From my understanding, it is simply the process of becoming one with the river of time, of being the star of your own science fiction story, or perhaps of discovering that you are madly in love with and are deeply loved by a Cordon Bleu cook with his or her own wine cellar. As a mere grasshopper I know nothing about any of this, but I hope Buddahood is something akin to simply living, perhaps even being, this Zen prayer:

To do goods,
To avoid evils,
To purify one's own heart:
This is the Buddha way.

Prajna: Wisdom From the Self

Thus far we have established that Zen talking-cure therapists must concern themselves with patients' ethical lives and moral conduct and must encourage patients to undertake the serious and disciplined practice of meditation. We can summarize these points by saying that Zen therapists must serve patients by doing everything in their power to encourage patients to keep their minds free from evil and fully devoted to good. The third element in the Zen therapy equation is the development of *prajna*. How and from what does wisdom develop? One might better ask from whence comes the Buddha's profound love of all living things.

Christianity's answer is that love comes directly as a gift from God. For Rollo May, in *Love and Will*, this love is akin to the biological love that mother (and some father) animals display for their young. May also said that it is the New Testament notion of "charity" (1969, p. 316), which a Zen master would not dispute. But has May fully explained enlightened love? In *Psychotherapy East and West*, Watts (1961) ducked the issue by saying it is simply a form of "insight," attained through "discipline" (p. 83). Which leaves us with Fromm, who wrote *The Art of Loving*:

Love is *union under the conditions of preserving one's integrity,* one's individuality. *Love is the active power in man;* a power which breaks through the walls which separate man from his fellow man, which unites him with others; love makes him overcome the sense of isolation and separateness, yet it permits him to be himself, to regain his integrity. (1956, p. 17)

But Zen is perhaps more Calvinist than this answer will allow. Zen is almost preoccupied with the suffering that exists in the world; it stands face to face with the destruction of the human heart that is wreaked by the three fires. It is almost a doctrine of irredeemable original sin. *Prajna* is the product of the experience of spontaneous, universal, unconditional love. In Buddhism it comes directly from one's experience in the world, which to Western eyes is probably the last place on earth you would think to look for it.

De Martino (1960), in an essay titled "The Human Situation and Zen Buddhism," stated this point elegantly. He suggested that what we discover through the ethical and mental practice of Zen is a recognition of the universality of self. Under this · "awakened" definition of self, self-awareness becomes awareness of all creation. Through Zen practice, self recognizes "I am I, Thou art Thou. I am Thou, and Thou art I." So that "when I see the flower, I see my Self; the flower sees my Self; my Self sees its Self; its Self sees its Self."

> Here is living, creative Love in consummate activation and fulfillment, ever expressing its Self, ever that which is expressed. That which expresses is that which is expressed, that with which it is expressed, and that for which it is expressed. Here, alone, is total and unconditional affirmation of subject and object, of itself, of the other, of the world, of being, for here, alone, is total and unconditional affirmation of its Self, by its Self, through its Self, as Self-ego. (De Martino, 1960, pp. 170–171)

Beginner's Mind

Shunryu Suzuki, a Zen master (1905–1971), wrote an enchanting book on Zen titled *Zen Mind, Beginner's Mind* (1970), which invites the "beginner's mind" to learn more about Zen. (It is a beautifully constructed and printed little book and very inexpensive.) Suzuki Sensei (who was teased by his wife about not having experienced satori) stressed the practice of Zen over the intellectual grasping of its tenets. He regarded *zazen* as a therapeutic practice, one that can help the practitioner attain a significant sense of freedom in daily life. His book is a gentle and compassionate guide for the beginning student.

Which is not to say that S. Suzuki was inviting you to any sort of couch-potato Zen practice:

> *When you do something, if you fix your mind on the activity with some confidence, the quality of the state of your mind is the activity itself. When you are concentrated on the quality of your being, you are prepared for activity.* (1970, p. 104)

I am not altogether sure the venerable master would appreciate all the intellection I have brought to this chapter. All I have written is words, but understanding Zen *"is not just an intellectual understanding. True understanding is actual practice itself"* (p. 97). Just to make sure that I get the point, Suzuki went on to say that Zen is about

"EXPERIENCE, NOT PHILOSOPHY. *There is something blasphemous in talking about how Buddhism is perfect as a philosophy or teaching without knowing what it actually is*" (p. 123).

Community

S. Suzuki went on to say:

> To practice zazen with a group is the most important thing . . . because this practice is the original way of life. One must not isolate one's self from the rest of humanity when practicing zazen. For to do so is to risk not understanding or knowing the *meaning* of the effort that one has to exert in practicing zazen. That meaning derives from the function of Zen of creating and maintaining one's connection to the community. This is the reason that in Japan companies often send their employees off together on weekend Zen retreats. Those who practice zazen all alone risk becoming "attached only to the result of their effort" and will [therefore] not have any chance to appreciate it, because the result will never come. (1970, p. 23)

In other words, the presence of a group of fellow practitioners of *zazen* minimizes the temptation to "take pride in your attainment or become discouraged because of your idealistic effort"—in which case "your practice will confine you by a thick wall" (p. 131).

So first gather a group together. Make sure you have an ample supply of munchies and drinks for later, and don't forget the music for the post-*zazen* karaoke. Eliminate any somber or serious ideas in your head. *Zazen* is a celebration of awareness. I have already written that Zen frowns on clouding the mind with intoxicants, and I would certainly extend that prohibition to the chemicals you get from the pharmacy that block or attenuate your grasp of reality. Further, in *zazen* as in the rest of your life, you should surely refrain from any substance with which you have had a negative relationship.

Keep in mind, however, that the principle of moderation is violated if you become too somber and pious about this whole exercise. How can you be moderate *and* sanctimonious? What is essential is the development of a sense of occasion and a feeling for the relativism of everything in life.

This relativism is richly illustrated in the tale of Wei-ching, a pious Chinese monk, and his young disciple Hsun-ching. They once went on a pilgrimage to southeast China to study some ancient Buddhist *sutras*. On their way back home, they happened to stay at an inn where the innkeeper had learned the art of cooking from a French chef. After a fine meal and a generous sample of the local brandy, which Wei-ching described as "simply miraculous," they retired to their room. There the boy posed the following question to his master:

"Master—I thought Buddhist monks never eat meat or drink. But tonight we had fish, ham, and liquor. What will happen to us now?"

Wei-ching picked at his teeth for a moment then said, "It is true that one should not eat meat or drink liquor. But it is even more true that a Buddhist must be compassionate. That man needed to prepare us a good meal, to redeem himself for ignoring religion during his life. If we had refused, we would have prevented him from carrying out a pious act and gaining merit. So you see, we soiled ourselves temporarily, that he might be cleansed." (Salzman, 1991, p. 27)

Any questions?

Having prepared the biological environment, we can now turn to the social environment. You must gather around you a group of equally thoughtful persons with whom you share a significant sense of community. For students, this step shouldn't be too hard. Nonstudents might inquire among their coworkers or neighbors. The only important rule is that you must, in Fromm's words, stay away from the "bad company" of people who occupy their time with trivial conversation, unworthy occupations, and unethical conduct. Fromm (1956) was quite instructive on this point:

By bad company I do not refer only to people who are vicious and destructive; one should avoid their company because their orbit is poisonous and depressing. I mean also the company of zombies, of people whose soul is dead, although their body is alive; of people whose thoughts and conversation are trivial; who chatter instead of talk, and who assert cliche opinions instead of thinking. (pp. 95–96)

Dogen's Exercise

At this point I will turn the podium over to Dogen, the monk who brought the principles of Zen to Japan from China 750 years ago. First, he would say, find a quiet room. It doesn't need to be a soundproof chamber; the ordinary sounds of the world will not interfere with your practice. But it should be free of television and radio, and people should not be coming and going through the room while you practice. Spend some time quietly sitting in the room and focus on trying to

free yourself from all attachments, and bring to rest the ten thousand things. Think of neither good nor evil and judge not right or wrong. Maintain the flow of mind, of will, and of consciousness; bring to an end all desires, all concepts [especially all the "concepts" in this and the previous chapter] and judgments. *Do not think about how to become a Buddha.* (Dogen, ca. 1231, quoted in Dumoulin, 1940, p. 161; italics added)

Second, put down a thick pillow on the floor; then add a round cushion on top of it. Make sure you are dressed comfortably—no shoes—but dress with care. This is not an opportunity for the "grunge" look, unless "grunge" is your normal mode of dress on important occasions. If you are fairly limber, assume the "full lotus" position by placing the right foot on the left thigh and the left foot on the right thigh (in that order). If you are not so limber, try the half-lotus position: Place only the left foot on the right thigh. Rest your right hand palm up in the general neighborhood of where your left foot is resting, and let your left hand rest in the palm of the right. Your thumbs should be lightly touching.

Third, sit upright, without inclining to the left or the right, forward or backward. Ears and shoulders, nose and navel must be kept in alignment. Keep your tongue against the palate, lips and jaw firmly closed, eyes always open.

Now regulate your breathing. As wishes and images arise, take note of them—almost as if you are seeing them in a museum—and then dismiss them. Accept that in *zazen,* as S. Suzuki (1970) told us, "your mind and body have great power to accept things as they are, whether agreeable or disagreeable" (p. 38); "to realize pure mind in [the midst of] your delusion is practice. If you try to expel the delusion it will only persist the more. Just say, 'Oh, this is just delusion', and do not be bothered by it" (p. 127).

Most masters suggest that beginners practice this simple form of *zazen,* known as *bonpu* or "ordinary" meditation, for just a few minutes a day, perhaps twice a day. The purpose of the exercise is practice, not enlightenment. It is to help us discover that random thoughts arise out of our unconscious and that if we make no special effort to retain them, they simply float away, bringing us no harm. Those thoughts vanish with no effort. Conversely—and as a cognitive therapist I recommend that you test this notion experimentally—when we make serious efforts to expel thoughts, they persist and grow in importance, empowered by the energy they have gathered from our struggle with them.

Finally, before you head off to the post-*zazen* party, reflect a bit on what you have just experienced and accomplished. Try to understand how you are now feeling. This is a crucial step for most novice Western meditators. As S. Suzuki (1970) warned, "If your practice [has been] good, you may become proud of it. What you *do* is good, but something more has been added to it. Pride is extra. *Right effort* is to get rid of something extra" (p. 59; italics added).

> This kind of bad effort [pride] is called being "Dharma-ridden" or "practice-ridden." You are involved in some idea of practice or attainment, and you can not get out of it. When you are involved in some dualistic idea, it means your practice is not pure. . . . If you think you will get something from practicing zazen, already you are involved in impure practice. . . . When you practice zazen, just practice zazen. If enlightenment comes, it just comes. We should not attach to the attainment. The true quality of zazen is always there, even if you are not aware of it, so forget about what you think you may have gained from it. Just do it. The quality of zazen will express itself; then you will have it. (pp. 59–60)

Now you are ready for the little party.

Seiza: "Quiet Sitting Therapy"

At least one formal Japanese therapeutic approach is based on *zazen*. It is called *seiza,* or "quiet sitting therapy." Reynolds (1980), whose work we will explore in greater detail in Chapter 22, described *seiza* as a "rest cure" whose origins can be traced back more than a thousand years in classic Chinese texts.

The essential aspect of *seiza* is learning to sit, not in the lotus position but in the traditional Japanese pattern, with the legs tucked under the buttocks and feet crossed. (Caution: Non-Japanese persons over the age of 35 should not attempt this sitting position without assistance; otherwise you may spend the rest of your life as a human pretzel.) Rest your left hand gently on top of your right hand, with the left thumb tucked inside the right palm. Alternatively, Reynolds advised that old codgers like me may use a straightback chair for *seiza*. In this case, sit forward in the chair with feet on the floor and separated slightly, head erect, hands clasped in your lap, eyes and mouth closed.

Posture is critically important. The posture is neither rigidly erect nor relaxed in a slouch. There should be a slightly forward, leaning, gentle S curve to the spine.

Breathing is equally important but slightly more complicated:

> The focus of seiza breathing is a point several inches below the navel, the point at which the center of gravity of the body, the *tanden,* is said to be found. When doing seiza properly, the upper chest does not expand and contract; the shoulders do not rise and fall. (Reynolds, 1980, p. 82)*

The key to *seiza* breathing is how you exhale. While sitting, focus on your lower abdomen while slowly, silently exhaling air through the nose. Your goal is to breathe in such a way that, as one of Reynolds's sources told him, "if a rabbit's hair were placed on the tip of one's nose it would not blow away" (1980, p. 84). The result is a dramatic reduction in the rate of breathing. Breathing is accomplished by expanding and contracting the diaphragm rather than the ordinary process of sucking in and blowing out air.

The main point of *seiza* is for patients to recapture control over their mind and attention by giving them an ordinary albeit vital task to concentrate on. They become attuned to the inner world of their biological processes,

> not passively resigned to some inexorable fate, nor tuned out from reality. Rather [they are] tuned in to an ongoing inner reality through an exercise that is designed to leave [them] better able to respond to the composite of inner and outer worlds that make up [their] everyday phenomenological reality. (Reynolds, 1980, p. 85)

---

*This and all following quotations from *The Quiet Therapies: Japanese Pathways to Personal Growth,* by D. K. Reynolds. Copyright © 1980 by the University of Hawaii Press. Reprinted by permission.

Practitioners of *seiza* claim it to be an effective response to a wide range of physical, emotional, and psychological ailments, including

> neuroses, poor appetite, digestive and eliminative problems, poor circulation, headaches, stiff neck and shoulders, and various chronic diseases. And they report positive results [including] necessary weight gain, fewer colds, better control of temper, increased patience and endurance, clearer thinking, and attainment of a more peaceful outlook on life. (Reynolds, 1980, p. 79)

These changes are said to occur when patients commit themselves to between two and three 30-minute sessions of *seiza* a day over the course of several weeks. The psychological explanation of the cure is that when patients engage in quiet sitting they come face to face with all the dissatisfactions they feel with their own body as a consequence of their desires for what might be or what ought to be.

Reynolds characterized this conflict as existing between the real and the ideal. His understanding of the psychological changes that take place in *seiza* was that they reflect the process of coming to accept the futility of trying to overcome various conflicts.

> In the end [the patient] is likely to arrive at a simple acceptance that he is sitting. His mind becomes less cluttered by the "mights" and "coulds" and "ought-to-bes." He simply sits. . . . His goals do not disappear entirely . . . but the goals are now accepted as part of [his] reality. There is no wishing that I had this goal instead of that one, and even if there were, there would be acceptance of wishing. . . . The purpose of sitting is to sit. And when it isn't, it isn't. (1980, p. 87)

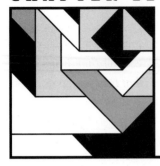

CHAPTER 22

Contemporary Japanese Psychotherapies: Morita and Naikan

Right Thought

The Japanese see the individually structured social system of North Americans as a series of problems waiting to happen. The Japanese system is significantly more group oriented; communal groups such as the family, coworkers, and the nation as a whole take precedence in everyday life over the needs and desires of the individual. In cross-cultural psychology, this social structure and way of viewing the world has been given a name: collectivism.

Collectivism and individualism are opposite ways of organizing a society. Why then would we think that psychotherapies might be transferable between cultures? The answer is that, although large-scale social systems may appear as different as night and day, in actuality the individuals within each culture have to find their own solutions to the dilemmas and para- doxes of human life. The Japanese term Nihonjinron, *belief in the complete uniqueness of the Japanese people, is thus treated as a myth in this chapter.*

It may be possible to use some Japanese approaches to psychotherapy cross-culturally, even to apply some of its collectivist assumptions in our more individualist context. Two Japanese therapies based on the principles of Zen, Morita and Naikan, are presented here. Morita is a therapy for the "misfocused mind." It encourages clients to accept the world and themselves exactly as they are, to make neurotic symptoms insignificant by absorbing them into the overall pattern of one's life. Naikan therapy helps individuals relocate their "misplaced minds." Naikan is a more introspective form of therapy than Morita, aiming to help people reconnect to the values and relationships that give life its meaning and purpose.

Perhaps if Western therapists asked the same sorts of questions of their clients that Morita and Naikan therapists ask theirs, we would discover that at the root all talking cures are concerned with human feelings and that human relationships are the source of virtually all these feelings.

Values and Psychotherapy: West Meets East

From what we have explored so far, we might generalize that regardless of historical and cultural context, the true function of the talking cure is to awaken human awareness in order to give human beings a fuller grasp of the range and extent of their potential. A significant advantage of thinking about the talking cure in these terms is that it permits both the client and the practitioner to consider the merits of psychotherapy in the absence of any conscious or overt suffering or mental, emotional, or physical disturbance. Although any strategy that calls itself a therapy should try to reduce human suffering, it does not necessarily have to address "mental illness." Talking cures, in short, ought also to be useful to ordinary people who seek to function more effectively and experience life more directly.

Certain universal principles can be applied to any such endeavor. In Chapter 21 I suggested that every therapy should ideally confront the totality of an individual's life. A therapy that ignores immoral or unethical conduct, therefore, would not by this definition be worthy of serious study. Such a "therapy" would be little more than a technology, and I would immediately distrust it because I would have no way of assessing the range of uses to which it could be put. In fact, this lack of moral or ethical grounding is the reason one seldom hears the term *behavior modification* any more; that purely instrumental term got many applied behaviorists into a great deal of trouble. Rodney King, for example, had his behavior modified by the Los Angeles police department, but no therapist would claim that the police actions were therapeutic. These days, behaviorally trained clinicians call themselves behavior therapists instead of behavior modification therapists. The distinction is important.

Practitioners of the talking cure have not always been candid about the values they promote in psychotherapy, but I think they have the responsibility of declaring those values in a fashion that permits everyone to hear and judge their biases.

Individualism and Its Discontents

By and large, the dominant values in Western psychotherapy are the supremacy of reason, an action-oriented will, the validity of science and the scientific method in human affairs, and the autonomy of the individual within the overall social context. In chapter after chapter, you have seen how Western psychotherapies strive to empower the individual to actualize her or his unique potential, to break free from instinctual and experiential bonds with the past, to be released into an autonomous present. Western psychotherapists want to see clients become autonomous, effective, decision-making, willful beings with the personal power to "be here now."

Any force on earth or in nature that limits, distracts, or otherwise impedes people from becoming everything they have the potential, will, and passion to become is the irresolute foe of members of the "party of hope." Therapists strive to develop explanations for the human condition that our clients can use to release themselves from nature, from their childhood, and from the perceived threats posed by the future. We therapists dispute every one of our clients' beliefs that prevent them from aspiring to be something better tomorrow. We are the latter-day Philosophes of individual experience and personal transformation.

Because this Western ideology is so central to our thinking, it is entirely possible that the last two chapters created the impression that the Tao and the doctrines and practices of Zen are culturally variant prescriptions for the same ends that Western therapists pursue. But when it comes to the Japanese, at least, this impression is seriously ethnocentric. In fact, a thoughtful Japanese observer would probably question every value I listed in the previous two paragraphs.

It's not that the Japanese don't understand our Western ideals of individualism, autonomy, and self-actualization. Rather, they find these assumptions both somewhat appalling and completely alien. Just as a reviewer in *The New York Times* accused a behaviorist of writing a book more appropriate to poodles than to children, so too does the Japanese observer wonder at the utility of a set of philosophical assumptions and therapeutic procedures that seem directed at creating "ill-smelling dirt sticks," as the venerable D. T. Suzuki might have phrased it. Most Japanese can barely conceive of a world where the concepts of individualism, alienation, and selfishness are distinct and separate; they think of these concepts as essentially interchangeable. Such a profound difference between cultures makes the possibility of misunderstanding a virtual certainty. Let me illustrate with a powerful example.

Maggie's Quest for Solitude

A student-friend named Maggie was spending the year as an exchange student in Japan. Maggie was excited when she received an invitation to spend several weeks with a family in radically rural Japan, especially because she had already spent six months in Tokyo and was ready for a break from that intensely crowded and urban scene. It was early spring, and Maggie looked forward to experiencing the blooming of the cherry blossoms in the countryside and seeing something of Japan that had not yet been paved. She packed her hiking boots, her journal, and a fresh shipment of trashy novels from home in the United States and traveled hopefully to the little village where she would spend a month or so with her "rural host family," as her study-program organization called it.

My wife and I, who were then living in Japan, arrived several weeks later to see how things were going with Maggie and the other students staying with families across the countryside. We drove and drove and drove to get to Maggie's host family's secluded country home. When we finally arrived, kilometers away from any other dwelling, Maggie virtually tackled us with joy. "It's like being in prison!" she cried. "Every time I put my hiking boots on, every person in the family stops what they are doing and prepares to 'go hiking' with me.

"Every time I take out my journal, my host sister and my host mother and my host grandmother and even my host great grandmother come up with some chore they need help with around the house or in the barn. Last night they 'caught' me reading in bed, and they insisted that we have a family sing-along.

"I'm going crazy! I can't take another three weeks of this. What do these people want from me?"

Meanwhile, Nagayama-san, our noble program coordinator, was imprisoned in the kitchen, getting the lowdown from the host family. "Maggie-chan is so lonely! We are all exhausted from taking care of her. Even great grandmother has to help by finding ways to keep Maggie-chan busy with the chickens.

"She keeps writing in her book, and Papa-san is sure the writing is a sign of her unhappiness here. We're at our wits end. We thought perhaps we ought to talk to our [Buddhist] priest about it, but perhaps that would offend Maggie-chan's other parents. We have never seen a child so lonely and withdrawn."

If you recall from Chapter 20 my experience in being inducted into our son's Japanese host family, which was in the same district as Maggie's family, you might begin to figure out the situation. Maggie had expected her rural sojourn to be something out of Ralph Waldo Emerson, Robert Frost, and Henry David Thoreau. She thought by leaving Tokyo she would find peace and solitude in the quiet, beautiful forests of rural Japan. However, every step she took to actualize this vision was a step away from her host family's equally intense dream of bringing an American student into the web of their extended Japanese family.

The more the family reached out to Maggie, the more determined she became to secure herself some privacy. The more desperate the grandmothers became to "keep her busy to keep her mind off her homesickness," the more Maggie craved a minute's solitude and quiet reflection. It was a complete cross-cultural standoff.

The wise and wily program coordinator, Nagayama-san, explained to the family that Maggie just needed more time to get used to being out of Tokyo and that she thought possibly Maggie had been "spoiled" by her Tokyo host family. You know how those people in the city are! People take showers anytime they want instead of enjoying the (life-threatening) ritual of the nightly scalding family bath

("Visitors always go first"). And probably the Tokyo family had been so busy that they ignored poor Maggie.

The kind yet assertive and all-knowing Nagayama-san explained to Maggie, "Well, you know how these country people are. You are just lucky they haven't arranged a marriage for you—yet. You are going to have to keep a better 'face.' Your family can read your concern, and the more aggravated you look, the more worried they feel. They are blaming themselves for your unhappiness. They believe you feel left out, alone, and isolated. In a few weeks you will be back as one among 14 million. But for now you are one among 12. *Gambatte, kudasai!*" (*Gambatte, kudasai* is the all-inclusive Japanese exhortation to "hang in there," persevere, endure—please!" Whenever anyone is confronted by the impossible in Japan—say, eating unimaginable things for breakfast or passing the college entrance examinations—"*Gambatte imasuyō,*" or "I will prevail," is sure to be heard in reply. Demonstrating this sort of character strength is the most important way of showing the world that you are not selfish and that you have a good heart.)

Maggie and her host family had fallen into a trap created by what I think is the widest gap between Japanese culture and the cultures of Western Europe and North America. Maggie needed to be alone, to have some privacy, to process the world in ways essential to her as an adventurous young American off in a foreign land to learn about the world and herself.

Her family needed even more desperately (because they were constantly talking themselves into it) to fulfill their human and moral obligation to Nagayama-san, to the university in Tokyo, and most crucially in their eyes, to Maggie's parents in Minnesota. That obligation was to welcome Maggie into the family with all their hearts and without reservation. They had agreed to become Maggie's "family," and this was an obligation neither accepted lightly nor ever fully discharged. For that Japanese family, Maggie's well-being came to be a test of their character and integrity. Of course, that is why Nagayama-san went out of her way to lay the "deep" responsibility for Maggie's "problem" on those anonymous people in Tokyo—people who, because they were city people, probably weren't doing a proper job of meeting their responsibility as Maggie's other host family.

Nagayama-san had to walk a fine line to restore good feelings among everyone involved. But that was her job, her formal responsibility in life (if one could ever accept that a married woman could have genuine responsibilities outside her marriage). She had to deliver separate messages to the family and to Maggie-chan that would enable both parties to save face and, hopefully, to create a better and more relaxed living situation for everyone.

The Japanese Perspective. Imagine for a moment that Maggie's rural Japanese host family had acted on their first impulse and called in the local Zen priest for his advice and counsel. That venerable gentleman probably would have expressed his deep sympathy for the family, and because a number of other people in the valley had also had experience with American students, the priest would probably have confessed to having at least a little expertise in these matters. I can imagine him analyzing the Maggie problem along something like the following lines:

Dear friends: As you know, this is a very serious problem, and you were right to ask for advice. But I am afraid there is little you can do to change the situation. It is hard for us to imagine, but the chances are that Maggie cannot accept the great honor and kindness you are bestowing upon her. You have to remember that Maggie-chan is not Japanese and that therefore she cannot possibly know all the joys of the human heart the way we Japanese people can.

It is perhaps hard to believe, and hard to accept without judging, that Maggie-chan's parents raised her to be exactly the way you describe her. Americans think it is very important for children to grow up to be independent and lacking in deep connections to others. It is very sad, both because Americans are so isolated and because they are blind to the selfishness that keeps them from ever knowing true peace of mind. Perhaps over the next few weeks, if you truly persist, Maggie-chan will begin to bloom, as the cherry blossoms are beginning to do in the valley. You must have faith in yourselves and not give up on her, for she is a living creature who needs the *dharma* of your love.

We see this problem all through the township, wherever an American student is staying with a Japanese family. And my advice is always the same: First, all the members of this family must redouble their efforts to preserve the *wa* (harmony) of this family. This task is difficult when one member wants to go her own way, but her alienation makes your task all the more important.

Second, you must understand that Americans have almost no intuitive or natural sense of *giri;* they think of obligation as a burden, they strive to pay off the debts they incur in relation to others. They are made uncomfortable when they discover that one can never fully discharge the obligations of a lifetime. This belief may sound nonsensical to us Japanese, but for Americans, living in society requires constant vigilance against getting "trapped" by obligation. They consider *giri* to be the opposite of true freedom. They believe their greatest happiness comes from living in isolation from their fellow humans and from nature.

So now you see why Maggie-chan shies away from embracing the kindnesses you have offered her. She experiences each aspect of her *on* (intuitively experienced obligation) as the opposite of what is intended. For you it is pure kindness; for her it is a hopelessly tangled web from which she cannot emerge in the same state of isolation as when she entered it. Your kindness threatens her most basic sense of well-being.

Yes, sadly, you are right. The person who shuns the benefits of *on*, of course, cannot experience *giri*. She can never know the deep human assurance of belonging to a group. So that is why we say that Americans are spiritually incapable of *ninjyo*. They cannot experience the human feeling that is the common emotional heritage of the Japanese people. Americans live as if in a house with no inner lights and only small clouded windows. Much of their life is an illusion, for they have no one with whom they share the deepest and most profound aspects of human feeling.

You know we Japanese have a saying: "*Giri* aspires continually to *ninjyo.*" We understand that the sorrow of life is broken only by our feelings of connectedness with one another because of the countless kindnesses each of us gives and receives every day. That is why we always say "*Sumanai!*" ("It is not finished") when we are in receipt of a great kindness. The Americans say "Thank you" and then rush off to repay their debt before it accrues any interest.

Having this American child in your home is something like having a wild animal with you. I am sure her heart is good and that she is very kind. But she wants to run away to be "free," and she fears that your kindness will cause her such a debt of obligation that she will never again be free. But we all must work together to show her the error of her ways and the wisdom of the human heart.

The path ahead is difficult but simple. As a family you must not give in to her fear of human bonding. You must continue to do her kindnesses in the hope that she will learn something of *ninjyo.* Be sure to give her plenty of responsibility and tasks. Surely she can learn to appreciate the joy of making her contribution to the good of the whole. Perhaps when she feels that she is contributing to the common good, she will experience some of the joy of *giri.*

And most importantly, you women must continue to mother Maggie-chan as if she were your own daughter, just born into the world. The power of the mother's love is the greatest power in the universe. Maggie-chan's initial responses will be wild and erratic, as are the instincts of any wild thing brought into a loving home. But in time the many kindnesses of the mother and the grandmothers will overwhelm her doubts and cause her to become a true daughter. Gradually her awareness of her gratitude to you will grow and grow within her. When this happens she too will say "*sumanai*" instead of "thank you." On that day you will know that *ninjyo* has been born in her heart. From that day forward she will have the joy of human responsibility in her heart. She will be able to let the delusions of her separateness blow away like the clouds over Mount Fuji. The disruptive interference of self-doubt and self-consciousness will clear from her eyes, and a true child of the family will be born.

It wouldn't hurt at all either if she received some instruction from *Otosan* (Father) in *zazen.* But perhaps, if she is as outwardly troubled as you describe, this instruction should be left for later. At any rate, the presence of Maggie-chan in this house is a great test of the moral strength of every member of this household. *Gamanshite-yo! Gambatte, kudasai!* (You have to work hard at it, you know? But I wish you good fortune in your endeavor. Please be successful in your undertaking!)

The Western Perspective. Now imagine that Maggie has taken her version of the problem to a Western psychotherapist; the contrast is instructive. Most therapists would be very sympathetic to Maggie's dilemma and would assure her that psychotherapy could help her reach a satisfactory resolution to the difficulties she was experiencing.

A dynamically oriented therapist would most likely want to explore the unconscious dynamics of Maggie's pulling away from intimacy. A true Freudian would understand that Maggie's unresolved oedipal conflicts with respect to her American family are erecting an impossible barrier to intimacy with any secondary family unit. Such a therapist might even see Maggie's "resistance" to her rural Japanese family operating as a sort of transference phenomenon: She is working out the dynamic oedipal issues concerning her American parents in the relatively safe and neutral arena of her relationship in this "fantasy" family situation. If the therapy is successful, Maggie will soon give up her resistances to the intimacy being expressed in her new family and thus take a major step toward greater psychosocial maturity.

A behaviorally oriented therapist would probably focus on two closely related issues. Maggie and her therapist would probably first agree that Maggie needs to work on gaining more emotional self-control under the stress of living in an unfamiliar culture, away from all her support systems, and with a family that violates her privacy boundaries. But the behavior therapist might also offer to help Maggie find ways to "adjust" to the demands placed on her by her Japanese family. I can well imagine sitting down with Maggie to work out strategies for overcoming her interfering emotional reactions and putting in their place a well-rehearsed set of assertive behaviors that would enable her to better present herself within the family context. Both strategies, better emotional self-control and more effective social behavior, are essential to increasing Maggie's sense of personal efficacy in her day-to-day life. If the behaviorist is successful, Maggie will soon be fully adapted to the expectations of her new culture.

A humanistic therapist would help Maggie gain greater clarity about the nature and depth of her feelings in this situation. Such a therapist would help Maggie find greater powers within herself to cope with this difficult and demanding time in her life. They would explore ways in which going through this experience is helping Maggie grow and understand herself as a person. I can well imagine Maggie's humanistic therapist starting a support group for other people in Maggie's situation, wherein people could reach out to one another with empathy and positive self-regard.

If we can really let our imaginations go, we can imagine that a successful course of Gestalt therapy would have Maggie confronting her Japanese family with what she feels, what she perceives her alternatives to be, and the conditions under which she can continue to live with this family. If they can make the relationship work, then great. But if not, then so be it: Maggie didn't come to Japan to tell the natives how to live their lives, and she certainly didn't come to Japan to have other people tell her how to live hers.

Cultural Metamessages. If we compare the "metamessages" that the Japanese host family received from the Buddhist priest with those that Maggie received from her

Western psychotherapists, we begin to see the differences between East and West more clearly.

The priest explained the dilemma in terms of unresolvable issues of character. He perceives that Americans grow up in a deeply flawed culture in which the children are not taught the essential things at the heart of taking one's place in society. He perceives Maggie as lacking all the important moral and emotional (and these cannot be separated) sensitivities that permit people to live in harmony with one another. You cannot give a person *ninjyo;* it is a fundamental human feeling that arises only out of the profoundly human experience of *giri.* You cannot bring a person to experience *giri,* because *giri* requires a lifetime of reciprocally experienced "obligations," countless thousands of one-sided kindnesses that each contribute a single blossom of *on.* Perhaps a person raised in a different culture could eventually experience *on,* but what an overwhelming and thankless task it would be to teach such a thing. The family must have courage, be strong, and persevere. They are trying to bring something wild and frightened into the middle of their lives, so they must not set their initial expectations too high.

The Western therapists, on the other hand, explained the situation in terms of Maggie's need to be restored to health and full functioning. She needs to recover her self-control and her emotional stability. If her will can be strengthened and her humanity reaffirmed, then she will find the courage to go forward. She is confronted with a very difficult situation, but she needs to understand that no one will fault her if that situation proves too difficult for her. Nobody will suggest that her character is deficient or that the problem is that she is selfish. Whereas the Japanese theory places responsibility for the problem inside the person, the Western approach places it in the situation. To be sure, the Western therapists recognize the necessity for change, and most recognize the importance of having Maggie do some if not most of that changing. But the central notion is that she must change to meet the demands of a harsh and competitive world; she is a good person with inadequate resources. Or as Albert Ellis (see Chapter 14) might say: "OK, Maggie, it would be nice, it would be preferable, if you could have a lovely homestay in rural Japan. But you can't. And that is *not* a world-class tragedy! Sure, you can blame yourself forever, or you can accept that some things are beyond your control, and then you can move on to try something new."

The Anatomy of Dependence

A Japanese psychiatrist, Takeo Doi (1971), wrote a book, *The Anatomy of Dependence,* that attempts to explain the reasons for the deep structural difference between Japanese and Western approaches to understanding the human psyche.

Amae and *Jibun*

Doi's primary focus was *amae,* the need for passive love. In at least one sense, *amae* is a universal phenomenon. All infants at birth have *amae,* which is to say all infants need to receive indulgent, protective, nurturing love and attention. An infant that fails to *amaeru* (the verb form) is said to have a problem with attachment. Such infants almost always live deeply troubled lives. I have seen suggestions that children who fail to attach may be showing the first signs of childhood autism or brain damage from fetal stress caused by the mother's substance abuse. We also know that if a baby's *amae* is not met—even if all other needs are met—the baby will not flourish and may soon die. This deep need for human love and acceptance is the reason that in a well-run hospital neonatal ward you will see the nurses and aides touching, massaging, and talking to newborns. *Amae*-like human contact is a biological necessity for survival.

In his work, Doi extended the concept of *amae* into childhood, adolescence, and event adulthood among Japanese people. He contended that this special form of human interaction is what makes the Japanese people emotionally and psychologically Japanese. Through his observations of mental patients in Japan, Doi developed the hypothesis that most emotional disorders are caused by a "frustrated desire to *amaeru*" (1971, p. 19); emotionally disturbed people are frustrated in their unconscious wish to be "the passive object" of other people's love and nurture.

Such people, said Doi, primarily lack *jibun,* or a conscious awareness of self or ego. *Jibun* serves to "check" *amae:*

> In a paper I read [in 1961 to] the Japanese Psychiatric and Neurological Association, I emphasized that this awareness of *jibun* presumed the existence of an inner desire to *amaeru,* and made itself felt in opposition to that desire. To put it briefly, the man who has a *jibun* is capable of checking *amae,* while a man who is at the mercy of *amae* has no *jibun.* This is true of so called normal people. (Doi, 1971, p. 19)

We all have friends who are *amai* (adjective form), which is to say friends who "behave self-indulgently, presuming on some special relationship that exists between the two" (Doi, 1971, p. 29). Perhaps we have relationships in which we are *amai.* In the West, it seems to me, this is more a quality of adolescent and young adult romantic relationships than it is of friendships, but I think you get the meaning.

I have known therapists who tolerate incredible amounts of *amae* in therapeutic relationships. They usually justify their tolerance as "allowing the patient to test the limits of the relationship"; this tolerance may even be a special quality of the patient-therapist relationship in Rogerian psychotherapy. (As we saw in Chapter 18, therapists' needs to *amaeru* seem to be the primary self-justification for molesting patients.) *Amae* seems a very obvious component in many of the cases I have recounted in this book. Luke (Chapter 7), for example, had never had his emotional needs met at home, had experienced severe frustration in his desire to *amaeru,* and then at the height of his emotional despair alternated wildly between expressing and suppressing *amae.*

In the vocabulary of Adlerian psychotherapy (see Chapter 8), pampering, neglect, and abuse profoundly interfere with children's normal psychological development. Pampered children never develop a reliable *jibun.* Neglected children never know the security and connection that other children learn from being the passive objects of their parents' love. Abused children have more than a frustrated desire to *amaeru;* they also know that to trust anyone with their most important needs opens them up to brutal abuse.

Psychological Foundations of Japanese Society

I want to try now to put the various pieces of this chapter together into a coherent whole. Please try to consume it in one big gulp. If you dissect it, Western style, it won't make as much sense as it will if you can accept its gestalt. The problem is primarily that I have been compelled to oversimplify some concepts and leave out other important concepts, such as the crucial Japanese distinction between inside and outside, regarded by Johnson (1993) as the nexus of Japanese selfhood. Your job is also made difficult by the fact that many of these ideas are tied together by, and are central to, the concept of *Nihonjinron,* the myth of Japanese uniqueness. Regarded by many Western social scientists as a "value laden perspective about Japanese life that voices an inflated, self-laudatory affirmation of cultural factors presumed as exclusive and outstanding in Japanese society" (Johnson, 1993, p. 11), *Nihonjinron* is shorthand for the cultural myth system that posits Japanese people as genetically unique and homogeneous within themselves. However, this idea largely falls apart when you start examining it carefully. Here, then, is a brief psychoanthropological interpretation of the psychological foundations of Japanese society.

It is natural for children to *amaeru* with their mother, to demonstrate natural dependency as infants (Johnson, 1993). It is natural for mothers to welcome and support this dependency. Children are born wild and unconnected beings. Their biological and emotional needs are their only contact with civilization. If mothers behave selfishly and self-indulgently, their children's entire future is put at risk. To be good mothers, indeed perfect mothers, they must become the wellspring for everything their children need.

For the first few years of life, children cannot imagine living without the constant presence of their mothers. Mothers anticipate their children's every need, meet their every demand, and ignore their every act of antisocial behavior. As you can imagine, traveling on a crowded bus or train in the company of mothers with young children is one of the most unpleasant experiences you can have in Japan.

As children grow, their *jibun* begins naturally to emerge. They venture out to play with their friends, learn their first Japanese characters, and exhibit the first signs of polite behavior around older people and persons in authority. At home they are still indulged, and their every wish is attended to. In mothers' eyes their infantile dependency at home is just as normal and "healthy" as their growing awareness of what is expected of them in the outside world.

The 4- or 5-year-old Japanese child is an enigma to Western eyes because of the radical split between what we would think of as intolerable behavior at home or with a parent and exceptionally mature and task-focused behavior while in the social group. Preschool children who scream at their mothers if they do not fill the children's rice bowls immediately turn around and are honored to serve the daily snack to their playmates. When these children become frustrated with a task at home, they throw the project at their mothers in petulant rage; when they become frustrated in play groups, a gentle "*Gaman suru*" ("Please persevere") will put them back on task in an instant.

These children would never throw a frustrating toy at the teacher. Why? Because she is "outside." With recognized outsiders, *tanin*, (almost any "public" persons, such as government officials, teachers, village or neighborhood elders, nonintimate coworkers), one must behave with *enryō*, or self-restraint. Children's behavior in a teacher's presence is all she knows about their families, especially their mothers. To mess up in public would bring shame on the children, and on their mothers, and on their entire families. At home children know no shame. "No *enryō* among *miuichi*" is a golden rule of Japanese childhood; no self-restraint is required among the members of one's inner circle. But, the teacher occupies some middle ground; she is clearly sanctioned by the family, yet she is an outsider. Such a situation calls for an elaborate and formal system of interaction, a system we think of as Japanese politeness.

But what happens on the train or in a restaurant or store? Here children appear to Westerners to be complete little monsters; there is no sign of the fabled *enryō* politeness. Doi (1971) explained that

> in the case of relatives . . . the absence of *enryō* is due to *amae,* whereas the same can not be said of the absence of *enryō* towards "strangers." In the former case, there is no holding back because the relationship of *amae* means there are no barriers, whereas in the latter case [the train, restaurant, or shop] barriers exist but there is no holding back since the barriers are not consciously felt. It is significant that both a high degree of *amae* and its total absence should give rise to a total lack of concern for others. Indeed, one often finds [in clinical practice] that it is precisely the man showing the most self-indulgent *amae* toward his family who shows the greatest coldness and indifference towards strangers. . . . [I]n brief, the man who is normally accustomed to *amae* behaves in a superior or contemptuous way when he finds himself in a position where he cannot *amaeru.* (p. 41)

The great indulgence that Japanese infants, children, and men find at home connects them in a powerful way with their mothers and wives. A newly married Japanese woman probably fears few things more than not getting along with her new mother-in-law. A newly married man asked to choose between a lifelong *amai* relationship with his mother and a brand-new relationship with a woman more or less his own age is put in an impossible situation; in most cases, I believe, the new wife in such a triangle is bound to lose. In fact, one of my closest friends in Japan is the object of intense envy among her same-age women friends because she married a man whose parents both died prior to their son's marriage.

As I hope you can see, to the Japanese to *amaeru* is to accept responsibility for a thousand small kindnesses a week and a million kindnesses over the course of our life. Because we have *jibun,* even at home, we can scarcely escape conscious recognition of our obligation to our mother (and of course to a lesser degree to our father and older siblings). Thus *amaeru* creates *on,* which is an intuitively experienced obligation.

By the time children become teenagers, the *on* has begun to coalesce into *giri.* They "belong" to their family not simply because they can *amaeru* there but because the family is the very center of the web of their obligations, which in fact are the most important structures in their life. And, if you remember from the priest's talk with Maggie's host family, *giri* continually aspires to *ninjyo.*

The Emotional Ties Created by Obligation

Students, reflect a bit on the "sacrifices" your parents have made for you to go to college. Reflect on how the money they spent on your orthodontia could have helped them live a little more comfortably. Think about the hours and hours they spent taking you shopping, watching you give recitals, sewing on your scouting badges, putting up with your emotional catastrophes as an adolescent. The memories of these fundamental instances of *amae* within your family relationships are the raw material that generates within your heart feelings of love, gratitude, connection, admiration, and appreciation. If you truly feel something emotional when you think about these instances (and I suspect most of us do), then you are experiencing *ninjyo*— even if *Nihonjinron*-crazed Japanese social scientists say it is impossible for Americans to feel these things.

Parents, dry that tear from your eye with that worn and threadbare handkerchief. What do you want from your children in return? Why all you want is . . . I expect that everyone over the age of 12 in this country can finish that sentence. It is one of the most genuinely manipulative (and possibly untrue) statements in our entire culture. Some mothers finish this sentence in language that curls their offsprings' toes, makes them clench their teeth and swear that they must have been switched at birth. You know the speech by heart: "I don't want anything for myself; I just want you to be happy and . . ." What she is saying is: "Live with the guilt, kid. I am never going to let you off the emotional hook. You may live to be 90, but if I am still around, then you will still be 'the kid,' and you will never fully discharge your obligations to me. I am so utterly selfless that I will never release you from that obligation—because I will never acknowledge that it is there."

When Japanese psychologists tell me that North Americans can't understand *on, giri,* and *ninjyo,* I just laugh. We haven't, however, built our entire culture around these concepts. We don't worship them. Moreover, we live in a society where slightly more than half the African American kids and between 20 and 30 percent of other kids grow up in single-parent households. When I go to the market in my hometown, most of the people carting babies and toddlers around are women younger than most of my college students. We Americans experience rates of physical, emotional, and sexual abuse of children that in all likelihood are the highest in the world. I want to hope the Japanese are wrong to think of us as emotional robots all trying to live out Marlboro Man fantasies, but you can see where they might get that impression.

For the Japanese, *amae* is the critical cultural practice that glues their society together. The average Japanese person never has to confront "the illusion of separateness," as Erich Fromm might have called it. The Japanese each have three or four lifetimes of obligations, duties, and responsibilities to discharge to express most fully their gratitude to those who have loved them. For them *sumanai* (it is not finished) is a promissory note, testimony to their integrity as human beings.

The world of *amae* creates among the Japanese a certain passivity (Bester, 1971). They recognize that if they interfere with the reality that exists outside their immediate domain, in truth they are interfering with something in someone else's domain. They might thus disrupt the harmony of that other person's situation or end up generating more *on* in that person's life and therefore in their own. Interference in someone else's life is disruptive, primarily of their own equilibrium but potentially of the harmony of the whole, the *wa.*

In Maggie's case, the family could never, never, never directly interfere with Maggie's private *on.* They could not tell her how to behave, except in the most superficial "right conduct" sort of way. But they could perceive, interpret, and feel Maggie's unhappiness. Poor thing! She had no one she could *amaeru* to. She could not experience the joy of connection. She needed company, lots and lots of company. If she couldn't *amaeru* with mom, then perhaps she could with grandmother. If that didn't work, then perhaps great grandmother knew some magic that she could put to use. They were not interfering; they were just trying to give nature a little nudge.

How could anyone bear to live without *ninjyo*? The United States must be a very sad and lonely place. No wonder it has so much crime and violence and child abuse. For Americans, all the world must be a terribly cold and almost commercial place. "Is it true," I have been asked dozens of times in Japan, "that American parents do not give a 'plan' to their children so that they will know how to lead their lives?" "Quite true, however unbelievably," I reply. "How then do Americans gain any satisfactions from their actions? Whom does it please when they make right decisions? Are their lives just random?"

Gentle reader: Look around you carefully. What is the most honest answer to that question?

When you come from a world where it is widely accepted that, as in an ancient Japanese proverb, you necessarily "incur *on* on a single night's stay," you can quickly become entangled in a complex web of not necessarily congruous social relations. In my wish to be a good son, husband, father, employee, teacher, therapist, colleague, and neighborhood man, I am going to often disappoint and fail to meet the expectations of a lot of people. In such a case,

> *on* means that one has incurred a kind of psychological burden as a result of receiving a favor, while *giri* means that *on* has brought about a relationship of interdependence. Now, what is usually referred to as the clash of *giri* and *ninjyo* can surely be seen as a case where there is an opposition between a number of persons from whom one has received, so that to fulfill one's *giri* towards one of them will mean neglecting it toward another. For the person concerned, of course, the ideal thing would be to keep the good will of all concerned, and it is the difficulty or impossibility of doing so that causes the conflict. The essence of the conflict, in other words, is not so much that one has to retain one and reject the other, but that one is forced to make the choice against one's own will. In other words, the motive force behind the inner conflict is the desire to retain the good will: which means, of course, one's *amae*. An interesting fact in this connection is that the emotion expressed in the word *sumanai is experienced most often in giri relationships*. . . . [T]he word *sumanai* is used as a means of holding on to the other's good will. (Doi, 1971, p. 35)

I can only imagine how much better or at least more interesting things would have been for Maggie if I had known enough about all this a few years ago to suggest that she respond to her family's desperate efforts for her to *amaeru* with a heartfelt "*Sumanai!*"

Right Thought: Morita and Naikan Therapies

Two uniquely Japanese psychotherapies operate on a theoretical model in accord with these concepts. At their base, both therapies are supported by the ideas from Asian philosophy that we explored in Chapters 20 and 21—that is, principles drawn from the Tao, Confucian ethics, and Zen practice. In the back of my mind I think of Morita therapy and Naikan therapy as a sort of "samurai psychology," and it is fairly obvious that neither is a therapy for the timid. In the remainder of this chapter we will look at them in some depth, and I will try to show how they can be applied to a wide range of psychosocial and emotional symptoms and complaints.

I have to confess that I have never actually seen either of these therapies in action, so I am relying completely on what I have been told and read in books. But I believe you can accept my report with credulity, especially since both therapies rely extensively on common sense—once you understand what that term means within a Japanese context.

Rampant "Homophobia"?

One of my primary interests when I went to Japan for the first time in 1980 was to explore how psychopathology differs in Japan from what I am accustomed to in North America. I knew that some Japanese people develop schizophrenia, mania, and depression. I had learned that they report relatively low rates of alcoholism, according to their definition of that term, and that most of their addictions involve various forms of licit and illicit amphetamines.

I had heard that in general the Japanese are vastly less intrusive into other people's sex lives than we Americans are, and I had read that mental health professionals in Japan don't wring their hands with anxiety when they encounter patients whose sexual orientation is atypical. So I wasn't at all prepared for the mass of psychological literature I found in Japan on the problem of "homophobia." The list of titles in the library on this subject ran on for pages. I knew that homophobia is an American obsession, but it appeared that in Japan it is considered a major form of mental illness. In fact, I learned from several sources that three-fourths of all mental health treatments in Japan are oriented toward removing homophobic reactions. I wasn't amazed quite so much by the prevalence of the diagnosis as I was by the idea of tens of thousands of middle-class Japanese people turning themselves over to mental health authorities for treatment for an antisocial prejudice. Imagine if everyone in the United States who harbors hatred for members of some other group suddenly showed up for treatment!

Alas, the problem was one of translation. I learned that the term *homophobia* is used in Japan, and throughout most of the rest of the world evidently, to refer to undue or irrational anxiety, fear, and discomfort in or in prospect of interaction with fellow human beings. Our American homophobia would thus be a subtype of this more generic disorder—except that to qualify as true homophobia, the presenting American client would have to experience something more akin to panic and anxiety, rather than simple bigotry, around homosexually oriented persons and stimuli.

In Japan people are somewhat unlikely to go to any sort of practitioner to make themselves feel better. They visit a physician's office or mental health clinic so their "illness" will not disrupt their ability to perform their job and relate smoothly and harmoniously with others. Often in the United States I wish I could wear a surgical mask when I teach or do counseling. Throughout the school year, seriously and infectiously ill students and patients gag, choke, wheeze, sneeze, and snort all over me. I spend most of the winter recovering from the colds and flus that my beloved students and precious patients inflict on me. In Japan, people with contagious ailments always wear surgical masks to protect those with whom they come into close physical contact. They take responsibility for the welfare of their teachers, fellow workers, and family members.

So why do Japanese people turn themselves in for homophobia? The problem with homophobia, I learned, is not that it causes the patients discomfort or embarrassment. It is because when their homophobia generates a strong anxiety reaction, they become generally agitated and nervous—they exhibit signs of *shin-keishitsu,* or "nervosity"—which distracts them and others from important responsibilities. The result is *toraware;* they become preoccupied with their symptoms and therefore with themselves. My "homophobia"—let's say my fear of being offensive in my speech—makes me apprehensive and nervous (*shinkeishitsu*) as I try to carry out my daily responsibilities. I don't hold up my piece of the sky, I let my family and my work group and my college down, because I have become selfishly preoccupied (*toraware*) with my petty obsession about saying a wrong word or using the wrong tone of voice in a conversation with a colleague, student, or dean.

Nervous people regress to become spoiled, pampered, self-indulgent, isolated, egotistical, uncooperative burdens on the rest of society. They are free, in their own eyes at least, to accept kindnesses without accepting responsibility. They have turned their backs on their *jibun* and in so doing think they can avoid or escape *on.*

I am sure that for the Japanese there is nothing new about this problem, but the idea that such people should be the responsibility of "therapy" is probably a radical proposition. In a paper published in 1958, Professor K. Sato offered his professional colleagues the idea that such people need some fundamental "Zen therapy."

Morita Therapy: To Cure Preoccupation With Self

Sato suggested that preoccupied nervous people are trying to resist having their "ego dissolve in the world." Such people cling to the false individualism that their nervous condition symbolizes, and thus resist living their life in the flow of the "eternal present." What such patients need, Sato declared, is "an awakening of the Real Self"—that is, to identify their very essence with "the creative dynamic of the whole." In other words, neurotic people are trying to escape their suffering by craving for separation; what they really need is to regain their character and to discipline themselves back into reality.

Sato-sensei recommended a course of *seiza* (quiet sitting therapy), described in Chapter 21, as a first step. But if *seiza* fails to bring people back to full awareness, if they remain mired in the illusions and shadows of their preoccupations, then sterner actions are called for. Patients must be actively discouraged from their craving for pity, the self-defeating cycle of preoccupation with the self that can only lead to further intensification of the symptoms of nervousness. Something more must be done "to require the patient to affirm and become one with the real situation."

Sato-sensei and his colleague T. Kora-sensei immediately presented such an alternative in the form of *Morita therapy* (Kora & Sato, 1958). This treatment is aimed at making patients aware that their symptoms are entirely the result of the conflict they have generated within themselves in the fruitless struggle to avoid inevitable and natural psychological and physiological reactions. We all experience these reactions, but preoccupied people experience them as embarrassing and entitling.

Homophobic patients experience intense feelings of unease and bashfulness when they appear before other people. They seize on these uncomfortable feelings and turn them into "an obsessive *idea* and an agony which increases more and more as one tries to escape from it" (Kora & Sato, 1958, p. 221). This idea quickly becomes a mental habit, and then patients begin to live in dread anticipation of the uncomfortable feelings. This anticipation, in time, develops into the highly generalized pathology the therapist sees in the clinic.

Hints for Patients. Kora and Sato provided a list of ten "hints for patients" that serves well as an introduction to the process of Morita therapy. I have paraphrased the hints from Kora and Sato's original list (1958, p. 223):

- Let the therapist explain the functional psychic nature of your situation. Make sure you understand why you are feeling the way you feel.
- Leave your symptoms completely as they are. You must accept that your symptoms—a stutter, a blush, a burning feeling of embarrassment, or anything else—are fully integrated into your larger identity.
- Throw yourself absolutely and unreservedly into your work. You need to be of service and need to make up for your failure to do your fair share during the period of your preoccupation.
- Complain about absolutely nothing. You are never to mention or draw attention to any of your symptoms.
- Anticipate and be prepared to vanquish the temptation to "escape into sickness." Your symptoms may get somewhat more severe at first, but this development is simply to be ignored as meaningless nonsense.
- Begin examining yourself for the sources of your abnormal behavior. When did you first learn how to think in these unproductive and selfish ways? What were your models for such disrespectful conduct?
- Immediately cease not trying things you are not sure about.
- As in rational emotive behavior therapy (see Chapter 14), you must realize that human beings rarely if ever experience complete peace of mind. "To live with worries!" must become your daily motto. You must make uneasiness your abode.
- Adjust your outer appearance so you do not appear to the world as a nervous patient. Wear a good "face"; project seriousness of purpose and commitment to the tasks before you. In a short time, the inner self will come to match the outer self.
- Come to recognize and trust in homeostasis. Your recovery will be natural, as you recover your ability to behave and think naturally.

Kora and Sato accepted that many North Americans would reject Morita therapy as "Japanese conformity"—but only, they concluded, because Americans don't understand the concept of living one's life with strong character. Morita therapy, they declared, is "character education," and the essence of character is learning to accept the world as it is—not as you would like, hope, wish, or force it to be.

Morita therapy, then, is a matter of adopting a sort of samurai code of personal behavior. Its Zen emphasis has to do with the central idea of *focusing the misfocused mind* away from preoccupation with self and toward the accomplishment of what needs to be done. As DeVos (1980) noted, the task before Japanese psychotherapy patients is to recover a renewed capacity to perform the duties of their life in full accord with the highest expectations they have for themselves.

Morita therapy is not for everyone. It is designed to address the problems of people who already possess "a strong will and a desire to recover" and who are "preoccupied with somatic complaints and problems relating to other people. More often than not [these] problems center around an over-sensitivity to others, shyness, feelings of inferiority, and other social tensions" (Reynolds, 1980, p. 6).

The heart of the "cure" in Morita therapy is in *arugamama* (a great word to be able to drop at a cocktail party), which means "accepting one's self, one's symptoms, and reality as they are; lit., 'as it is' " (Reynolds, 1980, p. 22). By tolerating the heretofore intolerable, you will gain immunity to it, and it will then cease to be a controlling factor in your life. A Morita therapist might say you become "wiser" to it (Reynolds, 1980) and ignore it, and instead of going away, it becomes just another piece of your cosmic scenery.

A Western Application of Morita Therapy. I have worked with this idea with patients who came to the clinic with severe PMS (premenstrual syndrome). Realize that few women come to a mental health clinic as a first stop for help with this problem. They usually have made the rounds of various medical specialists and end up on a psychologist's doorstep only as a last resort. Evidently, medical science and pharmacology can do nothing for them. So what can I do that "real" science can't?

I usually begin by giving the patients a lot of literature to read. Most of it takes the position that PMS is a "made-up" disorder. Here, for example, are selections from a book by Carol Tavris, quoted in a textbook in the field of human sexuality:

> Biomedical researchers have taken a set of bodily-changes that are normal to women over the menstrual cycle, packaged them into a "Premenstrual Syndrome," and sold them back to women as a disorder, a problem that needs treatment and attention. . . . [I]f you give men the same checklist of symptoms (reduced or increased energy, irritability and other negative moods, back pain, sleeplessness, headaches, confusion, etc.), men report having as many "premenstrual symptoms" as women do—when the symptoms aren't called PMS. If the identical checklist is titled "Menstrual Distress Questionnaire," however, men miraculously lose their headaches, food cravings, and insomnia. . . . Maybe the real question is not why some women become irritable before menstruation, but why they aren't angry the rest of the month, and why they (and others) are so quick to dismiss their irritations as being mere symptoms of PMS. (1992, quoted in McCammon, Knox, & Schacht, 1993, p. 173)

I then show my clients literature that relates PMS to repressive sex-role training, negative attitudes toward women and negative views of women's place in society, and hostile and negative attitudes toward sex (Brooks-Gunn & Ruble, 1986; Ruble, 1977).

From a quasi-Morita perspective, I ask them if they can accept the possibility that their "suffering" is just another way the patriarchal male medical establishment belittles women. "Don't fight your symptoms! Go with them! If you are feeling a little tense, then maybe this is a good day for people not to mess up their responsibilities while you are around. Get used to your monthly variations of mood. Anticipate them and welcome them. Have a friendly feeling about them. Become the world's most famous PMS-person! Show the world that your moods can chart the days of the month more accurately than a lunar telescope."

You get the point: The PMS patient is misfocusing her mind on her symptoms instead of on her total being. She needs to become better able to affirm her own experience as part of her unique identity, part of the situation as she experiences it. I am encouraging her to "accept life as it is," to "live life without a theory." Why? Not in the service of some stoic ideal, not because I or anyone else commands it, not in order to gain some extrinsic reward, but because that is the way her life is.

The odd thing to me is that none of my clients has ever complained about being told these things. Of course, this technique is "therapy" only if they discover six months later that their life is significantly better as a function of these new ways of seeing things.

Advocates for Morita therapy agree that their approach does not result in much overt behavior change. The stutterer still stutters, the person with headaches still has headaches, the shy person still looks shy when talking with strangers. But, these Morita therapists argue, profound changes occur within patients. They no longer fight their condition; they no longer shirk their responsibilities. They are now able to meet the obligations that heretofore had weighed them down so much. They no longer flee from *on* and thus from *giri*. Thus they are once again able to experience *ninjyo,* which is after all what makes life worth living.

Naikan Therapy: For Those Who Have Misplaced Their Minds

Morita therapy is often described as the ideal therapy for nervous, introverted people who worry a lot and are prone to convert their anxiety into physical symptoms. It might have been an effective treatment for my patient Martin, whose somatization disorder was described in Chapter 13. It is perhaps the treatment of choice for people with physical disabilities as well as people whose physical symptoms are the result of emotional and hysterical disorders. It is certainly an intriguing possibility for people who are very obsessive in their thinking and very self-conscious.

Naikan therapy, by contrast, is often described as a treatment for extroverted people, people who have lost touch with their inner world, people who are too caught up in the pounding routines of everyday life. The Japanese say that Naikan is treatment for *relocating a misplaced mind.* The essence of Naikan therapy is the recovery of the past, especially the past one encountered while indulging in *amae* within the security of one's family.

Reynolds (1980) describes Naikan as a form of introspection therapy. In the course of Naikan, patients are instructed to remember how they have conducted themselves with other people. A typical session begins with the therapist asking the patient to reveal whom the patient has been thinking or meditating about. The therapeutic conversation then focuses on three issues (adapted from Reynolds, 1980, p. 47):

- What does the patient remember about the things this person has done for her or him in the past? What acts of kindness, gifts, and services has the patient received from this person? Essentially, what is in the patient's "*on* file" from this relationship?

- What has the patient done to repay the obligations thus encountered? What kindnesses has the patient done for this person? Has the patient tried to deepen and enrich the relationship, or has she or he tried perhaps to discharge all obligations with one large gift, in the American fashion? Or perhaps the patient has only done *amaeru* in this relationship?

- The most important part of the interview is to explore "what troubles, inconveniences, deceit, pettiness, and the like the patient is responsible for in this relationship.

Reynolds described his experience as he meditated (albeit in Morita therapy at the time) in classic Naikan terms:

> By the fifth day (of intense self-reflection in an atmosphere of quiet isolation) I had come to realize that I was the product of the concern and kindness of other people in my life. Life, food, lodging, and the like had been given me by my parents; knowledge had been passed on to me by my family, peers, and teachers. Every skill, every possession, every idea that I considered "mine" had been created, developed, or given me by others or by "nothingness." . . . [T]ears of gratitude rolled down my cheeks at this revelation. How much I owe my mentors! How important it is to begin to repay them by passing on what was given to me by others. (1980, p. 9)

When Reynolds then underwent the more confession-oriented approach of Naikan therapy, his experience appears to have deepened even further:

> By the afternoon of the third day my self-analysis was at its deepest. I was remorseful about the periods of wasted energy and unconcern for others. I saw the need for renewed efforts in behalf of those around me. I rededicated myself to such goals. (p. 59).

Spontaneous Execution of What Is Expected

Morita and Naikan therapies are both based on the assumption that the individual is entirely self-correcting. They assume that what has been "misfocused" can be brought back into focus and that what has been "misplaced" can be recovered. What both approaches give the individual is an opportunity to withdraw from the world (in Morita one withdraws quite radically at first, shunning anything more than minimal sensory stimulation), to engage in a carefully structured self-examination process. The therapist serves a primarily spiritual role. In Morita the therapist reads a patient's journal entries, responds to them in writing, and "advances" the patient back to everyday life by supervising a process of gradual exposure to increasingly complex and "normal" environments (from a bare room to a wing of the hospital to the dining room of the hospital and so on). In Naikan the therapist serves as a probing father-confessor and provides an "agenda" for the patient's silent meditations.

Both types of therapy assume that the neurotic patient has abandoned his or her responsibilities and "fled" into illness as a consequence of having lost contact with "natural mind." Japanese quiet therapies are designed, in DeVos's (1980) terms, to address problems caused by

> weakness of will [in] individuals who lack the will to mobilize their energy to perform what is expected of them by others as well as by themselves. They come to therapy not simply because they have symptoms such as shyness, or fear of people . . . but because they are incapacitated in the performance of their daily occupations by such symptoms. . . . The solution to [this] malaise [is] to remove the observational ego's interference with the performance of one particular destiny. That is . . . to reduce the disruptive influence of doubt and self-consciousness, an interference that might have *prevented the spontaneous execution of what was expected.* (pp. 123–124; italics added)

The question I am left with as a Western psychologist, however, is, what happens in this process with clients who don't understand "what is expected"? What happens when clients discover that there is not one path that lies before them, but instead a range of mutually exclusive choices? This dilemma would be unlikely in traditional Japanese society, but in both our culture and the increasingly internationalized Japanese culture, choices have largely replaced obligations as paralyzers of the will.

Cultural Chauvinism

It is probably far too easy for Western psychotherapists to disregard or even deny such concepts as *on, giri,* and *ninjyo* in psychotherapy with Western clients, simply because our culture doesn't have as extensive a specialized vocabulary of interpersonal relationships as we find among the Japanese. Because the Japanese are vastly more sensitive to the complexities and nuances of human relationships and because they are significantly more attuned to the sources of human emotion and the causes of human suffering than we are, they have been better able to describe a social-emotional world common to all human beings.

When I first encountered the common *Nihonjinron* assertion that only Japanese people can experience *ninjyo*, because only Japanese people experience *giri*, I was contemptuous of the chauvinism embedded in the Japanese worldview. Today I still think the Japanese are wrong about their assumption of moral, spiritual, and emotional uniqueness, but I can see how they could conclude that the rest of the world does not experience human relationships with the sensitivity and even reverence that the Japanese do.

Indeed, as you have read your way through this book, you have not discovered much sensitivity to these matters in European and North American psychotherapies. They do tend to view each patient as an isolated skin bag, and they rarely consider the complexities of human connection, obligation, and feeling as they conceptualize what is wrong with a person and what changes will be necessary to restore a person to full functioning.

With the notable exception of Fromm's formulations, Western psychotherapies have turned a blind eye to questions of human separateness and isolation. The quest for union is certainly not uniquely Japanese, yet the Japanese quiet therapies are the only ones that actively encourage neurotic individuals to assess their personal situation within the context of complex, reciprocal human relationships. So I would argue with my Japanese friends and colleagues who try to understand North American life by looking at it through the lens of Western psychotherapies. I would suggest to them that they may be coming to mistaken conclusions about the nature of the non-Japanese heart because they are using the wrong instruments in the examination.

Perhaps if Western therapists asked the same sorts of questions of their patients that Morita and Naikan therapists ask theirs, we would discover that at their root all talking cures are concerned with human feelings and that human relationships are the source of virtually all these feelings. Perhaps this is the great discovery that awaits the next century of Western thinking about the talking cure.

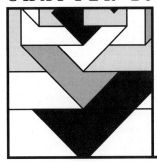

CHAPTER 23

Therapies Based on Behavioral Self-Regulation: Yoga and Other Techniques

Right Practice

Remember the Mad Hatter's tea party in Chapter 2? Welcome again to the wonderful world of tea. This time, however, we will view tea from a purely Eastern point of view. Tea first became popular with Buddhist monks in the early years of this millennium and eventually came to be the drink of choice among the Japanese upper social strata and finally among the common folk. The "art of tea" has a long historical lineage in Japan and is at the center of many of the cultural rituals of that nation. Learning the art of tea is still considered a highly respectable practice among the inhabitants of the island nation, and it has even spread to some parts of the United States.

Among the many aspects of the tea ceremony that must be just right are the floral arrangements. Over time, ikebana developed into a ritual all its own. The art of calligraphy has also had a large impact on the notion of "right practice" in Japan. The philosophy underlying right practice is reflected in shadan, *or isolation therapy, which was developed in the 1930s by two Japanese psychotherapists.* Shadan *therapy makes sharp distinctions between the "natural" and "cultural" worlds, with the natural world of mental processes being their only focus.*

Another interesting therapeutic orientation based on right practice is yoga, which is based on an ancient Hindu philosophy from India. Yoga made its way into Japan from China around the same time as Zen Buddhism. Especially when combined, Zen and yoga offer a slow, smooth, deliberate, and focused approach to life. Other Eastern self-practicing techniques, such as tai chi chuan, yield improved self-awareness and self-control.

Right Practice in Daily Life

You saw in Chapters 20, 21, and 22 how meditation-based therapies bring selfish, egocentric, self-conscious, "misfocused" minds back into focus and recover isolated, tormented, impulsive, "misplaced" minds. The practitioners of these techniques maintain that when troubled people faithfully devote themselves to rediscovering their natural minds—by following the various meditational and consciousness-focusing practices involved with Morita, Naikan, and *seiza* therapies—they experience increased attention, responsiveness, and interpersonal awareness. These techniques are understood as a form of remedial education of the whole person.

Traditional Eastern approaches to psychological and physical well-being also include a wide variety of techniques that are somewhat less well known in the West. The common element among these practices is recognition of the connection between mental and physical self-regulation and emotional and physiological well-being. In marked contrast to the implicit subject/object (mind/body) split that Western psychology inherited from the European philosophic tradition, traditional Eastern practices emphasize continuity between mental and physical life and teach techniques for bringing these systems into increased harmony.

The approaches described in this chapter belong to two interrelated traditions. The first set emphasizes carefully honed perceptual and motor skills and a highly refined aesthetic sensibility. The second set of traditions focuses on exercises that foster physical self-regulation and autonomic self-control.

Although distinct, these two traditions represent complementary strategies. They are ideally combined with the sorts of consciousness-enhancing, meditative strategies discussed in previous chapters. People who devote a significant measure of their energies to these practices experience holistic health, spiritual stability, and psychological well-being.

The Cult of Tea

Chanoyu, the Japanese tea ceremony, is devoted to "the art of tea." Tea was brought to Japan from China in 805 c.e. by a Buddhist priest called Saicho. He planted the tea at the foot of a sacred mountain and then built the great Buddhist temple Enryaku-ji to commemorate the event. The Japanese emperor drank the first tea from these plants in 815. For the next several hundred years, tea was a sacred drink reserved for Buddhist monks, who used its magical powers to help them stay awake during lengthy periods of meditation. Eventually it was discovered that tea also had medicinal uses, and its popularity spread throughout the Japanese aristocracy.

With the introduction of Zen Buddhism to Japan from China in the year 1191 and its dramatic spread throughout Japan in the century that followed, tea became a substance of great cultural and economic importance for the Japanese people. The 13th-century Zen priest Eisai wrote a two-volume philosophical and medical treatise on tea, in which he disclosed that the bitterness of tea is essential to life. People who do not drink tea, he said, have afflicted hearts and brief lives. Tea drinkers, on the other hand, grasp the secrets for the prolongation of life and have healthy hearts. Eisai essentially turned tea drinking into a holy sacrament of Zen. His views received the widest possible dissemination after it was revealed that he had saved the shogun Sanatomo's life by ceremoniously preparing tea for him during a long and serious illness.

Eisai's disciple Myoe Shonin was responsible for development of the Zen rituals surrounding the making and drinking of tea. Another disciple, Eison, began the practice of brewing vast cauldrons of tea to be handed out to the masses on festival days. Another of Eisai's disciples combined what he had learned about the art of tea from his fellow Zen monks with the "pure rules of Pai Chang," which he learned while studying Buddhism in China. That disciple was the monk Dogen, who is usually regarded as the greatest teacher of Zen who ever lived. Dogen's rules for tea were essentially a meditation on the Tao of preparing and serving the sacred beverage.

For a while, members of the aristocracy sponsored elaborate tea tournaments, in which aspiring Zen warrior-students would prepare and serve up to 100 bowls of tea, naming the exact place where each tea variety had been grown. Points were awarded for correct answers and flawless performances, and of course points were taken away for mistakes in ritual or knowledge. Fabulous prizes and great fame went to the winners of these competitions, which were contested primarily by aspiring military men who wanted to demonstrate that their skills in piety and decorum were equal to their skills in battle.

The Deeper Significance of Tea. A man by the name of Shuko became one of the great tea masters of Japan late in the 15th century. Shuko began his career in tea as a tournament champion but then discovered a richer and deeper significance in tea:

> Shuko was enlightened during his austerities when it appeared to him that even the Law of Buddha may be discovered in the gestures of filling an ordinary tea bowl with hot water. That is he was enlightened not just in drinking tea but in trying to involve himself in the philosophy of the act of drinking tea. (Iguchi, 1981, p. 108)

Shuko became interested in the character of the person serving tea. As Iguchi (1981) pointed out, Shuko brought a Confucian sensibility to the tea ceremony. He expressed admiration for "the heart" of a person humbled by serving tea. He taught, "Admonish egotism, be the teacher of your heart, do not let it be the teacher" (quoted in Iguchi, 1981, p. 109).

In Korea, the art of tea is said to aid in cultivation of the classical virtues of "equanimity, tranquility, harmony, purity, clarity, simplicity, decorum, and 'cleaving to the mean.'" (Blofeld, 1985). This is what two Korean tea masters say about the virtues of devoting oneself to the art of tea:

Tea is said to be the "Way" (Tao). This is because it is something one learns to appreciate through feeling, not through verbal instruction. If a person maintains a state of quietness, only then will he appreciate the quietness inherent in tea. If he is excited, he will never recognize the tea's quietness. For this reason it is said that "tea and meditation are one taste." If one's meditation is not single-pointed, one will fail to appreciate the true qualities of tea. (Pŏpchŏng Sŭnim quoted in Blofeld, 1985, p. 112)

How can one truly talk about tea without understanding meditation? For tea and meditation are of one taste—the taste of love and compassion, which are the final outcome of harmony and equanimity. The essence is to cultivate the six aspects of harmony; only then can one become a true "man of tea."

1. Living together in physical harmony.
2. Being harmonious in one's speech and not creating discord.
3. Working in harmony to accomplish common aims.
4. In accordance with one's religion or outlook on life, behaving in harmony with the prescribed rules of ethical conduct.
5. Maintaining harmony of outlook by being open and receptive to the views of others.
6. Distributing equally whatever benefits are gained. (An Kwangsŏk, quoted in Blofeld, 1985, p. 112–113)

The Zen of Serving Others. As an expression of the server's quest for inner harmony and enlightenment, Zen tea masters introduced the concepts of simple and natural into the vocabulary of tea. Both the teahouse itself and the bowls and implements used in the ceremony are fashioned from the most simple materials—straw, clay, and wood. But the simple, unpretentious natural elements have both profound beauty and rich significance. A potter, for example, may dedicate the most perfect bowl of his career to the use of a great tea master. The family that makes the charcoal used to heat the water accepts the importance of their task with great solemnity, for the charcoal is of no less significance than the tea itself.

In the 16th century, the Zen master Rikyu completed the transformation of the art of tea into the contemplative practice it remains today. Rikyu's tea ceremony contains "seven secrets":

Make the tea so that your guest will enjoy it; place charcoal so that it will boil water; arrange the flower in a way suited to it; keep the atmosphere of the tea room cool in summer and warm in winter; be ahead of time; prepare an umbrella even if no rain falls; attune your heart to the other guests. (Iguchi, 1981, p. 120)

To properly serve tea, Rikyu said, one must observe four rules: harmony, reverence, purity, and tranquility. Learning the art of tea, then, is fundamentally the art of learning about one's inner nature.

The same is ideally true if one is to receive tea as a guest at a tea ceremony:

When life becomes restless we seek the quietness of things and beg for time to think. If etiquette is abused, ceremonious deportment will be thought beautiful. The way of tea is therefore still essential today. But it is not only a way inside the tea room. Its purpose can be attained in the future because its spirit will revitalize our daily lives. (Iguchi, 1981, p. 122)

The enlightenment and composure offered by the tea ceremony is a reward that comes only after enrolling as a student of a tea master and exerting considerable effort. The formal lessons of tea can last a lifetime. It is still something of a status symbol in Japan for parents to enroll their children in a first-rank tea master's school.

Chanoyu is definitely not everyone's "cup of tea," however. A very good guide book to Japan has this to say about the ceremony:

The average Westerner, along with the average untutored Japanese, finds *chanoyu* hopelessly slow and head bobbingly boring. The greatest difficulty is in trying to keep awake as the interminable ceremony creeps along in what seems to be the almost bare and noiseless main room. . . . At first, the tea ceremony has some novel interest, but unless you are particularly interested in it, don't expect to be dazzled. You're expected to sit Japanese fashion . . . for a very long time which most Westerners will find tearfully excruciating. . . . A classical tea ceremony has 5 guests . . . and the atmosphere is ultra dignified and solemn. There are a number of schools of *chanoyu* with varying philosophies and with differing ceremonies depending upon the occasion and the time of year. Basically at a *sukiya* (tea house), you slowly walk along a garden path to begin your introspection and then you are led into a tiny anteroom where the tea ceremony utensils have been arranged. At this point you are expected to go into rapture concerning the artistry of the arrangement. Anything less than ecstasy is considered a slight. . . . If it all seems a bit much, it is that the subtle refinements of *chanoyu* can only be appreciated with years of study. Most Westerners don't even like the taste of the tea. (Bisignani, 1983, p. 65)

Perhaps so, but on December 9, 1992, *The Wall Street Journal* ran a story on the tea ceremony in which its beneficial effects were extolled for high-powered U.S. executives and professionals (Valente, 1992). The article reported that tea schools in Chicago, New York, and San Francisco are doing a brisk business, with long waiting lists for people who want to take lessons.

Ikebana: The Zen of Arranging Nature

The principles of "right practice" extend into every aspect of life in cultures that have been influenced by Confucian and Buddhist teachings. Consider, for example, the Japanese art of flower arranging, ikebana. Ikebana originally was an offshoot of the tea ceremony. Today Japan has more than 3,000 schools of ikebana. Senei Ikenobo, the head of one of the largest of these schools, wrote:

> Resisting wind and rain, a tiny flowering plant keeps breathing dreaming its bright future. Its serious activity to live is powerful enough to move people. The fundamental aims of the flower arrangement that stand above the shape, the color, and the beauty of forma-tion, are to express men's sympathy towards the tiny life of the plant and their expecta-tion for its future. *Ikebana* is created being based upon the noble and spiritual inter-change between men and flowers. (1981)

Recall that Rikyu's third rule of tea was to "arrange the flower in a way suited to it," which is a matter of selecting the right flower for the season and the occasion, the correct container for the flower, and then displaying that flower at precisely the right height and angle with precisely the right amount of foliage and background materi-als. Written instructions about arranging flowers to accompany the serving of tea go back at least 1,000 years, but it became a serious discipline in its own right only about 600 years ago with the development of *kuge*, the offering of flowers to the Buddha.

The philosophical core of *ikebana* is a well-crafted arrangement's ability to cap-ture the essence of a fleeting moment of feeling or a season. Ikenobo (1981) explained:

> Ikebana is not only beautiful to look at but also inspiring. The inspiring element is the very one which our predecessors fervently sought after in *Ikebana*. Tenshin's saying [Tenshin was an artist who wrote about flower arranging in *The Book of Tea* "restores to us our waning confidence in the universe" does not aim at the prettiness of the flower, but at the vitality and the movement of mind resonant with life. There we feel a joy in arranging flowers, and then we find the clue which leads us to [a particular arrange-ment]. The most important significance of *Ikebana* is in the blending into daily life and in EXISTING JUST NOW. (p. 3)

> In consequence, *Ikebana* must always be formed from the arranger's own will. It must result in one's own enjoyment. It must not be a difficult composition for the sake of hardship. When the flexible mind is reflected in the arrangement, a room is filled with brightness and *Ikebana* gives us hope for tomorrow and enjoyment. Daily-life *Ikebana* need not be called "art." If we have a clear mind, [we] will not fail to create a pretty form. (p. 30)

The basic structure of an ikebana arrangement represents the eternal harmony of the three plains of existence, "ten-chi-jin." *Ten*, which is heaven, is symbolized by a main upward branch of the arrangement. *Jin*, which is humankind, inhabits the plain between heaven and earth (*chi*) and is represented by a branch or branches that are a third shorter than the *ten*, and that extend to the right of the arrangement. The branch representing *chi* is a third shorter still and extends to the left of the overall arrangement.

I have found that beginning ikebana students generally want to work with blossoms—they want one tall rose, followed by a middle rose, followed by a short rose—with the result that although they have dutifully followed the form of ikebana, they have lost its essence. A better way to proceed is to abandon preconceived notions of what is beautiful—for example, roses—and go out into nature to find some objects with hidden elegance and grace, such as strands of tall grass or roadside weeds. Then work on revealing that beauty to observers by uncovering "the vitality and the movement of mind resonant with life" (Ikenobo, 1981, p. 3), which have been given expression through the arranger's own will. Ultimately the display "must result in one's own enjoyment" (Ikenobo, 1981, p. 30), a criterion that many students find extraordinarily difficult to meet.

Giving male students ikebana lessons has been an enlightening experience for me. As they struggle to clarify their own definitions of beauty and harmony, they have to struggle with their preconceptions of what is beautiful and what a flower arrangement should look like. In one class, every student created a little tiny miniature arrangement. Each was perfectly designed in terms of height, of course—young men really like to measure how big things are—but most of the arrangements looked like they came out of a brochure for a commercial florist. Finally, the ikebana *sensei* who was guiding the class couldn't hold back her dismay. She went around the room impaling the mini-ikebanas with tall reeds and great bushy branches. The students were initially stunned by what they feared was aesthetic disorder. But by the end, everyone had created something.

Perhaps the most eye-opening aspect of the entire exercise for me was that only three students dared to take their arrangements back to their residence halls after class. And one courageous student carried his to the rest of his classes and to chemistry lab that day. To my serious-minded psychologist colleagues, teaching in a classroom festooned with a dozen ikebana displays was disconcerting. I don't know what the chemistry teachers thought of the student's ikebana. They may not be used to such a revelation of will and inner mind in a college classroom.

The Zen of Calligraphy and Other Practices in Daily Life

Other aspects of Zen practice in daily life include *shodo,* the art of calligraphy; *bonsai,* the art of miniaturizing nature; *bonkei,* miniature landscape design; *chinzo,* ink painting; *haiku,* poetry writing; and the design and maintenance of contemplative gardens. As with the tea ceremony and flower arranging, each of these arts demands years and years of exacting practice, and each serves as a mirror to the souls of both its creator and its audience.

Consider, for example, what Yoshioka (1981) had to say about the art of writing with an ink brush:

[In Zen] the realm of enlightenment [is] accessible to one's own exertion. . . . Many techniques for expressing greater freedom within the utter simplicity of narrow limits . . . evolved in order to communicate the teachings of Zen which took *practice* as its core. This is the major characteristic of Zen culture.

The unique character of Zen calligraphy lies in its philosophy that "the writing is the man." Boldly revealing the individual personality with utter freedom, a style of calligraphy which disregarded the [Chinese] traditional style. An exquisite spiritual freedom and savor pours forth from the writing of Zen monks who have undergone the tempering of rigorous practice and attained enlightenment. For example in the [calligraphy] of Ryokan addressed to his younger brother, his fraternal sympathy is expressed in his warm hearted brush strokes. Such free expression of individual feeling can not be seen in earlier calligraphic styles. (pp. 32–33; italics added).

We can find this same profoundly humanistic emphasis in every aspect of Zen practice in daily life. Within each discipline resides a deep faith in the possibility of salvation from a life of emptiness and despair. Each of us already possesses the Buddha nature, but few of us possess the strength of character and the determination of will to achieve enlightenment. Conducting the tea ceremony, writing poetry, arranging flowers, and doing all the rest are sources of education, formally instructed mental habits to give our minds discipline and character.

A Zen proverb says, "There is no sense in trying to shovel away our shadows." The following poem is an instructive tale of a man who tried to run away from his shadow:

There was a man
who was so disturbed
by the sight of his own shadow
and so displeased with his own footsteps
that he determined to get rid of both.

The method he hit upon was to run away from them.
So he got up and ran.

But every time he put his foot down
there was another step,
while his shadow kept up with him
without the slightest difficulty.

He attributed his failure
to the fact that he was not running fast enough.
So he ran faster and faster, without stopping,
until finally he dropped dead.

He failed to realize
that if he merely stepped into the shade,

his shadow would vanish,
and if he sat down and stayed still,
there would be no more footsteps.
(Chuang-tzu, quoted in Merton, 1965, p. 155)*

Zen practice blocks the impulse to run away from reality. It provides us with "shade," it lets us examine the moment perfectly so we might realize that the footsteps we are running from are our own.

Shadan: A Zen Rest Cure

One school of psychotherapy in Japan combines some of the elements of Naikan and Morita therapies (see Chapter 22) with the notion of right practice. *Shadan,* or isolation therapy (Reynolds, 1980), was developed as a sort of rest cure by two Japanese psychiatrists in the 1930s. *Shadan* therapists make a sharp distinction between a client's "natural" world of biological processes (which includes all feelings, moods, and brain functions) and the "cultural and ideological" world (which comprises the client's beliefs, opinions, memories, and perceptions).

Shadan psychotherapists focus exclusively on the natural aspects of being. They feel they have no legitimate business tampering with the patient's ideological and cultural position, which they regard as the exclusive domain of teachers and parents.

> The psychotherapist appropriately turns to the disorders that are common to human beings and are subject to natural law. In other words, unhealthy thought processes, unhealthy fixation of attention, unhealthy moods, and the like are illnesses in the same [way] that a cold or measles are illnesses. What is the *natural* treatment for almost any sickness of the body? . . . The natural process of healing is advanced through *resting.*
> (Reynolds, 1980, p. 67; italics added)

"Food for Your Head." *Shadan* therapy begins with complete rest and more or less total social isolation for up to 30 days. During this period, the patient often may be permitted to communicate directly with only one person, the therapist, and then only in the form of written notes, which the therapist does not answer. Meanwhile, the *shadan* therapist has been prescribing "mental work" to the patient on a daily basis:

> Just as rest without exercise eventually weakens the body, so the mind must be exercised with what the shadan therapist calls mental work to avoid sluggishness. He may be asked to copy a page from a book, work simple arithmetic problems or write a daily diary

---

*"Flight From the Shadow," by Chuang Tzu, translated by Thomas Merton, from *The Way of Chuang Tzu.* Copyright © 1965 by The Abbey of Gethsemani. Reprinted by permission of New Directions Publishing Corp.

on both sides of a single page. The therapist silently collects the results during his daily visit to check the patient's general condition. . . .

[Over] time, the daily mental work assignments progress . . . to reading popular works about nature, . . . and then to readings about human beings. . . . [N]ovels, television comedies, light magazines, and the like are forbidden. . . . [C]asual conversation, arguing and complaining by the patient, and scolding by the therapist are considered stimulating and are forbidden. (Reynolds, 1980, pp. 68–69)

The point of the mental exercises is to give the patient a great deal of practice in using his or her mind in a constructive and focused manner. A popular U.S. television news magazine advertises by calling its contents "food for your head." *Shadan* therapy takes this metaphor quite seriously. The therapist becomes explicitly concerned that the patient's brain has just the right amount of nutrition to make and keep it strong. This is an intriguing idea. I wonder how North American psychotherapy patients would react if I proposed a treatment consisting solely of intellectually stimulating work. The closest I have come, perhaps, is in my patented premarital partner-compatibility do-it-yourself test.

Dr. Bankart's Relationship Challenge. To take this test, arrange to spend several days completely alone with the person you are considering marrying. The summer cottage of a family member or friend or a cabin in a state park is an ideal location, provided you visit in the off season. Agree that you will eat very simple meals and that, as budget allows, you will take those meals in restaurants. Take any games, books, or music that you particularly enjoy. But you may not bring "work" from office or school. A little wine either with or after dinner is OK, but this is not a weekend for artificially altering your consciousness with alien substances.

The first thing you do when you arrive at your retreat is to locate and disable all televisions, VCRs, radios, and electronic games. Hide the keys to any boats, mopeds, trailbikes, skimobiles, chainsaws, lawnmowers, or other internal combustion machines. As best you can, avoid all clocks, watches, timers, beepers, and other reminders of elapsed time. Unplug the phone. Turn up your hearing aid.

Now comes the hard part—or the easy part. Just be. If you are like most people, you will make love several times, and that is a fine thing to do. But you will also discover yourself sending and receiving a lot of important self-disclosure about everything under the sun. This experience is what we highly trained professional mind doctors call intimacy. You will encounter each other's deepest personal feelings about everything from Bartok to Yahtzee, and you will have no place to hide from any of them. At the end of a good long weekend you will know each other better than you ever thought possible. You will even have a private knowledge of those aspects of the personality and behavioral repertoire of this wonderful other that you absolutely must set about changing for the sake of your own sanity.

People who have been crazy enough to try this exercise have come away from it with genuinely new knowledge about the prospects for a lifelong commitment to their partner. Some people have discovered that their differences were much greater than they had previously comprehended. Others discovered dimensions of their partner that they never knew existed. But everyone I know who has tried this exercise has been surprised by what a challenge it is to keep their brains going continuously without refuge for several days. They discover that television really is a drug in their lives and that it is hard to get through an entire day without escaping into the electronic abyss. Of course, not everyone is ready for a Zen relationship, but it's good to know that the opportunity is there should the need ever arise.

Yoga and Related Practices

Earlier in the chapter I said that self-practicing techniques could be grouped on the basis of two fundamental traditions. As you have seen, the first set of practices is intimately connected with the traditions and practices of Zen Buddhism. The second set of practices is in the tradition of the Yoga, a school of Hindu philosophy. Yogic teachings focus on the union of the individual with the universal. Yogic practices encourage the development of physical self-regulation and autonomic self-control through prescribed exercises. This enhanced voluntary control over physiological states and processes is believed to be the key to self-realization. Yoga is based on a view of the self similar to that held by Carl Jung: an eternal, unchanging essence that is the common inheritance of all people.

The classic text on Yoga, the *Bhagavad-Gita,* was written as a dialogue between a warrior ego named Arjuna and his charioteer Krishna, who is self as an incarnation of God. Throughout the text, Krishna teaches Arjuna lessons of the eternal Yogic principles that make up a worthy life. These include devotion, self-control, meditation, and the practices that will ultimately unite the ego with the self.

Among the several central concepts in Yoga, we will explore only two: *purusha* and *chitta.* First among these is *purusha* (spirit), which is changeless, eternal, blissful, pure consciousness—akin to the Christian concept of the "mind of god." Spirit is infinite and fills the void of the universe. What makes me a self is that my being is suffused with *purusha.* There is no distinction between the two; I possess a body and a mind, but I am the essence of *purusha.* It is common human folly to seek spirit as something outside oneself, something that can be gained and possessed like wealth or knowledge, but in Yoga this common belief is considered common delusion.

Chitta (mind) refers to all thought processes. The practice of yoga involves learning to master mind; for when mind is agitated, it creates a great and stormy sea of conscious thought that obscures knowledge of self. We are told that when our minds become chaotic, "self is obscured, like a bright light suspended in churning water" (Frager & Fadiman, 1984, p. 411). All yogic practices serve the aim of calming and regulating the flow of mind. Once this goal has been accomplished, awareness of self is possible.

Mind is controlled by our actions. Right actions lead to a calm and disciplined mind. Harmful actions cloud mind with anger and sorrow. This is the essence of the notion of *karma:* Good actions produce good karma; unworthy actions produce bad karma. Good karma regulates and disciplines mind and makes self apparent; bad karma, of course, does just the opposite. By looking inward, however, the devoted student of yoga can, discover the sources of negative karma in thoughts and actions and through self-discipline, right action, and devotion transform the bad karma into good karma.

Take, for example, the experience of greed. By looking inward, greedy individuals may, discover that resentment of others stems from their own fear of inadequacy. Thus fear and resentment drive good feelings from their mind and their good actions from their behavior. In the vocabulary of yoga, we would say that their greed has created great waves of disturbance in their mind and led them to live as if they were not possessed of spirit. Greed has become an unconscious habit (*samskaras*) that generates bad karma and locks them away from awareness of how to redeem their situation and themselves. Soon they bring this greed into every aspect of life. They become greedy in public life as they once were greedy in personal life. They may become greedy in their spiritual life as well and harbor fantasies of being immune to the devastating effects of bad karma on one's spiritual well-being.

Greedy persons' salvation lies in coming face to face with the sources of their greed and bad karma. In the vocabulary of yoga, they must confront and destroy the seeds of their past actions in "the fires of wisdom and meditation" (Yogananda, 1968, quoted in Frager & Fadiman, 1984, p. 411).

> The discipline of Yoga must include a *complete* reformation of consciousness. Otherwise the subconscious tendencies eventually will seek to actualize themselves, sprouting suddenly like dormant seeds. Through meditation, self-analysis, and other powerful inner disciplines, it is possible to "roast" such seeds, to destroy their potential for further activity; that is, through fundamental inner change we can grow free of the influence of the past. (Frager & Fadiman, 1984, p. 411)

Eastern Self-Practicing Techniques: *Gyohos*

The *gyohos,* or self-practicing techniques, are the mainstay of the holistic approach to physical and mental health that Japanese practitioners have borrowed from yoga. The distinctive feature of these practices is that they actively transcend dichotomies between the psychological-mental-emotional-spiritual domain and the corporeal-physical-medical-bodily dimension of being.

Especially as they were imported to Japan, the practices of Zen and yoga have a great many similarities. But when we compare the self-practicing techniques associated with Zen with those associated with the *gyohos,* some important differences become apparent. From a yogic perspective, Zen practices are very one-sided. Zen appears to focus almost exclusively on developing and cleansing one's mind. Passions are all to be eradicated. Mind is to overwhelm matter. Zen practitioners become free to spontaneously do and be what is expected. They become the absolute masters of self-discipline, as they are no longer plagued by interfering doubts or self-consciousness (DeVos, 1980). The Zen gardener does not, indeed cannot, garden for the sake of something else. The tea ceremony is about serving tea, not about discovering something universal. As I mentioned in Chapters 21 and 22, many people seem to want to read into the idea of satori something "extra" in the human condition. But without exception, all such intimations of this alleged "something else" are dismissed as illusion by Zen masters.

In yoga, however, the "something else" is really the starting point. The spirit and the body and the mind are all of a piece. In yoga, to a far greater extent than in Zen, physical illness may be perceived as the result of mental or spiritual defect as much as the result of a germ or a virus. Confronting the demands of the body is an important part of the yogic tradition. So although the rules for living are roughly the same for both Zen and yoga—when hungry, eat; when thirsty, drink; but always do both in moderation—these goals would be arrived at by quite different routes.

In Zen you would attempt to overcome or transcend the obsessive and interfering cravings for food or drink that compel you to eat or drink too much. In yoga you would meditate on your cravings, to try to find their spiritual root, in order to reverse the source of the craving for food into an energy to do good for others. In Zen a hungry person might eat a bowl of rice and use hunger as a focus of meditation on the "meaning" of the rice. In yoga the hungry person might commit himself or herself to a fast in order to come to terms with the craving the body has generated.

This interrelatedness between body and mind is at the center of the *gyohos*. The person practicing these techniques is engaged in a process designed to overcome obstacles to the realization of self. The aim of the practice is to reverse the process wherein the energy and consciousness of self is distorted by unconscious habits (such as greed).

> Then the self which is pure joy, pure love and bliss, cannot manifest within our consciousness or in the world. The aim of yoga practice is to reduce the distortion and direct the flow of consciousness back to its source, the Self. To reduce distortion, we can cleanse our bodies and our personality tendencies. In hatha-yoga this cleansing is accomplished primarily through physical disciplines and concentration exercises. (Frager & Fadiman, 1984, p. 429)

Breathing Exercises

Foremost among these practices are yogic breathing exercises. Breathing exercises have a direct and profound effect on the state of the physical body. By slowing down and deepening one's breathing it is possible to slow the heart rate and to induce deep muscular relaxation. This deep muscular relaxation is accompanied by a calmness of mood and a quieting of the mind.

It is almost routine when working with panic-disorder patients to spend a fair amount of session time and a lot of homework time practicing breathing. Patients who begin to feel the onset of a panic attack are instructed to shift their attention from whatever they were doing to a deep conscious awareness of their own breathing patterns. One implication of this exercise, of course, is that the panic sensations thus receive no focused attention. With practice, the panic attacks become shorter, less frequent, and markedly less severe. This technique is also more or less routine for patients who experience either public-speaking or test-taking anxiety.

Note carefully, please, what is happening here: The instruction to focus on breathing is in essence an instruction to attend to self-regulation. By focusing on taking long, slow, deep breaths, patients start to look closer to the source of the unpleasant feelings—that is, something within the self. Before treatment, in contrast, they experienced the beginning symptoms of panic or anxiety in such a way that all their attention was directed outward to the world, away from self-regulation and self-control.

Kikoho, or recuperative breathing exercises (*Qigong* in Chinese), have been practiced in Asian societies for health reasons for more than 2,000 years (Haruki, 1990). Haruki identified five basic categories of breathing *gyohos:*

- *Static breathing.* Breathing is practiced without moving any part of the body. Static breathing is usually accompanied by a variety of images and is usually associated with advanced meditative practices. The Japanese name for this practice is *Sei-kiko.*
- *Dynamic breathing.* Breathing is coordinated with other bodily motions or movements. Thus breathing is activated when other bodily motions are activated. The Japanese call this practice *Do-kiko.*
- *Internal breathing.* The practice that the Japanese call *Nai-kiko* involves a transfer of life energy within oneself.
- *External breathing. Gai-kiko,* like internal breathing, is a more advanced breathing practice. Life energy is transferred externally as a way of influencing other persons.
- *Abdominal breathing.* This Japanese self-practice involves extremely powerful, intense breathing that emphasizes exhalation:

    The breathing is performed while bending the upper part of the body forward in a line 2 to 3 cm above the navel. This breathing includes two ways of expiration, i.e. short intense exhalation and long slow exhalation. The purpose of doing this is [to] relax the upper part of the body and strengthen the lower part of the body. (Haruki, 1990, p. 9)

    Abdominal breathing is said to produce mental relaxation and physical sedation and to foster physical relaxation and attentional stability among those who practice it.

Sex as Sacrament

Many readers of this book may be aware of another karmic tradition, one taught in the *Kama Sutra,* the 1,500-year-old illustrated guide to making love. Although it is no longer widely followed, for a thousand years the *Kama Sutra* was a popular reflection of the wider Hindu belief that, as a part of life, sex is essentially a religious duty, not a source of shame or guilt. Sex is to be celebrated and enjoyed in moderation. Allegedly written by the gods, the *Kama Sutra* advised all men and women to become serious students of the erotic arts as part of their preparation for marriage (Francoeur, 1991).

Under these teachings, karma can be gained by engaging in the dutiful practice of Tantric sex. "The greatest source of energy in the universe is sexual," and thus it is possible to gain great spiritual power by engaging in sexual intercourse. The experience of orgasm has very special significance because it affects the flow of spiritual energy, or kundalini (Francoeur, 1991).

The *Kama Sutra* provides graphic instruction in a wide variety of sexual positions and practices:

> [There are] four kinds of mild embrace, and four that are more passionate; eight kinds of love bites, eight stages of oral intercourse, and nine ways of moving the lingam [penis] inside the yoni [vagina]; four parts of the body that might be individually embraced; three ways of kissing an innocent maiden, and four angles from which it might be done. There were moderate kisses, contracted kisses, pressed ones, and soft ones, and there was also the clasping kiss, when one lover took "both the lips of the other" between his or her own. (Tannahill, 1980, p. 206)

Hatha Yoga: The Dance of the Buddha

If you walk through any Chinese, Korean, or Japanese village, town, city, or metropolis early in the morning, you will see and perhaps hear hundreds and hundreds of people outside, in all sorts of weather, practicing their morning gymnastics. In China, Korea, and Japan, millions of people practice tai chi chuan on a daily basis, and in Japan you may also see them practicing four-movement gymnastics, or *makkoho.*

These forms of gymnastics, derived from ancient martial arts, are very similar to hatha yoga, a form of yoga known for the extraordinary physical prowess of its adherents. Classical hatha yoga, in addition to gymnastics, requires sexual celibacy, vegetarianism, and complex routines for maintaining the purity of the body. The full hatha yoga regimen even requires following strict procedures for cleansing the nasal passages and the alimentary canal from the throat to the intestines (Frager & Fadiman, 1984). True Freudians would have a field day with that level of anal fixation if they encountered it in their consulting room.

Four-movement gymnastics has a specifically social context as well as a focus on the joints and muscles (Haruki, 1990). Because it is difficult for persons just learning four-movement gymnastics to assume the required body postures, another person may help and support the practicing person to assume these postures. We will come back to this social dimension later, but you should note that the social dimension is one of the reasons four-movement gymnastics is popular among the Japanese.

The gymnastic dimension of hatha yoga, which Buddhist practitioners like to call *"The Dancing of the Buddha,"* is probably the most widely practiced yoga in the world today. The purpose of the gymnastic exercises is to purify, cleanse, and strengthen the body as preparation for meditation. The goal of the exercises is to strengthen vital life-force energies (*pranas*) and then bring them under conscious control. These vital forces can then be redirected back into the body to create physical strength and health. The overall well-being of an individual is a reflection of the availability of well controlled and highly developed *pranas*. Yogic beliefs about the importance of developing and controlling *pranas* bear a striking resemblance to Sigmund Freud's early notions about sexual energy, or libido.

Levels of Practice. Hatha yoga practice stresses the transformation and purification of the person through intentional and systematic conserving and harnessing of the body's vital energies. The actual practice of yoga involves several progressive steps, or "limbs" (adapted from the organizational scheme delineated by Frager and Fadiman, 1984):

1. *Abstentions and observances* are the keys to living a calm and disciplined outer life. These are the moral and ethical rules that govern a person's daily conduct. They represent a purification of the mind through abstention from all the acts that weaken a person's character and thus the body as well. The heart of this moral code is nonviolence, which is fostered by destroying the seeds of violence—greed, hate, aversion, anger, lust, and the like—within our unconscious minds. This, I believe, is what Fritz Perls (see Chapter 16) was referring to when he talked about "finishing unfinished situations" from our past. The key notion is that one's inner and outer life must be continuous. A person cannot have a virtuous inner life while leading a corrupt outer life; purity, austerity, devotion, contemplation, and receptiveness must be a way of life for the follower of yoga. A disciple who does not accept the regimen of abstentions and observances as a total way of being has no hope of fully benefiting from any of the other practices of yoga, because his or her character will not be strong enough to direct and control the vital forces that these practices will put the disciple in touch with.

2. *Posture* refers to the disciple's ability to remain calm and steadfast during long hours of meditative practice. Good posture requires physical and ethical strength and is the result of concentration and devoted practice. To realize

the full flow of energy through the body, the spine must be straight and the muscles relaxed. Yet posture must not occupy the conscious attention of the practitioner.

3. *Control of vital energy* is probably the aspect of yogic practice that has received the most attention in the literature of Western psychology. The dramatic abilities of some yogis to control their heart rate, respiration, body temperature, brain waves, and other biological processes are well documented. In one published case, a yoga practitioner survived several hours confined in a sealed metal box by reducing his oxygen consumption and carbon dioxide elimination. Other yogis have demonstrated an impressive ability to reduce their blood lactate levels, an indication of powerful voluntary control over the norepinephrine output of the sympathetic nervous system, the major neurophysiological indicator of stress associated with anxiety, hypertension, and environmental stress. But their attentional and perceptual abilities are not sacrificed and even show some sharpening while the yogis are engaged in the process of calming their nervous systems so effectively. (For a fascinating review of some of this literature, see Wallace and Benson, 1972.)

4. *Interiorization* refers to the yogic ability to completely shut down the externally focused sensory systems. The accomplished yogi can withdraw completely from this world and restore awareness of what I have called in this book natural mind. Yogis refer to this process as renouncing the world and its objects, which is a nicely descriptive way of thinking about it. The purpose of interiorization is to turn one's energy flow inward to the brain and the rest of the nervous system. Consciousness can then be invested in its source rather than in the external objects in the world.

5. *Concentration* involves the selective focusing of all one's attention on the object of one's choice while withdrawing it from all other sources of stimulation. It is being able to concentrate on the call of a particular object in the universe while shutting out all the competing noise. Concentration is at the heart of the command "Be here now!" in the Gestalt and existential psychotherapies. One of the fascinating things about yogic concentration is that the full attentional system remains intact throughout the period of concentration. Normally we all become habituated to stimuli that we experience over an extended period. But the yogi shows a "freshness" of perceptual attention to stimuli even after extended concentration on a very narrow stimulus, such as a tone or a light. This phenomenon has been observed in demonstrations of concentration that measure both central nervous system activity, as through electroencephalographic recordings of alpha waves, and galvanic skin responses, which reflect autonomic nervous system activity.

6. *Meditation* in the yogic tradition has a more tightly defined meaning than it does in Zen practice. Within yoga, meditation is an advanced form of

concentration. Yogic meditation is a form of "fixation" (Spiegelberg, 1962), wherein a single stimulus or object becomes the sole source of the meditator's attention. The goal of this exercise is for the yogi to learn how to subjugate completely the sentient being—to bring all of his or her life energy to bear on a single point.

7. *Illumination,* or *samadhi,* is the functional equivalent of satori or enlightenment in Zen Buddhism. Those who have attained illumination are true yogis; all others are aspiring students of yoga. Illumination is a state of being; it is the achievement of union so profound that all formerly perceived separateness (perhaps what we in the West would call alienation) appears to be an illusion. Illumination is the total realization of self. The mind is absolutely at peace, attention is fully concentrated, and perception is infinite. Most importantly, perhaps, consciousness exists only of the experience of profoundly deep joy and peace. All aspects of being are at one. All of creation is known and accepted.

Earth *Kasina* Exercise. *Kasina* exercises, which relate to the sixth step, meditation, are extended exercises in developing and clarifying highly focused attention. One such exercise called earth *kasina,* is drawn from practices that lead the yogi along "the path of purity" (Spiegelberg, 1962).

Only a student who has passed through the first five levels of hatha yoga practice can undertake the earth *kasina* exercise. Then,

after choosing a proper place, and practicing [previously learned] posture and breathing exercises, the student should erect a sort of low table in his place of meditation by fixing four stakes in the ground and stretching a cloth or mat across them. On this he should then lay some light brown loam and spread it out with a perfectly smooth stone into a round, level disk (about 28 centimeters [11 inches] in diameter). People who are inclined to selfishness, obstinacy, and obsessively fixed ideas will do well to make the disk a little larger in circumference, whereas those who are inclined to be absent minded and those whose thoughts are easily scattered should make the disk smaller. The loam that is used for this purpose must be thoroughly kneaded, and all grass, roots, sand, and gravel removed from it. Next the place should be carefully cleaned; and then he should go away and purify himself as well. Returning, he should [sit] down about two meters away, on a low chair. The kasina disk must not be so far away that it can not be perceived distinctly; but at the same time it must not be so close that the unavoidable little unevennesses of its surface are visible. One's sitting posture must be comfortable, just as the Asana exercises prescribe; his knees should not ache, even if he stays in one position for a fairly long time, and his neck is not to be bent. He should be seated, filled with confidence and faith in the efficacy of the exercise, and begin to practice [meditation], letting no disturbing thoughts interrupt his [practice].

The aim is now to evolve the "spiritual image" of the kasina disk. To do this he must contemplate the disk continuously over a long period of time, seated in an attitude of serene, motionless concentration. He will find that it is no waste of time repeatedly to give up hours, even, of his leisure to this contemplation. His eyes should be kept only partly open, and he should gaze at the disk in a calm, relaxed manner, somewhat as though he were looking at his face in the mirror. (Spiegelberg, 1962, p. 44)

The student can deepen this meditation progressively and keep the spirit from growing weary in a number of ways. Eventually, the disk "will appear to him just as distinctly when his eyes are closed as when they are open" (Spiegelberg, 1962, p. 47). Once this result can be achieved on a regular basis, the student continues to practice until he or she can keep the disk in mind even when walking around and leaving the place of meditation.

> Through this exercise [the student] finally succeeds in unfolding the "Counterpart," which exists entirely within him, and in which, consequently, there no longer appear any of the imperfections of the disk that is being meditated on. It is free from earth and all other material attributes, and is pure and luminous as the disk of the moon. He should bear this image within him henceforth as a jewel, guarding it tirelessly as the "Embryo of a World Conqueror." It is the Golden Gem, to the attainment of which the Chinese Taoists aspired with the same zeal as the alchemists of the Middle Ages. (Spiegelberg, 1962, pp. 45–46)

Tai Chi and Shiatsu Massage

Tai chi chuan is derived from a very old form of martial arts in China. It is more behavioral than yoga in that it involves much more movement. The person practicing tai chi assumes a half-standing posture, with the upper part of the body straight, while slowly and smoothly moving arms, legs, neck, and torso, all coordinated with his or her breathing. If you have never seen tai chi, try to imagine a group of swordless swordsmen dueling invisible opponents in slow motion, with the grace of ballet dancers. To make the movements as fluid and smooth as possible, the practitioner must attain great mental stability. His or her eyes must be perfectly coordinated with the movement of the body (the *gyohos* for eye movements is called in Japanese *ganpo*) so that the practitioner "can feel and sense that his movements are becoming increasingly dynamic" (Haruki, 1990).

The *gyohos* that increases interpersonal awareness and sensitivity is *shiatsu,* or finger-pressure massage, an "Eastern *cooperative* self-practicing technique" (Haruki, 1990). Experienced shiatsu therapists know precisely where to apply pressure for each muscle group. Shiatsu follows a general principle very similar to acupuncture. The critical part of each muscle is known as its *keiraku,* and the locations of the *keiraku* are taught to students within the context of traditional Eastern medicine.

But the essential point of *shiatsu* is the education it provides the patient about the social or interpersonal domain. Genuine shiatsu is a product of the flexible interpersonal relationship between the patient and the massager, mutually relaxed in their minds and bodies. This relaxation should be understood as involving the entire aspect of their two persons, including not only touch but also bodily motions and breathing. Through this interaction, the two people develop a deep awareness of each other and of their relationship. Indeed, in shiatsu the effects of the massage are at least as transpersonal and emotional as they are physical (as we also saw in Chapter 17).

> An important distinction [to be made with reference to shiatsu] is that this therapeutic technique is different from the Western style massage for comfort or consolation, the so called *Anma*. The reason for this is that the conventional *Anma* is considered for the therapist as well as the patient, to be produced by mechanically applied pressure, which does not interact with the patient, and in this sense the therapist or massagist can be replaced by a non-responsive machine. [In shiatsu] both the patient and the therapist can feel and sense the genuine human aspects of each other person in the course of this therapeutic practice. In order to achieve such an interaction, both persons breathe together slowly and match their modes of breathing to each other, while they are relaxing completely their other muscles. In this way, the *shiatsu* is a kind of relaxation technique incorporated with the bodily motion and breathing practices, which can be performed by the two persons through the sensations and feelings of the other person as well as of oneself. (Haruki, 1990)

Consciousness and Silence

Self-practicing techniques promote the active integration of the physical, social, spiritual, and behavioral domains of being. The result is that practitioners completely overcome any one-sidedness in thought, perception, or feeling. Physical health is not considered separately from spiritual well-being, interpersonal awareness, or emotional-psychological stability.

A central feature of all the techniques covered in this chapter, especially as they are viewed by a Westerner, is that they all involve a slow, smooth, deliberate, and focused approach to life. Whether in the slow, fluid movements of tai chi, the concentrated focus on slow and regular breathing, the deliberately transpersonal interaction in shiatsu massage, or the rather elaborate sexual practices prescribed in the *Kama Sutra*, bodily movements, conscious thought processes, emotional state, and interpersonal relationships become the focus of a penetrating consciousness. In this state of consciousness, body, mind, emotion, and social relations become inseparable and thus unified into a dynamic, coherent whole. Consciousness is thus expanded, and the barriers separating the individual from union are at least momentarily overcome.

Such consciousness enables practitioners to understand the deepest aspects of their own being. With this understanding, Eastern psychologists believe, practitioners gain the ability to "intervene and influence" (Haruki, 1990) in every aspect of their being. Eastern psychologists thus use terms like *activate, awaken,* and *enrich* to describe the purpose and function of their therapies. When they speak of developing awareness of the conscious mind, they are referring to this comprehensive, global emphasis on the sources of one's entire being.

I am unaware of any Western therapeutic approach that even approximates such a position. It seems to me entirely possible that in Western psychology's unrelenting search for the keys to the unconscious mind in dreams, reflexes, and cognitions we have completely missed the point. After studying Eastern approaches to psychology for a decade or so, I would agree with William James that the really interesting stuff of psychology lies in the dynamics of conscious experience.

Perhaps if Western psychologists focused a bit more on what human beings know (or perhaps can know), they might have a better chance of making a substantial contribution to the improvement of the human condition. Instead of touting the psychology of "tricks and games," which every Introductory Psychology student has had to experience as a participant in our pseudoscientific "experiments," we might do a great deal more good by investing our energy in a serious, scholarly, and real exploration of natural mind.

It is also quite instructive, if not humbling, that all of Eastern psychology's wisdom is accomplished in relative silence. Perhaps the reason that the Western search for the "talking cure" has proved so elusive is that it asks all the right questions but listens for answers in all the wrong ways. Rollo May once observed that Western psychology, having lost its mind, seemed intent on abandoning its soul. I hope that these last few chapters have given you some feel for the profundity of that observation.

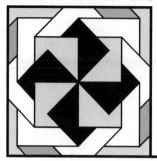

CHAPTER 24

Final Thoughts

If You Meet the Buddha on the Road, Kill Him!

A study of non-Western psychology invites us to make deep structural changes in our lives. This is neither an empty promise nor one held out only to an elite or wealthy few. We must work toward resolving the difficulties of understanding and application that separate East from West so we may overcome the repression that limits our full awareness of the possibilities of life.

Healthy Respect

Solitude, the safeguard of mediocrity,
is to genius the stern friend.
(Ralph Waldo Emerson)

I must close the discussion of Eastern approaches to mental and physical well-being on a cautionary note. Eastern psychological techniques are very powerful and rely, probably to a much greater degree than Western techniques, on a profound relationship between the student-patient and the teacher-therapist. The *sensei* in Zen and the guru in Yoga occupy positions of enormous responsibility and thus must be worthy of enormous trust.

Under the right conditions, Eastern approaches can be extraordinarily more personal, immediate, and transformative than any of the Western therapeutic techniques described in this book. To plunge into the depths of one's consciousness is an infinitely more immediate, dramatic, and powerful venture than to recover bits and pieces of one's unconscious. Sigmund Freud called on us all to be archaeologists of our own lives, a task that can be quite difficult and give rise to conscious awareness of powerful emotions and memories. But to me, becoming the architect of one's own consciousness is potentially even more devastating. I would want a trusted guide next to me in either case, but how much more would I want a guide in the process of designing my own consciousness.

Shapiro (1982), one of the West's leading researchers and writers on the psychological benefits of Zen meditation, called on Western therapists to use "extreme caution" when applying Eastern techniques with Western psychotherapy patients. Similarly, Reynolds (1980) advised "serious caution that this treatment may be dangerous for psychotic and depressive patients" (p. 70). Even deep relaxation has been noted to have a potential for adverse effects in some types of patients (Lazarus & Mayne, 1990). Virtually every resource I used in preparing Chapters 20 through 23 repeatedly warned of the dangers of approaching Eastern psychology without great care and emphasized the importance of experiencing its treasures with an experienced and trusted guide. There is substantial literature on this point in Western psychology, which I have commented on at length in two publications addressing the integration of Eastern techniques into Western psychotherapies (Bankart, 1993, Bankart, Koshikawa, Nedate, & Haruki, 1992).

In a carefully designed study, Shapiro (1992) assessed the adverse effects of meditation among a group of long-term meditators (average length of meditation 4.27 years). Sixty-three percent of his participants had experienced at least mildly aversive affects, and 2 of his subjects (out of 27 in the sample) suffered "profound aversive effects." One subject described the effects of meditation as leaving him "totally disoriented, confused, and spaced out." Another person said,

> My experience of returning from the [meditation] retreat was a difficult one. The mind set values that the retreat cultivated felt out of synch with the world I came back to and I've been slowly digesting the transformative changes that the retreat generated. Lots of depression, confusion, struggle during the last six months . . . experienced some severe shaking and energy releasing; eventually injured my back and stopped [meditation] practice. (Shapiro, 1992, p. 65)

Most of the negative effects reported by Shapiro's subjects described intrapersonal outcomes, but a few mentioned adverse interpersonal and social outcomes. Increased negativity about one's personal qualities, more emotional pain, increased fears and anxiety, disorientation, confusion, loss of self, feelings of incompleteness, and in one case "addiction to meditation" were mentioned as negative outcomes.

For almost all these people, however, the negative effects were vastly outweighed by the positive benefits of their meditative practice. At various points during the collection of data, between 81% and 92% of the participants reported enjoying the benefits of meditation, including "greater happiness and joy; more positive thinking; more self-confidence; greater ability to get things done; better problem solving; more accepting, compassionate, and tolerant of self and others; more relaxed; less stressed; more resilient; and better able to control feelings" (Shapiro, 1992, p. 64).

Several of Shapiro's (1992) respondents explained the apparent contradiction between these results with exceptional clarity:

> For me meditation is by far the most effective form of therapy. . . . [I]t is not a palliative; rather it eliminates the cause of mental suffering at its very roots. However, I have found in my own experience that I needed a certain amount of mental health and stability *before* I could undertake intensive meditation. Most psychotherapy seems to me to be a way of strengthening the ego. Meditation is a way of tearing it down. (p. 64)

> The paradox is that one seems to need a relatively strong ego in order to endure its removal. . . . Three months of intensive uninterrupted meditation seemed to me very much like a controlled breakdown, paralleling in many marked ways my own breakdown four years ago. (p. 65)

> In order to reach a deeper stability, one becomes fundamentally destabilized. To undergo this, one needs considerable preliminary strength and faith. If that strength and faith do not exist, intensive meditation can be dangerous. One of my colleagues during the three month retreat was asked to leave early because he was becoming seriously unstable and delusive. Degeneration continued at home for a month and a half. Eventually he attempted suicide because he had "failed" to become enlightened. He is now hospitalized and is seriously mentally ill. (p. 65)

The Power of Transformation

These findings are important and speak to the prodigious power of psychotherapeutic techniques derived from Zen and Yoga. They reinforce the great importance of the *interpersonal* realm in these approaches. This is a point that Haruki (1990) stressed in his writing about the *gyohos,* but it is widely applicable throughout the full range of the "quiet" therapies. The "patient" and the "therapist" in these endeavors must share an extraordinary bond of trust, perceptiveness, and even love. Considering the track record of Western therapists in this regard, especially with respect to women patients (see Chapter 18), this is not a trivial concern.

What is equally significant is that in Japanese and other Asian cultures the "therapists" are themselves accomplished masters of the practices they are teaching. Such advanced consciousness gives these *senseis* and gurus very evident perceptual and ethical advantages. The only two approximate Western parallels I can think of are the commitment of traditionally trained psychoanalysts to undergo training analysis with an experienced senior analyst and the great interpersonal warmth and deep understanding of client-centered therapists. In both these cases, the therapists' professional training and experience permit them a knowledge of or a joining with the other that a behaviorist like myself finds awesome. I've never talked with a real psychoanalyst, but as I recounted in Chapter 15, in my one face-to-face meeting with Carl Rogers I had the profound feeling that I had encountered a man who could truly understand the emotional lives of other human beings.

The Eastern techniques are potentially even more profound than those used by orthodox psychoanalysts and humanistic psychologists. Thus these newly discovered techniques can help Western therapists increase their perceptual sensitivity, empathic sensitivity and accuracy, and compassion for the pain of others (Walsh, 1989). This promise is all the more remarkable considering how much graduate training in Western psychology does to discourage, impede, and reduce these therapeutic qualities in students in training.

Western psychologists interested in Eastern techniques are a part of something akin to a movement (I hope not an ideology) that has the potential to extend our knowledge of human beings further than any Western psychology, with the possible exception of Jungian analytical therapy. Eastern psychology claims a power to transcend knowledge of the particular individual, to reach an understanding of or at least to encounter a force that is universal and all-encompassing—a psychology of the cosmic, more powerful and more potentially revolutionary than anything that has come before.

This is the psychology of transformation, of profound spiritual change as well as behavioral, social, cognitive, and emotional change. Indeed, the claims for Eastern techniques that we in the West have been reading about for the past 15 to 20 years are of a different kind and of a different order of magnitude—even of a different dimension—than the claims of the most enthusiastic, radical, and revolutionary behavior therapists of the 1960s and 1970s. In fact, even after discounting effects attributable to client population differences between East and West, and even discounting claims that may be difficult to replicate systematically within our reductionistic scientific models, practitioners of Eastern techniques seem to be offering the world the promise of human breakthroughs beyond anything known to our materialist, scientific, secular world.

A List of Cautions

Even if these claims can be only partially validated or prove to be less than universally applicable, there are potential dangers in widespread adoption of Eastern therapeutic techniques. So I want to raise several questions that will provide an opportunity for us to reflect a bit on some serious concerns. Of course, at some level I am talking about making sure that we don't mismatch our clients with our techniques. There is some literature on this issue (for example, Lazarus, 1976), but matching particular Eastern approaches to specific clients doesn't seem any more problematic than applying any powerful therapeutic technique in a client population. However, several issues specific to importing Eastern psychotherapy techniques into Western culture seem important:

- What are the safeguards that the extraordinary power of the teacher/student relationship will be honored and treasured, not abused, neglected, exploited for personal gain, or vandalized out of malice, ignorance, and greed or in the service of a corporate or national state? It is not sufficient to argue that the power of Eastern therapies is in its own nature purely benign or that it cannot be betrayed or perverted. The duties of the teacher are carefully laid out in all the great ancient Eastern texts, but what is their modern equivalent?

- Powerful techniques for influencing human behavior create economic, social, and political realities of their own. The history of psychoanalysis and the ideologically focused breakup of the American Psychological Association several years ago provide examples of this sort of development. What are the safeguards against patients being damaged by the corrosive effects of ideology from within the ranks of Eastern therapies?

- Can "science," in its usual form, coexist and advance with these techniques? One can argue, as many feminists do, that our ideas about science require fundamental revision if not complete transformation; and I would agree fully. But can the attitudes of the universal scientist, the professional skeptic, the disquieting pursuer of knowable truth coexist with, and even help advance, the integration of Eastern techniques into Western psychotherapy? This is a particularly difficult issue for a group of techniques derived out of thousands of years of spiritual teachings, but it is one that, from the Western perspective, must be addressed.

- When I call for "extreme caution" in employing Eastern techniques with Western client populations, I am also reminding myself that the selection criteria we use for training psychiatrists, clinical psychologists, social workers, and even pastoral counselors is intellectual, academic, competitive, and scholarly—without reference to spiritual qualities or even humanistic orientation. Can we ever hope to reconcile training focused on technique, metatheory, and objective assessment with practice founded on discipline, character, mystery, and faith?

- Finally, how are we to consider the question of therapeutic effectiveness? Is it possible to conduct something like a meaningful Western "psychotherapy outcome study" without either so distorting the whole idea of a reliable set of outcome variables or so reducing the Eastern practices that nothing is left of either?

Can we long avoid the question that has been shadowing the discussion of Eastern therapies in *Talking Cures*? As we reflect on how to approach a "scientific" understanding of the human condition, do the paths of Eastern and Western therapists inevitably diverge? Sorry though we may be that we cannot travel both paths, must we as scientist-practitioners and human beings ultimately make a decision between the material and the spiritual?

The negative case has been put most powerfully by Albert Ellis (1984), who reminded us of the harmful legacy of spiritualist teachings. Their doctrines of sin and vengeance have left many people with a spiritual legacy of fear and defenselessness. These are burdens borne by a great many of our clients and, I suspect, not a few of us. Is another belief system, no matter how powerful or organic, an appropriate solace for persons seeking help with the problems they are having with living?

The problem with this question is that if you answer by saying yes, as a great many Western practitioners of Eastern techniques would, you may not be practicing psychology any more. Because I have spent the last 20 years of my life in what some people call the Bible Belt of the United States, I am perhaps overly sensitized to claims of spiritually based knowledge. I fear that, as with "creationist science" or the new "pro-life science," the question is not whether such claims have essential worth but whether matters of faith and enlightenment can be meaningfully addressed in a scientific context and vice versa.

Many Japanese scholars perhaps rightly, reject employing Western scientific tools of analysis to reduce, measure, and analyze the effects of practices that represent thousands of years of collective wisdom and culture. I am mindful, of course, that these techniques have been applied for centuries for the benefit of countless thousands of people. But I am also mindful that an equivalent level of effectiveness and safety has not yet been demonstrated in a non-Eastern culture or setting.

Nor can we wish away the simple fact that in the Western world psychotherapy is big business. A National Institute for Mental Health study (Narrow, Regier, Rae, Manderscheid, & Locke, 1993) reported that 325.9 million ambulatory visits are made to outpatient mental health facilities each year. Assuming that each of these visits is billed at $75, outpatient mental health services are at the very minimum a $25-billion-a-year industry, one that influences the lives of hundreds of thousands of consumers and employs tens of thousands of practitioners drawn from virtually every community in the nation.

New Age Charlatans and Other Acts of Nature

I ran into a powerful reminder of the seriousness of my concern during a recent trip to Santa Fe, New Mexico. The city was hosting "The First Whole Life Expo," billed as "the world's largest exposition for holistic health and New Age awareness." The highlight of the expo would have been a 2-hour workshop by the late Dr. Timothy Leary (of LSD fame from the 1960s) on how to "produce self-induced trance states [with "inexpensive multi-media electronic image processors"] to reprogram minds [to] empower individuals to think for themselves and question authority."

To be honest, I have a soft place in my heart for Dr. Leary and favor anything that encourages folks to question authority. But how about Laurie Allen Grant's workshop to help you "make a quantum leap in your consciousness by becoming one with your Higher self [and] see and hear clairvoyantly . . . and live your higher purpose"? Or how about spending a few dollars to hear Terry Lynn Taylor, who lectured on "angel awareness" and "the implications of angel awareness for personal transformation"? Or a workshop by Tim Simmerman on "recovering your past-life through hypnosis" (Simmerman proclaims himself a "past-life therapist")? Several programs offered spiritual therapy based on "intergalactic communication," and at least one New Age therapist offered a workshop on therapy based on being able to "communicate with the animal, plant, and mineral kingdoms." The ultimate New Age moment at the expo must have been the several presentations by Ariel and Shya Kane, who offered lectures, demonstrations, and workshops on what they call "instantaneous transformation"—the therapy that promises "discovering fulfillment in their lives without working on themselves." You just know that this system was even better than the one offered by Dannion Howell, who "discovered the secrets to personal development after being struck by lightning in 1975." Incidentally, much like their intellectual predecessors, the French magnetists of old (see Chapter 3), many of these New Age spiritual healers also advertise themselves as "available for parties." Talk about convenience!

Is New Age therapy just harmless foolishness, God's way of redistributing income in favor of the outrageously creative? Perhaps. But I keep thinking about the 22.8 million people who seek professional help for mental, emotional, and addictive disorders every year and the 1.4 million people who were admitted to psychiatric inpatient services last year (Narrow et al., 1993). Then I wonder how innocent and wondrous New Age therapy is. Although the subtitle of this chapter—"If You Meet the Buddha on the Road, Kill Him"—is most assuredly a metaphor, the wisdom it champions has perhaps never been more important or current.

A Meditation on East and West

In my practice here in the United States, I most often work with clients from the rural heartland. Most have never heard of meditation and are suspicious of its nonChristian roots when I explain it to them. The ideas and ideals at the center of

Chapters 20 through 23 are alien to these people. They accept them, to the degree that they do, only because they have learned to trust me as a therapist and because as a person I am essentially similar to them.

Many of these clients are women, and most of them are single heads of households with one or more young children. Many of my clients are minorities—racial, ethnic, sexual, and religious. Most of them are mixed up with chemical substances, and many have been on the wrong side of the law at least once or twice. (In one study from my part of the country, 100% of all convicted repeat offenders in the criminal justice system have been identified as chemical abusers.) Their most frequent diagnosis is depression, but this term covers a wide range of problems, including ingestive disorders, psychosomatic disorders, and chronic illness. I have come to think of many of my clients as involuntary nonconformists.

"A Radical Environmentalist Psychology of Help"

With this point of reference, I want to argue that psychotherapeutic interventions must be essentially nonideological and must help the persons in our milieu who have the least power and the greatest needs. It is not enough to offer these clients a philosophy of transcendence. Courage and authenticity may be essential to a life worth living, but they are luxuries to a jobless, single parent in a postindustrial economy.

I largely agree with English psychologist David Smail (1991), who has called for a "radical environmentalist psychology of help," and with Charles Taylor (1989), who noted that

> the "triumph of the therapeutic" can also mean an abdication of autonomy, where the lapse of traditional standards, coupled with belief in technique, makes people cease to trust their own instincts about happiness fulfillment, and how to bring up their children. The "helping professions" take over their lives. (p. 508)

Perhaps we need to return to North American psychology's original concerns for practices and prescriptions that will strengthen the will, sharpen the intellect, and heighten the sensibilities, all of which were championed in Upham's *Mental Philosophy* (1851), which all the boys in my college were required to read for many years (see Chapter 11).

Upham, Taylor, and Smail all seem to call for a psychology that

> will bear implications for a whole range of measures which might improve the lot of people at the mercy of a harsh world.
>
> Such a psychology would seek to locate and explicate psychological phenomena within and by reference to the structures of the real, material world; it would not deny meaning to, say, "mentalistic" concepts . . . but would rather theorize about them in terms of a "harder" materiality in which individuals are seen, most essentially, as organisms . . . embodied in a (social) space-time maintained and organized by forms of power. (Smail, 1991, pp. 62–63)

Such a psychology would be empowering, because it would reveal the forces of "culture, ideology, and [social] class" (Smail, 1991, p. 63) that shape and maintain our perceptual realities. It would exercise its beneficial effects by raising awareness of the ultimate power of human choice in the everyday world. It speaks metaphorically of the possibility of a "liberation" of the self (Taylor, 1989, p. 520) by recovery of the power of the human spirit.

This psychology requires a new way of looking at and understanding human experience. As a physicist recommended,

> We need a new way of looking at culture, society and politics, and modern science, with its relativity, quantum, chaos, and complexity theories. [This new approach] requires some mental delicacy to operate with a more complex . . . concept of [human] identity, but quantum theory shows that it can be done consistently. (Zohar, 1994, pp. 14–15).

If psychology can more convincingly describe human behavior by taking into account both its Newtonian (anti-vitalist) determinants and its spontaneous autopoietic creativity, psychology will lay a truer claim to being the legacy of William James's "party of hope."

I find it relatively easy to accept the notion that Eastern approaches and techniques, with their emphasis on character and increased awareness, may be at the heart of this transformation. How much further can our Western psychotherapies take us if they don't recognize and incorporate the profoundly personal ethical and characterological changes prescribed by their Eastern counterparts? Those Eastern approaches posit that "lying, stealing, sexual misconduct, killing, and taking mind clouding intoxicants is motivated by states of mind such as greed, anger, and aversion [which in turn] leave the mind more agitated, anxious, and trapped" (Walsh, 1989, p. 550).

The Interference of Doubt

Does anyone seriously challenge the assertion that a fundamental change in consciousness is required to replace common, everyday unhappiness with "qualities such as the emotions of love and compassion, states of peace and joy, reduction of greed and anger, motives of generosity and service" (Walsh, 1989, p. 550)? Probably not, but the problem is, as George DeVos (1986) observed, a profound disconnect between Eastern and Western conceptions of human nature. Western approaches seem to require that "a person can create personal meaning for himself independent of social considerations . . . divested from its own emotional heritage [capable of] dispassionate objectivity; to uncover basic drives in order to control them" (DeVos, 1986, p. 123). Eastern approaches require not only self-discipline and to some degree self-denial but also a reconciliation of the individual with authority and the status quo. I would have a hard time persuading the majority of my colleagues, let alone my clients, that their ultimate liberation lies in uncovering the sources of "the disruptive interference of doubt and self-consciousness which *interferes with the spontaneous execution of what is expected*" (DeVos, 1980, p. 124, italics added).

Nowhere is this skepticism of the applicability of Eastern philosophy to Western life more apparent than in the contemporary writing of the so-called Japan bashers, popular writers who have focused attention on the dissimilarities between East and West historically, culturally, and philosophically. In one of the most widely read of these books, van Wolferen (1989) declared Zen to be the foundation for "a grand ethic of submission." He said that "Zen Buddhism . . . is totally amoral and idealizes an anti-intellectual approach to life" that is "profoundly contrary to the idea of an individual self" (p. 328). Van Wolferen went on to say that Zen training is "designed to break down any resistance to commands" (p. 332), allowing the individual to develop the ability "to remain mentally calm while unconditionally submitting to authority . . . the result of lifelong training of people to be submissive and compliant to the aims and demands of powerful men, even when these demands reach absurd proportions" (pp. 332–333). Lest anyone think that van Wolferen's target is "the system" and not the actual practices we have examined in the last few chapters, he wrote:

> If against all odds Japanese individuals nevertheless question their sociopolitical environment, they are constantly prodded to stop doing it. Japanese clinical treatments for sociogenic psychological disorders . . . suppress the human hankering to establish one's identity as an individual. Patients are led to alter their attitudes towards the outside world rather than come to terms with themselves. "Healing" begins when they empty their minds of personal ways of reasoning and personal emotions. (p. 357)

I would enjoy dismissing this criticism as a gross misinterpretation of non-Western psychotherapy, but I am not sure the task is so easy. Each psychology (East and West) appears to the observer on the other side—and especially the neurotic observer, whom we may think of as especially vigilant to any threat to the fragile structure of self from which he or she is operating—as offering precisely that which is most frightening and most evidently destructive of the self. The Westerner fears the loss of individuation inherent in Eastern approaches, just as the Easterner fears the threat of perceived loss of connection to family and group embedded in Western talking cures.

The Promise of Renewal

Surely, however, we can all strive for the eloquence, humanity, self-control, character, and creativity so highly valued in Eastern approaches. The reintegration of body and mind of which they speak holds the same promise of renewal, wholeness, and spontaneity for all persons, regardless of culture or circumstance.

What we are offered in a study of non-Western psychology is an invitation to deep structural changes in our lives. This is neither an empty promise nor one held out only to an elite or wealthy few. Our task as therapists and as human beings must be to work toward a resolution of the difficulties of understanding and application that separate East from West. Our goal should be to overcome the repression that limits our full awareness of the possibilities of life, regardless of the methods we use.

Bibliography

Adler, A. (1904). Hygiene of sexual life. *Aerztliche Standezeitung, 3* (18), 1–2.

Adler, A. (1912). *The neurotic constitution.* New York: Greenberg [English edition, 1927].

Adler, A. (1919). *The other side.* Vienna: Leopold Heidrich.

Adler, A. (1927). *Understanding human nature.* Garden City, NY: Garden City Publishing.

Adler, A. (1929). Position in family influences lifestyle. *International Journal of Individual Psychology, 3,* 211–222.

Adler, A. (1931). *What life should mean to you.* Boston: Little, Brown.

Adler, A. (1932). The structure of neuroses. In H. L. Ansbacher & R. R. Ansbacher (Eds.), *Superiority and social interest: A collection of later writings.* New York: Viking Compass.

Adler, A. (1933). The meaning of life. In H. L. Ansbacher and R. R. Ansbacher (Eds.), *The individual psychology of Alfred Adler.* New York: Harper, 1956.

Adler, A. (1968). *The practice and theory of individual psychology.* Totowa, NJ: Littlefield, Adams, & Co.

Adler, A. (1969). *The science of living.* New York: Doubleday.

Akamatsu, T. J. (1988). Intimate relationships with former clients: National survey of attitudes and behavior among practitioners. *Professional Psychology: Research and Practice, 19,* 454–458.

Alexander, F. G., & Selesnick, S. T. (1966). *The history of psychiatry: An evaluation of psychiatric thought and practice from prehistoric times to the present.* New York: Harper & Row.

Allport, G. W. (1955). *Becoming: Basic considerations for a psychology of personality.* New Haven, CT: Yale University Press.

Allport, G. W. (1961). *Pattern and growth in personality.* New York: Holt, Rinehart, and Winston.

Allport, G. W. (1967). Autobiography. In E. G. Boring & G. Lindzey (Eds.), *A history of psychology in autobiography* (Vol. 5, pp. 1–25). New York: Appleton.

American Psychological Association. (1975). Report of the task force on sex bias and sex-role stereotyping in psychotherapeutic practice. *American Psychologist, 30,* 1169–1175.

American Psychological Association. (1977, March). Ethical standards of psychologists. *APA Monitor,* 22–23.

Angelou, M. (1993). *On the pulse of morning.* New York: Random House.

Ariès, P. (1985). Thoughts on the history of homosexuality. In P. Ariès & A. Bejin (Eds.), *Western sexuality: Practice and precept in past and present times* (pp. 62–75). Blackwood, NJ: B. Blackwell.

Arnkoff, D. B., & Glass, C. R. (1992). Cognitive therapy and psychotherapy integration. In D. K. Freedheim (Ed.), *History of psychotherapy: A century of change* (pp. 657–694). Washington, DC: American Psychological Association.

Ayllon, T. (1989). *Stopping baby's colic.* New York: Perigee Books.

Bakan, D. (1966). *The duality of human existence: Isolation and communion in Western man.* Boston: Beacon Press.

Bakan, D. (1990). *Sigmund Freud and the Jewish mystical tradition.* London: Free Association. (Originally published in New York: Shocken Books, 1958. With new introduction.)

Bandura, A. (1969). *Principles of behavior modification.* New York: Holt, Rinehart, and Winston.

Bandura, A. (1977). Self efficacy: Toward a unifying theory of behavioural change. *Psychological Review, 84,* 191–215.

Bankart, B. (1978, February). Searching for woman's place in the History of Psychology course. Lecture presented during Women's Week at Wabash College, Crawfordsville, IN.

Bankart, B. M., Bankart, C. P., & Franklin, J. P. (1988). Adolescent values as predictors of self-reported achievement in young men. *Journal of Social Psychology, 128,* 249–257.

Bankart, C. P. (1993). Some Western questions for an Eastern psychology. *Japanese Health Psychology, 1* (1), 103–112.

Bankart, C. P., Koshikawa, F., Nedate, K., & Haruki, Y. (1992). When West meets East: Contributions of Eastern traditions to the future of psychotherapy. *Psychotherapy, 29,* 141–149.

Bankart, C. P., & Vincent, M. A. (1988). Beyond individualism and isolation: A study of communion in adolescent males. *Journal of Social Psychology, 128,* 675–683.

Bean, O. (1971). *Me and the orgone.* New York: St. Martin's Press.

Beck, A. T., Rush, A., Shaw, B., & Emery, G. (1979). *Cognitive therapy of depression.* New York: Guilford.

Beck, A. T., & Weishaar, M. E. (1989). Cognitive therapy. In R. J. Corsini & D. Wedding (Eds.), *Current psychotherapies* (4th ed., pp. 241–284). Itasca, IL: F. E. Peacock.

Bellah, R. N., Sullivan, W. M., Swindler, A., & Tipton, S. M. (1985). *Habits of the heart: Individualism and commitment in American life.* Berkeley: University of California Press.

Benjamin, L. T. (1986). Why don't they understand us? A history of psychology's public image. *American Psychologist, 43,* 703–712.

Benjamin, L. T. (1993). *A history of psychology in letters.* Dubuque, IA: W. C. B. Brown & Benchmark.

Bester, J. (1971). Foreword. In T. Doi, *The anatomy of dependence* (pp. 7–10). New York: Kodansha International.

Bisignani, J. D. (1983). *Japan handbook.* Chico, CA: Moon Publications.

Bleich, H. L., Moore, M. J., Benson, H., & McCallie, D. P. (1979). Angina pectoris and the placebo effect. *New England Journal of Medicine, 300,* 1424–1429.

Blofeld, J. (1985). *The Chinese art of tea.* Boston: Shamhala.

Bloom, C., Eichenbaum, L., & Orbach, S. (1982). A decade of women's oriented therapy. *Issues in Radical Therapy, 10,* 7–11.

Bolles, R. C. (1993). *The story of psychology: A thematic history.* Pacific Grove, CA: Brooks/Cole.

Bottome, P. (1939). *Alfred Adler, apostle of freedom.* London: Faber and Faber.

Bottome, P. (1957). *Alfred Adler: A portrait from life.* New York: Vanguard.

Bottome, P. (1962). *The goal.* New York: Vanguard Press.

Braginsky, D. D. (1985). Psychology: Handmaiden to society. In S. Koch & D. E. Leary (Eds.), *A century of psychology as a science* (pp. 880–891). New York: McGraw-Hill.

Breuer, J., & Freud, S. (1955a). On the psychical mechanisms of hysterical phenomena: A preliminary communication. In J. Strachey (Ed. and Trans.), *The standard edition of the complete psychological works of Sigmund Freud* (Vol. 2). London: Hogarth Press. (Original work published 1893)

Breuer, J., & Freud, S. (1955b). Studies in hysteria. In J. E. Strachey (Ed. and Trans.), *The standard edition of the complete psychological works of Sigmund Freud* (Vol. 2). London: Hogarth Press. (Original work published 1893)

Brodsky, A. M. (1980). A decade of feminist influence on psychotherapy. *Psychology of Women Quarterly, 4,* 331–344.

Brooks-Gunn, J., & Ruble, D. N. (1986). Men's and women's attitudes and beliefs about the menstrual cycle. *Sex Roles, 14,* 287–299.

Broverman, I. K., Broverman, D. M., Clarkson, F. E., Rosenkrantz, P. S., & Vogel, S. R. (1970). Sex role stereotypes and clinical judgments of mental health. *Journal of Consulting and Clinical Psychology, 45,* 250–256.

Brown, L. M., & Gilligan, C. (1992). *Meeting at the crossroads: Women's psychology and girl's development.* Cambridge, MA: Harvard University Press.

Bruner, J. (1990). *Acts of meaning.* Cambridge, MA: Harvard University Press.

Calkins, M. W. (1912). *A first book in psychology* (3rd ed.). New York: Macmillan.

Calkins, M. W. (1930). Mary Whinton Calkins. In C. Murchison (Ed.), *A history of psychology in autobiography* (Vol. 1, pp. 31–62). Worcester, MA: Clark University Press.

Callender, C., & Kochems, L. M. (1987). The North American berdache. *Current Anthropology, 24,* 443–456, 467–470.

Chesler, P. (1972). *Women and madness.* New York: Avon Books.

Chodorow, N. J. (1989). *Feminism and psychoanalytic theory.* New Haven, CT: Yale University Press.

Christensen, A., & Jacobson, N. S. (1995). Who (or what) can do psychotherapy: The status and challenge of nonprofessional therapies. *Psychological Science, 5,* 8–14.

Cleary, T. (Trans. and Presenter). (1991). *The essential Tao.* New York: Harper Collins.

Cleary, T. (Trans. and Presenter). (1992). *The essential Confucius.* New York: Harper Collins.

Cliadakis, W. C. (1989). Sexual abuse of clients in psychotherapy: A non-professional perspective. In G. R. Schoener, J. H. Milgrom, J. C. Gonsiorek, E. T. Luepker, & R. M. Conroe (Eds.), *Psychotherapists' sexual involvement with clients: Intervention and prevention* (pp. 367–374). Minneapolis: Walk-In Counseling Center.

Coan, R. W. (1977). *Hero, artist, sage, or saint?* New York: Columbia University Press.

Corsini, R. J. (1989). Introduction. In R. J. Corsini & D. Wedding (Eds.), *Current psychotherapies* (4th ed., pp. 1–16). Itasca, IL: F. E. Peacock.

Cushman, P. (1992). Psychotherapy: Economic and environmental influences. In D. K. Freedheim (Ed.), *History of psychotherapy: A century of change* (pp. 21–64). Washington, DC: American Psychological Association.

Dai, B. (1981). Zen and psychotherapy. *Asia 2000, 1* (1), 22–24.

Daly, M. (1978). *GYN/ECOLOGY.* Boston: Beacon Press.

Davison, G. C. (1976). Homosexuality: The ethical challenge. *Journal of Consulting and Clinical Psychology, 44,* 157–162.

Davison, G. C. (1978). Not can but ought: The treatment of homosexuality. *Journal of Consulting and Clinical Psychology, 46,* 170–172.

Davison, G. C., & Friedman, S. (1981). Sexual orientation stereotypy in the distortion of clinical judgment. *Journal of Homosexuality, 6* (3), 37–44.

Davison, G. C., & Neale, J. M. (1982). *Abnormal psychology: An experimental clinical approach* (3rd ed.). New York: John Wiley & Sons.

Dawes, R. M. (1994). *House of cards: Psychology and psychotherapy built on myth.* New York: Free Press.

De Bary, W. T., Chan, W. T., & Watson, B. (1960). *Sources of the Chinese tradition* (Vol. 1). New York: Columbia University Press.

Decker, H. S. (1991). *Freud, Dora, and Vienna 1900.* New York: Free Press.

Deikman, A. J. (1966). Deautomatization and the mystic experience. *Psychiatry, 29,* 324–338.

De Martino, R. (1960). The human situation and Zen Buddhism. In D. T. Suzuki, E. Fromm, & R. De Martino (Eds.), *Zen Buddhism and psychoanalysis* (pp. 142–171). New York: Harper & Row.

Desmond, A., & Moore, J. (1991). *Darwin: The life of a tormented evolutionist.* New York: Warner Books.

Deutsch, A. (1949). *The mentally ill in America.* New York: Columbia University Press.

DeVos, G. (1980). Afterword. In D. K. Reynolds, *The quiet therapies: Japanese pathways to personal growth* (pp. 113–132). Honolulu: University of Hawaii Press.

Doi, T. (1971). *The anatomy of dependence.* New York: Kodansha International.

Dollard, J., & Miller, N. (1950). *Personality and psychotherapy: An analysis in terms of learning, thinking, and culture.* New York: McGraw-Hill.

Donovan, J. (1985). *Feminist theory: The intellectual traditions of American feminism.* New York: Frederick Ungar.

Dostoyevsky, F. (1912). *The brothers Karamazov.* New York: Macmillan.

Dumoulin, H. (1969). *A history of Zen Buddhism.* Boston: Beacon Press.

Dyer, R. (1983). *The work of Anna Freud.* New York: Aronson.

Eagle, M. N., & Wolitzky, D. L. (1992). Psychoanalytic therapies of psychotherapy. In D. K. Freedheim (Ed.), *History of psychotherapy: A century of change* (pp. 109–158). Washington, DC: American Psychological Association.

Ellenberger, H. F. (1965). Charcot and the Salpêtrière school. *Journal of Psychotherapy, 19,* 253–267.

Ellenberger, H. F. (1970). *The discovery of the unconscious: The history and evolution of dynamic psychiatry.* New York: Basic Books.

Ellenberger, H. F. (1972). The story of "Anna O.": A critical review with new data. *Journal of the History of the Behavioral Sciences, 8,* 267–279.

Ellis, A. (1975). The rational-emotive approach to sex-therapy. *Counseling Psychologist, 5,* 14–22.

Ellis, A. (1984). The place of meditation in cognitive and rational emotive therapy. In D. H. Shapiro & R. N. Walsh (Eds.), *Meditation: Classic and contemporary perspectives* (pp. 671–673). New York: Aldine.

Ellis, A. (1989). Rational-emotive therapy. In R. J. Corsini & D. Wedding (Eds.), *Current psychotherapies* (4th ed., pp. 197–238). Itasca, IL: F. E. Peacock.

Ellis, A. (1993). Changing rational emotive therapy (RET) to rational emotive behavior therapy (REBT). *The Behavior Therapist, 16,* 257–258.

Enns, C. Z. (1993). Twenty years of feminist counseling and therapy: From naming biases to implementing multifaceted practice. *The Counseling Psychologist, 21* (1), 3–87.

Erikson, E. H. (1950). *Childhood and society.* New York: W. W. Norton.

Erikson, E. H. (1959). *Identity and the life-cycle: Selected papers* (Psychological Issues Monograph No. 1, Vol. 1). New York: International Universities Press.

Erikson, E. H. (1963). Youth: Fidelity and diversity. In E. Erikson (Ed.), *The challenge of youth* (pp. 1–28). New York: Doubleday.

Erikson, E. H. (1964). *Insight and responsibility.* New York: W. W. Norton.

Erikson, E. H. (1968). *Identity youth and crisis.* New York: W. W. Norton.

Erikson, E. H. (1974). *Dimensions of a new identity: The Jefferson lectures, 1973.* New York: W. W. Norton.

Evans, R. I. (1969). *Dialogue with Erik Erikson.* New York: Harper & Row.

Ewen, R. B. (1988). *An introduction to theories of personality* (3rd ed.). Hillsdale, NJ: Lawrence Erlbaum Associates.

Eysenck, H. J. (1952). The effects of psychotherapy: An evaluation. *Journal of Consulting and Clinical Psychology, 16,* 319–324.

Eysenck, H. J. (1961). *The handbook of abnormal psychology: An experimental approach.* New York: Basic Books.

Eysenck, H. J. (Ed.). (1964). *Experiments in behavior therapy; readings in modern methods of treatment of mental disorders derived from learning theory.* New York: Pergamon Press.

Eysenck, H. J. (1966). *The effects of psychotherapy.* New York: International Science Press.

Fancher, R. E. (1990). *Pioneers of psychology* (2nd ed.). New York: W. W. Norton.

Faulconer, J. E., & Williams, R. N. (1990). Reconsidering psychology. In J. E. Faulconer & R. N. Williams (Eds.), *Reconsidering psychology: Perspectives from continental philosophy* (pp. 9–60). Pittsburgh: Duquesne University Press.

Firestone, S. (1970). *The dialectic of sex: The case for feminist revolution.* New York: Bantam.

Fischer, C. T. (1993, March). Review of the book *Feminist perspectives in therapy: An empowerment model for women. Choice, 30,* (7), 1249.

Fishman, D. B., & Franks, C. M. (1992). Evolution and differentiation within behavior therapy: A theoretical and epistemological view. In D. K. Freedheim (Ed.), *History of psychotherapy: A century of change* (pp. 159–196). Washington, DC: American Psychological Association.

Frager, R., & Fadiman, J. (1984). *Personality and personal growth* (2nd ed.). New York: Harper & Row.

Francoeur, R. T. (1991). *Becoming a sexual person* (2nd ed.). New York: Macmillan.

Frankl, V. (1959). The spiritual dimension in existential analysis and logotherapy. *Journal of Individual Psychology, 15,* 157–165.

Frankl, V. (1962). *Man's search for meaning.* New York: Simon & Schuster.

Freedheim, D. K. (1992). Index. In D. K. Freedheim (Ed.), *History of psychotherapy: A century of change.* Washington, DC: American Psychological Association.

Freud, A. (1968). The contributions of psychoanalysis to genetic psychology. In *The writings of Anna Freud: Vol. 4* (pp. 107–142). New York: International Universities Press.

Freud, A. (1971). Difficulties in the path of psychoanalysis: A confrontation with present viewpoints. In *The writings of Anna Freud: Vol. 7* (pp. 124–146). New York: International Universities Press.

Freud, S. (1953). The interpretation of dreams. In J. Strachey (Ed. and Trans.), *The standard edition of the complete psychological works of Sigmund Freud* (Vols. 4 and 5). London: Hogarth Press. (Original work published 1900)

Freud, S. (1957a). On the history of the psychoanalytic movement. In J. Strachey (Ed. and Trans.), *The standard edition of the complete psychological works of Sigmund Freud* (Vol. 14, pp. 1–66). London: Hogarth Press. (Original work published 1914)

Freud, S. (1957b). Repression. In J. Strachey (Ed. and Trans.), *The standard edition of the complete psychological works of Sigmund Freud* (Vol. 14, pp. 141–158). London: Hogarth Press. (Original work published 1915)

Freud, S. (1958a). Observations on transference-love: Further recommendations on technique III—Transference-love. In J. Strachey (Ed. and Trans.), *The standard edition of the complete psychological works of Sigmund Freud* (Vol. 12, pp. 157–171). London: Hogarth Press. (Original work published 1912 and 1915)

Freud, S. (1958b). The disposition to obsessional neurosis: A contribution to the problem of choice of neurosis. In J. Strachey (Ed. and Trans.), *The standard edition of the complete psychological works of Sigmund Freud* (Vol. 12, pp. 311–326). London: Hogarth Press. (Original work published 1913)

Freud, S. (1958c). The dynamics of transference. In J. Strachey (Ed. and Trans.), *The standard edition of the complete psychological works of Sigmund Freud* (Vol. 12, pp. 97–108). London: Hogarth Press. (Original work published 1914)

Freud, S. (1958d). Remembering, repeating, and working through. In J. Strachey (Ed. and Trans.), *The standard edition of the complete psychological works of Sigmund Freud* (Vol. 12, pp. 145–156). London: Hogarth Press. (Original work published 1914)

Freud, S. (1959a). The question of lay analysis: Conversations with an impartial person. In J. Strachey (Ed. and Trans.), *The standard edition of the complete psychological works of Sigmund Freud* (Vol. 20, pp. 177–258). London: Hogarth Press. (Original work published 1926)

Freud, S. (1959b). Postscript to an autobiographical study. In J. Strachey (Ed. and Trans.), *The standard edition of the complete psychological works of Sigmund Freud* (Vol. 20, pp. 1–74). London: Hogarth Press. (Original work published 1935)

Freud S. (1960). In E. L. Freud (Ed.), *The letters of Sigmund Freud.* New York: McGraw-Hill.

Freud, S. (1961a). *Civilization and its discontents.* New York: W. W. Norton. (Original work published 1930)

Freud, S. (1961b). The future of an illusion. In J. Strachey (Ed. and Trans.), *The standard edition of the complete psychological works of Sigmund Freud* (Vol. 21, pp. 3–56).

Freud, S. (1962). Charcot. In *Complete psychological works of Sigmund Freud* (Vol. 3). London: Hogarth Press. (Original work published 1893)

Freud, S. (1964a). An autobiographical study. In J. Strachey (Ed. and Trans.), *The standard edition of the complete psychological works of Sigmund Freud* (Vol. 20, pp. 1–74). London: Hogarth Press. (Original work published 1925)

Freud, S. (1964b). New introductory lectures on psychoanalysis. In J. Strachey (Ed. and Trans.), *The standard edition of the complete psychological works of Sigmund Freud* (Vol. 22, pp. 1–182). London: Hogarth Press. (Original work published 1933)

Freud, S. (1985). *The complete letters of Sigmund Freud to Wilhelm Fliess, 1887–1904* (J. M. Masson, Ed. and Trans.). Cambridge, MA: Harvard University Press.

Freud, S., & Jung, C. G. (1974). *The Freud/Jung letters: The correspondence between Sigmund Freud and C. G. Jung* (W. McGuire, Ed.). Princeton, NJ: Princeton University Press.

Friedan, B. (1963). *The feminine mystique.* New York: Dell.

Fromm, E. (1941). *Escape from freedom.* New York: Avon Books.

Fromm, E. (1944). Individual and social origins of neurosis. *American Sociological Review, 9,* 380–384.

Fromm, E. (1955). *The sane society.* New York: Holt, Rinehart, and Winston.

Fromm, E. (1956). *The art of loving.* New York: Harper & Row.

Fromm, E. (1960). Psychoanalysis and Zen Buddhism. In D. T. Suzuki, E. Fromm, & R. De Martino, *Zen Buddhism and psychoanalysis* (pp. 77–141). New York: Harper & Row.

Fromm, E. (1962). *Sigmund Freud's mission: An analysis of his personality and mission.* New York: Simon & Schuster.

Fromm, E. (1973). *The anatomy of human destructiveness.* New York: Holt, Rinehart, and Winston.

Frost, R. (1967). *Complete poems of Robert Frost.* New York: Holt, Rinehart, and Winston.

Furumoto, L. (1991). From "paired-associates" to psychology of self: The intellectual odyssey of Mary White Calkins. In G. A. Kimble, M. Wertheimer, & C. L. White (Eds.), *Portraits of pioneers in psychology* (pp. 57–72). Hillsdale, NJ, and Washington, DC: Lawrence Erlbaum Associates and American Psychological Association.

Gamwell, L., & Tomes, N. (1995). *Madness in America: Cultural and medical perceptions of mental illness before 1914.* Ithaca, NY: Cornell University Press.

Gay, P. E. (1988). *Freud: A life for our time.* New York: W. W. Norton.

Gay, P. E. (1989). *The Freud reader.* New York: W. W. Norton.

Gilbert, L. A. (1980). Feminist therapy. In A. M. Brodsky & R. T. Hare-Mustin (Eds.), *Women and psychotherapy: An assessment of research and practice* (pp. 245–266). New York: Guilford Press.

Gilligan, C. (1982). *In a different voice: Psychological theory and women's development.* Cambridge, MA: Harvard University Press.

Glass, C. R., & Arnkoff, D. B. (1992). Behavior therapy. In D. K. Freedheim (Ed.), *History of psychotherapy: A century of change* (pp. 587–628). Washington, DC: American Psychological Association.

Glen, A. (1978). The psychoanalysis of prelatency children. In J. Glen (Ed.), *Child analysis and therapy* (pp. 164–203). New York: Jason Aronson.

Goldstein, J. (1987). *Console and classify: The French psychiatric profession in the nineteenth century.* Cambridge, England: Cambridge University Press.

Goleman, D. (1993, March 17). Each year, more than 1 in 4 U.S. adults suffers a mental disorder. *The New York Times,* p. B7.

Gould, S. J. (1989). Punctuated equilibrium in fact and theory. *Journal of Social and Biological Structures, 12,* 117–136.

Greenspan, M. (1986). Should therapists be personal? Self-disclosure and therapeutic distance in feminist therapy. In D. Howard (Ed.), *The dynamics of feminist therapy* (pp. 5–17). New York: Haworth Press.

Grunbaum, A. (1983). Freud's theory: The perspective of a philosopher of science. *American Philosophical Association Proceedings, 57,* 5–31.

Gurman, A. S., & Razin, A. M. (Eds.). (1977). *Effective psychotherapy: A handbook of research.* New York: Pergamon Press.

Haley, A. (1965). *The autobiography of Malcolm X.* New York: Ballantine Books.

Halleck, S. L. (1971). *The politics of therapy.* New York: Science House.

Halligan, F. R., & Shea, J. J. (Eds.). (1992). *The fires of desire: Erotic energies and the spiritual quest.* New York: Crossroad Press.

Hare-Mustin, R. T. (1983). An appraisal of the relationship between women and psychotherapy: 80 years after the case of Dora. *American Psychologist, 38,* 593–601.

Haruki, Y. (1990). Tōyō teki gyōhō no bunrui to tōkuchō [Classification of Eastern self-practicing techniques (*gyohos*) and their characteristics.] *Waseda Psychological Reports, 22,* 7–14.

Hayes, S. C., & Wilson, K. G. (1993). Some applied implications of a contemporary behavior-analytic account of verbal events. *The Behavior Analyst, 16,* 283–301.

Heidegger, M. (1977). On the essence of truth. In D. F. Krell (Ed.), *Martin Heidegger: Basic writings* (p. 130). New York: Harper & Row.

Hilgard, E. R. (1987). *Psychology in America: A historical survey.* New York: Harcourt Brace Jovanovich.

Hite, S. (1981). *The Hite report on male sexuality.* New York: Harcourt, Brace & World.

Holroyd, J. C., & Brodsky, A. M. (1977). Psychologists' attitudes and practices regarding erotic and nonerotic physical contact with patients. *American Psychologist, 32,* 843–849.

Horney, K. (1939). *New ways in psychoanalysis.* New York: W. W. Norton.

Horney, K. (1945). *Our inner conflicts: A constructive theory of neurosis.* New York: W. W. Norton.

Horney, K. (1946). *Are you considering psychoanalysis?* New York: W. W. Norton.

Horney, K. (1950). *Neurosis and human growth.* New York: W. W. Norton.

Horney, K. (1951). *Neurosis and human growth: The struggle toward self-realization.* London: Routledge & Kegan Paul.

Horney, K. (1967). *Feminine psychology.* New York: W. W. Norton.

Houts, P. S., & Serber, M. (Eds.). (1972). After the yturn on, What? Learning perspectives on humanistic groups. Champaign, IL: Research Press.

Howard, D. H. (1986). *The dynamics of feminist therapy.* New York: Haworth Press.

Hufford, D. J. (1982). *The terror that comes in the night.* Philadelphia: University of Pennsylvania Press.

Hurston, Z. N. (1935). *Mules and men.* Philadelphia: J. B. Lippincott.

Huxley, A. (1954). *The doors of perception.* New York: Harper & Row.

Hyde, J. S. (1991). *Half the human experience: The psychology of women* (4th ed.). Lexington, MA: D. C. Heath.

Iguchi, K. (1981). *Tea ceremony.* Osaka, Japan: Hoikusha's Color Books.

Ikenobo, S. (1981). *Ikebana* (Rev. ed.). Osaka, Japan: Hoikusha's Color Books.

James, W. (1890). *The principles of psychology* (2 vols). New York: Holt, Rinehart, and Winston.

James, W. (1929). *The varieties of religious experience.* New York: Modern Library.

James, W. (1992a). *William James, writings 1878–1899.* New York: Library of America.

James, W. (1992b). *William James, writings 1902–1910.* New York: Library of America.

Johnson, F. A. (1993). *Dependency and Japanese socialization: Psychoanalytic and anthropological investigations into* amae. New York: New York University Press.

Jones, E. (1953). *The life and work of Sigmund Freud: The formative years and the great discoveries* (Vol. 1). New York: Basic Books.

Jones, E. (1955). *The life and work of Sigmund Freud: Years of maturity* (Vol. 2). New York: Basic Books.

Jones, M. C. (1924). The elimination of children's fears. *Journal of Experimental Psychology, 8,* 382–390.

Jung, C. G. (1938). *Psychology and religion.* New Haven, CT: Yale University Press.

Jung, C. G. (1945). On the nature of dreams. In H. Read, M. Fordham, & G. Adler (Eds.), *Collected works, Bollingen series XX* (Vol. 8, pp. 281–297). Princeton, NJ: Princeton University Press.

Jung, C. G. (1953a). Individuation. In H. Read, M. Fordham, & G. Adler (Eds.), *Collected works, Bollinger Series XX* (Vol. 7). Princeton, NJ: Princeton University Press. (Original work published 1917)

Jung, C. G. (1953b). New paths in psychology. In H. Read, M. Fordham, & G. Adler (Eds.), *Collected works, Bollingen Series XX* (Vol. 7). Princeton, NJ: Princeton University Press. (Original work published 1912)

Jung, C. G. (1954a). Marriage as a psychological relationship. In H. Read, M. Fordham, & G. Adler (Eds.), *Collected works, Bollingen series XX* (Vol. 17, pp. 187–201). New York: Pantheon Books. (Original work published 1931)

Jung, C. G. (1954b). Analytical psychology and education. In H. Read, M. Fordham, & G. Adler (Eds.), *Collected works, Bollingen series XX* (Vol. 17, pp. 63–132). New York: Pantheon Books. (Original work published 1938)

Jung, C. G. (1965). *Memories, dreams, reflections.* New York: Vintage Books.

Jung, C. G. (1968). *Analytical psychology: Its theory and practice.* Tavistock lectures. New York: Pantheon Books. (Original work published 1935)

Jung, C. G. (1973). *Letters* (G. Adler, Ed.). Princeton, NJ: Princeton University Press.

Jung, C. G. (1983). *The essential Jung* (A. Storr, Ed.). Princeton, NJ: Princeton University Press.

Kakar, S. (1991). *The analyst and the mystic: Psychoanalytic reflections on religion and mysticism.* Chicago: University of Chicago Press.

Kapleau, P. (1965). Zen meditation. In P. Kapleau (Ed.), *The three pillars of Zen* (pp. 10–15). New York: John Weatherhill.

Kaschak, E. (1992). *Engendered lives: A new psychology of women's experience.* New York: Basic Books.

Kaufmann, Y. (1989). Analytical psychotherapy. In R. J. Corsini & D. Wedding (Eds.), *Current Psychotherapies* (4th ed., pp. 119–152). Itasca, IL: F. E. Peacock.

Kendall, P. C., & Bemis, K. M. (1983). Thought and action in psychotherapy: The cognitive behavioral approaches. In M. Hersen, E. Kazdin, & A. S. Bellack (Eds.), *The clinical psychology handbook* (pp. 565–592). Elmsford, NY: Pergamon Press.

Kennett, J. (1977). *How to grow a lotus blossom, or how a Zen Buddhist prepares for death.* Mount Shasta, CA: Shasta Abbey.

Kernberg, O. F. (1976). *Object-relations theory and clinical psychoanalysis.* New York: Jason Aronson.

Kohlenberg, R. J., Hayes, S. C., & Tsai, M. (1993). Radical behavioral psychotherapy: Two contemporary examples. *Clinical Psychology Review, 13,* 579–592.

Kohut, H. (1971). *The analysis of the self.* New York: International Universities Press.

Kora, T., & Sato, K. (1958). Morita therapy: A psychotherapy in the way of Zen. *Psychologia, 1,* 219–225.

Kramer, H., & Sprenger, J. (1971). The malleus maleficarum. M. Summers (Trans.). New York: Dover Publications, Inc. (Original work published 1486)

Krech, D., & Cartwright, D. (1956). On SPSSI's first twenty years. *American Psychologist, 11,* 470–473.

Kuchan, A. (1989). Survey of incidence of psychotherapists' sexual contact with clients in Wisconsin. In G. R. Schoener, J. H. Milgrom, J. C. Gonsioreck, E. T. Luepker, & R. M. Conroe (Eds.), *Psychotherapists' sexual involvement with clients: Intervention and prevention* (pp. 51–64). Minneapolis: Walk-In Counseling Center.

Laing, R. D. (1967). *The politics of experience.* New York: Pantheon.

Laing, R. D. (1970). *Knots.* New York: Vintage Books.

Laing, R. D. (1976). *The facts of life.* New York: Pantheon.

Lakoff, G. (1987). *Women, fire, and dangerous things: What categories reveal about the mind.* Chicago: University of Chicago Press.

Lambert, M. J. (1989). The individual therapists' contribution to psychotherapy process and outcome. *Clinical Psychology Review, 9,* 469–485.

Langs, R. (1976). *The therapeutic interaction: Vol. 2. A critical overview and synthesis.* New York: Jason Aronson.

Lazarus, A. A. (1971). Where do behavior therapists take their troubles? *Psychological Reports, 28,* 349–350.

Lazarus, A. A. (1976). Psychiatric problems precipitated by transcendental meditation. *Psychological Reports, 39,* 601–602.

Lazarus, A. A., & Mayne, T. J. (1990). Relaxation: Some limitations, side effects, and proposed solutions. *Psychotherapy, 27,* 261–266.

Leahey, T. H. (1992). *A history of psychology: Main currents in psychological thought* (3rd ed.). Englewood Cliffs, NJ: Prentice-Hall.

Leguin, U. K. (1969). *The left hand of darkness.* New York: Ace Books.

Lerman, H. (1974, September). *What happens in feminist therapy.* Paper presented at the meeting of the American Psychological Association, New Orleans, LA.

Lerner, G. (1986). *The Creation of patriarchy.* New York: Oxford University Press.

Lewis, R. W. B. (1991). *The Jameses: A family narrative.* New York: Farrar, Straus and Giroux.

Liebson, I. (1967). Conversion reaction: A learning theory approach. *Behavioral Research and Therapy, 7,* 217–218.

Lipsey, M. W., & Wilson, D. B. (1993). The efficacy of psychological, educational, and behavioral treatment. *American Psychologist, 48,* 1181–1209.

Maddi, S. R. (1967). The existential neurosis. *Journal of Abnormal Psychology, 72,* 311–325.

Madigan, S., & O'Hara, R. (1992). Short-term memory at the turn of the century. *American Psychologist, 47,* 170–174.

Mahoney, M. J. (1989). Scientific psychology and radical behaviorism: Important distinctions based in scientism and objectivism. *American Psychologist, 44,* 1372–1377.

Mahoney, M. J. (1991). *Human change processes: The scientific foundations of psychotherapy.* New York: Basic Books.

Margolis, J. (1992). Psychotherapy vs. morality. In R. B. Miller (Ed.), *The restoration of dialogue: Readings in the philosophy of clinical psychology* (pp. 85–97). Washington, DC: American Psychological Association. (Original work published 1966)

May, R. (1953). *Man's search for himself.* New York: W. W. Norton.

May, R. (1958). Contributions of existential psychotherapy. In R. May, E. Angel, &. H. F. Ellenberger (Eds.), *Existence: A new dimension in psychiatry and psychology* (pp. 37–91). New York: Basic Books.

May, R. (1967). *Psychology and the human dilemma.* New York: W. W. Norton.

May, R. (1969). *Love and will.* New York: W. W. Norton.

May, R. (1973). *Paulus: A personal portrait of Paul Tillich.* New York: Harper & Row.

May, R. (1985). *My quest for beauty.* Dallas: Saybrook.

May, R., & Yalom, I. (1989). Existential psychotherapy. In R. J. Corsini & D. Wedding (Eds.), *Current psychotherapies* (4th ed., pp. 363–402). Itasca, IL: F. E. Peacock.

McCammon, S. L., Knox, D., & Schacht, C. (1993). *Choices in sexuality.* Minneapolis: West.

Meichenbaum, D. (1977). *Cognitive-behavior modification: An integrative approach.* New York: Plenum.

Melendy, M. R. (1903). *Maiden, wife, and mother: How to attain health—beauty—happiness.* Chicago: A. B. Kuhlman.

Merton, T. (Trans.). (1965). Flight from the shadow. In *The way of Chuang Tzu* (p. 155). New York: New Directions.

Midelfort, H. C. (1972). *Witch hunting in south western Germany 1562–1684: The social and intellectual foundations.* Stanford, CA: University Press.

Miller, G. A. (1969). Psychology as a means of promoting human welfare. *American Psychologist, 24,* 1063–1075.

Mischel, W. (1973). Toward a cognitive social learning reconceptualization of personality. *Psychological Review, 80,* 252–283.

Mitchell, J. (1974). *Psychoanalysis and feminism.* New York: Random House.

Monte, C. F. (1991). *Beneath the mask: An introduction to theories of personality* (4th ed.). Fort Worth, TX: Holt, Rinehart, and Winston.

Naranjo, C. (1970). Present-centeredness in Gestalt therapy. In J. Fagan & I. L. Shepherd (Eds.), *Gestalt therapy now* (pp. 47–69). New York: Science and Behavior Books.

Narrow, W. E., Regier, D. A., Rae, D. S., Manderscheid, R. W., & Locke, B. Z. (1993). Use of medical services by persons with mental and addictive disorders: Findings from the National Institute of Mental Health epidemiologic catchment area program. *Archives of General Psychiatry, 50,* 95–107.

Neugebauer, R. (1979). Medieval and early modern theories of mental illness. *Archives of General Psychiatry, 36,* 477–483.

Nietzsche, F. (1961). *Thus spake Zarathustra: A book for everyone and no one.* Baltimore: Penguin Books.

Norcross, J. C., & Freedheim, D. K. (1992). Into the future: Retrospect and prospect in psychotherapy. In D. K. Freedheim (Ed.), *History of psychotherapy: A century of change* (pp. 881–900). Washington, DC: American Psychological Association.

Norcross, J. C., & Prochaska, J. O. (1984). Where do behavior therapists take their troubles?: II. *The Behavior Therapist, 7,* 26–27.

Norcross, J. C., & Prochaska, J. O. (1988). A study of eclectic (and integrative) views revisited. *Professional Psychology: Research and Practice, 19,* 170–174.

O'Doherty, B. (1992). *The strange case of Mademoiselle P.* New York: Pantheon Books.

Ohnuki-Tierney, E. (1993). *Rice as self: Japanese identities through time.* Princeton, NJ: Princeton University Press.

O'Leary, K. D., & Wilson, G. T. (1987). *Behavior therapy: Application and outcome* (2nd ed.). Englewood Cliffs, NJ: Prentice-Hall.

Ornstein, R. E. (1977). *The psychology of consciousness* (2nd ed.). New York: Harcourt Brace Jovanovich.

Pasons, W. B. (1993). *Psychoanalysis and mysticism: The Freud–Rolland correspondence.* Unpublished doctoral dissertation, University of Chicago. (Available on microfilm from the Joseph Regenstein Library, University of Chicago.)

Pattie, F. A. (1994). *Mesmer and animal magnetism: A chapter in the history of medicine.* Hamilton, NY: Edmonston.

Paul, G. L., & Lentz, R. J. (1977). *Psychosocial treatment of chronic mental patients.* Cambridge, MA: Harvard University Press.

Perls, F. S. (1969a). *Gestalt therapy verbatim.* Lafayette, CA: Real People Press.

Perls, F. S. (1969b). *In and out of the garbage pail.* Lafayette, CA: Real People Press.

Pirsig, R. M. (1974). *Zen and the art of motorcycle maintenance.* New York: Morrow.

Police blotter. (1989, January 9). *Crawfordsville* (Indiana) *Messenger-Crier,* p. 2.

Pollitt, K. (1992, December 28). Marooned on Gilligan's Island: Are women morally superior to men? *The Nation, 255* (22), 799–807.

Raskin, N. J., & Rogers, C. R. (1989). Person centered therapy. In R. J. Corsini & D. Wedding (Eds.), *Current psychotherapies* (4th ed., pp. 155–194). Itasca, IL: F. E. Peacock.

Rawlings, E. I. (1993). Reflections on "Twenty years of feminist counseling and therapy." *The Counseling Psychologist, 21* (1), 88–91.

Rawlings, E. I., & Carter, D. K. (1977). Feminist and non-sexist psychotherapy. In E. I. Rawlings & D. K. Carter (Eds.), *Psychotherapy for women: Treatment toward equality* (pp. 19–100). Springfield, IL: Charles C. Thomas.

Regier, D. A., Narrow, W. E., Rae, D. S., Manderscheid, R. W., Locke, B. Z., & Goodwin, F. K. (1993). The de facto U.S. mental and addictive system: Epidemiologic catchment area prospective 1-year prevalence rates of disorders and services. *Archives of General Psychiatry, 50,* 85–94.

Reich, W. (1961). *Selected writings.* New York: Farrar, Straus & Giroux.

Reich, W. (1970). *The mass psychology of fascism.* New York: Farrar, Straus & Giroux.

Reich, W. (1973). *The function of the orgasm.* New York: Touchstone.

Reich, W. (1988). *Passion of youth: An autobiography, 1897–1922* (M. B. Higgins & C. M. Raphael, Eds.). New York: Farrar, Straus and Giroux.

Reiff, P. (1966). *The triumph of the therapeutic: Uses of faith after Freud.* Chicago: University of Chicago Press.

Reynolds, D. K. (1980). *The quiet therapies: Japanese pathways to personal growth.* Honolulu: University of Hawaii Press.

Ricks, D. F., & Wessman, A. E. (1966, Spring). Winn: A case study of a happy man. *Humanistic Psychology,* pp. 2–16.

Ricoeur, P. (1992). The question of proof in Freud's psychoanalytic writings. In R. B. Miller (Ed.), *The restoration of dialogue: Readings in the philosophy of clinical psychology* (pp. 347–365). Washington, DC: American Psychological Association. (Reprinted from *Journal of the American Psychoanalytic Association, 25,* 1977, 835–871)

Ridley, C. R. (1984). Clinical treatment of the non-disclosing black client. *American Psychologist, 39,* 1234–1244.

Rigby-Weinberg, D. N. (1986). A future direction for radical feminist therapy. In D. Howard (Ed.), *The dynamics of feminist therapy* (pp. 191–205). New York: Haworth Press.

Roazen, P. (1971). *Freud and his followers.* New York: Meridian Books.

Roazen, P. (1976). *Erik Erikson: The power and limits of a vision.* New York: Free Press.

Rogers, C. R. (1942). *Counseling and psychotherapy.* Boston: Houghton Mifflin.

Rogers, C. R. (1951). *Client-centered therapy.* Boston: Houghton Mifflin.

Rogers, C. R. (1955). Persons or science? A philosophical question. *American Psychologist, 10,* 267–278.

Rogers, C. R. (1964). Toward a science of the person. In T. W. Wann (Ed.), *Behaviorism and phenomenology: Contrasting bases for modern psychology* (pp. 109–140). Chicago: University of Chicago Press.

Rogers, C. R. (1965). Client centered therapy: Part I. In E. Shostrom (Producer), *Three approaches to psychotherapy* [Film]. (Available from Psychological Films, Santa Anna, CA).

Rogers, C. R. (1967). Autobiography. In E. G. Boring & G. Lindzey (Eds.), *A history of psychology in autobiography* (Vol. 5, pp. 341–384). New York: Appleton.

Rogers, C. R. (1969). *Freedom to learn: A view of what education might become.* Columbus, OH: Charles E. Merrill.

Rogers, C. R. (1970). *Carl Rogers on encounter groups.* New York: Harper & Row.

Rogers, C. R. (1973). My philosophy of interpersonal relationships and how it grew. *Journal of Humanistic Psychology, 13,* 3–16.

Rogers, C. R. (1980). *A way of being.* Boston: Houghton Mifflin.

Rogers, C. R. (1983). *Freedom to learn for the 80's.* Columbus, OH: Charles E. Merrill.

Rogers, C. R. (1992). The necessary and sufficient conditions of therapeutic personality change. *Journal of Consulting and Clinical Psychology, 60,* 827–832. (Reprinted from *Journal of Consulting Psychology, 21,* 1957, 95–103)

Rosenbaum, R. (1995, May 1). Explaining Hitler. *The New Yorker,* pp. 50–73.

Rossiter, S. (1981). *Blue guide Greece.* Chicago: Rand McNally.

Rubins, J. L. (1978). *Karen Horney: Gentle rebel of psychoanalysis.* New York: Dial.

Ruble, D. N. (1977). Premenstrual symptoms: A reinterpretation. *Science, 197,* 291–292.

Rychlak, J. F. (1981). *Introduction to personality and psychotherapy: A theory construction approach.* (2nd ed.). Boston: Houghton Mifflin.

Rycroft, C. (1971). *Wilhelm Reich.* New York: Viking Press.

Salzman, M. (1991). *The laughing sutra.* New York: Random House.

Sato, K. (1958). Psychotherapeutic implications of Zen. *Psychologia, 1,* 213–218.

Schoener, W. C. (1989). A look at the literature. In G. R. Schoener, J. H. Milgrom, J. C. Gonsiorek, E. T. Luepker, & R. M. Conroe (Eds.), *Psychotherapists' sexual involvement with clients: Intervention and prevention* (pp. 11–50). Minneapolis: Walk-In Counseling Center.

Schopenhauer, A. (1819). *World as will and representation.* London: K. Paul, Trench, Trübner & Co.

Schultz, D. (1977). *Growth psychology: Models of the healthy personality.* New York: D. Van Nostrand.

Selling, L. S. (1940). *Men against madness.* New York: Greenberg.

Shaftesbury, E. (1925). *Universal magnetism: A private training course in the magnetic control of others by the most powerful of all known methods* (Vol. 1). Meriden, CT: Ralston University Press.

Shah, I. (1966). *The exploits of the incomparable mulla Nasrudin.* New York: Simon & Schuster.

Shapiro, D. H. (1982). Overview: Clinical and physiological comparison of meditation and other self-control strategies. *American Journal of Psychiatry, 139,* 267–274.

Shapiro, D. H. (1992). Adverse effects of meditation: A preliminary investigation of long term meditators. *International Journal of Psychosomatics, 39,* (Special Issue Nos. 1–4), 62–67.

Shepard, M. (1975). *Fritz: An intimate portrait of Fritz Perls and Gestalt therapy.* New York: Dutton.

Shibayama, Z. (1974). *Zen comments on the mumonkan.* New York: Harper & Row.

Showalter, E. (1987). *The female malady.* London: Virago.

Skinner, B. F. (1948). *Walden two.* New York: Macmillan.

Skinner, B. F. (1961). *Cumulative record.* New York: Appleton-Century-Crofts.

Skinner, B. F. (1964). Behaviorism at fifty. In T. W. Wann (Ed.), *Behaviorism and phenomenology: Contrasting bases for modern psychology* (pp. 79–108). Chicago: University of Chicago Press.

Skinner, B. F. (1971). *Beyond freedom and dignity.* New York: Knopf.

Skinner, B. F. (1975). The steep and thorny way to a science of behavior. *American Psychologist, 30,* 42–49.

Skinner, B. F. (1987). Whatever happened to psychology as the science of behavior? *American Psychologist, 42,* 780–786.

Skinner, B. F. (1990). Can psychology be a science of mind? *American Psychologist, 45,* 1206–1210.

Smail, D. (1991). Towards a radical environmentalist psychology of help. *The Psychologist, 2,* 61–65.

Smith, H. (1970). Preface. In S. Suzuki, *Zen mind, beginner's mind* (pp. 9–11). New York: Weatherhill.

Smith-Rosenberg, C. (1972, Winter). The hysterical woman: Sex roles and role conflict in 19th century America. *Social Research, 39,* 652–678.

Spencer, H. (1907). *First principles.* London: Williams and Norgate.

Spencer, S. B., & Hemmer, R. C. (1993). Therapeutic bias with gay and lesbian clients: A functional analysis. *The Behavior Therapist, 16* (4), 93–97.

Sperry, R. W. (1988). Psychology's mentalist paradigm and the religion/science tension. *American Psychologist, 43,* 607–613.

Spiegelberg, F. (1962). *Spiritual practices of India.* Secaucus, NJ: The Citadel Press.

Spotnitz, A. (1984). The case of Anna O.: Aggression and the narcissistic transference. In M. Rosenbaum and M. Muroff (Eds.), *Anna O.: Fourteen contemporary reinterpretations* (pp. 132–140). New York: The Free Press.

Sprecher, S., & McKinney, K. (1993). *Sexuality.* Newbury Park, CA: Sage.

Stewart, D. (1792). *Elements of the philosophy of the human mind.* London: Strahan & Caddell.

Stiles, W. B, Shapiro, D. A., & Elliott, R. (1986). Are all psychotherapies equivalent? *American Psychologist, 41,* 165–180.

Strupp, H. H. (1980). Humanism and psychotherapy: A personal statement of the therapist's essential values. *Psychotherapy: Theory, Research, and Practice, 17,* 396–400.

Sulloway, F. J. (1979). *Freud: Biologist of the mind.* New York: Basic Books.

Summers, M. (1971). Introduction to the 1928 edition. In H. Kramer & J. Sprenger (Eds.), *The malleus maleficarum* (pp. v–xl). New York: Dover Publications Inc. (Original introduction published 1928)

Suzuki, D. T. (1960). Lectures on Zen Buddhism. In D. T. Suzuki, E. Fromm, & R. De Martino (Eds.), *Zen Buddhism and psychoanalysis* (pp. 1–76). New York: Harper & Row.

Suzuki, S. (1970). *Zen mind, beginner's mind.* New York: Weatherhill.

Szasz, T. S. (1970). *The manufacture of madness.* New York: Dell.

Szasz, T. S. (1974). *The myth of mental illness* (Rev. ed). New York: Harper & Row.

Szasz, T. S. (1978). *The myth of psychotherapy: Mental healing as religion, rhetoric, and repression.* Garden City, NY: Anchor Press/Doubleday.

Tannahill, R. (1980). *Sex in history.* New York: Stein and Day.

Tavris, C. (1992). *The mismeasure of woman.* New York: Simon & Schuster.

Taylor, C. (1989). *Sources of the self: The making of the modern identity.* Cambridge, MA: Harvard University Press.

Thoreau, H. D. (1937). *Walden and other writings.* New York: Modern Library.

Thorndike, E. L. (1911). *Animal intelligence.* New York: Hafner.

Truax, C. B. (1963). Effective ingredients in psychotherapy: An approach to unraveling the patient-therapist interaction. *Journal of Counseling Psychology, 10,* 256–263.

Truax, C. B. (1966). Reinforcement and nonreinforcement in Rogerian psychotherapy. *Journal of Abnormal Psychology, 71,* 1–9.

Upham, T. C. (1851). *Upham's mental philosophy: A philosophical and practical treatise on the will.* New York: Harper Brothers.

Ussher, J. (1991). *Women's madness: Misogyny or mental illness?* Amherst: University of Massachusetts Press.

Vaihinger, H. (1911). *The philosophy of "as if."* New York: Harcourt, Brace and World.

Valente, J. (1992, December 9). Learning to drink tea takes time, and much humility. *Wall Street Journal,* pp. A1, A17.

Van Den Berg, J. H. (1971). What is psychotherapy? *Humanitas, 7* (3), 321–370.

Vandenbos, G. R., Cummings, N., & Deleon, P. H. (1992). A century of psychotherapy: Economic and environmental influences. In D. K. Freedheim (Ed.), *History of psychotherapy: A century of change* (pp. 65–102). Washington, DC: American Psychological Association.

van Wolferen, K. (1989). *The enigma of Japanese power.* New York: Macmillan.

Wallace, R. K., & Benson, H. (1972, February). The physiology of meditation. *Scientific American, 226,* 85–90.

Walsh, R. (1989). Asian psychotherapies. In R. J. Corsini & D. Wedding (Eds.), *Current psychotherapies* (4th ed., pp. 547–559). Itasca, IL: F. E. Peacock.

Watchel, P. L. (1992). On theory, practice, and the nature of integration. In R. B. Miller (Ed.), *The restoration of dialogue: Readings in the philosophy of clinical psychology* (pp. 418–432). Washington, DC: American Psychological Association. (Original work published 1984)

Watson, J. B. (1913). Psychology as a behaviorist views it. *Psychological Review, 20,* 158–177.

Watson, J. B. (1924). *Behaviorism.* Chicago: University of Chicago Press.

Watson, J. B. (1928). *Psychological care of infant and child.* New York: Norton.

Watson, J. B., & Raynor, R. (1920). Conditioned emotional reactions. *Journal of Experimental Psychology, 3,* 1–14.

Watts, A. W. (1961). *Psychotherapy East and West.* New York: Pantheon Books.

Weil, A. (1995, May 15). The new politics of cocoa. *The New Yorker,* pp. 70–80.

Whitman, W. (1950). *Leaves of grass and selected prose.* New York: Modern Library.

Wiesel, E. (1960). *Night.* New York: Bantam Books.

Wiggam, A. E. (1928). *Exploring your mind with the psychologists.* New York: Norton.

Williams, R. N. (1992). The human context of agency. *American Psychologist, 47,* 752–760.

Wilson, G. T. (1989). Behavior therapy. In R. J. Corsini & D. Wedding (Eds.), *Current psychotherapies* (4th ed., pp. 241–282). Itasca, IL: F. E. Peacock.

Wolpe, J. (1958). *Psychotherapy by reciprocal inhibition.* Stanford, CA: Stanford University Press.

Wordsworth, W. (1904). Intimations of immortality from recollections of early childhood. In *Complete poetical works of William Wordsworth.* (Vol. V, pp. 52–55). New York: Houghton Mifflin, Riverside Press.

Worell, J., & Remer, P. (1992). *Feminist perspectives in therapy: An empowerment model for women.* New York: John Wiley & Sons.

Yalom, I. D. (1989). *Love's executioner.* New York: Basic Books.

Yoshioka, T. (1981). *Zen.* Osaka, Japan: Hoikusha's Color Books.

Zohar, D. (1994, February 6). Forces of reaction. *The Sunday Times* [London, England], pp. 9:14–15.

Author Index

Subject Index

AABT. *See* Association for the Advancement of Behavior Therapy
Abdominal breathing, 476
Abreaction
    explained, 114–115
    necessity of, 146
    pathogenic secrets and, 170
    psychoanalytic case study on, 122–123
Abstentions, 478
Acceptance
    as aspect of ACT therapy, 256–257
    tactical, 301–302
Acceptance and commitment therapy (ACT), 256–258
Achilles (case study), 73–76
ACT. *See* Acceptance and commitment therapy
Addictions, 275
Adler, Alfred
    challenges Freud, 129–130
    childhood of, 131–132
    early professional life of, 132–135
    enduring influence of, 146
    fellow feeling and, 142–143
    parenting and, 139, 143–144
    personality complexes and, 139–141
    prototype of self and, 141–142
    psychotherapeutic method of, 144–145
    quest for meaning and, 138–139
    as revolutionary, 136–137
    as women's rights advocate, 135–136, 370
Adler, Leopold, 131, 132
Adler, Sigmund, 131

African Americans, 204, 273
After the Turn On, What? (Houts and Serber), 300
Agency
    college men and, 381–382
    defined, 381
    ideals of normalcy and, 382–384
Aggasiz, Louis, 43, 212
Aggressiveness, 193
Albert (case study). *See* Little Albert
Alexander, Franz, 419
Alice in Wonderland (Carroll), 40
Alienation, 193
Allport, Gordon
    biographical sketch of, 286–287
    process-oriented view of, 287–289
    proprium idea of, 289–291
Amadeus (film), 37
Amae, 449–454, 460
American Institute for Psychoanalysis, 195
American Philosophical Association, 284
American Psychiatric Association, 267
American Psychological Association, 19, 20, 189, 228, 242–243, 284, 295, 360, 488
American Psychological Society, 19
American Psychologist, 17, 295, 390
Amnesia, 65
Anal stage, 187
Analytical psychotherapy
    levels of human awareness in, 168–174
    origins of, 157–167

psychology of archetypes in, 163–167
Anatomy-is-destiny formulation, 190, 191, 355, 363–364, 371, 375
Anatomy of Dependence, The (Doi), 448
Anatomy of Human Destructiveness, The (Fromm), 423
Angelou, Maya, 385
Anger, 350–351
Anima archetype, 171–172
Animal magnetism, 47, 50–52, 222
Animal psychology, 227–230
Animus archetype, 171–172
Anna O. case
    cause of symptoms in, 89
    controversy over, 90–91
    historical significance of, 92–94
    overview of, 82
    phases of illness in, 82–87
    sexual motive in, 109–110
    transference in, 93, 110
Anomic dislocation, 399
Anorexia nervosa, 83, 84, 102
Antidepressants, 249
Antigone (Sophocles), 184
Antihero, 340
Antivitalism, 61–62, 71, 102–104
Antoinette, Marie, 45, 49
Anxiety. *See also* Fear
    basic, 192–193
    breathing exercises and, 476
    defined, 244
    Japanese culture and, 455–456
    ontological, 341
Apolitical interiority, 224
Apperception, 12
Aquinas, St. Thomas, 138
Arbitrary inference, 278

514

Women *(continued)*
communalism and, 381
cult of pure womanhood and, 135, 210–211
feminist psychotherapy and, 365–372
Freud's treatment of, 347–355
gender politics and, 190–192, 347, 358–364
journeying process and, 365
Mesmer's magnetism treatments and, 53–54
neurotic fictions of, 191–192
psychoanalytic treatment of, 352–355
psychotherapeutic bias against, 358–365
therapist sex with, 361–362
treatments for hysteria in, 31, 91–92, 352
witch hunts against, 27–30
Women and Therapy, 360
Women's Christian Temperance Union, 210
Wordsworth, William, 177

World Student Christian Federation, 292
Wundt, Wilhelm, 77

Yang archetype, 171
Yeibichai chant, 203
Yellow Wallpaper, The (Gillman), 91
Yin archetype, 171
Yoga tradition
breathing exercises in, 475–476
hatha yoga practices in, 477–481
overview of, 473–474
self-practicing techniques in, 474–475
sexual practices in, 477
shiatsu massage and, 481–482
tai chi practices and, 481

Zazen, 430–431, 434–437
Zen and the Art of Motorcycle Maintenance (Pirsig), 167
Zen Buddhism
aim of, 422–423
beginner's mind in, 434–439

calligraphy and, 469–470
case study illustrating, 423–424
contaminated mind in, 420–421
critique of, 493
doctrine of the Unborn in, 419–420
flower arranging and, 467–469
meditation in, 430–432
Morita therapy and, 456–459
natural mind in, 421–422
overview of, 412–417
right practice in, 464–473
role of the *sensei* in, 424–426
satori in, 432–433
seiza therapy and, 438–439, 456
tea ceremony and, 464–467
teachings of, 427–428
unconditional love and, 433–434
Zen Mind, Beginner's Mind (S. Suzuki), 434
Zone of awareness, 319
Zoroaster, 31

TO THE OWNER OF THIS BOOK:

We hope that you have found *Talking Cures: A History of Western and Eastern Psychotherapies* useful. So that this book can be improved in a future edition, would you take the time to complete this sheet and return it? Thank you.

School and address: ———————————————————————————

Department: ————————————————————————————————

Instructor's name: ————————————————————————————

1. What I like most about this book is: ——————————————————

——

——

2. What I like least about this book is: ——————————————————

——

——

3. My general reaction to this book is: ———————————————————

——

4. The name of the course in which I used this book is: ————————————

——

5. Were all of the chapters of the book assigned for you to read? ———————

   If not, which ones weren't? ———————————————————————

6. In the space below, or on a separate sheet of paper, please write specific suggestions for improving this book and anything else you'd care to share about your experience in using the book.

——

——

——

——

——

Optional:

Your name: _____ Date: _____

May Brooks/Cole quote you, either in promotion for *Talking Cures: A History of Western and Eastern Psychotherapies* or in future publishing ventures?

Yes: _____ No: _____

Sincerely,

C. Peter Bankart

Brooks/Cole is dedicated to publishing quality publications for education in the human services fields. If you are interested in learning more about our publications, please fill in your name and address and request our latest catalogue.

Name:_____

Street Address:_____

City, State, and Zip:_____

FOLD HERE

- -

NO POSTAGE
NECESSARY
IF MAILED
IN THE
UNITED STATES

BUSINESS REPLY MAIL
FIRST CLASS   PERMIT NO. 358   PACIFIC GROVE, CA

POSTAGE WILL BE PAID BY ADDRESSEE

ATT: *Human Services Catalogue*

**Brooks/Cole Publishing Company
511 Forest Lodge Road
Pacific Grove, California 93950-9968**

FOLD HERE